The Complete Works of
WASHINGTON
IRVING

Richard Dilworth Rust
General Editor

OLIVER GOLDSMITH:
A BIOGRAPHY

BIOGRAPHY
OF
THE LATE
MARGARET MILLER DAVIDSON

Washington Irving
c. 1859–60

*WASHINGTON
IRVING*

*OLIVER GOLDSMITH:
A BIOGRAPHY*

BIOGRAPHY
OF THE LATE
MARGARET MILLER DAVIDSON

*Edited by
Elsie Lee West*

Twayne Publishers

Boston

1978

Published by Twayne Publishers

A Division of G. K. Hall & Co.

Copyright © 1978 by

G. K. Hall & Co.

All Rights Reserved

The Complete Works of Washington Irving

Volume XVII

CENTER FOR EDITIONS OF
AMERICAN AUTHORS

AN APPROVED TEXT

MODERN LANGUAGE
ASSOCIATION OF AMERICA

Library of Congress Cataloging in Publication Data

Irving, Washington, 1783–1859.
Oliver Goldsmith : a biography.

(The complete works of Washington Irving ; v. 17)
Includes bibliographical references.
1. Goldsmith, Oliver, 1728–1774—Biography.
2. Authors, English—18th century—Biography.
3. Davidson, Margaret Miller, 1823–1838—Biography.
4. Poets, American—19th century—Biography.
I. Irving, Washington, 1783–1859. Biography of
the late Margaret Miller Davidson. 1978.
II. West, Elsie Lee.   III. Title.
PR3493.I7 1978   828'.6'09 [B]   78-2957
ISBN 0–8057–8521–3

Manufactured in the United States of America

ACKNOWLEDGMENTS

I owe a great debt to the many librarians who generously sent me copies of documents, provided information, or answered questions: notably, Robert H. Land, Chief of the Reference Department, Library of Congress; Robert W. Hill, former Keeper of Manuscripts, Mr. Paul Rugen of the Rare Book Room, and Miss Jean R. McNiece, First assistant of the Manuscripts and Archives Divisions of the New York Public Library; Donald A. Sinclair, Curator of Special Collections, Rutgers University Library; Mrs. Tsing S. Chu, Director, and Mrs. Florence Susman, Reference Librarian of the Saratoga Springs (New York) Public Library; Mrs. Elsie M. Maddaus, Librarian of the Ballston Spa (New York) Public Library; Mrs. Elizabeth Silvester, Head of the Reference Department, McLennon Library, McGill University (Montreal); Mr. M. Pollard, Rare Books Librarian of the Trinity College (Dublin) Library; Michael Plunkett, Assistant Curator of Manuscripts, University of Virginia Library; Egon A. Weiss, Librarian, Department of the Army, United States Military Academy, West Point; Kenneth Raymond, Head Librarian, and Mrs. Anna Dermody, Reference Librarian, Johnson (Vermont) State College Library; Mrs. Evelyn Shanley, Librarian, Morristown (Vermont) Centennial Library; and Miss Mary Jane Miller of the British Museum.

Many individuals also took time from their busy schedules to answer my questions or supply requested information. I gratefully acknowledge the help of James L. Clifford, professor emeritus, Columbia University; Professor Suzanne Nobbe, professor emeritus, Columbia University; Professor Donald Frame, French Department, Columbia University; Clifford E. Rugg, Saratoga County Historian, Schuylerville, New York; Fred E. Steele III, Director of the Public Records Division of the Vermont Department of Administration; and W. E. K. Anderson, Headmaster, Abingdon School, Berkshire, England.

Finally, my thanks go to many relatives and friends who lent their services in one way or another: to Kenneth J. Blume of Whitestone, Queens, New York, for frequent trips to libraries in New York City on my behalf and for typing assistance; to Seth Hubbard, Esq., of Riverhead, New York, for clarifying a legal term; to Morris Diamond of Riverhead, New York, for translating Latin phrases for me; to Professors Paul Silver and Ralph Carter, both of Johnson State College (Vermont), the former for assistance in proofreading and the latter for offering valuable suggestions.

E. L. W.

Morrisville, Vermont

CONTENTS

OLIVER GOLDSMITH: A BIOGRAPHY

ix

CONTENTS

BIOGRAPHY OF THE LATE
MARGARET MILLER DAVIDSON

EDITORIAL APPENDICES

OLIVER GOLDSMITH: A BIOGRAPHY

BIOGRAPHY OF THE LATE MARGARET MILLER DAVIDSON

ILLUSTRATIONS

INTRODUCTION

In several of the complete editions of the works of Washington Irving published after his death, the biographies of Oliver Goldsmith and Margaret Miller Davidson appeared in a single volume. Aside from the fact that both are biographies, the two works, published eight years apart, have very little to do with each other in terms of subject, style or literary excellence. The decision to publish the two biographies in the same volume must have been made on some other basis, and the most obvious consideration was that of length: in the Irving canon *Oliver Goldsmith: A Biography* is a relatively brief work, and the Davidson essay appeared as an introduction to a collection of her poetry entitled *Biography and Poetical Remains of the Late Margaret Miller Davidson.* Together they fit into one volume without undue strain. The present edition of Irving's works follows precedent in assigning the two works to a single volume.

While the yoking of these two biographies is an artificial one, it probably would not have displeased Irving. He possessed what could be called a biographical curiosity, an intelligence that was attracted to individuals and incidents of supernormal stature. The two authors depicted in these works fascinated Irving, each for different reasons, and his interest in Goldsmith and Davidson was not a mere passing one, as the following historical introductions to each work should make clear.

OLIVER GOLDSMITH: A BIOGRAPHY

Oliver Goldsmith: A Biography (1849) is the third of three versions of the life of the Irish writer which Washington Irving wrote in the course of twenty-five years. In contrast to the two earlier essays, published in 1825 and 1840 as prefaces to collections of Goldsmith's works, this is a full-length treatment of the author whom Irving acknowledged to be his favorite.

Irving's lifelong interest in Goldsmith was not unique. Indeed, Goldsmith enjoyed an unparalleled vogue in the United States in the last decades of the eighteenth century and well into the nineteenth. "Parson" Weems, the itinerant book peddler, is said to have sold close to a thousand copies of *Animated Nature* between Alexandria and Norfolk, Virginia, in a single year; and he regarded *The Vicar of Wakefield* as "one of the two titles in his 'sundry *best* novels' that sold most rapidly in Virginia during 1803."[1] During the Revolutionary period Goldsmith's historical compilations were among the favored titles of American readers, who were also partial to "The Deserted Village" and *She Stoops to Conquer.*[2] Later between 1801 and 1811 scarcely an issue of the *Port-Folio* failed to carry an article about Goldsmith or an excerpt from his works, and the constant admonition of this periodical to its readers was to study his style in order to eradicate barbarisms from American writing.

Almost from the beginning of Irving's literary career, critics linked his name with Goldsmith's.[3] Although as early as 1860 William Cullen Bryant expressed a dissenting view,[4] many writers have continued to find parallels between them; but a study of his early work has demonstrated that Irving adopted a style already developed in America: ". . . a blending of the style used by Addison in the *Spectator* in which exaggeration was the chief means of satire with the style used by Goldsmith in *The Citizen of the World* in which irony was the chief means of satire. The basis of the style might be said, then, to consist of a blending of exaggeration and irony to produce humor."[5]

Whether or not this settles the question of the similarity between the two men as writers, in the preface to *Goldsmith* Irving called this Life " 'a labor of love'; for it is a tribute to the memory of an author whose writings were the delight of my childhood, and have been a source of enjoyment to me throughout life." Several months after the publication of the book when a reviewer referred to the author as "a self-acknowledged imitator" of Goldsmith, Pierre M. Irving questioned his uncle about this matter of influence and paraphrased his reply:

1. James D. Hart, *The Popular Book: A History of America's Literary Taste* (Berkeley, Calif., 1961), pp. 32, 61. According to Frank Luther Mott, *Golden Multitudes, The Story of Best Sellers in the United States* (New York, 1947), p. 40, *The Vicar of Wakefield* was first published in America in 1772, and "it had at least nine different editions in various American cities before 1800."

2. Allan Nevins, *The Gateway to History* (Garden City, N. Y., 1962), p. 16; Hart, pp. 28–29.

3. See, e.g., John Neal, *American Writers, a Series of Papers Contributed to Blackwood's Magazine (1824–1825),* ed. Fred Lewis Pattee (Durham, N.C., 1937), p. 126; "Washington Irving's Tales," *The Quarterly Review* 31 (March, 1825), 483–84.

4. *A Discourse on the Life, Character and Genius of Washington Irving* (New York, 1860), pp. 11, 15.

5. Robert Stevens Osborne, "A Study of Washington Irving's Development as a Man of Letters to 1825" (Ph.D. diss., University of North Carolina, 1947), pp. 71–72.

He smiled; said he meant only to express his affectionate admiration of Goldsmith, but it would never do for an author to acknowledge anything. Was never conscious of an attempt to write after any model. No man of genius ever did. From his earliest attempts, everything fell naturally from him. His style, he believed, was as much his own as though Goldsmith had never written—as much his own as his voice.[6]

Whether or not Irving's playful response was a valid disclaimer, there can be little doubt that his "affectionate admiration of Goldsmith" was genuine.

In 1824 when Irving, then living in Paris, was approached by the French publisher Galignani with a proposal that he edit an edition of British classics, the young American was not a complete novice in the field of life-writing. In 1810 he had published a biographical sketch of the poet Thomas Campbell, whom he later came to know; and during his brief editorship of the *Analectic* (1812–1814) he wrote biographical essays on four naval heroes of the War of 1812 and on Lord Byron.

There is little probability that Galignani, who knew Irving as the author of the *Sketch Book* and the *Knickerbocker History,* was aware of these apprentice essays when he made his offer, which Irving recorded in his journal on February 20: "at 4 oclock go to Galignanis. Galg: Proposes my editing an Edition of British Classics—promise to think of it. He is about publishing Knickerbocker."[7] A period of negotiation followed with Peter Irving acting as agent for his brother.[8] Then on March 14 Irving noted: "Write Prospectus & terms for Collection of British Literature—Galignani calls—& agrees to my terms. 250 francs a vol. 2500 fr in advance—"[9] Irving accepted the offer because he was in need of funds;[10] and this promised to be a painless way of replenishing his purse since, according to the Articles of Agreement dated March 14, 1824, "it is expressly understood that he does not obligate

6. Pierre M. Irving, *The Life and Letters of Washington Irving* (New York, 1869), III, 166; hereafter cited as PMI.

7. Washington Irving, *Journals and Notebooks,* Vol. III, ed. Walter A. Reichart (Madison, Wisc., 1970), p. 292; hereafter cited as *Journals.*

8. References to the project appear in the *Journals* on February 21, 23, 24, March 1, 11, and 13.

9. The original contract, dated March 14, 1824, is in the possession of the Clifton Waller Barrett Library, University of Virginia Library, which has kindly given permission for the following quotation. The prospectus was published in *The United States Literary Gazette* 1 (November 1, 1824), 123.

10. Thatcher T. Payne Luquer, ed., "Correspondence of Washington Irving and John Howard Payne," *Scribner's Magazine* 48 (October, 1910), 480.

himself to contribute any original matter. This is left entirely to his own discretion." On March 22 Irving recorded that he was writing "at Goldsmith's life."[11] Then, surprisingly, on April 14 he again wrote that Galignani and Didot, a printer, called on him to arrange terms, which were agreed upon, and that the publisher had paid him twenty-five hundred francs down. After noting on April 16 that he had delivered part of the Goldsmith manuscript to Galignani and on May 5 that he had written the conclusion of the Life, Irving—again surprisingly—indicated on May 24 that Galignani called and that they signed an agreement.

Why only the first volume of the series was ever published is unknown. In a letter to Peter dated July 12, 1824, Irving, then visiting the Forster family in Bedfordshire, England, mentioned his intention of leaving for London where he would collect material for biographies of Samuel Rogers and Thomas Campbell prior to his return to Paris.[12] Galignani announced the publication of *Goldsmith* in his *Messenger* on October 26, 1824, and on October 28 Irving recorded in his journal that he had received copies of *Goldsmith* and *Tales of a Traveller* from Galignani. In a letter to Payne dated December 15 Irving said: "I have written no preface to the English Authors. The Galignanis have as yet only published the works of Goldsmith & the Biography is not by me; I have merely pruned & touched up a little Biography published at Edinburgh."[13] Then on February 21, 1825, he again mentioned the Life in a letter to Payne: "The Galignani enterprize stands still for want of sufficient encouragement & at present I am doing nothing but devouring my means, and studying hard."[14] Finally, on August 13, 1825, Irving recorded in his journal that Galignani had spoken to him about a new collection of English literature; and on March 15 he offered to do twenty volumes for five hundred pounds. There the matter appears to rest.

Irving was both misleading and overly modest in his statement to Payne and in a footnote on the first page of the 1825 essay[15] that "The present biography is principally taken from the Scotch edition of Goldsmith's works, published in 1821." The primary source of this essay was in fact the memoir attributed to Bishop Thomas Percy, which was prefixed to *The Miscellaneous Works of Oliver Goldsmith, M. B.* (Lon-

---

11. *Journals*, p. 306.
12. PMI, II, 34
13. *Journals*, p. 439, n. 135.
14. *Ibid.*, p. 458, n. 39.
15. The edition used here is *The Miscellaneous Works of Oliver Goldsmith, with an Account of his Life and Writings, stereotyped from the Paris Edition*, ed. Washington Irving, complete in one volume (Philadelphia: Crissy & Markley, 1849).

don, 1801).[16] Nevertheless, although the essay is largely a paraphrase of Percy's memoir, it is much more than that, for Irving drew upon other sources, notably Croker's Boswell,[17] to fill in the gaps in Percy's information, to enlarge upon his statements, and to add illustrative anecdotes and quotations from both Goldsmith's works and periodical articles. Irving himself said in the second paragraph of the essay that he had been "curious therefore in gathering together all the heterogenous particulars concerning poor Goldsmith that still exist."

After the first two paragraphs, in which Irving expresses his own thoughts about Goldsmith, he begins a fairly straight paraphrase of Percy's essay. As he proceeds, however, he adds more and more information from other sources and discards some of Percy's strategies. For example, early in his memoir Percy quoted the written account of Goldsmith's life which had been prepared for him by Catherine Hodson, Goldsmith's sister. When, therefore, he came to the end of the long quotation, he had to backtrack in order to include other information he had collected. Since Irving did not quote the Hodson memorandum, he was free to follow a strictly chronological order in dealing with Goldsmith's early years.

For the most part Irving paraphrases those passages of Percy which he incorporates into his own essay, but his paraphrasing varies in quality. Sometimes it is unconscionably close to the original as in the following example:

Percy (82): They all exhibit ingenious proofs of his talents as a composer, and generally give a better display of the subjects than could have been done by their own authors. But herein he is rather to be considered as an advocate pleading the cause of another, than delivering his own sentiments, for he often recommends the peculiarities, if not the defects of a work; which, if his pen were engaged on the other side, he would with equal ability and eloquence detect.

1825 (39): These exhibit ingenious proofs of his ready talent at general writing, and for the most part gave a much better display

16. The Reverend Thomas Percy (1729–1811) was an English clergyman, antiquary, and poet. In 1765 he published his *Reliques of Ancient English Poetry.* He became the dean of Carlisle in 1778 and the bishop of Dromore in 1782. Percy was originally to have been the official biographer of Goldsmith. See Sir Joshua Reynolds, *Portraits,* ed. Frederick W. Hilles (New York, 1952), p. 32; Katharine C. Balderston, *The History & Sources of Percy's Memoir of Goldsmith* (Cambridge, 1926).

17. James Boswell, *The Life of Samuel Johnson, LL.D. including a Journal of a Tour to the Hebrides,* 5 vols., ed. John Wilson Croker (London, 1831).

of the subjects treated of than could have been done by their own authors. But in this view he is rather to be considered as an advocate pleading the cause of another, than as delivering the sentiments of his own mind; for he often recommends the doubtful peculiarities, and even the defects of a work, which it is obvious, had [they] been engaged on the other side, he could with equal ability have detected and exposed.

Sometimes his paraphrasing shows considerable skill. Consider the following:

Percy (38): Subsequent to his attempt as an usher, his want of present subsistence induced him to apply to several apothecaries, to be admitted a journeyman: but his threadbare coat, his uncouth figure and Hibernian dialect caused him to meet with repeated refusals. . . .

1825 (17): Having thrown up this wretched employment, he was obliged to cast about for one more congenial to his mind. In this, however, he again found considerable difficulty. His personal appearance and address were never prepossessing, but at that particular period were still less so from the threadbare state of his wardrobe. He applied to several of the medical tribe, but had the mortification to meet with repeated refusals; and on more than one occasion was jeered with the mimicry of his broad Irish accent.

Not everything that appeared in the Percy memoir found its way into the 1825 essay. Irving omitted such material as the paragraph on the tradition that Goldsmith traced his ancestry from a "Spanish gentleman named Juan Romeiro" (2); and the lurid account of the murder of James Lawder, who married Jane Contarine, Goldsmith's cousin (18 n.). He also left out several letters[18] as well as the apothecary's published vindication of his treatment of Goldsmith in his last illness (114–15). Irving ignored Percy's expressed doubt (36) of the authenticity of the story of Goldsmith's becoming traveling tutor to an avaricious young man, and told it with added detail (16). In one instance he accepted Percy's long footnote (70–71) on Samuel Dyer, all except the last sentence, which made clear why Percy had used it: he was rebutting an "ill-natured, unfounded, and malignant account" of Dyer by Sir John Hawkins. Irving's omission of the sentence (30) leaves his reader won-

---

18. For example, those to Bryanton (22–26), from Oglethorpe (95–96), and from Thomas Paine (96–98).

dering why, of all members of the Club, Dyer merited the detailed footnote.

There can be little doubt that Irving had a copy of Boswell's *Life of Johnson* at his elbow as he wrote his essay. Concerning the Club he writes (30): "This literary association is said by Mr. Boswell to have been founded in 1764, but Dr. Percy is of opinion that its institution was not so early." Percy (72) merely mentions the election of Garrick and Boswell to the Club; Irving (30–31) goes to Boswell (I, 492–93) for added details, and he includes two pages (32–33) of material from Boswell on the activities of the Club, some of which is irrelevant to the subject of the biography. He also includes a number of anecdotes, not found in Percy, such as the visit of Boswell and Mickle to the farm where Goldsmith was living (45–46) and the Malagrida incident (35).

Irving's lifelong habit of reading periodicals served him well in preparing his essay. One journal which proved useful to him at this time was *The European Magazine*, which serialized from August to October, 1793, in its "Table Talk" column a series of anecdotes about Goldsmith written, it is said, by William Cooke.[19] From the August number (91) he took an anecdote and a footnote concerning Dr. Sleigh (18); and from the same issue (94) the account of Goldsmith's friendship with Bott (35). The names of the pallbearers chosen for the public funeral which never took place do not appear in Percy (115); they do in 1825 (52). Irving found them in the October issue, where Lord Lowth's name is misspelled as it is in the 1825 essay. Irving also found material in the *Annual Register* of 1774.[20] While Percy (66) refers indirectly to Goldsmith's account of his interview with the earl of Northumberland, Irving (28–29) gives Goldsmith's first-person account as it appears in this periodical (32). In the same number (31) he found details of Goldsmith's relationship with Newbery. In the *New Monthly Magazine and Literary Journal* for 1821 appeared an article entitled "Modern Pilgrimages—Auburn" (449–53). Irving used a long passage from this article as a footnote (42–43).

In discussing the first performance of *She Stoops to Conquer* Sir Walter Scott in his essay on Goldsmith included a footnote: "For a humorous account of the first performance of this play, see Cumberland's *Memoirs*, vol. i., p. 365–9."[21] The 1825 essay (46–47) includes a

19. The attribution to Cooke was made by John Forster, *The Life and Times of Oliver Goldsmith*, rev. ed., Library Edition (New York, 1900), III, 120.

20. Among the books listed at Sunnyside are nine volumes of the *Annual Register* (1780–1790), with only the 1782 volume missing.

21. *The Miscellaneous Prose Works of Sir Walter Scott, Bart.* (Edinburgh, 1854), I, 292.

long quotation from these pages of Cumberland. In addition, Irving quotes a number of other Cumberland passages, such as his remarks on critics—"a nest of vipers in league against every name to which any degree of celebrity was attached;" (36)—and his account (50–51) of the occasion that precipitated Goldsmith's "Retaliation." Whether or not he took the clue from Scott, Irving probably picked up a footnote on Contarine (16) which Scott (289) had borrowed from Thomas Campbell's essay on Goldsmith.[22] Yet Irving was undoubtedly familiar with the Campbell essay also, since to the statement "Sir Joshua is of opinion, that he owed no less than two thousand pounds." (52) Irving adds the footnote: "4000 £.—Campbell's Biography of Goldsmith."

There are other passages in the 1825 essay not found in Percy, such as the footnote on Gaubius (14), the long footnote on the tulip mania (15), and Dr. Johnson's comments on Goldsmith's *Life of Parnell* in the *Lives of the Poets* (44). Irving also includes quotations from Goldsmith's works: from the dedication to "The Traveller" and the poem itself, from *The Vicar of Wakefield*, and from the introduction to *Essays*.

Finally, a number of passages appear to be original. Of most interest are Irving's critical comments on the various works. One of the longest concerns "The Traveller," for which he wrote a three-paragraph precis and an added paragraph of commentary. This last paragraph is notable because Irving transferred part of it to his introductory paragraph in 1840 and 1849:

In this poem, we may particularly remark a quality which distinguishes the writings of Goldsmith; it perpetually presents the author to our minds. He is one of the few writers who are inseparably identified with their works. We think of him in every page; we grow intimate with him as a man, and learn to love him as we read. A general benevolence glows throughout this poem. It breathes the liberal spirit of a true citizen of the world. And yet how beautifully does it inculcate and illustrate that local attachment, that preference to native land, which, in spite of every disadvantage of soil or climate, pleads so eloquently to every bosom; which calls out with maternal voice from the sandy desert or the stormy rock, appealing irresistibly to the heart in the midst of foreign luxuries and delights, and calling the wanderer home. (27)

In addition, Irving wrote long critical passages on "The Deserted Village" (40) and *The Vicar of Wakefield* (34) and shorter bits on other

22. *Specimens of the British Poets; with Biographical and Critical Notices, and an Essay on English Poetry in Seven Volumes* (London, 1819), VI, 252.

works of Goldsmith. In his final evaluation of his subject he also wrote a long discussion of the poetry but ignored the prose (55).

Goldsmith the man occasionally comes in for brief commentary. Irving speculates on Goldsmith's motives for giving a false name when he applied for a job as tutor (17) and on the reasons for Goldsmith's having given up plans to go to India (23). In his paragraph on the collection of poems which failed because Goldsmith "marked off one of the most indecent tales in Prior," Irving comments: "It has been said, that the error in this instance must have arisen from inadvertency or carelessness; but the inadvertency must have been excessive, as the tale is actually introduced with a criticism" (45).

In the final paragraph of the essay he wrote: "Such is the amount of information which we have procured concerning Goldsmith; and we have given it almost precisely in the words in which we found it" (56). He had, indeed, "procured" material from various sources and had either quoted or paraphrased them; but he had also shown originality in his commentary on both the life and the works of his subject.

The Galignani volume named Irving as editor but not specifically as author of the introductory essay. Neither was he indicated as author in the American edition published in Philadelphia by J. Crissy and J. Grigg in 1830 or the many reprints that followed, nor in the Baudry 1837 impression of the Galignani 1825 edition.

In publicizing Galignani's projected series of English authors *The Port Folio* announced that Carey & Lea of Philadelphia were to receive subscriptions for the forthcoming volumes in this country.[23] According to *BAL*, however, no copy of the Goldsmith volume bearing the Carey & Lea imprint has been found.[24] An edition stereotyped from the Paris edition was published in Philadelphia by Crissy & Grigg in 1830; and there were many reprintings of the work, including those of Crissy in 1833, 1835, 1836, 1837, and 1840, as well as one reprint by Crissy & Markley.

The last-mentioned edition, the one referred to in the present volume, indicates on the title page that it was "stereotyped from the Paris edition" (Philadelphia: Crissy & Markley, 1849). What "stereotyped" meant to the publisher is a question, for this American edition varies in format from the Paris edition, the original being set in single column as compared with the double column in the "stereotyped" edition, and having larger type. Furthermore, a comparison of the two texts reveals approximately 465 variations, of which about fifteen are substantive

23. 18 (July–December, 1824), 259.
24. Jacob Blanck, *Bibliography of American Literature* (New Haven, Conn., 1969), V, 26; hereafter cited as *BAL*.

in nature. In some instances a word was omitted ("tidings came"/
"tidings"); in others they were added ("and as few" / "and as a few")
or changed ("the seeming" / "this seeming"). More than half of the
variations in accidentals are accounted for by the fact that in the Paris
edition abbreviations such as "Mr." and "Dr." do not have periods.
About forty others represent hyphenated words in the original changed
to two-word form in the American edition. Differences in spelling and
punctuation account for the remainder.

No reviews of this early essay have been found; but in 1837 in an
article on James Prior's recently published *The Life of Oliver Goldsmith,
M.B. from a Variety of Original Sources, The New York Review* commented on it as "rather an accumulation of facts and criticism than,
properly speaking, a classic biography." In contrast, said the *Review*:
"The sketch prefixed to the Paris edition of Goldsmith's works edited
by Washington Irving, approaches (for it is in many respects imper-
fect) what the life of the Poet should be,—a just and elegant narrative
of facts, with occasional reflection, where we gather the cream of the
whole story without the trouble of the tedious process of investigation."[25]

At this time when Prior's biography was stimulating renewed interest in the Irish writer, the Harper Brothers invited Irving to provide
a biographical preface for a two-volume edition of Goldsmith's works.
Basing this second version on the 1825 sketch, Irving added anecdotes
he found in Prior's Life and corrected misstatements earlier derived from
Percy. It was published in 1840 as *The Life of Oliver Goldsmith, with
Selections from His Writings* in Harper's *Family Library*. In this version
the biography is attributed to Irving.

If Irving's claims for the 1825 essay had been too modest, those for
the second version were overstated. In a footnote early in the essay
he said:

Some of the above remarks were introductory to a biography of
Goldsmith which the author edited in Paris in 1825. That biography
was not given as original, and was, in fact, a mere modification
of an interesting Scottish memoir published in 1821. In the present
article the author has undertaken, as a "labour of love," to collect
from various sources materials for a tribute to the memory of one
whose writings were the delight of his childhood, and have been
a source of enjoyment to him throughout life. He has principally
been indebted for his facts, however, to a recent copious work of
Mr. James Prior, who has collected and collated the most minute

25. 1 (October, 1837), 293. Prior's biography was published in London by
John Murray in 1837.

particulars of Goldsmith's history with unwearied research and scrupulous fidelity, and given them in a voluminous form to the world. (10)

Irving revised and expanded his 1825 essay by drawing extensively on Prior's work. There is no evidence that he drew on other sources.

Prior had spent ten years in his search for Goldsmith material. He had studied the periodicals and other published works of Goldsmith's time, had gone to Ireland to examine the Goldsmith country and talk to survivors of the family and friends, and had pursued collateral materials through a study of various other members of the Johnson circle.[26] Irving took full advantage of Prior's findings. He borrowed a number of new letters published here for the first time, such as those to Contarine (44–45) and Griffiths (67–68), and Judge Day's letter to Prior concerning Day's relationship with Goldsmith (125). He found many new anecdotes: for instance, the story of Pilkington and the white mouse (67–68), and an incident in which Sir Joshua Reynolds discovered Goldsmith writing a poem and training a dog at the same time (95). He was able to draw upon Prior for specific details to add to material already used in 1825, such as the names of Goldsmith's schoolteachers (14, 15), and the facts of the college riot that Goldsmith became involved in (27–28). Most congenial to Irving's nature must have been the traditions that had grown up about the house in which Goldsmith was born (11). Even new material from Boswell can also be found in Prior.

Not all the material in the 1825 essay was included in the second version. Irving deleted the footnote on Contarine (16), which was a quotation from Campbell's essay; and he discarded Cumberland's account of how "Retaliation" came to be written (50–51), though he retained that author's version of the first-night performance of *She Stoops to Conquer* (1840: 165–67). Several famous anecdotes, such as the Malagrida *faux pas* and the Fantoccini incident, were dropped in 1840 but would be restored in 1849.

Irving also reduced considerably the length of some passages. He omitted the long paragraph and the footnote on the tulip mania (15) and substituted a mere sentence: "The tulip mania was still prevalent in Holland, and some species of that splendid flower brought immense prices" (48). He reduced the long passage on the Club (30–32) to a manageable paragraph, and omitted the irrelevant examples of conversation at the meetings (33–34). The most unfortunate omissions were, perhaps, his own original critical evaluations of Goldsmith's

26. *The Literary World* 5 (September 1, 1849), 173.

works. He had ventured into criticism early in his career, but the truth
is that he "hated to write criticism, preferred to tell the truth but
'could not bear to inflict pain.' "[27] There is also evidence that Irving
regarded criticism as a lesser form of art.[28]

Nevertheless, he did add several new original passages. He adapted
the account of his visit to Green Arbour Court, which had originally
appeared in his sketch "The Club of Queer Fellows" in *Tales of a
Traveller,* for inclusion here (67); and for the first time he told of
his own visit to Canonbury House (124). Probably original are the
paragraph on nursery rhymes (103) and his comments on Goldsmith's
trip to the continent with the Hornecks (161–62).

There are three puzzling quoted passages. One concerns the economi-
cal landlady (43), another Goldsmith's "good constitution" (49), and
the third *The Citizen of the World* (87). The only source found for
the three quotations is the 1825 essay (13, 15, 25–26), which Irving
appears to have quoted.

Comparing the two early essays, one can trace Irving's changing
attitudes. In 1825 (37) he accepted the consensus that Goldsmith
tended to be jealous of other people. He wrote: "We find it difficult to
reconcile the possession of so odious a quality with affectionate habits
and benevolent propensities like his. True it is, however, that he was
prone to indulge this unamiable passion to so ridiculous an excess, that
the instances of it are hardly credible." To illustrate the point, he narrated the stock anecdotes. By 1840, however, he could scoff at such
"absurdities, evidently misconceptions of Goldsmith's peculiar vein of
humor, by which the charge of envious jealousy has been attempted
to be fixed upon him" (159.39–41).

Early writers had made much of Goldsmith's proclivity for gambling.
In 1825 Irving tells the story of how the poet "fell by accident into the
company of a sharper in Dublin" and lost his money (12). In Holland
he is unable to resist the gaming tables; and, having quoted Dr. Ellis's
account of how he exhorted Goldsmith not to gamble, Irving moralizes:
"The votary of play, however, is never to be so easily cured. Reason and
ridicule are equally impotent against that unhappy passion. To those
infected with it, the charms of the gaming table may be said to be
omnipotent" (15). As the end of Goldsmith's life draws near, his
"passion for gaming" is cited as the major cause of his financial embarrassment (50). In 1840 this emphasis on gambling is almost com-

---

27. Henry Boynton in *American Writers on American Literature by Thirty-
Seven 'Contemporary Writers,* ed. John Macy (New York, 1931), p. 65.

28. See, e.g., his biographical essay "Thomas Campbell" in *Biographies and
Miscellanies,* Knickerbocker Edition (New York, 1869), pp. 134–35. In the Knickerbocker Edition the volumes are not numbered.

pletely missing. The Dublin sharper becomes "one whose wits had been sharpened about town, who beguiled him into a gambling-house" (42), and in Holland "sometimes, unfortunately he resorted to the gambling-tables" (48). In the final discussion of his financial condition (177) nothing is said of gaming.[29]

Irving's attitude toward Boswell changes considerably also. In 1825 he shows respect for the Scot, whose "conversational anecdotes ... have conrtibuted to give so much interest to the pages of that gentleman's biography of Johnson" (30). Boswell's election to the Club is recorded with no adverse commentary (30, 31). Mr. Boswell rectifies Hawkins's misstatements about Garrick's election (31). The conversation of the Club members is of great interest; "Happily, Mr. Boswell has supplied such a desideratum..." (32). Nor is Boswell castigated for instigating an unpleasant argument with the clergyman Toplady (37; compare T 215). By 1840 Irving has begun to shift his stance. "It is difficult," he writes of the anecdote in which Goldsmith is labeled as jealous of the Horneck ladies, "to conceive the obtuseness of intellect necessary to misconstrue so obvious a piece of mock petulance and dry humour into an instance of mortified vanity and jealous self-conceit." The story, he adds, "even out-Boswells Boswell" (146). The Scot is given short shrift in the reduced passage on the history of the Club: "Boswell, who was admitted into it some few years after its institution, affords us a few tantalizing gleams; but his scraps of conversation are given merely to set forth his hero, Dr. Johnson, and contain but few of the choice sayings of his fellow-members. Above all, he had almost uniformly a disposition to underrate Goldsmith, and to place him in an absurd point of view" (99). In 1825 Irving has nothing to say of the meeting of Boswell and Goldsmith, but in 1840 he writes: "About the beginning of 1763 Goldsmith became acquainted with Boswell, whose literary gossippings were destined to have a deleterious effect upon his reputation. Boswell was at that time a young man, light, buoyant, pushing, and pre-sumptuous. He had a morbid passion for mingling in the society of men noted for wit and learning..." (88). The jealousy which Irving attributes to Goldsmith in the earlier essay is now transferred to Boswell: "The lurking hostility to Goldsmith discernible throughout Boswell's writings, has been attributed by some to a silly spirit of jealousy of the superior esteem evinced for the poet by Dr. Johnson" (89). Nevertheless, although Prior (I, 436) includes the anecdote about the "Scotch cur," Irving does not pick it up until 1849 (87.38–42); but he does include the paragraph of exasperated commentary on Boswell that precedes the anecdote.

29. See T 230.28–231.5, where Irving defends Goldsmith against the charge of being "an habitual gamester." See Explanatory Notes, 231.5.

Harper & Brothers republished the 1840 essay in 1844, again as part of the Harpers' Family Library.

Several New York periodicals commented briefly on this essay. *The New-Yorker* devoted most of its space to mentioning the "many qualities in common" of Irving and Goldsmith. Of the sketch itself the reviewer said, "It is an admirable and interesting performance"; but he regretted the lack of an additional volume of excerpts from Goldsmith, which "would have made the work more complete, and added greatly to the value of the collection."[30] *The New World* admired the selections chosen for the volumes and added, "It is almost superfluous to say, that Mr. Irving has succeeded to admiration in portraying the life of his favorite author."[31] *The Iris, or Literary Messenger* commented on the "liberal use of materials" taken from Prior, but the reivewer particularly praised "the chaste and beautiful style which so eminently distinguishes the classic American."[32]

In 1849, while Irving was engaged in revising his own works for the edition Putnam had contracted to publish, he conceived the idea of rewriting his 1840 essay. George Palmer Putnam recorded the incident:

Sitting at my desk one day, he was looking at Forster's clever work, which I proposed to reprint. He remarked that it was a favorite theme of his, and he had half a mind to pursue it, and extend into a volume a sketch he had once made for an edition of Goldsmith's works. I expressed the hope that he would do so, and within sixty days the first sheets of Irving's "Goldsmith" were in the printer's hands. The press (as he says) was "dogging at his heels," for in two or three weeks the work was published.[33]

In the preface to the 1849 version Irving acknowledged his indebtedness to Prior and Forster and admitted that, after the publication of Forster's Life, "executed with a spirit, a feeling, a grace, and an eloquence, that leave nothing to be desired," he himself might be regarded as presumptuous in offering another. Since, however, he was in the process of revising his works for Putnam's complete edition, he had either to include what he now regarded as the inadequate 1840 sketch or to revise it. In choosing the latter course he professed the haste with which he had executed his *Life* and urged those readers who sought greater detail and "critical disquisitions" to consult Prior's and Forster's versions.

30. 10 (February 6, 1841), 333.
31. 2 (February 6, 1841), 94.
32. 1 (April, 1841), 293–94.
33. *The Atlantic Monthly* 6 (November, 1860), 605.

During that summer of 1849 he complained to his nephew Pierre about "fagging at the 'Life of Goldsmith,' two or three chapters of which he had still to write, said it had taken more time than he could afford—had plucked the heart out of his summer; and after all he could only play with the subject. He had no time to finish it off as he wished."[34] This was a particularly busy time for Irving. Not only was he revising his works for the Putnam edition, but he was also working on *Mahomet*, the first volume of which was published in December. At the same time he was involved in settling John Jacob Astor's estate and organizing the Astor Library, and always in the background to haunt him was the life of George Washington, which he had contemplated writing for many years and which he said must be his "great and crowning labor."[35] The man was sixty-six years old and had only ten more years to live.

Oliver Goldsmith was published by Putnam, probably in August, 1849. On August 25 Irving wrote a letter, still extant, requesting Putnam to make a number of changes in the first edition.[36] *Holden's Dollar Magazine* commented briefly on the new work and published an extract from it in its issue of September, 1849; then in the October issue appeared a review with this opening sentence: "We made a brief allusion last month to the Life of Goldsmith by Geoffrey Crayon, and gave an extract from the work, it being then in sheets."[37] As early as July 21, 1849, *The Literary World* published "Goldsmith on his Travels: A chapter from the forthcoming new Life of the Poet and Humorist, by Washington Irving" and then included a full review in its September 1 issue.[38]

The author's manuscript for the biography is in the Seligman Collection of the New York Public Library. The two folio volumes bound in gold-tooled brown morocco contain 512 pages, of which approximately two-thirds are in Irving's handwriting and the other third in print. Most of these printed passages were taken from the 1840 essay, but a dozen of them were taken from John Forster's life of Goldsmith and several from other sources. Also extant are twenty-eight pages of author's corrections, which were bound in with an 1853 illustrated edition. Copies of twenty-six of these pages were preserved with the manuscript.[39]

According to Irving's own admission, there is little in his *Life* that

---

34. PMI, III, 158–59.

35. *Ibid.*, II, 188; *Mahomet and His Successors*, ed. Henry A. Pochmann and E. N. Feltskog (Madison, Wisc., 1970), pp. 519–20.

36. The original is in the possession of the Sleepy Hollow Restoration.

37. 4 (September, 1849), 573, 633.

38. 5 (July 21, 1849), 50–51; (September 1, 1849), 173–74.

39. For a fuller description of the manuscript see Textual Commentary, pp. 430–35.

does not appear in either Prior's or Forster's work. Asked by Pierre whether he had "introduced any new anecdotes," Irving replied:

> "No," playfully; "I could not invent any new ones; but I have altered the setting, and have introduced—not in their biography— Madame Darblay's anecdote about Boswell and Johnson, which is capital. I have also made more of the Jessamy Bride, by adverting to the dates in the tailor's bill, and fixing thereby the dates of certain visits to her."[40]

Despite his heavy reliance on sources, Irving did not in every instance use them unquestioningly. He accepted, for example, Prior's statement that Goldsmith had made Voltaire's acquaintance in Paris, even though Forster had pointed out that the French sage was at that time in exile.[41] On the other hand, he was more discerning than Forster in dealing with the Fiddleback incident (Chapter III). Because it was a good story, he used it for all it was worth; but he recognized it as a "story given by the poet-errant . . . here and there touched up a little with the fanciful pen of the future essayist . . ." (27.20–22). Without questioning the probability of the tale itself, Irving did indicate an awareness of its fictional quality.[42] Irving's haste also resulted in "occasional traces of carelessness."[43]

In his treatment of Goldsmith's relationship with Mary Horneck, according to Dana Kinsman Merrill, "Irving made one inexcusable digression in the biography by crossing the line of sheer invention."[44] Just how culpable was he? Irving took his hint from Forster, who wrote that Mary Horneck "exerted strange fascination over Goldsmith. Heaven knows what impossible dreams may at times have visited the awkward, unattractive man of letters! But whether at any time aspiring to other regard than his genius and simplicity might claim, at least for these the sisters heartily liked him; and perhaps the happiest hours of the later years of his life were passed in their society."[45]

40. PMI, III, 164.

41. T 39.39–41; Forster (50).

42. Katharine C. Balderston, ed., *The Collected Letters of Oliver Goldsmith* (Cambridge, 1928), p. xxix, commented: "It seems safe to conclude that the surprising story of Fiddleback was Goldsmith's first fiction."

43. *North American Review* 70 (April, 1850), 289. For an example see Explanatory Notes, 138.3.

44. *American Biography, Its Theory and Practice* (Portland, Maine, 1957), pp. 131–32.

45. John Forster, *The Life and Adventures of Oliver Goldsmith. A Biography: in Four Books.* (London, 1848), 501. See also Explanatory Notes, 140.31.

In introducing the Hornecks Irving stressed their kindness to the poet and their willingness to look beyond his ugly exterior. Then, without citing Forster, he added: "It has been intimated that the intimacy of poor Goldsmith with the Miss Hornecks, which began in so sprightly a vein, gradually assumed something of a more tender nature, and that he was not insensible to the fascinations of the younger sister" (140.28–31). Irving had noted that the dates on extant tailor bills showed that Goldsmith's increased interest in flamboyant clothing occurred just about the time of his meeting with the Hornecks, and he speculated as to whether the poet was trying "to win favor in the eyes of the Jessamy Bride!" (141.6–7).

In his revised edition Forster (III, 151–52) took Irving to task for going "somewhat too far in accepting the suggestion as if it were an ascertained fact"; and Forster collected every reference to Mary from Irving's *Life* into a single paragraph, which gives as distorted a view of Irving's interpretation as Irving himself was charged with. Rather, Irving reverted to the subject sporadically in speculative terms. In his final evaluation of Goldsmith's character (240.33–36), Irving suggested that the poet's "lurking sentiment of tenderness" for Mary, "kept down by conscious poverty and a humiliating idea of personal defects," might account in part for "much of that fitfulness of conduct" that marked his last years. This passage suggests that Irving was not merely romanticizing the story but was, instead, trying to understand and interpret his subject.

Oliver Goldsmith is not, like Forster's work, a "life and times" biography. The focus is seldom diverted from the subject. In occasional brief digressions the author deftly sketches in the backgrounds of Goldsmith's acquaintances, such as Dr. Johnson, Hugh Kelly, Tom Davies, and in the longest such passage the original members of the Club. For the benefit of his American readers he devoted a page to General Oglethorpe, whose name "has become historical, chiefly from his transactions in America, and the share he took in the settlement of the colony of Georgia" (174.14–16).

The one luminary of the age to whom Irving gave short shrift in introducing him to the reader is James Boswell (85–87). This was not an unconscious oversight for, if Irving had any purpose beyond retelling the story of a fascinating life, it was to rescue Goldsmith from Boswell. He was not without precedent in this respect. Prior thought that Boswell's character was "tinged with peculiarity" and that the Scotsman might not be "a high-minded man." He was, in fact, often "vain and credulous, inquisitive and communicative, bustling and occasionally assuming." Although he felt that Boswell had not been entirely just to Goldsmith in his *Life of Johnson*, Prior concluded that "if we cannot

altogether respect Boswell, it is difficult to dislike him."[46] Forster (259),
however, was vitriolic in his comments on Boswell, whom he characterized as "this wine-bibbing, tavern babbler, this meddling, conceited,
inquisitive, loquacious lion hunter, this bloated and vain young Scot."
Indeed, compared with Forster's constantly harsh assessment of Boswell, Irving's remarks seem almost innocuous. To him, Boswell is "the
obsequious satellite" to Johnson (86.29), "that literary magpie" (159.23),
and "the eternal meddler and busy body" (215.34–35).

Despite his bland treatment of Boswell in 1825, Irving's attitude
toward the Scot had actually been established long before he had
read either of his major sources. Americans in general had not taken
kindly to Boswell when he published his great *Life*, and their reaction
is reflected in a comment which appeared in the *Port-Folio*: "To the
labours of Boswell every admirer of Johnson owes great obligations;
but, whilst this gratitude renders a voluntary tribute of applause,
and dwells on the minutest lineaments in the character of the great
moralist, he is continually disgusted by the obtrusive egotism and
contemptible adulation of his fawning sycophant."[47] Indeed, many of
Boswell's close associates were critical of his portrait of Goldsmith, men
like Burke, Steevens, Percy, Wilkes, Malone, and even Reynolds.[48]
During his years abroad Irving was acquainted with people who had
little respect for Boswell: John Lockhart, Sir Egerton Brydges, Charles
Leslie, and even Boswell's own son Alexander.[49] Irving himself did not
record his own attitude toward the man; in fact, his journals and letters
reveal remarkably few adverse comments about other people; and his
published works are notable for an absence of such references.[50]
Furthermore, the fact that he was by nature averse to raising a laugh
at another's expense suggests that he could not accept with tranquillity

46. James Prior, *The Life of Oliver Goldsmith, M. B. from a Variety of Original Sources*, 2 vols. (London: John Murray, 1837), I, 446, 447.

47. N.s. 1 (March 15, 1806), 148.

48. See Reynolds, *Portraits*, pp. 38–39; *Letters of James Boswell*, ed. Chauncey Brewster Tinker (Oxford, 1924), II, 394, n. 1, for Percy's statement that Boswell was "studiously excluded from all decent company" after he published the *Life of Johnson*.

49. See, e.g., *Memoirs of the Life of Sir Walter Scott, Bart.* (Edinburgh, 1839), V, 336; *The Autobiography . . . of Sir Egerton Brydges, Bart.* (London, 1834), I, 134; Charles Robert Leslie, *Autobiographical Recollections*, ed. Tom Taylor (Boston, 1860), I, 155; F. L. Lucas, *The Search for Good Sense: Four Eighteenth-Century Characters: Johnson, Chesterfield, Boswell, Goldsmith* (London, 1958), p. 240.

50. George S. Hellman, *Washington Irving Esquire, Ambassador at Large from the New World to the Old* (New York, 1925), p. 75: "It was, I think, the *Edinburgh Review* that, after Irving's death, was the first to point out how, in all his writings (even under the stress of attack), there was never a caustic fling, a mean or bitter word."

what he regarded as Boswell's distorted picture of his favorite writer. Nowhere else in the writings of Irving is a person handled so harshly as is Boswell.

During a visit to his uncle some time after the book was published, Pierre "expressed to him my satisfaction with the work. He replied that he had been afraid to look at it since it was brought up, for he had never written anything in such a hurry. He wanted more time for it, and did not know but that his talents might be flagging. 'Are you sure it does not smell of the apoplexy?' he inquired, in playful allusion to Gil Blas and the Archbishop of Granada."[51]

Irving need not have worried, for even from critics who pointed out weaknesses in this *Life* it received generous praise. *The Gentleman's Magazine*, for instance, said that "it will bid fair to be the most popular as it is the most pleasing," and the reviewer presumed "that, for a considerable period at least, the biography of Goldsmith will close with this volume, for everything seems to have been done in the collection of facts that diligence could accomplish; and few writers could hope to surpass Mr. Washington Irving in the ease and gracefulness with which the narrative is composed." Then after listing a number of what he regarded as errors in fact, judgment, or taste, the reviewer concluded: "but these are only specks on the surface, easily removable, which do not injure the interior substance, nor detract from that general merit, which will ensure it a favourable reception with the public, and enable it to appear with confidence in the presence of its rivals."[52]

Many of the reviews compared the three recent biographies of Goldsmith: those of Prior, Forster, and Irving. There was general agreement that Prior's work was "too long" and Forster's "too discursive."[53] English reviewers took cognizance of the quarrel which had been precipitated by Prior's accusing Forster of plagiarism, but the tendency was to regard Prior as unreasonable in his charges.[54] As a result, they did not castigate Irving for his wholesale borrowing from sources; rather they regarded his *Life* as a more popular presentation which would appeal to a general reading public. Thomas Babington Macaulay's judgment possibly sums up the English point of view: "The diligence of Mr. Prior

51. PMI, III, 159–60.
52. N.s. 32 (December, 1849), 617, 620.
53. *Ibid.*, 617.
54. For details of the quarrel see *The Athenaeum*, no. 1076 (June 10, 1848), 577–80. An exception to the general view can be found in an unsigned letter published in pamphlet form (British Museum, 1414.i.1. [81]) by a man who protested that two writers had plagiarized from Prior's *Life*. He did not mention Forster by name, but he had harsh things to say of Irving, whom he apparently did not respect as a writer.

deserves great praise; the style of Mr. Washington Irving is always pleasing; but the highest place must in justice be assigned to the eminently interesting work of Mr. Forster."[55]

American reviews, on the other hand, reflect a more nationalistic viewpoint. *Graham's Magazine,* for example, thought that neither Prior's nor Forster's version was "equal to Irving's in respect to felicity in conveying to the reader a living impression of Goldsmith's character and life; and of depositing his image softly in the mind, as an object of good-natured affection."[56] According to *Holden's Dollar Magazine,* those who had read "the ponderous and particularizing history of Goldsmith by Prior, and the more recent and more ambitious biography by Forster" recognized their completeness in terms of factual material, but "every one must have felt that a true portrait was yet wanting, that the features of the subject, if truthfully delineated, did not give a just impression of the original, from a lack of an artistic arrangement of the back ground, and a proper disposition of lights and shadows." This reviewer asserted that Irving's *Life* supplied the lack: "Improvement on the picture which our own great literary limner has painted of the English humorist is beyond the reach of any hand that will be likely to make such an attempt."[57] In more flowery terms Mrs. C. M. Kirkland, reviewing Irving's *Life* and the first two volumes of Prior's in *The North American Review,* pronounced Prior as a "laborious collector of fact" who had written an unattractive life; while "Mr. Irving, selecting at will from the whole, has, with his usual taste, presented us with 'gems in order, fitly set,' from whose shifting and delicate hues flashes forth a daguerreotype, though not, like that, made of sunshine."[58]

Both English and American critics praised Irving's style. *The Critic* said: "To dwell here upon the well-known fascinations of Mr. Irving's style, as adding to the charms of this biography, would, indeed, be superfluous; and we are only led to allude to them, because he is so peculiarly impressed with the kindred beauties of that of Goldsmith."[59] Although in the opinion of *The Athenaeum,* "His book owes all that it has of novelty and charm to style, reflection, apposite illustration and arrangement," the reviewer qualified his praise by alluding to "its Americanisms."[60] *Graham's Magazine* praised "that 'polished want of polish' in the selection of the words, which indicates a master in diction";[61]

55. *Johnson and Goldsmith,* ed. William P. Trent (Boston, 1906), p. 92.
56. 35 (November, 1849), 311.
57. 4 (October, 1849), 633.
58. 70 (April, 1850), 266.
59. (December 1, 1849), 538.
60. No. 1151 (November 17, 1849), 1151.
61. 35 (November, 1849), 311.

while *The United States Magazine and Democratic Review*, somewhat less enthusiastic, admitted that "The grace of Irving's style throws around the subject-matter a charm, which it sometimes does not possess of itself."[62] *The Southern Literary Messenger* went so far as to claim that a line in Johnson's eulogy of Goldsmith was applicable equally to Irving: A poet who left scarcely any style of writing untouched, and touched nothing that he did not adorn.[63]

There were some differences of opinion as to whether Irving had dealt adequately with Goldsmith's weaknesses. *The Critic* thought that he had produced "a living image of Goldsmith, the man, as he actually was,"[64] but *Blackwood's* took both Forster and Irving to task for their "defence of Goldsmith from the charge of vanity."[65] Three years after the publication of the *Life* an article entitled "The Duty of a Biographer" appeared in *The United States Magazine and Democratic Review*, in which the anonymous author attacked the *de mortuis nil, nisi bonum* concept of nineteenth-century biography. Among the works criticized was Irving's *Goldsmith*, "so beautifully told, so full of the true spirit of candor in most respects, that one finds this excellent specimen of what biography should be, marred by a premeditated design of the author to, not only excuse, but deny, the faults which belong to Goldsmith's character."[66] Such criticism was, however, the exception. More typical was the verdict of George Washington Greene: "He tells you the story of his hero's errors as freely as he does that of his virtues, and in a way to make you feel that a man may have many a human weakness lie heavily at his door, and yet be worthy of our love and admiration still."[67]

Critics in general commented on Irving's treatment of Boswell. Some American periodicals expressed pleasure at it. *Holden's* thought it "truly delightful to see how he deals a blow to that poor driveller Boswell whenever the literary caitiff comes in his way,"[68] and *The Knickerbocker* was "glad to perceive that Mr. Irving has a due appreciation of that ineffable Scotch toady, Boswell."[69] The most incongruous anti-Boswell statement came from the writer who, having just castigated Irving for denying Goldsmith's faults of character, added curtly: "So far

62. 25 (September, 1849), 286.
63. 15 (September, 1849), 638.
64. (December 1, 1849), 537.
65. *The Eclectic*, May, 1850, p. 90.
66. 28 (March, 1851), 256.
67. *Biographical Studies* (New York, 186), p. 173. According to PMI, III, 162, this essay originally appeared in the *Christian Review*, April, 1850.
68. 4 (October, 1849), 633.
69. 34 (October, 1849), 349.

as the author has put a correct light upon the ungenerous criticisms of Boswell, he did well."[70] Less vehement than their American counterparts, English reviewers in general acquiesced in Irving's view of the Scot. *The Critic*, for instance, said: "Boswell was utterly incapable of comprehending a mind or character such as that of Goldsmith, and consequently misinterprets him on every possible occasion. Mr. Irving reads more truly that consciousness of ability yet diffidence of producing it, that anxiety to please yet distrust of his powers of pleasing, that perfect truth and child-like simplicity which lay at the root of all his actions."[71] On the other hand, the *Athenaeum* objected to Irving's "captious depreciation of Boswell's talents." Praising Boswell as "an author of deserved reputation," the reviewer commented: "Mr. Irving might have remembered, too, that some of the pages in his own 'Goldsmith' are lengthened and adulterated extracts from the flowing pages of Boswell."[72]

On balance, Irving must have been pleased with the critical reception of *Oliver Goldsmith*, "an almost perfect example of a well-written biography," in the opinion of *The Critic*.[73] Always eager for the good opinion of his countrymen, he would have felt content with George Ripley's comment in the *New York Tribune*: "Everything combines to make this one of the most fascinating pieces of biography in the English language."[74]

According to Pierre Irving, by September 19, 1849 the first edition of twenty-five hundred had been sold and Putnam was preparing "a second of 2,000."[75] The book was republished, presumably from the same plates, constantly corrected and repaired, in 1850, 1851, 1854, 1855, 1859, and 1860. In addition, there were illustrated editions in 1849 and 1853, only the table of contents being reset to accommodate pen drawings by W. Roberts.[76] Putnam also published the biography as part of the *Works* in various editions, including the Riverside (1864), Hudson (1864), Kinderhook (1864), and Knickerbocker (1869). In the latter *Goldsmith* appeared in a volume with *Margaret Davidson* as it also did in the Author's Autograph Edition (1897). After Irving's death in 1859 other editions were published in Philadelphia, Boston, Albany, and New York by various firms.

Since the first English impression, published by John Murray in 1849,

70. *The United States Magazine and Democratic Review* 28 (March, 1851), 256.
71. (January 1, 1850), 11–12.
72. (November 17, 1849), 1152.
73. (December 1, 1849), 537.
74. Quoted in PMI, III, 160.
75. PMI, III, 165.
76. According to *BAL*, vol. 5, p. 51, "Examination of typewear indicates that the trade edition was printed prior to the illustrated edition."

has the same text, type, and pagination as the first American edition, it is probable that the two were printed from the same or duplicate plates. Nevertheless, a handful of textual variations between the American and English editions indicate that Murray made a few changes. In the same year a pirated edition was published by G. Routledge (republished in 1850), and the following year, 1850, H. G. Bohn published the book in its Bohn's Shilling Series.[77] Other editions published in London were those of H. G. Clarke & Co. (1850) and W. Tweedie (1853). In 1850 an edition was published in Leipzig by B. Tauchnitz, Jr. as Volume 193 in its Collection of British Authors. The work was published in a French translation in Paris (1849), a German translation in Berlin (1858), and a Welsh translation in Edinburgh (1868). In the first decade of the twentieth century a number of edited editions appeared, presumably for the use of school children.

The many reprints of the book in both the United States and England testify to its popularity both here and abroad right into the twentieth century. Written more rapidly than any of Irving's other biographies, it represents no original research and no unique contribution to Goldsmith scholarship. The secret of its contemporary success lay in English pride in her adopted son, in the tremendous vogue of Goldsmith in America, and in the close relationship generally seen between Goldsmith and Irving as both men and writers. Its continuing popularity was due to its loving spirit, its charm, and the literary excellence of this little gem of nineteenth-century biography.

BIOGRAPHY OF THE LATE
MARGARET MILLER DAVIDSON

In a letter to Miss Ticknor William H. Prescott wrote, "You have read Irving's Memoirs of Miss Davidson, I believe. Did you ever meet with any novel half so touching? It is the most painful book I ever listened to. I hear it from the children, and we all cry over it together. What a little flower of Paradise! . . . Her whole life was one dying day,—one long heartbreak. How fitting that her beautiful character should be embalmed in the delicate composition of Irving!"[78]

77. For an account of the legal quarrel in London over international copyright pertaining to Irving's works, see *Washington Irving and the House of Murray: Geoffrey Crayon Charms the British, 1817–1856*, ed. Ben Harris McClary (Knoxville, Tenn., 1969), pp. 190–202.

78. George Ticknor, *Life of William Hickling Prescott* (Boston, 1864), pp. 187–88. See also *The Correspondence of William Hickling Prescott, 1833–1847*, ed. Roger Wolcott (Boston, 1825), pp. 239, 287. Prescott sent a copy of this memoir to

How well chosen is that word *embalmed*. Irving's memoir of Margaret Miller Davidson, the fifteen-year-old poet who had recently died of tuberculosis, may have caused Prescott to weep; but the modern reader is more likely to think of Emmeline Grangerford's tombstones and weeping willows, and to reckon with Huck Finn that "with her disposition, she was having a better time in the graveyard."[79] Such an attitude, however understandable, would reflect a failure to comprehend the prevailing mood of sentimentality and melancholy in the America of the 1840's. Of this lugubrious period Van Wyck Brooks asked: "What determines, in a given age, the meaning of a given mood?—the prestige of certain themes at certain times?—the power of peculiar images and situations to evoke, to affect, to inspire, to touch, to move?" And he replied to his own question: "A young woman dying of consumption had played a part in Irving's life that was almost as decisive perhaps as it played in Poe's; and this, one might say, was a typical reality of the time."[80]

Although the *Biography of the Late Margaret Miller Davidson* has stood the test of time less successfully than any other work in the Irving canon, it should be regarded as neither "a devastating proof that Irving had gone quite to seed"[81] nor an indication that he was too kindly "to withstand Mrs. Davidson's importunings."[82] Irving was perfectly sincere in publishing this memoir. Many years before, his family had known Mrs. Davidson as one of the Miller girls of Maiden Lane;[83] and like many other Americans he had read with great interest Samuel F. B. Morse's biography of young Margaret's celebrated sister Lucretia, another child genius, who in 1825 had died of consumption at the age of sixteen; and Irving had taken great pride in the review of Morse's book written by the English poet laureate, Robert Southey.[84] When in

Fanny Calderón de la Barca, who acknowledged it with the greatest delight. In 1844 Mme. Calderón became a close friend of Irving in Madrid.

79. Mark Twain, *The Adventures of Huckleberry Finn*, ed. Henry Nash Smith (Boston, 1958), p. 86.

80. *The World of Washington Irving* (Philadelphia, 1944), pp. 452–53.

81. Stanley T. Williams, *The Life of Washington Irving* (New York, 1935), II, 110.

82. John T. Winterich, "The Ladies of the Lake," *The Colophon*, part 8 (New York, 1931), unpaged.

83. Pierre M. Irving, *The Life and Letters of Washington Irving* (New York, 1869), II, 373; hereafter cited as PMI.

84. Morse's memoir was prefixed to *Amir Khan, and Other Poems: The Remains of Lucretia Maria Davidson, who died at Plattsburgh, N. Y., August 27, 1825, aged 16 years and 11 months*, with a biographical sketch, by Samuel F. B. Morse (New York, 1829). Southey's review published in *The Quarterly Review* 41 (November, 1829), 289–301, was a matter of great pride to Americans, though Poe

1833 Irving learned, possibly through his friend James Kent,[85] that
Mrs. Davidson was in New York City and wanted to talk to him about
a new edition of Lucretia's poems, he "lost no time in waiting upon her."[86]

Except for the details Irving gives us in the memoir, little is known of
his relationship with the Davidsons. During this first interview he met
Margaret, then eleven years old, and was struck by her "intellectual
beauty" (245.27–28) and "blushing diffidence" (245.29). Three years
later when he visited the Davidsons at their home in Ruremont, he
again saw Margaret, who by this time he felt certain "was not long for
this world" (246.20–21). That was the last time he saw her. Some time
after she died in 1838, he was given a number of her manuscripts, which
were "accompanied by copious memoranda concerning her, furnished
by her mother at my request" (246.24–25). He does not make clear
who took the initiative, but one suspects that he was asked to prepare
an edition of Margaret's poems. There is no reason to suppose that he
undertook the task unwillingly; in fact, he wrote to his sister Sally Van
Wart: "She was a beautiful little being, as bright and as fragile as a
flower, and like a flower she has passed away. Her poetical effusions
are surprising, and the spirit they breathe is heavenly. I think you will
find her biography one of the most affecting things you have ever read."[87]

If other reasons for his interest in this child are needed, they are
not far to seek. Americans in general appear to have been fascinated
by child prodigies, especially those who died young. As early as 1813,
during Irving's brief tenure as editor, the *Analectic* carried a short article
on an "infant prodigy," one Zerah Colburn from "Cabut, (a town at the
head of Onion river, in the United States of America)," who was then
being exhibited in London.[88] A few years later Irving himself jokingly
referred to the European theory that physical and mental powers declined in the New World: "I was anxious," he wrote in "The Author's
Account of Himself," in *The Sketch-Book*, "to see the great men of
Europe; for I had read in the works of various philosophers, that all
animals degenerated in America, and man among the number." That
this preoccupation with the intellectual competence of Americans still
flourished in the 1840's is evident from the fact that reviewers of *Mar-*

(*The Complete Works of Edgar Allan Poe*, ed. James A. Harrison [New York,
1902], X, 224) was inclined to regard such pride as a sign of "subserviency which
would have been disgusting had it not been ludicrous." Southey's review is, for
the most part, a poor paraphrase of Morse's memoir.

85. See Explanatory Notes, 267.36.
86. See T 245.22.
87. PMI, II, 373.
88. *The Analectic Magazine* 1 (January–June, 1813), 124–25.

garet Davidson inevitably commented on the child's "genius." Another reason for Irving's interest in Margaret may well be that he was touched to find he had inspired some of her poetry, such as "Boabdil El Chico's Farewell to Granada," to which she appended notes composed of quotations from the *Conquest of Granada*. Finally, Van Wyck Brooks's assessment may not be too far from the truth: Irving may, indeed, have seen the analogy between the early deaths of Margaret and his own fiancée, Matilda Hoffman, both from tuberculosis.

Regardless of his reason for undertaking the memoir, toward the end of February, 1841, Irving apparently sent a proposal to Mathew Carey, the Philadelphia publisher, offering him the biography he was then writing. On March 2, 1841, Carey replied that "We shd be pleased to give the volume to the public." However, pleading the adverse conditions in the publishing business as an excuse for offering less than Irving had asked, Carey made a counterproposal: "We think it would be better to print an edition of 2500 copies for a first ed for which we could allow twenty two cents per copy payable at 9 mos from publication & if it was sufficiently attractive could be stereotyped or set up again for 2000 copies at the same price per copy. Would this not be your best course? It may be that the work may prove more attractive than we suppose & many thousands may be wanted. We would of course push it with our best efforts."[89] Carey's terms seem to have been unacceptable to Irving, who by mid-March had completed the book and had submitted it to Wiley & Putnam to be forwarded to the Philadelphia publisher, Lea and Blanchard. In a letter from New York to the latter firm, dated March 14, 1841, he wrote:

> You will be able after looking over the Memoir, to judge what chance it has to make an impression, and what number of copies it will be advisable to publish. You may stereotype it or not as you think proper, and make an allowance at the rate you proposed in your letter. I wish ultimately, when it has had its run in a handsome edition, to put it in Harpers Family library, that it may yield as much profit as possible to the family of the deceased. I will thank you to put it to press as soon as possible and forward me proofs struck off while the type is in galleys, so that in case of any material corrections there will be no need of breaking forms. I should like very much to have the proofs, ↑of the Memoir,↓ within a fortnight, or three weeks at farthest. When I am informed you have determined upon the mode of bringing out the work, and we have

89. Reprinted in E. L. Bradsher, *Mathew Carey, Editor, Author and Publisher: A Study in American Literary Development* (New York, 1912), p. 90.

settled definitely as to the terms, we can draw up a memorandum—
I wish the work to be handsomely printed so as to make a very
presentable volume.[90]

By April 16 Irving was reading proof, for on that date he wrote
another letter to Lea and Blanchard chiding the publisher for tardiness
in keeping him supplied with copy. He was anxious, he said, to return
to Sunnyside and his "country avocations."[91] According to BAL, the
copyright deposit date is June 10, 1841.[92]

To his niece Sarah Storrow, Irving wrote on July 11, 1841: "I presume
before this you have received the volume containing Miss Davidson's
memoir and poetical remains, as I directed one to be forwarded to
you. . . . I remitted to the mother the note of hand given by the booksellers for the edition, and transferred to her the copyright, reserving
merely [the] right to publish at any time, the memoir, in connection
with my o[ther] writings."[93] His transfer of the copyright and proceeds
of the book to Mrs. Davidson appears to have been an act of charity.
Margaret's father, Dr. Oliver Davidson, was a charter member of the
Clinton County (New York) Medical Society, its president in 1825,
and a delegate to the New York State Medical Society in 1809.[94] Nevertheless, he has been described as "a doctor with cultivated tastes, . . .
barely able to support his family;"[95] and Samuel F. B. Morse, in his
biography of Lucretia, wrote: "The pecuniary state of her father's family, was such as to render it proper that much of her time should be
devoted to domestic duties."[96] Mrs. Davidson, a perennial invalid, had
nine children, of whom seven died before her death in 1844. As Winterich facetiously remarks, "One cannot escape the conviction that Dr.
Davidson was a singularly ineffectual practitioner."[97]

90. The original letter is in the possession of the Historical Society of Pennsylvania. The arrows used here indicate interlinear insertions, above or below the line,
in the document being quoted.

91. In this letter he also sent the four lines of verse which, he said, "I wish . . .
to be inserted as an epigraph on the title page." The original letter is in the possession of the Historical Society of Pennsylvania.

92. Jacob Blanck, comp., Bibliography of American Literature (New Haven,
1969), V, 46.

93. Washington Irving's Letters from Sunnyside and Spain, ed. Stanley T. Williams (New Haven, 1828), p. 15.

94. Henry R. Remson Coles, Genealogical Record of the Davison, Davidson,
Davisson Family of New England (New York, privately printed, 1899), p. 52.

95. Dictionary of American Biography, vol. 5, ed. Allen Johnson and Dumas
Malone (New York, 1930), p. 94.

96. Amir Khan, p. vii.

97. Winterich, "The Ladies of the Lake." In a holograph copy of an undated

In his letter to Sally Van Wart Irving said that the biography was "made up in a great degree from memorandums furnished by [Margaret's] mother, who is of almost as poetical a temperament as her children. The most affecting passages of the biography are quoted literally from her manuscript."[98] Neither Mrs. Davidson's notes nor Irving's manuscript has been located. Since Irving transferred the copyright to Mrs. Davidson, he may very well have returned her papers also. In a letter dated February 28, 1842, to Lewis J. Cist Irving complied with a request for an autograph and said: "I am sorry to say I have nothing in the handwriting of the Miss Davidsons to furnish you."[99]

One valuable document that has survived is a journal kept by Margaret in 1833, which contains a twenty-six page account of her trip from Canada to Plattsburgh, then to Saratoga Springs and Schenectady, and finally to New York City. The journal begins on May 31, 1833; and the last passage was entered on August 7, 1833.[100] Although one passage from the journal, in altered form, appears in the biography (258.8–22) as do several factual details,[101] there is no way of knowing whether Irving ever saw the journal or whether Mrs. Davidson supplied him with extracts from it. In light of the fact that the journal contains vivid material not included in the biography, the latter would seem to be the more probable. For example, Margaret told of a fishing trip she enjoyed, a fourth of July celebration parade she saw, a visit to Hoboken, where the notorious Hamilton-Burr duel was fought, a trip to Coney Island, and several visits to Niblo's, the famous pleasure garden in New York, where she heard concerts and saw fireworks displays and a ventriloquist perform. Although a writer like Irving would welcome such specific detail, a mother interested in elevating her daughter to sainthood would be more likely to suppress it. One of the most fascinating passages in the journal is an account of Irving's first visit to Mrs. Davidson, in which Margaret gives her impression of the great author and a description of him.[102] This section alone might have kept the mother, out of a sense of delicacy, from showing the journal to Irving. Of the play that Margaret wrote Irving says, "The little drama lies before us . . . (259.19)." Had he seen the original journal, one suspects he would have made a similar comment.

---

letter to her son Matthias at Ossining Mrs. Davidson referred to another son, Morris, as "almost our sole support." This document is in the possession of the Rutgers University Library.

98. PMI, II, 373.

99. In the possession of the New York Public Library.

100. In the possession of the Rutgers University Library.

101. See Explanatory Notes, 257.34, 258.2.

102. "Journal," pp. 24–25. See Explanatory Notes, 245.30.

How Irving used the material from Mrs. Davidson is a question. Did he prepare a manuscript in which he had copied quotations from the source? Or did he use the scissors and paste method he was later to follow in the *Goldsmith* manuscript?[103] With no evidence at hand it is impossible to determine how exact his quotations are or how well he paraphrased the unquoted passages. One might ask, for instance, whether it was the mother or Irving who, in speaking of Lucretia as the baby Margaret's "fond attendant," failed to perceive the incongruity of Lucretia's writing poetry "with the infant sporting in her arms" (246.41). As a matter of fact, Irving quoted so liberally from Mrs. Davidson's material that the biography ought to be judged as a collaborative work.

Nevertheless, one need only compare this *Life* with Catharine Maria Sedgwick's life of Lucretia[104] to realize Irving's greater skill in using even mediocre material. Though he rises to the "melancholy interest"[105] of his subject, he avoids the sort of moralizing that Miss Sedgwick freely indulges in. He seizes upon the child's pitifully few objective experiences and presents them vividly and, by including several of her letters, succeeds in mitigating the effect of Mrs. Davidson's mournful prose. Occasionally, too, Irving's own common sense asserts itself. Of Margaret's religious education he comments somewhat wryly, "There is nothing more truly poetical than religion when properly inculcated (249.9–10). Within the limitations of his subject and his source, Irving even tried to probe the child's motives. She had, he explained, an "ardent desire for literary distinction," which had been aroused by the fame of her sister (287.10). Yet one senses the author's decreasing interest in the work as he progresses. At the beginning he intersperses his paraphrase of the material with occasional judiciously chosen quotations, but gradually the ratio of quotation to paraphrase increases until finally he no longer maintains his own identity as biographer. Had the mother's lachrymose account of the decline and death of Margaret been, at last, too much even for Washington Irving? After all, spring was coming to Sunnyside.

In his letter to Sarah Storrow, Irving said that the biography "has met with great success; which I do not attribute to any merit of mine: but to the extreme interest and pathos of the materials placed in my hands."[106] Although he had assessed his biography correctly, he was himself universally praised for his "delicate pen" in tastefully preparing the

103. See Textual Commentary for *Goldsmith,* p. 431.
104. *Poetical Remains of the Late Lucretia Maria Davidson, Collected and Arranged by Her Mother: with a Biography, by Miss Sedgwick* (Philadelphia, 1841).
105. *The North American Review* 112 (July, 1841), 141.
106. *Letters from Sunnyside,* p. 15.

volume.[107] "It is enough," said the reviewer of *The New World*, "for the lover of literature that an author, so distinguished and so esteemed, should have undertaken this task; we sit down to the book with a confident feeling of being gratified—but gratification rises into delight when we find with what simple yet admirable skill the duty has been performed. Mr. Irving has arranged the little treasures, deposited in his keeping, with a taste not inferior to that which has marked his more prominent performances."[108] Succinctly the *North American Review* pronounced the memoir "as feeling and graceful as we should naturally expect to find any thing from his pen."[109]

Of much greater interest to the reviewers, however, were Margaret's life, death, and "genius" and Mrs. Davidson's suffering and sensibility. *The New-Yorker* began its review in typical fashion:

> The records of genius present no more remarkable instances of high poetical ability in very infancy than those of Lucretia Maria and her sister Margaret Miller Davidson. More emphatically than that of Pope might it be said of them that they "lisped in numbers for the numbers came," and their earliest breathings seemed to come from a land of more than human love and of a higher than mortal life. Angel visitants from the spirit-land—bright beings of seraphic purity—they breathed the uncongenial air of this lower world but for a season and then broke the "strong affections of earth" which bound them here and flew aloft with joy to their homes in heaven.[110]

Pope's was not the only famous name mentioned. *The New World* commented on the fact that "true genius adorns whatsoever it touches.... Its truth has never struck us more forcibly than in looking over this tribute to the memory of a marvellous child, who perished, not like Chatterton, in *pride*, but in all humility.[111] The *Arcturus* likened Margaret to Mrs. Hemans in her ability to write down poetry even before she was conscious of "the rhythmical process" and in her "early talent of story-telling," and the reviewer thought too that the story of Margaret's "illness and death may remind the reader of similar scenes in the touching portrait of Nell."[112] Indeed, *Waldie's Select Circulating Library* saw "the same affinity between the character and genius of this youthful poetess and her biographer, which existed in the case of Kirke

107. *Arcturus, A Journal of Books and Opinion* 2 (July, 1841), 126.
108. *The New World* 2 (June 5, 1841), 238.
109. 112 (July, 1841), 138.
110. 11 (June 5, 1841), 178.
111. 2 (June 5, 1841), 381.
112. 2 (July, 1841), 126.

White and his biographer, Southey. In each case the task of recovering and embalming the remains of a deceased favourite, encasing them in the amber of their own beautiful creations, has been executed with an affectionate solicitude which does honour to the author's heart."[113]

In general Mrs. Davidson came in for high praise as "a mother, not unworthy of such daughters."[114] Only the North American Review suggested the possibility that she, like most parents of geniuses, might have been guilty of "accelerating the progress which ought to be checked, and feeding the flame which ought to be quenched."[115] Several of the reviewers were particularly impressed by Mrs. Davidson's final letter to Miss Sedgwick (338–342). Writing in Graham's Magazine, Poe called it "a letter so full of all potent nature, so full of minute beauty, and truth and pathos, that to read it without tears would be to prove one's self less than human."[116] And The New-Yorker confessed that its comments on the book were "merely . . . an introduction to the following account of her death contained in a letter from her mother to Miss Sedgwick."[117]

Several of the reviews dignified Margaret's poetry with commentary on it. The New World regarded her poems as more astonishing than Lucretia's and added that they "are sometimes marked by an originality of idea and a felicity of expression which would surprise and delight us in the productions of an established author—but, when we come to reflect that they are the emanations of the immature mind of a child, . . . we regard them as inspired and the direct expression of thoughts sent from Heaven."[118] The North American Review said that the poems "are certainly remarkable specimens of early ripening genius, and awaken admiration and astonishment"; and of her work as a whole, including her studies, the reviewer exclaimed: "Have the annals of recorded genius any thing to show more remarkable than this?"[119]

As might be expected, Poe devoted most of his essay to a consideration of the poetry. Of "Lenore" he wrote: "But although as indicative of her future power, it is the most important, as it is the longest of her products, yet, as a whole, it is not equal to some of her shorter compositions." Nevertheless, he added, "Its length, viewed in connection with its keeping, its unity, its adaptation, and completeness, will impress the

---

113. Part 1, no. 26 (June, 1841), unpaged.
114. From a squib from the New York American, published in the end-matter of Poetical Remains.
115. 112 (July, 1841), 141.
116. Works, X, 175.
117. 11 (June 5, 1841), 178.
118. 2 (June 5, 1841), 381.
119. 112 (July, 1841), 142.

metaphysician most forcibly when surveying the capacities of its author. Powers are here brought into play which are the last to be matured. For fancy we might have looked, and for the lower evidences of skill in a perfect versification and the like, but hardly for what we see in Lenore." Of the short poems he singled out two, of which he said, "we look around us in vain for anything composed at eight years, which can bear comparison with the lines subjoined." Then, unable to see the beam in his own eye, he seized upon Irving's remarks on Margaret's poem "To My Sister Lucretia" (287.19–24) for supercilious comment: "The nature of inspiration is disputable, and we will not pretend to assert that Mr. Irving is in the wrong. His words, however, in their hyperbole, do wrong to his subject, and would be hyperbole still, if applied to the most exalted poets of all time."[120] Four months later in a review of a new edition of Lucretia's poems, also in *Graham's Magazine*, Poe, still unaware of his own hyperbole, insisted that the tone of his remarks on Margaret's poetry "was not fully in accordance with that of the mass of our contemporaries." He thought that he had been forced "to dissent from the extravagant eulogium which had its origin, beyond doubt, in a confounding of the interest felt in the poetess and her sad fortunes, with a legitimate admiration of her works."[121]

In this last remark Poe had hit upon a truth: the general reaction to the biography and to the poetry reflected the reviewer's emotional experience in reading the book. Poe himself said, "Few books have interested us more profoundly"; and he commented on "the exquisite loveliness of the picture here presented to view."[122] The point is all the more obvious in the words of another reviewer, who admitted unashamedly that "Seldom have we let fall the tears of sympathy over more true pathos than that which breathes in the stanzas, 'On the death of my sister Anna Eliza;' 'To my mother oppressed with sorrow;' 'On the corpse of my little brother, Kent.' The very title of the latter is heart-breaking—and how we grieve with the poor girl when she exclaims, with an agony as deep as that of the King of Israel when he mourned for Absalom—'But thou art gone! and this cold clay / Is all that now remains of thee.' "[123]

One result of the success of this book was a revival of interest in Lucretia, whose volume of poetry containing the Morse biography, published in 1829, had not been a success. In 1841 Lea and Blanchard published the *Poetical Remains of the Late Lucretia Maria Davidson*, which included a new biography by Catherine Maria Sedgwick and

120. *Works*, X, 176, 178.
121. *Ibid.*, p. 221.
122. *Ibid.*, pp. 174, 175.
123. *The New World* 2 (June 5, 1841), 381.

a seventeen-page dedication to Irving written by Mrs. Davidson. In it she thanked him for "the truly touching and elegant manner in which you have executed your voluntary task."[124]

On July 21, 1841, Irving wrote to Lea and Blanchard in acknowledgment of Lea's letter to him of July 17 "Relative to a Second of Miss Davidsons Memoir &c." He continued: "You will use your discretion as to the number of copies &c of the edition, on the same terms as the first edition. The note for the amount in payt, as before, you will make out in favor of Mrs Davidson. I am not aware of any alterations ⟨to be made⟩ necessary or advisable in the second edition; if there are any corrections they will be very trifling and may be specified in a letter, but I do not think there will be any. You may proceed with the edition therefore at your convenience."[125]

No explanatory details concerning the publication of a second edition have survived; nevertheless such an edition was advertised in an unnumbered end page of the *Poetical Remains*.[126] Two of Irving's letters to Lea and Blanchard written about this time, which may bear on the subject, have not been located. One, mentioned by Williams[127] as dated August 7, 1841, from Tarrytown, was in 1935 in the possession of Marston Drake of New York City. The other, according to Ralph M. Aderman,[128] was dated August 9, 1841. It was sold at auction in 1946. No second edition is listed in *BAL* or in the bibliographies of William R. Langfeld and Stanley T. Williams and Mary Ellen Edge although Williams and Edge do list two issues in 1841.[129] Not until 1974 was a copy of this second edition discovered. Dr. Edwin T. Bowden, textual editor of the Twayne edition, found it listed under the subject rather than the author in the Library of Congress Catalog. Although no major revisions were

---

124. *Poetical Remains*, p. ix.

125. Quoted by permission of The Carl H. Pforzheimer Library. On July 26, 1841, Irving again wrote to his niece, Sarah Storrow: "I sent you some time since a copy of Miss Davidsons works & memoir, which I trust you have received before this. It has been well received and meets with so good a sale that a new edition is about to be put to press. I hand all the profits of the work to Mrs Davidson" (original letter in the Collection of American Literature, Beinecke Library, Yale University). The angle brackets indicate crossed out words in the document being quoted.

126. According to Williams (*Life*, II, 109), "Before the end of the year the volume had passed through its second edition."

127. *Life*, II, 361, n. 114.

128. In a letter to the editor, August 31, 1972.

129. William R. Langfeld, comp., *Washington Irving: A Bibliography* (New York, 1933); Stanley T. Williams and Mary Ellen Edge, comps., *A Bibliography of the Writings of Washington Irving: A Check List* (New York, 1936).

made in the second edition, twenty-three substantive variations and more than four hundred variations in accidentals are found in it.

Lea and Blanchard published a "Third Edition" in 1842, and "A New Edition, revised" in 1843. The only major revision, an addition of a paragraph and a four-stanza poem, was effected in the 1842 edition. The "New Edition, revised" was republished in 1845, 1846, 1847, and 1848; and it was also published by Clark, Austin & Co., New York, in 1851, 1852, and 1854; and by P. Sampson and Co., Boston, in 1857. Pierre M. Irving included the biography in his *Biographies and Miscellanies,* published by G. P. Putnam & Son in 1869 and by J. B. Lippincott & Co. in 1873.

The earliest English edition noted in *BAL* was advertised by Wiley and Putnam as the third edition in the *Athenaeum,* May 14, 1842. It was also published by Tilt & Bogue in 1842 and 1843, by David Bogue in 1843 and 1850, by T. Allman in 1846, and by Knight and Son, 1854. There was also an edition which combined the poetry and memoirs of the two sisters: *Life and Recollections of Margaret Davidson and Her Poetical Remains with a Biography of Lucretia Davidson by Miss Sedgwick*; [second title page] *Margaret and Lucretia Davidson with Poetical Remains by Washington Irving and Miss Sedgwick,* published by N. Tegg and Co. and by Aylott & Jones in 1848. F. A. Brockhaus, Leipzig, published a German translation of the *Biography and Poetical Remains of the Late Margaret Miller Davidson* in 1843 and a German translation of the combined biographies in 1848.

After 1873 the vogue for the mournful poetry of the Davidson sisters seems to have ended.[130] Had they really been poetic geniuses, modern scholars would owe a debt of gratitude to Samuel F. B. Morse, Catharine Maria Sedgwick, and Washington Irving for recording the scant details of their lives; and of the three, Irving would be acknowledged as the most artistic biographer. Since, however, these two young poets have passed into a well-deserved oblivion, the *Biography of Margaret Davidson* retains only a historical interest for the literary scholar.

---

130. "What of [their] verse? There is little to choose between the two, and little to be said once a choice has been made. Their work is almost interchangeable in theme, treatment, and mediocrity of performance. Lucretia Maria seems to have been a shade the sprightlier, but I am afraid that this is to the credit of her first editor, and that her mother suppressed any gay little fragments of Margaret's that might have survived on the theory that her innocently pompous little elegies and facile paraphrases of psalms and invocations to spring were more nearly attuned to the lyric mode of the day, which indeed they were." Their work is "on a par with the effusions of Maria Brooks, Emma C. Embury, Amelia B. Welby, Anne C. Lynch, Mrs. M. St. Leon Loud, and most of the rest of that forgotten sisterhood of song who made the pre-bellum anthology business so profitable" (Winterich, "The Ladies of the Lake").

OLIVER GOLDSMITH:
A BIOGRAPHY

Oliver Goldsmith

PREFACE

In the course of a revised edition of my works I have come to a biographical sketch of Goldsmith, published several years since. It was written hastily, as introductory to a selection from his writings; and, though the facts contained in it were collected from various sources, I was chiefly indebted for them to the voluminous work of Mr. James Prior, who had collected and collated the most minute particulars of the poet's history with unwearied research and scrupulous fidelity; but had rendered them, as I thought, in a form too cumbrous and overlaid with details and disquisitions, and matters uninteresting to the general reader.

When I was about of late to revise my biographical sketch, preparatory to republication, a volume was put into my hands, recently given to the public by Mr. John Forster, of the Inner Temple, who, likewise availing himself of the labors of the indefatigable Prior, and of a few new lights since evolved, has produced a biography of the poet, executed with a spirit, a feeling, a grace and an eloquence that leave nothing to be desired. Indeed it would have been presumption in me to undertake the subject after it had been thus felicitously treated, did I not stand committed by my previous sketch. That sketch now appeared too meager and insufficient to satisfy public demand; yet it had to take its place in the revised series of my works unless something more satisfactory could be substituted. Under these circumstances I have again taken up the subject, and gone into it with more fullness than formerly, omitting none of the facts which I considered illustrative of the life and character of the poet, and giving them in as graphic a style as I could command. Still the hurried manner in which I have had to do this amidst the pressure of other claims on my attention, and with the press dogging at my heels, has prevented me from giving some parts of the subject the thorough handling I could have wished. Those who would like to see it treated still more at large, with the addition of critical disquistions and the advantage of collateral facts, would do well to refer themselves to Mr. Prior's circumstantial volumes, or to the eloquent and discursive pages of Mr. Forster.

For my own part, I can only regret my short comings in what to me is a 'labor of love'; for it is a tribute of gratitude to the memory of an author whose writings were the delight of my childhood, and have

3

been a source of enjoyment to me throughout life; and to whom, of all others, I may address the beautiful apostrophe of Dante to Virgil:

Tu se' lo mio maestro, e 'l mio autore;
Tu se' solo colui, da cu' io tolsi
Lo bello stile, che m' ha fatto onore.

W. I.

SUNNYSIDE, Aug. 1, 1849.

CHAPTER I

There are few writers for whom the reader feels such personal kindness as for Oliver Goldsmith, for few have so eminently possessed the magic gift of identifying themselves with their writings. We read his character in every page, and grow into familiar intimacy with him as we read. The artless benevolence that beams throughout his works; the whimsical yet amiable views of human life and human nature; the unforced humor, blended so happily with good feeling and good sense, and singularly dashed at times with a pleasing melancholy; even the very nature of his mellow, and flowing, and softly-tinted style, all seem to bespeak his moral as well as his intellectual qualities, and make us love the man at the same time that we admire the author. While the productions of writers of loftier pretension and more sounding names are suffered to moulder on our shelves, those of Goldsmith are cherished and laid in our bosoms. We do not quote them with ostentation, but they mingle with our minds, sweeten our tempers, and harmonize our thoughts; they put us in good humor with ourselves and with the world, and in so doing they make us happier and better men.

An acquaintance with the private biography of Goldsmith lets us into the secret of his gifted pages. We there discover them to be little more than transcripts of his own heart and picturings of his fortunes. There he shows himself the same kind, artless, good humored, excursive, sensible, whimsical, intelligent being that he appears in his writings. Scarcely an adventure or character is given in his works that may not be traced to his own parti-colored story. Many of his most ludicrous scenes and ridiculous incidents have been drawn from his own blunders and mischances, and he seems really to have been buffeted into almost every maxim imparted by him for the instruction of his reader.

Oliver Goldsmith was born on the 10th of November, 1728, at the hamlet of Pallas, or Pallasmore, county of Longford, in Ireland. He sprang from a respectable, but by no means a thrifty stock. Some families seem to inherit kindliness and incompetency, and to hand down virtue and poverty from generation to generation. Such was the case with the Goldsmiths. "They were always," according to their own accounts, "a strange family; they rarely acted like other people; their hearts were

5

in the right place, but their heads seemed to be doing any thing
but what they ought."—"They were remarkable," says another statement,
"for their worth, but of no cleverness in the ways of the world." Oliver
Goldsmith will be found faithfully to inherit the virtues and weaknesses
of his race.

His father, the Rev. Charles Goldsmith, with hereditary improvidence,
married when very young and very poor, and starved along for several
years on a small country curacy and the assistance of his wife's friends.
His whole income, eked out by the produce of some fields which he
farmed, and of some occasional duties performed for his wife's uncle,
the rector of an adjoining parish, did not exceed forty pounds.

And passing rich with forty pounds a year.

He inhabited an old, half rustic mansion, that stood on a rising ground
in a rough, lonely part of the country, overlooking a low tract occasionally
flooded by the river Inny. In this house Goldsmith was born, and it
was a birthplace worthy of a poet; for, by all accounts, it was haunted
ground. A tradition handed down among the neighboring peasantry states
that, in after years, the house, remaining for some time untenanted,
went to decay, the roof fell in, and it became so lonely and forlorn as
to be a resort for the "good people" or fairies, who in Ireland are
supposed to delight in old, crazy, deserted mansions for their midnight
revels. All attempts to repair it were in vain; the fairies battled stoutly
to maintain possession. A huge misshapen hobgoblin used to bestride
the house every evening with an immense pair of jackboots, which, in
his efforts at hard riding, he would thrust through the roof, kicking
to pieces all the work of the preceding day. The house was therefore
left to its fate, and went to ruin.

Such is the popular tradition about Goldsmith's birthplace. About
two years after his birth a change came over the circumstances of his
father. By the death of his wife's uncle he succeeded to the rectory of
Kilkenny West; and, abandoning the old goblin mansion, he removed
to Lissoy, in the county of Westmeath, where he occupied a farm of
seventy acres, situated on the skirts of that pretty little village.

This was the scene of Goldsmith's boyhood, the little world whence
he drew many of those pictures, rural and domestic, whimsical and
touching, which abound throughout his works, and which appeal so
eloquently both to the fancy and the heart. Lissoy is confidently cited
as the original of his "Auburn" in the "Deserted Village;" his father's
establishment, a mixture of farm and parsonage, furnished hints, it is
said, for the rural economy of the Vicar of Wakefield; and his father
himself, with his learned simplicity, his guileless wisdom, his amiable

piety, and utter ignorance of the world, has been exquisitely portrayed in the worthy Dr. Primrose. Let us pause for a moment, and draw from Goldsmith's writings one or two of those pictures which, under feigned names, represent his father and his family, and the happy fireside of his childish days.

"My father," says the Man in Black, who, in some respects, is a counterpart of Goldsmith himself, "my father, the younger son of a good family, was possessed of a small living in the church. His education was above his fortune, and his generosity greater than his education. Poor as he was, he had his flatterers poorer than himself: for every dinner he gave them, they returned him an equivalent in praise; and this was all he wanted. The same ambition that actuates a monarch at the head of his army, influenced my father at the head of his table: he told the story of the ivy-tree, and that was laughed at; he repeated the jest of the two scholars and one pair of breeches, and the company laughed at that; but the story of Taffy in the sedan-chair was sure to set the table in a roar. Thus his pleasure increased in proportion to the pleasure he gave; he loved all the world, and he fancied all the world loved him.

"As his fortune was but small, he lived up to the very extent of it: he had no intention of leaving his children money, for that was dross; he resolved they should have learning, for learning, he used to observe, was better than silver or gold. For this purpose he undertook to instruct us himself, and took as much care to form our morals as to improve our understanding. We were told that universal benevolence was what first cemented society: we were taught to consider all the wants of mankind as our own; to regard the *human face divine* with affection and esteem; he wound us up to be mere machines of pity, and rendered us incapable of withstanding the slightest impulse made either by real or fictitious distress. In a word, we were perfectly instructed in the art of giving away thousands before we were taught the necessary qualifications of getting a farthing."

In the Deserted Village we have another picture of his father and his father's fireside:

> His house was known to all the vagrant train,
> He chid their wanderings, but relieved their pain;
> The long-remembered beggar was his guest,
> Whose beard, descending, swept his aged breast;
> The ruin'd spendthrift, now no longer proud,
> Claim'd kindred there, and had his claims allow'd;
> The broken soldier, kindly bade to stay,
> Sat by his fire, and talk'd the night away;

Wept o'er his wounds, or tales of sorrow done,
Shoulder'd his crutch, and show'd how fields were won.
Pleased with his guests, the good man learned to glow,
And quite forgot their vices in their woe;
Careless their merits or their faults to scan,
His pity gave ere charity began.

The family of the worthy pastor consisted of five sons and three daughters. Henry, the eldest, was the good man's pride and hope, and he tasked his slender means to the utmost in educating him for a learned and distinguished career. Oliver was the second son, and seven years younger than Henry, who was the guide and protector of his childhood, and to whom he was most tenderly attached throughout life.

Oliver's education began when he was about three years old; that is to say, he was gathered under the wings of one of those good old motherly dames, found in every village, who cluck together the whole callow brood of the neighborhood to teach them their letters and keep them out of harm's way. Mistress Elizabeth Delap, for that was her name, flourished in this capacity for upward of fifty years, and it was the pride and boast of her declining days, when nearly ninety years of age, that she was the first that had put a book (doubtless a hornbook) into Goldsmith's hands. Apparently he did not much profit by it, for she confessed he was one of the dullest boys she had ever dealt with, insomuch that she had sometimes doubted whether it was possible to make any thing of him: a common case with imaginative children, who are apt to be beguiled from the dry abstractions of elementary study by the picturings of the fancy.

At six years of age he passed into the hands of the village schoolmaster, one Thomas (or, as he was commonly and irreverently named, Paddy) Byrne, a capital tutor for a poet. He had been educated for a pedagogue, but had enlisted in the army, served abroad during the wars of Queen Anne's time, and risen to the rank of quartermaster of a regiment in Spain. At the return of peace, having no longer exercise for the sword, he resumed the ferule, and drilled the urchin populace of Lissoy. Goldsmith is supposed to have had him and his school in view in the following sketch in the Deserted Village:

Beside yon straggling fence that skirts the way,
With blossom'd furze unprofitably gay,
There, in his noisy mansion, skill'd to rule,
The village master taught his little school;

> A man severe he was, and stern to view,
> I knew him well, and every truant knew:
> Well had the boding tremblers learn'd to trace
> The day's disasters in his morning face;
> Full well they laugh'd with counterfeited glee
> At all his jokes, for many a joke had he;
> Full well the busy whisper circling round,
> Convey'd the dismal tidings when he frown'd:
> Yet he was kind, or, if severe in aught,
> The love he bore to learning was in fault;
> The village all declared how much he knew,
> 'Twas certain he could write and cipher too;
> Lands he could measure, terms and tides presage,
> And e'en the story ran that he could gauge:
> In arguing, too, the parson own'd his skill,
> For, e'en though vanquished, he could argue still;
> While words of learned length and thund'ring sound
> Amazed the gazing rustics ranged around—
> And still they gazed, and still the wonder grew,
> That one small head could carry all he knew.

There are certain whimsical traits in the character of Byrne not given in the foregoing sketch. He was fond of talking of his vagabond wanderings in foreign lands, and had brought with him from the wars a world of campaigning stories, of which he was generally the hero, and which he would deal forth to his wondering scholars when he ought to have been teaching them their lessons. These travellers' tales had a powerful effect upon the vivid imagination of Goldsmith, and awakened an unconquerable passion for wandering and seeking adventure.

Byrne was, moreover, of a romantic vein, and exceedingly superstitious. He was deeply versed in the fairy superstitions which abound in Ireland, all which he professed implicitly to believe. Under his tuition Goldsmith soon became almost as great a proficient in fairy lore. From this branch of good-for-nothing knowledge, his studies, by an easy transition, extended to the histories of robbers, pirates, smugglers, and the whole race of Irish rogues and rapparees. Every thing, in short, that savored of romance, fable, and adventure, was congenial to his poetic mind, and took instant root there; but the slow plants of useful knowledge were apt to be overrun, if not choked, by the weeds of his quick imagination.

Another trait of his motley preceptor, Byrne, was a disposition to dabble in poetry, and this likewise was caught by his pupil. Before he was eight years old Goldsmith had contracted a habit of scribbling verses on small scraps of paper, which in a little while he would throw into the fire. A few of these sibylline leaves, however, were rescued from the flames and conveyed to his mother. The good woman read them with a mother's delight, and saw at once that her son was a genius and a poet. From that time she beset her husband with solicitations to give the boy an education suitable to his talents. The worthy man was already straitened by the costs of instruction of his eldest son Henry, and had intended to bring his second son up to a trade; but the mother would listen to no such thing; as usual, her influence prevailed, and Oliver, instead of being instructed in some humble, but cheerful and gainful handicraft, was devoted to poverty and the Muse.

A severe attack of the smallpox caused him to be taken from under the care of his story-telling preceptor, Byrne. His malady had nearly proved fatal, and his face remained pitted throughout life. On his recovery he was placed under the charge of the Rev. Mr. Griffin, schoolmaster of Elphin, in Roscommon, and became an inmate in the house of his uncle, John Goldsmith, Esq., of Ballyoughter, in that vicinity. He now entered upon studies of a higher order, but without making any uncommon progress. Still a careless, easy facility of disposition, an amusing eccentricity of manners, and a vein of quiet and peculiar humor, rendered him a general favorite, and a trifling incident soon induced his uncle's family to concur in his mother's opinion of his genius.

A number of young folks had assembled at his uncle's to dance. One of the company, named Cummings, played on the violin. In the course of the evening Oliver undertook a hornpipe. His short and clumsy figure, and his face pitted and discolored with the smallpox, rendered him a ludicrous figure in the eyes of the musician, who made merry at his expense, dubbing him his little Æsop. Goldsmith was nettled by the jest, and, stopping short in the hornpipe, exclaimed,

> "Our herald hath proclaimed this saying,
>   See Æesop dancing, and his monkey playing."

The repartee was thought wonderful for a boy of nine years old, and Oliver became forthwith the wit and the bright genius of the family. It was thought a pity he should not receive the same advantages with his elder brother Henry, who had been sent to the University; and, as his father's circumstances would not afford it, several of his relatives, spurred on by the representations of his mother, agreed to contribute towards the expense. The greater part however was borne by his uncle, the Rev. Thomas Contarine. This worthy man had been the college companion of Bishop Berkeley, and was possessed of moderate means, holding the living of Carrick-on-Shannon. He had married the sister of Goldsmith's father but was now a widower with an only child, a daughter named Jane. Contarine was a kind hearted man, with a generosity beyond his means. He took Goldsmith into favor from his infancy; his house was open to him during the holydays; his daughter Jane, two years older than the poet, was his early playmate: and uncle Contarine continued to the last one of his most active, unwavering and generous friends.

Fitted out in a great measure by this considerate relative, Oliver was now transferred to schools of a higher order, to prepare him for the University; first to one at Athlone, kept by the Rev. Mr. Campbell, and, at the end of two years, to one at Edgeworthstown, under the superintendence of the Rev. Patrick Hughes.

Even at these schools his proficiency does not appear to have been brilliant. He was indolent and careless, however, rather than dull, and, on the whole, appears to have been well thought of by his teachers. In his studies he inclined towards the Latin poets and historians; relished Ovid and Horace, and delighted in Livy. He exercised himself with pleasure in reading and translating Tacitus, and was brought to pay attention to style in his compositions by a reproof from his brother Henry, to whom he had written brief and confused letters, and who told him in reply, that if he had but little to say, to endeavor to say that little well.

The career of his brother Henry at the University was enough to stimulate him to exertion. He seemed to be realizing all his father's hopes, and was winning collegiate honors that the good man considered indicative of his future success in life.

In the mean while, Oliver, if not distinguished among his teachers, was popular among his schoolmates. He had a thoughtless generosity extremely captivating to young hearts: his temper was quick and sensitive, and easily offended; but his anger was momentary, and it was impossible for him to harbor resentment. He was the leader of all boyish sports and athletic amusements, especially ball-playing, and he was foremost in all mischievous pranks. Many years afterward, an old man, Jack Fitzimmons, one of the directors of the sports and keeper of the ball-court at Ballymahon, used to boast of having been schoolmate of "Noll Goldsmith," as he called him, and would dwell with vainglory on one of their exploits, in robbing the orchard of Tirlicken, an old family residence of Lord Annaly. The exploit, however, had nearly involved disastrous consequences; for the crew of juvenile depredators were captured, like Shakspeare and his deer-stealing colleagues; and nothing but the respectability of Goldsmith's connections saved him from the punishment that would have awaited more plebeian delinquents.

An amusing incident is related as occurring in Goldsmith's last journey homeward from Edgeworthstown. His father's house was about twenty miles distant; the road lay through a rough country, impassable for carriages. Goldsmith procured a horse for the journey, and a friend furnished him with a guinea for travelling expenses. He was but a stripling of sixteen, and being thus suddenly mounted on horseback, with money in his pocket, it is no wonder that his head was turned. He determined to play the man, and to spend his money in independent traveller's style. Accordingly, instead of pushing directly for home, he halted for the night at the little town of Ardagh, and, accosting the first person he met, inquired, with somewhat of a consequential air, for the best house in the place. Unluckily, the person he had accosted was one Kelly, a notorious wag, who was quartered in the family of one Mr. Featherstone, a gentleman of fortune. Amused with the self-consequence of the stripling, and willing to play off a practical joke at his expense, he directed him to what was literally "the best house in the place," namely, the family mansion of Mr. Featherstone. Goldsmith accordingly rode up to what he supposed to be an inn, ordered his horse to be taken to the stable, walked into the parlor, seated himself by the fire, and demanded what he could have for supper. On ordinary occasions he was diffident and even awkward in his manners, but here he was "at ease in his inn," and felt called upon to show his manhood and enact the experienced traveller. His person was by no means calculated to play off his pretensions, for he was short and thick, with a pock-marked face, and an air and carriage by no means of a distinguished cast. The owner of the house, however, soon discovered his whimsical mistake, and, being a man of humor, determined to indulge it, especially as he accidentally learned that this intruding guest was the son of an old acquaintance.

Accordingly, Goldsmith was "fooled to the top of his bent," and permitted to have full sway throughout the evening. Never was schoolboy more elated. When supper was served, he most condescendingly insisted that the landlord, his wife and daughter should partake, and ordered a bottle of wine to crown the repast and benefit the house. His last flourish was on going to bed, when he gave especial orders to have a hot cake at breakfast. His confusion and dismay, on discovering the next morning that he had been swaggering in this free and easy way in the house of a private gentleman, may be readily conceived. True to his habit of turning the events of his life to literary account, we find this chapter of ludicrous blunders and cross purposes dramatized many years afterward in his admirable comedy of "She Stoops to Conquer, or the Mistakes of a Night."

CHAPTER II

While Oliver was making his way somewhat negligently through the schools, his elder brother Henry was rejoicing his father's heart by his career at the University. He soon distinguished himself at the examinations, and obtained a scholarship in 1743. This is a collegiate distinction which serves as a stepping-stone in any of the learned professions, and which leads to advancement in the University should the individual choose to remain there. His father now trusted that he would push forward for that comfortable provision, a fellowship, and thence to higher dignities and emoluments. Henry, however, had the improvidence or the "unworldliness" of his race: returning to the country during the succeeding vacation, he married for love, relinquished, of course, all his collegiate prospects and advantages, set up a school in his father's neighborhood, and buried his talents and acquirements for the remainder of his life in a curacy of forty pounds a year.

Another matrimonial event occurred not long afterward in the Goldsmith family, to disturb the equanimity of its worthy head. This was the clandestine marriage of his daughter Catherine with a young gentleman of the name of Hodson, who had been confided to the care of her brother Henry to complete his studies. As the youth was of wealthy parentage, it was thought a lucky match for the Goldsmith family; but the tidings of the event stung the bride's father to the soul. Proud of his integrity, and jealous of that good name which was his chief possession, he saw himself and his family subjected to the degrading suspicion of having abused a trust reposed in them to promote a mercenary match. In the first transports of his feelings, he is said to have uttered a wish that his daughter might never have a child to bring like shame and sorrow on her head. The hasty wish, so contrary to the usual benignity of the man, was recalled and repented of almost as soon as uttered; but it was considered baleful in its effects by the superstitious neighborhood; for, though his daughter bore three children, they all died before her.

A more effectual measure was taken by Mr. Goldsmith to ward off the apprehended imputation, but one which imposed a heavy burden on his family. This was to furnish a marriage portion of four hundred pounds, that his daughter might not be said to have entered her husband's family empty-handed. To raise the sum in cash was impossible;

but he assigned to Mr. Hodson his little farm and the income of his tithes until the marriage portion should be paid. In the mean time, as his living did not amount to £200 per annum, he had to practise the strictest economy to pay off gradually this heavy tax incurred by his nice sense of honor.

The first of his family to feel the effects of this economy was Oliver. The time had now arrived for him to be sent to the University; and, accordingly, on the 11th June, 1745, when seventeen years of age, he entered Trinity College, Dublin; but his father was no longer able to place him there as a pensioner, as he had done his eldest son Henry; he was obliged, therefore, to enter him as a sizer, or "poor scholar." He was lodged in one of the top rooms adjoining the library of the building, numbered 35, where it is said his name may still be seen, scratched by himself upon a window frame.

A student of this class is taught and boarded gratuitously, and has to pay but a very small sum for his room. It is expected, in return for these advantages, that he will be a diligent student, and render himself useful in a variety of ways. In Trinity College, at the time of Goldsmith's admission, several derogatory, and, indeed, menial offices were exacted from the sizer, as if the college sought to indemnify itself for conferring benefits by inflicting indignities. He was obliged to sweep part of the courts in the morning; to carry up the dishes from the kitchen to the fellows' table, and to wait in the hall until that body had dined. His very dress marked the inferiority of the "poor student" to his happier classmates. It was a black gown of course stuff without sleeves, and a plain black cloth cap without a tassel. We can conceive nothing more odious and ill judged than these distinctions, which attached the idea of degradation to poverty, and placed the indigent youth of merit below the worthless minion of fortune. They were calculated to wound and irritate the noble mind, and to render the base mind baser.

Indeed, the galling effect of these servile tasks upon youths of proud spirits and quick sensibilities became at length too notorious to be disregarded. About fifty years since, on a Trinity Sunday, a number of persons were assembled to witness the college ceremonies; and as a sizer was carrying up a dish of meat to the fellows' table, a burly citizen in the crowd made some sneering observation on the servility of his office. Stung to the quick, the high-spirited youth instantly flung the dish and its contents at the head of the sneerer. The sizer was sharply reprimanded for this outbreak of wounded pride, but the degrading task was from that day forward very properly consigned to menial hands.

It was with the utmost repugnance that Goldsmith entered college in this capacity. His shy and sensitive nature was affected by the inferior station he was doomed to hold among his gay and opulent fellow-students, and he became, at times, moody and despondent. A recollection of these early mortifications induced him, in after years, most strongly to dissuade his brother Henry, the clergyman, from sending a son to college on a like footing. "If he has ambition, strong passions, and an exquisite sensibility of contempt, do not send him there, unless you have no other trade for him except your own."

To add to his annoyances, the fellow of the college who had the peculiar control of his studies, the Rev. Theaker Wilder, was a man of violent and capricious temper, and of diametrically opposite tastes. The tutor was devoted to the exact sciences; Goldsmith was for the classics. Wilder endeavored to force his favorite studies upon the student by harsh means suggested by his own coarse and savage nature. He abused him in presence of the class as ignorant and stupid; ridiculed him as awkward and ugly, and at times in the transports of his temper indulged in personal violence. The effect was to aggravate a passive distaste into a positive aversion. Goldsmith was loud in expressing his contempt for mathematics and his dislike of ethics and logic; and the prejudices thus imbibed continued through life. Mathematics he always pronounced as a science to which the meanest intellects were competent.

A truer cause of this distaste for the severer studies may probably be found in his natural indolence and his love of convivial pleasures. "I was a lover of mirth, good humour, and even sometimes of fun," said he, "from my childhood." He sang a good song, was a boon companion, and could not resist any temptation to social enjoyment. He endeavored to persuade himself that learning and dulness went hand in hand, and that genius was not to be put in harness. Even in riper years, when the consciousness of his own deficiencies ought to have convinced him of the importance of early study, he speaks slightingly of college honors.

"A lad," says he, "whose passions are not strong enough in youth to mislead him from that path of science which his tutors, and not his inclination, have chalked out, by four or five years' perseverance will probably obtain every advantage and honour his college can bestow. I would compare the man whose youth has been thus passed in the tranquillity of dispassionate prudence, to liquors that never ferment, and, consequently, continue always muddy."

The death of his worthy father, which took place early in 1747, rendered Goldsmith's situation at college extremely irksome. His mother was left with little more than the means of providing for the wants of her household, and was unable to furnish him any remittances. He would have been compelled, therefore, to leave college, had it not been for the occasional contributions of friends, the foremost among whom was his generous and warm-hearted uncle Contarine. Still these supplies were so scanty and precarious, that in the intervals between them he was put to great straits. He had two college associates from whom he would occasionally borrow small sums; one was an early schoolmate by the name of Beatty; the other a cousin and the chosen companion of his frolicks, Robert (or rather Bob) Bryanton of Bally-mulvey House near Ballymahon. When these casual supplies failed him he was more than once obliged to raise funds for his immediate wants by pawning his books. At times he sank into despondency, but he had what he termed "a knack at hoping," which soon buoyed him up again. He began now to resort to his poetical vein as a source of profit, scribbling street-ballads, which he privately sold for five shillings each at a shop which dealt in such small wares of literature. He felt an author's affection for these unowned bantlings, and we are told that he would stroll privately through the streets at night to hear them sung, listening to the comments and criticisms of by-standers, and observing the degree of applause which each received.

Edmund Burke was a fellow-student with Goldsmith at the college. Neither the statesman nor the poet gave promise of their future celebrity, though Burke certainly surpassed his contemporary in industry and application, and evinced more disposition for self-improvement, associating himself with a number of his fellow students in a debating club, in which they discussed literary topics, and exercised themselves in composition.

Goldsmith may likewise have belonged to this association, but his propensity was rather to mingle with the gay and thoughtless. On one occasion we find him implicated in an affair that came nigh produc-ing his expulsion. A report was brought to college that a scholar was in the hands of the bailiffs. This was an insult in which every gownsman felt himself involved. A number of the scholars flew to arms, and sallied forth to battle, headed by a hair-brained fellow nicknamed Gallows Walsh, noted for his aptness at mischief and fondness for riot. The stronghold of the bailiff was carried by storm, the scholar set at liberty, and the delinquent catchpole borne off captive to the college, where, having no pump to put him under, they satisfied the demands of collegiate law by ducking him in an old cistern.

Flushed with this signal victory, Gallows Walsh now harangued his followers, and proposed to break open Newgate, or the Black Dog, as the prison was called, and effect a general jail delivery. He was answered by shouts of concurrence, and away went the throng of madcap youngsters, fully bent upon putting an end to the tyranny of law. They were joined by the mob of the city, and made an attack upon the prison with true Irish precipitation and thoughtlessness, never having provided themselves with cannon to batter its stone walls. A few shots from the prison brought them to their senses, and they beat a hasty retreat, two of the townsmen being killed and several wounded.

A severe scrutiny of this affair took place at the University. Four students, who had been ringleaders, were expelled; four others, who had been prominent in the affray, were publicly admonished; among the latter was the unlucky Goldsmith.

To make up for this disgrace, he gained, within a month afterward, one of the minor prizes of the college. It is true it was one of the very smallest, amounting in pecuniary value to but thirty shillings, but it was the first distinction he had gained in his whole collegiate career. This turn of success and sudden influx of wealth proved too much for the head of our poor student. He forthwith gave a supper and dance at his chamber to a number of young persons of both sexes from the city, in direct violation of college rules. The unwonted sound of the fiddle reached the ears of the implacable Wilder. He rushed to the scene of unhallowed festivity, inflicted corporal punishment on the "father of the feast," and turned his astonished guests neck and heels out of doors.

This filled the measure of poor Goldsmith's humiliations; he felt degraded both within college and without. He dreaded the ridicule of his fellow students for the ludicrous termination of his orgie, and he was ashamed to meet his city acquaintances after the degrading chastisement received in their presence, and after their own ignominious expulsion. Above all, he felt it impossible to submit any longer to the insulting tyranny of Wilder: he determined, therefore, to leave, not merely the college, but also his native land, and to bury what he conceived to be his irretrievable disgrace in some distant country. He accordingly sold his books and clothes, and sallied forth from the college walls the very next day, intending to embark at Cork for—he scarce knew where—America, or any other part beyond sea. With his usual heedless imprudence, however, he loitered about Dublin until his finances were reduced to a shilling; with this amount of specie he set out on his journey.

For three whole days he subsisted on his shilling; when that was spent, he parted with some of the clothes from his back, until, reduced almost to nakedness, he was four-and-twenty hours without food, insomuch that he declared a handful of gray pease, given to him by a girl at a wake, was one of the most delicious repasts he had ever tasted. Hunger, fatigue, and destitution brought down his spirit and calmed his anger. Fain would he have retraced his steps, could he have done so with any salvo for the lingerings of his pride. In his extremity he conveyed to his brother Henry information of his distress, and of the rash project on which he had set out. His affectionate brother hastened to his relief; furnished him with money and clothes; soothed his feelings with gentle counsel; prevailed upon him to return to college, and effected an indifferent reconciliation between him and Wilder.

After this irregular sally upon life he remained nearly two years longer at the University, giving proofs of talent in occasional translations from the classics, for one of which he received a premium, awarded only to those who are the first in literary merit. Still he never made much figure at college, his natural disinclination to study being increased by the harsh treatment he continued to experience from his tutor.

Among the anecdotes told of him while at college is one indicative of that prompt, but thoughtless and often whimsical benevolence which throughout life formed one of the most eccentric, yet endearing points of his character. He was engaged to breakfast one day with a college intimate, but failed to make his appearance. His friend repaired to his room, knocked at the door, and was bidden to enter. To his surprise, he found Goldsmith in his bed, immersed to his chin in feathers. A serio-comic story explained the circumstance. In the course of the preceding evening's stroll he had met with a woman with five children, who implored his charity. Her husband was in the hospital; she was just from the country, a stranger, and destitute, without food or shelter for her helpless offspring. This was too much for the kind heart of Goldsmith. He was almost as poor as herself, it is true, and had no money in his pocket; but he brought her to the college gate, gave her the blankets from his bed to cover her little brood, and part of his clothes for her to sell and purchase food; and, finding himself cold during the night, had cut open his bed and buried himself among the feathers.

At length, on the 27th of February, 1749, O. S., he was admitted to the degree of Bachelor of Arts, and took his final leave of the University. He was freed from college rule, that emancipation so ardently coveted by the thoughtless student, and which too generally launches him amid the cares, the hardships, and vicissitudes of life. He was freed too from the brutal tyranny of Wilder. If his kind and placable nature could retain any resentment for past injuries, it might have been gratified by learning subsequently that the passionate career of Wilder was terminated by a violent death in the course of a dissolute brawl; but Goldsmith took no delight in the misfortunes even of his enemies.

He now returned to his friends, no longer the student to sport away the happy interval of vacation, but the anxious man, who is henceforth to shift for himself and make his way through the world. In fact, he had no legitimate home to return to. At the death of his father,

the paternal house at Lissoy, in which Goldsmith had passed his childhood, had been taken by Mr. Hodson, who had married his sister Catherine. His mother had removed to Ballymahon, where she occupied a
small house, and had to practice the severest frugality. His elder brother
Henry served the curacy and taught the school of his late father's parish,
and lived in narrow circumstances at Goldsmith's birthplace, the old
goblin-house at Pallas.

None of his relatives were in circumstances to aid him with any thing
more than a temporary home, and the aspect of every one seemed
somewhat changed. In fact, his career at college had disappointed his
friends, and they began to doubt his being the great genius they had
fancied him. He whimsically alludes to this circumstance in that piece
of autobiography, "The Man in Black," in the Citizen of the World.

"The first opportunity my father had of finding his expectations disappointed was in the middling figure I made at the University: he had
flattered himself that he should soon see me rising into the foremost
rank in literary reputation, but was mortified to find me utterly unnoticed and unknown. His disappointment might have been partly
ascribed to his having overrated my talents, and partly to my dislike
of mathematical reasonings at a time when my imagination and memory, yet unsatisfied, were more eager after new objects than desirous
of reasoning upon those I knew. This, however, did not please my
tutors, who observed, indeed, that I was a little dull, but at the same
time allowed that I seemed to be very good-natured, and had no
harm in me."*

The only one of his relatives who did not appear to lose faith in him
was his uncle Contarine. "This kind and considerate man," it is said,
"saw in him a warmth of heart requiring some skill to direct, and a
latent genius that wanted time to mature, and these impressions none of
his subsequent follies and irregularities wholly obliterated." His purse
and affection, therefore, as well as his house, were now open to him,
and he became his chief counsellor and director after his father's death.
He urged him to prepare for holy orders, and others of his relatives
concurred in the advice. Goldsmith had a settled repugnance to a
clerical life. This has been ascribed by some to conscientious scruples,
not considering himself of a temper and frame of mind for such a
sacred office: others attributed it to his roving propensities, and his
desire to visit foreign countries; he himself gives a whimsical objection
in his biography of the "Man in Black:"—"To be obliged to wear a
long wig when I liked a short one, or a black coat when I generally

* Citizen of the World, letter xxvii.

dressed in brown, I thought such a restraint upon my liberty that I absolutely rejected the proposal."

In effect, however, his scruples were overruled, and he agreed to qualify himself for the office. He was now only twenty one, and must pass two years of probation. They were two years of rather loitering unsettled life. Sometimes he was at Lissoy, participating with thoughtless enjoyment in the rural sports and occupations of his brother-in-law, Mr. Hodson; sometimes he was with his brother Henry, at the old goblin mansion at Pallas, assisting him occasionally in his school. The early marriage and unambitious retirement of Henry, though so subversive of the fond plans of his father, had proved happy in their results. He was already surrounded by a blooming family; he was contented with his lot, beloved by his parishioners, and lived in the daily practice of all the amiable virtues, and the immediate enjoyment of their reward. Of the tender affection inspired in the breast of Goldsmith by the constant kindness of this excellent brother, and of the longing recollection with which, in the lonely wanderings of after years, he looked back upon this scene of domestic felicity, we have a touching instance in the well-known opening to his poem of "The Traveller:"

> Remote, unfriended, melancholy, slow,
> Or by the lazy Scheld or wandering Po;
>
> ❋   ❋   ❋   ❋   ❋   ❋
>
> Where'er I roam, whatever realms to see,
> My heart untravell'd fondly turns to thee;
> Still to my brother turns with ceaseless pain,
> And drags at each remove a lengthening chain.
>
> Eternal blessings crown my earliest friend,
> And round his dwelling guardian saints attend;
> Bless'd be that spot, where cheerful guests retire
> To pause from toil, and trim their evening fire;
> Bless'd that abode, where want and pain repair,
> And every stranger finds a ready chair:
> Bless'd be those feasts with simple plenty crown'd,
> Where all the ruddy family around
> Laugh at the jests or pranks that never fail,
> Or sigh with pity at some mournful tale;
> Or press the bashful stranger to his food,
> And learn the luxury of doing good.

During this loitering life Goldsmith pursued no study, but rather amused himself with miscellaneous reading; such as biography, travels,

poetry, novels, plays—every thing, in short, that administered to the
imagination. Sometimes he strolled along the banks of the river Inny;
where in after years when he had become famous, his favorite seats
and haunts used to be pointed out. Often he joined in the rustic sports
of the villagers and became adroit at throwing the sledge, a favorite
feat of activity and strength in Ireland. Recollections of these "healthful
sports" we find in his "Deserted Village:"

> How often have I bless'd the coming day,
> When toil remitting lent its turn to play,
> And all the village train, from labour free,
> Led up their sports beneath the spreading tree;
> And many a gambol frolicked o'er the ground,
> And sleights of art and feats of strength went round.

A boon companion in all his rural amusements was his cousin and
college crony, Robert Bryanton, with whom he sojourned occasionally
at Ballymulvey House in the neighborhood. They used to make excursions about the country on foot, sometimes fishing, sometimes hunting
otter in the Inny. They got up a country club at the little inn of Ballymahon, of which Goldsmith soon became the oracle and prime wit;
astonishing his unlettered associates by his learning, and being considered capital at a song and a story. From the rustic conviviality of
the inn at Ballymahon and the company which used to assemble there
it is surmised that he took some hints in after life for his picturing
of Tony Lumpkin and his associates: "Dick Muggins the exciseman,
Jack Slang the horse doctor, little Aminidab that grinds the music box
and Tom Twist that spins the pewter platter." Nay, it is thought that
Tony's drinking song at the "Three Jolly Pigeons" was but a revival of
one of the convivial catches at Ballymahon:

> Then come put the jorum about,
>   And let us be merry and clever,
> Our hearts and our liquors are stout,
>   Here's the Three Jolly Pigeons for ever.
> Let some cry of woodcock or hare,
>   Your bustards, your ducks, and your widgeons;
> But of all the gay birds in the air,
>   Here's a health to the Three Jolly Pigeons.
>   Toroddle, toroddle, toroll.

Notwithstanding all these accomplishments and this rural popularity,
his friends began to shake their heads and shrug their shoulders

when they spoke of him; and his brother Henry noted with any thing but satisfaction his frequent visits to the club at Ballymahon. He emerged however unscathed from this dangerous ordeal more fortunate in this respect than his comrade Bryanton; but he retained throughout life a fondness for clubs: often too in the course of his checkered career he looked back to this period of rural sports and careless enjoyments, as one of the few sunny spots of his cloudy life; and though he ultimately rose to associate with birds of a finer feather, his heart would still yearn in secret after the THREE JOLLY PIGEONS.

CHAPTER III

The time was now arrived for Goldsmith to apply for orders, and he presented himself accordingly before the Bishop of Elphin for ordination. We have stated his great objection to clerical life, the obligation to wear a black coat; and, whimsical as it may appear, dress seems in fact to have formed an obstacle to his entrance into the church. He had ever a passion for clothing his sturdy but awkward little person in gay colors; and on this solemn occasion, when it was to be supposed his garb would be of suitable gravity, he appeared luminously arrayed in scarlet breeches! He was rejected by the bishop: some say for want of sufficient studious preparation; his rambles and frolicks with Bob Bryanton and his revels with the club at Ballymahon having been much in the way of his theological studies; others attribute his rejection to reports of his college irregularities, which the Bishop had received from his old tyrant Wilder; but those who look into the matter with more knowing eyes pronounce the scarlet breeches to have been the fundamental objection. "My friends," says Goldsmith speaking through his humorous representative, the "Man in Black"—"my friends were now perfectly satisfied I was undone; and yet they thought it a pity for one that had not the least harm in him, and was so very good natured." His uncle Contarine, however, still remained unwavering in his kindness, though much less sanguine in his expectations. He now looked round for a humbler sphere of action, and through his influence and exertions Oliver was received as tutor in the family of a Mr. Flinn, a gentleman of the neighborhood. The situation was apparently respectable; he had his seat at the table; and joined the family in their domestic recreations and their evening game at cards. There was a servility however in his position, which was not to his taste: nor did his deference for the family increase upon familiar intercourse. He charged a member of it with unfair play at cards. A violent altercation ensued, which ended in his throwing up his situation as tutor. On being paid off he found himself in possession of an unheard of amount of money. His wandering propensity and his desire to see the world were instantly in the ascendency. Without communicating his plans or intentions to his friends he procured a good horse, and with thirty pounds in his pocket made his second sally forth into the world.

The worthy niece and housekeeper of the hero of La Mancha could not have been more surprised and dismayed at one of the Don's clandestine expeditions, than were the mother and friends of Goldsmith when they heard of his mysterious departure. Weeks elapsed, and nothing was seen or heard of him. It was feared that he had left the country on one of his wandering freaks, and his poor mother was reduced almost to despair, when one day he arrived at her door almost as forlorn in plight as the prodigal son. Of his thirty pounds not a shilling was left; and, instead of the goodly steed on which he had issued forth on his errantry, he was mounted on a sorry little pony, which he had nicknamed Fiddle-back. As soon as his mother was well assured of his safety, she rated him soundly for his inconsiderate conduct. His brothers and sisters, who were tenderly attached to him, interfered, and succeeded in mollifying her ire; and whatever lurking anger the good dame might have, was no doubt effectually vanquished by the following whimsical narrative which he drew up at his brother's house and dispatched to her:

"My dear mother, if you will sit down and calmly listen to what I say, you shall be fully resolved in every one of those many questions you have asked me. I went to Cork and converted my horse, which you prize so much higher than Fiddle-back, into cash, took my passage in a ship bound for America, and, at the same time, paid the captain for my freight and all the other expenses of my voyage. But it so happened that the wind did not answer for three weeks; and you know, mother, that I could not command the elements. My misfortune was, that, when the wind served, I happened to be with a party in the country, and my friend the captain never inquired after me, but set sail with as much indifference as if I had been on board. The remainder of my time I employed in the city and its environs, viewing every thing curious, and you know no one can starve while he has money in his pocket.

"Reduced, however, to my last two guineas, I began to think of my dear mother and friends whom I had left behind me, and so bought that generous beast Fiddle-back, and bade adieu to Cork with only five shillings in my pocket. This, to be sure, was but a scanty allowance for man and horse towards a journey of above a hundred miles; but I did not despair, for I knew I must find friends on the road.

"I recollected particularly an old and faithful acquaintance I made at college, who had often and earnestly pressed me to spend a summer with him, and he lived but eight miles from Cork. This circumstance of vicinity he would expatiate on to me with peculiar emphasis. 'We shall,' says he, 'enjoy the delights of both city and country, and you shall command my stable and my purse.'

"However, upon the way I met a poor woman all in tears, who told me her husband had been arrested for a debt he was not able to pay, and that his eight children must now starve, bereaved as they were of his industry, which had been their only support. I thought myself at home, being not far from my good friend's house, and therefore parted with a moiety of all my store; and pray, mother, ought I not to have given her the other half crown, for what she got would be of little use to her? However, I soon arrived at the mansion of my affectionate friend, guarded by the vigilance of a huge mastiff, who flew at me and would have torn me to pieces but for the assistance of a woman, whose countenance was not less grim than that of the dog; yet she with great humanity relieved me from the jaws of this Cerberus, and was prevailed on to carry up my name to her master.

"Without suffering me to wait long, my old friend, who was then recovering from a severe fit of sickness, came down in his nightcap, nightgown, and slippers, and embraced me with the most cordial welcome, showed me in, and, after giving me a history of his indisposition, assured me that he considered himself peculiarly fortunate in having under his roof the man he most loved on the earth, and whose stay with him must, above all things, contribute to perfect his recovery. I now repented sorely I had not given the poor woman the other half crown, as I thought all my bills of humanity would be punctually answered by this worthy man. I revealed to him my whole soul; I opened to him all my distresses; and freely owned that I had but one half crown in my pocket; but that now, like a ship after weathering out the storm, I considered myself secure in a safe and hospitable harbour. He made no answer, but walked about the room, rubbing his hands as one in deep study. This I imputed to the sympathetic feelings of a tender heart, which increased my esteem for him, and, as that increased, I gave the most favourable interpretation to his silence. I construed it into delicacy of sentiment, as if he dreaded to wound my pride by expressing his commiseration in words, leaving his generous conduct to speak for itself.

"It now approached six o'clock in the evening; and as I had eaten no breakfast, and as my spirits were raised, my appetite for dinner grew uncommonly keen. At length the old woman came into the room with two plates, one spoon, and a dirty cloth, which she laid upon the table. This appearance, without increasing my spirits, did not diminish my appetite. My protectress soon returned with a small bowl of sago, a small porringer of sour milk, a loaf of stale brown bread, and the heel of an old cheese all over crawling with mites. My friend apologized that his illness obliged him to live on slops, and that better fare was not in the house; observing, at the same time, that a milk diet

was certainly the most healthful; and at eight o'clock he again recommended a regular life, declaring that for his part he would *lie down
with the lamb and rise with the lark.* My hunger was at this time so
exceedingly sharp that I wished for another slice of the loaf, but was
obliged to go to bed without even that refreshment.

"The lenten entertainment I had received made me resolve to depart
as soon as possible; accordingly, next morning, when I spoke of going,
he did not oppose my resolution; he rather commended my design,
adding some very sage counsel upon the occasion. 'To be sure,' said he,
'the longer you stay away from your mother, the more you will grieve
her and your other friends; and possibly they are already afflicted at
hearing of this foolish expedition you have made.' Notwithstanding all
this, and without any hope of softening such a sordid heart, I again
renewed the tale of my distress, and asking 'how he thought I could
travel above a hundred miles upon one half crown?' I begged to borrow
a single guinea, which I assured him should be repaid with thanks.
'And you know, sir,' said I, 'it is no more than I have done for you.'
To which he firmly answered, 'Why, look you, Mr. Goldsmith, that is
neither here nor there. I have paid you all you ever lent me, and this
sickness of mine has left me bare of cash. But I have bethought myself
of a conveyance for you; sell your horse, and I will furnish you a
much better one to ride on.' I readily grasped at his proposal, and
begged to see the nag; on which he led me to his bedchamber, and from
under the bed he pulled out a stout oak stick. 'Here he is,' said he;
'take this in your hand, and it will carry you to your mother's with
more safety than such a horse as you ride.' I was in doubt, when I
got it into my hand, whether I should not, in the first place, apply it
to his pate; but a rap at the street door made the wretch fly to it, and
when I returned to the parlour, he introduced me, as if nothing
of the kind had happened, to the gentleman who entered, as Mr.
Goldsmith, his most ingenious and worthy friend, of whom he had so
often heard him speak with rapture. I could scarcely compose myself;
and must have betrayed indignation in my mien to the stranger, who
was a counsellor at law in the neighbourhood, a man of engaging aspect
and polite address.

"After spending an hour, he asked my friend and me to dine with him
at his house. This I declined at first, as I wished to have no farther
communication with my old hospitable friend; but at the solicitation of
both I at last consented, determined as I was by two motives; one, that I
was prejudiced in favour of the looks and manner of the counsellor; and
the other, that I stood in need of a comfortable dinner. And there,
indeed, I found every thing I could wish, abundance without profusion,
and elegance without affectation. In the evening, when my old friend,

who had eaten very plentifully at his neighbour's table, but talked again of lying down with the lamb, made a motion to me for retiring, our generous host requested I should take a bed with him, upon which I plainly told my old friend that he might go home and take care of the horse he had given me, but that I should never re-enter his doors. He went away with a laugh, leaving me to add this to the other little things the counsellor already knew of his plausible neighbour.

"And now, my dear mother, I found sufficient to reconcile me to all my follies; for here I spent three whole days. The counsellor had two sweet girls to his daughters, who played enchantingly on the harpsichord; and yet it was but a melancholy pleasure I felt the first time I heard them; for that being the first time also that either of them had touched the instrument since their mother's death, I saw the tears in silence trickle down their father's cheeks. I every day endeavoured to go away, but every day was pressed and obliged to stay. On my going, the counsellor offered me his purse, with a horse and servant to convey me home; but the latter I declined, and only took a guinea to bear my necessary expenses on the road.

"OLIVER GOLDSMITH.

"To Mrs. Anne Goldsmith, Ballymahon."

Such is the story given by the poet-errant of this his second sally in quest of adventures. We cannot but think it was here and there touched up a little with the fanciful pen of the future essayist, with a view to amuse his mother and soften her vexation; but even in these respects it is valuable as showing the early play of his humor, and his happy knack of extracting sweets from that worldly experience which to others yields nothing but bitterness.

CHAPTER IV

A new consultation was held among Goldsmith's friends as to his future course, and it was determined he should try the law. His uncle Contarine agreed to advance the necessary funds, and actually furnished him with fifty pounds, with which he set off for London to enter on his studies at the Temple. Unfortunately, he fell in company at Dublin with a Roscommon acquaintance, one whose wits had been sharpened about town, who beguiled him into a gambling house, and soon left him as penniless as when he bestrode the redoubtable Fiddle-back.

He was so ashamed of this fresh instance of gross heedlessness and imprudence, that he remained some time in Dublin without communicating to his friends his destitute condition. They heard of it, however, and he was invited back to the country, and indulgently forgiven by his generous uncle, but less readily by his mother, who was mortified and disheartened at seeing all her early hopes of him so repeatedly blighted. His brother Henry, too, began to lose patience at these successive failures, resulting from thoughtless indiscretion; and a quarrel took place, which for some time interrupted their usually affectionate intercourse.

The only home where poor erring Goldsmith still received a welcome was the parsonage of his affectionate forgiving uncle. Here he used to talk of literature with the good simple hearted man and delight him and his daughter with his verses. Jane, his early playmate, was now the woman grown; their intercourse was of a more intellectual kind than formerly; they discoursed of poetry and music; she played on the harpsichord, and he accompanied her with his flute. The music may not have been very artistic, as he never performed but by ear; it had probably as much merit as the poetry which, if we may judge by the following specimen, was as yet but juvenile:

TO A YOUNG LADY ON VALENTINE'S DAY,

WITH THE DRAWING OF A HEART.

With submission at your shrine,
Comes a heart your Valentine;

From the side where once it grew,
See it panting flies to you.
Take it, fair one, to your breast,
Sooth the fluttering thing to rest;
Let the gentle, spotless toy,
Be your sweetest, greatest joy;
Every night when wrapp'd in sleep,
Next your heart the conquest keep;
Or if dreams your fancy move,
Hear it whisper me and love;
Then in pity to the swain,
Who must heartless else remain,
Soft as gentle dewy show'rs,
Slow descend on April flow'rs;
Soft as gentle riv'lets glide,
Steal unnoticed to my side;
If the gem you have to spare,
Take your own and place it there.

If this Valentine was intended for the fair Jane, and expressive of a tender sentiment indulged by the stripling poet, it was unavailing; as not long afterwards she was married to a Mr. Lawder. We trust however it was but a poetical passion of that transient kind which grows up in idleness and exhales itself in rhyme. While Oliver was thus piping and poetizing at the parsonage, his uncle Contarine received a visit from Dean Goldsmith of Cloyne; a kind of magnate in the wide but improvident family connection, throughout which his word was law and almost gospel. This august dignitary was pleased to discover signs of talent in Oliver, and suggested that, as he had attempted divinity and law without success, he should now try physic. The advice came from too important a source to be disregarded, and it was determined to send him to Edinburgh to commence his studies. The Dean having given the advice added to it, we trust, his blessing, but no money; that was furnished from the scantier purses of Goldsmith's brother, his sister (Mrs. Hodson) and his ever ready uncle Contarine.

It was in the autumn of 1752 that Goldsmith arrived in Edinburgh. His outset in that city came near adding to the list of his indiscretions and disasters. Having taken lodgings at haphazard, he left his trunk there, containing all his worldly effects, and sallied forth to see the town. After sauntering about the streets until a late hour, he thought of returning home, when, to his confusion, he found he had not acquainted himself with the name either of his landlady or the street in which she lived. Fortunately, in the height of his whimsical perplexity, he

met the cawdy or porter who had carried his trunk, and who now
served him as a guide.

He did not remain long in the lodgings in which he had put up.
The hostess was too adroit at that hocus-pocus of the table which
often is practised in cheap boarding houses. No one could conjure a
single joint through a greater variety of forms. A loin of mutton,
according to Goldsmith's account, would serve him and two fellow
students a whole week. "A brandered chop was served up one day,
a fried steak another, collops with onion sauce a third, and so on
until the fleshy parts were quite consumed, when finally a dish of broth
was manufactured from the bones on the seventh day, and the landlady rested from her labours." Goldsmith had a good humored mode
of taking things, and for a short time amused himself with the shifts
and expedients of his landlady, which struck him in a ludicrous manner; he soon, however, fell in with fellow-students from his own country,
whom he joined at more eligible quarters.

He now attended medical lectures, and attached himself to an association of students called the Medical Society. He set out, as usual, with
the best intentions, but, as usual, soon fell into idle, convivial, thoughtless habits. Edinburgh was indeed a place of sore trial for one of his
temperament. Convivial meetings were all the vogue, and the tavern
was the universal rallying-place of good-fellowship. And then Goldsmith's intimacies lay chiefly among the Irish students, who were
always ready for a wild freak and frolic. Among them he was a prime
favorite and somewhat of a leader, from his exuberance of spirits, his
vein of humor, and his talent at singing an Irish song and telling an
Irish story.

His usual carelessness in money matters attended him. Though his
supplies from home were scanty and irregular, he never could bring
himself into habits of prudence and economy; often he was stripped
of all his present finances at play; often he lavished them away in fits
of unguarded charity or generosity. Sometimes among his boon companions he assumed a ludicrous swagger in money matters, which no
one afterward was more ready than himself to laugh at. At a convivial
meeting with a number of his fellow-students, he suddenly proposed
to draw lots with any one present which of the two should treat the
whole party to the play. The moment the proposition had bolted from
his lips, his heart was in his throat. "To my great though secret joy,"
said he, "they all declined the challenge. Had it been accepted, and
had I proved the loser, a part of my wardrobe must have been pledged
in order to raise the money."

At another of these meetings there was an earnest dispute on the
question of ghosts, some being firm believers in the possibility of

departed spirits returning to visit their friends and familiar haunts. One of the disputants set sail the next day for London, but the vessel put back through stress of weather. His return was unknown except to one of the believers in ghosts, who concerted with him a trick to be played off on the opposite party. In the evening at a meeting of the students the discussion was renewed, and one of the most strenuous opposers of ghosts was asked whether he considered himself proof against ocular demonstration? He persisted in his scoffing. Some solemn process of conjuration was performed, and the comrade supposed to be on his way to London made his appearance. The effect was fatal. The unbeliever fainted at the sight and ultimately went mad. We have no account of what share Goldsmith took in this transaction, at which he was present.

The following letter to his friend Bryanton contains some of Goldsmith's impressions concerning Scotland and its inhabitants, and gives indications of that humor which characterized some of his later writings.

"Robert Bryanton, at Ballymahon, Ireland.

"Edinburgh, September 26th, 1753.
"My dear Bob,

"How many good excuses (and you know I was ever good at an excuse) might I call up to vindicate my past shameful silence. I might tell how I wrote a long letter on my first coming hither, and seem vastly angry at my not receiving an answer; I might allege that business (with business you know I was always pestered) had never given me time to finger a pen. But I suppress those and twenty more as plausible, and as easily invented, since they might be attended with a slight inconvenience of being known to be lies. Let me then speak truth. An hereditary indolence (I have it from the mother's side) has hitherto prevented my writing to you, and still prevents my writing at least twenty-five letters more, due to my friends in Ireland. No turn-spit-dog gets up into his wheel with more reluctance than I sit down to write; yet no dog ever loved the roast meat he turns better than I do him I now address.

"Yet what shall I say now I am entered? Shall I tire you with a description of this unfruitful country; where I must lead you over their hills all brown with heath, or their valleys scarcely able to feed a rabbit? Man alone seems to be the only creature who has arrived to the natural size in this poor soil. Every part of the country presents the same dismal landscape. No grove, nor brook, lend their music to cheer the stranger, or make the inhabitants forget their poverty. Yet with all these disadvantages to call him down to humility, a Scotchman is one of the proudest things alive. The poor have pride ever ready to relieve them. If mankind should happen to despise them, they are masters of their own admiration; and that they can plentifully bestow upon themselves.

"From their pride and poverty, as I take it, results one advantage this country enjoys; namely, the gentlemen here are much better bred than among us. No such character here as our fox-hunters; and they have expressed great surprise when I informed them, that some men in Ireland of one thousand pounds a year, spend their whole lives in running after a hare, and drinking to be drunk. Truly if such a being, equipped in his hunting dress, came among a circle of Scotch gentry, they would behold him with the same astonishment that a countryman does King George on horseback.

"The men here have generally high cheek bones, and are lean and swarthy, fond of action, dancing in particular. Now that I have mentioned dancing, let me say something of their balls, which are very frequent here. When a stranger enters the dancing-hall, he sees one end of the room taken up by the ladies, who sit dismally in a group by themselves;—in the other end stand their pensive partners that are to be;—but no more intercourse between the sexes than there is between two countries at war. The ladies indeed may ogle, and the gentlemen sigh; but an embargo is laid on any closer commerce. At length, to interrupt hostilities, the lady directress, or intendant, or what you will, pitches upon a lady and gentleman to walk a minuet; which they perform with a formality that approaches to despondence. After five or six couple have thus walked the gauntlet, all stand up to country dances; each gentleman furnished with a partner from the aforesaid lady directress; so they dance much, say nothing, and thus concludes our assembly. I told a Scotch gentleman that such profound silence resembled the ancient procession of the Roman matrons in honour of Ceres; and the Scotch gentleman told me, (and, faith, I believe he was right) that I was a very great pedant for my pains.

"Now I am come to the ladies; and to show that I love Scotland, and every thing that belongs to so charming a country, I insist on it, and will give him leave to break my head that denies it—that the Scotch ladies are ten thousand times finer and handsomer than the Irish. To be sure, now, I see your sisters Betty and Peggy vastly surprised at my partiality,—but tell them flatly, I don't value them—or their fine skins, or eyes, or good sense, or ———, a potato;—for I say, and will maintain it; and as a convincing proof (I am in a great passion) of what I assert, the Scotch ladies say it themselves. But to be less serious; where will you find a language so prettily become a pretty mouth as the broad Scotch? And the women here speak it in its highest purity; for instance, teach one of your young ladies at home to pronounce the "Whoar wull I gong?" with a becoming widening of mouth, and I'll lay my life they'll wound every hearer.

"We have no such character here as a coquet, but alas! how many envious prudes! Some days ago I walked into my Lord Kilcoubry's (don't be surprised, my lord is but a glover,)* when the Duchess of Hamilton (that fair who sacrificed her beauty to her ambition, and her inward peace to a title and gilt equipage) passed by in her chariot; her battered husband, or more properly the guardian of her charms, sat by her side. Straight envy began, in the shape of no less than three ladies who sat with me, to find faults in her faultless form.—'For my part,' says the first, 'I think what I always thought, that the Duchess has too much of the red in her complexion.' 'Madam, I am of your opinion,' says the second; 'I think her face has a palish cast too much on the delicate order.' 'And, let me tell you,' added the third lady, whose mouth was puckered up to the size of an issue, 'that the Duchess has fine lips, but she wants a mouth.'—At this every lady drew up her mouth as if going to pronounce the letter P.

"But how ill, my Bob, does it become me to ridicule women with whom I have scarcely any correspondence? There are, 'tis certain, handsome women here; and 'tis certain they have handsome men to keep them company. An ugly and poor man is society only for himself; and such society the world lets me enjoy in great abundance. Fortune has given you circumstances, and nature a person to look charming in the eyes of the fair. Nor do I envy my dear Bob such blessings, while I may sit down and laugh at the world and at myself—the most ridiculous object in it. But you see I am grown downright splenetic, and perhaps the fit may continue till I receive an answer to this. I know you cannot send me much news from Ballymahon, but such as it is, send it all; every thing you send will be agreeable to me.

"Has George Conway put up a sign yet; or John Binley left off drinking drams; or Tom Allen got a new wig? But I leave you to your own choice what to write. While I live, know you have a true friend in yours, &c. &c. &c.

"OLIVER GOLDSMITH.

"P. S. Give my sincere respects (not compliments, do you mind) to your agreeable family, and give my service to my mother if you see her; for, as you express it in Ireland, I have a sneaking kindness for her still. Direct to me, ——, Student in Physic, in Edinburgh."

*William Maclellan, who claimed the title, and whose son succeeded in establishing the claim in 1773. The father is said to have voted at the election of the sixteen Peers for Scotland; and to have sold gloves in the lobby at this and other public assemblages.

Nothing worthy of preservation appeared from his pen during his residence in Edinburgh; and indeed his poetical powers, highly as they had been estimated by his friends, had not as yet produced any thing of superior merit. He made on one occasion a month's excursion to the Highlands. "I set out the first day on foot," says he in a letter to his uncle Contarine, "but an ill-natured corn I have on my toe has for the future prevented that cheap mode of travelling; so the second day I hired a horse, about the size of a ram, and he walked away (trot he could not) as pensive as his master."

During his residence in Scotland his convivial talents gained him at one time attentions in a high quarter, which however he had the good sense to appreciate correctly. "I have spent," says he in one of his letters, "more than a fortnight every second day at the Duke of Hamilton's; but it seems they like me more as a jester than as a companion, so I disdained so servile an employment as unworthy my calling as a physician." Here we again find the origin of another passage in his autobiography under the character of the Man in Black, wherein that worthy figures as a flatterer to a great man. "At first," says he, "I was surprised that the situation of a flatterer at a great man's table could be thought disagreeable; there was no great trouble in listening attentively when his lordship spoke, and laughing when he looked round for applause. This even good manners might have obliged me to perform. I found, however, too soon, his lordship was a greater dunce than myself, and from that moment flattery was at an end. I now rather aimed at setting him right, than at receiving his absurdities with submission: to flatter those we do not know is an easy task; but to flatter our intimate acquaintances, all whose foibles are strongly in our eyes, is drudgery insupportable. Every time I now opened my lips in praise, my falshood went to my conscience; his lordship soon perceived me to be very unfit for his service; I was therefore discharged; my patron at the same time being graciously pleased to observe that he believed I was tolerably good natured, and had not the least harm in me."

After spending two winters at Edinburgh Goldsmith prepared to finish his medical studies on the Continent, for which his uncle Contarine agreed to furnish the funds. "I intend," said he, in a letter to his uncle, "to visit Paris, where the great Farheim, Petit, and Du Hammel de Monceau instruct their pupils in all the branches of medicine. They speak French, and consequently I shall have much the advantage of most of my countrymen, as I am perfectly acquainted with that language, and few who leave Ireland are so. I shall spend the spring and summer in Paris, and the beginning of next winter go to Leyden. The great Albinus is still alive there, and 'twill be proper to go, though only to have it said that we have studied in so famous a university.

"As I shall not have another opportunity for receiving money from your bounty till my return to Ireland, so I have drawn for the last sum that I hope I shall ever trouble you for; 'tis £20. And now, dear Sir, let me here acknowledge the humility of the station in which you found me; let me tell how I was despised by most, and hateful to myself. Poverty, hopeless poverty, was my lot, and Melancholy was beginning to make me her own. When you ———— but I stop here, to inquire how your health goes on? How does my cousin Jenny, and has she recovered her late complaint? How does my poor Jack Goldsmith? I fear his disorder is of such a nature as he won't easily recover. I wish, my dear Sir, you would make me happy by another letter before I go abroad, for there I shall hardly hear from you. * * Give my—how shall I express it? Give my earnest love to Mr. and Mrs. Lawder."

Mrs. Lawder was Jane, his early playmate—the object of his valentine—his first poetical inspiration. She had been for some time married.

Medical instruction, it will be perceived, was the ostensible motive for this visit to the Continent, but the real one in all probability was his long cherished desire to see foreign parts. This, however, he would not acknowledge even to himself but sought to reconcile his roving propensities with some grand moral purpose. "I esteem the traveller who instructs the heart," says he in one of his subsequent writings, "but despise him who only indulges the imagination. A man who leaves home to mend himself and others is a philosopher; but he who goes from country to country, guided by the blind impulse of curiosity, is only a vagabond." He of course was to travel as a philosopher, and in truth his outfits for a Continental tour were in character. "I shall carry just £33 to France," said he, "with good store of clothes, shirts, &c., and that with economy will suffice." He forgot to make mention of his flute, which it will be found had occasionally to come in play when economy could not replenish his purse nor philosophy find him a supper. Thus slenderly provided with money, prudence or experience, and almost as slightly guarded against "hard knocks" as the hero of La Mancha, whose head piece was half iron, half pasteboard, he made his final sally forth upon the world; hoping all things; believing all things: little anticipating the checkered ills in store for him; little thinking when he penned his valedictory letter to his good uncle Contarine, that he was never to see him more; never to return after all his wandering to the friends of his infancy; never to revisit his early and fondly remembered haunts at 'sweet Lissoy' and Ballymahon.

CHAPTER V

His usual indiscretions attended Goldsmith at the very outset of his
foreign enterprise. He had intended to take shipping at Leith for Holland; but on arriving at that port he found a ship about to sail for
Bordeaux, with six agreeable passengers, whose acquaintance he had
probably made at the inn. He was not a man to resist a sudden impulse;
so, instead of embarking for Holland, he found himself ploughing the
seas on his way to the other side of the continent. Scarcely had the ship
been two days at sea when she was driven by stress of weather to
Newcastle-upon-Tyne. Here 'of course' Goldsmith and his agreeable
fellow passengers found it expedient to go on shore and "refresh themselves after the fatigues of the voyage." 'Of course' they frolicked and
made merry until a late hour in the evening when, in the midst of their
hilarity, the door was burst open, and a serjeant and twelve grenadiers
entered with fixed bayonets and took the whole convivial party prisoners.

It seems that the agreeable companions with whom our green horn
had struck up such a sudden intimacy were Scotchmen in the French
service, who had been in Scotland enlisting recruits for the French army.

In vain Goldsmith protested his innocence; he was marched off with
his fellow revellers to prison, whence he with difficulty obtained his
release at the end of a fortnight. With his customary facility, however,
at palliating his misadventures, he found every thing turn out for the
best. His imprisonment saved his life, for during his detention the ship
proceeded on her voyage, but was wrecked at the mouth of the Garonne
and all on board perished.

Goldsmith's second embarkation was for Holland direct, and in nine
days he arrived at Rotterdam, whence he proceeded without any more
deviations to Leyden. He gives a whimsical picture, in one of his letters,
of the appearance of the Hollanders. "The modern Dutchman is quite
a different creature from him of former times: he in every thing imitates
a Frenchman but in his easy, disengaged air. He is vastly ceremonious,
and is, perhaps, exactly what a Frenchman might have been in the
reign of Louis XIV. Such are the better bred. But the downright Hol-
lander is one of the oddest figures in nature. Upon a lank head of
hair he wears a half-cocked narrow hat, laced with black riband; no

coat, but seven waistcoats and nine pair of breeches, so that his hips reach up almost to his armpits. This well-clothed vegetable is now fit to see company or make love. But what a pleasing creature is the object of his appetite! why, she wears a large fur cap, with a deal of Flanders lace; and for every pair of breeches he carries, she puts on two petticoats.

"A Dutch lady burns nothing about her phlegmatic admirer but his tobacco. You must know, sir, every woman carries in her hand a stove of coals, which, when she sits, she snugs under her petticoats, and at this chimney dozing Strephon lights his pipe."

In the same letter he contrasts Scotland and Holland. "There hills and rocks intercept every prospect; here it is all a continued plain. There you might see a well-dressed Duchess issuing from a dirty close and here a dirty Dutchman inhabiting a palace. The Scotch may be compared to a tulip planted in dung; but I can never see a Dutchman in his own house but I think of a magnificent Egyptian temple dedicated to an ox."

The country itself awakened his admiration. "Nothing," said he, "can equal its beauty; wherever I turn my eyes, fine houses, elegant gardens, statues, grottoes, vistas present themselves; but when you enter their towns you are charmed beyond description. No misery is to be seen here; every one is usefully employed." And again, in his noble description in "The Traveller:"

> To men of other minds my fancy flies,
> Imbosom'd in the deep where Holland lies.
> Methinks her patient sons before me stand,
> Where the broad ocean leans against the land,
> And, sedulous to stop the coming tide,
> Lift the tall rampire's artificial pride.
> Onward, methinks, and diligently slow,
> The firm connected bulwark seems to grow;
> Spreads its long arms amid the watery roar,
> Scoops out an empire, and usurps the shore.
> While the pent ocean, rising o'er the pile,
> Sees an amphibious world beneath him smile;
> The slow canal, the yellow blossom'd vale,
> The willow-tufted bank, the gliding sail,
> The crowded mart, the cultivated plain,
> A new creation rescued from his reign.

He remained about a year at Leyden, attending the lectures of Gaubius on chemistry and Albinus on anatomy; though his studies are said to have been miscellaneous, and directed to literature rather than science. The thirty-three pounds with which he had set out on his travels were soon consumed, and he was put to many a shift to meet his expenses until his precarious remittances should arrive. He had a good friend on these occasions in a fellow student and countryman named Ellis, who afterwards rose to eminence as a physician. He used frequently to loan small sums to Goldsmith, which were always scrupulously paid. Ellis discovered the innate merits of the poor awkward student and used to declare in after life "that it was a common remark in Leyden, that in all the peculiarities of Goldsmith an elevation of mind was to be noted; a philosophical tone and manner; the feelings of a gentleman and the language and information of a scholar."

Sometimes in his emergencies, Goldsmith undertook to teach the English language. It is true he was ignorant of the Dutch, but he had a smattering of the French, picked up among the Irish priests at Ballymahon. He depicts his whimsical embarrassment in this respect in his account in the Vicar of Wakefield of the *philosophical vagabond* who went to Holland to teach the natives English, without knowing a word of their own language. Sometimes when sorely pinched, and sometimes, perhaps, when flush, he resorted to the gambling tables, which in those days abounded in Holland. His good friend Ellis repeatedly warned him against this unfortunate propensity but in vain. It brought its own cure, or rather its own punishment, by stripping him of every shilling.

Ellis once more stepped in to his relief with a true Irishman's generosity, but with more considerateness than generally characterizes an Irishman, for he only granted pecuniary aid on condition of his quitting the sphere of danger. Goldsmith gladly consented to leave Holland, being anxious to visit other parts. He intended to proceed to Paris and pursue his studies there, and was furnished by his friend with money for the journey. Unluckily, he rambled into the garden of a florist just before quitting Leyden. The tulip mania was still prevalent in Holland, and some species of that splendid flower brought immense prices. In wandering through the garden Goldsmith recollected that his uncle Contarine was a tulip fancier. The thought suddenly struck him that here was an opportunity of testifying, in a delicate manner, his sense of that generous uncle's past kindnesses. In an instant his hand was in his pocket; a number of choice and costly tulip-roots were purchased and packed up for Mr. Contarine; and it was not until he had paid for them that he bethought himself that he had spent all the money borrowed for his travelling expenses. Too proud, however, to give up his journey, and too shamefaced to make another appeal to his friend's liberality, he determined to travel on foot, and depend upon chance and good luck for the means of getting forward; and it is said that he

actually set off on a tour of the Continent, in February, 1755, with but
one spare shirt, a flute, and a single guinea.

"Blessed," says one of his biographers, "with a good constitution,
an adventurous spirit, and with that thoughtless, or, perhaps, happy
disposition which takes no care for to-morrow, he continued his travels
for a long time in spite of innumerable privations." In his amusing
narrative of the adventures of a "Philosophic Vagabond" in the "Vicar
of Wakefield," we find shadowed out the expedients he pursued. "I had
some knowledge of music, with a tolerable voice; I now turned what
was once my amusement into a present means of subsistence. I passed
among the harmless peasants of Flanders, and among such of the French
as were poor enough to be very merry, for I ever found them sprightly
in proportion to their wants. Whenever I approached a peasant's house
towards nightfall, I played one of my merriest tunes, and that procured
me not only a lodging, but subsistence for the next day; but in truth
I must own, whenever I attempted to entertain persons of a higher
rank, they always thought my performance odious, and never made me
any return for my endeavours to please them."

At Paris he attended the chemical lectures of Rouelle, then in great
vogue, where he says he witnessed as bright a circle of beauty as
graced the court of Versailles. His love of theatricals also led him to
attend the performances of the celebrated actress Mademoiselle Clairon,
with which he was greatly delighted. He seems to have looked upon
the state of society with the eye of a philosopher but to have read
the signs of the times with the prophetic eye of a poet. In his rambles
about the environs of Paris he was struck with the immense quantities
of game running about almost in a tame state; and saw in those costly
and rigid preserves for the amusement and luxury of the privileged few,
a sure "badge of the slavery of the people." This slavery he predicted
was drawing towards a close. "When I consider that these parliaments,
the members of which are all created by the court and the presidents
of which can only act by immediate direction, presume even to mention
privileges and freedom, who till of late received directions from the
throne with implicit humility; when this is considered, I cannot help
fancying that the genius of Freedom has entered that kingdom in disguise. If they have but three weak monarchs more successively on the
throne, the mask will be laid aside, and the country will certainly once
more be free." Events have testified to the sage forecast of the poet.

During a brief sojourn in Paris, he appears to have gained access to
valuable society and to have had the honor and pleasure of making
the acquaintance of Voltaire, of whom in after years he wrote a memoir.
"As a companion," says he, "no man ever exceeded him when he pleased
to lead the conversation; which, however, was not always the case. In

company which he either disliked or despised, few could be more
reserved than he; but when he was warmed in discourse, and got over
a hesitating manner, which sometimes he was subject to, it was rapture
to hear him. His meagre visage seemed insensibly to gather beauty; every
muscle in it had meaning, and his eye beamed with unusual brightness.
The person who writes this memoir," continues he, "remembers to have
seen him in a select company of wits of both sexes at Paris, when the
subject happened to turn upon English taste and learning. Fontenelle,
[then nearly a hundred years old,] who was of the party, and who being
unacquainted with the language or authors of the country he undertook
to condemn, with a spirit truly vulgar began to revile both. Diderot,
who liked the English, and knew something of their literary pretensions,
attempted to vindicate their poetry and learning, but with unequal
abilities. The company quickly perceived that Fontenelle was superior
in the dispute, and were surprised at the silence which Voltaire had
preserved all the former part of the night, particularly as the conversation happened to turn upon one of his favorite topics. Fontenelle
continued his triumph till about twelve o'clock, when Voltaire appeared
at last roused from his reverie. His whole frame seemed animated. He
began his defence with the utmost elegance mixed with spirit, and now
and then let fall the finest strokes of raillery upon his antagonist; and
his harangue lasted till three in the morning. I must confess, that, whether
from national partiality, or from the elegant sensibility of his manner,
I never was so charmed, nor did I ever remember so absolute a victory
as he gained in this dispute."

Goldsmith's ramblings took him into Germany and Switzerland, from
which last mentioned country he sent to his brother in Ireland the first
brief sketch, afterwards amplified into his poem of the "Traveller."

At Geneva he became travelling tutor to a mongrel young gentleman,
son of a London pawnbroker, who had been suddenly elevated into
fortune and absurdity by the death of an uncle. The youth, before
setting up for a gentleman, had been an attorney's apprentice, and was
an arrant pettifogger in money matters. Never were two beings more
illy assorted than he and Goldsmith. We may form an idea of the tutor
and the pupil from the following extract from the narrative of the
Philosophic Vagabond.

"I was to be the young gentleman's governor, but with a proviso that
he should always be permitted to govern himself. My pupil, in fact,
understood the art of guiding in money concerns much better than I.
He was heir to a fortune of about two hundred thousand pounds, left
him by an uncle in the West Indies; and his guardians, to qualify him
for the management of it, had bound him apprentice to an attorney.
Thus avarice was his prevailing passion; all his questions on the road

were, how money might be saved—which was the least expensive course of travel—whether any thing could be bought that would turn to account when disposed of again in London? Such curiosities on the way as could be seen for nothing, he was ready enough to look at; but if the sight of them was to be paid for, he usually asserted that he had been told that they were not worth seeing. He never paid a bill that he would not observe how amazingly expensive travelling was: and all this though not yet twenty-one."

In this sketch Goldsmith undoubtedly shadows forth his annoyances as travelling tutor to this concrete young gentleman, compounded of the pawnbroker, the pettifogger and the West Indian heir with an overlaying of the city miser. They had continual difficulties on all points of expense until they reached Marseilles, where both were glad to separate.

Once more on foot but freed from the irksome duties of 'bear leader,' and with some of his pay as tutor in his pocket, Goldsmith continued his half vagrant peregrinations through part of France and Piedmont and some of the Italian States. He had acquired, as has been shown, a habit of shifting along and living by expedients, and a new one presented itself in Italy. "My skill in music," says he, in the Philosophic Vagabond, "could avail me nothing in a country where every peasant was a better musician than I; but by this time I had acquired another talent, which answered my purpose as well, and this was a skill in disputation. In all the foreign universities and convents there are, upon certain days, philosophical theses maintained against every adventitious disputant: for which, if the champion opposes with any dexterity, he can claim a gratuity in money, a dinner, and a bed for one night." Though a poor wandering scholar, his reception in these learned piles was as free from humiliation as in the cottages of the peasantry. "With the members of these establishments," said he, "I could converse on topics of literature, *and then I always forgot the meanness of my circumstances."*

At Padua where he remained some months, he is said to have taken his medical degree. It is probable he was brought to a pause in this city by the illness of his uncle Contarine; who had hitherto assisted him in his wanderings by occasional though of course slender remittances. Deprived of this source of supplies, he wrote to his friends in Ireland, and especially to his brother in law, Hodson, describing his destitute situation. His letters brought him neither money nor reply. It appears, from subsequent correspondence, that his brother in law actually exerted himself to raise a subscription for his assistance among his relatives, friends and acquaintance, but without success. Their faith and hope in him were most probably at an end; as yet he had disappointed them at every point, he had given none of the anticipated proofs of talent,

and they were too poor to support what they may have considered the
wandering propensities of a heedless spendthrift.

Thus left to his own precarious resources, Goldsmith gave up all
further wandering in Italy, without visiting the south, though Rome
and Naples must have held out powerful attractions to one of his
poetical cast. Once more resuming his pilgrim staff, he turned his face
toward England, "walking along from city to city, examining mankind
more nearly and seeing both sides of the picture." In traversing France
his flute—his magic flute!—was once more in requisition, as we may
conclude by the following passage in his Traveller:

> Gay sprightly land of mirth and social ease,
> Pleased with thyself, whom all the world can please,
> How often have I led thy sportive choir
> With tuneless pipe beside the murmuring Loire!
> Where shading elms along the margin grew,
> And freshened from the wave the zephyr flew;
> And haply though my harsh note falt'ring still,
> But mocked all tune, and marr'd the dancer's skill;
> Yet would the village praise my wondrous power,
> And dance forgetful of the noontide hour.
> Alike all ages. Dames of ancient days
> Have led their children through the mirthful maze,
> And the gay grandsire, skill'd in gestic lore,
> Has frisk'd beneath the burden of threescore.

CHAPTER VI

After two years spent in roving about the continent, "pursuing novelty," as he said, "and losing content," Goldsmith landed at Dover early in 1756. He appears to have had no definite plan of action. The illness of his uncle Contarine and the neglect of his relatives and friends to reply to his letters, seem to have produced in him a temporary feeling of loneliness and destitution, and his only thought was to get to London and throw himself upon the world. But how was he to get there? His purse was empty. England was to him as completely a foreign land as any part of the continent, and where on earth is a penniless stranger more destitute? His flute and his philosophy were no longer of any avail; the English boors cared nothing for music; there were no convents; and as to the learned and the clergy, not one of them would give a vagrant scholar a supper and night's lodging for the best thesis that ever was argued. "You may easily imagine," says he in a subsequent letter to his brother in law, "what difficulties I had to encounter, left as I was without friends, recommendations, money, or impudence, and that in a country where being born an Irishman was sufficient to keep me unemployed. Many, in such circumstances, would have had recourse to the friar's cord or the suicide's halter. But, with all my follies, I had principle to resist the one, and resolution to combat the other."

He applied at one place, we are told, for employment in the shop of a country apothecary; but all his medical science gathered in foreign universities could not gain him the management of a pestle and mortar. He even resorted, it is said, to the stage as a temporary expedient and figured in low comedy at a country town in Kent. This accords with his last shift of the Philosophic Vagabond and with the knowledge of country theatricals displayed in his "Adventures of a Strolling Player" or may be a story suggested by them. All this part of his career, however, in which he must have trod the lowest paths of humility, are only to be conjectured from vague traditions or scraps of autobiography gleaned from his miscellaneous writings.

At length we find him launched on the great metropolis, or rather drifting about its streets, at night, in the gloomy month of February with but a few half pence in his pocket. The deserts of Arabia are not

43

more dreary and inhospitable than the streets of London at such a time, and to a stranger in such a plight. Do we want a picture as an illustration? We have it in his own works and furnished doubtless from his own experience.

"The clock has just struck two; what a gloom hangs all around! no sound is heard but of the chiming clock, or the distant watch-dog. How few appear in those streets, which but some few hours ago were crowded! But who are those who make the streets their couch, and find a short repose from wretchedness at the doors of the opulent? They are strangers, wanderers, and orphans, whose circumstances are too humble to expect redress, and whose distresses are too great even for pity. Some are without the covering even of rags, and others emaciated with disease; the world has disclaimed them; society turns its back upon their distress, and has given them up to nakedness and hunger. *These poor shivering females have once seen happier days, and been flattered into beauty.* They are now turned out to meet the severity of winter. Perhaps, now lying at the doors of their betrayers, they sue to wretches whose hearts are insensible, or debauchees who may curse, but will not relieve them.

"Why, why was I born a man, and yet see the sufferings of wretches I cannot relieve! Poor houseless creatures! The world will give you reproaches, but will not give you relief."

Poor houseless Goldsmith! we may here ejaculate—to what shifts he must have been driven to find shelter and sustenance for himself in this his first venture into London. Many years afterwards, in the days of his social elevation, he startled a polite circle at Sir Joshua Reynolds's by humorously dating an anecdote about the time he "lived among the beggars of Axe Lane." Such may have been the desolate quarters with which he was fain to content himself when thus adrift upon the town with but a few half pence in his pocket.

The first authentic trace we have of him in this new part of his career is filling the situation of an usher to a school, and even this employ he obtained with some difficulty, after a reference for a character to his friends in the University of Dublin. In the Vicar of Wakefield he makes George Primrose undergo a whimsical catechism concerning the requisites for an usher. "Have you been bred apprentice to the business?" "No." "Then you won't do for a school. Can you dress the boys hair?" "No." "Then you won't do for a school. Can you lie three in a bed?" "No." "Then you will never do for a school. Have you a good stomach?" "Yes." "Then you will by no means do for a school. I have been an usher in a boarding school myself and may I die of an anodyne necklace, but I had rather be under turnkey in Newgate.

I was up early and late: I was brow beat by the master, hated for my ugly face by the mistress, worried by the boys."

Goldsmith remained but a short time in this situation, and to the mortifications experienced there we doubtless owe the picturings given in his writings of the hardships of an usher's life. "He is generally," says he, "the laughing stock of the school. Every trick is played upon him; the oddity of his manner, his dress, or his language, is a fund of eternal ridicule; the master himself now and then cannot avoid joining in the laugh; and the poor wretch, eternally resenting this ill usage, lives in a state of war with all the family."———"He is obliged perhaps to sleep in the same bed with the French teacher, who disturbs him for an hour every night in papering and filleting his hair, and stinks worse than a carrion with his rancid pomatums when he lays his head beside him on the bolster."

His next shift was as assistant in the laboratory of a chemist near Fish Street Hill. After remaining here a few months, he heard that Dr. Sleigh, who had been his friend and fellow student at Edinburgh, was in London. Eager to meet with a friendly face in this land of strangers, he immediately called on him; "but though it was Sunday, and it is to be supposed I was in my best clothes, Sleigh scarcely knew me—such is the tax the unfortunate pay to poverty. However, when he did recollect me, I found his heart as warm as ever, and he shared his purse and friendship with me during his continuance in London."

Through the advice and assistance of Dr. Sleigh, he now commenced the practice of medicine, but in a small way, in Bankside, Southwark, and chiefly among the poor; for he wanted the figure, address, polish and management to succeed among the rich. His old schoolmate and college companion Beatty, who used to aid him with his purse at the university, met him about this time decked out in the tarnished finery of a secondhand suit of green and gold with a shirt and neckcloth of a fortnight's wear.

Poor Goldsmith endeavored to assume a prosperous air in the eyes of his early associate. "He was practising physic," he said, "and *doing very well!*" At this moment poverty was pinching him to the bone in spite of his practise and his dirty finery. His fees were necessarily small and ill paid, and he was fain to seek some precarious assistance from his pen. Here his quondam fellow student Dr. Sleigh was again of service, introducing him to some of the booksellers, who gave him occasional though starveling employment. According to tradition, however, his most efficient patron just now was a journeyman printer, one of his poor patients of Bankside; who had formed a good opinion of his talents and perceived his poverty and his literary shifts. The printer was in the employ of Mr. Samuel Richardson, the author of Pamela,

Clarissa and Sir Charles Grandison; who combined the novelist and the publisher and was in flourishing circumstances. Through the journeyman's intervention Goldsmith is said to have become acquainted with Richardson, who employed him as reader and corrector of the press at his printing establishment in Salisbury Court; an occupation which he alternated with his medical duties.

Being admitted occasionally to Richardson's parlor, he began to form literary acquaintances, among whom the most important was Dr. Young, the author of Night Thoughts, a poem in the height of fashion. It is not probable, however, that much familiarity took place at the time between the literary lion of the day and the poor Æsculapius of Bankside, the humble corrector of the press. Still the communion with literary men had its effect to set his imagination teeming. Dr. Farr, one of his Edinburgh fellow students, who was at London about this time attending the hospitals and lectures, gives us an amusing account of Goldsmith in his literary character.

"Early in January he called upon me one morning before I was up, and, on my entering the room, I recognised my old acquaintance, dressed in a rusty, full-trimmed black suit, with his pockets full of papers, which instantly reminded me of the poet in Garrick's farce of Lethe. After we had finished our breakfast, he drew from his pocket part of a tragedy, which he said he had brought for my correction. In vain I pleaded inability, when he began to read; and every part on which I expressed a doubt as to the propriety was immediately blotted out. I then most earnestly pressed him not to trust to my judgment, but to take the opinion of persons better qualified to decide on dramatic compositions. He now told me he had submitted his production, so far as he had written, to Mr. Richardson, the author of Clarissa, on which I peremptorily declined offering another criticism on the performance."

From the graphic description given of him by Dr. Farr, it will be perceived that the tarnished finery of green and gold had been succeeded by a professional suit of black, to which we are told were added the wig and cane indispensable to medical doctors in those days. The coat was a secondhand one of rusty velvet, with a patch on the left breast, which he adroitly covered with his three cornered hat during his medical visits; and we have an amusing anecdote of his contest of courtesy with a patient who persisted in endeavoring to relieve him from the hat, which only made him press it more devoutly to his heart.

Nothing further has ever been heard of the tragedy mentioned by Dr. Farr; it was probably never completed. The same gentleman speaks of a strange Quixotic scheme which Goldsmith had in contemplation at the time "of going to decipher the inscriptions on the *written mountains,* though he was altogether ignorant of Arabic, or the language in which they might be supposed to be written. The salary of three hundred pounds," adds Dr. Farr, "which had been left for the purpose, was the temptation." This was probably one of many dreamy projects with which his fervid brain was apt to teem. On such subjects he was prone to talk vaguely and magnificently, but inconsiderately, from a kindled imagination rather than a well instructed judgment. He had always a great notion of expeditions to the East, and wonders to be seen and effected in the oriental countries.

CHAPTER VII

Life of a pedagogue—Kindness to schoolboys; pertness in return—
Expensive charities—The Griffiths and the "Monthly Review"—Toils
of a literary hack—Rupture with the Griffiths

Among the most cordial of Goldsmith's intimates in London during this
time of precarious struggle were certain of his former fellow students
in Edinburgh. One of these was the son of a Dr. Milner, a dissenting
minister, who kept a classical school of eminence at Peckham in Surrey.
Young Milner had a favorable opinion of Goldsmith's abilities and
attainments and cherished for him that good will which his genial
nature seems ever to have inspired among his school and college associates. His father falling ill, the young man negotiated with Goldsmith
to take temporary charge of the school. The latter readily consented;
for he was discouraged by the slow growth of medical reputation and
practice, and as yet had no confidence in the coy smiles of the muse.
Laying by his wig and cane therefore and once more wielding the
ferule, he resumed the character of the pedagogue, and for some time
reigned as vicegerent over the academy at Peckham. He appears to
have been well treated by both Dr. Milner and his wife; and became
a favorite with the scholars from his easy, indulgent good nature. He
mingled in their sports, told them droll stories; played on the flute for
their amusement, and spent his money in treating them to sweetmeats
and other schoolboy dainties. His familiarity was sometimes carried
too far; he indulged in boyish pranks and practical jokes, and drew
upon himself retorts in kind which, however, he bore with great good
humor. Once indeed he was touched to the quick by a piece of schoolboy pertness. After playing on the flute he spoke with enthusiasm of
music as delightful in itself and as a valuable accomplishment for a
gentleman, whereupon a youngster with a glance at his ungainly person
wished to know if he considered himself a gentleman. Poor Goldsmith,
feelingly alive to the awkwardness of his appearance and the humility
of his situation, winced at this unthinking sneer, which long rankled
in his mind.

As usual while in Dr. Milner's employ, his benevolent feelings were
a heavy tax upon his purse, for he never could resist a tale of distress
and was apt to be fleeced by every sturdy beggar; so that, between his
charity and his munificence, he was generally in advance of his slender
salary. "You had better, Mr. Goldsmith, let me take care of your
money," said Mrs. Milner one day, "as I do for some of the young

48

gentlemen."—"In truth, madam, there is equal need!" was the good humored reply.

Dr. Milner was a man of some literary pretensions and wrote occasionally for the "Monthly Review," of which a bookseller by the name of Griffiths was proprietor. This work was an advocate for Whig principles and had been in prosperous existence for nearly eight years. Of late, however, periodicals had multiplied exceedingly, and a formidable Tory rival had started up in the "Critical Review," published by Archibald Hamilton, a bookseller, and aided by the powerful and popular pen of Dr. Smollett. Griffiths was obliged to recruit his forces. While so doing he met Goldsmith, a humble occupant of a seat at Dr. Milner's table, and was struck with remarks on men and books which fell from him in the course of conversation. He took occasion to sound him privately as to his inclination and capacity as a reviewer, and was furnished by him with specimens of his literary and critical talents. They proved satisfactory. The consequence was that Goldsmith once more changed his mode of life and in April 1757 became a contributor to the "Monthly Review" at a small fixed salary with board and lodging: and accordingly took up his abode with Mr. Griffiths at the sign of the Dunciad, Paternoster Row. As usual we trace this phase of his fortunes in his semifictitious writings; his sudden transmutation of the pedagogue into the author being humorously set forth in the case of George Primrose in the "Vicar of Wakefield." "Come," says George's adviser, "I see you are a lad of spirit and some learning, what do you think of commencing author like me? You have read in books, no doubt, of men of genius starving at the trade: at present I'll show you forty very dull fellows about town that live by it in opulence. All honest, jog trot men, who go on smoothly and dully, and write history and politics, and are praised: men, sir, who had they been bred cobblers, would all their lives have only mended shoes, but never made them." "Finding" (says George) "that there was no great degree of gentility affixed to the character of an usher, I resolved to accept his proposal; and, having the highest respect for literature, hailed the *antiqua mater* of Grub Street with reverence. I thought it my glory to pursue a track which Dryden and Otway trod before me." Alas, Dryden struggled with indigence all his days; and Otway, it is said, fell a victim to famine in his thirty fifth year, being strangled by a roll of bread, which he devoured with the voracity of a starving man.

In Goldsmith's experience the track soon proved a thorny one. Griffiths was a hard business man, of shrewd, worldly good sense but little refinement or cultivation. He meddled or rather muddled with literature too in a business way, altering and modifying occasionally the writings of his contributors, and in this he was aided by his wife, who, according to Smollett, was "an antiquated female critic and a dabbler in the 'Review.' " Such was the literary vassalage to which Goldsmith had unwarily subjected himself. A diurnal drudgery was imposed on him, irksome to his indolent habits and attended by circumstances humiliating to his pride. He had to write daily from nine o'clock until two and often throughout the day; whether in the vein or not, and on subjects dictated by his task master, however foreign to his taste; in a word, he was treated as a mere literary hack. But this was not the worst; it was the critical supervision of Griffiths and his wife which grieved him: the "illiterate, bookselling Griffiths," as Smollett called them, "who presumed to revise, alter and amend the articles contributed to their 'Review.' Thank heaven," crowed Smollett, "the 'Critical Review' is not written under the restraint of a bookseller and his wife. Its principal writers are independent of each other, unconnected with booksellers and unawed by old women!"

This literary vassalage, however, did not last long. The bookseller became more and more exacting. He accused his hack writer of idleness; of abandoning his writing desk and literary work shop at an early hour of the day; and of assuming a tone and manner *above his situation.* Goldsmith in return charged him with impertinence, his wife with meanness and parsimony in her household treatment of him, and both of literary meddling and marring. The engagement was broken off at the end of five months, by mutual consent, and without any violent rupture, as it will be found they afterwards had occasional dealings with each other.

Though Goldsmith was now nearly thirty years of age, he had produced nothing to give him a decided reputation. He was as yet a mere writer for bread. The articles he had contributed to the "Review" were anonymous and were never avowed by him. They have since been for the most part ascertained; and though thrown off hastily, often treating on subjects of temporary interest, and marred by the Griffith interpolations, they are still characterized by his sound, easy good sense and the genial graces of his style. Johnson observed that Goldsmith's genius flowered late; he should have said it flowered early, but was late in bringing its fruit to maturity.

CHAPTER VIII

Being now known in the publishing world, Goldsmith began to find casual employment in various quarters; among others he wrote occasionally for the Literary Magazine, a production set on foot by Mr. John Newbery, bookseller, St. Paul's Churchyard, renowned in nursery literature throughout the latter half of the last century for his picture books for children. Newbery was a worthy, intelligent, kind hearted man and a seasonable, though cautious friend to authors, relieving them with small loans when in pecuniary difficulties, though always taking care to be well repaid by the labor of their pens. Goldsmith introduces him in a humorous yet friendly manner in his novel of the Vicar of Wakefield. "This person was no other than the philanthropic bookseller in St. Paul's Churchyard, who has written so many little books for children; he called himself their friend; but he was the friend of all mankind. He was no sooner alighted but he was in haste to be gone; for he was ever on business of importance, and was at that time actually compiling materials for the history of one Mr. Thomas Trip. I immediately recollected this good-natured man's red-pimpled face."

Besides his literary job work, Goldsmith also resumed his medical practice, but with very trifling success. The scantiness of his purse still obliged him to live in obscure lodgings somewhere in the vicinity of Salisbury Square, Fleet Street; but his extended acquaintance and rising importance caused him to consult appearances. He adopted an expedient, then very common, and still practised in London among those who have to tread the narrow path between pride and poverty; while he burrowed in lodgings suited to his means, he "hailed," as it is termed, from the Temple Exchange Coffee House near Temple Bar. Here he received his medical calls; hence he dated his letters, and here he passed much of his leisure hours, conversing with the frequenters of the place. Thirty pounds a year, said a poor Irish painter, who understood the art of shifting, is enough to enable a man to live in London without being contemptible. Ten pounds will find him in clothes and linen; he can live in a garret on eighteen pence a week; hail from a coffee house, where by occasionally spending threepence he may pass some hours each day in good company; he may breakfast on bread and milk for a penny; dine for six pence; do without supper; and on *clean-shirt-day* he may go abroad and pay visits.

Goldsmith seems to have taken a leaf out of this poor devil's manual in respect to the coffee house at least. Indeed, coffee houses in those days were the resorts of wits and literati; where the topics of the day were gossiped over, and the affairs of literature and the drama discussed and criticised. In this way he enlarged the circle of his intimacy, which now embraced several names of notoriety.

Do we want a picture of Goldsmith's experience in this part of his career? We have it in his observations on the life of an author in the *Enquiry into the state of polite learning*, published some years afterwards.

"The author, unpatronized by the Great, has naturally recourse to the bookseller. There cannot, perhaps, be imagined a combination more prejudicial to taste than this. It is the interest of the one to allow as little for writing, and for the other to write as much as possible; accordingly, tedious compilations and periodical magazines are the result of their joint endeavours. In these circumstances the author bids adieu to fame; writes for bread; and for that only, imagination is seldom called in. He sits down to address the venal muse with the most phlegmatic apathy; and, as we are told of the Russian, courts his mistress by falling asleep in her lap."

Again. "Those who are unacquainted with the world are apt to fancy the man of wit as leading a very agreeable life. They conclude, perhaps, that he is attended with silent admiration, and dictates to the rest of mankind with all the eloquence of conscious superiority. Very different is his present situation. He is called an author, and all know that an author is a thing only to be laughed at. His person, not his jest, becomes the mirth of the company. At his approach the most fat unthinking face brightens into malicious meaning. Even aldermen laugh, and avenge on him the ridicule which was lavished on their forefathers. * * * * The poet's poverty is a standing topic of contempt. His writing for bread is an unpardonable offence. Perhaps of all mankind, an author in these times is used most hardly. We keep him poor, and yet revile his poverty. We reproach him for living by his wit, and yet allow him no other means to live. His taking refuge in garrets and cellars has of late been violently objected to him, and that by men who, I dare hope, are more apt to pity than insult his distress. Is poverty the writer's fault? No doubt he knows how to prefer a bottle of champagne to the nectar of the neighboring ale house, or a venison pasty to a plate of potatoes. Want of delicacy is not in him, but in those who deny him the opportunity of making an elegant choice. Wit certainly is the property of those who have it, nor should we be displeased if it is the only property a man sometimes has. We must not under-rate him who uses it for subsistence, and flees from the ingratitude of the age, even to a bookseller for redress." * * * *

"If the author be necessary among us, let us treat him with proper consideration as a child of the public, not as a rent-charge on the community. And indeed a child of the public he is in all respects; for while so well able to direct others, how incapable is he frequently found of guiding himself. His simplicity exposes him to all the insidious approaches of cunning; his sensibility, to the slightest invasions of contempt. Though possessed of fortitude to stand unmoved the expected bursts of an earthquake, yet of feelings so exquisitely poignant, as to agonize under the slightest disappointment. Broken rest, tasteless meals, and causeless anxieties shorten life and render it unfit for active employments; prolonged vigils and intense application still farther contract his span, and make his time glide insensibly away."

While poor Goldsmith was thus struggling with the difficulties and discouragements which in those days beset the path of an author, his friends in Ireland received accounts of his literary success and of the distinguished acquaintances he was making. This was enough to put the wise heads at Lissoy and Ballymahon in a ferment of conjectures. With the exaggerated notions of provincial relatives concerning the family great man in the metropolis, some of Goldsmith's poor kindred pictured him to themselves seated in high places, clothed in purple and fine linen, and hand and glove with the givers of gifts and dispensers of patronage. Accordingly, he was one day surprised at the sudden apparition, in his miserable lodging, of his younger brother Charles, a raw youth of twenty-one, endowed with a double share of the family heedlessness, and who expected to be forthwith helped into some snug by-path to fortune by one or other of Oliver's great friends. Charles was sadly disconcerted on learning that, so far from being able to provide for others, his brother could scarcely take care of himself. He looked round with a rueful eye on the poet's quarters, and could not help expressing his surprise and disappointment at finding him no better off. "All in good time, my dear boy," replied poor Goldsmith, with infinite good humor; "I shall be richer by-and-by. Addison, let me tell you, wrote his poem of the Campaign in a garret in the Haymarket, three stories high, and you see I am not come to that yet, for I have only got to the second story."

Charles Goldsmith did not remain long to embarrass his brother in London. With the same roving disposition and inconsiderate temper of Oliver, he suddenly departed in an humble capacity to seek his fortune in the West Indies, and nothing was heard of him for above thirty years, when, after having been given up as dead by his friends, he made his reappearance in England.

Shortly after his departure Goldsmith wrote a letter to his brother in law, Daniel Hodson, Esq., of which the following is an extract; it was partly intended, no doubt, to dissipate any further illusions concerning his fortunes which might float on the magnificent imagination of his friends in Ballymahon.

"I suppose you desire to know my present situation. As there is nothing in it at which I should blush or which mankind could censure, I see no reason for making it a secret. In short, by a very little practice as a physician, and a very little reputation as a poet, I make a shift to live. Nothing is more apt to introduce us to the gates of the muses than poverty; but it were well if they only left us at the door. The mischief is, they sometimes choose to give us their company to the entertainment; and want, instead of being gentleman-usher, often turns master of the ceremonies.

"Thus, upon learning I write, no doubt you imagine I starve; and the name of an author naturally reminds you of a garret. In this particular I do not think proper to undeceive my friends. But, whether I eat or starve, live in a first floor or four pairs of stairs high, I still remember them with ardour; nay, my very country comes in for a share of my affection. Unaccountable fondness for country, this *maladie du pais,* as the French call it! Unaccountable that he should still have an affection for a place, who never, when in it, received above common civility; who never brought any thing out of it except his brogue and his blunders. Surely my affection is equally ridiculous with the Scotchman's, who refused to be cured of the itch because it made him unco' thoughtful of his wife and bonny Inverary.

"But, now, to be serious: let me ask myself what gives me a wish to see Ireland again. The country is a fine one, perhaps? No. There are good company in Ireland? No. The conversation there is generally made up of a smutty toast or a bawdy song; the vivacity supported by some humble cousin, who had just folly enough to earn his dinner. Then perhaps there's more wit and learning among the Irish? Oh, Lord, no! There has been more money spent in the encouragement of the Padareen mare there one season, than given in rewards to learned men since the time of Usher. All their productions in learning amount to perhaps a translation, or a few tracts in divinity; and all their productions in wit to just nothing at all. Why the plague, then, so fond of Ireland? Then, all at once, because you, my dear friend, and a few more who are exceptions to the general picture, have a residence there. This it is that gives me all the pangs I feel in separation. I confess I carry this spirit sometimes to the souring the pleasures I at present possess. If I go to the opera, where Signora Columba pours out all the mazes of melody, I sit and sigh for Lishoy fireside, and Johnny Armstrong's 'Last Good-night' from Peggy Golden. If I climb Hampstead Hill, than where nature never exhibited a more magnificent prospect,

I confess it fine; but then I had rather be placed on the little mount before Lishoy gate, and there take in, to me, the most pleasing horizon in nature.

"Before Charles came hither, my thoughts sometimes found refuge from severer studies among my friends in Ireland. I fancied strange revolutions at home; but I find it was the rapidity of my own motion that gave an imaginary one to objects really at rest. No alterations there. Some friends, he tells me, are still lean, but very rich; others very fat, but still very poor. Nay, all the news I hear of you is, that you sally out in visits among the neighbours, and sometimes make a migration from the blue bed to the brown. I could from my heart wish that you and she (Mrs. Hodson), and Lishoy and Ballymahon, and all of you, would fairly make a migration into Middlesex; though, upon second thoughts, this might be attended with a few inconveniences. Therefore, as the mountain will not come to Mohammed, why Mohammed shall go to the mountain; or, to speak plain English, as you cannot conveniently pay me a visit, if next summer I can contrive to be absent six weeks from London, I shall spend three of them among my friends in Ireland. But first, believe me, my design is purely to visit, and neither to cut a figure nor levy contributions; neither to excite envy nor solicit favour; in fact, my circumstances are adapted to neither. I am too poor to be gazed at, and too rich to need assistance."

CHAPTER IX

*Hackney authorship—Thoughts of literary suicide—Return to Peck-
ham—Oriental projects—Literary enterprise to raise funds—Letter
to Edward Mills; to Robert Bryanton—Death of uncle Contarine—
Letter to cousin Jane*

For some time Goldsmith continued to write miscellaneously, for reviews
and other periodical publications, but without making any decided
hit, to use a technical term. Indeed as yet he appeared destitute of the
strong excitement of literary ambition, and wrote only on the spur
of necessity and at the urgent importunity of his bookseller. His indolent
and truant disposition, ever averse from labor and delighting in holyday,
had to be scourged up to its task; still it was this very truant disposition
which threw an unconscious charm over every thing he wrote; bringing
with it honeyed thoughts and pictured images which had sprung up
in his mind in the sunny hours of idleness: these effusions, dashed off
on compulsion in the exigency of the moment, were published anonymously; so that they made no collective impression on the public and
reflected no fame on the name of their author.

In an essay published some time subsequently in the "Bee," Goldsmith
adverts, in his own humorous way, to his impatience at the tardiness
with which his desultory and unacknowledged essays crept into notice.
"I was once induced," says he, "to shew my indignation against the
public by discontinuing my efforts to please; and was bravely resolved,
like Raleigh, to vex them by burning my manuscripts in a passion. Upon
reflection, however, I considered what set or body of people would
be displeased at my rashness. The sun after so sad an accident, might
shine next morning as bright as usual; men might laugh and sing
the next day, and transact business as before; and not a single creature
feel any regret but myself. Instead of having Apollo in mourning or
the Muses in a fit of the spleen; instead of having the learned world
apostrophising at my untimely decease; perhaps all Grub Street might
laugh at my fate, and self-approving dignity be unable to shield me
from ridicule."

Circumstances occurred about this time to give a new direction to
Goldsmith's hopes and schemes. Having resumed for a brief period
the superintendence of the Peckham school during a fit of illness of
Dr. Milner, that gentleman in requital for his timely services promised
to use his influence with a friend, an East India director, to procure
him a medical appointment in India.

There was every reason to believe that the influence of Dr. Milner would be effectual; but how was Goldsmith to find the ways and means of fitting himself out for a voyage to the Indies? In this emergency he was driven to a more extended exercise of the pen than he had yet attempted. His skirmishing among books as a reviewer, and his disputatious ramble among the schools and universities and literati of the Continent had filled his mind with facts and observations which he now set about digesting into a treatise of some magnitude to be entitled "An Inquiry into the Present State of Polite Learning in Europe." As the work grew on his hands his sanguine temper ran ahead of his labors. Feeling secure of success in England, he was anxious to forestall the piracy of the Irish press; for as yet, the union not having taken place, the English law of copy right did not extend to the other side of the Irish Channel. He wrote therefore to his friends in Ireland, urging them to circulate his proposals for his contemplated work and obtain subscriptions payable in advance, the money to be transmitted to a Mr. Bradley, an eminent bookseller in Dublin, who would give a receipt for it and be accountable for the delivery of the books. The letters written by him on this occasion are worthy of copious citation as being full of character and interest. One was to his relative and college intimate, Edward Mills, who had studied for the bar, but was now living at ease on his estate at Roscommon. "You have quitted," writes Goldsmith, "the plan of life which you once intended to pursue, and given up ambition for domestic tranquillity. I cannot avoid feeling some regret that one of my few friends has declined a pursuit in which he had every reason to expect success. I have often let my fancy loose when you were the subject, and have imagined you gracing the bench, or thundering at the bar: while I have taken no small pride to myself, and whispered to all that I could come near that this was my cousin. Instead of this, it seems you are merely contented to be a happy man; to be esteemed by your acquaintances; to cultivate your paternal acres; to take unmolested a nap under one of your own hawthorns, or in Mrs. Mills's bedchamber, which even a poet must confess is rather the more comfortable place of the two. But however your resolutions may be altered with regard to your situation in life, I persuade myself they are unalterable with respect to your friends in it. I cannot think the world has taken such entire possession of that heart (once so susceptible of friendship) as not to have left a corner there for a friend or two, but I flatter myself that even I have a place among the number. This I have a claim to from the similitude of our dispositions; or setting that aside, I can demand it as a right by the most equitable law of nature; I mean that of retaliation; for indeed you have more than your share in mine. I am a man of few professions; and yet at this very instant I cannot avoid the painful apprehension that my present professions (which speak not half my feelings) should be considered only as a pretext to cover a request, as I have a request to make. No, my dear Ned, I know you are too generous to think so, and you know me too proud to stoop to unnecessary insincerity—I have a request, it is true, to make; but as I know to whom I am a petitioner, I make it without diffidence or confusion. It is in short this, I am going to publish a book in London," &c. The residue of the letter specifies the nature of the request, which was merely to aid in circulating his proposals and obtaining subscriptions. The letter of the poor author however was unattended to and unacknowledged by the prosperous Mr. Mills of Roscommon, though in after years he was proud to claim relationship to Dr. Goldsmith when he had risen to celebrity.

Another of Goldsmith's letters was to Robert Bryanton, with whom he had long ceased to be in correspondence. "I believe," writes he, "that they who are drunk, or out of their wits, fancy every body else in the same condition. Mine is a friendship that neither distance nor time can efface, which is probably the reason that, for the soul of me, I can't avoid thinking yours of the same complexion; and yet I have many reasons for being of a contrary opinion, else why in so long an absence was I never made a partner in your concerns? To hear of your success would have given me the utmost pleasure; and a communication of your very disappointments would divide the uneasiness I too frequently feel for my own. Indeed, my dear Bob, you don't conceive how unkindly you have treated one whose circumstances afford him few prospects of pleasure, except those reflected from the happiness of his friends. However, since you have not let me hear from you, I have in some measure disappointed your neglect by frequently thinking of you. Every day do I remember the calm anecdotes of your life, from the fireside to the easy chair; recall the various adventures that first cemented our friendship; the school, the college, or the tavern; preside in fancy over your cards; and am displeased at your bad play when the rubber goes against you, though not with all that agony of soul as when I was once your partner. Is it not strange that two of such like affections should be so much separated and so differently employed as we are? You seem placed at the centre of fortune's wheel, and, let it revolve never so fast, are insensible of the motion. I seem to have been tied to the circumference, and whirled disagreeably round as if on a whirligig."

He then runs into a whimsical and extravagant tirade about his future prospects, the wonderful career of fame and fortune that awaits him, and after indulging in all kinds of humorous gasconades concludes: "Let me, then, stop my fancy to take a view of my future self,—and, as the boys say, light down to see myself on horseback. Well, now that

I am down, where the d——l *is I*? Oh gods! gods! here in a garret, writing for bread, and expecting to be dunned for a milk score!"

He would on this occasion have doubtless written to his uncle Contarine, but that generous friend was sunk into a helpless hopeless state from which death soon released him.

Cut off thus from the kind co-operation of his uncle, he addresses a letter to his daughter Jane, the companion of his schoolboy and happy days, now the wife of Mr. Lawder. The object was to secure her interest with her husband in promoting the circulation of his proposals. The letter is full of character.

"If you should ask," he begins, "why, in an interval of so many years, you never heard from me, permit me, Madam, to ask the same question. I have the best excuse in recrimination. I wrote to Kilmore from Leyden in Holland, from Louvain in Flanders, and Rouen in France, but received no answer. To what could I attribute this silence but to displeasure or forgetfulness? Whether I was right in my conjecture I do not pretend to determine; but this I must ingenuously own, that I have a thousand times in my turn endeavoured to forget *them*, whom I could not but look upon as forgetting *me*. I have attempted to blot their names from my memory, and, I confess it, spent whole days in efforts to tear their image from my heart. Could I have succeeded, you had not now been troubled with this renewal of a discontinued correspondence; but, as every effort the restless make to procure sleep serves but to keep them waking, all my attempts contributed to impress what I would forget deeper on my imagination. But this subject I would willingly turn from, and yet, 'for the soul of me,' I can't till I have said all. I was, Madam, when I discontinued writing to Kilmore, in such circumstances, that all my endeavours to continue your regards might be attributed to wrong motives. My letters might be looked upon as the petitions of a beggar, and not the offerings of a friend; while all my professions, instead of being considered as the result of disinterested esteem, might be ascribed to venal insincerity. I believe, indeed, you had too much generosity to place them in such a light, but I could not bear even the shadow of such a suspicion. The most delicate friendships are always most sensible of the slightest invasion, and the strongest jealousy is ever attendant on the warmest regard. I could not—I own I could not—continue a correspondence in which every acknowledgment for past favours might be considered as an indirect request for future ones; and where it might be thought I gave my heart from a motive of gratitude alone, when I was conscious of having bestowed it on much more disinterested principles. It is true, this conduct might have been simple enough; but yourself must confess it was in character. Those who know me at all, know that I have always

been actuated by different principles from the rest of mankind; and while
none regarded the interest of his friend more, no man on earth regarded
his own less. I have often affected bluntness to avoid the imputation
of flattery; have frequently seemed to overlook those merits too obvious
to escape notice, and pretended disregard to those instances of good
nature and good sense, which I could not fail tacitly to applaud; and
all this lest I should be ranked among the grinning tribe, who say
'very true' to all that is said; who fill a vacant chair at a tea-table;
whose narrow souls never moved in a wider circle than the circumference
of a guinea; and who had rather be reckoning the money in your
pocket than the virtue in your breast. All this, I say, I have done, and
a thousand other very silly, though very disinterested, things in my
time; and for all which no soul cares a farthing about me.   *   *   *   *
Is it to be wondered that he should once in his life forget you, who
has been all his life forgetting himself? However, it is probable you
may one of these days see me turned into a perfect hunks, and as dark
and intricate as a mouse-hole. I have already given my landlady orders
for an entire reform in the state of my finances. I declaim against hot
suppers, drink less sugar in my tea, and check my grate with brick-bats.
Instead of hanging my room with pictures, I intend to adorn it with
maxims of frugality. Those will make pretty furniture enough, and
won't be a bit too expensive; for I will draw them all out with my
own hands, and my landlady's daughter shall frame them with the
parings of my black waistcoat. Each maxim is to be inscribed on a
sheet of clean paper, and wrote with my best pen; of which the following
will serve as a specimen. *Look sharp: Mind the main chance: Money is
money now: If you have a thousand pounds you can put your hands by
your sides, and say you are worth a thousand pounds every day of the
year: Take a farthing from a hundred and it will be a hundred no longer.*
Thus, which way soever I turn my eyes, they are sure to meet one of
those friendly monitors; and as we are told of an actor who hung his
room round with looking-glass to correct the defects of his person,
my apartment shall be furnished in a peculiar manner, to correct the
errors of my mind. Faith! Madam, I heartily wish to be rich, if it were
only for this reason, to say without a blush how much I esteem you.
But, alas! I have many a fatigue to encounter before that happy time
comes, when your poor old simple friend may again give a loose to the
luxuriance of his nature; sitting by Kilmore fire-side, recount the various
adventures of a hard-fought life; laugh over the follies of the day; join
his flute to your harpsichord; and forget that ever he starved in those
streets where Butler and Otway starved before him. And now I mention
those great names—my Uncle! he is no more that soul of fire as when
I once knew him. Newton and Swift grew dim with age as well as he.

But what shall I say? His mind was too active an inhabitant not to disorder the feeble mansion of its abode: for the richest jewels soonest wear their settings. Yet who but the fool would lament his condition! He now forgets the calamities of life. Perhaps indulgent Heaven has given him a foretaste of that tranquillity here, which he so well deserves hereafter. But I must come to business; for business, as one of my maxims tells me, must be minded or lost. I am going to publish in London a book entitled *The Present State of Taste and Literature in Europe.* The booksellers in Ireland republish every performance there without making the author any consideration. I would, in this respect, disappoint their avarice, and have all the profits of my labour to myself. I must therefore request Mr. Lawder to circulate among his friends and acquaintances a hundred of my proposals, which I have given the bookseller, Mr. Bradley in Dame Street, directions to send to him. If, in pursuance of such circulation, he should receive any subscriptions, I entreat, when collected, they may be sent to Mr. Bradley, as aforesaid, who will give a receipt, and be accountable for the work, or a return of the subscription. If this request (which, if it be complied with, will in some measure be an encouragement to a man of learning) should be disagreeable or troublesome, I would not press it; for I would be the last man on earth to have my labours go a-begging; but if I know Mr. Lawder (and sure I ought to know him), he will accept the employ-ment with pleasure. All I can say—if he writes a book, I will get him two hundred subscribers, and those of the best wits in Europe. Whether this request is complied with or not, I shall not be uneasy; but there is one petition I must make to him and to you, which I solicit with the warmest ardour, and in which I cannot bear a refusal. I mean, dear Madam, that I may be allowed to subscribe myself, your ever affectionate and obliged kinsman, OLIVER GOLDSMITH. Now see how I blot and blunder, when I am asking a favour."

CHAPTER X

While Goldsmith was yet laboring at his treatise, the promise made him by Dr. Milner was carried into effect, and he was actually appointed physician and surgeon to one of the factories on the coast of Coromandel. His imagination was immediately on fire with visions of Oriental wealth and magnificence. It is true the salary did not exceed one hundred pounds, but then, as appointed physician, he would have the exclusive practice of the place, amounting to one thousand pounds per annum; with advantages to be derived from trade and from the high interest of money—twenty per cent; in a word, for once in his life the road to fortune lay broad and straight before him.

Hitherto, in his correspondence with his friends, he had said nothing of his India scheme; but now he imparted to them his brilliant prospects, urging the importance of their circulating his proposals and obtaining him subscriptions and advances on his forthcoming work, to furnish funds for his outfit.

In the mean time he had to task that poor drudge, his muse, for present exigencies. Ten pounds were demanded for his appointment-warrant. Other expenses pressed hard upon him. Fortunately, though as yet unknown to fame, his literary capability was known to "the trade," and the coinage of his brain passed current in Grub Street. Archibald Hamilton, proprietor of the "Critical Review," the rival to that of Griffiths, readily made him a small advance on receiving three articles for his periodical. His purse thus slenderly replenished, Goldsmith paid for his warrant, wiped off the score of his milk maid, abandoned his garret and moved into a shabby first floor in a forlorn court near the Old Bailey; there to await the time for his migration to the magnificent coast of Coromandel.

Alas! poor Goldsmith! ever doomed to disappointment. Early in the gloomy month of November, that month of fog and despondency in London, he learnt the shipwreck of his hope. The great Coromandel enterprise fell through; or rather the post promised to him, was transferred to some other candidate. The cause of this disappointment it is now impossible to ascertain. The death of his quasi patron, Dr. Milner, which happened about this time, may have had some effect in producing it; or there may have been some heedlessness and blundering on his own part; or some obstacle arising from his insuperable indigence; whatever may have been the cause, he never mentioned it, which gives some ground to surmise that he himself was to blame. His friends learnt with surprise that he had suddenly relinquished his appointment to India, about which he had raised such sanguine expectations: some accused him of fickleness and caprice; others supposed him unwilling to tear himself from the growing fascinations of the literary society of London.

In the mean time cut down in his hopes and humiliated in his pride by the failure of his Coromandel scheme, he sought, without consulting his friends, to be examined at the College of Physicians for the humble situation of hospital mate. Even here poverty stood in his way. It was necessary to appear in a decent garb before the examining committee; but how was he to do so? He was literally out at elbows as well as out of cash. Here again the muse, so often jilted and neglected by him, came to his aid. In consideration of four articles furnished to the "Monthly Review," Griffiths, his old task master, was to become his security to the tailor for a suit of clothes. Goldsmith said he wanted them but for a single occasion, on which depended his appointment to a situation in the army; as soon as that temporary purpose was served they would either be returned or paid for. The books to be reviewed were accordingly lent to him; the muse was again set to her compulsory drudgery; the articles were scribbled off and sent to the bookseller, and the clothes came in due time from the tailor.

From the records of the College of Surgeons it appears that Goldsmith underwent his examination at Surgeons' Hall on the 21st of December, 1758. Either from a confusion of mind incident to sensitive and imaginative persons on such occasions, or from a real want of surgical science, which last is extremely probable, he failed in his examination and was rejected as unqualified. The effect of such a rejection was to disqualify him for every branch of public service, though he might have claimed a reexamination after the interval of a few months devoted to further study. Such a reexamination he never attempted, nor did he ever communicate his discomfiture to any of his friends.

On Christmas Day, but four days after his rejection by the College of Surgeons, while he was suffering under the mortification of defeat and disappointment, and hard pressed for means of subsistence, he was surprised by the entrance into his room of the poor woman from whom he hired his wretched apartment and to whom he owed some small arrears of rent. She had a piteous tale of distress and was clamorous in her afflictions. Her husband had been arrested in the night for debt

and thrown into prison. This was too much for the quick feelings of
Goldsmith; he was ready at any time to help the distressed, but in
this instance he was himself in some measure a cause of the distress.
What was to be done? He had no money it is true; but there hung
the new suit of clothes in which he had stood his unlucky examination
at Surgeons' Hall. Without giving himself time for reflection, he sent
it off to the pawnbroker's and raised thereon a sufficient sum to pay off
his own debt and to release his landlord from prison.

Under the same pressure of penury and despondency he borrowed
from a neighbor a pittance to relieve his immediate wants, leaving as a
security the books which he had recently reviewed. In the midst of
these straits and harassments he received a letter from Griffiths demanding in peremptory terms the return of the clothes and books, or immediate payment for the same. It appears that he had discovered the
identical suit at the pawnbroker's. The reply of Goldsmith is not known;
it was out of his power to furnish either the clothes or the money;
but he probably offered once more to make the muse stand his bail.
His reply only increased the ire of the wealthy man of trade and drew
from him another letter still more harsh than the first; using the
epithets of knave and sharper and containing threats of prosecution
and a prison.

The following letter from poor Goldsmith gives the most touching
picture of an inconsiderate but sensitive man, harassed by care, stung
by humiliations, and driven almost to despondency.

SIR,—"I know of no misery but a jail to which my own imprudences
and your letter seem to point. I have seen it inevitable these three or
four weeks, and, by heavens! request it as a favour—as a favour that may
prevent somewhat more fatal. I have been some years struggling with
a wretched being—with all that contempt that indigence brings with it
—with all those passions which make contempt insupportable. What,
then, has a jail that is formidable? I shall at least have the society of
wretches, and such is to me true society. I tell you, again and again,
that I am neither able nor willing to pay you a farthing, but I will be
punctual to any appointment you or the tailor shall make; thus far, at
least, I do not act the sharper, since, unable to pay my own debts one
way, I would generally give some security another. No, sir; had I been
a sharper—had I been possessed of less good-nature and native generosity,
I might surely now have been in better circumstances.

"I am guilty, I own, of meannesses which poverty unavoidably brings
with it: my reflections are filled with repentance for my imprudence,
but not with any remorse for being a villain: that may be a character
you unjustly charge me with. Your books, I can assure you, are neither

pawned nor sold, but in the custody of a friend, from whom my necessities obliged me to borrow some money: whatever becomes of my person, you shall have them in a month. It is very possible both the reports you have heard and your own suggestions may have brought you false information with respect to my character; it is very possible that the man whom you now regard with detestation may inwardly burn with grateful resentment. It is very possible that, upon a second perusal of the letter I sent you, you may see the workings of a mind strongly agitated with gratitude and jealousy. If such circumstances should appear, at least spare invective till my book with Mr. Dodsley shall be published, and then, perhaps, you may see the bright side of a mind, when my professions shall not appear the dictates of necessity, but of choice.

"You seem to think Dr. Milner knew me not. Perhaps so; but he was a man I shall ever honour; but I have friendships only with the dead! I ask pardon for taking up so much time; nor shall I add to it by any other professions than that I am, sir, your humble servant,

"OLIVER GOLDSMITH.

"P. S.—I shall expect impatiently the result of your resolutions."

The dispute between the poet and the publisher was afterward imperfectly adjusted, and it would appear that the clothes were paid for by a short compilation advertised by Griffiths in the course of the following month; but the parties were never really friends afterward, and the writings of Goldsmith were harshly and unjustly treated in the Monthly Review.

We have given the preceding anecdote in detail, as furnishing one of the many instances in which Goldsmith's prompt and benevolent impulses outran all prudent forecast, and involved him in difficulties and disgraces, which a more selfish man would have avoided. The pawning of the clothes, charged upon him as a crime by the grinding bookseller and apparently admitted by him as one of "the meannesses which poverty unavoidably brings with it," resulted, as we have shown, from a tenderness of heart and generosity of hand in which another man would have gloried; but these were such natural elements with him that he was unconscious of their merit. It is a pity that wealth does not oftener bring such 'meannesses' in its train.

And now let us be indulged in a few particulars about these lodgings in which Goldsmith was guilty of this thoughtless act of benevolence. They were in a very shabby house, No. 12 Green Arbour Court, between the Old Bailey and Fleet Market. An old woman was still living in 1820 who was a relative of the identical landlady whom Goldsmith relieved by the money received from the pawnbroker. She was a child about seven years of age at the time that the poet rented his apartment of her relative, and used frequently to be at the house in Green Arbour Court. She was drawn there, in a great measure, by the good humored kindness of Goldsmith, who was always exceedingly fond of the society of children. He used to assemble those of the family in his room, give them cakes and sweetmeats, and set them dancing to the sound of his flute. He was very friendly to those around him, and cultivated a kind of intimacy with a watchmaker in the Court, who possessed much native wit and humor. He passed most of the day, however, in his room, and only went out in the evenings. His days were no doubt devoted to the drudgery of the pen, and it would appear that he occasionally found the booksellers urgent task-masters. On one occasion a visitor was shown up to his room, and immediately their voices were heard in high altercation, and the key was turned within the lock. The landlady, at first, was disposed to go to the assistance of her lodger; but a calm succeeding, she forbore to interfere.

Late in the evening the door was unlocked; a supper ordered by the visitor from a neighboring tavern, and Goldsmith and his intrusive guest finished the evening in great good humor. It was probably his old task master Griffiths, whose press might have been waiting, and who found no other mode of getting a stipulated task from Goldsmith than by locking him in, and staying by him until it was finished.

But we have a more particular account of these lodgings in Green Arbour Court from the Rev. Thomas Percy, afterward Bishop of Dromore, and celebrated for his relics of ancient poetry, his beautiful ballads, and other works. During an occasional visit to London, he was introduced to Goldsmith by Grainger, and ever after continued one of his most steadfast and valued friends. The following is his description of the poet's squalid apartment: "I called on Goldsmith at his lodgings in March, 1759, and found him writing his 'Inquiry,' in a miserable, dirty-looking room, in which there was but one chair; and when, from civility, he resigned it to me, he himself was obliged to sit in the window. While we were conversing together some one tapped gently at the door, and, being desired to come in, a poor, ragged little girl, of a very becoming demeanour, entered the room, and, dropping a courtesy, said, 'My mamma sends her compliments, and begs the favour of you to lend her a chamber-pot full of coals.'"

We are reminded in this anecdote of Goldsmith's picture of the lodgings of Beau Tibbs, and of the peep into the secrets of a make shift establishment given to a visitor by the blundering old Scotch woman.

"By this time we were arrived as high as the stairs would permit us to ascend, till we came to what he was facetiously pleased to call the first floor down the chimney; and, knocking at the door, a voice from within demanded 'who's there?' My conductor answered that it was him. But this not satisfying the querist, the voice again repeated the demand, to which he answered louder than before; and now the door was opened by an old woman with cautious reluctance.

"When we got in he welcomed me to his house with great ceremony; and, turning to the old woman, asked where was her lady. 'Good troth,' replied she, in a peculiar dialect, 'she's washing your twa shirts at the next door, because they have taken an oath against lending the tub any longer.' 'My two shirts,' cried he, in a tone that faltered with confusion; 'what does the idiot mean?' 'I ken what I mean weel enough,' replied the other; 'she's washing your twa shirts at the next door, be-cause—' 'Fire and fury! no more of thy stupid explanations,' cried he; 'go and inform her we have company. Were that Scotch hag to be for ever in my family, she would never learn politeness, nor forget that absurd poisonous accent of hers, or testify the smallest specimen of breeding or high life; and yet it is very surprising too, as I had her from a Parliament man, a friend of mine from the Highlands, one of the politest men in the world; but that's a secret.' "*

Let us linger a little in Green Arbour Court, a place consecrated by the genius and the poverty of Goldsmith, but recently obliterated in the course of modern improvements. The writer of this memoir visited it not many years since on a literary pilgrimage, and may be excused for repeating a description of it which he has heretofore inserted in another publication. "It then existed in its pristine state, and was a small square of tall and miserable houses, the very intestines of which seemed turned inside out, to judge from the old garments and frippery that fluttered from every window. It appeared to be a region of washerwomen, and lines were stretched about the little square, on which clothes were dangling to dry.

"Just as we entered the square, a scuffle took place between two viragoes about a disputed right to a washtub, and immediately the whole community was in a hubbub. Heads in mob caps popped out of every window, and such a clamor of tongues ensued that I was fain to stop my ears. Every amazon took part with one or other of the disputants, and brandished her arms, dripping with soapsuds, and fired away from her window as from the embrasure of a fortress; while the swarms of children nestled and cradled in every procreant chamber of this hive, waking with the noise, set up their shrill pipes to swell the general concert."†

While in these forlorn quarters, suffering under extreme depression

* Citizen of the World, letter lv.
† Tales of a Traveller, vol. i.

of spirits, caused by his failure at Surgeons' Hall, the disappointment of his hopes, and his harsh collisions with Griffiths, Goldsmith wrote the following letter to his brother Henry, some parts of which are most touchingly mournful.

"DEAR SIR,

"Your punctuality in answering a man whose trade is writing, is more than I had reason to expect; and yet you see me generally fill a whole sheet, which is all the recompense I can make for being so frequently troublesome. The behaviour of Mr. Mills and Mr. Lawder is a little extraordinary. However, their answering neither you nor me is a sufficient indication of their disliking the employment which I assigned them. As their conduct is different from what I had expected, so I have made an alteration in mine. I shall, the beginning of next month, send over two hundred and fifty books,* which are all that I fancy can be well sold among you, and I would have you make some distinction in the persons who have subscribed. The money, which will amount to sixty pounds, may be left with Mr. Bradley as soon as possible. I am not certain but I shall quickly have occasion for it.

"I have met with no disappointment with respect to my East India voyage, nor are my resolutions altered; though, at the same time, I must confess, it gives me some pain to think I am almost beginning the world at the age of thirty-one. Though I never had a day's sickness since I saw you, yet I am not that strong, active man you once knew me. You scarcely can conceive how much eight years of disappointment, anguish, and study have worn me down. If I remember right, you are seven or eight years older than me, yet I dare venture to say, that, if a stranger saw us both, he would pay me the honours of seniority. Imagine to yourself a pale, melancholy visage, with two great wrinkles between the eyebrows, with an eye disgustingly severe, and a big wig; and you may have a perfect picture of my present appearance. On the other hand, I conceive you as perfectly sleek and healthy, passing many a happy day among your own children, or those who knew you a child.

"Since I knew what it was to be a man, this is a pleasure I have not known. I have passed my days among a parcel of cool, designing beings, and have contracted all their suspicious manner in my own behaviour. I should actually be as unfit for the society of my friends at home, as I detest that which I am obliged to partake of here. I can now neither partake of the pleasure of a revel, nor contribute to raise

---

* The Inquiry into Polite Literature. His previous remarks apply to the subscription.

its jollity. I can neither laugh nor drink; have contracted a hesitating, disagreeable manner of speaking, and a visage that looks ill-nature itself; in short, I have thought myself into a settled melancholy, and an utter disgust of all that life brings with it. Whence this romantic turn that all our family are possessed with? Whence this love for every place and every country but that in which we reside—for every occupation but our own? this desire of fortune, and yet this eagerness to dissipate? I perceive, my dear sir, that I am at intervals for indulging this splenetic manner, and following my own taste, regardless of yours.

"The reasons you have given me for breeding up your son a scholar are judicious and convincing; I should, however, be glad to know for what particular profession he is designed. If he be assiduous and divested of strong passions (for passions in youth always lead to pleasure), he may do very well in your college; for it must be owned that the industrious poor have good encouragement there, perhaps better than in any other in Europe. But if he has ambition, strong passions, and an exquisite sensibility of contempt, do not send him there, unless you have no other trade for him but your own. It is impossible to conceive how much may be done by proper education at home. A boy, for instance, who understands perfectly well Latin, French, arithmetic, and the principles of the civil law, and can write a fine hand, has an education that may qualify him for any undertaking; and these parts of learning should be carefully inculcated, let him be designed for whatever calling he will.

"Above all things, let him never touch a romance or novel: these paint beauty in colours more charming than nature, and describe happiness that man never tastes. How delusive, how destructive are those pictures of consummate bliss! They teach the youthful mind to sigh after beauty and happiness that never existed; to despise the little good which fortune has mixed in our cup, by expecting more than she ever gave; and, in general, take the word of a man who has seen the world, and who has studied human nature more by experience than precept: take my word for it, I say, that books teach us very little of the world. The greatest merit in a state of poverty would only serve to make the possessor ridiculous—may distress, but cannot relieve him. Frugality, and even avarice, in the lower orders of mankind, are true ambition. These afford the only ladder for the poor to rise to preferment. Teach then, my dear sir, to your son, thrift and economy. Let his poor wandering uncle's example be placed before his eyes. I had learned from books to be disinterested and generous, before I was taught from experience the necessity of being prudent. I had contracted the habits and notions of a philosopher, while I was exposing myself to the approaches of insidious cunning; and often by being, even with my narrow finances, charitable to excess, I forgot the rules of justice, and placed myself in the very situation of the wretch who thanked me for my bounty. When I am in the remotest part of the world, tell him this, and perhaps he may improve from my example. But I find myself again falling into my gloomy habits of thinking.

"My mother, I am informed, is almost blind; even though I had the utmost inclination to return home, under such circumstances I could not, for to behold her in distress without a capacity of relieving her from it would add much to my splenetic habit. Your last letter was much too short; it should have answered some queries I had made in my former. Just sit down as I do, and write forward until you have filled all your paper. It requires no thought, at least from the ease with which my own sentiments rise when they are addressed to you. For, believe me, my head has no share in all I write; my heart dictates the whole. Pray give my love to Bob Bryanton, and entreat him from me not to drink. My dear sir, give me some account about poor Jenny.* Yet her husband loves her: if so, she cannot be unhappy.

"I know not whether I should tell you—yet why should I conceal these trifles, or, indeed, any thing from you? There is a book of mine will be published in a few days: the Life of a very extraordinary man; no less than the great Voltaire. You know already by the title that it is no more than a catchpenny. However, I spent but four weeks on the whole performance, for which I received twenty pounds. When published, I shall take some method of conveying it to you, unless you may think it dear of the postage, which may amount to four or five shillings. However, I fear you will not find an equivalent of amusement.

"Your last letter, I repeat it, was too short; you should have given me your opinion of the design of the heroi-comical poem which I sent you. You remember I intended to introduce the hero of the poem as lying in a paltry alehouse. You may take the following specimen of the manner, which I flatter myself is quite original. The room in which he lies may be described somewhat in this way:

> "The window, patched with paper, lent a ray
> That feebly show'd the state in which he lay;
> The sanded floor that grits beneath the tread,
> The humid wall with paltry pictures spread;
> The game of goose was there exposed to view,
> And the twelve rules the royal martyr drew;

---

* His sister, Mrs. Johnston; her marriage, like that of Mrs. Hodson, was private, but in pecuniary matters much less fortunate.

> The Seasons, framed with listing, found a place,
> And Prussia's monarch show'd his lamp-black face.
> The morn was cold: he views with keen desire
> A rusty grate unconscious of a fire;
> An unpaid reckoning on the frieze was scored,
> And five crack'd teacups dress'd the chimney board."

"And now imagine, after his soliloquy, the landlord to make his appearance in order to dun him for the reckoning:

> "Not with that face, so servile and so gay,
> That welcomes every stranger that can pay:
> With sulky eye he smoked the patient man,
> Then pull'd his breeches tight, and thus began," &c.*

"All this is taken, you see, from nature. It is a good remark of Montaign's, that the wisest men often have friends with whom they do not care how much they play the fool. Take my present follies as instances of my regard. Poetry is a much easier and more agreeable species of composition than prose; and, could a man live by it, it were not unpleasant employment to be a poet. I am resolved to leave no space, though I should fill it up only by telling you, what you very well know already, I mean that I am your most affectionate friend and brother,

"OLIVER GOLDSMITH."

The Life of Voltaire, alluded to in the latter part of the preceding letter, was the literary job undertaken to satisfy the demands of Griffiths. It was to have preceded a translation of the Henriade by Ned Purdon, Goldsmith's old schoolmate, now a Grub Street writer, who starved rather than lived by the exercise of his pen, and often tasked Goldsmith's scanty means to relieve his hunger. His miserable career was summed up by our poet in the following lines written some years after the time we are treating of, on hearing that he had suddenly dropped dead in Smithfield:

> Here lies poor Ned Purdon, from misery freed,
>   Who long was a bookseller's hack;
> He led such a damnable life in this world,
>   I don't think he'll wish to come back.

* The projected poem, of which the above were specimens, appears never to have been completed.

The memoir and translation, though advertised to form a volume, were not published together; but appeared separately in a magazine.

As to the "heroi-comical poem" also cited in the foregoing letter, it appears to have perished in embryo. Had it been brought to maturity we should have had further traits of autobiography; the room already described was probably his own squalid quarters in Green Arbour Court; and in a subsequent morsel of the poem we have the poet himself, under the euphonious name of Scroggen:

> Where the Red Lion peering o'er the way,
> Invites each passing stranger that can pay;
> Where Calvert's butt, and Parson's black champagne,
> Regale the drabs and bloods of Drury Lane:
> There, in a lonely room, from bailiffs snug,
> The muse found Scroggen stretch'd beneath a rug.
> A night cap deck'd his brows instead of bay,
> A cap by night, a stocking all the day!

It is to be regretted that this poetical conception was not carried out. Like the author's other writings it might have abounded with pictures of life and touches of nature drawn from his own observation and experience and mellowed by his own humane and tolerant spirit; and might have been a worthy companion or rather contrast to his "Traveller" and "Deserted Village," and have remained in the language a first rate specimen of the mock heroic.

CHAPTER XI

Towards the end of March, 1759, the treatise on which Goldsmith had laid so much stress, on which he at one time had calculated to defray the expense of his outfit to India, and to which he had adverted in his correspondence with Griffiths, made its appearance. It was published by the Dodsleys, and entitled "An Inquiry into the Present State of Polite Learning in Europe."

In the present day, when the whole field of contemporary literature is so widely surveyed and amply discussed, and when the current productions of every country are constantly collated and ably criticised, a treatise like that of Goldsmith would be considered as extremely limited and unsatisfactory; but at that time it possessed novelty in its views and wideness in its scope, and being indued with the peculiar charm of style inseparable from the author, it commanded public attention and a profitable sale. As it was the most important production that had yet come from Goldsmith's pen, he was anxious to have the credit of it; yet it appeared without his name on the title page. The authorship, however, was well known throughout the world of letters, and the author had now grown into sufficient literary importance to become an object of hostility to the underlings of the press. One of the most virulent attacks upon him was in a criticism on this treatise, and appeared in the Monthly Review, to which he himself had been recently a contributor. It slandered him as a man while it decried him as an author, and accused him, by innuendo, of "labouring under the infamy of having, by the vilest and meanest actions, forfeited all pretensions to honour and honesty," and of practising "those acts which bring the sharper to the cart's tail or the pillory."

It will be remembered that the Review was owned by Griffiths the bookseller, with whom Goldsmith had recently had a misunderstanding. The criticism, therefore, was no doubt dictated by the lingerings of resentment; and the imputations upon Goldsmith's character for honor and honesty, and the vile and mean actions hinted at, could only allude to the unfortunate pawning of the clothes. All this, too, was after Griffiths had received the affecting letter from Goldsmith, drawing a picture of his poverty and perplexities, and after the latter had made him a literary compensation. Griffiths, in fact, was sensible of the falsehood and extravagance of the attack, and tried to exonerate himself by declaring that the criticism was written by a person in his employ; but we see no difference in atrocity between him who wields the knife and him who hires the cutthroat. It may be well, however, in passing, to bestow our mite of notoriety upon the miscreant who launched the slander. He deserves it for a long course of dastardly and venomous attacks, not merely upon Goldsmith, but upon most of the successful authors of the day. His name was Kenrick. He was originally a mechanic, but, possessing some degree of talent and industry, he applied himself to literature as a profession. This he pursued for many years, and tried his hand in every department of prose and poetry; he wrote plays and satires, philosophical tracts, critical dissertations, and works on philology; nothing from his pen ever rose to first rate excellence, or gained him a popular name, though he received from some university the degree of Doctor of Laws. Dr. Johnson characterized his literary career in one short sentence. "Sir, he is one of the many who have made themselves *public* without making themselves *known*."

Soured by his own want of success, jealous of the success of others, his natural irritability of temper increased by habits of intemperance, he at length abandoned himself to the practice of reviewing, and became one of the Ishmaelites of the press. In this his malignant bitterness soon gave him a notoriety which his talents had never been able to attain. We shall dismiss him for the present with the following sketch of him by the hand of one of his contemporaries:

> Dreaming of genius which he never had,
> Half wit, half fool, half critic, and half mad;
> Seizing, like Shirley, on the poet's lyre,
> With all his rage, but not one spark of fire;
> Eager for slaughter, and resolved to tear
> From other's brows that wreath he must not wear—
> Next Kenrick came: all furious, and replete
> With brandy, malice, pertness, and conceit;
> Unskill'd in classic lore, through envy blind
> To all that's beauteous, learned, or refined;
> For faults alone behold the savage prowl,
> With reason's offal glut his ravening soul;
> Pleased with his prey, its inmost blood he drinks,
> And mumbles, paws, and turns it—till it stinks.

The British press about this time was extravagantly fruitful of periodical publications. That "oldest inhabitant," the Gentleman's Magazine, almost coeval with St. John's gate which graced its title page, had long been elbowed by magazines and reviews of all kinds; Johnson's Rambler had introduced the fashion of periodical essays, which he had followed up in his Adventurer and Idler. Imitations had sprung up on every side under every variety of name; until British literature was entirely overrun by a weedy and transient efflorescence. Many of these rival periodicals choked each other almost at the outset, and few of them have escaped oblivion.

Goldsmith wrote for some of the most successful, such as the Bee, the Busy Body, and the Lady's Magazine. His essays, though characterized by his delightful style, his pure, benevolent morality, and his mellow, unobtrusive humor, did not produce equal effect at first with more garish writings of infinitely less value; they did not "strike," as it is termed; but they had that rare and enduring merit which rises in estimation on every perusal. They gradually stole upon the heart of the public, were copied into numerous contemporary publications, and now they are garnered up among the choice productions of British literature.

In his Inquiry into the State of Polite Learning Goldsmith had given offense to David Garrick, at that time the autocrat of the Drama, and was doomed to experience its effect. A clamor had been raised against Garrick for exercising a despotism over the stage and bringing forward nothing but old plays to the exclusion of original productions. Walpole joined in this charge. "Garrick," said he, "is treating the town as it deserves and likes to be treated; with scenes, fireworks, and *his own writings*. A good new play I never expect to see more; nor have seen since the *Provoked Husband*, which came out when I was at school." Goldsmith, who was extremely fond of the theatre, and felt the evils of this system, inveighed in his treatise against the wrongs experienced by authors at the hands of managers. "Our poet's performance," said he, "must undergo a process truly chemical before it is presented to the public. It must be tried in the manager's fire; strained through a licenser, suffer from repeated corrections, till it may be a mere *caput mortuum* when it arrives before the public." Again.—"Getting a play on even in three or four years is a privilege reserved only for the happy few who have the arts of courting the Manager as well as the Muse; who have adulation to please his vanity, powerful patrons to support their merit, or money to indemnify disappointment. Our Saxon ancestors had but one name for a wit and a witch. I will not dispute the propriety of uniting those characters then; but the man who under present discouragements ventures to write for the stage, whatever claim he may have to the appellation of a wit, at least has no right to be called a conjuror." But a passage which perhaps touched more sensibly than all the rest on the sensibilities of Garrick was the following:

"I have no particular spleen against the fellow who sweeps the stage with the besom, or the hero who brushes it with his train. It were a matter of indifference to me, whether our heroines are in keeping, or our candle-snuffers burn their fingers, did not such make a great part of public care and polite conversation. Our actors assume all that state off the stage which they do on it; and, to use an expression borrowed from the green-room, every one is *up* in his part. I am sorry to say it, they seem to forget their real characters."

These strictures were considered by Garrick as intended for himself, and they were rankling in his mind when Goldsmith waited upon him and solicited his vote for the vacant secretaryship of the Society of Arts, of which the manager was a member. Garrick, puffed up by his dramatic renown and his intimacy with the great and knowing Goldsmith only by his budding reputation, may not have considered him of sufficient importance to be conciliated. In reply to his solicitations he observed that he could hardly expect his friendly exertions after the unprovoked attack he had made upon his management. Goldsmith replied that he had indulged in no personalities, and had only spoken what he believed to be the truth. He made no further apology nor application; failed to get the appointment, and considered Garrick his enemy. In the second edition of his treatise he expunged or modified the passages which had given the manager offense; but though the author and actor became intimate in after years, this false step at the outset of their intercourse was never forgotten.

About this time Goldsmith engaged with Dr. Smollett, who was about to launch the British Magazine. Smollett was a complete schemer and speculator in literature, and intent upon enterprises that had money rather than reputation in view. Goldsmith has a good humored hit at this propensity in one of his papers in the Bee, in which he represents Johnson, Hume, and others taking seats in the stagecoach bound for Fame, while Smollett prefers that destined for Riches.

Another prominent employer of Goldsmith was Mr. John Newbery, who engaged him to contribute occasional essays to a newspaper entitled the Public Ledger, which made its first appearance on the 12th of January, 1760. His most valuable and characteristic contributions to this paper were his Chinese Letters, subsequently modified into the Citizen of the World. These lucubrations attracted general attention; they were reprinted in the various periodical publications of the day, and met with great applause. The name of the author, however, was as yet but little known.

Being now easier in circumstances, and in the receipt of frequent sums from the booksellers, Goldsmith, about the middle of 1760, emerged from his dismal abode in Green Arbour Court, and took respectable apartments in Wine Office Court, Fleet Street.

Still he continued to look back with considerate benevolence to the poor hostess whose necessities he had relieved by pawning his gala coat, for we are told that "he often supplied her with food from his own table, and visited her frequently with the sole purpose to be kind to her."

He now became a member of a debating club, called the Robin Hood, which used to meet near Temple Bar and in which Burke, while yet a Temple student, had first tried his powers. Goldsmith spoke here occasionally, and is recorded in the Robin Hood archives as "a candid disputant, with a clear head and an honest heart, though coming but seldom to the society." His relish was for clubs of a more social, jovial nature, and he was never fond of argument. An amusing anecdote is told of his first introduction to the club, by Samuel Derrick, an Irish acquaintance of some humor. On entering, Goldsmith was struck with the self important appearance of the chairman ensconced in a large gilt chair. "This," said he, "must be the Lord Chancellor at least." "No, no," replied Derrick, "he's only master of the *rolls.*"— The chairman was a *baker.*

CHAPTER XII

New lodgings—Visits of ceremony—Hangers on—Pilkington and the white mouse—Introduction to Dr. Johnson—Davies and his bookshop—Pretty Mrs. Davies—Foote and his projects—Criticism of the cudgel

In his new lodgings in Wine Office Court Goldsmith began to receive visits of ceremony and to entertain his literary friends. Among the latter he now numbered several names of note, such as Guthrie, Murphy, Christopher Smart, and Bickerstaffe. He had also a numerous class of hangers on, the small fry of literature; who, knowing his almost utter incapacity to refuse a pecuniary request, were apt, now that he was considered flush, to levy continual taxes upon his purse.

Among others, one Pilkington, an old college acquaintance, but now a shifting adventurer, duped him in the most ludicrous manner. He called on him with a face full of perplexity. A lady of the first rank having an extraordinary fancy for curious animals, for which she was willing to give enormous sums, he had procured a couple of white mice to be forwarded to her from India. They were actually on board of a ship in the river. Her grace had been apprized of their arrival, and was all impatience to see them. Unfortunately, he had no cage to put them in, nor clothes to appear in before a lady of her rank. Two guineas would be sufficient for his purpose, but where were two guineas to be procured!

The simple heart of Goldsmith was touched; but, alas! he had but half a guinea in his pocket. It was unfortunate; but, after a pause, his friend suggested, with some hesitation, "that money might be raised upon his watch: it would but be the loan of a few hours." So said, so done; the watch was delivered to the worthy Mr. Pilkington to be pledged at a neighboring pawnbroker's, but nothing farther was ever seen of him, the watch, or the white mice. The next that Goldsmith heard of the poor shifting scapegrace, he was on his death bed, starving with want, upon which, forgetting or forgiving the trick he had played upon him, he sent him a guinea. Indeed he used often to relate with great humor the foregoing anecdote of his credulity, and was ultimately in some degree indemnified by its suggesting to him the amusing little story of Prince Bonbennin and the White Mouse in the Citizen of the World.

In this year Goldsmith became personally acquainted with Dr. Johnson, toward whom he was drawn by strong sympathies, though their natures were widely different. Both had struggled from early life with poverty but had struggled in different ways. Goldsmith, buoyant, heedless, sanguine, tolerant of evils and easily pleased, had shifted along by any temporary expedient; cast down at every turn but rising again with indomitable good humor and still carried forward by his talent at hoping. Johnson, melancholy and hypochondriacal, and prone to apprehend the worst, yet sternly resolute to battle with and conquer it, had made his way doggedly and gloomily but with a noble principle of self reliance and a disregard of foreign aid. Both had been irregular at college, Goldsmith, as we have shown, from the levity of his nature and his social and convivial habits; Johnson from his acerbity and gloom. When in after life the latter heard himself spoken of as gay and frolicsome at college because he had joined in some riotous excesses there, "Ah, sir!" replied he, "I was mad and violent. It was bitterness which they mistook for frolic. *I was miserably poor, and I thought to fight my way by my literature and my wit.* So I disregarded all power and all authority."

Goldsmith's poverty was never accompanied by bitterness; but neither was it accompanied by the guardian pride which kept Johnson from falling into the degrading shifts of poverty. Goldsmith had an unfortunate facility at borrowing, and helping himself along by the contributions of his friends; no doubt trusting, in his hopeful way, of one day making retribution. Johnson never hoped and therefore never borrowed. In his sternest trials he proudly bore the ills he could not master. In his youth when some unknown friend, seeing his shoes completely worn out, left a new pair at his chamber door, he disdained to accept the boon and threw them away.

Though like Goldsmith an immethodical student, he had imbibed deeper draughts of knowledge, and made himself a riper scholar. While Goldsmith's happy constitution and genial humors carried him abroad into sunshine and enjoyment, Johnson's physical infirmities and mental gloom drove him upon himself; to the resources of reading and meditation; threw a deeper though darker enthusiasm into his mind and stored a retentive memory with all kinds of knowledge.

After several years of youth passed in the country as usher, teacher, and an occasional writer for the press, Johnson, when twenty eight years of age, came up to London with a half written tragedy in his pocket; and David Garrick, late his pupil, and several years his junior, as a companion, both poor and penniless, both, like Goldsmith, seeking their fortune in the metropolis. "We rode and tied," said Garrick sportively in after years of prosperity, when he spoke of their humble wayfaring. "I came to London," said Johnson, "with twopence halfpenny in my pocket."—"Eh, what's that you say?" cried Garrick, "with twopence halfpenny in your pocket?" "Why, yes: I came with twopence halfpenny in *my* pocket, and thou, Davy, with but three halfpence in thine." Nor was there much exaggeration in the picture; for so poor were they in purse and credit that after their arrival they had with difficulty raised five pounds by giving their joint note to a bookseller in the Strand.

Many, many years had Johnson gone on obscurely in London, "fighting his way by his literature and his wit;" enduring all the hardships and miseries of a Grub Street writer: so destitute at one time that he and Savage the poet had walked all night about St. James's Square, both too poor to pay for a night's lodging, yet both full of poetry and patriotism and determined to stand by their country; so shabby in dress at another time that when he dined at Cave his bookseller's, when there was prosperous company, he could not make his appearance at table but had his dinner handed to him behind a screen.

Yet through all the long and dreary struggle, often diseased in mind as well as in body, he had been resolutely self dependent, and proudly self respectful; he had fulfilled his college vow, he had "fought his way by his literature and his wit." His "Rambler" and "Idler" had made him the great moralist of the age, and his "Dictionary and History of the English Language," that stupendous monument of individual labor, had excited the admiration of the learned world. He was now at the head of intellectual society; and had become as distinguished by his conversational as his literary powers. He had become as much an autocrat in his sphere as his fellow wayfarer and adventurer Garrick had become of the stage, and had been humorously dubbed by Smollett, "The Great Cham of Literature."

Such was Dr. Johnson when on the 31st of May, 1761, he was to make his appearance as a guest at a literary supper given by Goldsmith to a numerous party at his new lodgings in Wine Office Court. It was the opening of their acquaintance. Johnson had felt and acknowledged the merit of Goldsmith as an author and been pleased by the honorable mention made of himself in the Bee and the Chinese Letters. Dr. Percy called upon Johnson to take him to Goldsmith's lodgings; he found Johnson arrayed with unusual care in a new suit of clothes, a new hat, and a well-powdered wig; and could not but notice his uncommon spruceness. "Why, sir," replied Johnson, "I hear that Goldsmith, who is a very great sloven, justifies his disregard of cleanliness and decency by quoting my practice, and I am desirous this night to show him a better example."

The acquaintance thus commenced ripened into intimacy in the course of frequent meetings at the shop of Davies, the bookseller, in Russell Street, Covent Garden. As this was one of the great literary gossiping places of the day, especially to the circle over which Johnson presided, it is worthy of some specification. Mr. Thomas Davies, noted in after times as the biographer of Garrick, had originally been on the stage, and though a small man, had enacted tyrannical tragedy, with a pomp and magniloquence beyond his size, if we may trust the description given of him by Churchill in the Rosciad:

> Statesman all over—in plots famous grown,
> *He mouths a sentence as curs mouth a bone.*

This unlucky sentence is said to have crippled him in the midst of his tragic career, and ultimately to have driven him from the stage. He carried into the bookselling craft somewhat of the grandiose manner of the stage and was prone to be mouthy and magniloquent.

Churchill had intimated that while on the stage he was more noted for his pretty wife than his good acting:

> With him came mighty Davies; on my life,
> That fellow has a very pretty wife.

'Pretty Mrs. Davies' continued to be the lode star of his fortunes. Her tea table became almost as much a literary lounge as her husband's shop. She found favor in the eyes of the Ursa Major of literature by her winning ways, as she poured out for him cups without stint of his favorite beverage. Indeed it is suggested that she was one leading cause of his habitual resort to this literary haunt. Others were drawn thither for the sake of Johnson's conversation, and thus it became a resort of many of the notorieties of the day. Here might occasionally be seen Bennet Langton, George Steevens, Dr. Percy, celebrated for his ancient ballads, and sometimes Warburton in prelatic state. Garrick resorted to it for a time, but soon grew shy and suspicious, declaring that most of the authors who frequented Mr. Davies's shop went merely to abuse him.

Foote, the Aristophanes of the day, was a frequent visitor; his broad face beaming with fun and waggery, and his satirical eye ever on the look out for characters and incidents for his farces. He was struck with the odd habits and appearance of Johnson and Goldsmith, now so often brought together in Davies's shop. He was about to put on the stage a farce called The Orators, intended as a hit at the Robin Hood debating club, and resolved to show up the two doctors in it for the entertainment of the town.

"What is the common price of an oak stick, sir?" said Johnson to Davies. "Sixpence," was the reply. "Why then, sir, give me leave to send your servant to purchase a shilling one. I'll have a double quantity;

for I am told Foote means to take me off as he calls it, and I am determined the fellow shall not do it with impunity."

Foote had no disposition to undergo the criticism of the cudgel wielded by such potent hands, so the farce of The Orators appeared without the caricatures of the lexicographer and the essayist.

CHAPTER XIII

Oriental projects—Literary jobs—The Cherokee chiefs—Merry Isling-
ton and the White Conduit House—Letters on the History of Eng-
land—James Boswell—Dinner of Davies—Anecdotes of Johnson and
Goldsmith

Notwithstanding his growing success, Goldsmith continued to consider literature a mere make shift, and his vagrant imagination teemed with schemes and plans of a grand but indefinite nature. One was for visiting the East and exploring the interior of Asia. He had, as has been before observed, a vague notion that valuable discoveries were to be made there, and many useful inventions in the arts brought back to the stock of European knowledge. "Thus, in Siberian Tartary," observes he, in one of his writings, "the natives extract a strong spirit from milk, which is a secret probably unknown to the chymists of Europe. In the most savage parts of India they are possessed of the secret of dying vegetable substances scarlet, and that of refining lead into a metal which, for hardness and colour, is little inferior to silver."

Goldsmith adds a description of the kind of person suited to such an enterprise, in which he evidently had himself in view.

"He should be a man of philosophical turn, one apt to deduce consequences of general utility from particular occurrences; neither swoln with pride, nor hardened by prejudice; neither wedded to one particular system, nor instructed only in one particular science; neither wholly a botanist, nor quite an antiquarian; his mind should be tinctured with miscellaneous knowledge, and his manners humanized by an intercourse with men. He should be in some measure an enthusiast to the design; fond of travelling, from a rapid imagination and an innate love of change; furnished with a body capable of sustaining every fatigue, and a heart not easily terrified at danger."

In 1761, when Lord Bute became prime minister on the accession of George the Third, Goldsmith drew up a memorial on the subject, suggesting the advantages to be derived from a mission to those countries solely for useful and scientific purposes; and, the better to insure success, he preceded his application to the government by an ingenious essay to the same effect in the Public Ledger.

His memorial and his essay were fruitless, his project most probably being deemed the dream of a visionary. Still it continued to haunt his mind, and he would often talk of making an expedition to Aleppo some time or other, when his means were greater, to inquire into the arts peculiar to the East, and to bring home such as might be valuable.

Johnson, who knew how little poor Goldsmith was fitted by scientific lore for this favorite scheme of his fancy, scoffed at the project when it was mentioned to him. "Of all men," said he, "Goldsmith is the most unfit to go out upon such an inquiry, for he is utterly ignorant of such arts as we already possess, and, consequently, could not know what would be accessions to our present stock of mechanical knowledge. Sir, he would bring home a grinding barrow, which you see in every street in London, and think that he had furnished a wonderful improvement."

His connection with Newbery the bookseller now led him into a variety of temporary jobs, such as a pamphlet on the Cock-lane Ghost, a Life of Beau Nash, the famous Master of Ceremonies at Bath, &c.: one of the best things for his fame, however, was the remodelling and republication of his Chinese Letters under the title of "the Citizen of the World," a work which has long since taken its merited stand among the classics of the English language. "Few works," it has been observed by one of his biographers, "exhibit a nicer perception, or more delicate delineation of life and manners. Wit, humour, and sentiment pervade every page; the vices and follies of the day are touched with the most playful and diverting satire; and English characteristics, in endless variety, are hit off with the pencil of a master."

In seeking materials for his varied views of life, he often mingled in strange scenes and got involved in whimsical situations. In the summer of 1762 he was one of the thousands who went to see the Cherokee chiefs, whom he mentions in one of his writings. The Indians made their appearance in grand costume, hideously painted and besmeared. In the course of the visit Goldsmith made one of the chiefs a present, who, in the ecstasy of his gratitude, gave him an embrace that left his face well bedaubed with oil and red ochre.

Towards the close of 1762 he removed to "merry Islington," then a country village, though now swallowed up in omnivorous London. He went there for the benefit of country air, his health being injured by literary application and confinement, and to be near his chief employer, Mr. Newbery, who resided in the Canonbury House. In this neighborhood he used to take his solitary rambles, sometimes extending his walks to the gardens of the "White Conduit House," so famous among the essayists of the last century. While strolling one day in these gardens, he met three females of the family of a respectable tradesman to whom he was under some obligation. With his prompt disposition to oblige, he conducted them about the garden, treated them to tea, and ran up a bill in the most open-handed manner imaginable; it was only when he came to pay that he found himself in one of his old dilemmas—he had not the wherewithal in his pocket. A scene of perplexity now took place between him and the waiter, in the midst of which came up some of his acquaintances, in whose eyes he wished to stand particularly well. This completed his mortification. There was no concealing the awkwardness of his position. The sneers of the waiter revealed it. His acquaintances amused themselves for some time at his expense, professing their inability to relieve him. When, however, they had enjoyed their banter, the waiter was paid, and poor Goldsmith enabled to convoy off the ladies with flying colors.

Among the various productions thrown off by him for the booksellers during this growing period of his reputation, was a small work in two volumes, entitled "the History of England, in a series of Letters from a Nobleman to his Son." It was digested from Hume, Rapin, Carte, and Kennet. These authors he would read in the morning; make a few notes; ramble with a friend into the country about the skirts of "merry Islington;" return to a temperate dinner and cheerful evening; and, before going to bed, write off what had arranged itself in his head from the studies of the morning. In this way he took a more general view of the subject, and wrote in a more free and fluent style than if he had been mousing at the time among authorities. The work, like many others written by him in the earlier part of his literary career, was anonymous. Some attributed it to Lord Chesterfield, others to Lord Orrery, and others to Lord Lyttleton. The latter seemed pleased to be the putative father, and never disowned the bantling thus laid at his door; and well might he have been proud to be considered capable of producing what has been well-pronounced "the most finished and elegant summary of English history in the same compass that has been or is likely to be written."

The reputation of Goldsmith, it will be perceived, grew slowly; he was known and estimated by a few; but he had not those brilliant though fallacious qualities which flash upon the public, and excite loud but transient applause. His works were more read than cited; and the charm of style, for which he was especially noted, was more apt to be felt than talked about. He used often to repine, in a half humorous, half querulous manner, at his tardiness in gaining the laurels which he felt to be his due. "The public," he would exclaim, "will never do me justice; whenever I write any thing, they make a point to know nothing about it."

About the beginning of 1763 he became acquainted with Boswell, whose literary gossipings were destined to have a deleterious effect upon his reputation. Boswell was at that time a young man, light, buoyant, pushing and presumptuous. He had a morbid passion for mingling in the society of men noted for wit and learning, and had just arrived from Scotland, bent upon making his way into the literary circles

of the metropolis: an intimacy with Dr. Johnson, the great literary luminary of the day, was the crowning object of his aspiring and somewhat
ludicrous ambition. He expected to meet him at a dinner to which he
was invited at Davies the bookseller's but was disappointed. Goldsmith was present, but he was not as yet sufficiently renowned
to excite the reverence of Boswell. "At this time," says he in his notes,
"I think he had published nothing with his name, though it was pretty
generally understood that one Dr. Goldsmith was the author of 'An
Inquiry into the present State of Polite Learning in Europe,' and of
'The Citizen of the World,' a series of letters supposed to be written
from London, by a Chinese."

A conversation took place at table between Goldsmith and Mr.
Robert Dodsley, compiler of the well known collection of modern
poetry, as to the merits of the current poetry of the day. Goldsmith
declared there was none of superior merit. Dodsley cited his own
collection in proof of the contrary. "It is true," said he, "we can boast
of no palaces nowadays, like Dryden's Ode to St. Cecilia's Day, but
we have villages composed of very pretty houses." Goldsmith, however,
maintained that there was nothing above mediocrity, an opinion in
which Johnson, to whom it was repeated, concurred, and with reason,
for the era was one of the dead levels of British poetry.

Boswell has made no note of this conversation; he was a unitarian
in his literary devotion and disposed to worship none but Johnson. Little
Davies endeavored to console him for his disappointment and to stay
the stomach of his curiosity, by giving him imitations of the great
lexicographer; mouthing his words, rolling his head and assuming as
ponderous a manner as his petty person would permit. Boswell was
shortly afterwards made happy by an introduction to Johnson, of whom
he became the obsequious satellite. From him he likewise imbibed a
more favorable opinion of Goldsmith's merits, though he was fain to
consider them derived in a great measure from his Magnus Apollo.
"He had sagacity enough," says he, "to cultivate assiduously the
acquaintance of Johnson, and his faculties were gradually enlarged by
the contemplation of such a model. To me and many others it appeared
that he studiously copied the manner of Johnson, though, indeed, upon
a smaller scale." So on another occasion he calls him "one of the
brightest ornaments of the Johnsonian school." "His respectful attachment to Johnson," adds he, "was then at its height; for his own literary
reputation had not yet distinguished him so much as to excite a vain
desire of competition with his great master."

What beautiful instances does the garrulous Boswell give of the
goodness of heart of Johnson and the passing homage to it by Goldsmith. They were speaking of a Mr. Levett, long an inmate of John-

son's house and a dependent on his bounty; but who, Boswell thought, must be an irksome charge upon him. "He is poor and honest," said Goldsmith, "which is recommendation enough to Johnson."

Boswell mentioned another person of a very bad character, and wondered at Johnson's kindness to him. "He is now become miserable," said Goldsmith, "and that insures the protection of Johnson." Encomiums like these speak almost as much for the heart of him who praises as of him who is praised.

Subsequently, when Boswell had become more intense in his literary idolatry, he affected to undervalue Goldsmith, and a lurking hostility to him is discernible throughout his writings, which some have attributed to a silly spirit of jealousy of the superior esteem evinced for the poet by Dr. Johnson. We have a gleam of this in his account of the first evening he spent in company with those two eminent authors at their famous resort, the Mitre Tavern in Fleet Street. This took place on the 1st of July, 1763. The trio supped together, and passed some time in literary conversation. On quitting the tavern, Johnson, who had now been sociably acquainted with Goldsmith for two years, and knew his merits, took him with him to drink tea with his blind pensioner, Miss Williams; a high privilege among his intimates and admirers. To Boswell, a recent acquaintance, whose intrusive sycophancy had not yet made its way into his confidential intimacy, he gave no invitation. Boswell felt it with all the jealousy of a little mind. "Dr. Goldsmith," says he, in his memoirs, "being a privileged man, went with him, strutting away, and calling to me with an air of superiority, like that of an esoteric over an exoteric disciple of a sage of antiquity, 'I go to Miss Williams.' I confess I then envied him this mighty privilege, of which he seemed to be so proud; but it was not long before I obtained the same mark of distinction."

Obtained! but how? not like Goldsmith, by the force of unpretending but congenial merit, but by a course of the most pushing, contriving, and spaniel-like subserviency. Really, the ambition of the man to illustrate his mental insignificance, by continually placing himself in juxtaposition with the great lexicographer, has something in it perfectly ludicrous. Never, since the days of Don Quixote and Sancho Panza, has there been presented to the world a more whimsically contrasted pair of associates than Johnson and Boswell.

"Who is this Scotch cur at Johnson's heels?" asked some one when Boswell had worked his way into incessant companionship. "He is not a cur," replied Goldsmith, "you are too severe. He is only a bur. Tom Davies flung him at Johnson in sport, and he has the faculty of sticking."

CHAPTER XIV

Hogarth a visitor at Islington; his character—Street studies—Sympathies between authors and painters—Sir Joshua Reynolds; his character; his dinners—The Literary Club; its members—Johnson's revels with Lanky and Beau—Goldsmith at the Club

Among the intimates who used to visit the poet occasionally in his retreat at Islington was Hogarth the painter. Goldsmith had spoken well of him in his essays in the Public Ledger, and this formed the first link in their friendship. He was at this time upwards of sixty years of age and is described as a stout, active, bustling little man, in a sky blue coat, satirical and dogmatic, yet full of real benevolence and the love of human nature. He was the moralist and philosopher of the pencil; like Goldsmith he had sounded the depths of vice and misery without being polluted by them; and though his picturings had not the pervading amenity of those of the essayist, and dwelt more on the crimes and vices than the follies and humors of mankind, yet they were all calculated in like manner, to fill the mind with instruction and precept, and to make the heart better.

Hogarth does not appear to have had much of the rural feeling with which Goldsmith was so amply endowed, and may not have accompanied him in his strolls about hedges and green lanes; but he was a fit companion with whom to explore the mazes of London, in which he was continually on the look out for character and incident. One of Hogarth's admirers speaks of having come upon him in Castle Street, engaged in one of his street studies, watching two boys who were quarrelling; patting one on the back who flinched, and endeavoring to spirit him up to a fresh encounter. "At him again! D——— him, if I would take it of him! at him again!"

A frail memorial of this intimacy between the painter and the poet exists in a portrait in oil, called 'Goldsmith's Hostess.' It is supposed to have been painted by Hogarth in the course of his visits to Islington and given by him to the poet as a means of paying his landlady. There are no friendships among men of talents more likely to be sincere than those between painters and poets. Possessed of the same qualities of mind, governed by the same principles of taste and natural laws of grace and beauty, but applying them to different yet mutually illustrative arts, they are constantly in sympathy, and never in collision with each other.

A still more congenial intimacy of the kind was that contracted by Goldsmith with Mr. afterwards Sir Joshua Reynolds. The latter was

now about forty years of age, a few years older than the poet, whom
he charmed by the blandness and benignity of his manners and the
nobleness and generosity of his disposition, as much as he did by the
graces of his pencil and the magic of his coloring. They were men of
kindred genius, excelling in corresponding qualities of their several
arts, for style in writing is what color is in panting; both are innate
endowments, and equally magical in their effects. Certain graces and
harmonies of both may be acquired by diligent study and imitation,
but only in a limited degree; whereas by their natural possessors they
are exercised spontaneously, almost unconsciously, and with ever-vary-
ing fascination. Reynolds soon understood and appreciated the merits
of Goldsmith, and a sincere and lasting friendship ensued between
them.

At Reynolds's house Goldsmith mingled in a higher range of company
than he had been accustomed to. The fame of this celebrated artist
and his amenity of manners were gathering round him men of talents
of all kinds, and the increasing affluence of his circumstances enabled
him to give full indulgence to his hospitable disposition. Poor Goldsmith had not yet like Dr. Johnson acquired reputation enough to
atone for his external defects and his want of the air of good society.
Miss Reynolds used to inveigh against his personal appearance, which
gave her the idea, she said, of a low mechanic, a journeyman tailor.
One evening at a large supper party, being called upon to give as a
toast, the ugliest man she knew, she gave Dr. Goldsmith, upon which
a lady who sat opposite, and whom she had never met before, shook
hands with her across the table and "hoped to become better acquainted."

We have a graphic and amusing picture of Reynolds's hospitable
but motley establishment in an account given by a Mr. Courtenay to
Sir James Mackintosh; though it speaks of a time after Reynolds had
received the honor of knighthood. "There was something singular,"
said he, "in the style and economy of Sir Joshua's table that contributed to pleasantry and good-humour, a course inelegant plenty,
without any regard to order and arrangement. At five o'clock precisely
dinner was served, whether all the invited guests were arrived or not.
Sir Joshua was never so fashionably ill-bred as to wait an hour perhaps
for two or three persons of rank or title, and put the rest of the company out of humour by this invidious distinction. His invitations,
however, did not regulate the number of his guests. Many dropped
in uninvited. A table prepared for seven or eight was often compelled
to contain fifteen or sixteen. There was a consequent deficiency of
knives, forks, plates, and glasses. The attendance was in the same
style, and those who were knowing in the ways of the house took care
on sitting down to call instantly for beer, bread or wine, that they

might secure a supply before the first course was over. He was once prevailed on to furnish the table with decanters and glasses at dinner, to save time and prevent confusion. These gradually were demolished in the course of service and were never replaced. These trifling embarrassments however only served to enhance the hilarity and singular pleasure of the entertainment. The wine, cookery and dishes were but little attended to; nor was the fish or venison ever talked of or recommended. Amidst this convivial, animated bustle among his guests, our host sat perfectly composed; always attentive to what was said, never minding what was eat or drank, but left every one at perfect liberty to scramble for himself."

Out of the casual but frequent meetings of men of talent at this hospitable board rose that association of wits, authors, scholars and statesmen renowned as the Literary Club. Reynolds was the first to propose a regular association of the kind and was eagerly seconded by Johnson, who proposed as a model a club which he had formed many years previously in Ivy Lane, but which was now extinct. Like that club the number of members was limited to nine. They were to meet and sup together once a week on Monday night at the Turk's Head on Gerard Street, Soho, and two members were to constitute a meeting. It took a regular form in the year 1764 but did not receive its literary appellation until several years afterwards.

The original members were Reynolds, Johnson, Burke, Dr. Nugent, Bennet Langton, Topham Beauclerc, Chamier, Hawkins and Goldsmith; and here a few words concerning some of the members may be acceptable. Burke was at that time about thirty three years of age; he had mingled a little in politics and been Under Secretary to Hamilton at Dublin, but was again a writer for the booksellers and as yet but in the dawning of his fame. Dr. Nugent was his father in law, a Roman Catholic and a physician of talent and instruction. Mr. afterwards Sir John Hawkins was admitted into this association from having been a member of Johnson's Ivy Lane club. Originally an attorney, he had retired from the practice of the law in consequence of a large fortune which fell to him in right of his wife, and was now a Middlesex magistrate. He was moreover a dabbler in literature and music, and was actually engaged on a history of music, which he subsequently published in five ponderous volumes. To him we are also indebted for a biography of Johnson, which appeared after the death of that eminent man. Hawkins was as mean and parsimonious as he was pompous and conceited. He forebore to partake of the suppers at the Club and begged, therefore, to be excused from paying his share of the reckoning. "And was he excused?" asked Dr. Burney of Johnson. "Oh yes, for no man is angry at another for being inferior to himself.

We all scorned him and admitted his plea. Yet I really believe him to be an honest man at bottom, though to be sure he is penurious, and he is mean, and it must be owned he has a tendency to savageness." He did not remain above two or three years in the club; being in a manner elbowed out in consequence of his rudeness to Burke.

Mr. Anthony Chamier was Secretary in the war office and a friend of Beauclerc, by whom he was proposed. We have left our mention of Bennet Langton and Topham Beauclerc until the last, because we have most to say about them. They were doubtless induced to join the club through their devotion to Johnson, and the intimacy of these two very young and aristocratic young men with the stern and somewhat melancholy moralist is among the curiosities of literature.

Bennet Langton was of an ancient family, who held their ancestral estate of Langton in Lincolnshire, a great title to respect with Johnson. "Langton, sir," he would say, "has a grant of free-warren from Henry the Second; and Cardinal Stephen Langton, in King John's reign, was of this family."

Langton was of a mild, contemplative, enthusiastic nature. When but eighteen years of age he was so delighted with reading Johnson's Rambler, that he came to London chiefly with a view to obtain an introduction to the author. Boswell gives us an account of his first interview, which took place in the morning. It is not often that the personal appearance of an author agrees with the preconceived ideas of his admirer. Langton, from perusing the writings of Johnson, expected to find him "a decent, well drest, in short a remarkably decorous philosopher. Instead of which, down from his bedchamber about noon, came, as newly risen, a huge uncouth figure, with a little dark wig which scarcely covered his head, and his clothes hanging loose about him. But his conversation was so rich, so animated, and so forcible, and his religious and political notions so congenial with those in which Langton had been educated, that he conceived for him that veneration and attachment which he ever preserved."

Langton went to pursue his studies at Trinity College, Oxford, where Johnson saw much of him during a visit which he paid to the University. He found him in close intimacy with Topham Beauclerc, a youth two years older than himself, very gay and dissipated, and wondered what sympathies could draw two young men together of such opposite characters. On becoming acquainted with Beauclerc he found that, rake though he was, he possesed an ardent love of literature, an acute understanding, polished wit, innate gentility and high aristocratic breeding. He was moreover the only son of Lord Sidney Beauclerc and grandson of the Duke of St. Albans, and was thought in some particulars to have a resemblance to Charles the Second. These were high recommendations with Johnson, and when the youth testified a profound respect for him and an ardent admiration of his talents the conquest was complete, so that in a "short time," says Boswell, "the moral pious Johnson and the gay dissipated Beauclerc were companions."

The intimacy begun in college chambers was continued when the youths came to town during the vacations. The uncouth, unwieldy moralist was flattered at finding himself an object of idolatry to two high born, high bred, aristocratic young men and, throwing gravity aside, was ready to join in their vagaries and play the part of a 'young man upon town.' Such at least is the picture given of him by Boswell on one occasion when Beauclerc and Langton, having supped together at a tavern, determined to give Johnson a rouse at three o'clock in the morning. They accordingly rapped violently at the door of his chambers in the Temple. The indignant sage sallied forth in his shirt, poker in hand and a little black wig in the top of his head instead of helmet; prepared to wreak vengeance on the assailants of his castle: but when his two young friends, *Lanky* and *Beau,* as he used to call them, presented themselves, summoning him forth to a morning ramble, his whole manner changed. "What, is it you, ye dogs!" cried he. "Faith, I'll have a frisk with you!"

So said so done. They sallied forth together into Covent Garden; figured among the green grocers and fruit women, just come in from the country with their hampers; repaired to a neighboring tavern, where Johnson brewed a bowl of *bishop,* a favorite beverage with him, grew merry over his cups and anathematized sleep in two lines from Lord Lansdowne's drinking song:

> Short, very short, be then thy reign,
> For I'm in haste to laugh and drink again.

They then took boat, rowed to Billingsgate, and Johnson and Beauclerc determined like "mad wags" to "keep it up" for the rest of the day. Langton, however, the most sober minded of the three, pleaded an engagement to breakfast with some young ladies; whereupon the great moralist reproached him with "leaving his social friends to go and sit with a set of wretched *un-idea'd* girls."

This madcap freak of the great lexicographer made a sensation, as may well be supposed, among his intimates. "I heard of your frolic t'other night," said Garrick to him; "you'll be in the Chronicle." He uttered worse forebodings to others. "I shall have my old friend to bail out of the round-house," said he. Johnson, however, valued himself upon having thus enacted a chapter in the Rake's Progress, and crowed over Garrick on the occasion. "*He* durst not do such a thing!" chuckled he, "his *wife* would not *let* him!"

When these two young men entered the Club, Langton was about twenty two, and Beauclerc about twenty four years of age, and both were launched on London life. Langton, however, was still the mild, enthusiastic scholar, steeped to the lips in Greek, with fine conversational powers and an invaluable talent for listening. He was upwards of six feet high, and very spare. "Oh! that we could sketch him," exclaims Miss Hawkins in her Memoirs, "with his mild countenance, his elegant features, and his sweet smile, sitting with one leg twisted round the other, as if fearing to occupy more space than was equitable; his person inclining forward as if wanting strength to support his weight and his arms crossed over his bosom or his hands locked together on his knee." Beauclerc on such occasions sportively compared him to a stork in Raphael's Cartoons, standing on one leg. Beauclerc was more a "man upon town," a lounger in St. James's Street, an associate with George Selwyn, with Walpole and other aristocratic wits; a man of fashion at court; a casual frequenter of the gaming table; yet with all this he alternated in the easiest and happiest manner the scholar and the man of letters; lounged into the club with the most perfect self possession, bringing with him the careless grace and polished wit of high bred society but making himself cordially at home among his learned fellow members.

The gay yet lettered rake maintained his sway over Johnson, who was fascinated by that air of the world, that ineffable tone of good society in which he felt himself deficient, especially as the possessor of it always paid homage to his superior talent. "Beauclerc," he would say, using a quotation from Pope, "has a love of folly but a scorn of fools; every thing he does shows the one, and every thing he says the other." Beauclerc delighted in rallying the stern moralist of whom others stood in awe, and no one, according to Boswell, could take equal liberty with him with impunity. Johnson, it is well known, was often shabby and negligent in his dress and not overcleanly in his person. On receiving a pension from the crown, his friends vied with each other in respectful congratulations. Beauclerc simply scanned his person with a whimsical glance and hoped that, like Falstaff, "he'd in future purge and live cleanly like a gentleman." Johnson took the hint with unexpected good humor, and profited by it.

Still Beauclerc's satirical vein, which darted shafts on every side, was not always tolerated by Johnson. "Sir," said he on one occasion, "you never open your mouth but with intention to give pain; and you have often given me pain, not from the power of what you have said, but from seeing your intention."

When it was at first proposed to enroll Goldsmith among the members of this association, there seems to have been some demur; at least so says the pompous Hawkins. "As he wrote for the booksellers, we of the club looked on him as a mere literary drudge, equal to the task of compiling and translating, but little capable of original and still less of poetical composition."

Even for some time after his admission he continued to be regarded in a dubious light by some of the members. Johnson and Reynolds of course were well aware of his merits, nor was Burke a stranger to them; but to the others he was as yet a sealed book, and the outside was not prepossessing. His ungainly person and awkward manners were against him with men accustomed to the graces of society, and he was not sufficiently at home to give play to his humors and to that bonhommie which won the hearts of all who knew him. He felt strange and out of place in this new sphere; he felt at times the cool satirical eye of the courtly Beauclerc scanning him, and the more he attempted to appear at his ease, the more awkward he became.

CHAPTER XV

Johnson had now become one of Goldsmith's best friends and advisers. He knew all the weak points of his character, but he knew also his merits; and while he would rebuke him like a child, and rail at his errors and follies, he would suffer no one else to undervalue him. Goldsmith knew the soundness of his judgment and his practical benevolence, and often sought his counsel and aid amid the difficulties into which his heedlessness was continually plunging him.

"I received one morning," says Johnson, "a message from poor Goldsmith that he was in great distress, and, as it was not in his power to come to me, begging that I would come to him as soon as possible. I sent him a guinea, and promised to come to him directly. I accordingly went as soon as I was dressed, and found that his landlady had arrested him for his rent, at which he was in a violent passion: I perceived that he had already changed my guinea, and had a bottle of Madeira and a glass before him. I put the cork into the bottle, desired he would be calm, and began to talk to him of the means by which he might be extricated. He then told me that he had a novel ready for the press, which he produced to me. I looked into it and saw its merit; told the landlady I should soon return; and, having gone to a bookseller, sold it for sixty pounds. I brought Goldsmith the money, and he discharged his rent, not without rating his landlady in a high tone for having used him so ill."

The novel in question was the "Vicar of Wakefield:" the bookseller to whom Johnson sold it was Francis Newbery, nephew to John. Strange as it may seem, this captivating work, which has obtained and preserved an almost unrivalled popularity in various languages, was so little appreciated by the bookseller, that he kept it by him for nearly two years unpublished!

Goldsmith had, as yet, produced nothing of moment in poetry. Among his literary jobs, it is true, was an Oratorio entitled "The Captivity," founded on the bondage of the Israelites in Babylon. It was one of those unhappy offsprings of the muse ushered into existence amid the distortions of music. Most of the Oratorio has passed into oblivion; but the following song from it will never die.

The wretch condemned from life to part,
    Still, still on hope relies
And every pang that rends the heart
    Bids expectation rise.

Hope like the glimmering taper's light,
    Illumes and cheers our way;
And still as darker grows the night
    Emits a brighter ray.

Goldsmith distrusted his qualifications to succeed in poetry and doubted the disposition of the public mind in regard to it. "I fear," said he, "I have come too late into the world; Pope and other poets have taken up the places in the temple of Fame; and as few at any period can possess poetical reputation, a man of genius can now hardly acquire it." Again, on another occasion, he observes: "Of all kinds of ambition, as things are now circumstanced, perhaps that which pursues poetical fame is the wildest. What from the increased refinement of the times, from the diversity of judgment produced by opposing systems of criticism, and from the more prevalent divisions of opinion influenced by party, the strongest and happiest efforts can expect to please but in a very narrow circle."

At this very time he had by him his poem of "The Traveller." The plan of it, as has already been observed, was conceived many years before, during his travels in Switzerland, and a sketch of it sent from that country to his brother Henry in Ireland. The original outline is said to have embraced a wider scope; but it was probably contracted through diffidence, in the process of finishing the parts. It had laid by him for several years in a crude state, and it was with extreme hesitation and after much revision that he at length submitted it to Dr. Johnson. The frank and warm approbation of the latter encouraged him to finish it for the press; and Dr. Johnson himself contributed a few lines towards the conclusion.

We hear much about "poetic inspiration," and the "poet's eye in a fine phrensy rolling;" but Sir Joshua Reynolds gives an anecdote of Goldsmith while engaged upon his poem, calculated to cure our notions about the ardor of composition. Calling upon the poet one day, he opened the door without ceremony, and found him in the double occupation of turning a couplet and teaching a pet dog to sit upon his haunches. At one time he would glance his eye at his desk, and at another shake his finger at the dog to make his retain his position. The last lines on the page were still wet; they form a part of the description of Italy:

> By sports like these are all their cares beguiled,
> The sports of children satisfy the child.

Goldsmith, with his usual good humor, joined in the laugh caused by his whimsical employment, and acknowledged that his boyish sport with the dog suggested the stanza.

The poem was published on the 19th of December, 1764, in a quarto form, by Newbery, and was the first of his works to which Goldsmith prefixed his name. As a testimony of cherished and well merited affection, he dedicated it to his brother Henry. There is an amusing affectation of indifference as to its fate expressed in the dedication. "What reception a poem may find," says he, "which has neither abuse, party, nor blank verse to support it, I cannot tell, nor am I solicitous to know." The truth is, no one was more emulous and anxious for poetic fame; and never was he more anxious than in the present instance, for it was his grand stake. Dr. Johnson aided the launching of the poem by a favorable notice in the Critical Review; other periodical works came out in its favor. Some of the author's friends complained that it did not command instant and wide popularity; that it was a poem to win, not to strike: it went on rapidly increasing in favor; in three months a second edition was issued; shortly afterwards, a third; then a fourth; and, before the year was out, the author was pronounced the best poet of his time.

The appearance of "The Traveller" at once altered Goldsmith's intellectual standing in the estimation of society; but its effect upon the club, if we may judge from the account given by Hawkins, was almost ludicrous. They were lost in astonishment that a "newspaper essayist" and "bookseller's drudge" should have written such a poem. On the evening of its announcement to them Goldsmith had gone away early, after "rattling away as usual," and they knew not how to reconcile his heedless garrulity with the serene beauty, the easy grace, the sound good sense, and the occasional elevation of his poetry. They could scarcely believe that such magic numbers had flowed from a man to whom in general, says Johnson, "it was with difficulty they could give a hearing." "Well," exclaimed Chamier, "I do believe he wrote this poem himself, and let me tell you, that is believing a great deal."

At the next meeting of the Club Chamier sounded the author a little about his poem. "Mr. Goldsmith," said he, "what do you mean by the last word in the first line of your Traveller, 'remote, unfriended, melancholy, *slow?*' Do you mean tardiness of locomotion?"—"Yes," replied Goldsmith inconsiderately, being probably flurried at the moment. "No, sir," interposed his protecting friend Johnson, "you did not mean tardiness of locomotion; you meant that sluggishness of mind which comes upon a man in solitude."—"Ah," exclaimed Goldsmith, "*that* was what I meant." Chamier immediately believed that Johnson himself had written the line, and a rumor became prevalent that he was the author of many of the finest passages. This was ultimately set at rest by Johnson himself, who marked with a pencil all the verses he had contributed, nine in number, inserted towards the conclusion, and by no means the best in the poem. He moreover with generous warmth pronounced it the finest poem that had appeared since the days of Pope.

But one of the highest testimonials to the charm of the poem was given by Miss Reynolds, who had toasted poor Goldsmith as the ugliest man of her acquaintance. Shortly after the appearance of "The Traveller" Dr. Johnson read it aloud from beginning to end in her presence. "Well," exclaimed she, when he had finished, "I never more shall think Dr. Goldsmith ugly!"

On another occasion when the merits of "The Traveller" were discussed at Reynolds's, Bennet Langton declared "there was not a bad line in the poem, not one of Dryden's careless verses." "I was glad," observed Reynolds, "to hear Charles Fox say it was one of the finest poems in the English language." "Why was you glad?" rejoined Langton, "you surely had no doubt of this before." "No," interposed Johnson decisively; "the merit of 'The Traveller' is so well established that Mr. Fox's praise cannot augment it, nor his censure diminish it."

Boswell, who was absent from England at the time of the publication of the Traveller, was astonished on his return to find Goldsmith, whom he had so much undervalued, suddenly elevated almost to a par with his idol. He accounted for it by concluding that much both of the sentiments and expression of the poem had been derived from conversations with Johnson. "He imitates you, sir," said this incarnation of toadyism. "Why no, sir," replied Johnson, "Jack Hawksworth is one of my imitators; but not Goldsmith. Goldy, sir, has great merit." "But, sir, he is much indebted to you for his getting so high in the public estimation." "Why, sir, he has perhaps got *sooner* to it by his intimacy with me."

The poem went through several editions in the course of the first year, and received some few additions and corrections from the author's pen. It produced a golden harvest to Mr. Newbery, but all the remuneration on record doled out by his niggard hand to the author was twenty guineas!

CHAPTER XVI

New lodgings—Johnson's compliment—A titled patron—The poet at Northumberland House—His independence of the great—The Countess of Northumberland—Edwin and Angelina—Gosfield and Lord Clare—Publication of Essays—Evils of a rising reputation—Hangers on—Job writing—Goody Two Shoes—A medical campaign—Mrs. Sidebotham

Goldsmith, now that he was rising in the world and becoming a notoriety, felt himself called upon to improve his style of living. He accordingly emerged from Wine Office Court and took chambers in the Temple. It is true they were but of humble pretensions, situated on what was then the library stair case, and it would appear that he was a kind of inmate with Jeffs, the butler of the society. Still he was in the Temple, that classic region, rendered famous by the Spectator and other essayists, as the abodes of gay wits and thoughtful men of letters; and which, with its retired courts and embowered gardens in the very heart of a noisy metropolis, is to the quiet-seeking student and author an oasis freshening with verdure in the midst of a desert. Johnson, who had become a kind of growling supervisor of the poet's affairs, paid him a visit soon after he had installed himself in his new quarters, and went prying about the apartment in his near sighted manner, examining every thing minutely. Goldsmith was fidgeted by this curious scrutiny and, apprehending a disposition to find fault, exclaimed, with the air of a man who had money in both pockets, "I shall soon be in better chambers than these." The harmless bravado drew a reply from Johnson, which touched the chord of proper pride. "Nay, sir," said he, "never mind that. Nil te quæsiveris extra"—implying that his reputation rendered him independent of outward show. Happy would it have been for poor Goldsmith could he have kept this consolatory compliment perpetually in mind, and squared his expenses accordingly.

Among the persons of rank who were struck with the merits of the Traveller was the Earl (afterwards Duke) of Northumberland. He procured several other of Goldsmith's writings, the perusal of which tended to elevate the author in his good opinion and to gain for him his good will. The earl held the office of Lord Lieutenant of Ireland, and understanding Goldsmith was an Irishman, was disposed to extend to him the patronage which his high post afforded. He intimated the same to his relative Dr. Percy, who he found was well acquainted with the poet, and expressed a wish that the latter should wait upon him. Here then was another opportunity for Goldsmith to better his fortune,

had he been knowing and worldly enough to profit by it. Unluckily the
path to fortune lay through the aristocratical mazes of Northumberland House, and the poet blundered at the outset. The following is the
account he used to give of his visit:—"I dressed myself in the best
manner I could, and, after studying some compliments I thought necessary on such an occasion, proceeded to Northumberland House, and
acquainted the servants that I had particular business with the duke.
They showed me into an antechamber, where, after waiting some time,
a gentleman very elegantly dressed made his appearance. Taking him
for the duke, I delivered all the fine things I had composed in order
to compliment him on the honour he had done me; when, to my great
astonishment, he told me I had mistaken him for his master, who would
see me immediately. At that instant the duke came into the apartment,
and I was so confounded on the occasion, that I wanted words barely
sufficient to express the sense I entertained of the duke's politeness,
and went away exceedingly chagrined at the blunder I had committed."

Sir John Hawkins, in his life of Dr. Johnson, gives some farther
particulars of this visit, of which he was, in part, a witness. "Having
one day," says he, "a call to make on the late Duke, then Earl, of Northumberland, I found Goldsmith waiting for an audience in an outer
room: I asked him what had brought him there; he told me, an
invitation from his lordship. I made my business as short as I could,
and, as a reason, mentioned that Dr. Goldsmith was waiting without.
The earl asked me if I was acquainted with him. I told him I was,
adding what I thought was most likely to recommend him. I retired,
and stayed in the outer room to take him home. Upon his coming out,
I asked him the result of his conversation. 'His lordship,' said he, 'told
me he had read my poem, meaning the Traveller, and was much delighted with it; that he was going to be lord-lieutenant of Ireland, and
that, hearing I was a native of that country, he should be glad to do
me any kindness.' 'And what did you answer,' said I, 'to this gracious
offer?' 'Why,' said he, 'I could say nothing but that I had a brother
there, a clergyman, that stood in need of help: as for myself, I have
no great dependence on the promises of great men; I look to the
booksellers for support; they are my best friends, and I am not inclined
to forsake them for others.'" "Thus," continues Sir John, "did this
idiot in the affairs of the world trifle with his fortunes, and put back
the hand that was held out to assist him."

We cannot join with Sir John in his worldly sneer at the conduct
of Goldsmith on this occasion. While we admire that honest independence of spirit which prevented him from asking favors for himself,
we love that warmth of affection which instantly sought to advance
the fortunes of a brother: but the peculiar merits of poor Goldsmith

seem to have been little understood by the Hawkinses, the Boswells, and the other biographers of the day.

After all, the introduction to Northumberland House did not prove so complete a failure as the humorous account given by Goldsmith and the cynical account given by Sir John Hawkins might lead one to suppose. Dr. Percy, the heir male of the ancient Percies, brought the poet into the acquaintance of his kinswoman, the countess; who, before her marriage with the earl, was in her own right heiress of the House of Northumberland. "She was a lady," says Boswell, "not only of high dignity of spirit, such as became her noble blood, but of excellent understanding and lively talents." Under her auspices a poem of Goldsmith's had an aristocratical introduction to the world. This was the beautiful ballad of "the Hermit," originally published under the name of "Edwin and Angelina." It was suggested by an old English ballad beginning "Gentle Herdsman," shown him by Dr. Percy, who was at that time making his famous collection entitled "Reliques of Ancient English Poetry," which he submitted to the inspection of Goldsmith prior to publication. A few copies only of the Hermit were printed at first, with the following title-page: "Edwin and Angelina: a Ballad. By Mr. Goldsmith. Printed for the Amusement of the Countess of Northumberland."

All this, though it may not have been attended with any immediate pecuniary advantage, contributed to give Goldsmith's name and poetry the high stamp of fashion, so potent in England: the circle at Northumberland House, however, was of too stately and aristocratical a nature to be much to his taste, and we do not find that he became familiar in it.

He was much more at home at Gosfield, the seat of his countryman Robert Nugent, afterwards Baron Nugent and Viscount Clare, who appreciated his merits even more heartily than the Earl of Northumberland, and occasionally made him his guest both in town and country. Nugent is described as a jovial voluptuary, who left the Roman Catholic for the Protestant religion with a view to bettering his fortunes; he had an Irishman's inclination for rich widows and an Irishman's luck with the sex; having been thrice married and gained a fortune with each wife. He was now nearly sixty, with a remarkably loud voice, broad Irish brogue and ready but somewhat coarse wit. With all his occasional coarseness he was capable of high thought and had produced poems which showed a truly poetic vein. He was long a member of the House of Commons, where his ready wit, his fearless decision and good humored audacity of expression always gained him a hearing, though his tall person and awkward manner gained him the nickname of Squire Gawkey among the political scribblers of the day. With a patron of this jovial temperament Goldsmith probably felt more at ease than with those of higher refinement.

The celebrity which Goldsmith had acquired by his poem of "The Traveller," occasioned a resuscitation of many of his miscellaneous and anonymous tales and essays from the various newspapers and other transient publications in which they lay dormant. These he published in 1765, in a collected form, under the title of "Essays by Mr. Goldsmith." "The following Essays," observes he in his preface, "have already appeared at different times, and in different publications. The pamphlets in which they were inserted being generally unsuccessful, these shared the common fate, without assisting the bookseller's aims, or extending the author's reputation. The public were too strenuously employed with their own follies to be assiduous in estimating mine; so that many of my best attempts in this way have fallen victims to the transient topic of the times—the Ghost in Cock-Lane, or the Siege of Ticonderoga.

"But, though they have passed pretty silently into the world, I can by no means complain of their circulation. The magazines and papers of the day have indeed been liberal enough in this respect. Most of these essays have been regularly reprinted twice or thrice a year, and conveyed to the public through the kennel of some engaging compilation. If there be a pride in multiplied editions, I have seen some of my labours sixteen times reprinted, and claimed by different parents as their own. I have seen them flourished at the beginning with praise, and signed at the end with the names of Philautos, Philalethes, Phileleutheros, and Philanthropos. It is time, however, at last to vindicate my claims; and as these entertainers of the public, as they call themselves, have partly lived upon me for some years, let me now try if I cannot live a little upon myself."

It was but little, in fact, for all the pecuniary emolument he received from the volume was twenty guineas. It had a good circulation, however, was translated into French, and has maintained its stand among the British classics.

Notwithstanding that the reputation of Goldsmith had greatly risen, his finances were often at a very low ebb, owing to his heedlessness as to expense, his liability to be imposed upon, and a spontaneous and irresistible propensity to give to every one who asked. The very rise in his reputation had increased these embarrassments. It had enlarged his circle of needy acquaintances, authors poorer in pocket than himself, who came in search of literary counsel; which generally meant a guinea and a breakfast. And then his Irish hangers on! "Our Doctor," said one of these sponges, "had a constant levee of his distressed countrymen, whose wants, as far as he was able, he always relieved;

and he has often been known to leave himself without a guinea, in order to supply the necessities of others."

This constant drainage of the purse therefore obliged him to undertake all jobs proposed by the booksellers and to keep up a kind of running account with Mr. Newbery; who was his banker on all occasions, sometimes for pounds, sometimes for shillings; but who was a rigid accountant and took care to be amply repaid in manuscript. Many effusions, hastily penned in these moments of exigency, were published anonymously, and never claimed. Some of them have but recently been traced to his pen; while of many the true authorship will probably never be discovered. Among others, it is suggested, and with great probability, that he wrote for Mr. Newbery the famous nursery story of "Goody Two Shoes," which appeared in 1765, at a moment when Goldsmith was scribbling for Newbery, and much pressed for funds. Several quaint little tales introduced in his Essays show that he had a turn for this species of mock history; and the advertisement and title-page bear the stamp of his sly and playful humor.

"We are desired to give notice, that there is in the press, and speedily will be published, either by subscription or otherwise as the public shall please to determine, the History of Little Goody Two Shoes, otherwise Mrs. Margery Two Shoes; with the means by which she acquired learning and wisdom, and, in consequence thereof, her estate; set forth at large for the bentfit of those

> Who, from a state of rags and care,
> And having shoes but half a pair,
> Their fortune and their fame should fix,
> And gallop in a coach and six.

The world is probably not aware of the ingenuity, humor, good sense, and sly satire contained in many of the old English nursery-tales. They have evidently been the sportive productions of able writers, who would not trust their names to productions that might be considered beneath their dignity. The ponderous works on which they relied for immortality have perhaps sunk into oblivion, and carried their names down with them; while their unacknowledged offspring, Jack the Giant Killer, Giles Gingerbread, and Tom Thumb, flourish in wide-spreading and never-ceasing popularity.

As Goldsmith had now acquired popularity and an extensive acquaintance, he attempted, with the advice of his friends, to procure a more regular and ample support by resuming the medical profession. He accordingly launched himself upon the town in style; hired a man-servant; replenished his wardrobe at considerable expense, and appeared in a professional wig and cane, purple silk small-clothes, and a scarlet roquelaure buttoned to the chin: a fantastic garb, as we should think at the present day, but not unsuited to the fashion of the times.

With his sturdy little person thus arrayed in the unusual magnificence of purple and fine linen and his scarlet roquelaure flaunting from his shoulders, he used to strut into the apartments of his patients swaying his three cornered hat in one hand and his medical sceptre, the cane, in the other, and assuming an air of gravity and importance suited to the solemnity of his wig; at least, such is the picture given of him by the waiting gentlewoman who let him into the chamber of one of his lady patients.

He soon, however, grew tired and impatient of the duties and restraints of his profession; his practice was chiefly among his friends, and the fees were not sufficient for his maintenance; he was disgusted with attendance on sick chambers and capricious patients, and looked back with longing to his tavern haunts and broad convivial meetings, from which the dignity and duties of his medical calling restrained him. At length, on prescribing to a lady of his acquaintance who, to use a hackneyed phrase, "rejoiced" in the aristocratical name of Sidebotham, a warm dispute arose between him and the apothecary as to the quantity of medicine to be administred. The doctor stood up for the rights and dignities of his profession and resented the interference of the compounder of drugs. His rights and dignities, however, were disregarded; his wig and cane and scarlet roquelaur were of no avail; Mrs. Sidebotham sided with the hero of the pestle and mortar; and Goldsmith flung out of the house in a passion. "I am determined henceforth," said he to Topham Beauclerc, "to leave off prescribing for my friends." "Do so, my dear Doctor," was the reply; "whenever you undertake to kill, let it be only your enemies."

This was the end of Goldsmith's medical career.

CHAPTER XVII

Publication of the Vicar of Wakefield; opinions concerning it; of Dr. Johnson; of Rogers the poet; of Goethe; its merits—Exquisite extract— Attack by Kenrick—Reply—Book building—Project of a comedy

The success of the poem of "The Traveller" and the popularity which it had conferred on its author, now roused the attention of the bookseller in whose hands the novel of "The Vicar of Wakefield" had been slumbering for nearly two long years. The idea has generally prevailed that it was Mr. John Newbery to whom the manuscript had been sold, and much surprise has been expressed that he should be insensible to its merit and suffer it to remain unpublished while putting forth various inferior writings by the same author. This, however, is a mistake; it was his nephew, Francis Newbery, who had become the fortunate purchaser. Still the delay is equally unaccountable. Some have imagined that the uncle and nephew had business arrangements together, in which this work was included, and that the elder Newbery, dubious of its success, retarded the publication until the full harvest of "The Traveller" should be reaped. Booksellers are prone to make egregious mistakes as to the merit of works in manuscript; and to undervalue, if not reject, those of classic and enduring excellence, when destitute of that false brilliancy commonly called "effect." In the present instance an intellect vastly superior to that of either of the booksellers was equally at fault. Dr. Johnson, speaking of the work to Boswell, some time subsequent to its publication, observed, "I myself did not think it would have had much success. It was written and sold to a bookseller before 'The Traveller' but published after, so little expectation had the bookseller from it. Had it been sold after 'The Traveller,' he might have had twice as much money; *though sixty guineas was no mean price.*"

Sixty guineas for the Vicar of Wakefield! and this could be pronounced *no mean price* by Dr. Johnson, at that time the arbiter of British talent, and who had had an opportunity of witnessing the effect of the work upon the public mind; for its success was immediate. It came out on the 27th of March, 1766; before the end of May a second edition was called for; in three months more a third; and so it went on, widening in a popularity that has never flagged. Rogers, the Nestor of British literature, whose refined purity of taste and exquisite mental organization, rendered him eminently calculated to appreciate a work of the kind, declared that of all the books which through the fitful changes of three generations he had seen rise and fall, the charm of the Vicar of Wakefield had alone continued as at first; and, could he revisit the world after an interval of many more generations, he should as surely look to find it undiminished. Nor has its celebrity been confined to Great Britain. Though so exclusively a picture of British scenes and manners, it has been translated into almost every language, and every where its charm has been the same. Goethe, the great genius of Germany, declared in his eighty first year, that it was his delight at the age of twenty, that it had in a manner formed a part of his education, influencing his taste and feelings throughout life, and that he had recently read it again from beginning to end—with renewed delight and with a grateful sense of the early benefit derived from it.

It is needless to expatiate upon the qualities of a work which has thus passed from country to country and language to language, until it is now known throughout the whole reading world and is become a household book in every hand. The secret of its universal and enduring popularity is undoubtedly its truth to nature but to nature of the most amiable kind; to nature such as Goldsmith saw it. The author, as we have occasionally shown in the course of this memoir, took his scenes and characters in this, as in his other writings, from originals in his own motley experience; but he has given them as seen through the medium of his own indulgent eye and has set them forth with the colorings of his own good head and heart. Yet how contradictory it seems that this, one of the most delightful pictures of home and homefelt happiness should be drawn by a homeless man; that the most amiable picture of domestic virtue and all the endearments of the married state should be drawn by a bachelor, who had been severed from domestic life almost from boyhood; that one of the most tender, touching and affecting appeals on behalf of female loveliness should have been made by a man whose deficiency in all the graces of person and manner seemed to mark him out for a cynical disparager of the sex.

We cannot refrain from transcribing from the work a short passage illustrative of what we have said, and which within a wonderfully small compass comprises a world of beauty of imagery, tenderness of feeling, delicacy and refinement of thought, and matchless purity of style. The two stanzas which conclude it, in which are told a whole history of woman's wrongs and sufferings, is for pathos, simplicity and euphony a gem in the language. The scene depicted is where the poor Vicar is gathering around him the wrecks of his shattered family and endeavoring to rally them back to happiness.

"The next morning the sun arose with peculiar warmth for the season, so that we agreed to breakfast together on the honeysuckle bank; where, while we sat, my youngest daughter at my request joined her voice to the concert on the trees about us. It was in this place my

poor Olivia first met her seducer, and every object served to recall her
sadness. But that melancholy which is excited by objects of pleasure,
or inspired by sounds of harmony, soothes the heart instead of corroding
it. Her mother, too, upon this occasion, felt a pleasing distress, and
wept, and loved her daughter as before. 'Do, my pretty Olivia,' cried she,
'let us have that melancholy air your papa was so fond of; your sister
Sophy has already obliged us. Do, child, it will please your old father.'
She complied in a manner so exquisitely pathetic as moved me.

> When lovely woman stoops to folly,
>   And finds too late that men betray,
> What charm can soothe her melancholy,
>   What art can wash her guilt away?
>
> The only art her guilt to cover,
>   To hide her shame from every eye,
> To give repentance to her lover,
>   And wring his bosom—is to die."

Scarce had the Vicar of Wakefield made its appearance and been
received with acclamation than its author was subjected to one of
the usual penalties that attend success. He was attacked in the newspapers. In one of the chapters he had introduced his ballad of the
Hermit, of which, as we have mentioned, a few copies had been printed
some considerable time previously for the use of the Countess of
Northumberland. This brought forth the following article in a fashionable journal of the day:

"To the Printer of the St. James's Chronicle.

"Sir,—In the Reliques of Ancient Poetry, published about two years
ago, is a very beautiful little ballad, called 'A Friar of Orders Gray.' The
ingenious editor, Mr. Percy, supposes that the stanzas sung by Ophelia
in the play of Hamlet were parts of some ballad well known in Shakspeare's time, and from these stanzas, with the addition of one or two
of his own to connect them, he has formed the above-mentioned ballad;
the subject of which is, a lady comes to a convent to inquire for her
love who had been driven there by her disdain. She is answered by a
friar that he is dead:

> 'No, no, he is dead, gone to his death's bed.
>   He never will come again.'

The lady weeps and laments her cruelty; the friar endeavours to comfort her with morality and religion, but all in vain; she expresses the deepest grief and the most tender sentiments of love, till at the last the friar discovers himself:

'And lo! beneath this gown of gray
Thy own true love appears.'

"This catastrophe is very fine, and the whole, joined with the greatest tenderness, has the greatest simplicity; yet, though this ballad was so recently published in the Ancient Reliques, Dr. Goldsmith has been hardy enough to publish a poem called 'the Hermit,' where the circumstances and catastrophe are exactly the same, only with this difference, that the natural simplicity and tenderness of the original are almost entirely lost in the languid smoothness and tedious paraphrase of the copy, which is as short of the merits of Mr. Percy's ballad as the insipidity of negus is to the genuine flavour of Champagne.

"I am, sir, yours, &c.,
"DETECTOR."

This attack, supposed to be by Goldsmith's constant persecutor, the malignant Kenrick, drew from him the following note to the editor:

"SIR,—As there is nothing I dislike so much as newspaper controversy, particularly upon trifles, permit me to be as concise as possible in informing a correspondent of yours that I recommended Blainville's travels because I thought the book was a good one; and I think so still. I said I was told by the bookseller that it was then first published; but in that it seems I was misinformed, and my reading was not extensive enough to set me right.

"Another correspondent of yours accuses me of having taken a ballad I published some time ago from one by the ingenious Mr. Percy. I do not think there is any great resemblance between the two pieces in question. If there be any, his ballad was taken from mine. I read it to Mr. Percy some years ago; and he, as we both considered these things as trifles at best, told me, with his usual good-humour, the next time I saw him, that he had taken my plan to form the fragments of Shakspeare into a ballad of his own. He then read me his little Cento, if I may so call it, and I highly approved it. Such petty anecdotes as these are scarcely worth printing; and, were it not for the busy disposition of some of your correspondents, the public should never have known that

he owes me the hint of his ballad, or that I am obliged to his friendship
and learning for communications of a much more important nature.

"I am, sir, yours, &c.,

"OLIVER GOLDSMITH."

The unexpected circulation of the "Vicar of Wakefield" enriched the
the publisher, but not the author. Goldsmith no doubt thought himself
entitled to participate in the profits of the repeated editions; and a
memorandum, still extant, shows that he drew upon Mr. Francis Newbery, in the month of June, for fifteen guineas, but that the bill was
returned dishonored. He continued, therefore, his usual job work for
the booksellers, writing introductions, prefaces, and head and tail pieces
for new works; revising, touching up, and modifying travels and voyages;
making compilations of prose and poetry, and "building books," as he
sportively termed it. These tasks required little labor or talent, but
that taste and touch which are the magic of gifted minds. His terms
began to be proportioned to his celebrity. If his price was at any time
objected to, "Why, sir," he would say, "it may seem large; but then a
man may be many years working in obscurity before his taste and
reputation are fixed or estimated; and then he is, as in other professions,
only paid for his previous labours."

He was however prepared to try his fortune in a different walk of
literature from any he had yet attempted. We have repeatedly adverted
to his fondness for the drama; he was a frequent attendant at the
theatres; though, as we have shown, he considered them under gross
mismanagement. He thought, too, that a vicious taste prevailed among
those who wrote for the stage. "A new species of dramatic composition,"
says he in one of his essays, "has been introduced under the name of
Sentimental Comedy, in which the virtues of private life are exhibited
rather than the vices exposed; and the distresses rather than the faults
of mankind make our interest in the piece. In these plays almost all
the characters are good, and exceedingly generous; they are lavish
enough of their tin money on the stage; and though they want humour,
have abundance of sentiment and feeling. If they happen to have faults
or foibles, the spectator is taught not only to pardon, but to applaud
them in consideration of the goodness of their hearts; so that folly,
instead of being ridiculed, is commended, and the comedy aims at
touching our passions, without the power of being truly pathetic. In
this manner we are likely to lose one great source of entertainment on
the stage; for while the comic poet is invading the province of the tragic
muse, he leaves her lively sister quite neglected. Of this, however, he is no
ways solicitous, as he measures his fame by his profits.   *   *   *   *

"Humour at present seems to be departing from the stage; and it will soon happen that our comic players will have nothing left for it but a fine coat and a song. It depends upon the audience whether they will actually drive those poor merry creatures from the stage, or sit at a play as gloomy as at the tabernacle. It is not easy to recover an art when once lost; and it will be a just punishment, that when, by our being too fastidious, we have banished humour from the stage, we should ourselves be deprived of the art of laughing."

Symptoms of reform in the drama had recently taken place. The comedy of the *Clandestine Marriage*, the joint production of Colman and Garrick, and suggested by Hogarth's inimitable pictures of *Marriage à la mode*, had taken the town by storm, crowded the theatre with fashionable audiences, and formed one of the leading literary topics of the year. Goldsmith's emulation was roused by its success. The new comedy was in what he considered the legitimate line, totally different from the sentimental school; it presented pictures of real life, delineations of character and touches of humor, in which he felt himself calculated to excel. The consequence was that in the course of this year (1766) he commenced a comedy of the same class, to be entitled the Good Natured Man, at which he diligently wrought whenever the hurried occupation of 'book building' allowed him leisure.

CHAPTER XVIII

Social position of Goldsmith—His colloquial contests with Johnson—Anecdotes and illustrations

The social position of Goldsmith had undergone a material change since the publication of The Traveller. Before that event he was but partially known as the author of some clever anonymous writings, and had been a tolerated member of the club and the Johnson circle without much being expected from him. Now he had suddenly risen to literary fame and become one of the *lions* of the day. The highest regions of intellectual society were now open to him; but he was not prepared to move in them with confidence and success. Ballymahon had not been a good school of manners at the outset of life; nor had his experience as a 'poor student' at colleges and medical schools contributed to give him the polish of society. He had brought from Ireland, as he said, nothing but his "brogue and his blunders," and they had never left him. He had travelled, it is true; but the Continental tour which in those days gave the finishing grace to the education of a patrician youth had with poor Goldsmith been little better than a course of literary vagabondizing. It had enriched his mind, deepened and widened the benevolence of his heart, and filled his memory with enchanting pictures, but it had contributed little to disciplining him for the polite intercourse of the world. His life in London had hitherto been a struggle with sordid cares and sad humiliations. "You scarcely can conceive," wrote he some time previously to his brother, "how much eight years of disappointment, anguish, and study, have worn me down." Several more years had since been added to the term during which he had trod the lowly walks of life. He had been a tutor, an apothecary's drudge, a petty physician of the suburbs, a bookseller's hack, drudging for daily bread. Each separate walk had been beset by its peculiar thorns and humiliations. It is wonderful how his heart retained its gentleness and kindness through all these trials; how his mind rose above the "meannesses of poverty," to which, as he says, he was compelled to submit; but it would be still more wonderful, had his manners acquired a tone corresponding to the innate grace and refinement of his intellect. He was near forty years of age when he published The Traveller and was lifted by it into celebrity. As is beautifully said of him by one of his biographers, "he has fought his way to consideration and esteem; but he bears upon him the scars of his twelve years' conflict; of the mean sorrows through which he has passed; and of the cheap indulgences he has sought relief and

111

help from. There is nothing plastic in his nature now. His manners and habits are completely formed; and in them any further success can make little favourable change, whatever it may effect for his mind or genius."*

We are not to be surprised therefore at finding him make an awkward figure in the elegant drawing rooms which were now open to him, and disappointing those who had formed an idea of him from the fascinating ease and gracefulness of his poetry.

Even the literary club and the circle of which it formed a part, after their surprise at the intellectual flights of which he showed himself capable, fell into a conventional mode of judging and talking of him, and of placing him in absurd and whimsical points of view. His very celebrity operated here to his disadvantage. It brought him into continual comparison with Johnson, who was the oracle of that circle and had given it a tone. Conversation was the great staple there, and of this Johnson was a master. He had been a reader and thinker from childhood: his melancholy temperament, which unfitted him for the pleasures of youth, had made him so. For many years past the vast variety of works he had been obliged to consult in preparing his Dictionary had stored an uncommonly retentive memory with facts on all kinds of subjects; making it a perfect colloquial armory. "He had all his life," says Boswell, "habituated himself to consider conversation as a trial of intellectual vigour and skill. He had disciplined himself as a talker as well as a writer, making it a rule to impart whatever he knew in the most forcible language he could put it in, so that by constant practice and never suffering any careless expression to escape him, he had attained an extraordinary accuracy and command of language."

His common conversation in all companies, according to Sir Joshua Reynolds, was such as to secure him universal attention, something above the usual colloquial style being always expected from him.

"I do not care," said Orme, the historian of Hindostan, "on what subject Johnson talks; but I love better to hear him talk than any body. He either gives you new thoughts or a new colouring."

A stronger and more graphic eulogium is given by Dr. Percy. "The conversation of Johnson," said he, "is strong and clear, and may be compared to an antique statue, where every vein and muscle is distinct and clear."

Such was the colloquial giant with which Goldsmith's celebrity and his habits of intimacy brought him into continual comparison; can we wonder that he should appear to disadvantage? Conversation grave, discursive and disputatious, such as Johnson excelled and delighted in,

* Forster's Goldsmith, p. 437.

was to him a severe task, and he never was good at a task of any kind. He had not like Johnson a vast fund of acquired facts to draw upon; nor a retentive memory to furnish them forth when wanted. He could not like the great lexicographer mould his ideas and balance his periods while talking. He had a flow of ideas, but it was apt to be hurried and confused, and as he said of himself, he had contracted a hesitating and disagreeable manner of speaking. He used to say that he always argued best when he argued alone; that is to say, he could master a subject in his study, with his pen in his hand; but, when he came into company, he grew confused and was unable to talk about it. Johnson made a remark concerning him to somewhat of the same purport. "No man," said he, "is more foolish than Goldsmith when he has not a pen in his hand, or more wise when he has." Yet with all this conscious deficiency he was continually getting involved in colloquial contests with Johnson and other prime talkers of the literary circle. He felt that he had become a notoriety; that he had entered the lists and was expected to make fight; so with that heedlessness which characterized him in every thing else he dashed on at a venture; trusting to chance in this as in other things, and hoping occasionally to make a lucky hit. Johnson perceived his haphazard temerity but gave him no credit for the real diffidence which lay at bottom. "The misfortune of Goldsmith in conversation," said he, "is this, he goes on without knowing how he is to get off. His genius is great, but his knowledge is small. As they say of a generous man it is a pity he is not rich, we may say of Goldsmith it is a pity he is not knowing. He would not keep his knowledge to himself." And, on another occasion, he observes: "Goldsmith, rather than not talk, will talk of what he knows himself to be ignorant, which can only end in exposing him. If in company with two founders, he would fall a talking on the method of making cannon, though both of them would soon see that he did not know what metal a cannon is made of." And again: "Goldsmith should not be for ever attempting to shine in conversation; he has not temper for it, he is so much mortified when he fails. Sir, a game of jokes is composed partly of skill, partly of chance; a man may be beat at times by one who has not the tenth part of his wit. Now Goldsmith, putting himself against another, is like a man laying a hundred to one, who cannot spare the hundred. It is not worth a man's while. A man should not lay a hundred to one unless he can easily spare it, though he has a hundred chances for him; he can get but a guinea, and he may lose a hundred. Goldsmith is in this state. When he contends, if he gets the better, it is a very little addition to a man of his literary reputation; if he does not get the better, he is miserably vexed."

Johnson was not aware how much he was himself to blame in producing this vexation. "Goldsmith," said Miss Reynolds, "always appeared to be overawed by Johnson, particularly when in company with people of any consequence; always as if impressed with fear of disgrace; and indeed well he might. I have been witness to many mortifications he has suffered in Dr. Johnson's company."

It may not have been disgrace that he feared, but rudeness. The great lexicographer, spoiled by the homage of society, was still more prone than himself to lose temper when the argument went against him. He could not brook appearing to be worsted; but would attempt to bear down his adversary by the rolling thunder of his periods; and, when that failed, would become downright insulting. Boswell called it "having recourse to some sudden mode of robust sophistry;" but Goldsmith designated it much more happily. "There is no arguing with Johnson," said he, *"for, when his pistol misses fire, he knocks you down with the butt end of it."* *

In several of the intellectual collisions recorded by Boswell as triumphs of Dr. Johnson, it really appears to us that Goldsmith had the best both of the wit and the argument, and especially of the courtesy and good nature.

On one occasion he certainly gave Johnson a capital reproof as to his own colloquial peculiarities. Talking of fables, Goldsmith observed that the animals introduced in them seldom talked in character. "For instance," said he, "the fable of the little fishes, who saw birds fly over their heads, and, envying them, petitioned Jupiter to be changed into birds. The skill consists in making them talk like little fishes." Just then observing that Dr. Johnson was shaking his sides and laughing, he immediately added, "Why, Dr. Johnson, this is not so easy as you seem to think; for, if you were to make little fishes talk, they would talk like whales."

But though Goldsmith suffered frequent mortifications in society from the overbearing and sometimes harsh conduct of Johnson, he always did justice to his benevolence. When royal pensions were granted to Dr. Johnson and Dr. Shebbeare, a punster remarked that the king had pensioned a *She-bear* and a *He-bear*; to which Goldsmith replied, "Johnson, to be sure, has a roughness in his manner, but no man alive has a more tender heart. *He has nothing of the bear but the skin.*"

Goldsmith in conversation shone most when he least thought of shining; when he gave up all effort to appear wise and learned or to

---

* The following is given by Boswell as an instance of 'robust sophistry':—"Once when I was pressing upon him with visible advantage, he stopped me thus—'My dear Boswell, let's have no more of this; you'll make nothing of it. I'd rather hear you whistle a Scotch tune.' "

cope with the oracular sententiousness of Johnson and gave way to his natural impulses. Even Boswell could perceive his merits on these occasions. "For my part," said he condescendingly, "I like very well to hear *honest Goldsmith* talk away carelessly;" and many a much wiser man than Boswell delighted in those outpourings of a fertile fancy and a generous heart. In his happy moods, Goldsmith had an artless simplicity and buoyant good humor, that led to a thousand amusing blunders and whimsical confessions, much to the entertainment of his intimates; yet, in his most thoughtless garrulity, there was occasionally the gleam of the gold and the flash of the diamond.

CHAPTER XIX

Social resorts—The shilling whist club—A practical joke—The Wednesday club—The 'tun of man'—The pig butcher—Tom King—Hugh Kelly—Glover and his characteristics

Though Goldsmith's pride and ambition led him to mingle occasionally with high society, and to engage in the colloquial conflicts of the learned circle, in both of which he was ill at ease and conscious of being undervalued, yet he had some social resorts in which he indemnified himself for their restraints by indulging his humor without control. One of them was a shilling whist club, which held its meetings at the Devil Tavern near Temple Bar, a place rendered classic, we are told, by a club held there in old times, to which "rare Ben Jonson" had furnished the rules. The company was of a familiar, unceremonious kind, delighting in that very questionable wit which consists in playing off practical jokes upon each other. Of one of these Goldsmith was made the butt. Coming to the club one night in a hackney coach, he gave the coachman by mistake a guinea instead of a shilling, which he set down as a dead loss, for there was no likelihood, he said, that a fellow of this class would have the honesty to return the money. On the next club evening he was told a person at the street door wished to speak with him. He went forth but soon returned with a radiant countenance. To his surprise and delight the coachman had actually brought back the guinea. While he launched forth in praise of this unlooked for piece of honesty, he declared it ought not to go unrewarded. Collecting a small sum from the club and no doubt increasing it largely from his own purse, he dismissed the Jehu with many encomiums on his good conduct. He was still chanting his praises, when one of the club requested a sight of the guinea thus honestly returned. To Goldsmith's confusion it proved to be a counterfeit. The universal burst of laughter which succeeded, and the jokes by which he was assailed on every side, showed him that the whole was a hoax and the pretended coachman as much a counterfeit as the guinea. He was so disconcerted, it is said, that he soon beat a retreat for the evening.

Another of those free and easy clubs met on Wednesday evenings at the Globe Tavern in Fleet Street. It was somewhat in the style of the Three Jolly Pigeons: songs, jokes, dramatic imitations, burlesque parodies and broad sallies of humor formed a contrast to the sententious morality, pedantic casuistry and polished sarcasm of the learned circle. Here a huge 'tun of man,' by the name of Gordon, used to delight

Goldsmith by singing the jovial song of Nottingham Ale, and looking like a butt of it. Here too a wealthy pig butcher, charmed no doubt by the mild philanthropy of The Traveller, aspired to be on the most sociable footing with the author, and here was Tom King, the comedian, recently risen to consequence by his performance of Lord Ogleby in the new comedy of the Clandestine Marriage.

A member of more note was one Hugh Kelly, a second rate author, who, as he became a kind of competitor of Goldsmith's, deserves particular mention. He was an Irishman about twenty eight years of age, originally apprentice to a staymaker in Dublin; then writer to a London attorney; then a Grub Street hack; scribbling for magazines and newspapers. Of late he had set up for theatrical censor and satirist, and, in a paper called Thespis, in emulation of Churchill's Rosciad, had harassed many of the poor actors without mercy and often without wit; but had lavished his incense on Garrick, who in consequence took him into favor. He was the author of several works of superficial merit, but which had sufficient vogue to inflate his vanity. This however must have been mortified on his first introduction to Johnson; after sitting a short time he got up to take leave, expressing a fear that a longer visit might be troublesome. "Not in the least, sir," said the surly moralist, "I had forgotten you were in the room." Johnson used to speak of him as a man who had written more than he had read.

A prime wag of this club was one of Goldsmith's poor countrymen and hangers on by the name of Glover. He had originally been educated for the medical profession, but had taken in early life to the stage, though apparently without much success. While performing at Cork, he undertook, partly in jest, to restore life to the body of a malefactor, who had just been executed. To the astonishment of every one, himself among the number, he succeeded. The miracle took wind. He abandoned the stage, resumed the wig and cane, and considered his fortune as secure. Unluckily, there were not many dead people to be restored to life in Ireland; his practice did not equal his expectation, so he came to London, where he continued to dabble indifferently, and rather unprofitably, in physic and literature.

He was a great frequenter of the Globe and Devil taverns, where he used to amuse the company by his talent at story-telling and his powers of mimicry, giving capital imitations of Garrick, Foote, Colman, Sterne, and other public characters of the day. He seldom happened to have money enough to pay his reckoning, but was always sure to find some ready purse among those who had been amused by his humors. Goldsmith of course was one of the readiest. It was through him that Glover was admitted to the Wednesday Club, of which his theatrical imitations became the delight. Glover, however, was a little anxious for the dignity of his patron, which appeared to him to suffer from the overfamiliarity of some of the members of the club. He was especially shocked by the free and easy tone in which Goldsmith was addressed by the pig butcher: "Come, Noll," would he cry, as he pledged him, "here's my service to you, old boy!"

Glover whispered to Goldsmith that he "should not allow such liberties." "Let him alone," was the reply, "you'll see how civilly I'll let him down." After a time he called out, with marked ceremony and politeness, "Mr. B., I have the honor of drinking your good health." Alas! dignity was not poor Goldsmith's forte: he could keep no one at a distance. "Thank'ee, thank'ee, Noll," nodded the pig butcher, scarce taking the pipe out of his mouth. "I don't see the effect of your reproof," whispered Glover. "I give it up," replied Goldsmith with a good humored shrug, "I ought to have known before now there is no putting a pig in the right way."

Johnson used to be severe upon Goldsmith for mingling in these motley circles, observing that, having been originally poor, he had contracted a love for low company. Goldsmith, however, was guided not by a taste for what was low, but for what was comic and characteristic. It was the feeling of the artist; the feeling which furnished out some of his best scenes in familiar life; the feeling with which "rare Ben Jonson" sought these very haunts and circles in days of yore to study "Every Man in his Humour."

It was not always, however, that the humor of these associates was to his taste: as they became boisterous in their merriment, he was apt to become depressed. "The company of fools," says he in one of his essays, "may at first make us smile, but at last never fails of making us melancholy." Often he would become moody, says Glover, and would leave the party abruptly "to go home and brood over his misfortune."

It is possible however that he went home for quite a different purpose; to commit to paper some scene or passage suggested for his comedy of "The Good Natured Man." The elaboration of humor is often a most serious task; and we have never witnessed a more perfect picture of mental misery than was once presented to us by a popular dramatic writer—still, we hope, living—whom we found in the agonies of producing a farce which subsequently set the theatres in a roar.

CHAPTER XX

The Great Cham of literature and the King—Scene at Sir Joshua Reynolds's—Goldsmith accused of jealousy—Negotiations with Garrick—The author and the actor—Their correspondence

The comedy of "The Good Natured Man" was completed by Goldsmith early in 1767 and submitted to the perusal of Johnson, Burke, Reynolds and others of the literary club, by whom it was heartily approved. Johnson, who was seldom half way either in censure or applause, pronounced it the best comedy that had been written since "The Provoked Husband," and promised to furnish the prologue. This immediately became an object of great solicitude with Goldsmith, knowing the weight an introduction from 'the Great Cham of literature' would have with the public; but circumstances occurred which he feared might drive the comedy and the prologue from Johnson's thoughts. The latter was in the habit of visiting the royal library at the Queen's (Buckingham) House, a noble collection of books, in the formation of which he had assisted the librarian, Mr. Bernard, with his advice. One evening as he was seated there by the fire reading, he was surprised by the entrance of the King (George III.), then a young man; who sought this occasion to have a conversation with him. The conversation was varied and discursive; the King shifting from subject to subject according to his wont; "during the whole interview," says Boswell, "Johnson talked to his majesty with profound respect, but still in his open, manly manner, with a sonorous voice, and never in that subdued tone which is commonly used at the levee and in the drawing room. 'I found his majesty wished I should talk,' said he, 'and I made it my business to talk. I find it does a man good to be talked to by his sovereign. In the first place, a man cannot be in a passion—.' " It would have been well for Johnson's colloquial disputants, could he have often been under such decorous restraint. Profoundly monarchical in his principles, he retired from the interview highly gratified with the conversation of the King and with his gracious behavior. "Sir," said he to the librarian, "they may talk of the King as they will, but he is the finest gentleman I have ever seen."— "Sir," said he subsequently to Bennet Langton, "his manners are those of as fine a gentleman as we may suppose Louis the Fourteenth or Charles the Second."

While Johnson's face was still radiant with the reflex of royalty, he was holding forth one day to a listening group at Sir Joshua Reynolds's, who were anxious to hear every particular of this memorable conversation. Among other questions the King had asked him whether he was writing any thing. His reply was that he thought he had already done his part as a writer. "I should have thought so too," said the King, "if you had not written so well."—"No man," said Johnson, commenting on this speech, "could have made a handsomer compliment; and it was fit for a King to pay. It was decisive."—"But did you make no reply to this high compliment?" asked one of the company. "No, sir," replied the profoundly deferential Johnson, "when the King had said it, it was to be so. It was not for me to bandy civilities with my sovereign."

During all the time that Johnson was thus holding forth, Goldsmith, who was present, appeared to take no interest in the royal theme but remained seated on a sofa at a distance in a moody fit of abstraction; at length recollecting himself, he sprang up, and advancing, exclaimed, with what Boswell calls his usual "frankness and simplicity," "Well, you acquitted yourself in this conversation better than I should have done, for I should have bowed and stammered through the whole of it." He afterwards explained his seeming inattention by saying that his mind was completely occupied about his play and by fears lest Johnson, in his present state of royal excitement, would fail to furnish the much desired prologue.

How natural and truthful is this explanation. Yet Boswell presumes to pronounce Goldsmith's inattention affected; and attributes it to jealousy. "It was strongly suspected," says he, "that he was fretting with chagrin and envy at the singular honour Dr. Johnson had lately enjoyed." It needed the littleness of mind of Boswell to ascribe such pitiful motives to Goldsmith and to entertain such exaggerated notions of the honor paid to Dr. Johnson.

"The Good Natured Man" was now ready for performance, but the question was how to get it upon the stage. The affairs of Covent Garden, for which it had been intended, were thrown in confusion by the recent death of Rich, the manager. Drury Lane was under the management of Garrick, but a feud, it will be recollected, existed between him and the poet, from the animadversions of the latter on the mismanagement of theatrical affairs, and the refusal of the former to give the poet his vote for the secretaryship of the Society of Arts. Times however were changed. Goldsmith when that feud took place was an anonymous writer, almost unknown to fame and of no circulation in society. Now he had become a literary lion; he was a member of the Literary Club; he was the associate of Johnson, Burke, Topham Beauclerc and other magnates— in a word, he had risen to consequence in the public eye and of course was of consequence in the eyes of David Garrick. Sir Joshua Reynolds saw the lurking scruples of pride existing between the author and actor, and thinking it a pity that two men of such congenial talents, and who might be so serviceable to each other should be kept asunder by a worn out pique, exerted his friendly offices to bring them together. The meeting took place in Reynolds's house in Leicester Square. Garrick however could not entirely put off the mock majesty of the stage; he meant to be civil, but he was rather too gracious and condescending. Tom Davies in his "Life of Garrick" gives an amusing picture of the coming together of these punctilious parties. "The manager," says he, "was fully conscious of his (Goldsmith's) merit, and perhaps more ostentatious of his abilities to serve a dramatic author than became a man of his prudence; Goldsmith was, on his side, as fully persuaded of his own importance and independent greatness. Mr. Garrick, who had been so long treated with the complimentary language paid to a successful patentee and admired actor, expected that the writer would esteem the patronage of his play a favour; Goldsmith rejected all ideas of kindness in a bargain that was intended to be of mutual advantage to both parties, and in this he was certainly justifiable; Mr. Garrick could reasonably expect no thanks for the acting a new play, which he would have rejected if he had not been convinced it would have amply rewarded his pains and expense. I believe the manager was willing to accept the play, but he wished to be courted to it; and the doctor was not disposed to purchase his friendship by the resignation of his sincerity." They separated, however, with an understanding on the part of Goldsmith that his play would be acted. The conduct of Garrick subsequently proved evasive, not through any lingerings of past hostility, but from habitual indecision in matters of the kind, and from real scruples of delicacy. He did not think the piece likely to succeed on the stage and avowed that opinion to Reynolds and Johnson; but hesitated to say as much to Goldsmith, through fear of wounding his feelings. A further misunderstanding was the result of this want of decision and frankness; repeated interviews and some correspondence took place without bringing matters to a point, and in the meantime the theatrical season passed away.

Goldsmith's pocket, never well supplied, suffered grievously by this delay, and he considered himself entitled to call upon the manager, who still talked of acting the play, to advance him forty pounds upon a note of the younger Newbery. Garrick readily complied, but subsequently suggested certain important alterations in the comedy as indispensable to its success; these were indignantly rejected by the author but pertinaciously insisted on by the manager. Garrick proposed to leave the matter to the arbitration of Whitehead, the laureate, who officiated as his "reader" and elbow critic. Goldsmith was more indignant than ever, and a violent dispute ensued, which was only calmed by the interference of Burke and Reynolds.

Just at this time order came out of confusion in the affairs of Covent

Garden. A pique having risen between Colman and Garrick in the course of their joint authorship of "The Clandestine Marriage," the former had become manager and part proprietor of Covent Garden, and was preparing to open a powerful competition with his former colleague. On hearing of this, Goldsmith made overtures to Colman; who, without waiting to consult his fellow proprietors, who were absent, gave instantly a favorable reply. Goldsmith felt the contrast of this warm, encouraging conduct to the chilling delays and objections of Garrick. He at once abandoned his piece to the discretion of Colman. "Dear Sir," says he in a letter dated Temple, Garden Court, July 19th, "I am very much obliged to you for your kind partiality in my favour, and your tenderness in shortening the interval of my expectation. That the play is liable to many objections I well know, but I am happy that it is in hands the most capable in the world of removing them. If then Dear Sir, you will complete your favors by putting the piece into such a state as it may be acted, or of directing me how to do it I shall ever retain a sense of your goodness to me. And indeed though most probably this be the last I shall ever write yet I can't help feeling a secret satisfaction that poets for the future are likely to have a protector who declines taking advantage of their dependent situation; and scorns that importance which may be acquired by trifling with their anxieties."

The next day Goldsmith wrote to Garrick, who was at Litchfield, informing him of his having transferred his piece to Covent Garden, for which it had been originally written and by the patentee of which it was claimed, observing, "as I found you had very great difficulties about that piece, I complied with his desire. * * * * * * * * I am extremely sorry that you should think me warm at our last meeting; your judgment certainly ought to be free, especially in a matter which must in some measure concern your own credit and interest. I assure you, sir, I have no disposition to differ with you on this or any other account, but am with an high opinion of your abilities and a very real esteem, Sir, your most obedient humble servant. OLIVER GOLDSMITH."

In his reply Garrick observed, "I was indeed much hurt that your warmth at our last meeting mistook my sincere and friendly attention to your play for the remains of a former misunderstanding which I had as much forgot as if it had never existed. What I said to you at my own house I now repeat, that I felt more pain in giving my sentiments than you possibly would in receiving them. It has been the business, and ever will be, of my life to live on the best terms with men of genius; and I know that Dr. Goldsmith will have no reason to change his previous friendly disposition towards me, as I shall be glad of every future opportunity to convince him how much I am his obedient servant and well-wisher. D. GARRICK."

CHAPTER XXI

More hack authorship—Tom Davies and the Roman History—Canon-bury Castle—Political authorship—Pecuniary temptation—Death of Newbery the elder

Though Goldsmith's comedy was now in train to be performed, it could not be brought out before Christmas; in the mean time he must live. Again, therefore, he had to resort to literary jobs for his daily support. These obtained for him petty occasional sums, the largest of which was ten pounds, from the elder Newbery for a historical compilation; but this scanty rill of quasi patronage, so sterile in its products, was likely soon to cease; Newbery being too ill to attend to business, and having to transfer the whole management of it to his nephew.

At this time Tom Davies, the sometime Roscius, sometime bibliopole, stepped forward to Goldsmith's relief and proposed that he should undertake an easy popular history of Rome in two volumes. An arrangement was soon made. Goldsmith undertook to complete it in two years, if possible, for two hundred and fifty guineas, and forthwith set about his task with cheerful alacrity. As usual, he sought a rural retreat during the summer months, where he might alternate his literary labors with strolls about the green fields. "Merry Islington" was again his resort, but he now aspired to better quarters than formerly, and engaged the chambers occupied occasionally by Mr. Newbery in Canonbury House, or Castle, as it is popularly called. This had been a hunting lodge of Queen Elizabeth, in whose time it was surrounded by parks and forests. In Goldsmith's day nothing remained of it but an old brick tower; it was still in the country amid rural scenery; and was a favorite nestling place of authors, publishers and others of the literary order.*
A number of these he had for fellow occupants of the castle; and they formed a temporary club, which held its meetings at the Crown Tavern, in the Islington lower road; and here he presided in his own genial style and was the life and delight of the company.

* See on the distant slope, majestic shows
  Old Canonbury's tower, an ancient pile
  To various fates assign'd; and where by turns
  Meanness and grandeur have alternate reign'd,
  Thither, in latter days, hath genius fled
  From yonder city to respire and die.
  There the sweet bard of Auburn sat, and tuned
  The plaintive moanings of his village dirge.
  There learned Chambers treasured lore for *men*
  And Newbery there his A B C's for *babes.*

The writer of these pages visited old Canonbury Castle some years since out of regard to the memory of Goldsmith. The apartment was still shown which the poet had inhabited, consisting of a sitting room and small bedroom, with panelled wainscots and Gothic windows. The quaintness and quietude of the place were still attractive. It was one of the resorts of citizens on their Sunday walks, who would ascend to the top of the tower and amuse themselves with reconnoitring the city through a telescope. Not far from this tower were the gardens of the White Conduit House, a Cockney Elysium, where Goldsmith used to figure in the humbler days of his fortune. In the first edition of his Essays he speaks of a stroll in these gardens, where he at that time no doubt thought himself in perfectly genteel society. After his rise in the world however he became too knowing to speak of such plebeian haunts. In a new edition of his Essays, therefore, the White Conduit House and its garden disappear, and he speaks of "a stroll in the Park."

While Goldsmith was literally living from hand to mouth by the forced drudgery of the pen, his independence of spirit was subjected to a sore pecuniary trial. It was the opening of Lord North's administration, a time of great political excitement. The public mind was agitated by the question of American taxation, and other questions of like irritating tendency. Junius and Wilkes and other powerful writers were attacking the administration with all their force; Grub Street was stirred up to its lowest depths; inflammatory talent of all kinds was in full activity, and the kingdom was deluged with pamphlets, lampoons and libels of the grossest kinds. The Ministers were looking anxiously round for literary support. It was thought that the pen of Goldsmith might be readily enlisted. His hospitable friend and countryman, Robert Nugent, politically known as Squire Gawkey, had come out strenuously for colonial taxation, had been selected for a lordship of the board of trade and raised to the rank of Baron Nugent and Viscount Clare. His example, it was thought, would be enough, of itself, to bring Goldsmith into the ministerial ranks; and then what writer of the day was proof against a full purse or a pension? Accordingly one Parson Scott, chaplain to Lord Sandwich, and author of Anti Sejanus Panurge, and other political libels in support of the administration, was sent to negotiate with the poet, who at this time was returned to town. Dr. Scott, in after years, when his political subserviency had been rewarded by two fat crown livings, used to make what he considered a good story out of this embassy to the poet. "I found him," said he, "in a miserable sett of chambers in the Temple. I told him my authority: I told how I was empowered to pay most liberally for his exertions; and, would you believe it! he was so absurd as to say 'I can earn as much as will supply my wants without writing for any party; the assistance you offer is therefore unnecessary to me;'—and so I left him in his garret!" Who does not admire the sturdy independence of poor Goldsmith toiling 'in his garret' for nine guineas the job, and smile with contempt at the indignant wonder of the political divine, albeit his subserviency *was* repaid by two fat crown livings?

Not long after this occurrence Goldsmith's old friend, though frugal handed employer, Newbery of picture book renown, closed his mortal career. The poet has celebrated him as 'the friend of all mankind'; he certainly lost nothing by his friendship. He coined the brains of his authors in the times of their exigency and made them pay dear for the plank put out to keep them from drowning. It is not likely his death caused much lamentation among the scribbling tribe; we may express decent respect for the memory of the just, but we shed tears only at the grave of the generous.

CHAPTER XXII

The comedy of "The Good Natured Man" was doomed to experience delays and difficulties to the very last. Garrick, notwithstanding his professions, had still a lurking grudge against the author and tasked his managerial arts to thwart him in his theatrical enterprise. For this purpose he undertook to build up Hugh Kelly, Goldsmith's boon companion of the Wednesday Club, as a kind of rival. Kelly had written a comedy called *False Delicacy*, in which were embodied all the meretricious qualities of the sentimental school. Garrick, though he had decried that school and had brought out his comedy of "The Clandestine Marriage" in opposition to it, now lauded "False Delicacy" to the skies and prepared to bring it out at Drury Lane with all possible stage effect. He even went so far as to write a prologue and epilogue for it and to touch up some parts of the dialogue. He had become reconciled to his former colleague, Colman, and it is intimated that one condition in the treaty of peace between these potentates of the realms of pasteboard (equally prone to play into each other's hand with the confederate potentates on the great theatre of life) was, that Goldsmith's play should be kept back until Kelly's had been brought forward.

In the mean time the poor author, little dreaming of the deleterious influence at work behind the scenes, saw the appointed time arrive and pass by without the performance of his play; while "False Delicacy" was brought out at Drury Lane (January 23, 1768) with all the trickery of managerial management. Houses were packed to applaud it to the echo; the newspapers vied with each other in their venal praises, and night after night seemed to give it a fresh triumph.

While "False Delicacy" was thus borne on the full tide of fictitious prosperity, "The Good Natured Man" was creeping through the last rehearsals at Covent Garden. The success of the rival piece threw a damp upon author, manager and actors. Goldsmith went about with a face full of anxiety; Colman's hopes in the piece declined at each rehearsal; as to his fellow proprietors, they declared they had never entertained any. All the actors were discontented with their parts, excepting Ned Shuter, an excellent low comedian, and a pretty actress named Miss Walford; both of whom the poor author ever afterward held in grateful recollection.

Johnson, Goldsmith's growling monitor and unsparing castigator in times of heedless levity, stood by him at present with that protecting kindness with which he ever befriended him in time of need. He attended the rehearsals; he furnished the prologue according to promise; he pish'd and pshaw'd at any doubts and fears on the part of the author but gave him sound counsel and held him up with a steadfast and manly hand. Inspirited by his sympathy, Goldsmith plucked up new heart and arrayed himself for the grand trial with unusual care. Ever since his elevation into the polite world he had improved in his wardrobe and toilet. Johnson could no longer accuse him of being shabby in his appearance; he rather went to the other extreme. On the present occasion there is an entry in the books of his tailor, Mr. William Filby, of a suit of "Tyrian bloom, satin grain, and garter blue silk breeches, £8 2s. 7d." Thus magnificently attired, he attended the theatre and watched the reception of the play and the effect of each individual scene with that vicissitude of feeling incident to his mercurial nature.

Johnson's prologue was solemn in itself, and being delivered by Bensley in lugubrious tones suited to the ghost in Hamlet, seemed to throw a portentous gloom over the audience. Some of the scenes met with great applause, and at such times Goldsmith was highly elated; others went off coldly, or there were slight tokens of disapprobation, and then his spirits would sink. The fourth act saved the piece; for Shuter, who had the main comic character of Croaker, was so varied and ludicrous in his execution of the scene in which he reads an incendiary letter that he drew down thunders of applause. On his coming behind the scenes Goldsmith greeted him with an overflowing heart; declaring that he exceeded his own idea of the character, and made it almost as new to him as to any of the audience.

On the whole, however, both the author and his friends were disappointed at the reception of the piece, and considered it a failure. Poor Goldsmith left the theatre with his towering hopes completely cut down. He endeavored to hide his mortification, and even to assume an air of unconcern while among his associates; but, the moment he was alone with Dr. Johnson, in whose rough but magnanimous nature he reposed unlimited confidence, he threw off all restraint and gave way to an almost childlike burst of grief. Johnson, who had shown no want of sympathy at the proper time, saw nothing in the partial disappointment of overrated expectations to warrant such ungoverned emotions and rebuked him sternly for what he termed a silly affectation, saying that "no man should be expected to sympathize with the sorrows of vanity."

When Goldsmith had recovered from the blow, he, with his usual unreserve, made his past distress a subject of amusement to his friends. Dining one day, in company with Dr. Johnson, at the chaplain's table at

St. James's Palace, he entertained the company with a particular and comic account of all his feelings on the night of representation, and his despair when the piece was hissed. How he went, he said, to the Literary Club; chatted gayly, as if nothing had gone amiss; and, to give a greater idea of his unconcern, sang his favorite song about an old woman tossed in a blanket seventeen times as high as the moon.... "All this while," added he, "I was suffering horrid tortures, and, had I put a bit in my mouth, I verily believe it would have strangled me on the spot, I was so excessively ill: but I made more noise than usual to cover all that; so they never perceived my not eating, nor suspected the anguish of my heart; but, when all were gone except Johnson here, I burst out a-crying, and even swore that I would never write again."

Dr. Johnson sat in amaze at the odd frankness and childlike self accusation of poor Goldsmith. When the latter had come to a pause, "All this, doctor," said he dryly, "I thought had been a secret between you and me, and I am sure I would not have said any thing about it for the world." But Goldsmith had no secrets: his follies, his weaknesses, his errors were all thrown to the surface; his heart was really too guileless and innocent to seek mystery and concealment. It is too often the false, designing man that is guarded in his conduct and never offends proprieties.

It is singular, however, that Goldsmith, who thus in conversation could keep nothing to himself, should be the author of a maxim which would inculcate the most thorough dissimulation. "Men of the world," says he in one of the papers of the Bee, "maintain that the true end of speech is not so much to express our wants as to conceal them." How often is this quoted as one of the subtle remarks of the fine witted Talleyrand!

"The Good Natured Man" was performed for ten nights in succession; the third, sixth and ninth nights were for the author's benefit; the fifth night it was commanded by their majesties; after this it was played occasionally, but rarely, having always pleased more in the closet than on the stage.

As to Kelly's comedy, Johnson pronounced it entirely devoid of character, and it has long since passed into oblivion. Yet it is an instance how an inferior production, by dint of puffing and trumpeting, may be kept up for a time on the surface of popular opinion or rather of popular talk. What had been done for "False Delicacy" on the stage was continued by the press. The booksellers vied with the manager in launching it upon the town. They announced that the first impression of three thousand copies was exhausted before two o'clock on the day of publication; four editions, amounting to ten thousand copies,

were sold in the course of the season; a public breakfast was given to
Kelly at the Chapter Coffee House, and a piece of plate presented to
him by the publishers. The comparative merits of the two plays were
continual subjects of discussion in green rooms, coffee houses, and other
places where theatrical questions were discussed.

Goldsmith's old enemy, Kenrick, that "viper of the press," endeavored
on this as on many other occasions to detract from his well earned
fame; the poet was excessively sensitive to these attacks and had not
the art and self command to conceal his feelings.

Some scribblers on the other side insinuated that Kelly had seen
the manuscript of Goldsmith's play, while in the hands of Garrick or
elsewhere, and had borrowed some of the situations and sentiments.
Some of the wags of the day took a mischievous pleasure in stirring
up a feud between the two authors. Goldsmith became nettled, though
he could scarcely be deemed jealous of one so far his inferior. He
spoke disparagingly, though no doubt sincerely, of Kelly's play: the
latter retorted. Still, when they met one day behind the scenes of
Covent Garden, Goldsmith, with his customary urbanity, congratulated
Kelly on his success. "If I thought you sincere, Mr. Goldsmith," replied
the other, abruptly, "I should thank you." Goldsmith was not a man
to harbor spleen or ill will, and soon laughed at this unworthy rivalship:
but the jealousy and envy awakened in Kelly's mind long continued.
He is even accused of having given vent to his hostility by anonymous
attacks in the newspapers, the basest resource of dastardly and malignant spirits; but of this there is no positive proof.

CHAPTER XXIII

Burning the candle at both ends—Fine apartments—Fine furniture—Fine clothes—Fine acquaintances—Shoemaker's holyday and jolly pigeon associates—Peter Barlow, Glover and the Hampstead hoax—Poor friends among great acquaintances

The profits resulting from "The Good Natured Man" were beyond any that Goldsmith had yet derived from his works. He netted about four hundred pounds from the theatre and one hundred pounds from his publisher.

Five hundred pounds! And all at one miraculous draught! It appeared to him wealth inexhaustible. It at once opened his heart and hand and led him into all kinds of extravagance. The first symptom was ten guineas sent to Shuter for a box ticket for his benefit when "The Good Natured Man" was to be performed. The next was an entire change in his domicil. The shabby lodgings with Jeffs, the butler, in which he had been worried by Johnson's scrutiny, were now exchanged for chambers more becoming a man of his ample fortune. The apartment consisted of three rooms on the second floor of No. 2 Brick Court, Middle Temple, on the right hand ascending the stair case, and overlooked the umbrageous walks of the Temple garden. The lease he purchased for £400, and then went on to furnish his rooms with mahogany sofas, card tables and bookcases; with curtains, mirrors and Wilton carpets. His awkward little person was also furnished out in a style befitting his apartment, for in addition to his suit of "Tyrian bloom, satin grain" we find another charged about this time in the books of Mr. Filby in no less gorgeous terms, being "lined with silk and furnished with gold buttons." Thus lodged and thus arrayed, he invited the visits of his most aristocratic acquaintances and no longer quailed beneath the courtly eye of Beauclerc. He gave dinners to Johnson, Reynolds, Percy, Bickerstaffe and other friends of note and supper parties to young folks of both sexes. These last were preceded by round games of cards, at which there was more laughter than skill and in which the sport was to cheat each other; or by romping games of forfeits and blind man's buff, at which he enacted the lord of misrule. Blackstone, whose chambers were immediately below, and who was studiously occupied on his *Commentaries*, used to complain of the racket made overhead by his revelling neighbor.

Sometimes Goldsmith would make up a rural party composed of four or five of his "jolly pigeon" friends, to enjoy what he humorously called a "shoemaker's holyday." These would assemble at his chambers in the morning, to partake of a plentiful and rather expensive breakfast; the remains of which, with his customary benevolence, he generally gave to some poor woman in attendance. The repast ended, the party would set out on foot in high spirits, making extensive rambles by footpaths and green lanes to Blackheath, Wandsworth, Chelsea, Hampton Court, Highgate, or some other pleasant resort, within a few miles of London. A simple but gay and heartily-relished dinner at a country inn crowned the excursion. Sometimes it was at Highbury Barn, where there was a very good ordinary of two dishes and pastry at ten pence a head, including a penny to the waiter. In the evening they strolled back to town, all the better in health and spirits for a day spent in rural and social enjoyment. Occasionally, when extravagantly inclined, they adjourned from dinner to drink tea at the White Conduit House, and now and then concluded their festive day by supping at the Grecian or Temple Exchange Coffee Houses, or at the Globe Tavern in Fleet Street. The whole expenses of the day never exceeded a crown and were oftener from three and six pence to four shillings; for the best part of their entertainment, sweet air and rural scenes, excellent exercise and joyous conversation, cost nothing.

One of Goldsmith's humble companions on these excursions was his occasional amanuensis, Peter Barlow, whose quaint peculiarities afforded much amusement to the company. Peter was poor but punctilious, squaring his expenses according to his means. He always wore the same garb; fixed his regular expenditure for dinner at a trifling sum, which, if left to himself, he never exceeded, but which he always insisted on paying. His oddities always made him a welcome companion on the "shoemaker's holydays." The dinner on these occasions generally exceeded considerably his tariff; he put down, however, no more than his regular sum, and Goldsmith made up the difference.

Another of these hangers on, for whom on such occasions he was content to "pay the shot," was his countryman, Glover, of whom mention has already been made, as one of the wags and sponges of the Globe and Devil taverns, and a prime mimic at the Wednesday Club.

This vagabond genius has bequeathed us a whimsical story of one of his practical jokes upon Goldsmith, in the course of a rural excursion in the vicinity of London. They had dined at an inn on Hampstead Heights, and were descending the hill, when, in passing a cottage, they saw through the open window a party at tea. Goldsmith, who was fatigued, cast a wistful glance at the cheerful tea table. "How I should like to be of that party," exclaimed he. "Nothing more easy," replied Glover; "allow me to introduce you." So saying, he entered the house with an air of the most perfect familiarity, though an utter stranger, and was followed by the unsuspecting Goldsmith, who supposed, of

course, that he was a friend of the family. The owner of the house
rose on the entrance of the strangers. The undaunted Glover shook
hands with him in the most cordial manner possible, fixed his eye
on one of the company who had a peculiarly good natured physiognomy,
muttered something like a recognition, and forthwith launched into an
amusing story, invented at the moment, of something which he pretended
had occurred upon the road. The host supposed the new-comers were
friends of his guests; the guests that they were friends of the host.
Glover did not give them time to find out the truth. He followed one
droll story with another; brought his powers of mimicry into play, and
kept the company in a roar. Tea was offered and accepted; an hour
went off in the most sociable manner imaginable, at the end of which
Glover bowed himself and his companion out of the house with many
facetious last words, leaving the host and his company to compare
notes, and to find out what an impudent intrusion they had experienced.

Nothing could exceed the dismay and vexation of Goldsmith when
triumphantly told by Glover that it was all a hoax, and that he did not
know a single soul in the house. His first impulse was to return instantly
and vindicate himself from all participation in the jest; but a few
words from his free and easy companion dissuaded him. "Doctor," said
he, coolly, "we are unknown; you quite as much as I; if you return
and tell the story, it will be in the newspapers to-morrow; nay, upon
recollection, I remember in one of their offices the face of that squinting
fellow who sat in the corner as if he was treasuring up my stories for
future use, and we shall be sure of being exposed; let us therefore
keep our own counsel."

This story was frequently afterward told by Glover with rich dramatic
effect, repeating and exaggerating the conversation, and mimicking in
ludicrous style the embarrassment, surprise, and subsequent indignation
of Goldsmith.

It is a trite saying that a wheel cannot run in two ruts; nor a man
keep two opposite sets of intimates. Goldsmith sometimes found his
old friends of the 'jolly pigeon' order turning up rather awkwardly
when he was in company with his new aristocratic acquaintances. He
gave a whimsical account of the sudden apparition of one of them
at his gay apartments in the Temple, who may have been a welcome
visitor at his squalid quarters in Green Arbour Court. "How do you
think he served me?" said he to a friend. "Why, sir, after staying away
two years, he came one evening into my chambers, half drunk, as I was
taking a glass of wine with Topham Beauclerc and General Oglethorpe;
and sitting himself down, with most intolerable assurance inquired after
my health and literary pursuits, as if we were upon the most friendly
footing. I was at first so much ashamed of ever having known such a

fellow, that I stifled my resentment, and drew him into a conversation on such topics as I knew he could talk upon; in which, to do him justice, he acquitted himself very reputably: when all of a sudden, as if recollecting something, he pulled two papers out of his pocket, which he presented to me with great ceremony, saying, 'Here, my dear friend, is a quarter of a pound of tea, and a half pound of sugar, I have brought you; for though it is not in my power at present to pay you the two guineas you so generously lent me, you, nor any man else, shall ever have it to say that I want gratitude.' This," added Goldsmith, "was too much. I could no longer keep in my feelings, but desired him to turn out of my chambers directly; which he very coolly did, taking up his tea and sugar; and I never saw him afterwards."

CHAPTER XXIV

Reduced again to book building—Rural retreat at Shoemaker's paradise—Death of Henry Goldsmith; tributes to his memory in the Deserted Village

The heedless expenses of Goldsmith, as may easily be supposed, soon brought him to the end of his 'prize money,' but when his purse gave out he drew upon futurity, obtaining advances from his booksellers and loans from his friends in the confident hope of soon turning up another trump. The debts which he thus thoughtlessly incurred in consequence of a transient gleam of prosperity embarrassed him for the rest of his life; so that the success of "The Good Natured Man" may be said to have been ruinous to him.

He was soon obliged to resume his old craft of book building, and set about his History of Rome, undertaken for Davies.

It was his custom, as we have shown, during the summer time, when pressed by a multiplicity of literary jobs or urged to the accomplishment of some particular task, to take country lodgings a few miles from town, generally on the Harrow or Edgeware Roads, and bury himself there for weeks and months together. Sometimes he would remain closely occupied in his room, at other times he would stroll out along the lanes and hedge rows, and taking out paper and pencil, note down thoughts to be expanded and connected at home. His summer retreat for the present year, 1768, was a little cottage with a garden, pleasantly situated about eight miles from town on the Edgeware Road. He took it in conjunction with a Mr. Edmund Bott, a barrister and man of letters, his neighbor in the Temple, having rooms immediately opposite him on the same floor. They had become cordial intimates, and Bott was one of those with whom Goldsmith now and then took the friendly but pernicious liberty of borrowing.

The cottage which they had hired belonged to a rich shoemaker of Piccadilly, who had embellished his little domain of half an acre with statues, and jets, and all the decorations of landscape gardening; in consequence of which Goldsmith gave it the name of The Shoemaker's Paradise. As his fellow occupant Mr. Bott drove a gig, he sometimes in an interval of literary labor accompanied him to town, partook of a social dinner there and returned with him in the evening. On one occasion when they had probably lingered too long at the table, they came near breaking their necks on their way homeward by driving against a post on the side walk, while Bott was proving by the force

of legal eloquence that they were in the very middle of the broad
Edgeware Road.

In the course of this summer Goldsmith's career of gayety was suddenly brought to a pause by intelligence of the death of his brother
Henry, then but forty five years of age. He had led a quiet and blameless
life amid the scenes of his youth, fulfilling the duties of village pastor
with unaffected piety; conducting the school at Lissoy with a degree
of industry and ability that gave it celebrity, and acquitting himself
in all the duties of life with undeviating rectitude and the mildest
benevolence. How truly Goldsmith loved and venerated him is evident
in all his letters and throughout his works; in which his brother continually forms his model for an exemplification of all the most endearing
of the Christian virtues; yet his affliction at his death was embittered
by the fear that he died with some doubt upon his mind of the warmth
of his affection. Goldsmith had been urged by his friends in Ireland,
since his elevation in the world, to use his influence with the great,
which they supposed to be all powerful, in favor of Henry to obtain
for him church preferment. He did exert himself, as far as his diffident
nature would permit, but without success; we have seen that, in the
case of the Earl of Northumberland, when, as Lord Lieutenant of
Ireland, that nobleman proffered him his patronage, he asked nothing
for himself but only spoke on behalf of his brother. Still some of his
friends, ignorant of what he had done and of how little he was able
to do, accused him of negligence. It is not likely however that his
amiable and estimable brother joined in the accusation.

To the tender and melancholy recollections of his early days awakened
by the death of this loved companion of his childhood, we may attribute
some of the most heartfelt passages in his Deserted Village. Much of
that poem we are told was composed this summer, in the course of
solitary strolls about the green lanes and beautifully rural scenes of
the neighborhood; and thus much of the softness and sweetness of
English landscape became blended with the ruder features of Lissoy.
It was in these lonely and subdued moments, when tender regret was
half mingled with self upbraiding, that he poured forth that homage
of the heart rendered as it were at the grave of his brother. The
picture of the village pastor in this poem, which we have already hinted
was taken in part from the character of his father, embodied likewise
the recollections of his brother Henry; for the natures of the father
and son seem to have been identical. In the following lines, however,
Goldsmith evidently contrasted the quiet settled life of his brother,
passed at home in the benevolent exercise of the Christian duties, with
his own restless vagrant career:

> Remote from towns he ran his godly race,
> Nor e'er had changed, nor wished to change his place.

To us the whole character seems traced as it were in an expiatory spirit; as if, conscious of his own wandering restlessness, he sought to humble himself at the shrine of excellence which he had not been able to practise:

> At church with meek and unaffected grace,
> His looks adorn'd the venerable place;
> Truth from his lips prevail'd with double sway,
> And fools, who came to scoff, remain'd to pray.
> The service past, around the pious man,
> With steady zeal, each honest rustic ran;
> Even children follow'd, with endearing wile,
> And pluck'd his gown, to share the good man's smile:
> His ready smile a parent's warmth express'd,
> Their welfare pleas'd him, and their cares distress'd;
> To them his heart, his love, his griefs were given,
> But all his serious thoughts had rest in heaven.
>
> ❖   ❖   ❖   ❖   ❖   ❖   ❖
>
> And, as a bird each fond endearment tries
> To tempt its new-fledged offspring to the skies,
> He tried each art, reprov'd each dull delay,
> Allur'd to brighter words, *and led the way.*

CHAPTER XXV

*Dinner at Bickerstaffe's—Hiffernan and his impecuniosity—Kenrick's
epigram—Johnson's consolation—Goldsmith's toilet—The bloom colored
coat—New acquaintances—The Hornecks—A touch of poetry and
passion—The Jessamy Bride*

In October Goldsmith returned to town and resumed his usual haunts.
We hear of him at a dinner given by his countryman Isaac Bickerstaffe,
author of "Love in a Village," "Lionel and Clarissa" and other successful
dramatic pieces. The dinner was to be followed by the reading by
Bickerstaffe of a new play. Among the guests was one Paul Hiffernan,
likewise an Irishman; somewhat idle and intemperate; who lived no
body knew how nor where, sponging wherever he had a chance, and
often of course upon Goldsmith, who was ever the vagabond's friend
or rather victim. Hiffernan was something of a physician and elevated
the emptiness of his purse into the dignity of a disease, which he termed
impecuniosity and against which he claimed a right to call for relief
from the healthier purses of his friends. He was a scribbler for the
newspapers and latterly a dramatic critic, which had probably gained
him an invitation to the dinner and reading. The wine and wassail
however befogged his senses. Scarce had the author got into the second
act of his play when Hiffernan began to nod and at length snored
outright. Bickerstaffe was embarrassed but continued to read in a
more elevated tone. The louder he read, the louder Hiffernan snored;
until the author came to a pause. "Never mind the brute, Bick, but go
on," cried Goldsmith. "He would have served Homer just so, if he
were here and reading his own works."

Kenrick, Goldsmith's old enemy, travestied this anecdote in the
following lines, pretending that the poet had compared his countryman
Bickerstaffe to Homer.

> What are your Bretons, Romans, Grecians,
> Compared with thorough-bred Milesians.
> Step into Griffin's shop, he'll tell ye
> Of Goldsmith, Bickerstaffe, and Kelly * * *
> And take one Irish evidence for t'other,
> Ev'n Homer's self is but their foster brother.

Johnson was a rough consoler to a man when wincing under an attack
of this kind. "Never mind, sir," said he to Goldsmith, when he saw
that he felt the sting. "A man whose business it is to be talked of is

137

much helped by being attacked. Fame, sir, is a shuttlecock; if it be struck only at one end of the room, it will soon fall to the ground; to keep it up, it must be struck at both ends."

Bickerstaffe at the time of which we are speaking was in high vogue, the associate of the first wits of the day; a few years afterwards he was obliged to fly the country to escape the punishment of an infamous crime. Johnson expressed great astonishment at hearing the offence for which he had fled. "Why, sir?" said Thrale; "he had long been a suspected man." Perhaps there was a knowing look on the part of the eminent brewer, which provoked a somewhat contemptuous reply. "By those who look close to the ground," said Johnson, "dirt will sometimes be seen; I hope I see things from a greater distance."

We have already noticed the improvement, or rather the increased expense of Goldsmith's wardrobe since his elevation into polite society. "He was fond," says one of his contemporaries, "of exhibiting his muscular little person in the gayest apparel of the day, to which was added a bag wig and sword." Thus arrayed, he used to figure about in the sunshine in the Temple Gardens, much to his own satisfaction but to the amusement of his acquaintances.

Boswell in his memoirs has rendered one of his suits for ever famous. That worthy, on the 16th of October in this same year, gave a dinner to Johnson, Goldsmith, Reynolds, Garrick, Murphy, Bickerstaffe and Davies. Goldsmith was generally apt to bustle in at the last moment, when the guests were taking their seats at table, but on this occasion he was unusually early. While waiting for some lingerers to arrive, "he strutted about," says Boswell, "bragging of his dress, and I believe, was seriously vain of it, for his mind was undoubtedly prone to such impressions. 'Come, come,' said Garrick, 'talk no more of that. You are perhaps the worst—eh, eh?' Goldsmith was eagerly attempting to interrupt him, when Garrick went on, laughing ironically. 'Nay, you will always *look* like a gentleman; but I am talking of your being well or *ill dressed.*' 'Well, let me tell you,' said Goldsmith, 'when the tailor brought home my bloom-coloured coat, he said, "Sir, I have a favour to beg of you; when any body asks you who made your clothes, be pleased to mention John Filby, at the Harrow, in Water Lane." 'Why, sir,' cried Johnson, 'that was because he knew the strange colour would attract crowds to gaze at it, and thus they might hear of him, and see how well he could make a coat of so absurd a colour.' "

But though Goldsmith might permit this raillery on the part of his friends, he was quick to resent any personalities of the kind from strangers. As he was one day walking the Strand in grand array with bag wig and sword, he excited the merriment of two coxcombs, one of whom called to the other to "look at that fly with a long pin stuck through it." Stung to the quick, Goldsmith's first retort was to caution the passers by to be on their guard against "that brace of disguised pickpockets"—his next was to step into the middle of the street, where there was room for action, half draw his sword, and beckon the joker, who was armed in like manner, to follow, him. This was literally a war of wit which the other had not anticipated. He had no inclination to push the joke to such an extreme, but abandoning the ground, sneaked off with his brother wag amid the hootings of the spectators.

This proneness to finery in dress, however, which Boswell and others of Goldsmith's contemporaries, who did not understand the secret plies of his character, attributed to vanity, arose, we are convinced, from a widely different motive. It was from a painful idea of his own personal defects, which had been cruelly stamped upon his mind in his boyhood, by the sneers and jeers of his playmates, and which had been ground deeper into it by rude speeches made to him in every step of his struggling career, until it had become a constant cause of awkwardness and embarrassment. This he had experienced the more sensibly since his reputation had elevated him into polite society; and he was constantly endeavoring by the aid of dress to acquire that personal *acceptability*, if we may use the phrase, which nature had denied him. If ever he betrayed a little self complacency on first turning out in a new suit, it may perhaps have been because he felt as if he had achieved a triumph over his ugliness.

There were circumstances too about the time of which we are treating which may have rendered Goldsmith more than usually attentive to his personal appearance. He had recently made the acquaintance of a most agreeable family from Devonshire, which he met at the house of his friend Sir Joshua Reynolds. It consisted of a Mrs. Horneck, widow of Captain Kane Horneck; two daughters, seventeen and nineteen years of age, and an only son, Charles, *the Captain in Lace* as his sisters playfully and somewhat proudly called him, he having lately entered the Guards. The daughters are described as uncommonly beautiful, intelligent, sprightly and agreeable. Catharine, the eldest, went among her friends by the name of *Little Comedy*, indicative very probably of her disposition. She was engaged to William Henry Bunbury, second son of a Suffolk baronet. The hand and heart of her sister Mary were yet unengaged, although she bore the byname among her friends of the *Jessamy Bride*. This family was prepared by their intimacy with Reynolds and his sister to appreciate the merits of Goldsmith. The poet had always been a chosen friend of the eminent painter, and Miss Reynolds, as we have shown, ever since she had heard his poem of The Traveller read aloud, had ceased to consider him ugly. The Hornecks were equally capable of forgetting his person in admiring his works.

On becoming acquainted with him too they were delighted with his
guileless simplicity; his buoyant good nature and his innate benevolence,
and an enduring intimacy soon sprang up between them. For once
poor Goldsmith had met with polite society with which he was perfectly
at home and by which he was fully appreciated; for once he had met
with lovely women to whom his ugly features were not repulsive. A
proof of the easy and playful terms on which he was with them remains
in a whimsical epistle in verse, of which the following was the occasion.
A dinner was to be given to their family by a Dr. Baker, a friend of
their mother's, at which Reynolds and Angelica Kauffman were to be
present. The young ladies were eager to have Goldsmith of the party,
and their intimacy with Dr. Baker allowing them to take the liberty,
they wrote a joint invitation to the poet at the last moment. It came
too late, and drew from him the following reply; on the top of which
was scrawled, This *is* a poem! This *is* a copy of verses!

Your mandate I got,
You may all go to pot;
Had your senses been right,
You'd have sent before night—
So tell Horneck and Nesbitt,
And Baker and his bit,
And Kauffman beside,
And the *Jessamy Bride*,
With the rest of the crew,
The Reynoldses two,

Little Comedy's face,
And the *Captain in Lace*—
Tell each other to rue
Your Devonshire crew,
For sending so late
To one of my state.
But 'tis Reynolds's way
From wisdom to stray,
And Angelica's whim
To be frolick like him;

But, alas! your good worships, how could they be wiser
When both have been spoil'd in to-day's *Advertiser?**

It has been intimated that the intimacy of poor Goldsmith with
the Miss Hornecks, which began in so sprightly a vein, gradually
assumed something of a more tender nature and that he was not

---

* The following lines had appeared in that day's Advertiser on the portrait of
Sir Joshua by Angelica Kauffman:—

While fair Angelica, with matchless grace,
Paints Conway's lovely form and Stanhope's face;
Our hearts to beauty willing homage pay,
We praise, admire, and gaze our souls away.
But when the likeness she hath done for thee,
O Reynolds! with astonishment we see,
Forced to submit, with all our pride we own,
Such strength, such harmony excelled by none,
And thou art rivall'd by thyself alone.

insensible to the fascinations of the younger sister. This may account for some of the phenomena which about this time appeared in his wardrobe and toilet. During the first year of his acquaintance with these lovely girls the tell tale book of his tailor, Mr. William Filby, displays entries of four or five full suits, beside separate articles of dress. Among the items we find a green half trimmed frock and breeches, lined with silk; a queen's-blue dress suit; a half dress suit of ratteen lined with satin; a pair of silk stocking breeches and another pair of a bloom color. Alas! poor Goldsmith! how much of this silken finery was dictated, not by vanity, but humble consciousness of thy defects; how much of it was to atone for the uncouthness of thy person, and to win favor in the eyes of the Jessamy Bride!

CHAPTER XXVI

Goldsmith in the Temple—Judge Day and Grattan—Labor and dissipation—Publication of the Roman History—Opinions of it—History of Animated Nature—Temple rookery—Anecdotes of a spider

In the winter of 1768–69 Goldsmith occupied himself at his quarters in the Temple, slowly "building up" his Roman History. We have pleasant views of him in this learned and half cloistered retreat of wits and lawyers and legal students, in the reminiscences of Judge Day of the Irish Bench, who in his advanced age delighted to recall the days of his youth when he was a templar and to speak of the kindness with which he and his fellow student Grattan were treated by the poet. "I was just arrived from College," said he, "full freighted with Academic gleanings, and our Author did not disdain to receive from me some opinions and hints towards his Greek and Roman histories. Being then a young man I felt much flattered by the notice of so celebrated a person. He took great delight in the conversation of Grattan, whose brilliancy in the morning of life furnished full earnest of the unrivalled splendor which awaited his meridian; and finding us dwelling together in Essex Court near himself, where he frequently visited my immortal friend, his warm heart became naturally prepossessed towards the associate of one whom he so much admired."

The judge goes on in his reminiscences to give a picture of Goldsmith's social habits, similar in style to those already furnished. He frequented much the Grecian Coffee House, then the favorite resort of the Irish and Lancashire Templars. He delighted too in collecting his friends around him at evening parties at his chambers, where he entertained them with a cordial and unostentatious hospitality. "Occasionally," adds the judge, "he amused them with his flute, or with whist, neither of which he played well, particularly the latter, but in losing his money, he never lost his temper. In a run of bad luck and worse play, he would fling his cards upon the floor and exclaim '*Bye-fore* George, I ought for ever to renounce thee, fickle, faithless fortune.'"

The judge was aware at the time that all the learned labor of poor Goldsmith upon his Roman History was mere hack work to recruit his exhausted finances. "His purse replenished," adds he, "by labours of this kind, the season of relaxation and pleasure took its turn, in attending the theatres, Ranelagh, Vauxhall, and other scenes of gayety and amusement. Whenever his funds were dissipated—and they fled more rapidly from being the dupe of many artful persons, male and female, who practised upon his benevolence—he returned to his literary labours, and shut himself up from society to provide fresh matter for his bookseller and fresh supplies for himself."

How completely had the young student discerned the characteristics of poor genial, generous, drudging, holyday loving Goldsmith; toiling that he might play; earning his bread by the sweat of his brains and then throwing it out of the window.

The Roman History was published in the middle of May in two volumes of five hundred pages each. It was brought out without parade or pretension and was announced as for the use of schools and colleges; but, though a work written for bread, not fame, such is its ease, perspicuity, good sense and the delightful simplicity of its style that it was well received by the critics, commanded a prompt and extensive sale and has ever since remained in the hands of young and old.

Johnson, who, as we have before remarked, rarely praised or dispraised things by halves, broke forth in a warm eulogy of the author and the work in a conversation with Boswell, to the great astonishment of the latter. "Whether we take Goldsmith," said he, "as a poet, as a comic writer, or as an historian, he stands in the first class." Boswell.— "An historian! My dear sir, you surely will not rank his compilation of the Roman History with the works of other historians of this age." Johnson.—"Why, who are before him?" Boswell.—"Hume—Robertson— Lord Lyttleton." Johnson (his antipathy against the Scotch beginning to rise).—"I have not read Hume; but doubtless Goldsmith's History is better than the *verbiage* of Robertson, or the foppery of Dalrymple." Boswell.—"Will you not admit the superiority of Robertson, in whose history we find such penetration, such painting?" Johnson.—"Sir, you must consider how that penetration and that painting are employed. It is not history, it is imagination. He who describes what he never saw, draws from fancy. Robertson paints minds, as Sir Joshua paints faces, in a history-piece; he imagines an heroic countenance. You must look upon Robertson's work as romance, and try it by that standard. History it is not. Besides, sir, it is the great excellence of a writer to put into his book as much as his book will hold. Goldsmith has done this in his history. Now Robertson might have put twice as much in his book. Robertson is like a man who has packed gold in wool; the wool takes up more room than the gold. No, sir; I always thought Robertson would be crushed with his own weight—would be buried under his own ornaments. Goldsmith tells you shortly all you want to know; Robertson detains you a great deal too long. No man will read Robertson's cumbrous detail a second time; but Goldsmith's plain narrative will please again and again. I would say to Robertson, what an old tutor of a college said to one of his pupils, 'Read over your compositions, and, whenever you meet with a passage which you think is particularly fine, strike it out!' Goldsmith's abridgment is better than that of Lucius Florus or Eutropius; and I will venture to say, that if you compare him with Vertot in the same places of the Roman History, you will find that he excels Vertot. Sir, he has the art of compiling, and of saying every thing he has to say in a pleasing manner. He is now writing a Natural History, and will make it as entertaining as a Persian tale."

The Natural History to which Johnson alluded was the "History of Animated Nature," which Goldsmith commenced in 1769, under an engagement with Griffin, the bookseller, to complete it as soon as possible in eight volumes, each containing upwards of four hundred pages in pica; a hundred guineas to be paid to the author on the delivery of each volume in manuscript.

He was induced to engage in this work by the urgent solicitations of the booksellers, who had been struck by the sterling merits and captivating style of an introduction which he wrote to Brookes's Natural History. It was Goldsmith's intention originally to make a translation of Pliny, with a popular commentary; but the appearance of Buffon's work induced him to change his plan, and make use of that author for a guide and model.

Cumberland, speaking of this work, observes: "Distress drove Goldsmith upon undertakings neither congenial with his studies nor worthy of his talents. I remember him when, in his chambers in the Temple, he showed me the beginning of his 'Animated Nature;' it was with a sigh, such as genius draws when hard necessity diverts it from its bent to drudge for bread, and talk of birds, and beasts, and creeping things, which Pidcock's showman would have done as well. Poor fellow, he hardly knows an ass from a mule, nor a turkey from a goose, but when he sees it on the table."

Others of Goldsmith's friends entertained similar ideas with respect to his fitness for the task, and they were apt now and then to banter him on the subject, and to amuse themselves with his easy credulity. The custom among the natives of Otaheite of eating dogs being once mentioned in company, Goldsmith observed that a similar custom prevailed in China; that a dog-butcher is as common there as any other butcher; and that, when he walks abroad, all the dogs fall on him. Johnson.—"That is not owing to his killing dogs; sir, I remember a butcher at Litchfield, whom a dog that was in the house where I lived always attacked. It is the smell of carnage which provokes this, let the animals he has killed be what they may." Goldsmith.—"Yes, there is a general abhorrence in animals at the signs of massacre. If you put a tub full of blood into a stable, the horses are likely to go mad."

Johnson.—"I doubt that." Goldsmith.—"Nay, sir, it is a fact well authenticated." Thrale.—"You had better prove it before you put it into your book on Natural History. You may do it in my stable if you will." Johnson.—"Nay, sir, I would not have him prove it. If he is content to take his information from others, he may get through his book with little trouble, and without much endangering his reputation. But if he makes experiments for so comprehensive a book as his, there would be no end to them; his erroneous assertions would fall then upon himself; and he might be blamed for not having made experiments as to every particular."

Johnson's original prediction, however, with respect to this work, that Goldsmith would make it as entertaining as a Persian tale, was verified; and though much of it was borrowed from Buffon, and but little of it written from his own observation; though it was by no means profound, and was chargeable with many errors, yet the charms of his style and the play of his happy disposition throughout have continued to render it far more popular and readable than many works on the subject of much greater scope and science. Cumberland was mistaken, however, in his notion of Goldsmith's ignorance and lack of observation as to the characteristics of animals. On the contrary he was a minute and shrewd observer of them; but he observed them with the eye of a poet and moralist as well as a naturalist. We quote two passages from his works illustrative of this fact, and we do so the more readily because they are in a manner a part of his history and give us another peep into his private life in the Temple; of his mode of occupying himself in his lonely and apparently idle moments and of another class of acquaintances which he made there.

Speaking in his "Animated Nature" of the habitudes of Rooks, "I have often amused myself," says he, "with observing their plans of policy from my window in the Temple, that looks upon a grove where they have made a colony in the midst of a city. At the commencement of spring the rookery, which, during the continuance of winter, seemed to have been deserted, or only guarded by about five or six, like old soldiers in a garrison, now begins to be once more frequented; and in a short time, all the bustle and hurry of business will be fairly commenced."

The other passage which we take the liberty to quote at some length is from an admirable paper in The Bee and relates to the House Spider.

"Of all the solitary insects I have ever remarked, the spider is the most sagacious, and its motions to me, who have attentively considered them, seem almost to exceed belief. * * * I perceived, about four years ago, a large spider in one corner of my room making its web; and, though the maid frequently levelled her fatal broom against the labours of the little animal, I had the good fortune then to prevent its destruction, and I may say it more than paid me by the entertainment it afforded.

"In three days the web was, with incredible diligence, completed; nor could I avoid thinking that the insect seemed to exult in its new abode. It frequently traversed it round, examined the strength of every part of it, retired into its hole, and came out very frequently. The first enemy, however, it had to encounter was another and a much larger spider, which, having no web of its own, and having probably exhausted all its stock in former labours of this kind, came to invade the property of its neighbour. Soon, then, a terrible encounter ensued, in which the invader seemed to have the victory, and the laborious spider was obliged to take refuge in its hole. Upon this I perceived the victor using every art to draw the enemy from its stronghold. He seemed to go off, but quickly returned; and when he found all arts in vain, began to demolish the new web without mercy. This brought on another battle, and, contrary to my expectations, the laborious spider became conqueror, and fairly killed his antagonist.

"Now, then, in peaceable possession of what was justly its own, it waited three days with the utmost impatience, repairing the breaches of its web, and taking no sustenance that I could perceive. At last, however, a large blue fly fell into the snare, and struggled hard to get loose. The spider gave it leave to entangle itself as much as possible, but it seemed to be too strong for the cobweb. I must own I was greatly surprised when I saw the spider immediately sally out, and in less than a minute weave a new net round its captive, by which the motion of its wings was stopped; and, when it was fairly hampered in this manner, it was seized and dragged into the hole.

"In this manner it lived, in a precarious state; and nature seemed to have fitted it for such a life, for upon a single fly it subsisted for more than a week. I once put a wasp into the net; but when the spider came out in order to seize it as usual, upon perceiving what kind of an enemy it had to deal with, it instantly broke all the bands that held it fast, and contributed all that lay in its power to disengage so formidable an antagonist. When the wasp was set at liberty, I expected the spider would have set about repairing the breaches that were made in its net; but those, it seems, were irreparable: wherefore the cobweb was now entirely forsaken, and a new one begun, which was completed in the usual time.

"I had now a mind to try how many cobwebs a single spider could furnish, wherefore I destroyed this, and the insect set about another. When I destroyed the other also, its whole stock seemed entirely exhausted, and it could spin no more. The arts it made use of to support itself, now deprived of its great means of subsistence, were indeed surprising. I have seen it roll up its legs like a ball, and lie motionless for hours together, but cautiously watching all the time: when a fly happened to approach sufficiently near, it would dart out all at once, and often seize its prey.

"Of this life, however, it soon began to grow weary, and resolved to invade the possession of some other spider, since it could not make a web of its own. It formed an attack upon a neighbouring fortification with great vigour, and at first was as vigorously repulsed. Not daunted, however, with one defeat, in this manner it continued to lay siege to another's web for three days, and at length, having killed the defendant, actually took possession. When smaller flies happen to fall into the snare, the spider does not sally out at once, but very patiently waits till it is sure of them; for, upon his immediately approaching, the terror of his appearance might give the captive strength sufficient to get loose; the manner, then, is to wait patiently, till, by ineffectual and impotent struggles, the captive has wasted all its strengh, and then he becomes a certain and easy conquest.

"The insect I am now describing lived three years; every year it changed its skin and got a new set of legs. I have sometimes plucked off a leg, which grew again in two or three days. At first it dreaded my approach to its web, but at last it became so familiar as to take a fly out of my hand; and, upon my touching any part of the web, would immediately leave its hole, prepared either for a defence or an attack."

CHAPTER XXVII

*Honors at the Royal Academy—Letter to his brother Maurice—Family
fortunes—Jane Contarine and the miniature—Portraits and engravings—
School associations—Johnson and Goldsmith in Westminster Abbey*

The latter part of the year 1768 had been made memorable in the world
of taste by the institution of the Royal Academy of Arts, under the
patronage of the King and the direction of forty of the most distinguished artists. Reynolds, who had been mainly instrumental in founding
it, had been unanimously elected president and had thereupon received
the honor of knighthood.* Johnson was so delighted with his friend's
elevation that he broke through a rule of total abstinence with respect
to wine, which he had maintained for several years, and drank bumpers
on the occasion. Sir Joshua eagerly sought to associate his old and valued
friends with him in his new honors, and it is supposed to be through
his suggestions that on the first establishment of professorships, which
took place in December, 1769, Johnson was nominated to that of Ancient
Literature and Goldsmith to that of History. They were mere honorary
titles, without emolument, but gave distinction from the noble institution to which they appertained. They also gave the possessors honorable
places at the annual banquet, at which were assembled many of the most
distinguished persons of rank and talent, all proud to be classed among
the patrons of the arts.

The following letter of Goldsmith to his brother alludes to the foregoing appointment and to a small legacy bequeathed to him by his
uncle Contarine:

*"To Mr. Maurice Goldsmith, at James Lawder's, Esq., at Kilmore, near
Carrick-on-Shannon.*

"January, 1770.

"DEAR BROTHER,—I should have answered your letter sooner, but, in
truth, I am not fond of thinking of the necessities of those I love, when
it is so very little in my power to help them. I am sorry to find you are
every way unprovided for; and what adds to my uneasiness is, that I have
received a letter from my sister Johnson, by which I learn that she is
pretty much in the same circumstances. As to myself, I believe I could

---

* We must apologize for the anachronism we have permitted ourselves in the
course of this memoir, in speaking of Reynolds as *Sir Joshua*, when treating of
circumstances which occurred prior to his being dubbed; but it is so customary
to speak of him by that title that we found it difficult to dispense with it.

get both you and my poor brother-in-law something like that which you desire, but I am determined never to ask for little things, nor exhaust any little interest I may have, until I can serve you, him, and myself more effectually. As yet, no opportunity has offered; but I believe you are pretty well convinced that I will not be remiss when it arrives.

"The king has lately been pleased to make me professor of Ancient History in a royal academy of painting which he has just established, but there is no salary annexed; and I took it rather as a compliment to the institution than any benefit to myself. Honours to one in my situation are something like ruffles to one that wants a shirt.

"You tell me that there are fourteen or fifteen pounds left me in the hands of my cousin Lawder, and you ask me what I would have done with them. My dear brother, I would by no means give any directions to my dear worthy relations at Kilmore how to dispose of money which is, properly speaking, more theirs than mine. All that I can say is, that I entirely, and this letter will serve to witness, give up any right and title to it; and I am sure they will dispose of it to the best advantage. To them I entirely leave it; whether they or you may think the whole necessary to fit you out, or whether our poor sister Johnson may not want the half, I leave entirely to their and your discrection. The kindness of that good couple to our shattered family demands our sincerest gratitude; and, though they have almost forgotten me, yet, if good things at last arrive, I hope one day to return and increase their good humour by adding to my own.

"I have sent my cousin Jenny a miniature picture of myself, as I believe it is the most acceptable present I can offer. I have ordered it to be left for her at George Faulkner's, folded in a letter. The face, you well know, is ugly enough, but it is finely painted. I will shortly also send my friends over the Shannon some mezzotinto prints of myself, and some more of my friends here, such as Burke, Johnson, Reynolds, and Colman. I believe I have written a hundred letters to different friends in your country, and never received an answer to any of them. I do not know how to account for this, or why they are unwilling to keep up for me those regards which I must ever retain for them.

"If, then, you have a mind to oblige me, you will write often, whether I answer you or not. Let me particularly have the news of our family and old acquaintances. For instance, you may begin by telling me about the family where you reside, how they spend their time, and whether they ever make mention of me. Tell me about my mother, my brother Hodson and his son, my brother Harry's son and daughter, my sister Johnson, the family of Ballyoughter, what is become of them, where they live, and how they do. You talked of being my only brother:

I don't understand you. Where is Charles? A sheet of paper occasionally filled with the news of this kind would make me very happy, and
would keep you nearer my mind. As it is, my dear brother, believe
me to be

"Yours, most affectionately,

"OLIVER GOLDSMITH."

By this letter we find the Goldsmiths the same shifting, shiftless race
as formerly; a "shattered family," scrambling on each other's back as
soon as any rise above the surface. Maurice is "every way unprovided
for;" living upon cousin Jane and her husband; and perhaps amusing
himself by hunting otter in the river Inny. Sister Johnson and her husband are as poorly off as Maurice, with perhaps no one at hand to
quarter themselves upon; as to the rest, "what is become of them; where
do they live; how do they do; what is become of Charles?" What forlorn,
haphazard life is implied by these questions! Can we wonder that, with
all the love for his native place which is shown throughout Goldsmith's
writings, he had not the heart to return there? Yet his affections are still
there. He wishes to know whether the Lawders (which means his cousin
Jane, his early Valentine) ever make mention of him; he sends Jane his
miniature; he believes "it is the most acceptable present he can offer;" he
evidently therefore does not believe she has almost forgotten him.
although he intimates that he does: in his memory she is still Jane
Contarine, as he last saw her, when he accompanied her harpsichord with
his flute. Absence, like death, sets a seal on the image of those we have
loved; we cannot realize the intervening changes which time may have
effected.

As to the rest of Goldsmith's relatives, he abandons his legacy of
fifteen pounds, to be shared among them. It is all he has to give. His
heedless improvidence is eating up the pay of the booksellers in advance.
With all his literary success he has neither money nor influence; but
he has empty fame, and he is ready to participate with them; he is
honorary professor, without pay; his portrait is to be engraved in mezzotinto in company with those of his friends, Burke, Reynolds, Johnson,
Colman and others, and he will send prints of them to his friends over
the Shannon, though they may not have a house to hang them up in.
What a motley letter! How indicative of the motley character of the
writer! By the by, the publication of a splendid mezzotinto engraving
of his likeness by Reynolds, was a great matter of glorification to Goldsmith, especially as it appeared in such illustrious company. As he was
one day walking the streets in a state of high elation from having just
seen it figuring in the print shop windows, he met a young gentleman
with a newly married wife hanging on his arm, whom he immediately

recognized for Master Bishop, one of the boys he had petted and treated with sweetmeats when a humble usher at Milner's school. The kindly feelings of old times revived, and he accosted him with cordial familiarity, though the youth may have found some difficulty in recognizing in the personage, arrayed perhaps in garments of Tyrian dye, the dingy pedagogue of the Milners. "Come, my boy," cried Goldsmith as if still speaking to a schoolboy, "Come, Sam, I am delighted to see you. I must treat you to something. What shall it be? Will you have some apples?" glancing at an old woman's stall; then, recollecting the print shop window: "Sam," said he, "have you seen my picture by Sir Joshua Reynolds? Have you seen it, Sam? Have you got an engraving?" Bishop was caught; he equivocated; he had not yet bought it; but he was furnishing his house, and had fixed upon the place where it was to be hung. "Ah, Sam!" rejoined Goldsmith reproachfully, "if your picture had been published, I should not have waited an hour without having it."

After all, it was honest pride, not vanity, in Goldsmith that was gratified at seeing his portrait deemed worthy of being perpetuated by the classic pencil of Reynolds and "hung up in history" beside that of his revered friend, Johnson. Even the great moralist himself was not insensible to a feeling of this kind. Walking one day with Goldsmith in Westminster Abbey, among the tombs of monarchs, warriors and statesmen, they came to the sculptured mementos of literary worthies in Poets' Corner. Casting his eye round upon these memorials of genius, Johnson muttered in a low tone to his companion,

Forsitan et nostrum nomen miscebitur istis.

Goldsmith treasured up the intimated hope and shortly afterwards, as they were passing by Temple Bar, where the heads of Jacobite rebels, executed for treason, were mouldering aloft on spikes, pointed up to the grizzly mementos and echoed the intimation,

Forsitan et nostrum nomen miscebitur *istis*.

CHAPTER XXVIII

Publication of the Deserted Village; notice and illustrations of it

Several years had now elapsed since the publication of The Traveller, and much wonder was expressed that the great success of that poem had not excited the author to further poetic attempts. On being questioned at the annual dinner of the Royal Academy by the Earl of Lisburn why he neglected the muses to compile histories and write novels, "My Lord," replied he, "by courting the muses I shall starve, but by my other labours I eat, drink, have good clothes, and can enjoy the luxuries of life." So also on being asked by a poor writer what was the most profitable mode of exercising the pen, "My dear fellow," replied he good humoredly, "pay no regard to the draggle-tailed muses; for my part I have found productions in prose much more sought after and better paid for."

Still, however, as we have heretofore shown, he found sweet moments of dalliance to steal away from his prosaic toils, and court the muse among the green lanes and hedge rows in the rural environs of London, and on the 26th of May, 1770, he was enabled to bring his Deserted Village before the public.

The popularity of The Traveller had prepared the way for this poem, and its sale was instantaneous and immense. The first edition was immediately exhausted; in a few days a second was issued; in a few days more a third, and by the 16th of August the fifth edition was hurried through the press. As is the case with popular writers, he had become his own rival, and critics were inclined to give the preference to his first poem; but with the public at large we believe the Deserted Village has ever been the greatest favorite. Previous to its publication the bookseller gave him in advance a note for the price agreed upon, one hundred guineas. As the latter was returning home he met a friend to whom he mentioned the circumstance, and who apparently judging of poetry by quantity rather than quality, observed that it was a great sum for so small a poem. "In truth," said Goldsmith, "I think so too; it is much more than the honest man can afford or the piece is worth. I have not been easy since I received it." In fact, he actually returned the note to the bookseller, and left it to him to graduate the payment according to the success of the work. The bookseller, as may well be supposed, soon repaid him in full with many acknowledgments of his disinterestedness. This anecdote has been called in question, we know not on what grounds; we see nothing in it incompatible with the character of Goldsmith, who was very impulsive and prone to acts of inconsiderate generosity.

As we do not pretend in this summary memoir to go into a criticism or analysis of any of Goldsmith's writings, we shall not dwell upon the peculiar merits of this poem; we cannot help noticing, however, how truly it is a mirror of the author's heart and of all the fond pictures of early friends and early life for ever present there. It seems to us as if the very last accounts received from home, of his "shattered family" and the desolation that seemed to have settled upon the haunts of his childhood, had cut to the roots one feebly cherished hope and produced the following exquisitely tender and mournful lines:

> In all my wand'rings round this world of care,
> In all my griefs—and God has giv'n my share—
> I still had hopes my latest hours to crown,
> Amid these humble bowers to lay me down;
> To husband out life's taper at the close,
> And keep the flame from wasting by repose;
> I still had hopes, for pride attends us still,
> Amid the swains to show my book-learn'd skill,
> Around my fire an ev'ning group to draw,
> And tell of all I felt and all I saw;
> And as a hare, whom hounds and horns pursue,
> Pants to the place from whence at first she flew,
> I still had hopes, my long vexations past,
> Here to return—and die at home at last.

How touchingly expressive are the succeeding lines, wrung from a heart which all the trials and temptations and buffetings of the world could not render worldly; which amid a thousand follies and errors of the head still retained its childlike innocence; and which, doomed to struggle on to the last amidst the din and turmoil of the metropolis, had ever been cheating itself with a dream of rural quiet and seclusion:

> Oh bless'd retirement! friend to life's decline,
> Retreats from care, that never must be mine,
> How blest is he who crowns, in shades like these,
> A youth of labour with an age of ease;
> Who quits a world where strong temptations try,
> And, since 'tis hard to combat, learns to fly!
> For him no wretches, born to work and weep,
> Explore the mine, or tempt the dangerous deep;
> Nor surly porter stands, in guilty state,
> To spurn imploring famine from the gate;
> But on he moves to meet his latter end,

Angels around befriending virtue's friend;
Sinks to the grave with unperceived decay,
While resignation gently slopes the way;
And all his prospects brightening to the last,
His heaven commences ere the world be past.

NOTE

The following article, which appeared in a London periodical, shows
the effect of Goldsmith's poem in renovating the fortunes of Lissoy:

"About three miles from Ballymahon, a very central town in the
sister kingdom, is the mansion and village of Auburn, so called by their
present possessor, Captain Hogan. Through the taste and improvement
of this gentleman, it is now a beautiful spot, although fifteen years since
it presented a very bare and unpoetical aspect. This, however, was owing
to a cause which serves strongly to corroborate the assertion, that
Goldsmith had this scene in view when he wrote his poem of 'The
Deserted Village.' The then possessor, General Napier, turned all his
tenants out of their farms that he might enclose them in his own private
domain. Littleton, the mansion of the general, stands not far off, a
complete emblem of the desolating spirit lamented by the poet, dilapi-
dated and converted into a barrack.

"The chief object of attraction is Lishoy, once the parsonage house of
Henry Goldsmith, that brother to whom the poet dedicated his 'Traveller,' and who is represented as the village pastor,

'Passing rich with forty pounds a year.'

"When I was in the country, the lower chambers were inhabited by
pigs and sheep, and the drawing-rooms by oats. Captain Hogan, however, has, I believe, got it since into his possession, and has, of course,
improved its condition.

"Though at first strongly inclined to dispute the identity of Auburn,
Lishoy House overcame my scruples. As I clambered over the rotten
gate, and crossed the grass-grown lawn or court, the tide of association became too strong for casuistry: here the poet dwelt and wrote,
and here his thoughts fondly recurred when composing his 'Traveller'
in a foreign land. Yonder was the decent church, that literally 'topped
the neighbouring hill.' Before me lay the little hill of Knockrue, on
which he declares, in one of his letters, he had rather sit with a book
in hand than mingle in the proudest assemblies. And, above all,
startlingly true, beneath my feet was

> 'Yonder copse, where once the garden smiled,
> And still where many a garden-flower grows wild.'

"A painting from the life could not be more exact. 'The stubborn currant-bush' lifts its head above the rank grass, and the proud holly-hock flaunts where its sisters of the flower-knot are no more.

"In the middle of the village stands the old 'hawthorn-tree,' built up with masonry to distinguish and preserve it; it is old and stunted, and suffers much from the depredations of post chaise travellers, who generally stop to procure a twig. Opposite to it is the village alehouse, over the door of which swings 'The Three Jolly Pigeons.' Within every thing is arranged according to the letter:

> 'The whitewash'd wall, the nicely-sanded floor,
> The varnish'd clock that click'd behind the door:
> The chest, contrived a double debt to pay,
> A bed by night, a chest of drawers by day;
> The pictures placed for ornament and use,
> The twelve good rules, the royal game of goose.'

"Captain Hogan, I have heard, found great difficulty in obtaining 'the twelve good rules,' but at length purchased them at some London book-stall to adorn the whitewashed parlour of 'The Three Jolly Pigeons.' However laudable this may be, nothing shook my faith in the reality of Auburn so much as this exactness, which had the disagreeable air of being got up for the occasion. The last object of pilgrimage is the quon-dam habitation of the schoolmaster,

> 'There, in his noisy mansion, skill'd to rule.'

It is surounded with fragrant proofs of its identity in

> 'The blossom'd furze, unprofitably gay.'

There is to be seen the chair of the poet, which fell into the hands of its present possessors at the wreck of the parsonage-house; they have frequently refused large offers of purchase; but more, I dare say, for the sake of drawing contributions from the curious than from any reverence for the bard. The chair is of oak, with back and seat of cane, which precluded all hopes of a secret drawer, like that lately discovered in Gay's. There is no fear of its being worn out by the devout earnestness of sitters—as the cocks and hens have usurped undisputed possession of it, and protest most clamorously against all attempts to get it cleansed or to seat one's self.

"The controversy concerning the identity of this Auburn was formerly a standing theme of discussion among the learned of the neighbourhood; but, since the pros and cons have been all ascertained, the argument has died away. Its abettors plead the singular agreement between the local history of the place and the Auburn of the poem, and the exactness with which the scenery of the one answers to the description of the other. To this is opposed the mention of the nightingale,

'And fill'd each pause the nightingale had made;'

there being no such bird in the island. The objection is slighted, on the other hand, by considering the passage as a mere poetical license: 'Besides,' say they, 'the robin is the Irish nightingale.' And if it be hinted how unlikely it was that Goldsmith should have laid the scene in a place from which he was and had been so long absent, the rejoinder is always, 'Pray, sir, was Milton in hell when he built Pandemonium?'

"The line is naturally drawn between; there can be no doubt that the poet intended England by

'The land to hast'ning ills a prey,
Where wealth accumulates and men decay.'

But it is very natural to suppose that, at the same time, his imagination had in view the scenes of his youth, which give such strong features of resemblance to the picture."

Best, an Irish clergyman, told Davis, the traveller in America, that the hawthorn-bush mentioned in the poem was still remarkably large. "I was riding once," said he, "with Brady, titular Bishop of Ardagh, when he observed to me, 'Ma foy Best, this huge overgrown bush is mightily in the way. I will order it to be cut down.'—'What, sir!' replied I, 'cut down the bush that supplies so beautiful an image in "The Deserted Village?"'—'Ma foy!' exclaimed the Bishop, 'is that the hawthorn-bush? Then let it be sacred from the edge of the axe, and evil be to him that should cut off a branch.'"—The hawthorn-bush, however, has long since been cut up, root and branch, in furnishing relics to literary pilgrims.

CHAPTER XXIX

The poet among the ladies; description of his person and manners—Expedition to Paris with the Horneck family—The traveller of twenty and the traveller of forty—Hickey, the special attorney—An unlucky exploit

The Deserted Village had shed an additional poetic grace round the homely person of the author; he was becoming more and more acceptable in ladies' eyes and finding himself more and more at ease in their society; at least in the society of those whom he met in the Reynolds circle, among whom he particularly affected the beautiful family of the Hornecks.

But let us see what were really the looks and manners of Goldsmith about this time and what right he had to aspire to ladies' smiles; and in so doing let us not take the sketches of Boswell and his compeers, who had a propensity to represent him in caricature; but let us take the apparently truthful and discriminating picture of him as he appeared to Judge Day when the latter was a student in the Temple.

"In person," says the judge, "he was short, about five feet five or six inches; strong, but not heavy in make; rather fair in complexion, with brown hair, such at least as could be distinguished from his wig. His features were plain, but not repulsive,—certainly not so when lighted up by conversation. His manners were simple, natural, and perhaps on the whole, we may say, not polished; at least without the refinement and good-breeding which the exquisite polish of his compositions would lead us to expect. He was always cheerful and animated, often, indeed, boisterous in his mirth; entered with spirit into convivial society; contributed largely to its enjoyments by solidity of information, and the naïveté and originality of his character; talked often without premeditation, and laughed loudly without restraint."

This, it will be recollected, represents him as he appeared to a young Templar, who probably saw him only in Temple coffee houses, at students' quarters or at the jovial supper parties given at the poet's own chambers; here of course his mind was in its rough dress; his laugh may have been loud and his mirth boisterous; but we trust all these matters became softened and modified when he found himself in polite drawing rooms and in female society.

But what say the ladies themselves of him; and here, fortunately, we have another sketch of him as he appeared at the time to one of the Horneck circle; in fact, we believe, to the Jessamy Bride herself. After admitting apparently with some reluctance, that "he was a very plain man," she goes on to say, "but had he been much more so, it was impossible not to love and respect his goodness of heart, which broke out on every occasion. His benevolence was unquestionable, and *his countenance bore every trace of it:* no one that knew him intimately could avoid admiring and loving his good qualities." When to all this we add the idea of intellectual delicacy and refinement associated with him by his poetry and the newly plucked bays that were flourishing round his brow, we cannot be surprised that fine and fashionable ladies should be proud of his attentions and that even a young beauty should not be altogether displeased with the thoughts of having a man of his genius in her chains.

We are led to indulge some notions of the kind from finding him in the month of July, but a few weeks after the publication of the Deserted Village, setting off on a six weeks' excursion to Paris in company with Mrs. Horneck and her two beautiful daughters. A day or two before his departure we find another new gala suit charged to him on the books of Mr. William Filby. Were the bright eyes of the Jessamy Bride responsible for this additional extravagance of wardrobe? Goldsmith had recently been editing the works of Parnell; had he taken courage from the example of Edwin in the Fairy Tale?—

> Yet spite of all that nature did
> To make his uncouth form forbid,
>   This creature dared to love.
> He felt the force of Edith's eyes,
> Nor wanted hope to gain the prize
>   *Could ladies look within*——

All this we throw out as mere hints and surmises, leaving it to our readers to draw their own conclusions. It will be found however that the poet was subjected to shrewd bantering among his contemporaries about the beautiful Mary Horneck, and that he was extremely sensitive on the subject.

It was in the month of June that he set out for Paris with his fair companions, and the following letter was written by him to Sir Joshua Reynolds, soon after the party landed at Calais:

"MY DEAR FRIEND,

"We had a very quick passage from Dover to Calais, which we performed in three hours and twenty minutes, all of us extremely sea-sick, which must necessarily have happened, as my machine to prevent sea-sickness was not completed. We were glad to leave Dover, because we hated to be imposed upon; so were in high spirits at coming to Calais, where we were told that a little money would go a great way.

"Upon landing two little trunks, which was all we carried with us, we were surprised to see fourteen or fifteen fellows all running down to the ship to lay their hands upon them; four got under each trunk, the rest surrounded and held the hasps; and in this manner our little baggage was conducted, with a kind of funeral solemnity, till it was safely lodged at the custom-house. We were well enough pleased with the people's civility till they came to be paid; every creature that had the happiness of but touching our trunks with their finger, expected six-pence; and they had so pretty and civil a manner of demanding it, that there was no refusing them.

"When we had done with the porters, we had next to speak with the custom-house officers, who had their pretty civil way too. We were directed to the Hôtel d'Angleterre, where a valet-de-place came to offer his service, and spoke to me ten minutes before I once found out that he was speaking English. We had no occasion for his services, so we gave him a little money because he spoke English, and because he wanted it. I cannot help mentioning another circumstance: I bought a new riband for my wig at Canterbury, and the barber at Calais broke it in order to gain sixpence by buying me a new one."

An incident which occurred in the course of this tour has been tortured by that literary magpie, Boswell, into a proof of Goldsmith's absurd jealousy of any admiration shown to others in his presence. While stopping at a hotel in Lisle, they were drawn to the windows by a military parade in front. The extreme beauty of the Miss Hornecks immediately attracted the attention of the officers, who broke forth with enthusiastic speeches and compliments intended for their ears. Goldsmith was amused for a while, but at length affected impatience at this exclusive admiration of his beautiful companions, and exclaimed, with mock severity of aspect, "Elsewhere I also would have my admirers."

It is difficult to conceive the obtuseness of intellect necessary to mis-construe so obvious a piece of mock petulance and dry humor into an instance of mortified vanity and jealous self-conceit.

Goldsmith jealous of the admiration of a group of gay officers for the charms of two beautiful young women! This even out-Boswells Boswell; yet this is but one of several similar absurdities, evidently mis-conceptions of Goldsmith's peculiar vein of humor, by which the charge of envious jealousy has been attempted to be fixed upon him. In the present instance it was contradicted by one of the ladies herself, who was annoyed that it had been advanced against him. "I am sure," said she, "from the peculiar manner of his humour and assumed frown of countenance, what was often uttered in jest was mistaken by those who did not know him, for earnest." No one was more prone to err on this point than Boswell. He had a tolerable perception of wit, but none of humor.

The following letter to Sir Joshua Reynolds was subsequently written:

"*To Sir Joshua Reynolds.*

"Paris, July 29 (1770).

"MY DEAR FRIEND,—I began a long letter to you from Lisle, giving a description of all that we had done and seen, but, finding it very dull, and knowing that you would show it again, I threw it aside and it was lost. You see by the top of this letter that we are at Paris, and (as I have often heard you say) we have brought our own amusement with us, for the ladies do not seem to be very fond of what we have yet seen.

"With regard to myself, I find that travelling at twenty and at forty are very different things. I set out with all my confirmed habits about me, and can find nothing on the Continent so good as when I formerly left it. One of our chief amusements here is scolding at every thing we meet with, and praising every thing and every person we left at home. You may judge, therefore, whether your name is not frequently bandied at table among us. To tell you the truth, I never thought I could regret your absence so much as our various mortifications on the road have often taught me to do. I could tell you of disasters and adventures without number; of our lying in barns, and of my being half poisoned with a dish of green peas; of our quarrelling with postillions, and being cheated by our landladies; but I reserve all this for a happy hour which I expect to share with you upon my return.

"I have little to tell you more but that we are at present all well, and expect returning when we have stayed out one month, which I did not care if it were over this very day. I long to hear from you all, how you yourself do, how Johnson, Burke, Dyer, Chamier, Colman, and every one of the club do. I wish I could send you some amusement in this letter, but I protest I am so stupified by the air of this country (for I am sure it cannot be natural) that I have not a word to say. I have been thinking of the plot of a comedy, which shall be entitled A Journey to Paris, in which a family shall be introduced with a full intention of going to France to save money. You know there is not a place in the world more promising for that purpose. As for the meat of this country, I can scarce eat it; and, though we pay two good shillings a head for our dinner, I find it all so tough that I have spent less time with my knife than my picktooth. I said this as a good thing at table, but it was not understood. I believe it to be a good thing.

"As for our intended journey to Devonshire, I find it out of my power to perform it; for, as soon as I arrive at Dover, I intend to let the ladies go on, and I will take a country lodging somewhere near that place in order to do some business. I have so outrun the constable that I must mortify a little to bring it up again. For God's sake, the night you receive this, take your pen in your hand and tell me something about yourself and myself, if you know of any thing that has happened. About Miss Reynolds, about Mr. Bickerstaffe, my nephew, or any body that you regard. I beg you will send to Griffin the bookseller to know if there be any letters left for me, and be so good as to send them to me at Paris. They may perhaps be left for me at the Porter's Lodge, opposite the pump in Temple Lane. The same messenger will do. I expect one from Lord Clare, from Ireland. As for the others, I am not much uneasy about.

"Is there any thing I can do for you at Paris? I wish you would tell me. The whole of my own purchases here is one silk coat, which I have put on, and which makes me look like a fool. But no more of that. I find that Colman has gained his lawsuit. I am glad of it. I suppose you often meet. I will soon be among you, better pleased with my situation at home than I ever was before. And yet I must say, that if any thing could make France pleasant, the very good women with whom I am at present would certainly do it. I could say more about that, but I intend showing them the letter before I send it away. What signifies teazing you longer with moral observations, when the business of my writing is over? I have one thing only more to say, and of that I think every hour in the day, namely that I am your most sincere and most affectionate friend,

"OLIVER GOLDSMITH.

"Direct to me at the Hotel de Danemarc, }
Rue Jacob, Fauxbourg St. Germains." }

A word of comment on this letter:
Travelling is indeed a very different thing with Goldsmith the poor student at twenty and Goldsmith the poet and professor at forty. At twenty, though obliged to trudge on foot from town to town and country to country, paying for a supper and a bed by a tune on the flute, every thing pleased, every thing was good; a truckle bed in a garret was a couch of down, and the homely fare of the peasant a feast fit for an epicure. Now at forty when he posts through the country in a carriage with fair ladies by his side, every thing goes wrong: he has to quarrel with postillions, he is cheated by landladies, the hotels are barns, the meat is too tough to be eaten, and he is half poisoned by green peas! A line in his letter explains the secret: "the ladies do not seem to

be very fond of what we have yet seen." "One of our chief amusements is scolding at every thing we meet with and praising every thing and every person we have left at home."—the true English travelling amusement. Poor Goldsmith! he has "all his *confirmed habits* about him;" that is to say, he has recently risen into high life and acquired high bred notions; he must be fastidious like his fellow travellers; he dare not be pleased with what pleased the vulgar tastes of his youth. He is unconsciously illustrating the trait so humorously satirized by him in Bill Tibbs, the shabby beau, who can find "no such dressing as he had at Lord Crumps or Lady Crimps;" whose very senses have grown genteel, and who no longer "smacks at wretched wine or praises detestable custard."

A lurking thorn too is worrying him throughout this tour; he has "outrun the constable;" that is to say, his expenses have outrun his means, and he will have to make up for this butterfly flight by toiling like a grub on his return.

Another circumstance contributes to mar the pleasure he had promised himself in this excursion. At Paris the party is unexpectedly joined by a Mr. Hickey, a bustling attorney, who is well acquainted with that metropolis and its environs and insists on playing the cicerone on all occasions. He and Goldsmith do not relish each other, and they have several petty altercations. The lawyer is too much a man of business and method for the careless poet and is disposed to manage every thing. He has perceived Goldsmith's whimsical peculiarities without properly appreciating his merits and is prone to indulge in broad bantering and raillery at his expense, particularly irksome if indulged in presence of the ladies. He makes himself merry on his return to England by giving the following anecdote as illustrative of Goldsmith's vanity:

"Being with a party at Versailles viewing the water-works, a question arose among the gentlemen present, whether the distance from whence they stood to one of the little islands was within the compass of a leap. Goldsmith maintained the affirmative; but, being bantered on the subject, and remembering his former prowess as a youth, attempted the leap, but, falling short, descended into the water, to the great amusement of the company."

Was the Jessamy Bride a witness of this unlucky exploit?

This same Hickey is the one of whom Goldsmith some time subsequently gave a good humored sketch in his poem of "The Retaliation."

> Here Hickey reclines, a most blunt, pleasant creature,
> And slander itself must allow him good nature;
> He cherish'd his friend, and he relish'd a bumper,
> Yet one fault he had, and that one was a thumper.
> Perhaps you may ask if the man was a miser;

> I answer, No, no, for he always was wiser;
> Too courteous, perhaps, or obligingly flat,
> His very worst foe can't accuse him of that;
> Perhaps he confided in men as they go,
> And so was too foolishly honest? Ah no!
> Then what was his failing? Come, tell it, and burn ye—
> He was, could he help it? a special attorney.

One of the few remarks extant made by Goldsmith during this tour is the following, of whimsical import, in his "Animated Nature."

"In going through the towns of France some time since, I could not help observing how much plainer their parrots spoke than ours, and how very distinctly I understood their parrots speak French, when I could not understand our own, though they spoke my native language. I at first ascribed it to the different qualities of the two languages, and was for entering into an elaborate discussion on the vowels and consonants; but a friend that was with me solved the difficulty at once, by assuring me that the French women scarce did any thing else the whole day than sit and instruct their feathered pupils; and that the birds were thus distinct in their lessons in consequence of continual schooling."

His tour does not seem to have left in his memory the most fragrant recollections; for, being asked after his return whether travelling on the Continent repaid "an Englishman for the privations and annoyances attendant on it," he replied, "I recommend it by all means to the rich, if they are without the sense of *smelling*, and to the poor if they are without the sense of *feeling*; and to both if they can discharge from their minds all idea of what in England we term comfort."

It is needless to say that the universal improvement in the art of living on the Continent has at the present day taken away the force of Goldsmith's reply, though even at the time it was more humorous than correct.

CHAPTER XXX

Death of Goldsmith's mother—Biography of Parnell—Agreement with Davies for the History of Rome—Life of Bolingbroke—The Haunch of Venison

On his return to England Goldsmith received the melancholy tidings of the death of his mother. Notwithstanding the fame as an author to which he had attained, she seems to have been disappointed in her early expectations for him. Like others of his family, she had been more vexed by his early follies than pleased by his proofs of genius; and in subsequent years, when he had risen to fame and to intercourse with the great, had been annoyed at the ignorance of the world and want of management, which prevented him from pushing his fortune. He had always, however, been an affectionate son, and in the latter years of her life, when she had become blind, contributed from his precarious resources to prevent her from feeling want.

He now resumed the labors of the pen, which his recent excursion to Paris rendered doubly necessary. We should have mentioned a Life of Parnell, published by him shortly after the Deserted Village. It was, as usual, a piece of job work, hastily got up for pocket money. Johnson spoke slightingly of it, and the author, himself, thought proper to apologize for its meagerness; yet, in so doing, used a simile which for beauty of imagery and felicity of language is enough of itself to stamp a value upon the essay.

"Such," says he, "is the very unpoetical detail of the life of a poet. Some dates and some few facts, scarcely more interesting than those that make the ornaments of a country tombstone, are all that remain of one whose labours now begin to excite universal curiosity. A poet, while living, is seldom an object sufficiently great to attract much attention; his real merits are known but to a few, and these are generally sparing in their praises. When his fame is increased by time, it is then too late to investigate the peculiarities of his disposition; *the dews of morning are past, and we vainly try to continue the chase by the meridian splendour.*"

He now entered into an agreement with Davies to prepare an abridgment in one volume duodecimo of his History of Rome; but first to write a work for which there was a more immediate demand. Davies was about to republish Lord Bolingbroke's *Dissertation on Parties,* which he conceived would be exceedingly applicable to the affairs of the day and make a probable *hit* during the existing state of violent political excitement; to give it still greater effect and currency he engaged Goldsmith to introduce it with a prefatory life of Lord Bolingbroke.

164

About this time Goldsmith's friend and countryman Lord Clare was in geat affliction, caused by the death of his only son, Colonel Nugent, and stood in need of the sympathies of a kind hearted friend. At his request, therefore, Goldsmith paid him a visit at his seat of Gosfield, taking his tasks with him. Davies was in a worry lest Gosfield Park should prove a Capua to the poet and the time be lost. "Dr. Goldsmith," writes he to a friend, "has gone with Lord Clare into the country, and I am plagued to get the proofs from him of his Life of Lord Bolingbroke." The proofs however were furnished in time for the publication of the work in December. The Biography, though written during a time of political turmoil, and introducing a work intended to be thrown into the arena of politics, maintained that freedom from party prejudice observable in all the writings of Goldsmith. It was a selection of facts drawn from many unreadable sources and arranged into a clear, flowing narrative, illustrative of the career and character of one who, as he intimates, "seemed formed by nature to take delight in struggling with opposition, whose most agreeable hours were passed in storms of his own creating; whose life was spent in a continual conflict of politics, and, as if that was too short for the combat, has left his memory as a subject of lasting contention." The sum received by the author for this memoir is supposed from circumstances to have been forty pounds.

Goldsmith did not find the residence among the great unattended with mortifications. He had now become accustomed to be regarded in London as a literary lion and was annoyed at what he considered a slight on the part of Lord Camden. He complained of it on his return to town at a party of his friends. "I met him," said he, "at Lord Clare's house in the country; and he took no more notice of me than if I had been an ordinary man." "The company," says Boswell, "laughed heartily at this piece of 'diverting simplicity.'" And foremost among the laughers was doubtless the rattle pated Boswell. Johnson, however, stepped forward as usual to defend the poet, whom he would allow no one to assail but himself; perhaps in the present instance he thought the dignity of literature itself involved in the question. "Nay, gentlemen," roared he, "Dr. Goldsmith is in the right. A nobleman ought to have made up to such a man as Goldsmith; and I think it is much against Lord Camden that he neglected him."

After Goldsmith's return to town he received from Lord Clare a present of game, which he has celebrated and perpetuated in his amusing verses entitled the "Haunch of Venison." Some of the lines pleasantly set forth the embarrassment caused by the appearance of such an aristocratic delicacy in the humble kitchen of a poet, accustomed to look up to mutton as a treat:

Thanks, my lord, for your venison; for finer or fatter
Never rang'd in a forest, or smok'd in a platter:
The haunch was a picure for painters to study,
The fat was so white, and the lean was so ruddy;
Though my stomach was sharp, I could scarce help regretting,
To spoil such a delicate picture by eating:
I had thought in my chambers to place it in view,
To be shown to my friends as a piece of virtù;
As in some Irish houses where things are so-so,
One gammon of bacon hangs up for a show;
But, for eating a rasher of what they take pride in,
They'd as soon think of eating the pan it was fry'd in.

   ❖   ❖   ❖   ❖   ❖   ❖   ❖

But hang it—to poets, who seldom can eat,
Your very good mutton's a very good treat;
Such dainties to them, their health it might hurt;
It's like sending them ruffles, when wanting a shirt.

We have an amusing anecdote of one of Goldsmith's blunders which took place on a subsequent visit to Lord Clare's, when that nobleman was residing in Bath.

Lord Clare and the Duke of Northumberland had houses next to each other, of similar architecture. Returning home one morning from an early walk, Goldsmith, in one of his frequent fits of absence, mistook the house, and walked up into the duke's dining-room, where he and the duchess were about to sit down to breakfast. Goldsmith, still supposing himself in the house of Lord Clare, and that they were visitors, made them an easy salutation, being acquainted with them, and threw himself on a sofa in the lounging manner of a man perfectly at home. The duke and duchess soon perceived his mistake, and, while they smiled internally, endeavored, with the considerateness of well-bred people, to prevent any awkward embarrassment. They accordingly chatted sociably with him about matters in Bath, until, breakfast being served, they invited him to partake. The truth at once flashed upon poor heedless Goldsmith; he started up from his free-and-easy position, made a confused apology for his blunder, and would have retired perfectly disconcerted had not the duke and duchess treated the whole as a lucky occurrence to throw him in their way, and exacted a promise from him to dine with them.

This may be hung up as a companion piece to his blunder on his first visit to Northumberland House.

CHAPTER XXXI

Dinner at the Royal Academy—The Rowley controversy—Horace Walpole's conduct to Chatterton—Johnson at Redcliffe Church—Goldsmith's History of England—Davies's criticism—Letter to Bennet Langton

On St. George's day of this year (1771) the first annual banquet of the Royal Academy was held in the exhibition room; the walls of which were covered with works of art, about to be submitted to public inspection. Sir Joshua Reynolds, who first suggested this elegant festival, presided in his official character; Drs. Johnson and Goldsmith of course were present as professors of the academy; and, beside the academicians, there was a large number of the most distinguished men of the day as guests. Goldsmith on this occasion drew on himself the attention of the company by launching out with enthusiasm on the poems recently given to the world by Chatterton as the works of an ancient author by the name of Rowley, discovered in the tower of Redcliffe Church at Bristol. Goldsmith spoke of them with rapture as a treasure of old English poetry. This immediately raised the question of their authenticity, they having been pronounced a forgery of Chatterton's. Goldsmith was warm for their being genuine. When he considered, he said, the merit of the poetry; the acquaintance with life and the human heart displayed in them, the antique quaintness of the language and the familiar knowledge of historical events of their supposed day, he could not believe it possible they could be the work of a boy of sixteen of narrow education and confined to the duties of an attorney's office. They must be the productions of Rowley.

Johnson, who was a stout unbeliever in Rowley as he had been in Ossian, rolled in his chair and laughed at the enthusiasm of Goldsmith. Horace Walpole, who sat near by, joined in the laugh and jeer as soon as he found that the *"trouvaille,"* as he called it, "of *his friend* Chatterton" was in question. This matter, which had excited the simple admiration of Goldsmith, was no novelty to him, he said. "He might, had he pleased, have had the honor of ushering the great discovery to the learned world." And so he might, had he followed his first impulse in the matter, for he himself had been an original believer; had pronounced some specimen verses sent to him by Chatterton wonderful for their harmony and spirit; and had been ready to print them and publish them to the world with his sanction. When he found however that his unknown correspondent was a mere boy, humble in sphere and indigent in circumstances, and when Gray and Mason pronounced the poems forgeries, he had changed his whole conduct towards the unfortunate author and by his neglect and coldness had dashed all his sanguine hopes to the ground.

Exulting in his superior discernment, this cold hearted man of society now went on to divert himself, as he says, with the credulity of Goldsmith, whom he was accustomed to pronounce "an inspired idiot;" but his mirth was soon dashed, for on asking the poet what had become of this Chatterton, he was answered, doubtless in the feeling tone of one who had experienced the pangs of despondent genius, that "he had been to London and had destroyed himself."

The reply struck a pang of self reproach even to the cold heart of Walpole; a faint blush may have visited his cheek at his recent levity. "The persons of honor and veracity who were present," said he in after years when he found it necessary to exculpate himself from the charge of heartless neglect of genius, "will attest with what surprise and concern I thus first heard of his death." Well might he feel concern. His cold neglect had doubtless contributed to madden the spirit of that youthful genius and hurry him towards his untimely end; nor have all the excuses and palliations of Walpole's friends and admirers been ever able entirely to clear this stigma from his fame.

But what was there in the enthusiasm and credulity of honest Goldsmith in this matter to subject him to the laugh of Johnson or the raillery of Walpole? Granting the poems were not ancient, were they not good? Granting they were not the productions of Rowley, were they the less admirable for being the productions of Chatterton? Johnson himself testified to their merits and the genius of their composer when some years afterwards he visited the tower of Redcliffe Church and was shown the coffer in which poor Chatterton had pretended to find them. "This," said he, "is the most extraordinary young man that has encountered my knowledge. *It is wonderful how the whelp has written such things.*"

As to Goldsmith, he persisted in his credulity and had subsequently a dispute with Dr. Percy on the subject, which interrupted and almost destroyed their friendship. After all, his enthusiasm was of a generous, poetic kind; the poems remain beautiful monuments of genius, and it is even now difficult to persuade one's self that they could be entirely the productions of a youth of sixteen.

In the month of August was published anonymously the History of England, on which Goldsmith had been for some time employed. It was in four volumes, compiled chiefly, as he acknowledged in the preface, from Rapin, Carte, Smollett and Hume, each of whom, says he, "have their peculiar admirers, in proportion as the reader is studious of political antiquities, fond of minute anecdote, a warm partizan, or a deliberate reasoner." It possessed the same kind of merit as his other historical compilations; a clear, succinct narrative, a simple, easy and graceful style, and an agreeable arrangement of facts; but was not remarkable for either depth of observation or minute accuracy of research. Many passages were transferred with little if any alteration from his "Letters from a Nobleman to his Son" on the same subject. The work, though written without party feeling, met with sharp animadversions from political scribblers. The writer was charged with being unfriendly to liberty, disposed to elevate monarchy above its proper sphere; a tool of ministers; one who would betray his country for a pension. Tom Davies, the publisher, the pompous little bibliopole of Russell Street, alarmed lest the book should prove unsaleable, undertook to protect it by his pen and wrote a long article in its defense in "The Public Advertiser." He was vain of his critical effusion, and sought by nods and winks and inuendoes to intimate his authorship. "Have you seen," said he in a letter to a friend, "an impartial account of Goldsmith's History of England? If you want to know who was the writer of it, you will find him in Russell Street;— *but mum!*"

The history on the whole, however, was well received; some of the critics declared that English history had never before been so usefully, so elegantly and agreeably epitomized, "and, like his other historical writings, it has kept its ground" in English literature.

Goldsmith had intended this summer in company with Sir Joshua Reynolds to pay a visit to Bennet Langton at his seat in Lincolnshire, where he was settled in domestic life, having the year previously married the Countess Dowager of Rothes. The following letter however, dated from his chambers in the Temple on the 7th of September, apologizes for putting off the visit, while it gives an amusing account of his summer occupations and of the attacks of the critics on his History of England:

"My dear Sir,

"Since I had the pleasure of seeing you last, I have been almost wholly in the country at a farmer's house, quite alone, trying to write a comedy. It is now finished; but when or how it will be acted, or whether it will be acted at all, are questions I cannot resolve. I am therefore so much employed upon that, that I am under the necessity of putting off my intended visit to Lincolnshire for this season. Reynolds is just returned from Paris, and finds himself now in the case of a truant that must make up for his idle time by diligence. We have therefore agreed to postpone our journey till next summer, when we hope to have the honour of waiting upon Lady Rothes, and you, and staying double the time of our late intended visit. We often meet, and never without remembering you. I see Mr. Beauclerc very often both in town and country. He is now going directly forward to become a second Boyle: deep in chemistry and physics. Johnson has been down on a visit to a country parson, Doctor Taylor; and is returned to his old haunts at Mrs. Thrale's. Burke is a farmer, *en attendant* a better place; but visiting about too. Every soul is a visiting about and merry but myself. And that is hard too, as I have been trying these three months to do something to make people laugh. There have I been strolling about the hedges, studying jests with a most tragical countenance. The *Natural History* is about half finished, and I will shortly finish the rest. God knows I am tired of this kind of finishing, which is but bungling work; and that not so much my fault as the fault of my scurvy circumstances. They begin to talk in town of the Opposition's gaining ground; the cry of liberty is still as loud as ever. I have published, or Davies has published for me, an *Abridgement of the History of England,* for which I have been a good deal abused in the newspapers, for betraying the liberties of the people. God knows I had no thought for or against liberty in my head; my whole aim being to make up a book of a decent size, that, as 'Squire Richard says, would do no harm to nobody. However, they set me down as an arrant Tory, and consequently an honest man. When you come to look at any part of it, you'll say that I am a sore Whig. God bless you, and with my most respectful compliments to her Ladyship, I remain, dear Sir, your most affectionate humble servant,

"OLIVER GOLDSMITH."

CHAPTER XXXII

Marriage of Little Comedy—Goldsmith at Barton—Practical jokes at the expense of his toilet—Amusements at Barton—Aquatic misadventure

Though Goldsmith found it impossible to break from his literary occupations to visit Bennet Langton in Lincolnshire, he soon yielded to attractions from another quarter, in which somewhat of sentiment may have mingled. Miss Catherine Horneck, one of his beautiful fellow travellers, otherwise called *Little Comedy*, had been married in August to Henry William Bunbury, Esq., a gentleman of fortune, who has become celebrated for the humorous productions of his pencil. Goldsmith was shortly afterwards invited to pay the newly married couple a visit at their seat at Barton in Suffolk. How could he resist such an invitation—especially as the Jessamy Bride would of course be among the guests? It is true, he was hampered with work; he was still more hampered with debt; his accounts with Newbery were perplexed; but all must give way. New advances are procured from Newbery on the promise of a new tale in the style of the Vicar of Wakefield, of which he showed him a few roughly sketched chapters; so, his purse replenished in the old way, "by hook or by crook," he posted off to visit the bride at Barton. He found there a joyous household and one where he was welcomed with affection. Garrick was there, and played the part of master of the revels, for he was an intimate friend of the master of the house. Notwithstanding early misunderstandings a social intercourse between the actor and the poet had grown up of late from meeting together continually in the same circle. A few particulars have reached us concerning Goldsmith while on this happy visit. We believe the legend has come down from Miss Mary Horneck herself. "While at Barton," she says, "his manners were always playful and amusing, taking the lead in promoting any scheme of innocent mirth, and usually prefacing the invitation by 'Come now and let us play the fool a little.' At cards, which was commonly a round game, and the stake small, he was always the most noisy, affected great eagerness to win, and teased his opponents of the gentler sex with continual jest and banter on their want of spirit in not risking the hazards of the game. But one of his most favourite enjoyments was to romp with the children, when he threw off all reserve, and seemed one of the most joyous of the group."

"One of the means by which he amused us was his songs, chiefly of the comic kind, which were sung with some taste and humour; several, I believe, were of his own composition, and I regret that I neither have copies, which might have been readily procured from him at the time, nor do I remember their names."

His perfect good humor made him the object of tricks of all kinds; often in retaliation of some prank which he himself had played off. Unluckily these tricks were sometimes made at the expense of his toilet, which, with a view peradventure to please the eye of a certain fair lady, he had again enriched to the impoverishment of his purse. "Being at all times gay in his dress," says this ladylike legend, "he made his appearance at the breakfast table in a smart black silk coat with an expensive pair of ruffles; the coat some one contrived to soil, and it was sent to be cleansed; but, either by accident, or probably by design, the day after it came home, the sleeves became daubed with paint, which was not discovered until the ruffles also, to his great mortification, were irretrievably disfigured.

"He always wore a wig, a peculiarity which those who judge of his appearance only from the fine poetical head of Reynolds would not suspect; and on one occasion some person contrived seriously to injure this important adjunct to dress. It was the only one he had in the country, and the misfortune seemed irreparable until the services of Mr. Bunbury's valet were called in, who, however, performed his functions so indifferently that poor Goldsmith's appearance became the signal for a general smile."

This was wicked waggery, especially when it was directed to mar all the attempts of the unfortunate poet to improve his personal appearance, about which he was at all times dubiously sensitive, and particularly when among the ladies.

We have in a former chapter recorded his unlucky tumble into a fountain at Versailles when attempting a feat of agility in presence of the fair Hornecks. Water was destined to be equally baneful to him on the present occasion. "Some difference of opinion," says the fair narrator, "having arisen with Lord Harrington respecting the depth of a pond, the poet remarked that it was not so deep but that, if anything valuable was to be found at the bottom, he would not hesitate to pick it up. His lordship, after some banter, threw in a guinea; Goldsmith, not to be outdone in this kind of bravado, in attempting to fulfil his promise without getting wet, accidentally fell in, to the amusement of all present, but persevered, brought out the money, and kept it, remarking that he had abundant objects on whom to bestow any farther proofs of his lordship's whim or bounty."

All this is recorded by the beautiful Mary Horneck, the Jessamy Bride herself; but while she gives these amusing pictures of poor Goldsmith's eccentricities and of the mischievous pranks played off upon him, she bears unqualified testimony, which we have quoted elsewhere, to the qualities of his head and heart, which shone forth in his countenance, and gained him the love of all who knew him.

Among the circumstances of this visit vaguely called to mind by this fair lady in after years, was that Goldsmith read to her and her sister the first part of a novel which he had in hand. It was doubtless the manuscript mentioned at the beginning of this chapter, on which he had obtained an advance of money from Newbery to stave off some pressing debts and to provide funds for this very visit. It never was finished. The bookseller, when he came afterwards to examine the manuscript, objected to it as a mere narrative version of "The Good Natured Man." Goldsmith, too easily put out of conceit of his writings, threw it aside, forgetting that this was the very Newbery who kept his Vicar of Wakefield by him nearly two years through doubts of its success. The loss of the manuscript is deeply to be regretted; it doubtless would have been properly wrought up before given to the press, and might have given us new scenes in life and traits of character, while it could not fail to bear traces of his delightful style. What a pity he had not been guided by the opinions of his fair listeners at Barton instead of that of the astute Mr. Newbery!

CHAPTER XXXIII

Dinner at General Oglethorpe's—Anecdotes of the general—Dispute about duelling—Ghost stories

We have mentioned old General Oglethorpe as one of Goldsmith's aristocratical acquaintances. This veteran, born in 1698, had commenced life early by serving when a mere stripling, under Prince Eugene against the Turks. He had continued in military life and been promoted to the rank of major general in 1745 and received a command during the Scottish rebellion. Being of strong Jacobite tendencies, he was suspected and accused of favoring the rebels; and though acquitted by a court of inquiry, was never afterwards employed; or, in technical language, was shelved. He had since been repeatedly a member of parliament, and had always distinguished himself by learning, taste, active benevolence and high Tory principles. His name, however, has become historical, chiefly from his transactions in America and the share he took in the settlement of the colony of Georgia. It lies embalmed in honorable immortality in a single line of Pope's:

> One, driven *by strong benevolence of soul,*
> Shall fly, like Oglethorpe, from pole to pole.

The veteran was now seventy four years of age but healthy and vigorous and as much the preux chevalier as in his younger days when he served with Prince Eugene. His table was often the gathering place of men of talent. Johnson was frequently there and delighted in drawing from the general details of his various "experiences." He was anxious that he should give the world his life. "I know no man," said he, "whose life would be more interesting." Still the vivacity of the general's mind and the variety of his knowledge made him skip from subject to subject too fast for the lexicographer. "Oglethorpe," growled he, "never completes what he has to say."

Boswell gives us an interesting and characteristic account of a dinner party at the general's, (April 10th, 1772,) at which Goldsmith and Johnson were present. After dinner, when the cloth was removed, Oglethorpe at Johnson's request gave an account of the siege of Belgrade in the true veteran style. Pouring a little wine upon the table, he drew his lines and parallels with a wet finger, describing the positions of the opposing forces. "Here were we—here were the Turks," to all which Johnson listened with the most earnest attention, pouring over the plans and diagrams with his usual purblind closeness.

174

In the course of conversation the general gave an anecdote of himself in early life, when serving under Prince Eugene. Sitting at table once in company with a prince of Würtemberg, the latter gave a fillip to a glass of wine so as to make some of it fly in Oglethorpe's face. The manner in which it was done was somewhat equivocal. How was it to be taken by the stripling officer? If seriously, he must challenge the prince; but in so doing he might fix on himself the character of a drawcansir. If passed over without notice, he might be charged with cowardice. His mind was made up in an instant. "Prince," said he smiling, "that is an excellent joke; but we do it much better in England." So saying, he threw a whole glass of wine in the prince's face. "Il a bien fait, mon prince," cried an old general present, "vous l'avez commencé." (He has done right, my prince; you commenced it.) The prince had the good sense to acquiesce in the decision of the veteran, and Oglethorpe's retort in kind was taken in good part.

It was probably at the close of this story that the officious Boswell, ever anxious to promote conversation for the benefit of his note book, started the question whether duelling were consistent with moral duty. The old general fired up in an instant. "Undoubtedly," said he, with a lofty air, "undoubtedly a man has a right to defend his honour." Goldsmith immediately carried the war into Boswell's own quarters and pinned him with the question, "what he would do if affronted?" The pliant Boswell, who for the moment had the fear of the general rather than of Johnson before his eyes, replied he should think it necessary to fight. "Why then that solves the question," replied Goldsmith. "No, sir!" thundered out Johnson; "it does not follow that what a man would do is therefore right." He however subsequently went into a discussion to show that there were necessities in the case arising out of the artificial refinement of society, and its proscription of any one who should put up with an affront without fighting a duel. "He then," concluded he, "who fights a duel does not fight from passion against his antagonist, but out of self-defence, to avert the stigma of the world, and to prevent himself from being driven out of society. I could wish there were not that superfluity of refinement; but while such notions prevail, no doubt a man may lawfully fight a duel."

Another question started was whether people who disagreed on a capital point could live together in friendship. Johnson said they might. Goldsmith said they could not, as they had not the idem velle atque idem nolle—the same likings and aversions. Johnson rejoined that they must shun the subject on which they disagreed. "But, sir," said Goldsmith, "when people live together who have something as to which they disagree, and which they want to shun, they will be in the situation mentioned in the story of Bluebeard: 'You may look into all the chambers but one.' But we should have the greatest inclination to look into that chamber, to talk of that subject." "Sir," thundered Johnson in a loud voice, "I am not saying that *you* could live in friendship with a man from whom you differ as to some point; I am only saying that *I* could do it."

Who will not say that Goldsmith had the best of this petty contest? How just was his remark! how felicitous the illustration of the blue chamber! how rude and overbearing was the argumentum ad hominem of Johnson, when he felt that he had the worst of the argument!

The conversation turned upon ghosts. General Oglethorpe told the story of a Colonel Prendergast, an officer in the Duke of Marlborough's army, who predicted among his comrades that he should die on a certain day. The battle of Malplaquet took place on that day. The colonel was in the midst of it but came out unhurt. The firing had ceased, and his brother officers jested with him about the fallacy of his prediction. "The day is not over," replied he gravely; "I shall die notwithstanding what you see." His words proved true. The order for a cessation of firing had not reached one of the French batteries, and a random shot from it killed the colonel on the spot. Among his effects was found a pocket book in which he had made a solemn entry that Sir John Friend, who had been executed for high treason, had appeared to him either in a dream or vision and predicted that he would meet him on a certain day (the very day of the battle). Colonel Cecil, who took possession of the effects of Colonel Prendergast and read the entry in the pocket book, told this story to Pope, the poet, in the presence of General Oglethorpe.

The story as related by the general appears to have been well received, if not credited, by both Johnson and Goldsmith, each of whom had something to relate in kind. Goldsmith's brother, the clergyman in whom he had such implicit confidence, had assured him of his having seen an apparition. Johnson also had a friend, old Mr. Edward Cave, the printer at St. John's Gate, "an honest man and a sensible man," who told him he had seen a ghost: he did not however like to talk of it and seemed to be in great horror whenever it was mentioned. "And pray, sir," asked Boswell, "what did he say was the appearance?" "Why, sir, something of a shadowy being."

The reader will not be surprised at this superstitious turn in the conversation of such intelligent men, when he recollects that, but a few years before this time, all London had been agitated by the absurd story of the Cock-lane ghost; a matter which Dr. Johnson had deemed worthy of his serious investigation and about which Goldsmith had written a pamphlet.

CHAPTER XXXIV

Mr. Joseph Cradock—An author's confidings—An amanuensis—Life at Edgeware—Goldsmith conjuring—George Colman—The Fantoccini

Among the agreeable acquaintances made by Goldsmith about this time was a Mr. Joseph Cradock, a young gentleman of Leicestershire, living at his ease, but disposed to "make himself uneasy" by meddling with literature and the theatre. In fact he had a passion for plays and players, and had come up to town with a modified translation of Voltaire's tragedy of Zobeide, in a view to get it acted. There was no great difficulty in the case, as he was a man of fortune, had letters of introduction to persons of note, and was altogether in a different position from the indigent man of genius whom managers might harass with impunity. Goldsmith met him at the house of Yates, the actor, and finding that he was a friend of Lord Clare, soon became sociable with him. Mutual tastes quickened the intimacy, especially as they found means of serving each other. Goldsmith wrote an epilogue for the tragedy of Zobeide; and Cradock, who was an amateur musician, arranged the music for the Threnodia Augustalis, a lament on the death of the Princess Dowager of Wales, the political mistress and patron of Lord Clare, which Goldsmith had thrown off hastily to please that nobleman. The tragedy was played with some success at Covent Garden. The lament was recited and sung at Mrs. Cornelys' rooms, a very fashionable resort in Soho Square, got up by a woman of enterprise of that name. It was in whimsical parody of those gay and somewhat promiscuous assemblages, that Goldsmith used to call the motley evening parties at his lodgings "little Cornelys."

The Threnodia Augustalis was not publicly known to be by Goldsmith until several years after his death.

Cradock was one of the few polite intimates who felt more disposed to sympathize with the generous qualities of the poet than to sport with his eccentricities. He sought his society whenever he came to town and occasionally had him to his seat in the country. Goldsmith appreciated his sympathy and unburthened himself to him without reserve. Seeing the lettered ease in which this amateur author was enabled to live, and the time he could bestow on the elaboration of a manuscript, "Ah! Mr. Cradock," cried he, "think of me, that must write a volume every month!" He complained to him of the attempts made by inferior writers, and by others who could scarcely come under that denomination, not only to abuse and depreciate his writings but to render him ridiculous as a man; perverting every harmless sentiment and action into charges of absurdity, malice or folly. "Sir," said he in the fulness of his heart, "I am as a lion baited by curs!"

Another acquaintance, which he made about this time, was a young countryman of the name of M'Donnell, whom he met in a state of destitution, and of course befriended. The following grateful recollections of his kindness and his merits were furnished by that person in after years:

"It was in the year 1772," writes he, "that the death of my elder brother when in London on our way to Ireland left me in a most forlorn situation; I was then about eighteen; I possessed neither friends nor money, nor the means of getting to Ireland, of which or of England I knew scarcely any thing, from having so long resided in France. In this situation I had strolled about for two or three days considering what to do, but unable to come to any determination, when Providence directed me to the Temple Gardens. I threw myself on a seat, and, willing to forget my miseries for a moment, drew out a book; that book was a volume of Boileau. I had not been there long when a gentleman, strolling about, passed near me, and observing, perhaps, something Irish or foreign in my garb or countenance, addressed me: 'Sir, you seem studious; I hope you find this a favourable place to pursue it.' 'Not very studious, sir; I fear it is the want of society that brings me hither; I am solitary and unknown in this metropolis;' and a passage from Cicero—Oratio pro Archia—occurring to me, I quoted it: 'Hæc studia pernoctant nobiscum, peregrinantur, rusticantur.' 'You are a scholar too, sir, I perceive.' 'A piece of one, sir; but I ought still to have been in the college where I had the good fortune to pick up the little I know.' A good deal of conversation ensued; I told him part of my history, and he, in return, gave his address in the Temple, desiring me to call soon, from which, to my infinite surprise and gratification, I found that the person who thus seemed to take an interest in my fate was my countryman, and a distinguished ornament of letters.

"I did not fail to keep the appointment, and was received in the kindest manner. He told me, smilingly, that he was not rich; that he could do little for me in direct pecuniary aid, but would endeavour to put me in the way of doing something for myself; observing, that he could at least furnish me with advice not wholly useless to a young man placed in the heart of a great metropolis. 'In London,' he continued, 'nothing is to be got for nothing: you must work; and no man who chooses to be industrious need be under obligations to another, for here labour of every kind commands its reward. If you think proper to assist me occasionally as amanuensis, I shall be obliged, and you will be placed under no obligation, until something more permanent can be secured for you.' This employment, which I pursued for some time, was to translate passages from Buffon, which was abridged or altered, according to circumstances, for his Natural History."

Goldsmith's literary tasks were fast getting ahead of him, and he began now to "toil after them in vain." Five volumes of the Natural History here spoken of had long since been paid for by Mr. Griffin, yet most of them were still to be written. His young amanuensis bears testimony to his embarrassments and perplexities, but to the degree of equanimity with which he bore them:

"It has been said," observes he, "that he was irritable. Such may have been the case at times; nay, I believe it was so; for what with the continual pursuit of authors, printers, and booksellers, and occasional pecuniary embarrassments, few could have avoided exhibiting similar marks of impatience. But it was never so towards me. I saw him only in his bland and kind moods, with a flow, perhaps an overflow, of the milk of human kindness for all who were in any manner dependent upon him. I looked upon him with awe and veneration, and he upon me as a kind parent upon a child.

"His manner and address exhibited much frankness and cordiality, particularly to those with whom he possessed any degree of intimacy. His good-nature was equally apparent. You could not dislike the man, although several of his follies and foibles you might be tempted to condemn. He was generous and inconsiderate: money with him had little value."

To escape from many of the tormentors just alluded to and to devote himself without interruption to his task, Goldsmith took lodgings for the summer at a farm house near the six-mile stone on the Edgeware Road and carried down his books in two returned post chaises. He used to say he believed the farmer's family thought him an odd character, similar to that in which the *Spectator* appeared to his landlady and her children; he was *The Gentleman*. Boswell tells us that he went to visit him at the place in company with Mickle, translator of the Lusiad. Goldsmith was not at home. Having a curiosity to see his apartment, however, they went in and found curious scraps of descriptions of animals scrawled upon the wall with a black-lead pencil.

The farm house in question is still in existence, though much altered. It stands upon a gentle eminence in Hyde Lane, commanding a pleasant prospect towards Hendon. The room is still pointed out in which "She Stoops to Conquer" was written; a convenient and airy apartment, up one flight of stairs.

Some matter of fact traditions concerning the author were furnished a few years since by a son of the farmer, who was sixteen years of age at the time Goldsmith resided with his father. Though he had engaged to board with the family, his meals were generally sent to him in his room, in which he passed the most of his time, negligently dressed, with his shirt collar open, busily engaged in writing. Sometimes, probably when in moods of composition, he would wander into the kitchen, without noticing any one, stand musing with his back to the fire and then hurry off again to his room; no doubt to commit to paper some thought which had struck him.

Sometimes he strolled about the fields, or was to be seen loitering and reading and musing under the hedges. He was subject to fits of wakefulness and read much in bed; if not disposed to read, he still kept the candle burning; if he wished to extinguish it, and it was out of his reach, he flung his slipper at it, which would be found in the morning near the overturned candlestick and daubed with grease. He was noted here, as every where else, for his charitable feelings. No beggar applied to him in vain, and he evinced on all occasions great commiseration for the poor.

He had the use of the parlor to receive and entertain company, and was visited by Sir Joshua Reynolds, Hugh Boyd, the reputed author of Junius, Sir William Chambers and other distinguished characters. He gave occasionally, though rarely, a dinner party; and on one occasion, when his guests were detained by a thunder shower, he got up a dance, and carried the merriment late into the night.

As usual, he was the promoter of hilarity among the young, and at one time took the children of the house to see a company of strolling players at Hendon. The greatest amusement to the party, however, was derived from his own jokes on the road and his comments on the performance, which produced infinite laughter among his youthful companions.

Near to his rural retreat at Edgeware a Mr. Seguin, an Irish merchant of literary tastes, had country quarters for his family, where Goldsmith was always welcome.

In this family he would indulge in playful and even grotesque humor, and was ready for any thing—conversation, music or a game of romps. He prided himself upon his dancing, and would walk a minuet with Mrs. Seguin, to the infinite amusement of herself and the children, whose shouts of laughter he bore with perfect good humor. He would sing Irish songs, and the Scotch ballad of Johnny Armstrong. He took the lead in the children's sports of blind man's buff, hunt the slipper, &c., or in their games at cards, and was the most noisy of the party, affecting to cheat and to be excessively eager to win; while with children of smaller size he would turn the hind part of his wig before, and play all kinds of tricks to amuse them.

One word as to his musical skill and his performance on the flute, which comes up so invariably in all his fireside revels. He really knew nothing of music scientifically; he had probably a good ear and may have played sweetly; but we are told he could not read a note of music. Roubillac, the statuary, once played a trick upon him in this respect. He pretended to score down an air as the poet played it, but put down crotchets and semibreves at random. When he had finished, Goldsmith cast his eyes over it and pronounced it correct! It is possible that his execution in music was like his style in writing; in sweetness and melody he may have 'snatched a grace beyond the reach of art!'

He was at all times a capital companion for children and knew how to fall in with their humors. "I little thought," said Miss Hawkins, the woman grown, "what I should have to boast, when Goldsmith taught me to play Jack and Jill by two bits of paper on his fingers." He entertained Mrs. Garrick, we are told, with a whole budget of stories and songs; delivered the *Chimney Sweep* with exquisite taste as a solo; and performed a duet with Garrick of Old Rose and Burn the Bellows.

"I was only five years old," says the late George Colman, "when Goldsmith one evening when drinking coffee with my father, took me on his knee and began to play with me, which amiable act I returned with a very smart slap in the face; it must have been a tingler, for I left the marks of my little spiteful paw upon his cheek. This infantile outrage was followed by summary justice, and I was locked up by my father in an adjoining room, to undergo solitary imprisonment in the dark. Here I began to howl and scream most abominably. At length a friend appeared to extricate me from jeopardy; it was the good-natured doctor himself, with a lighted candle in his hand, and a smile upon his countenance, which was still partially red from the effects of my petulance. I sulked and sobbed, and he fondled and soothed until I began to brighten. He seized the propitious moment, placed three hats upon the carpet, and a shilling under each; the shillings, he told me, were England, France, and Spain. 'Hey, presto, cockolorum!' cried the doctor, and, lo! on uncovering the shillings, they were all found congregated under one. I was no politician at the time, and therefore might not have wondered at the sudden revolution which brought England, France, and Spain all under one crown; but, as I was also no conjurer, it amazed me beyond measure. From that time, whenever the doctor came to visit my father,

'I pluck'd his gown to share the good man's smile;'

a game of romps constantly ensued, and we were always cordial friends and merry playfellows."

Although Goldsmith made the Edgeware farm house his headquarters for the summer, he would absent himself for weeks at a time on visits to Mr. Cradock, Lord Clare and Mr. Langton at their country seats. He would often visit town also to dine and partake of the public amusements. On one occasion he accompanied Edmund Burke to witness a performance of the Italian Fantoccini or Puppets, in Panton Street; an exhibition which had hit the caprice of the town and was in great vogue. The puppets were set in motion by wires, so well concealed as to be with difficulty detected. Boswell with his usual obtuseness with respect to Goldsmith accuses him of being jealous of the puppets! When Burke, said he, praised the dexterity with which one of them tossed a pike, "Pshaw," said Goldsmith *with some warmth*, "I can do it better myself." "The same evening," adds Boswell, "when supping at Burke's lodgings, he broke his shin by attempting to exhibit to the company how much better he could jump over a stick than the puppets."

Goldsmith jealous of puppets! This even surpasses in absurdity Boswell's charge upon him of being jealous of the beauty of the two Miss Hornecks.

The Panton Street puppets were destined to be a source of further amusement to the town and of annoyance to the little autocrat of the stage. Foote, the Aristophanes of the English drama, who was always on the alert to turn every subject of popular excitement to account, seeing the success of the Fantoccini, gave out that he should produce a Primitive Puppet-Shew at the Haymarket, to be entitled *The Handsome Chambermaid, or Piety in Pattens*: intended to burlesque the *sentimental comedy* which Garrick still maintained at Drury Lane. The idea of a play to be performed in a regular theatre by puppets excited the curiosity and talk of the town. "Will your puppets be as large as life, Mr. Foote?" demanded a lady of rank. "Oh, no, my lady," replied Foote, *"not much larger than Garrick."*

CHAPTER XXXV

Goldsmith returned to town in the autumn (1772) with his health much disordered. His close fits of sedentary application, during which he in a manner tied himself to the mast, had laid the seeds of a lurking malady in his system, and produced a severe illness in the course of the summer. Town life was not favorable to the health either of body or mind. He could not resist the siren voice of temptation which, now that he had become a notoriety, assailed him on every side. Accordingly we find him launching away in a career of social dissipation; dining and supping out; at clubs, at routs, at theatres; he is a guest with Johnson at the Thrales' and an object of Mrs. Thrale's lively sallies; he is a lion at Mrs. Vesey's and Mrs. Montagu's, where some of the high bred blue stockings pronounce him a "wild genius" and others, peradventure, a "wild Irishman." In the mean time his pecuniary difficulties are increasing upon him, conflicting with his proneness to pleasure and expense, and contributing by the harassment of his mind to the wear and tear of his constitution. His Animated Nature, though not finished, has been entirely paid for and the money spent. The money advanced by Garrick on Newbery's note still hangs over him as a debt. The tale on which Newbery had loaned from two to three hundred pounds previous to the excursion to Barton has proved a failure. The bookseller is urgent for the settlement of his complicated account; the perplexed author has nothing to offer him in liquidation but the copy right of the comedy which he has in his portfolio; "Though to tell you the truth, Frank," said he, "there are great doubts of its success." The offer was accepted, and, like bargains wrung from Goldsmith in times of emergency, turned out a golden speculation to the bookseller.

In this way Goldsmith went on "overrunning the constable" as he termed it; spending every thing in advance; working with an overtasked head and weary heart to pay for past pleasures and past extravagance, and at the same time incurring new debts, to perpetuate his struggles and darken his future prospects. While the excitement of society and the excitement of composition conspire to keep up a feverishness of the system, he has incurred an unfortunate habit of quacking himself with James's powders, a fashionable panacea of the day.

A farce produced this year by Garrick and entitled *The Irish Widow* perpetuates the memory of a practical joke played off a year or two previously upon the alleged vanity of poor, simple hearted Goldsmith. He was one evening at the house of his friend Burke when he was beset by a tenth muse, an Irish widow and authoress just arrived from Ireland, full of brogue and blunders and poetic fire and rantipole gentility. She was soliciting subscriptions for her poems; and assailed Goldsmith for his patronage; the great Goldsmith—her countryman and of course her friend. She overpowered him with eulogiums on his own poems and then read some of her own with vehemence of tone and gesture, appealing continually to the great Goldsmith to know how he relished them.

Poor Goldsmith did all that a kind hearted and gallant gentleman could do in such a case; he praised her poems as far as the stomach of his sense would permit: perhaps a little further; he offered her his subscription, and it was not until she had retired with many parting compliments to the great Goldsmith, that he pronounced the poetry which had been inflicted on him execrable. The whole scene had been a hoax got up by Burke for the amusement of his company, and the Irish widow, so admirably performed, had been personated by a Mrs. Balfour, a lady of his connection, of great sprightliness and talent.

We see nothing in the story to establish the alleged vanity of Goldsmith, but we think it tells rather to the disadvantage of Burke; being unwarrantable under their relations of friendship and a species of waggery quite beneath his genius.

Croker in his notes to Boswell gives another of these practical jokes perpetrated by Burke at the expense of Goldsmith's credulity. It was related to Croker by Colonel O'Moore, of Cloghan Castle in Ireland, who was a party concerned. The Colonel and Burke, walking one day through Leicester Square on their way to Sir Joshua Reynolds's, with whom they were to dine, observed Goldsmith, who was likewise to be a guest, standing and regarding a crowd which was staring and shouting at some foreign ladies in the window of a hotel. "Observe Goldsmith," said Burke to O'Moore, "and mark what passes between us at Sir Joshua's." They passed on and reached there before him. Burke received Goldsmith with unusual reserve and coldness: being pressed to explain the reason, "Really," said he, "I am ashamed to keep company with a person who could act as you have just done in the Square." Goldsmith protested he was ignorant of what was meant. "Why," said Burke, "did you not exclaim as you were looking up at those women, what stupid beasts the crowd must be for staring with such admiration at those *painted Jezebels*, while a man of your talents passed by unnoticed?" "Surely, surely, my dear friend," cried Goldsmith, with alarm, "surely I did not say so?" "Nay," replied Burke, "if you had not said so, how should I have known it?" "That's true," answered Goldsmith, "I am very sorry—it was very foolish: *I do recollect that something of the kind passed through my mind, but I did not think I had uttered it."*

It is proper to observe that these jokes were played off by Burke before he had attained the full eminence of his social position, and that he may have felt privileged to take liberties with Goldsmith as his countryman and college associate. It is evident, however, that the peculiarities of the latter and his guileless simplicity made him a butt for the broad waggery of some of his associates; while others, more polished, though equally perfidious, are on the watch to give currency to his bulls and blunders.

The Stratford jubilee, in honor of Shakespeare, where Boswell had made a fool of himself, was still in every one's mind. It was sportively suggested that a fête should be held at Litchfield in honor of Johnson and Garrick and that the Beaux' Stratagem should be played by the members of the Literary Club. "Then," exclaimed Goldsmith, "I shall certainly play Scrub. I should like of all things to try my hand at that character." The unwary speech, which any one else might have made without comment, has been thought worthy of record as whimsically characteristic. Beauclerc was extremely apt to circulate anecdotes at his expense, founded perhaps on some trivial incident but dressed up with the embellishments of his sarcastic brain. One relates to a venerable dish of peas served up at Sir Joshua's table, which should have been green, but were any other color. A wag suggested to Goldsmith in a whisper that they should be sent to Hammersmith, as that was the way to *turn-em-green* (Turnham Green). Goldsmith, delighted with the pun, endeavored to repeat it at Burke's table, but missed the point. "That is the way to *make* 'em green," said he. No body laughed. He perceived he was at fault. "I mean that is the *road* to turn 'em green." A dead silence and a stare; "whereupon," adds Beauclerc, "he started up disconcerted and abruptly left the table." This is evidently one of Beauclerc's caricatures.

On another occasion the poet and Beauclerc were seated at the theatre next to Lord Shelburne, the minister, whom political writers had thought proper to nickname Malagrida. "Do you know," said Goldsmith to his lordship in the course of conversation, "that I never could conceive why they call you Malagrida, *for* Malagrida was a very good sort of man." This was too good a trip of the tongue for Beauclerc to let pass: he serves it up in his next letter to Lord Charlemont as a specimen of a mode of turning a thought the wrong way peculiar to the poet. He makes merry over it with his witty and sarcastic compeer, Horace Walpole, who pronounces it "a picture of Goldsmith's whole life." Dr. Johnson alone, when he hears it bandied about as Goldsmith's last blunder, growls forth a friendly defence: "Sir," said he, "it was a mere blunder in emphasis. He meant to say I wonder they should use Malagrida as a term of reproach." Poor Goldsmith! On such points he was ever doomed to be misinterpreted. Rogers the poet, meeting in times long subsequent with a survivor from those days, asked him what Goldsmith really was in conversation. The old conventional character was too deeply stamped in the memory of the veteran to be effaced. "Sir," replied the old wiseacre, *"he was a fool.* The right word never came to him. If you gave him back a bad shilling, he'd say, Why it's as good a shilling as ever was *born.* You know he ought to have said *coined. Coined,* sir, never entered his head. *He was a fool, sir."*

We have so many anecdotes in which Goldsmith's simplicity is played upon, that it is quite a treat to meet with one in which he is represented playing upon the simplicity of others, especially when the victim of his joke is the "Great Cham" himself, whom all others are disposed to hold so much in awe. Goldsmith and Johnson were supping cosily together at a tavern in Dean Street, Soho, kept by Jack Roberts, a singer at Drury Lane and a protégé of Garrick's. Johnson delighted in these gastronomical tête-a-têtes, and was expatiating in high good humor on a dish of rumps and kidneys, the veins of his forehead swelling with the ardor of mastication. "These," said he, "are pretty little things; but a man must eat a great many of them before he is filled." "Aye, but how many of them," asked Goldsmith, with affected simplicity, "would reach to the moon?" "To the moon! Ah, sir, that, I fear, exceeds your calculation." "Not at all, sir; I think I could tell." "Pray, then, sir, let us hear." "Why, sir, one, *if it were long enough!"* Johnson growled for a time at finding himself caught in such a trite schoolboy trap. "Well, sir," cried he at length, "I have deserved it. I should not have provoked so foolish an answer by so foolish a question."

Among the many incidents related as illustrative of Goldsmith's vanity and envy is one which occurred one evening when he was in a drawing room with a party of ladies, and a ballad singer under the window struck up his favorite song of *Sally Salisbury.* "How miserably this woman sings!" exclaimed he. "Pray, doctor," said the lady of the house, "could you do it better?" "Yes, madam, and the company shall be judges." The company, of course, prepared to be entertained by an absurdity; but their smiles were well nigh turned to tears, for he acquitted himself with a skill and pathos that drew universal applause. He had in fact a delicate ear for music, which had been jarred by the false notes of the ballad singer; and there were certain pathetic ballads, associated with recollections of his childhood, which were sure to touch the springs of his heart. We have another story of him, connected with ballad singing, which is still more characteristic. He was one evening at the house of Sir William Chambers in Berners Street, seated at a whist table with Sir William, Lady Chambers and Baretti, when all at once he threw down his cards, hurried out of the room and into the street. He returned in an instant, resumed his seat, and the game went on. Sir William after a little hesitation ventured to ask the cause of his retreat, fearing he had been overcome by the heat of the room. "Not at all," replied Goldsmith; "but in truth I could not bear to hear that unfortunate woman in the street, half singing, half sobbing, for such tones could only arise from the extremity of distress; her voice grated painfully on my ear and jarred my frame, so that I could not rest until I had sent her away." It was in fact a poor ballad singer whose cracked voice had been heard by others of the party, but without having the same effect on their sensibilities. It was the reality of his fictitious scene in the story of the Man in Black; wherein he describes "a woman in rags, with one child in her arms and another on her back, attempting to sing ballads, but with such a mournful voice that it was difficult to determine whether she was singing or crying. A wretch," he adds, "who in the deepest distress still aimed at good humor, was an object my friend was by no means capable of withstanding." The Man in Black gave the poor woman all that he had—a bundle of matches; Goldsmith, it is probable, sent his ballad singer away rejoicing with all the money in his pocket.

Ranelagh was at that time greatly in vogue as a place of public entertainment. It was situated near Chelsea; the principal room was a Rotunda of great dimensions with an orchestra in the centre and tiers of boxes all round. It was a place to which Johnson resorted occasionally. "I am a great friend to public amusements," said he, "for they keep people from vice."* Goldsmith was equally a friend to them, though perhaps not altogether on such moral grounds. He was particularly fond of masquerades, which were then exceedingly popular and got up at Ranelagh with great expense and magnificence. Sir Joshua Reynolds, who had likewise a taste for such amusements, was sometimes his companion, at other times he went alone; his peculiarities of person and manner would soon betray him, whatever might be his disguise, and he would be singled out by wags, acquainted with his foibles, and more successful than himself in maintaining their incognito, as a capital

---

* "Alas, sir!" said Johnson, speaking, when in another mood, of grand houses, fine gardens and splendid places of public amusement; "alas, sir! these are only struggles for happiness. When I first entered Ranelagh it gave an expansion and gay sensation to my mind, such as I never experienced any where else. But, as Xerxes wept when he viewed his immense army and considered that not one of that great multitude would be alive a hundred years afterwards, so it went to my heart to consider that there was not one in all that brilliant circle that was not afraid to go home and think."

subject to be played upon. Some, pretending not to know him, would decry his writings and praise those of his contemporaries; others would laud his verses to the skies but purposely misquote and burlesque them; others would annoy him with parodies; while one young lady whom he was teasing, as he supposed, with great success and infinite humor silenced his rather boisterous laughter by quoting his own line about "the loud laugh that speaks the vacant mind." On one occasion he was absolutely driven out of the house by the persevering jokes of a wag whose complete disguise gave him no means of retaliation.

His name appearing in the newspapers among the distinguished persons present at one of these amusements, his old enemy, Kenrick, immediately addressed to him a copy of anonymous verses, to the following purport.

To Dr. Goldsmith; on seeing his name in the list of mummers at the late masquerade:

> How widely different, Goldsmith, are the ways
> Of Doctors now, and those of ancient days!
> Theirs taught the truth in academic shades,
> Ours in lewd hops and midnight masquerades.
> So changed the times! say, philosophic sage,
> Whose genius suits so well this tasteful age,
> Is the Pantheon, late a sink obscene,
> Become the fountain of chaste Hippocrene?
> Or do thy moral numbers quaintly flow,
> Inspired by th' *Aganippe* of Soho?
> Do wisdom's sons gorge cates and vermicelli,
> Like beastly Bickerstaffe or bothering Kelly?
> Or art thou tired of th' undeserved applause,
> Bestowed on bards affecting Virtue's cause?
> Is this the good that makes the humble vain,
> The good philosophy should not disdain?
> If so, let pride dissemble all it can,
> A modern sage is still much less than man.

Goldsmith was keenly sensitive to attacks of the kind, and meeting Kenrick at the Chapter Coffee House, called him to sharp account for taking such a liberty with his name, and calling his morals in question merely on account of his being seen at a place of general resort and amusement. Kenrick shuffled and sneaked, protesting that he meant nothing derogatory to his private character. Goldsmith let him know, however, that he was aware of his having more than once indulged in attacks of this dastard kind, and intimated that another such outrage would be followed by personal chastisement.

Kenrick having played the craven in his presence, avenged himself as soon as he was gone by complaining of his having made a wanton attack upon him, and by making coarse comments upon his writings, conversation and person.

The scurrilous satire of Kenrick, however unmerited, may have checked Goldsmith's taste for masquerades and given rise to the following incident. Sir Joshua Reynolds calling on the poet one morning, found him walking about his room in somewhat of a reverie, kicking a bundle of clothes before him like a foot-ball. It proved to be an expensive masquerade dress, which he said he had been fool enough to purchase, and as there was no other way of getting the worth of his money, he was trying to take it out in exercise.

CHAPTER XXXVI

*Invitation to Christmas—The spring velvet coat—The haymaking wig—
The mischances of Loo—The fair culprit—A dance with the Jessamy
Bride*

From the feverish dissipations of town Goldsmith is summoned away
to partake of the genial dissipations of the country. In the month of
December a letter from Mrs. Bunbury invites him down to Barton to
pass the Christmas holydays. The letter is written in the usual playful
vein which marks his intercourse with this charming family. He is to
come in his "smart spring velvet coat," to bring a new wig to dance
with the haymakers in, and above all to follow the advice of herself
and her sister (the Jessamy Bride) in playing Loo. This letter, which
plays so archly yet kindly with some of poor Goldsmith's peculiarities,
and bespeaks such real ladylike regard for him, requires a word or two
of annotation. The spring velvet suit alluded to, appears to have been
a gallant adornment, (somewhat in the style of the famous bloom
colored coat) in which Goldsmith had figured in the preceding month
of May—the season of blossoms—for on the 21st of that month we find
the following entry in the chronicle of Mr. William Filby, tailor: *To
your blue velvet suit*, £21 10s. 9d. Also about the same time, a suit of
livery and a crimson collar for the serving man. Again we hold the
Jessamy Bride responsible for this gorgeous splendor of wardrobe.

The new wig no doubt is a bag wig and solitaire, still highly the
mode, and in which Goldsmith is represented as figuring when in full
dress, equipped with his sword.

As to the dancing with the haymakers, we presume it alludes to
some gambol of the poet in the course of his former visit to Barton; when
he ranged the fields and lawns a chartered libertine and tumbled into
the fish ponds.

As to the suggestions about Loo, they are in sportive allusion to the
doctor's mode of playing that game in their merry evening parties;
affecting the desperate gambler and easy dupe; running counter to all
rule; making extravagant ventures; reproaching all others with cowardice;
dashing at all hazards at the pool, and getting himself completely loo'd,
to the great amusement of the company. The drift of the fair sisters'
advice was most probably to tempt him on and then leave him in
the lurch.

With these comments we subjoin Goldsmith's reply to Mrs. Bunbury,
a fine piece of off hand, humorous writing, which has but in late years

been given to the public, and which throws a familiar light on the social circle at Barton.

"MADAM, I read your letter with all that allowance which critical candour could require, but after all find so much to object to, and so much to raise my indignation, that I cannot help giving it a serious answer.—I am not so ignorant, madam, as not to see there are many sarcasms contained in it, and solecisms also. (Solecism is a word that comes from the town of Soleis in Attica, among the Greeks, built by Solon, and applied as we use the word Kidderminster for curtains from a town also of that name—but this is learning you have no taste for!)— I say, madam, there are many sarcasms in it, and solecisms also. But not to seem an ill-natured critic, I'll take leave to quote your own words, and give you my remarks upon them as they occur. You begin as follows:

'I hope my good Doctor, you soon will be here,
And your spring-velvet coat very smart will appear,
To open our ball the first day of the year.'

"Pray, madam, where did you ever find the epithet 'good,' applied to the title of Doctor? Had you called me 'learned Doctor,' or 'grave Doctor,' or 'noble Doctor,' it might be allowable, because they belong to the profession. But, not to cavil at trifles, you talk of my 'spring-velvet coat,' and advise me to wear it the first day in the year, that is, in the middle of winter!—a spring-velvet coat in the middle of winter!!! That would be a solecism indeed! and yet to increase the inconsistence, in another part of your letter you call me a beau. Now, on one side or other, you must be wrong. If I am a beau, I can never think of wearing a spring-velvet in winter: and if I am not a beau, why then, that explains itself. But let me go on to your two next strange lines:

'And bring with you a wig, that is modish and gay,
To dance with the girls that are makers of hay.'

"The absurdity of making hay at Christmas you yourself seem sensible of: you say your sister will laugh; and so indeed she well may! The Latins have an expression for a contemptuous kind of laughter, 'naso contemnere adunco;' that is, to laugh with a crooked nose. She may laugh at you in the manner of the ancients if she thinks fit. But now I come to the most extraordinary of all extraordinary propositions, which is, to take your and your sister's advice in playing at loo. The presumption of the offer raises my indignation beyond the bounds of prose; it inspires me at once with verse and resentment. I take advice! and from whom? You shall hear.

"First let me suppose, what may shortly be true,
The company set, and the word to be Loo:
All smirking, and pleasant, and big with adventure,
And ogling the stake which is fix'd in the centre.
Round and round go the cards, while I inwardly damn
At never once finding a visit from Pam.
I lay down my stake, apparently cool,
While the harpies about me all pocket the pool.
I fret in my gizzard, yet, cautious and sly,
I wish all my friends may be bolder than I:
Yet still they sit snugg, not a creature will aim
By losing their money to venture at fame.
'Tis in vain that at niggardly caution I scold,
'Tis in vain that I flatter the brave and the bold:
All play their own way, and they think me an ass.
'What does Mrs. Bunbury?'—'I, sir? I pass.'
'Pray what does Miss Horneck? take courage, come do.'
'Who, I? let me see, sir, why I must pass too.'
Mr. Bunbury frets, and I fret like the devil,
To see them so cowardly, lucky, and civil.
Yet still I sit snugg, and continue to sigh on,
'Till, made by my losses as bold as a lion,
I venture at all, while my avarice regards
The whole pool as my own.—'Come give me five cards.'
'Well done!' cry the ladies; 'Ah, Doctor, that's good!
The pool's very rich,—ah! the Doctor is loo'd!'
Thus foil'd in my courage, on all sides perplext,
I ask for advice from the lady that's next:
'Pray, ma'am, be so good as to give your advice;
Don't you think the best way is to venture for't twice?'
'I advise,' cries the lady, 'to try it, I own.
'Ah! the Doctor is loo'd! Come, Doctor, put down.'
Thus, playing, and playing, I still grow more eager,
And so bold, and so bold, I'm at last a bold beggar.
Now, ladies, I ask, if law-matters you're skill'd in,
Whether crimes such as yours should not come before Fielding:
For giving advice that is not worth a straw,
May well be call'd picking of pockets in law;
And picking of pockets, with which I now charge ye,
Is, by quinto Elizabeth, Death without Clergy.
What justice, when both to the Old Baily brought!
By the gods, I'll enjoy it, tho' 'tis but in thought!
Both are plac'd at the bar, with all proper decorum,

With bunches of fennel, and nosegays before 'em;
Both cover their faces with mobs and all that,
But the judge bids them, angrily, take off their hat.
When uncover'd, a buzz of inquiry runs round,
'Pray what are their crimes?'—'They've been pilfering found.'
'But, pray, who have they pilfer'd?'—'A Doctor, I hear.'
'What, yon solemn-faced, odd-looking man that stands near!'
'The same.'—'What a pity! how does it surprise one,
Two handsomer culprits I never set eyes on!'
Then their friends all come round me with cringing and leering,
To melt me to pity, and soften my swearing.
First Sir Charles advances with phrases well-strung,
'Consider, dear Doctor, the girls are but young.'
'The younger the worse,' I return him again,
'It shews that their habits are all dyed in grain.'
'But then they're so handsome, one's bosom it grieves.'
'What signifies *handsome*, when people are thieves?'
'But where is your justice? their cases are hard.'
'What signifies *justice*? I want the *reward*.

" 'There's the parish of Edmonton offers forty pounds; there's the parish of St. Leonard Shoreditch offers forty pounds; there's the parish of Tyburn, from the Hog-in-the-pound to St. Giles's watch-house, offers forty pounds,—I shall have all that if I convict them!'—

" 'But consider their case,—it may yet be your own!
And see how they kneel! Is your heart made of stone?'
This moves:—so at last I agree to relent,
For ten pounds in hand, and ten pounds to be spent.'

"I challenge you all to answer this: I tell you, you cannot. It cuts deep. But now for the rest of the letter: and next—but I want room—so I believe I shall battle the rest out at Barton some day next week.—I don't value you all!

                                                        "O. G."

We regret that we have no record of this Christmas visit to Barton; that the poet had no Boswell to follow at his heels and take note of all his sayings and doings. We can only picture him in our minds, casting off all care; enacting the lord of misrule; presiding at the Christmas revels; providing all kinds of merriment, keeping the card table in an uproar and finally opening the ball on the first day of the year in his spring velvet suit, with the Jessamy Bride for a partner.

CHAPTER XXXVII

*Theatrical delays—Negotiations with Colman—Letter to Garrick—
Croaking of the manager—Naming of the play—She Stoops to Conquer
—Foote's Primitive Puppet Shew, Piety on Pattens—First performance
of the comedy—Agitation of the author—Success—Colman squibbed out
of town*

The gay life depicted in the two last chapters, while it kept Goldsmith
in a state of continual excitement, aggravated the malady which was
impairing his constitution; yet his increasing perplexities in money
matters drove him to the dissipations of society as a relief from solitary
care. The delays of the theatre added to those perplexities. He had long
since finished his new comedy, yet the year 1772 passed away without
his being able to get it on the stage. No one, uninitiated in the interior
of a theatre, that little world of traps and trickery, can have any idea
of the obstacles and perplexities multiplied in the way of the most
eminent and successful author by the mismanagement of managers,
the jealousies and intrigues of rival authors and the fantastic and impertinent caprices of actors. A long and baffling negotiation was carried on
between Goldsmith and Colman, the manager of Covent Garden; who
retained the play in his hands until the middle of January (1773) without
coming to a decision. The theatrical season was rapidly passing away,
and Goldsmith's pecuniary difficulties were augmenting and pressing
on him. We may judge of his anxiety by the following letter:

> *"To George Colman, Esq.*
>
> "DEAR SIR,
>
> "I entreat you'll relieve me from that state of suspense in which I
> have been kept for a long time. Whatever objections you have made
> or shall make to my play, I will endeavour to remove and not argue
> about them. To bring in any new judges either of its merits or faults I
> can never submit to. Upon a former occasion, when my other play was
> before Mr. Garrick, he offered to bring me before Mr. Whitehead's
> tribunal, but I refused the proposal with indignation: I hope I shall not
> experience as harsh treatment from you as from him. I have, as you
> know, a large sum of money to make up shortly; by accepting my play,
> I can readily satisfy my creditor that way; at any rate, I must look about
> to some certainty to be prepared. For God's sake take the play, and let
> us make the best of it, and let me have the same measure, at least, which
> you have given as bad plays as mine.
>
> "I am your friend and servant,
>
> "OLIVER GOLDSMITH."

Colman returned the manuscript with the blank sides of the leaves scored with disparaging comments and suggested alterations, but with the intimation that the faith of the theatre should be kept and the play acted notwithstanding. Goldsmith submitted the criticisms to some of his friends, who pronounced them trivial, unfair and contemptible and intimated that Colman, being a dramatic writer himself, might be actuated by jealousy. The play was then sent, with Colman's comments written on it, to Garrick; but he had scarce sent it when Johnson interfered, represented the evil that might result from an apparent rejection of it by Covent Garden, and undertook to go forthwith to Colman and have a talk with him on the subject. Goldsmith, therefore, penned the following note to Garrick:

"Dear Sir,

"I ask many pardons for the trouble I gave you yesterday. Upon more mature deliberation, and the advice of a sensible friend, I began to think it indelicate in me to throw upon you the odium of confirming Mr. Colman's sentence. I therefore request you will send my play back by my servant; for having been assured of having it acted at the other house, though I confess yours in every respect more to my wish, yet it would be folly in me to forego an advantage which lies in my power of appealing from Mr. Colman's opinion to the judgment of the town. I entreat, if not too late, you will keep this affair a secret for some time.

"I am, dear Sir, your very humble servant,

"Oliver Goldsmith."

The negotiation of Johnson with the manager of Covent Garden was effective. Colman, he says, "was prevailed on at last by much solicitation, nay, a kind of force," to bring forward the comedy. Still the manager was ungenerous, or, at least, indiscreet enough to express his opinion that it would not reach a second representation. The plot, he said, was bad, and the interest not sustained; "it dwindled and dwindled, and at last went out like the snuff of a candle." The effect of his croaking was soon apparent within the walls of the theatre. Two of the most popular actors, Woodward and Gentleman Smith, to whom the parts of Tony Lumpkin and Young Marlow were assigned, refused to act them, one of them alleging in excuse the evil predictions of the manager. Goldsmith was advised to postpone the performance of his play until he could get these important parts well supplied. "No," said he, "I would sooner that my play were damned by bad players than merely saved by good acting."

Quick was substituted for Woodward in Tony Lumpkin and Lee

Lewes, the harlequin of the theatre, for Gentleman Smith in Young Marlow; and both did justice to their parts.

Great interest was taken by Goldsmith's friends in the success of his piece. The rehearsals were attended by Johnson, Cradock, Murphy, Reynolds and his sister and the whole Horneck connection, including of course the *Jessamy Bride*, whose presence may have contributed to flutter the anxious heart of the author. The rehearsals went off with great applause, but that Colman attributed to the partiality of friends. He continued to croak and refused to risk any expense in new scenery or dresses on a play which he was sure would prove a failure.

The time was at hand for the first representation, and as yet the comedy was without a title. "We are all in labour for a name for Goldy's play," said Johnson, who, as usual, took a kind of fatherly protecting interest in poor Goldsmith's affairs. "The Old House a New Inn" was thought of for a time, but still did not please. Sir Joshua Reynolds proposed "The Belle's Stratagem," an elegant title, but not considered applicable, the perplexities of the comedy being produced by the mistake of the hero, not the stratagem of the heroine. The name was afterwards adopted by Mrs. Cowley for one of her comedies. "The Mistakes of a Night" was the title at length fixed upon, to which Goldsmith prefixed the words, "She Stoops to Conquer."

The evil bodings of Colman still continued. They were even communicated in the box office to the servant of the Duke of Gloucester, who was sent to engage a box. Never did the play of a popular writer struggle into existence through more difficulties.

In the mean time Foote's *Primitive Puppet Shew*, entitled the *Handsome Housemaid, or Piety on Pattens*, had been brought out at the Haymarket on the 15th of February. All the world, fashionable and unfashionable, had crowded to the theatre. The street was thronged with equipages; the doors were stormed by the mob. The burlesque was completely successful, and sentimental comedy received its quietus. Even Garrick, who had recently befriended it, now gave it a kick as he saw it going down hill, and sent Goldsmith a humorous prologue to help his comedy of the opposite school. Garrick and Goldsmith, however, were now on very cordial terms, to which the social meetings in the circle of the Hornecks and Bunburys may have contributed.

On the 15th of March the new comedy was to be performed. Those who had stood up for its merits and been irritated and disgusted by the treatment it had received from the manager, determined to muster their forces, and aid in giving it a good launch upon the town. The particulars of this confederation, and of its triumphant success, are amusingly told by Cumberland in his memoirs.

"We were not over sanguine of success, but perfectly determined to struggle hard for our author. We accordingly assembled our strength at the Shakspeare Tavern, in a considerable body, for an early dinner, where Samuel Johnson took the chair at the head of a long table, and was the life and soul of the corps: the poet took post silently by his side, with the Burkes, Sir Joshua Reynolds, Fitzherbert, Caleb White-foord, and a phalanx of North British, predetermined applauders, under the banner of Major Mills, all good men and true. Our illustrious president was in inimitable glee; and poor Goldsmith that day took all his raillery as patiently and complacently as my friend Boswell would have done any day, or every day of his life. In the mean time, we did not forget our duty; and though we had a better comedy going, in which Johnson was chief actor, we betook ourselves in good time to our separate and allotted posts, and waited the awful drawing up of the curtain. As our stations were preconcerted, so were our signals for plaudits arranged and determined upon in a manner that gave every one his cue where to look for them, and how to follow them up.

"We had among us a very worthy and efficient member, long since lost to his friends and the world at large, Adam Drummond, of amiable memory, who was gifted by nature with the most sonorous, and at the same time, the most contagious laugh that ever echoed from the human lungs. The neighing of the horse of the son of Hystaspes was a whisper to it; the whole thunder of the theatre could not drown it. This kind and ingenious friend fairly forewarned us that he knew no more when to give his fire than the cannon did that was planted on a battery. He desired, therefore, to have a flapper at his elbow, and I had the honour to be deputed to that office. I planted him in an upper box, pretty nearly over the stage, in full view of the pit and galleries, and perfectly well situated to give the echo all its play through the hollows and recesses of the theatre. The success of our manœuvre was complete. All eyes were upon Johnson, who sat in a front row of a side box; and when he laughed, everybody thought themselves warranted to roar. In the mean time, my friend followed signals with a rattle so irresistibly comic that, when he had repeated it several times, the attention of the spectators was so engrossed by his person and performances, that the progress of the play seemed likely to become a secondary object, and I found it prudent to insinuate to him that he might halt his music without any prejudice to the author; but alas! it was now too late to rein him in; he had laughed upon my signal where he found no joke, and now, unluckily, he fancied that he found a joke in almost every thing that was said; so that nothing in nature could be more mal-a-propos than some of his bursts every now and then were. These were dangerous moments, for the pit began to take umbrage; but we carried our point through, and triumphed not only over Colman's judgment, but our own."

Much of this statement has been condemned as exaggerated or discolored. Cumberland's memoirs have generally been characterized as partaking of romance, and in the present instance he had particular motives for tampering with the truth. He was a dramatic writer himself, jealous of the success of a rival, and anxious to have it attributed to the private management of friends. According to various accounts, public and private, such management was unnecessary, for the piece was "received throughout with the greatest acclamations."

Goldsmith in the present instance had not dared, as on a former occasion, to be present at the first performance. He had been so overcome by his apprehensions that at the preparatory dinner he could hardly utter a word and was so choked that he could not swallow a mouthful. When his friends trooped to the theatre, he stole away to St. James's Park: there he was found, by a friend, between seven and eight o'clock wandering up and down the Mall like a troubled spirit. With difficulty he was persuaded to go to the theatre, where his presence might be important should any alteration be necessary. He arrived at the opening of the fifth act and made his way behind the scenes. Just as he entered there was a slight hiss at the improbability of Tony Lumpkin's trick on his mother in persuading her she was forty miles off, on Crack-skull Common, though she had been trundled about on her own grounds. "What's that? what's that!" cried Goldsmith to the manager in great agitation. "Pshaw! Doctor," replied Colman sarcastically, "don't be frightened at a squib when we've been sitting these two hours on a barrel of gunpowder!" Though of a most forgiving nature, Goldsmith did not easily forget this ungracious and ill timed sally.

If Colman was indeed actuated by the paltry motives ascribed to him in his treatment of this play, he was more amply punished by its success, and by the taunts, epigrams, and censures levelled at him through the press: in which his false prophecies were jeered at; his critical judgment called in question; and he was openly taxed with literary jealousy. So galling and unremitting was the fire, that he at length wrote to Goldsmith, entreating him "to take him off the rack of the newspapers;" in the mean time, to escape the laugh that was raised about him in the theatrical world of London, he took refuge in Bath during the triumphant career of the comedy.

The following is one of the many squibs which assailed the ears of the manager:

To George Colman, Esq.,

ON THE SUCCESS OF DR. GOLDSMITH'S NEW COMEDY.

Come, Coley, doff those mourning weeds,
    Nor thus with jokes be flamm'd;

Tho' Goldsmith's present play succeeds,
His next may still be damn'd.

As this has 'scaped without a fall,
To sink his next prepare;
New actors hire from Wapping Wall,
And dresses from Rag Fair.

For scenes let tatter'd blankets fly,
The prologue Kelly write;
Then swear again the piece must die
Before the author's night.

Should these tricks fail, the lucky elf,
To bring to lasting shame,
E'en write *the best you can yourself*,
And print it in *his name*.

The solitary hiss, which had startled Goldsmith, was ascribed by some of the newspaper scribblers to Cumberland himself, who was "manifestly miserable" at the delight of the audience, or to Ossian Macpherson, who was hostile to the whole Johnson clique, or to Goldsmith's dramatic rival, Kelly. The following is one of the epigrams which appeared:

At Dr. Goldsmith's merry play,
All the spectators laugh, they say;
The assertion, Sir, I must deny,
For Cumberland and Kelly cry.
Ride, si sapis.

Another, addressed to Goldsmith, alludes to Kelly's early apprenticeship to staymaking:

If Kelly finds fault with the *shape* of your muse,
And thinks that too loosely it plays,
He surely, dear Doctor, will never refuse
To make it a new *Pair of Stays!*

Cradock had returned to the country before the production of the play; the following letter of Goldsmith to Cradock, written just after the performance, gives an additional picture of the thorns which beset an author in the path of theatrical literature:

"MY DEAR SIR,

"The play has met with a success much beyond your expectations or mine. I thank you sincerely for your epilogue, which, however, could not be used, but with your permission shall be printed. The story in short is this. Murphy sent me rather the outline of an epilogue than an epilogue, which was to be sung by Miss Catley, and which she approved; Mrs. Bulkley hearing this, insisted on throwing up her part" (*Miss Hardcastle*) "unless, according to the custom of the theatre, she were permitted to speak the epilogue. In this embarrassment I thought of making a quarreling epilogue between Catley and her, debating *who* should speak the epilogue; but then Mrs. Catley refused after I had taken the trouble of drawing it out. I was then at a loss indeed; an epilogue was to be made, and for none but Mrs. Bulkley. I made one, and Colman thought it too bad to be spoken; I was obliged therefore to try a fourth time, and I made a very mawkish thing, as you'll shortly see. Such is the history of my Stage adventures, and which I have at last done with. I cannot help saying, that I am very sick of the stage; and though I believe I shall get three tolerable benefits, yet I shall on the whole be a loser, even in a pecuniary light; my ease and comfort I certainly lost while it was in agitation.

"I am, my dear Cradock, your obliged and obedient servant,

"OLIVER GOLDSMITH.

"P. S. Present my most humble respects to Mrs. Cradock."

Johnson, who had taken such a conspicuous part in promoting the interests of poor "Goldy," was triumphant at the success of the piece. "I know of no comedy for many years," said he, "that has so much exhilarated an audience; that has answered so much the great end of comedy—making an audience merry."

Goldsmith was happy also in gleaning applause from less authoritative sources. Northcote, the painter, then a youthful pupil of Sir Joshua Reynolds, and Ralph, Sir Joshua's confidential man, had taken their stations in the gallery to lead the applause in that quarter. Goldsmith asked Northcote's opinion of the play. The youth modestly declared he could not presume to judge in such matters. "Did it make you laugh?" "Oh, exceedingly!" "That is all I require," replied Goldsmith; and rewarded him for his criticism by box tickets for his first benefit night.

The comedy was immediately put to press and dedicated to Johnson in the following grateful and affectionate terms:

"In inscribing this slight performance to you, I do not mean so much to compliment you as myself. It may do me some honour to inform the public, that I have lived many years in intimacy with you. It may serve the interests of mankind also to inform them, that the greatest wit may be found in a character, without impairing the most unaffected piety."

The copy right was transferred to Mr. Newbery, according to agreement, whose profits on the sale of the work far exceeded the debts for which the author in his perplexities had preengaged it. The sum which accrued to Goldsmith from his benefit nights afforded but a slight palliation of his pecuniary difficulties. His friends, while they exulted in his success, little knew of his continually increasing embarrassments, and of the anxiety of mind which kept tasking his pen while it impaired the ease and freedom of spirit necessary to felicitous composition.

CHAPTER XXXVIII

A newspaper attack—The Evans affray—Johnson's comments

The triumphant success of She Stoops to Conquer brought forth of course those carpings and cavillings of the underling scribblers which are the thorns and briers in the path of successful authors. Goldsmith, though easily nettled by attacks of the kind, was at present too well satisfied with the reception of his comedy to heed them; but the following anonymous letter, which appeared in a public paper, was not to be taken with equal equanimity:

"*For the London Packet.*

"TO DR. GOLDSMITH.

"*Vous vous noyez par vanité.*

"Sir,—The happy knack which you have learned of puffing your own compositions, provokes me to come forth. You have not been the editor of newspapers and magazines not to discover the trick of literary *humbug*; but the gauze is so thin that the very foolish part of the world see through it, and discover the doctor's monkey face and cloven foot. Your poetic vanity is as unpardonable as your personal. Would man believe it, and will woman bear it, to be told that for hours the great Goldsmith will stand surveying his grotesque orang-outang's figure in a pier-glass? Was but the lovely H——k as much enamoured, you would not sigh, my gentle swain, in vain. But your vanity is preposterous. How will this same bard of Bedlam ring the changes in the praise of Goldy! But what has he to be either proud or vain of? 'The Traveller' is a flimsy poem, built upon false principles—principles diametrically opposite to liberty. What is 'The Good-natured Man' but a poor, water-gruel, dramatic dose? What is 'The Deserted Village' but a pretty poem, of easy numbers, without fancy, dignity, genius, or fire? And, pray, what may be the last *speaking* pantomime, so praised by the doctor himself, but an incoherent piece of stuff, the figure of a woman with a fish's tail, without plot, incident, or intrigue? We are made to laugh at stale, dull jokes, wherein we mistake pleasantry for wit, and grimace for humour; wherein every scene is unnatural and inconsistent with the rules, the laws of nature and of the drama; viz., two gentlemen come to a man of fortune's house, eat, drink, &c., and take it for an inn. The one is intended as a lover for the daughter; he talks with her for some hours; and, when he sees her again in a different dress, he treats her as a bar-girl, and swears she squinted. He abuses the master of the house, and threatens to kick him out of his own doors. The squire, whom we are told is to be a fool, proves to be the most sensible being of the piece; and he makes out a whole act by bidding his mother lie close behind a bush, persuading her that his father, her own husband, is a highwayman, and that he has come to cut their throats; and, to give his cousin an opportunity to go off, he drives his mother over hedges, ditches, and through ponds. There is not, sweet, sucking Johnson, a natural stroke in the whole play but the young fellow's giving the stolen jewels to the mother, supposing her to be the landlady. That Mr. Colman did no justice to this piece, I honestly allow; that he told all his friends it would be damned, I positively aver; and, from such ungenerous insinuations, without a dramatic merit, it rose to public notice, and it is now the ton to go and see it, though I never saw a person that either liked it or approved it, any more than the absurd plot of Home's tragedy of 'Alonzo.' Mr. Goldsmith, correct your arrogance, reduce your vanity, and endeavour to believe, as a man, you are of the plainest sort; and as an author, but a mortal piece of mediocrity.

> 'Brise le miroir infidèle
> Qui vous cache la vérité.
>
> "TOM TICKLE."

It would be difficult to devise a letter more calculated to wound the peculiar sensibilities of Goldsmith. The attacks upon him as an author, though annoying enough, he could have tolerated; but then the allusion to his "grotesque" person, to his studious attempts to adorn it, and above all to his being an unsuccessful admirer of the lovely H——k (the Jessamy Bride) struck rudely upon the most sensitive part of his highly sensitive nature. The paragraph, it is said, was first pointed out to him by an officious friend, an Irishman, who told him he was bound in honor to resent it; but he needed no such prompting. He was in a high state of excitement and indignation. Accompanied by his friend, who is said to have been a Captain Higgins of the marines, he repaired to Paternoster Row to the shop of Evans the publisher, whom he supposed to be the editor of the paper. Evans was summoned by his shopman from an adjoining room. Goldsmith announced his name. "I have called," added he, "in consequence of a scurrilous attack made upon me, and an unwarrantable liberty taken with the name of a young lady. As for myself I care little, but her name must not be sported with."
Evans professed utter ignorance of the matter, and said he would

speak to the editor. He stooped to examine a file of the paper in search of the offensive article, whereupon Goldsmith's friend gave him a signal that now was a favorable moment for the exercise of his cane. The hint was taken as quick as given, and the cane was vigorously applied to the back of the stooping publisher. The latter rallied in an instant and, being a stout, high blooded Welshman, returned the blows with interest. A lamp hanging overhead was broken and sent down a shower of oil upon the combatants, but the battle raged with unceasing fury. The shopman ran off for a constable; but Dr. Kenrick, who happened to be in the adjacent room, sallied forth, interfered between the combatants and put an end to the affray. He conducted Goldsmith to a coach in exceedingly battered and tattered plight and accompanied him home, soothing him with much mock commiseration, though he was generally suspected, and on good grounds, to be the author of the libel.

Evans immediately instituted a suit against Goldsmith for an assault, but was ultimately prevailed upon to compromise the matter, the poet contributing fifty pounds to the Welsh charity.

Newspapers made themselves, as may well be supposed, exceedingly merry with the combat. Some censured him severely for invading the sanctity of a man's own house; others accused him of having, in his former capacity of editor of a magazine, been guilty of the very offences that he now resented in others. This drew from him the following vindication:

"To the Public.

"Lest it should be supposed that I have been willing to correct in others an abuse of which I have been guilty myself, I beg leave to declare, that, in all my life, I never wrote or dictated a single paragraph, letter, or essay in a newspaper, except a few moral essays under the character of a Chinese, about ten years ago, in the Ledger, and a letter, to which I signed my name, in the St. James's Chronicle. If the liberty of the press, therefore, has been abused, I have had no hand in it.

"I have always considered the press as the protector of our freedom, as a watchful guardian, capable of uniting the weak against the encroachments of power. What concerns the public most properly admits of a public discussion. But, of late, the press has turned from defending public interest to making inroads upon private life; from combating the strong to overwhelming the feeble. No condition is now too obscure for its abuse, and the protector has become the tyrant of the people. In this manner the freedom of the press is beginning to sow the seeds of its own dissolution; the great must oppose it from principle, and the weak from fear; till at last every rank of mankind shall be found to give up its benefits, content with security from insults.

"How to put a stop to this licentiousness, by which all are indis-criminately abused, and by which vice consequently escapes in the general censure, I am unable to tell; all I could wish is, that, as the law gives us no protection against the injury, so it should give calum-niators no shelter after having provoked correction. The insults which we receive before the public, by being more open, are the more distressing; by treating them with silent contempt we do not pay a suffi-cient deference to the opinion of the world. By recurring to legal redress we too often expose the weakness of the law, which only serves to increase our mortification by failing to relieve us. In short, every man should singly consider himself as the guardian of the liberty of the press, and, as far as his influence can extend, should endeavour to pre-vent its licentiousness becoming at last the grave of its freedom.

"OLIVER GOLDSMITH."

Boswell, who had just arrived in town, met with this article in a news-paper which he found at Dr. Johnson's. The doctor was from home at the time, and Bozzy and Mrs. Williams, in a critical conference over the letter, determined from the style that it must have been written by the lexicographer himself. The latter on his return soon undeceived them. "Sir," said he to Boswell, "Goldsmith would no more have asked me to have wrote such a thing as that for him, than he would have asked me to feed him with a spoon, or do any thing else that denoted his imbecility. Sir, had he shown it to any one friend, he would not have been allowed to publish it. He has, indeed, done it very well; but it is a foolish thing well done. I suppose he has been so much elated with the success of his new comedy, that he has thought every thing that con-cerned him must be of importance to the public."

CHAPTER XXXIX

The return of Boswell to town to his task of noting down the conversations of Johnson enables us to glean from his journal some scanty
notices of Goldsmith. It was now Holy Week, a time during which Johnson was particularly solemn in his manner and strict in his devotions.
Boswell, who was the imitator of the great moralist in every thing,
assumed of course an extra devoutness on the present occasion. "He had
an odd mock solemnity of tone and manner," said Miss Burney (afterwards Madame D'Arblay) "which he had acquired from constantly
thinking of and imitating Dr. Johnson." It would seem that he undertook to deal out some secondhand homilies *a la Johnson,* for the edifica-
tion of Goldsmith during Holy Week. The poet, whatever might be his
religious feeling, had no disposition to be schooled by so shallow an
apostle. "Sir," said he in reply, "as I take my shoes from the shoemaker,
and my coat from the tailor, so I take my religion from the priest."

Boswell treasured up this reply in his memory or his memorandum
book. A few days afterwards, the 9th of April, he kept Good Friday with
Dr. Johnson in the orthodox style; breakfasted with him on tea and
crossbuns; went to church with him morning and evening; fasted in
the interval and read with him in the Greek Testament: then, in the
piety of his heart, complained of the sore rebuff he had met with in
the course of his religious exhortations to the poet, and lamented that
the latter should indulge in "this loose way of talking." "Sir," replied
Johnson, "Goldsmith knows nothing—he has made up his mind about
nothing."

This reply seems to have gratified the lurking jealousy of Boswell,
and he has recorded it in his journal. Johnson, however, with respect
to Goldsmith, and indeed with respect to every body else, blew hot
as well as cold, according to the humor he was in. Boswell, who was
astonished and piqued at the continually increasing celebrity of the
poet, observed some time after to Johnson in a tone of surprise, that
Goldsmith had acquired more fame than all the officers of the last war
who were not generals. "Why, sir," answered Johnson, his old feeling of
good will working uppermost, "you will find ten thousand fit to do what
they did, before you find one who does what Goldsmith has done. You
must consider that a thing is valued according to its rarity. A pebble

that paves the street is in itself more useful than the diamond upon a lady's finger."

On the 13th of April we find Goldsmith and Johnson at the table of old General Oglethorpe discussing the question of the degeneracy of the human race. Goldsmith asserts the fact and attributes it to the influence of luxury. Johnson denies the fact; and observes that even admitting it, luxury could not be the cause. It reached but a small proportion of the human race. Soldiers on six pence a day could not indulge in luxuries; the poor and laboring classes, forming the great mass of mankind, were out of its sphere. Wherever it could reach them, it strengthened them and rendered them prolific. The conversation was not of particular force or point as reported by Boswell; the dinner party was a very small one, in which there was no provocation to intellectual display.

After dinner they took tea with the ladies; where we find poor Goldsmith happy and at home singing Tony Lumpkin's song of the "Three Jolly Pigeons," and another called the "Humours of Ballamaguery" to a very pretty Irish tune. It was to have been introduced in She Stoops to Conquer but was left out, as the actress who played the heroine could not sing.

It was in these genial moments that the sunshine of Goldsmith's nature would break out and he would say and do a thousand whimsical and agreeable things that made him the life of the strictly social circle. Johnson, with whom conversation was every thing, used to judge Goldsmith too much by his own colloquial standard and undervalue him for being less provided than himself with acquired facts, the ammunition of the tongue and often the mere lumber of the memory; others, however, valued him for the native felicity of his thoughts, however carelessly expressed, and for certain good-fellow qualities, less calculated to dazzle than to endear. "It is amazing," said Johnson one day, after he himself had been talking like an oracle. "It is amazing how little Goldsmith knows; he seldom comes where he is not more ignorant than any one else." "Yet," replied Sir Joshua Reynolds with affectionate promptness, "there is no man whose company is more *liked*."

Two or three days after the dinner at General Oglethorpe's Goldsmith met Johnson again at the table of General Paoli, the hero of Corsica. Martinelli of Florence, author of an Italian History of England, was among the guests; as was Boswell, to whom we are indebted for minutes of the conversation which took place. The question was debated whether Martinelli should continue his history down to that day. "To be sure he should," said Goldsmith. "No, sir," cried Johnson, "it would give great offence. He would have to tell of almost all the living great what they did not wish told." Goldsmith. "It may, perhaps, be necessary for a native to be more cautious; but a foreigner who comes among us without prejudice may be considered as holding the place of a judge, and may speak his mind freely." Johnson. "Sir, a foreigner, when he sends a work from the press, ought to be on his guard against catching the error and mistaken enthusiasm of the people among whom he happens to be." Goldsmith. "Sir, he wants only to sell his history, and to tell truth; one an honest, the other a laudable motive." Johnson. "Sir, they are both laudable motives. It is laudable in a man to wish to live by his labours; but he should write so as he may *live* by them, not so as he may be knocked on the head. I would advise him to be at Calais before he publishes his history of the present age. A foreigner who attaches himself to a political party in this country, is in the worst state that can be imagined; he is looked upon as a mere intermeddler. A native may do it from interest." Boswell. "Or principle." Goldsmith. "There are people who tell a hundred political lies every day, and are not hurt by it. Surely, then, one may tell truth with perfect safety." Johnson. "Why, sir, in the first place, he who tells a hundred lies has disarmed the force of his lies. But besides; a man had rather have a hundred lies told of him, than one truth which he does not wish to be told." Goldsmith. "For my part, I'd tell truth, and shame the devil." Johnson. "Yes, sir, but the devil will be angry. I wish to shame the devil as much as you do, but I should choose to be out of the reach of his claws." Goldsmith. "His claws can do you no hurt where you have the shield of truth."

This last reply was one of Goldsmith's lucky hits, and closed the argument in his favor.

"We talked," writes Boswell, "of the king's coming to see Goldsmith's new play." "I wish he would," said Goldsmith, adding, however, with an affected indifference, "Not that it would do me the least good." "Well, then, Sir," cried Johnson laughing, "'let us say it would do *him* good. No, sir, this affection will not pass;—it is mighty idle. In such a state as ours, who would not wish to please the chief magistrate?"

"I *do* wish to please him," rejoined Goldsmith. "I remember a line in Dryden:

'And every poet is the monarch's friend.'

It ought to be reversed." "Nay," said Johnson, "there are finer lines in Dryden on this subject:

'For colleges on bounteous kings depend,
And never rebel was to arts a friend.'"

General Paoli observed that "successful rebels might be." "Happy rebellions," interjected Martinelli. "We have no such phrase," cried Goldsmith. "But have you not the thing?" asked Paoli. "Yes," replied Goldsmith, "all our *happy* revolutions. They have hurt our constitution, and *will* hurt it, till we mend it by another HAPPY REVOLUTION." This was a sturdy sally of Jacobitism, that quite surprised Boswell, but must have been relished by Johnson.

General Paoli mentioned a passage in the play which had been construed into a compliment to a lady of distinction, whose marriage with the Duke of Cumberland had excited a strong disapprobation of the king as a mesalliance. Boswell, to draw Goldsmith out, pretended to think the compliment unintentional. The poet smiled and hesitated. The general came to his relief. "Monsieur Goldsmith," said he, "est comme la mer, quit jette des perles et beaucoup d'autres belles choses, sans s'en appercevoir." (Mr. Goldsmith is like the sea, which casts forth pearls and many other beautiful things without perceiving it.)

"Tres-bien dit, et tres-élégamment," (very well said and very elegantly), exclaimed Goldsmith; delighted with so beautiful a compliment from such a quarter.

Johnson spoke disparagingly of the learning of Mr. Harris of Salisbury and doubted his being a good Grecian. "He is what is much better," cried Goldsmith with prompt good nature, "he is a worthy, humane man." "Nay, sir," rejoined the logical Johnson, "that is not to the purpose of our argument; that will prove that he can play upon the fiddle as well as Giardini, as that he is an eminent Grecian." Goldsmith found he had got into a scrape and seized upon Giardini to help him out of it. "The greatest musical performers," said he, dextrously turning the conversation, "have but small emoluments. Giardini, I am told, does not get above seven hundred a year." "That is indeed but little for a man to get," observed Johnson, "who does best that which so many endeavour to do. There is nothing, I think, in which the power of art is shown so much as in playing on the fiddle. In all other things we can do something at first. Any man will forge a bar of iron, if you give him a hammer; not so well as a smith, but tolerably. A man will saw a piece of wood, and make a box, though a clumsy one; but give him a fiddle and fiddle stick, and he can do nothing."

This upon the whole, though reported by the one sided Boswell, is a tolerable specimen of the conversations of Goldsmith and Johnson; the former heedless, often illogical, always on the kind hearted side of the question, and prone to redeem himself by lucky hits; the latter closely argumentative, studiously sententious, often profound and sometimes laboriously prosaic.

They had an argument a few days later at Mr. Thrale's table on the subject of suicide. "Do you think, sir," said Boswell, "that all who commit suicide are mad?" "Sir," replied Johnson, "they are not often universally disordered in their intellects, but one passion presses so upon them that they yield to it, and commit suicide, as a passionate man will stab another—I have often thought," added he, "that after a man has taken the resolution to kill himself, it is not courage in him to do any thing, however desperate, because he has nothing to fear." "I don't see that," observed Goldsmith. "Nay, but my dear sir," rejoined Johnson, "why should you not see what every one else sees?"—"It is," replied Goldsmith, "for fear of something that he has resolved to kill himself; and will not that timid disposition restrain him?" "It does not signify," pursued Johnson, "that the fear of something made him resolve; it is upon the state of his mind, after the resolution is taken, that I argue. Suppose a man, either from fear, or pride, or conscience, or whatever motive, has resolved to kill himself; when once the resolution is taken he has nothing to fear. He may then go and take the King of Prussia by the nose at the head of his army. He cannot fear the rack who is determined to kill himself." Boswell reports no more of the discussion, though Goldsmith might have continued it with advantage; for the very 'timid disposition' which through 'fear of something' was impelling the man to commit suicide, might restrain him from an act involving the punishment of the rack, more terrible to him than death itself.

It is to be regretted that in all these reports by Boswell we have scarcely any thing but the remarks of Johnson; it is only by accident that he now and then gives us the observations of others, or when they are necessary to explain or set off those of his hero. "When in *that presence*," says Miss Burney, "he was unobservant, if not contemptuous of every one else. In truth, when he met with Dr. Johnson, he commonly forbore even answering any thing that was said, or attending to any thing that went forward, lest he should miss the smallest sound from that voice to which he paid such exclusive, though merited, homage. But the moment that voice burst forth, the attention which it excited on Mr. Boswell amounted almost to pain. His eyes goggled wih eagerness; he leant his ear almost on the shoulder of the Doctor; and his mouth dropped open to catch every syllable that might be uttered; nay, he seemed not only to dread losing a word, but to be anxious not to miss a breathing; as if hoping from it latently, or mystically, some information."

On one occasion the doctor detected Boswell, or Bozzy as he called him, eavesdropping behind his chair as he was conversing with Miss Burney at Mr. Thrale's table. "What are you doing there, Sir?" cried he, turning round angrily and clapping his hand upon his knee. "Go to the table, Sir."

Boswell obeyed with an air of affright and submission, which raised a smile on every face. Scarce had he taken his seat, however, at a distance than, impatient to get again at the side of Johnson, he rose and was running off in quest of something to show him when the doctor roared after him authoritatively, "What are you thinking of, Sir? Why do you get up before the cloth is removed? Come back to your place, Sir;"—and the obsequious spaniel did as he was commanded.—"Running about in the middle of meals!" muttered the doctor, pursing his mouth at the same time to restrain his rising risibility.

Boswell got another rebuff from Johnson, which would have demolished any other man. He had been teasing him with many direct questions, such as What did you do, sir?—What did you say, sir? until the great philologist became perfectly enraged. "I will not be put to the *question!*" roared he. "Don't you consider, sir, that these are not the manners of a gentleman? I will not be baited with *what* and *why;* What is this? What is that? Why is a cow's tail long? Why is a fox's tail bushy?" "Why, sir," replied pill garlic, "you are so good that I venture to trouble you." "Sir," replied Johnson, "my being so *good* is no reason why you should be so *ill.*" "You have but two topics, sir;" exclaimed he on another occasion, "yourself and me, and I am sick of both."

Boswell's inveterate disposition to *toad* was a sore cause of mortification to his father, the old laird of Auchinleck (or Affleck.) He had been annoyed by his extravagant devotion to Paoli, but then he was something of a military hero; but this tagging at the heels of Dr. Johnson, whom he considered a kind of pedagogue, set his Scotch blood in a ferment. "There's nae hope for Jamie, mon," said he to a friend; "Jamie is gaen clean gyte. What do you think, mon? He's done wi' Paoli; he's off wi' the land-louping scoundrel of a Corsican; and whose tail do you think he has pinn'd himself to now, mon? A *dominie*, mon; an auld dominie: he keeped a schule, and cau'd it an acaadamy."

We shall show in the next chapter that Jamie's devotion to the dominie did not go unrewarded.

CHAPTER XL

Changes in the Literary Club—Johnson's objections to Garrick—Election of Boswell

The Literary Club (as we have termed the club in Gerard Street, though it took that name some time later) had now been in existence several years. Johnson was exceedingly chary at first of its exclusiveness, and opposed to its being augmented in number. Not long after its institution Sir Joshua Reynolds was speaking of it to Garrick. "I like it much," said little David briskly; "I think I shall be of you." "When Sir Joshua mentioned this to Dr. Johnson," says Boswell, "he was much displeased with the actor's conceit. *'He'll be of us?'* growled he. 'How does he know we will *permit* him? The first duke in England has no right to hold such language.'"

When Sir John Hawkins spoke favorably of Garrick's pretensions, "Sir," replied Johnson, "he will disturb us by his buffoonery." In the same spirit he declared to Mr. Thrale, that if Garrick should apply for admission, he would black-ball him. "Who, sir?" exclaimed Thrale with surprise; "Mr. Garrick—your friend, your companion—black-ball him!" "Why, sir," replied Johnson, "I love my little David dearly; better than all or any of his flatterers do; but surely one ought to sit in a society like ours,

'Unelbowed by a gamester, pimp, or player.'"

The exclusion from the club was a sore mortification to Garrick, though he bore it without complaining. He could not help continually to ask questions about it—what was going on there—whether he was ever the subject of conversation. By degrees the rigor of the club relaxed; some of the members grew negligent. Beauclerc lost his right of membership by neglecting to attend. On his marriage however with Lady Diana Spencer, daughter of the Duke of Marlborough and recently divorced from Viscount Bolingbroke, he had claimed and regained his seat in the club. The number of members had likewise been augmented. The proposition to increase it originated with Goldsmith. It would give, he thought, an agreeable variety to their meetings; "for there can be nothing new among us," said he; "we have travelled over each other's minds." Johnson was piqued at the suggestion. "Sir," said he, "you have not travelled over my mind, I promise you." Sir Joshua, less confident in the exhaustless fecundity of his mind, felt and acknowledged the force of

Goldsmith's suggestion. Several new members therefore had been added. The first, to his great joy, was David Garrick. Goldsmith, who was now on cordial terms with him, had zealously promoted his election, and Johnson had given it his warm approbation. Another new member was Beauclerc's friend Lord Charlemont; and a still more important one was Mr., afterwards Sir William Jones, the famous Orientalist, at that time a young lawyer of the Temple and a distinguished scholar.

To the great astonishment of the Club Johnson now proposed his devoted follower Boswell as a member. He did it in a note addressed to Goldsmith, who presided on the evening of the 23d of April. The nomination was seconded by Beauclerc. According to the rules of the Club, the ballot would take place at the next meeting (on the 30th); there was an intervening week, therefore, in which to discuss the pretensions of the candidate. We may easily imagine the discussions that took place. Boswell had made himself absurd in such a variety of ways that the very idea of his admission was exceedingly irksome to some of the members. "The honor of being elected into the Turk's Head Club," said the Bishop of St. Asaph, "is not inferior to that of being representative of Westminster and Surrey." What had Boswell done to merit such an honor: what chance had he of gaining it? The answer was simple: he had been the persevering worshipper, if not sycophant of Johnson. The great lexicographer had a heart to be won by apparent affection; he stood forth authoritatively in support of his vassal. If asked to state the merits of the candidate, he summed them up in an indefinable but comprehensive word of his own coining. He was *clubable*. He moreover gave significant hints that if Boswell were kept out he should oppose the admission of any other candidate. No further opposition was made; in fact none of the members had been so fastidious and exclusive in regard to the club as Johnson himself; and if he were pleased, they were easily satisfied. Beside, they knew that with all his faults, Boswell was a cheerful companion and possessed lively social qualities.

On Friday when the ballot was to take place, Beauclerc gave a dinner at his house in the Adelphi where Boswell met several of the members who were favorable to his election. After dinner the latter adjourned to the Club, leaving Boswell in company with Lady Di Beauclerc until the fate of his election should be known. He sat, he says, in a state of anxiety which even the charming conversation of Lady Di could not entirely dissipate. It was not long before tidings were brought of his election, and he was conducted to the place of meeting where, beside the company he had met at dinner, Burke, Dr. Nugent, Garrick, Goldsmith and Mr. William Jones were waiting to receive him. The club, notwithstanding all its learned dignity in the eyes of the world, could at times "unbend and play the fool" as well as less important bodies. Some of its jocose conversations have at times leaked out, and a society in which Goldsmith could venture to sing his song of "an old woman tossed in a blanket," could not be so very staid in its gravity. We may suppose therefore the jokes that had been passing among the members while awaiting the arrival of Boswell. Beauclerc himself could not have repressed his disposition for a sarcastic pleasantry. At least we have a right to presume all this from the conduct of Doctor Johnson himself.

With all his gravity he possessed a deep fund of quiet humor, and felt a kind of whimsical responsibility to protect the club from the absurd propensities of the very questionable associate he had thus inflicted on them. Rising, therefore, as Boswell entered, he advanced with a very doctorial air, placed himself behind a chair on which he leaned as on a desk or pulpit, and then delivered *ex cathedra* a mock solemn charge, pointing out the conduct expected from him as a good member of the Club; what he was to do and especially what he was to avoid; including in the latter no doubt all those petty, prying, questioning, gossiping, babbling habits which had so often grieved the spirit of the lexicographer. It is to be regretted that Boswell has never thought proper to note down the particulars of this charge, which, from the well known characters and positions of the parties, might have furnished a parallel to the noted charge of Launcelot Gobbo to his dog.

CHAPTER XLI

Dinner at Dilly's—Conversations on natural history—Intermeddling of Boswell—Dispute about toleration; Johnson's rebuff to Goldsmith; his apology—Man worship—Doctors Major and Minor—A farewell visit

A few days after the serio-comic scene of the elevation of Boswell into the Literary Club we find that indefatigable biographer giving particulars of a dinner at the Dillys, booksellers in the Poultry, at which he met Goldsmith and Johnson with several other literary characters. His anecdotes of the conversation of course go to glorify Dr. Johnson, for, as he observes in his biography, "his conversation alone, or what led to it, or was interwoven with it, is the business of this work." Still on the present, as on other occasions, he gives unintentional and perhaps unavoidable gleams of Goldsmith's good sense, which show that the latter only wanted a less prejudiced and more impartial reporter, to put down the charge of colloquial incapacity so unjustly fixed upon him. The conversation turned upon the natural history of birds, a beautiful subject on which the poet from his recent studies, his habits of observation, and his natural tastes, must have talked with instruction and feeling; yet, though we have much of what Johnson said, we have only a casual remark or two of Goldsmith. One was on the migration of swallows, which he pronounced partial; "the stronger ones," said he, "migrate, the others do not."

Johnson denied to the brute creation the faculty of reason. "Birds," said he, "build by instinct; they never improve; they build their first nest as well as any one they ever build." "Yet we see," observed Goldsmith, "if you take away a bird's nest with the eggs in it, she will make a slighter nest and lay again." "Sir," replied Johnson, "that is because at first she has full time, and makes her nest deliberately. In the case you mention she is pressed to lay, and must therefore make her nest quickly, and consequently it will be slight." "The nidification of birds," rejoined Goldsmith, "is what is least known in natural history, though one of the most curious things in it." While conversation was going on in this placid, agreeable and instructive manner, the eternal meddler and busy body Boswell must intrude to put it in a brawl. The Dillys were dissenters; two of their guests were dissenting clergymen; another, Mr. Toplady, was a clergyman of the established church. Johnson himself was a zealous, uncompromising churchman. None but a marplot like Boswell would have thought, on such an occasion and in such company, to broach the subject of religious toleration; but, as has

215

been well observed, "it was his perverse inclination to introduce subjects that he hoped would produce difference and debate." In the present instance he gained his point. An animated dispute immediately arose in which, according to Boswell's report, Johnson monopolized the greater part of the conversation; not always treating the dissenting clergymen with the greatest courtesy, and even once wounding the feelings of the mild and amiable Bennet Langton by his harshness.

Goldsmith mingled a little in the dispute and with some advantage, but was cut short by flat contradictions when most in the right. He sat for a time silent but impatient under such overbearing dogmatism, though Boswell, with his usual misinterpretation, attributes his "restless agitation" to a wish *to get in and shine*. "Finding himself excluded," continues Boswell, "he had taken his hat to go away, but remained for a time with it in his hand, like a gamester, who at the end of a long night, lingers for a little while to see if he can have a favourable opportunity to finish with success." Once he was beginning to speak when he was overpowered by the loud voice of Johnson, who was at the opposite end of the table and did not perceive his attempt; whereupon he threw down, as it were, his hat and his argument, and, darting an angry glance at Johnson, exclaimed in a bitter tone, *"Take it."*

Just then one of the disputants was beginning to speak, when Johnson uttering some sound as if about to interrupt him, Goldsmith, according to Boswell, seized the opportunity to vent his own *envy and spleen* under pretext of supporting another person. "Sir," said he to Johnson, "the gentleman has heard you patiently for an hour; pray allow us now to hear him." It was a reproof in the lexicographer's own style; and he may have felt that he merited it; but he was not accustomed to be reproved. "Sir," said he sternly, "I was not interrupting the gentleman. I was only giving him a signal of my attention. Sir, *you are impertinent*." Goldsmith made no reply, but after some time went away, having another engagement.

That evening as Boswell was on the way with Johnson and Langton to the club, he seized the occasion to make some disparaging remarks on Goldsmith, which he thought would just then be acceptable to the great lexicographer. "It was a pity," he said, "that Goldsmith would, on every occasion, endeavor to shine, by which he so often exposed himself." Langton contrasted him with Addison who, content with the fame of his writings, acknowledged himself unfit for conversation; and on being taxed by a lady with silence in company replied, "Madam, I have but nine pence in ready money, but I can draw for a thousand pounds." To this Boswell rejoined that Goldsmith had a great deal of gold in his cabinet, but was always taking out his purse. "Yes, sir," chuckled Johnson, "and that so often an empty purse."

By the time Johnson arrived at the Club however, his angry feelings had subsided, and his native generosity and sense of justice had got the uppermost. He found Goldsmith in company with Burke, Garrick and other members, but sitting silent and apart, "brooding," as Boswell says, "over the reprimand he had received." Johnson's good heart yearned towards him; and knowing his placable nature, "I'll make Goldsmith forgive me," whispered he. Then with a loud voice, "Dr. Goldsmith," said he, "something passed to-day where you and I dined. *I ask your pardon.*" The ire of the poet was extinguished in an instant, and his grateful affection for the magnanimous, though sometimes overbearing moralist, rushed to his heart. "It must be much from you, sir," said he, that I take ill!" "And so," adds Boswell, "the difference was over, and they were on as easy terms as ever, and Goldsmith rattled away as usual." We do not think these stories tell to the poet's disadvantage, even though related by Boswell.

Goldsmith with all his modesty could not be ignorant of his proper merit and must have felt annoyed at times at being undervalued and elbowed aside by light minded or dull men in their blind and exclusive homage to the literary autocrat. It was a fine reproof he gave to Boswell on one occasion for talking of Johnson as entitled to the honor of exclusive superiority. "Sir, you are for making a monarchy what should be a republic."

On another occasion when he was conversing in company with great vivacity and apparently to the satisfaction of those around him, an honest Swiss who sat near, one George Michael Moser, keeper of the Royal Academy, perceiving Dr. Johnson rolling himself as if about to speak, exclaimed, "Stay, stay! Toctor Shonson is going to say something." "And are you sure, sir," replied Goldsmith sharply, "that *you* can comprehend what he says?"

This clever rebuke, which gives the main zest to the anecdote, is omitted by Boswell, who probably did not perceive the point of it.

He relates another anecdote of the kind on the authority of Johnson himself. The latter and Goldsmith were one evening in company with the Rev. George Graham, a master of Eton, who, notwithstanding the sobriety of his cloth, had got intoxicated "to about the pitch of looking at one man and talking to another." "Doctor," cried he in an ecstasy of devotion and good will, but goggling by mistake upon Goldsmith, "I should be glad to see you at Eton." "I shall be glad to wait upon you," replied Goldsmith. "No, no!" cried the other eagerly; "'tis not you I mean, Doctor *Minor,* 'tis Doctor *Major* there." "You may easily conceive," said Johnson in relating the anecdote, "what effect this had upon Goldsmith, who was irascible as a hornet." The only comment however which he is said to have made partakes more of quaint and dry humor than bitterness: "That Graham," said he, "is enough to make one commit suicide." What more could be said to express the intolerable nuisance of a consummate *bore?*

We have now given the last scenes between Goldsmith and Johnson which stand recorded by Boswell. The latter called on the poet a few days after the dinner at Dilly's to take leave of him prior to departing for Scotland; yet even in this last interview he contrives to get up a charge of "jealousy and envy." Goldsmith, he would fain persuade us, is very angry that Johnson is going to travel with him in Scotland and endeavors to persuade him that he will be a dead weight "to lug along through the Highlands and Hebrides." Any one else, knowing the character and habits of Johnson, would have thought the same; and no one but Boswell would have supposed his office of bear leader to the ursa major a thing to be envied.*

---

* One of Peter Pindar's (Dr. Wolcot) most amusing *jeux d'esprit* is his congratulatory epistle to Boswell on this tour, of which we subjoin a few lines.

> O Boswell, Bozzy, Bruce, whate'er thy name,
> Thou mighty shark for anecdote and fame;
> Thou jackall, leading lion Johnson forth,
> To eat M'Pherson 'midst his native north;
> To frighten grave professors with his roar,
> And shake the Hebrides from shore to shore.

> ❋   ❋   ❋   ❋   ❋   ❋   ❋   ❋

> Bless'd be thy labors, most adventurous Bozzy,
> Bold rival of Sir John and Dame Piozzi;
> Heavens! with what laurels shall thy head be crown'd!
> A grove, a forest, shall thy ears surround!
> Yes! whilst the Rambler shall a comet blaze,
> And gild a world of darkness with his rays,
> Thee, too, that world with wonderment shall hail,
> A lively, bouncing cracker at his tail!

CHAPTER XLII

The works which Goldsmith had still in hand being already paid for and
the money gone, some new scheme must be devised to provide for the
past and the future—for impending debts which threatened to crush
him, and expenses which were continually increasing. He now projected a work of greater compass than he had yet undertaken; a
Dictionary of Arts and Sciences on a comprehensive scale, which was
to occupy a number of volumes. For this he received promises of
assistance from several powerful hands. Johnson was to contribute
an article on ethics; Burke an abstract of his Essay on the Sublime and
Beautiful, an essay on the Berkleyan system of philosophy, and others
on political science; Sir Joshua Reynolds an essay on painting; and
Garrick, while he undertook on his own part to furnish an essay on
acting, engaged Dr. Burney to contribute an article on music. Here
was a great array of talent positively engaged, while other writers of
eminence were to be sought for the various departments of science.
Goldsmith was to edit the whole. An undertaking of this kind, while
it did not incessantly task and exhaust his inventive powers by original
composition, would give agreeable and profitable exercise to his taste
and judgment in selecting, compiling and arranging, and he calculated to diffuse over the whole the acknowledged graces of his style.

He drew up a prospectus of the plan, which is said, by Bishop Percy
who saw it, to have been written with uncommon ability, and to have
had that perspicuity and elegance for which his writings are remarkable. This paper unfortunately is no longer in existence.

Goldsmith's expectations, always sanguine repecting any new plan,
were raised to an extraordinary height by the present project; and well
they might be, when we consider the powerful coajutors already pledged.
They were doomed, however, to complete disappointment. Davies, the
bibliopole of Russell Street, lets us into the secret of this failure.
"The booksellers," said he, "notwithstanding they had a very good
opinion of his abilities, yet were startled at the bulk, importance, and
expense of so geat an undertaking, the fate of which was to depend upon
the industry of a man with whose indolence of temper and method of
procrastination they had long been acquainted."

Goldsmith certainly gave reason for some such distrust by the heedlessness with which he conducted his literary undertakings. Those

219

unfinished, but paid for, would be suspended to make way for some job that was to provide for present necessities. Those thus hastily taken up would be as hastily executed; and the whole, however pressing, would be shoved aside and left "at loose ends" on some sudden call to social enjoyment or recreation.

Cradock tells us that on one occasion, when Goldsmith was hard at work on his Natural History, he sent to Dr. Percy and himself, entreating them to finish some pages of his work which lay upon his table and for which the press was urgent, he being detained by other engagements at Windsor. They met by appointment at his chambers in the Temple, where they found every thing in disorder and costly books lying scattered about on the tables and on the floor; many of the books on natural history which he had recently consulted lay open among uncorrected proofsheets. The subject in hand, and from which he had suddenly broken off, related to birds. "Do you know any thing about birds?" asked Dr. Percy smiling. "Not an atom," replied Cradock; "do you?" "Not I! I scarcely know a goose from a swan: however, let us try what we can do." They set to work and completed their friendly task. Goldsmith, however, when he came to revise it, made such alterations that they could neither of them recognize their own share. The engagement at Windsor, which had thus caused Goldsmith to break off suddenly from his multifarious engagements, was a party of pleasure with some literary ladies. Another anecdote was current, illustrative of the carelessness with which he executed works requiring accuracy and research. On the 22d day of June he had received payment in advance for a Grecian History in two volumes, though only one was finished. As he was pushing on doggedly at the second volume, Gibbon, the historian, called in. "You are the man of all others I wish to see," cried the poet, glad to be saved the trouble of reference to his books. "What was the name of that Indian king who gave Alexander the Great so much trouble?" "Montezuma," replied Gibbon sportively. The heedless author was about committing the name to paper without reflection, when Gibbon pretended to recollect himself, and gave the true name, Porus.

This story very probably was a sportive exaggeration; but it was a multiplicity of anecdotes like this and the preceding one, some true and some false, which had impaired the confidence of booksellers in Goldsmith as a man to be relied on for a task requiring wide and accurate research and close and long continued application. The project of the Universal Dictionary, therefore, met with no encouragement, and fell through.

The failure of this scheme, on which he had built such spacious hopes, sank deep into Goldsmith's heart. He was still further grieved and mortified by the failure of an effort made by some of his friends to obtain for him a pension from government. There had been a talk of the disposition of the ministry to extend the bounty of the crown to distinguished literary men in pecuniary difficulty, without regard to their political creed; when the merits and claims of Goldsmith, however, were laid before them, they met no favor. The sin of sturdy independence lay at his door. He had refused to become a ministerial hack when offered a *carte blanche* by Parson Scott, the cabinet emissary. The wondering parson had left him in poverty and *"his garret,"* and there the ministry were disposed to suffer him to remain.

In the mean time Dr. Beattie comes out with his Essay on Truth, and all the orthodox world are thrown into a paroxysm of contagious ecstasy. He is cried up as the great champion of Christianity against the attacks of modern philosophers and infidels; he is fêted and flattered in every way. He receives at Oxford the honorary degree of doctor of civil law at the same time with Sir Joshua Reynolds. The king sends for him, praises his Essay and gives him a pension of two hundred pounds.

Goldsmith feels more acutely the denial of a pension to himself, when one has thus been given unsolicited to a man he might without vanity consider so much his inferior. He was not one to conceal his feelings. "Here's such a stir," said he one day at Thrale's table, "about a fellow that has written one book, and I have written so many!"

"Ah, Doctor!" exclaimed Johnson, in one of his caustic moods, "there go two and forty sixpences you know, to one guinea." This is one of the cuts at poor Goldsmith in which Johnson went contrary to head and heart in his love for saying what is called a "good thing." No one knew better than himself the comparative superiority of the writings of Goldsmith; but the jingle of the sixpences and the guinea was not to be resisted.

"Every body," exclaimed Mrs. Thrale, "loves Dr. Beattie but Goldsmith, who says he cannot bear the sight of so much applause as they all bestow upon him. Did he not tell us so himself no one would believe he was so exceedingly ill-natured."

He told them so himself because he was too open and unreserved to disguise his feelings and because he really considered the praise lavished on Beattie extravagant, as in fact it was. It was all of course set down to sheer envy and uncharitableness. To add to his annoyance, he found his friend Sir Joshua Reynolds joining in the universal adulation. He had painted a full length portrait of Beattie decked in the doctor's robes in which he had figured at Oxford, with the Essay on Truth under his arm and the angel of truth at his side; while Voltaire figured as one of the demons of infidelity, sophistry, and falsehood, driven into utter darkness.

Goldsmith had known Voltaire in early life; he had been his admirer and his biographer; he grieved to find him receiving such an insult from the classic pencil of his friend. "It is unworthy of you," said he to Sir Joshua, "to debase so high a genius as Voltaire before so mean a writer as Beattie. Beattie and his book will be forgotten in ten years, while Voltaire's fame will last for ever. Take care it does not perpetuate this picture to the shame of such a man as you." This noble and high minded rebuke is the only instance on record of any reproachful words between the poet and the painter; and we are happy to find that it did not destroy the harmony of their intercourse.

CHAPTER XLIII

Toil without hope—The poet in the green room; in the flowergarden; at Vauxhall; dissipation without gayety—Cradock in town; friendly sympathy; a parting scene; an invitation to pleasure

Thwarted in the plans and disappointed in the hopes which had recently cheered and animated him, Goldsmith found the labor at his half finished tasks doubly irksome from the consciousness that the completion of them could not relieve him from his pecuniary embarrassments. His impaired health also rendered him less capable than formerly of sedentary application, and continual perplexities disturbed the flow of thought necessary for original composition. He lost his usual gayety and good humor and became at times peevish and irritable. Too proud of spirit to seek sympathy or relief from his friends for the pecuniary difficulties he had brought upon himself by his errors and extravagance, and unwilling perhaps to make known their amount, he buried his cares and anxieties in his own bosom and endeavored in company to keep up his usual air of gayety and unconcern. This gave his conduct an appearance of fitfulness and caprice, varying suddenly from moodiness to mirth and from silent gravity to shallow laughter; causing surprise and ridicule in those who were not aware of the sickness of heart which lay beneath.

His poetical reputation too was sometimes a disadvantage to him; it drew upon him a notoriety which he was not always in the mood or the vein to act up to . "Good heavens, Mr. Foote," exclaimed an actress at the Haymarket theatre, "what a humdrum kind of man Dr. Goldsmith appears in our green-room compared with the figure he makes in his poetry!" "The reason of that, madam," replied Foote, "is because the Muses are better company than the players."

Beauclerc's letters to his friend Lord Charlemont, who was absent in Ireland, give us now and then an indication of the whereabout of the poet during the present year. "I have been but once to the Club since you left England," writes he; "we were entertained, as usual, with Goldsmith's absurdity." With Beauclerc every thing was absurd that was not polished and pointed. In another letter he threatens, unless Lord Charlemont returns to England, to bring over the whole Club and let them loose upon him to drive him home by their peculiar habits of annoyance—Johnson shall spoil his books; Goldsmith shall *pull his flowers;* and last, and most intolerable of all, Boswell shall—talk to him. It would appear that the poet, who had a passion for flowers, was apt to pass much of his time in the garden when on a visit to a country seat, much to the detriment of the flower beds and the despair of the gardeners.

The summer wore heavily away with Goldsmith. He had not his usual solace of a country retreat; his health was impaired and his spirits depressed. Sir Joshua Reynolds, who perceived the state of his mind, kindly gave him much of his company. In the course of their interchange of thought Goldsmith suggested to him the story of Ugolino as a subject for his pencil. The painting founded on it remains a memento of their friendship.

On the 4th of August we find them together at Vauxhall; at that time a place in high vogue, and which had once been to Goldsmith a scene of oriental splendor and delight. We have, in fact, in the Citizen of the World a picture of it as it had struck him in former years and in his happier moods. "Upon entering the gardens," says the Chinese philosopher, "I found every sense occupied with more than expected pleasure; the lights every where glimmering through the scarcely moving trees; the full-bodied concert bursting on the stillness of the night; the natural concert of the birds in the more retired part of the grove, vying with that which was formed by art; the company gayly dressed looking satisfaction, and the tables spread with various delicacies, all conspired to fill my imagination with the visionary happiness of the Arabian lawgiver, and lifted me into an extacy of admiration."[*]

Every thing now however is seen with different eyes; with him it is dissipation without pleasure; and he finds it impossible any longer by mingling in the gay and giddy throng of apparently prosperous and happy beings to escape from the carking care which is clinging to his heart.

His kind friend Cradock came up to town towards autumn when all the fashionable world was in the country to give his wife the benefit of a skilful dentist. He took lodgings in Norfolk Street to be in Goldsmith's neighborhood and passed most of his mornings with him. "I found him," he says, "much altered and at times very low. He wished me to look over and revise some of his works; but, with a select friend or two, I was more pressing that he should publish by subscription his two celebrated poems of the Traveller and the Deserted Village, with notes." The idea of Cradock was that the subscription would enable wealthy persons favorable to Goldsmith, to contribute to his pecuniary relief without wounding his pride. "Goldsmith," said he, "readily gave up to me his private copies, and said, 'Pray do what you please with them.' But whilst he sat near me he rather submitted to than encouraged my zealous proceedings.

[*] Citizen of the World. Let. LXXI.

"I one morning called upon him, however, and found him infinitely better than I had expected; and in a kind of exulting style he exclaimed, 'Here are some of the best of my prose writings; *I have been hard at work since midnight*, and I desire you to examine them.' 'These,' said I, 'are excellent indeed.' 'They are,' replied he, 'intended as an introduction to a body of arts and sciences.'"

Poor Goldsmith was in fact gathering together the fragments of his shipwreck; the notes, and essays and memoranda collected for his dictionary, and proposed to found on them a work in two volumes to be entitled "A Survey of Experimental Philosophy."

The plan of the subscription came to nothing, and the projected survey never was executed. The head might yet devise, but the heart was failing him; his talent at hoping, which gave him buoyancy to carry out his enterprises, was almost at an end.

Cradock's farewell scene with him is told in a simple but touching manner.

"The day before I was to set out for Leicestershire I insisted upon his dining with us. He replied 'I will, but on one condition, that you will not ask me to eat any thing.' 'Nay,' said I, 'this answer is absolutely unkind, for I had hoped as we are supplied from the Crown and Anchor, that you would have named something you might have relished.' 'Well,' was the reply, 'if you will but explain it to Mrs. Cradock I will certainly wait upon you.'

"The Doctor found as usual at my apartments newspapers and pamphlets, and with a pen and ink he amused himself as well as he could. I had ordered from the tavern some fish, a roasted joint of lamb, and a tart; and the Doctor either sat down or walked about just as he pleased. After dinner he took some wine with biscuits, but I was obliged soon to leave him for a while, as I had matters to settle prior to my next day's journey. On my return coffee was ready, and the Doctor appeared more cheerful (for Mrs. Cradock was always rather a favorite with him) and in the evening he endeavored to talk and remark as usual, but all was force. He stayed till midnight, and I insisted on seeing him safe home, and we most cordially shook hands at the Temple gate." Cradock little thought that this was to be their final parting. He looked back to it with mournful recollections in after years, and lamented that he had not remained longer in town at every inconvenience, to solace the poor broken spirited poet.

The latter continued in town all the autumn. At the opening of the Opera House on the 20th of November Mrs. Yates, an actress whom he held in great esteem, delivered a poetical exordium of his composition. Beauclerc, in a letter to Lord Charlemont, pronounced it 'very good' and predicted that it would soon be in all the papers. It does not appear, however, to have been ever published. In his fitful state of mind Goldsmith may have taken no care about it, and thus it has been lost to the world, although it was received with great applause by a crowded and brilliant audience.

A gleam of sunshine breaks through the gloom that was gathering over the poet. Towards the end of the year he receives another Christmas invitation to Barton. A country Christmas! with all the cordiality of the fireside circle, and the joyous revelry of the oaken hall—what a contrast to the loneliness of a bachelor's chambers in the Temple! It is not to be resisted. But how is poor Goldsmith to raise the ways and means? His purse is empty; his booksellers are already in advance to him. As a last resource, he applies to Garrick. Their mutual intimacy at Barton may have suggested him as an alternative. The old loan of forty pounds has never been paid; and Newbery's note, pledged as a security, has never been taken up. An additional loan of sixty pounds is now asked for, thus increasing the loan to one hundred; to insure the payment, he now offers, besides Newbery's note, the transfer of the comedy of "The Good Natured Man" to Drury Lane, with such alterations as Garrick may suggest. Garrick in reply evades the offer of the altered comedy, alludes significantly to a new one which Goldsmith had talked of writing for him, and offers to furnish the money required on his own acceptance.

The reply of Goldsmith bespeaks a heart brimful of gratitude and overflowing with fond anticipations of Barton and the smiles of its fair residents. "My dear friend," writes he, "I thank you. I wish I could do something to serve you. I shall have a comedy for you in a season or two at farthest that I believe will be worth your acceptance, for I fancy I will make it a fine thing. You shall have the refusal. * * * * I will draw upon you one month after date for sixty pounds and your acceptance will be ready money, *part of which I want to go down to Barton with.* May God preserve my honest little man, for he has my heart. Ever,

"OLIVER GOLDSMITH."

And having thus scrambled together a little pocket money by hard contrivance, poor Goldsmith turns his back upon care and trouble and Temple quarters, to forget for a time his desolate bachelorhood in the family circle and a Christmas fireside at Barton.

CHAPTER XLIV

A return to drudgery—Forced gayety—Retreat to the country—The poem of Retaliation—Portrait of Garrick; of Goldsmith; of Reynolds—Illness of the poet; his death—Grief of his friends—A last work respecting the Jessamy Bride

The Barton festivities are over; Christmas with all its homefelt revelry of the heart has passed like a dream; the Jessamy Bride has beamed her last smile upon the poor poet, and the early part of 1774 finds him in his now dreary bachelor abode in the Temple, toiling fitfully and hopelessly at a multiplicity of tasks. His Animated Nature, so long delayed, so often interrupted, is at length announced for publication though it has yet to receive a few finishing touches. He is preparing a third History of England to be compressed and condensed in one volume for the use of schools. He is revising his Inquiry into Polite Learning, for which he receives the pittance of five guineas, much needed in his present scantiness of purse; he is arranging his Survey of Experimental Philosophy, and he is translating the Comic Romance of Scarron. Such is a part of the various labors of a drudging, depressing kind, by which his head is made weary and his heart faint. "If there is a mental drudgery," says Sir Walter Scott, "which lowers the spirits and lacerates the nerves, like the toil of a slave, it is that which is exacted by literary composition when the heart is not in unison with the work upon which the head is employed. Add to the unhappy author's task sickness, sorrow, or the pressure of unfavorable circumstances, and the labor of the bondsman becomes light in comparison."

Goldsmith again makes an effort to rally his spirits by going into gay society. "Our club," writes Beauclerc to Charlemont on the 12th of February, "has dwindled away to nothing. Sir Joshua and Goldsmith have got into such a round of pleasures that they have no time." This shows how little Beauclerc was the companion of the poet's mind, or could judge of him below the surface. Reynolds, the kind participator in joyless dissipation, could have told a different story of his companion's heartsick gayety.

In this forced mood Goldsmith gave entertainments in his chambers in the Temple; the last of which was a dinner to Johnson, Reynolds and others of his intimates, who partook with sorrow and reluctance of his imprudent hospitality. The first course vexed them by its needless profusion. When a second, equally extravagant, was served up, Johnson and Reynolds declined to partake of it; the rest of the company, understanding their motives, followed their example, and the dishes went from the table untasted. Goldsmith felt sensibly this silent and well intended rebuke.

The gayeties of society, however, cannot medicine for any length of time a mind diseased. Wearied by the distractions and harassed by the expenses of a town life, which he had not the discretion to regulate, Goldsmith took the resolution too tardily adopted, of retiring to the serene quiet, and cheap and healthful pleasures of the country and of passing only two months of the year in London. He accordingly made arrangements to sell his right in the Temple chambers and in the month of March retired to his country quarters at Hyde, there to devote himself to toil. At this dispirited juncture when inspiration seemed to be at an end and the poetic fire extinguished, a spark fell on his combustible imagination and set it in a blaze.

He belonged to a temporary association of men of talent, some of them members of the Literary Club, who dined together occasionally at the St. James's Coffee House. At these dinners as usual he was one of the last to arrive. On one occasion when he was more dilatory than usual, a whim seized the company to write epitaphs on him as "The late Dr. Goldsmith," and several were thrown off in a playful vein hitting off his peculiarities. The only one extant was written by Garrick and has been preserved very probably by its pungency:

> Here lies poet Goldsmith, for shortness called Noll,
> Who wrote like an angel but talked like poor poll.

Goldsmith did not relish the sarcasm, especially as coming from such a quarter. He was not very ready at repartee; but he took his time, and in the interval of his various tasks concocted a series of epigrammatic sketches, under the title of Retaliation, in which the characters of his distinguished intimates were admirably hit off, with a mixture of generous praise and good humored raillery. In fact the poem for its graphic truth; its nice discrimination; its terse good sense and its shrewd knowledge of the world must have electrified the Club almost as much as the first appearance of The Traveller, and let them still deeper into the character and talents of the man they had been accustomed to consider as their butt. Retaliation, in a word, closed his accounts with the Club and balanced all his previous deficiencies.

The portrait of David Garrick is one of the most elaborate in the poem. When the poet came to touch it off, he had some lurking piques to gratify, which the recent attack had revived. He may have forgotten David's cavalier treatment of him, in the early days of his comparative obscurity; he may have forgiven his refusal of his plays; but Garrick had been capricious in his conduct in the times of their recent intercourse: sometimes treating him with gross familiarity, at other times affecting dignity and reserve and assuming airs of superiority; frequently he had been facetious and witty in company at his expense, and lastly he had been guilty of the couplet just quoted. Goldsmith therefore touched off the lights and shadows of his character with a free hand, and, at the same time, gave a side hit at his old rival, Kelly, and his critical persecutor, Kenrick, in making them sycophantic satellites of the actor. Goldsmith, however, was void of gall even in his revenge, and his very satire was more humorous than caustic:

> Here lies David Garrick, describe him who can,
> An abridgment of all that was pleasant in man;
> As an actor, confess'd without rival to shine;
> As a wit, if not first, in the very first line:
> Yet, with talents like these, and an excellent heart,
> The man had his failings, a dupe to his art.
> Like an ill-judging beauty, his colours he spread,
> And beplaster'd with rouge his own natural red.
> On the stage he was natural, simple, affecting;
> 'Twas only that when he was off he was acting.
> With no reason on earth to go out of his way,
> He turn'd and he varied full ten times a day:
> Though secure of our hearts, yet confoundedly sick
> If they were not his own by finessing and trick:
> He cast off his friends as a huntsman his pack,
> For he knew, when he pleased, he could whistle them back.
> Of praise a mere glutton, he swallow'd what came,
> And the puff of a dunce he mistook it for fame;
> Till his relish, grown callous almost to disease,
> Who pepper'd the highest was surest to please.
> But let us be candid, and speak out our mind,
> If dunces applauded, he paid them in kind.
> Ye Kenricks, ye Kellys, and Woodfalls so grave,
> What a commerce was yours, while you got and you gave!
> How did Grub-street re-echo the shouts that you raised,
> While he was be-Rosciused and you were be-praised!
> But peace to his spirit, wherever it flies,
> To act as an angel and mix with the skies:
> Those poets who owe their best fame to his skill,
> Shall still be his flatterers, go where he will;
> Old Shakspeare receive him with praise and with love,
> And Beaumonts and Bens be his Kellys above.

This portion of Retaliation soon brought a retort from Garrick, which we insert as giving something of a likeness of Goldsmith, though in broad caricature:

> Here, Hermes, says Jove, who with nectar was mellow,
> Go fetch me some clay—I will make an odd fellow:
> Right and wrong shall be jumbled, much gold and some dross,
> Without cause be he pleased, without cause be he cross;
> Be sure, as I work, to throw in contradictions,
> A great love of truth, yet a mind turn'd to fictions;
> Now mix these ingredients, which, warm'd in the baking,
> Turn'd to *learning* and *gaming, religion* and *raking.*
> With the love of a wench let his writings be chaste;
> Tip his tongue with strange matter, his lips with fine taste;
> That the rake and the poet o'er all may prevail,
> Set fire to the head and set fire to the tail;
> For the joy of each sex on the world I'll bestow it,
> This scholar, rake, Christian, dupe, gamester, and poet.
> Though a mixture so odd, he shall merit great fame,
> And among brother mortals be Goldsmith his name;
> When on earth this strange meteor no more shall appear,
> You, *Hermes,* shall fetch him, to make us sport here.

The charge of raking, so repeatedly advanced in the foregoing lines, must be considered a sportive one, founded perhaps on an incident or two within Garrick's knowledge, but not borne out by the course of Goldsmith's life. He seems to have had a tender sentiment for the sex, but perfectly free from libertinism. Neither was he an habitual gamester. The strictest scrutiny has detected no settled vice of the kind. He was fond of a game of cards, but an unskilful and careless player. Cards in those days were universally introduced into society. High play was in fact a fashionable amusement, as, at one time, was deep drinking; and a man might occasionally lose large sums, and be beguiled into deep potations without incurring the character of a gamester or a drunkard. Poor Goldsmith on his advent into high society assumed fine notions with fine clothes. He was thrown occasionally among high play-ers, men of fortune who could sport their cool hundreds as carelessly as his early comrades at Ballymahon could their half crowns. Being at all times magnificent in money matters, he may have played with them in their own way without considering that what was sport to them to him was ruin. Indeed part of his financial embarrassments may have arisen from losses of the kind incurred inadvertently, not in the indul-gence of a habit. "I do not believe Goldsmith to have deserved the name of gamester," said one of his contemporaries; "he liked cards very well as other people do, and lost and won occasionally; but as far as I saw or heard, and I had many opportunities of hearing, never any considerable sums. If he gamed with any one, it was probably with Beauclerc, but I do not know that such was the case."

Retaliation, as we have already observed, was thrown off in parts, at intervals, and was never completed. Some characters, originally intended to be introduced, remained unattempted; others were but partially sketched. Such was the one of Reynolds, the friend of his heart, and which he commenced with a felicity which makes us regret that it should remain unfinished.

> Here Reynolds is laid, and to tell you my mind,
> He has not left a wiser or better behind.
> His pencil was striking, resistless and grand;
> His manners were gentle, complying and bland;
> Still born to improve us in every part,
> His pencil our faces, his manners our heart.
> To coxcombs averse, yet most civilly steering,
> When they judged without skill he was still hard of hearing:
> When they talked of their Raphaels, Corregios and stuff,
> He shifted his trumpet and only took snuff.
> By flattery unspoiled ———

The friendly portrait stood unfinished on the easel; the hand of the artist had failed! An access of a local complaint, under which he had suffered for some time past, added to a general prostration of health, brought Goldsmith back to town before he had well settled himself in the country. The local complaint subsided but was followed by a low nervous fever. He was not aware of his critical situation and intended to be at the Club on the 25th of March, on which occasion Charles Fox, Sir Charles Bunbury, one of the Horneck connection, and two other new members were to be present. In the afternoon, however, he felt so unwell as to take to his bed; and his symptoms soon acquired sufficient force to keep him there. His malady fluctuated for several days, and hopes were entertained of his recovery, but they proved fallacious. He had skilful medical aid and faithful nursing, but he would not follow the advice of his physicians and persisted in the use of James's powders, which he had once found beneficial but which were now injurious to him. His appetite was gone, his strength failed him, but his mind remained clear, and was perhaps too active for his frame. Anxieties and disappointments which had previously sapped his constitution doubtless aggravated his present complaint and rendered him sleepless. In reply to an inquiry of his physician he acknowledged that his mind was ill at ease. This was his last reply; he was too weak to talk and in general took no notice of what was said to him. He sank at last into a deep sleep, and it was hoped a favorable crisis had arrived. He awoke however in strong convulsions, which continued without intermission until he expired on the fourth of April at five o'clock in the morning; being in the forty sixth year of his age.

His death was a shock to the literary world and a deep affliction to a wide circle of intimates and friends; for, with all his foibles and peculiarities, he was fully as much beloved as he was admired. Burke on hearing the news burst into tears. Sir Joshua Reynolds threw by his pencil for the day and grieved more than he had done in times of great family distress. "I was abroad at the time of his death," writes Dr. M'Donnell, the youth whom when in distress he had employed as an amanuensis, "and I wept bitterly when the intelligence first reached me. A blank came over my heart as if I had lost one of my nearest relatives, and was followed for some days by a feeling of despondency." Johnson felt the blow deeply and gloomily. In writing some time afterwards to Boswell he observed, "Of poor Dr. Goldsmith there is little to be told more than the papers have made public. He died of a fever, made, I am afraid, more violent by uneasiness of mind. His debts began to be heavy, and all his resources were exhausted. Sir Joshua is of opinion that he owed no less than two thousand pounds. Was ever poet so trusted before?"

Among his debts were seventy nine pounds due to his tailor, Mr. William Filby, from whom he had received a new suit but a few days before his death. "My father," said the younger Filby, "though a loser to that amount, attributed no blame to Goldsmith; he had been a good customer, and had he lived, would have paid every farthing." Others of his tradespeople evinced the same confidence in his integrity notwithstanding his heedlessness. Two sister milliners in Temple Lane, who had been accustomed to deal with him, were concerned when told some time before his death of his pecuniary embarrassments. "Oh Sir," said they to Mr. Cradock, "sooner persuade him to let us work for him gratis than apply to any other; we are sure he will pay us when he can."

On the stairs of his apartment there was the lamentation of the old and infirm, and the sobbing of women; poor objects of his charity, to whom he had never turned a deaf ear, even when struggling himself with poverty.

But there was one mourner whose enthusiasm for his memory, could it have been foreseen, might have soothed the bitterness of death. After the coffin had been screwed down, a lock of his hair was requested for a lady, a particular friend, who wished to preserve it as a remembrance.

It was the beautiful Mary Horneck—the Jessamy Bride. The coffin was opened again, and a lock of hair cut off; which she treasured to her dying day. Poor Goldsmith! could he have foreseen that such a memorial of him was to be thus cherished!

One word more concerning this lady, to whom we have so often ventured to advert. She survived almost to the present day. Hazlitt met her at Northcote's painting room about twenty years since as Mrs. Gwyn, the widow of a General Gwyn of the army. She was at that time upwards of seventy years of age. Still, he said, she was beautiful, beautiful even in years. After she was gone, Hazlitt remarked how handsome she still was. "I dont know," said Northcote, "why she is so kind as to come to see me, except that I am the last link in the chain that connects her with all those she most esteemed when young, Johnson, Reynolds, Goldsmith—and remind her of the most delightful period of her life." "Not only so," observed Hazlitt, "but you remember what she was at twenty; and you thus bring back to her the triumphs of her youth—that pride of beauty which must be the more fondly cherished as it has no external vouchers, and lives chiefly in the bosom of its once lovely possessor. In her, however, the Graces had triumphed over time; she was one of Ninon de l'Enclos' people, of the last of the immortals. I could almost fancy the shade of Goldsmith in the room, looking round with complacency."

The Jessamy Bride survived her sister upwards of forty years and died in 1840 within a few days of completing her eighty eighth year. "She had gone through all the stages of life," said Northcote, "and had lent a grace to each." However gayly she may have sported with the half concealed admiration of the poor awkward poet in the heyday of her youth and beauty, and however much it may have been made a subject of teasing by her youthful companions, she evidently prided herself in after years upon having been an object of his affectionate regard; it certainly rendered her interesting throughout life in the eyes of his admirers, and has hung a poetical wreath above her grave.

CHAPTER XLV

The funeral—The monument—The epitaph—Concluding remarks

In the warm feeling of the moment while the remains of the poet were scarce cold, it was determined by his friends to honor them by a public funeral and a tomb in Westminster Abbey. His very pall bearers were designated: Lord Shelburne, Lord Lowth, Sir Joshua Reynolds; the Hon. Mr. Beauclerc, Mr. Burke and David Garrick. This feeling cooled down, however, when it was discovered that he died in debt, and had not left wherewithal to pay for such expensive obsequies. Five days after his death, therefore, at five o'clock of Saturday evening, the 9th of April, he was privately interred in the burying ground of the Temple Church; a few persons attending as mourners, among whom we do not find specified any of his peculiar and distinguished friends. The chief mourner was Sir Joshua Reynolds's nephew Palmer, afterwards Dean of Cashel. One person, however, from whom it was but little to be expected, attended the funeral and evinced real sorrow on the occasion. This was Hugh Kelly, once the dramatic rival of the deceased, and often, it is said, his anonymous assailant in the newspapers. If he had really been guilty of this basest of literary offences, he was punished by the stings of remorse, for we are told that he shed bitter tears over the grave of the man he had injured. His tardy atonement only provoked the lash of some unknown satirist, as the following lines will show:

> Hence Kelly, who years, without honour or shame,
> Had been sticking his bodkin in Oliver's fame,
> Who thought, like the Tartar, by this to inherit
> His genius, his learning, simplicity, spirit;
> Now sets every feature to weep o'er his fate,
> And acts as a mourner to blubber in state.

One base wretch deserves to be mentioned, the reptile Kenrick, who, after having repeatedly slandered Goldsmith while living, had the audacity to insult his memory when dead. The following distich is sufficient to show his malignancy, and to hold him up to execration:

> By his own art, who justly died,
> A blund'ring, artless suicide:
> Share, earthworms, share, since now he's dead,
> His megrim, maggot-bitten head.

234

This scurrilous epitaph produced a burst of public indignation, that awed for a time even the infamous Kenrick into silence. On the other hand, the press teemed with tributes in verse and prose to the memory of the deceased; all evincing the mingled feeling of admiration for the author and affection for the man.

Not long after his death the Literary Club set on foot a subscription and raised a fund to erect a monument to his memory, in Westminster Abbey. It was executed by Nollekens and consisted simply of a bust of the poet in profile, in high relief, in a medallion, and was placed in the area of a pointed arch, over the south door in Poets' Corner between the monuments of Gay and the Duke of Argyll. Johnson furnished a Latin epitaph, which was read at the table of Sir Joshua Reynolds, where several members of the Club and other friends of the deceased were present. Though considered by them a masterly composition, they thought the literary character of the poet not defined with sufficient exactness, and they preferred that the epitaph should be in English rather than Latin, as "the memory of so eminent an English writer ought to be perpetuated in the language to which his works were to be so lasting an ornament."

These objections were reduced to writing to be respectfully submitted to Johnson, but such was the awe entertained of his frown that every one shrank from putting his name first to the instrument; whereupon their names were written about it in a circle, making what mutinous sailors call a Round Robin. Johnson received it half graciously half grimly. He was willing, he said, to modify the sense of the epitaph in any manner the gentlemen pleased; *"but he never would consent to disgrace the walls of Westminster Abbey with an English inscription."* Seeing the names of Dr. Warton and Edmund Burke among the signers, "he wondered," he said, "that Joe Warton, a scholar by profession, should be such a fool; and should have thought that Mund Burke would have had more sense." The following is the epitaph as it stands inscribed on a white marble tablet beneath the bust:

"OLIVARII GOLDSMITH,

Poetæ, Physici, Historici,
Qui nullum ferè scribendi genus
Non tetigit,
Nullum quod tetigit non ornavit:
Sive risus essent movendi,
Sive lacrymæ,
Affectuum potens at lenis dominator:
Ingenio sublimis, vividus, versatilis,

Oratione grandis, nitidus, venustus:
Hoc monumento memoriam coluit
Sodalium amor,
Amicorum fides,
Lectorum veneratio.
Natus in Hiberniâ Forniæ Longfordiensis,
In loco cui nomen Pallas,
Nov. xxix. MDCCXXXI.;
Eblanæ literis institutus;
Obiit Londini,
April iv. MDCCLXXIV."*

We shall not pretend to follow these anecdotes of the life of Goldsmith with any critical dissertation on his writings; their merits have long since been fully discussed, and their station in the scale of literary merit permanently established. They have outlasted generations of works of higher power and wider scope, and will continue to outlast succeeding generations, for they have that magic charm of style by which works are embalmed to perpetuity. Neither shall we attempt a regular analysis of the character of the poet, but will indulge in a few desultory remarks in addition to those scattered throughout the preceding chapters.

Never was the trite, because sage apothegm, that "The child is father

---

* The following translation is from Croker's edition of Boswell's Johnson:

OF OLIVER GOLDSMITH—
A Poet, Naturalist, and Historian,
Who left scarcely any style of writing
untouched,
And touched nothing that he did not adorn;
Of all the passions,
Whether smiles were to be moved
or tears,
A powerful yet gentle master;
In genius, sublime, vivid, versatile,
In style, elevated, clear, elegant—
The love of companions,
The fidelity of friends,
And the veneration of readers,
Have by this monument honored the memory.
He was born in Ireland,
At a place called Pallas,
[In the parish] of Forney, [and county] of Longford,
On the 29th Nov., 1731,
Educated at [the University of] Dublin,
And died in London,
4th April, 1774.

to the man," more fully verified than in the case of Goldsmith. He is shy, awkward and blundering in childhood yet full of sensibility; he is a butt for the jeers and jokes of his companions, but apt to surprise and confound them by sudden and witty repartees; he is dull and stupid at his tasks, yet an eager and intelligent devourer of the travelling tales and campaigning stories of his half military pedagogue; he may be a dunce, but he is already a rhymer; and his early scintillations of poetry awaken the expectations of his friends. He seems from infancy to have been compounded of two natures, one bright, the other blundering; or to have had fairy gifts laid in his cradle by the "good people" who haunted his birthplace, the old goblin mansion on the banks of the Inny.

He carries with him the wayward elfin spirit, if we may so term it, throughout his career. His fairy gifts are of no avail at school, academy or college. They unfit him for close study and practical science, and render him heedless of every thing that does not address itself to his poetical imagination and genial and festive feelings; they dispose him to break away from restraint; to stroll about hedges, green lanes and haunted streams; to revel with jovial companions, or to rove the country like a gipsy in quest of odd adventures.

As if confiding in these delusive gifts, he takes no heed of the present nor care for the future, lays no regular and solid foundation of knowledge, follows out no plan, adopts and discards those recommended by his friends, at one time prepares for the ministry, next turns to the law, and then fixes upon medicine. He repairs to Edinburgh, the great emporium of medical science, but the fairy gifts accompany him. He idles and frolics away his time there, imbibing only such knowledge as is agreeable to him; makes an excursion to the poetical regions of the Highlands; and having walked the hospitals for the customary time, sets off to ramble over the Continent, in quest of novelty rather than knowledge. His whole tour is a poetical one. He fancies he is playing the philosopher while he is really playing the poet; and though professedly he attends lectures and visits foreign universities, so deficient is he on his return in the studies for which he set out, that he fails in an examination as a surgeon's mate; and while figuring as a doctor of medicine, is outvied on a point of practice by his apothecary. Baffled in every regular pursuit, after trying in vain some of the humbler callings of commonplace life, he is driven almost by chance to the exercise of his pen, and here the fairy gifts come to his assistance. For a long time however he seems unaware of the magic properties of that pen: he uses it only as a make shift, until he can find a *legitimate* means of support. He is not a learned man and can write but meagerly and at secondhand on learned subjects; but he has a quick convertible talent that seizes lightly on the points of knowledge necessary to the illustration of a theme: his writings for a time are desultory, the fruits of what he has seen and felt or what he has recently and hastily read; but his gifted pen transmutes every thing into gold, and his own genial nature reflects its sunshine through his pages.

Still unaware of his powers he throws off his writings anonymously, to go with the writings of less favored men; and it is a long time and after a bitter struggle with poverty and humiliation, before he acquires confidence in his literary talent as a means of support and begins to dream of reputation.

From this time his pen is a wand of power in his hand, and he has only to use it discreetly, to make it competent to all his wants. But discretion is not a part of Goldsmith's nature; and it seems the property of these fairy gifts to be accompanied by moods and temperaments to render their effect precarious. The heedlessness of his early days; his disposition for social enjoyment; his habit of throwing the present on the neck of the future still continue. His expenses forerun his means; he incurs debts on the faith of what his magic pen is to produce, and then, under the pressure of his debts, sacrifices its productions for prices far below their value. It is a redeeming circumstance in his prodigality that it is lavished oftener upon others than upon himself: he gives without thought or stint and is the continual dupe of his benevolence and his trustfulness in human nature. We may say of him as he says of one of his heroes, "He could not stifle the natural impulse which he had to do good, but frequently borrowed money to relieve the distressed; and when he knew not conveniently where to borrow, he has been observed to shed tears as he passed through the wretched suppliants who attended his gate."   *   *   *   *   *

"His simplicity in trusting persons whom he had no previous reasons to place confidence in, seems to be one of those lights of his character which, while they impeach his understanding, do honour to his benevolence. The low and the timid are ever suspicious; but a heart impressed with honorable sentiments, expects from others sympathetic sincerity."*

His heedlessness in pecuniary matters, which had rendered his life a struggle with poverty even in the days of his obscurity, rendered the struggle still more intense when his fairy gifts had elevated him into the society of the wealthy and luxurious, and imposed on his simple and generous spirit fancied obligations to a more ample and bounteous display.

"How comes it," says a recent and ingenious critic, "that in all the miry paths of life which he had trod, no speck ever sullied the robe of his modest and graceful muse. How amidst all that love of inferior

---

* Goldsmith's Life of Nashe.

company, which never to the last forsook him, did he keep his genius so free from every touch of vulgarity?"

We answer that it was owing to the innate purity and goodness of his nature; there was nothing in it that assimilated to vice and vulgarity. Though his circumstances often compelled him to associate with the poor, they never could betray him into companionship with the depraved. His relish for humor and for the study of character, as we have before observed, brought him often into convivial company of a vulgar kind; but he discriminated between their vulgarity and their amusing qualities, or rather wrought from the whole those familiar pictures of life which form the staple of his most popular writings.

Much too of this intact purity of heart may be ascribed to the lessons of his infancy under the paternal roof; to the gentle, benevolent, elevated, unworldly maxims of his father, who "passing rich with forty pounds a year," infused a spirit into his child which riches could not deprave nor poverty degrade. Much of his boyhood too had been passed in the household of his uncle, the amiable and generous Contarine; where he talked of literature with the good pastor and practised music with his daughter and delighted them both by his juvenile attempts at poetry. These early associations breathed a grace and refinement into his mind and toned it up, after the rough sports on the green or the frolics at the tavern. These led him to turn from the roaring glees of the club to listen to the harp of his cousin Jane; and from the rustic triumph of "throwing sledge" to a stroll with his flute along the pastoral banks of the Inny.

The gentle spirit of his father walked with him through life, a pure and virtuous monitor; and in all the vicissitudes of his career we find him ever more chastened in mind by the sweet and holy recollections of the home of his infancy.

It has been questioned whether he really had any religious feeling. Those who raise the question have never considered well his writings; his Vicar of Wakefield, and his pictures of the village pastor, present religion under its most endearing forms and with a feeling that could only flow from the deep convictions of the heart. When his fair travelling companions at Paris urged him to read the Church Service on a Sunday, he replied that "he was not worthy to do it." He had seen in early life the sacred offices performed by his father and his brother with a solemnity which had sanctified them in his memory; how could he presume to undertake such functions? His religion has been called in question by Johnson and by Boswell: he certainly had not the gloomy hypochondriacal piety of the one, nor the babbling mouth piety of the other; but the spirit of Christian charity breathed forth in his writings and illustrated in his conduct give us reason to believe he had the indwelling religion of the soul.

We have made sufficient comments in the preceding chapters on his conduct in elevated circles of literature and fashion. The fairy gifts which took him there were not accompanied by the gifts and graces necessary to sustain him in that artificial sphere. He can neither play the learned sage with Johnson nor the fine gentleman with Beauclerc; though he has a mind replete with wisdom and natural shrewdness and a spirit free from vulgarity. The blunders of a fertile but hurried intellect and the awkward display of the student assuming the man of fashion fix on him a character for absurdity and vanity which like the charge of lunacy it is hard to disprove, however weak the grounds of the charge and strong the facts in opposition to it.

In truth he is never truly in his place in these learned and fashionable circles, which talk and live for display. It is not the kind of society he craves. His heart yearns for domestic life; it craves familiar, confiding intercourse, family firesides, the guileless and happy company of children; these bring out the heartiest and sweetest sympathies of his nature.

"Had it been his fate," says the critic we have already quoted, "to meet a woman who could have loved him despite his faults, and respected him despite his foibles, we cannot but think that his life and his genius would have been much more harmonious; his desultory affections would have been concentred, his craving self-love appeased, his pursuits more settled, his character more solid. A nature like Goldsmith's, so affectionate, so confiding—so susceptible to simple innocent enjoyments— so dependent on others for the sunshine of existence, does not flower if deprived of the atmosphere of home."

The cravings of his heart in this respect are evident, we think, throughout his career; and if we have dwelt with more significancy than others upon his intercourse with the beautiful Horneck family, it is because we fancied we could detect, amid his playful attentions to one of its members, a lurking sentiment of tenderness, kept down by conscious poverty and a humiliating idea of personal defects. A hopeless feeling of this kind—the last a man would communicate to his friends—might account for much of that fitfulness of conduct and that gathering melancholy, remarked but not comprehended by his associates during the last year or two of his life; and may have been one of the troubles of the mind which aggravated his last illness and only terminated with his death.

We shall conclude these desultory remarks with a few which have been used by us on a former occasion. From the general tone of Goldsmith's biography, it is evident that his faults, at the worst, were but negative, while his merits were great and decided. He was no one's enemy but his own; his errors, in the main, inflicted evil on none but himself, and were so blended with humorous, and even affecting circumstances, as to disarm anger and conciliate kindness. Where eminent talent is united to spotless virtue, we are awed and dazzled into admiration, but our admiration is apt to be cold and reverential; while there is something in the harmless infirmities of a good and great, but erring individual, that pleads touchingly to our nature; and we turn more kindly towards the object of our idolatry, when we find that, like ourselves, he is mortal and is frail. The epithet so often heard, and in such kindly tones, of "poor Goldsmith," speaks volumes. Few, who consider the real compound of admirable and whimsical qualities which form his character, would wish to prune away its eccentricities, trim its grotesque luxuriance, and clip it down to the decent formalities of rigid virtue. "Let not his frailties be remembered," said Johnson; "he was a very great man." But, for our part, we rather say "Let them be remembered," since their tendency is to endear; and we question whether he himself would not feel gratified in hearing his reader, after dwelling with admiration on the proofs of his greatness, close the volume with the kind hearted phrase, so fondly and familiarly ejaculated, of "POOR GOLDSMITH."

THE END

BIOGRAPHY

OF

THE LATE

MARGARET MILLER DAVIDSON.

Thou wert unfit to dwell with clay,
  For sin too pure, for earth too bright!
And death, who call'd thee hence away,
  Placed on his brow a gem of light!

Margaret to her Sister.

Mrs. Margaret Miller Davidson

BIOGRAPHY

of

MISS MARGARET DAVIDSON.

The reading world has long set a cherishing value on the name of Lucretia Davidson, a lovely American girl, who, after giving early promise of rare poetic excellence, was snatched from existence in the seventeenth year of her age. An interesting biography of her by President Morse of the American Society of Arts, was published shortly after her death; another has since appeared from the classic pen of Miss Sedgwick, and her name has derived additional celebrity in Great Britain from an able article by Robert Southey, inserted some years since in the London Quarterly Review.

An intimate acquaintance in early life with some of the relatives of Miss Davidson had caused me, while in Europe, to read with great interest every thing concerning her; when, therefore, in 1833, about a year after my return to the United States, I was told, while in New York, that Mrs. Davidson, the mother of the deceased, was in the city and desirous of consulting me about a new edition of her daughter's works, I lost no time in waiting upon her. Her appearance corresponded with the interesting idea given of her in her daughter's biography; she was feeble and emaciated, and supported by pillows in an easy chair, but there were the lingerings of grace and beauty in her form and features, and her eye still gleamed with intelligence and sensibility.

While conversing with her on the subject of her daughter's works, I observed a young girl, apparently not more than eleven years of age, moving quietly about her; occasionally arranging a pillow, and at the same time listening earnestly to our conversation. There was an intellectual beauty about this child that struck me; and that was heightened by a blushing diffidence when Mrs. Davidson presented her to me as her daughter Margaret. Shortly afterwards, on her leaving the room, her mother, seeing that she had attracted my attention, spoke of her as having evinced the same early poetical talent that had distinguished her sister, and as evidence, showed me several copies of verses remarkable for such a child. On further inquiry I found that she had very nearly the same moral and physical constitution, and was prone to the same feverish excitement of the mind, and kindling of the imagination that had acted so powerfully on the fragile frame of her sister Lucretia. I cautioned the mother, therefore, against fostering her poetic vein, and

245

advised such studies and pursuits as would tend to strengthen her judgment, calm and regulate the sensibilities, and enlarge that common sense which is the only safe foundation for all intellectual superstructure.

I found Mrs. Davidson fully aware of the importance of such a course of treatment, and disposed to pursue it, but saw at the same time that she would have difficulty to carry it into effect; having to contend with the additional excitement produced in the mind of this sensitive little being by the example of her sister, and the intense enthusiasm she evinced concerning her.

Three years elapsed before I again saw the subject of this memoir. She was then residing with her mother at a rural retreat in the neighbourhood of New York. The interval that had elapsed had rapidly developed the powers of her mind, and heightened the loveliness of her person, but my apprehensions had been verified. The soul was wearing out the body. Preparations were making to take her on a tour for the benefit of her health, and her mother appeared to flatter herself that it might prove efficacious; but when I noticed the fragile delicacy of her form, the hectic bloom of her cheek, and the almost unearthly lustre of her eye, I felt convinced that she was not long for this world; in truth, she already appeared more spiritual than mortal. We parted, and I never saw her more. Within three years afterwards a number of manuscripts were placed in my hands, as all that was left of her. They were accompanied by copious memoranda concerning her, furnished by her mother at my request. From these I have digested and arranged the following particulars, adopting in many places the original manuscript, without alteration. In fact, the narrative will be found almost as illustrative of the character of the mother as of the child; they were singularly identified in taste, feelings, and pursuits; tenderly entwined together by maternal and filial affection; they reflected an inexpressibly touching grace and interest upon each other by this holy relationship, and, to my mind, it would be marring one of the most beautiful and affecting groups in the history of modern literature, to sunder them.

Margaret Miller Davidson, the youngest daughter of Dr. Oliver and Mrs. Margaret Davidson, was born at the family residence on Lake Champlain, in the village of Plattsburgh, on the 26th of March, 1823. She evinced fragility of constitution from her very birth. Her sister Lucretia, whose brief poetical career has been so celebrated in literary history, was her early and fond attendant, and some of her most popular lays were composed with the infant sporting in her arms. She used to gaze upon her little sister with intense delight, and, remarking the uncommon brightness and beauty of her eyes, would exclaim,

"She must, she will be a poet!" The exclamation was natural enough in an enthusiastic girl who regarded every thing through the medium of her ruling passion; but it was treasured up by her mother, and considered almost prophetic. Lucretia did not live to see her prediction verified. Her brief sojourn upon earth was over before Margaret was quite two years and a half old; yet, to use her mother's fond expressions, "On ascending to the skies, it seemed as if her poetic mantle fell, like a robe of light, on her infant sister."

Margaret, from the first dawnings of intellect, gave evidence of being no common child: her ideas and expressions were not like those of other children, and often startled by their precocity. Her sister's death had made a strong impression on her, and, though so extremely young, she already understood and appreciated Lucretia's character. An evidence of this, and of the singular precocity of thought and expression just noticed, occurred but a few months afterwards. As Mrs. Davidson was seated, at twilight, conversing with a female friend, Margaret entered the room with a light elastic step, for which she was remarked.

"That child never walks," said the lady; then turning to her, "Margaret, where are you flying now?" said she.

"To heaven!" replied she, pointing up with her finger, "to meet my sister Lucretia, when I get my new wings."

"Your new wings! When will you get them?"

"Oh soon, very soon; and then I shall fly!"

"She loved," says her mother, "to sit hour after hour on a cushion at my feet, her little arms resting upon my lap, and her full dark eyes fixed upon mine, listening to anecdotes of her sister's life and details of the events which preceded her death, often exclaiming, while her face beamed with mingled emotions, 'Oh mamma, I will try to fill her place! Oh teach me to be like her!'"

Much of Mrs. Davidson's time was now devoted to her daily instruction; noticing, however, her lively sensibility, the rapid developement of her mind, and her eagerness for knowledge, her lessons were entirely oral, for she feared for the present to teach her to read, lest, by too early and severe application, she should injure her delicate frame. She had nearly attained her fourth year before she was taught to spell. Ill health then obliged Mrs. Davidson, for the space of a year, to entrust her tuition to a lady in Canada, a valued friend, who had other young girls under her care. When she returned home she could read fluently, and had commenced lessons in writing. It was now decided that she should not be placed in any public seminary, but that her education should be conducted by her mother. The task was rendered delightful by the docility of the pupil; by her affectionate feelings, and quick kindling sensibilities. This maternal instruction, while it kept her apart from the world, and fostered a singular purity and innocence of thought, contributed greatly to enhance her imaginative powers, for the mother partook largely of the poetical temperament of the child; it was, in fact, one poetical spirit ministering to another.

Among the earliest indications of the poetical character in this child were her perceptions of the beauty of natural scenery. Her home was in a picturesque neighbourhood, calculated to awaken and foster such perceptions. The following description of it is taken from one of her own writings: "There stood on the banks of the Saranac a small neat cottage, which peeped forth from the surrounding foliage, the image of rural quiet and contentment. An old-fashioned piazza extended along the front, shaded with vines and honeysuckles; the turf on the bank of the river was of the richest and brightest emerald; and the wild rose and sweet briar, which twined over the neat enclosure, seemed to bloom with more delicate freshness and perfume within the bounds of this earthly paradise. The scenery around was wildly yet beautifully romantic; the clear blue river, glancing and sparkling at its feet, seemed only as a preparation for another and more magnificent view, when the stream, gliding on to the west, was buried in the broad white bosom of Champlain, which stretched back, wave after wave in the distance, until lost in faint blue mists that veiled the sides of its guardian mountains, seeming more lovely from their indistinctness."

Such were the natural scenes which presented themselves to her dawning perceptions, and she is said to have evinced, from her earliest childhood, a remarkable sensibility to their charms. A beautiful tree, or shrub, or flower would fill her with delight; she would note with surprising discrimination the various effects of the weather upon the surrounding landscape; the mountains wrapt in clouds; the torrents roaring down their sides in times of tempest; the "bright warm sunshine," the "cooling shower," the "pale cold moon," for such was already her poetical phraseology. A bright starlight night, also, would seem to awaken a mysterious rapture in her infant bosom, and one of her early expressions in speaking of the stars was, that they "shone like the eyes of angels."

One of the most beautiful parts of the maternal instruction was in guiding these kindling perceptions from nature up to nature's God.

"I cannot say," observes her mother, "at what age her religious impressions were imbibed. They seemed to be interwoven with her existence. From the very first exercise of reason she evinced strong devotional feelings, and, although she loved play, she would at any time prefer seating herself beside me, and, with every faculty absorbed in the subject, listen while I attempted to recount the wonders of Providence, and point out the wisdom and benevolence of God, as manifested in the works of creation. Her young heart would swell with rapture, and the tear would tremble in her eye, when I explained to her, that he who clothed the trees with verdure, and gave the rose its bloom, had also created her with capacities to enjoy their beauties: that the same power which clothed the mountains with sublimity, made her happiness his daily care. Thus a sentiment of gratitude and affection towards the Creator entered into all her emotions of delight at the wonders and beauties of creation."

There is nothing more truly poetical than religion when properly inculcated, and it will be found that this early piety, thus amiably instilled, had the happiest effect upon her throughout life; elevating and ennobling her genius; lifting her above every thing gross and sordid; attuning her thoughts to pure and lofty themes; heightening rather than impairing her enjoyments, and at all times giving an ethereal lightness to her spirit. To use her mother's words, "she was like a bird on the wing, her fairy form scarcely seemed to touch the earth as she passed." She was at times in a kind of ecstasy from the excitement of her imagination and the exuberance of her pleasurable sensations. In such moods every object of natural beauty inspired a degree of rapture always mingled with a feeling of gratitude to the Being "who had made so many beautiful things for her." In such moods too her little heart would overflow with love to all around; indeed, adds her mother, to love and be beloved was necessary to her existence. Private prayer became a habit with her at a very early age; it was almost a spontaneous expression of her feelings, the breathings of an affectionate and delighted heart.

"By the time she was six years old," says Mrs. Davidson, "her language assumed an elevated tone, and her mind seemed filled with poetic imagery, blended with veins of religious thought. At this period I was chiefly confined to my room by debility. She was my companion and friend, and, as the greater part of my time was devoted to her instruction, she advanced rapidly in her studies. She read not only well, but elegantly. Her love of reading amounted almost to a passion, and her intelligence surpassed belief. Strangers viewed with astonishment a child little more than six years old reading with enthusiastic delight Thomson's Seasons, the Pleasures of Hope, Cowper's Task, the writings of Milton, Byron, and Scott, and marking, with taste and discrimination, the passages which struck her. The sacred writings were her daily studies; with her little Bible on her lap, she usually seated herself near me, and there read a chapter from the holy volume. This was a duty which she was taught not to perform lightly, and we have frequently spent two hours in reading and remarking upon the contents of a chapter."

A tendency to "lisp in numbers," was observed in her about this time.

She frequently made little impromptus in rhyme, without seeming to be conscious that there was any thing peculiar in the habit. On one occasion, while standing by a window at which her mother was seated, and looking out upon a lovely landscape, she exclaimed—

> "See those lofty, those grand trees;
> Their high tops waving in the breeze;
> They cast their shadows on the ground,
> And spread their fragrance all around."

Her mother, who had several times been struck by little rhyming ejaculations of the kind, now handed her writing implements and requested her to write down what she had just uttered. She appeared surprised at the request, but complied; writing it down as if it had been prose, without arranging it in a stanza, or commencing the lines with capitals; not seeming aware that she had rhymed. The notice attracted to this impromptu, however, had its effect, whether for good or for evil. From that time she wrote some scraps of poetry, or rather rhyme, every day, which would be treasured up with delight by her mother, who watched with trembling, yet almost fascinated anxiety, these premature blossomings of poetic fancy.

On another occasion, towards sunset, as Mrs. Davidson was seated by the window of her bed-room, little Margaret ran in, greatly excited, exclaiming that there was an awful thundergust rising, and that the clouds were black as midnight.

"I gently drew her to my bosom," says Mrs. Davidson, "and after I had soothed her agitation, she seated herself at my feet, laid her head in my lap, and gazed at the rising storm. As the thunder rolled, she clung closer to my knees, and when the tempest burst in all its fury, I felt her tremble. I passed my arms around her, but soon found it was not fear that agitated her. Her eyes kindled as she watched the warring elements, until extending her hand, she exclaimed,

> "The lightning plays along the sky,
> The thunder rolls and bursts from high!
> Jehovah's voice amid the storm
> I heard—methinks I see his form,
> As riding on the clouds of even,
> He spreads his glory o'er the heaven."

This likewise her mother made her write down at the instant; thus giving additional impulse to this growing inclination.

I shall select one more instance of this early facility at numbers, especially as it involves a case of conscience, creditable to her early powers of self-examination. She had been reproved by her mother for some trifling act of disobedience, but aggravated her fault by attempting to justify it; she was, therefore, banished to her bed-room until she should become sensible of her error. Two hours elapsed, without her evincing any disposition to yield; on the contrary, she persisted in vindicating her conduct, and accused her mother of injustice.

Mrs. Davidson mildly reasoned with her; entreated her to examine the spirit by which she was actuated; placed before her the example of our Saviour in submitting to the will of his parents; and, exhorting her to pray to God to assist her, and to give her meekness and humility, left her again to her reflections.

"An hour or two afterwards," says Mrs. Davidson, "she desired I would admit her. I sent word that, when she was in a proper frame of mind, I would be glad to see her. The little creature came in, bathed in tears, threw her arms round my neck, and sobbing violently, put into my hands the following verses:

> "Forgiven by my Saviour dear,
>   For all the wrongs I've done,
> What other wish could I have here?
>   Alas there yet is one.
>
> I know my God has pardoned me,
>   I know he loves me still;
> I wish forgiven I may be,
>   By her I've used so ill.
>
> Good resolutions I have made,
>   And thought I loved my Lord;
> But ah! I trusted in myself,
>   And broke my foolish word.
>
> But give me strength, oh Lord, to trust
>   For help alone in thee;
> Thou knowest my inmost feelings best,
>   Oh teach me to obey."

We have spoken of the buoyancy of Margaret's feelings, and the vivid pleasure she received from external objects; she entered, however, but little into the amusements of the few children with whom she associated, nor did she take much delight in their society; she was conscious of a difference between them and herself, but scarce knew in what it consisted. Their sports seemed to divert for a while, but soon wearied her, and she would fly to a book, or seek the conversation of persons of maturer age and mind. Her highest pleasures were intellectual. She seemed to live in a world of her own creation, surrounded by the images of her own fancy. Her own childish amusements had originality and freshness, and called into action the mental powers, so as to render them interesting to persons of all ages. If at play with her little dog or kitten, she would carry on imaginary dialogues between them; always ingenious, and sometimes even brilliant. If her doll happened to be the plaything of the moment, it was invested with a character exhibiting knowledge of history, and all the powers of memory which a child can be supposed to exercise. Whether it was Mary, Queen of Scots, or her rival, Elizabeth, or the simple cottage maiden, each character was maintained with propriety. In telling stories (an amusement all children are fond of,) hers were always original, and of a kind calculated to elevate the minds of the children present, giving them exalted views of truth, honour, and integrity; and the sacrifice of all selfish feelings to the happiness of others was illustrated in the heroine of her story.

This talent for extemporaneous story-telling increased with exercise, until she would carry on a narrative for hours together; and in nothing was the precocity of her inventive powers more apparent than in the discrimination and individuality of her fictitious characters; the consistency with which they were sustained; the graphic force of her descriptions; the elevation of her sentiments, and the poetic beauty of her imagery.

This early gift caused her to be sought by some of the neighbours; who would lead her unconsciously into an exertion of her powers. Nothing was done by her from vanity or a disposition to "show off," but she would become excited by their attention and the pleasure they seemed to derive from her narrations. When thus excited, a whole evening would be occupied by one of her stories; and when the servant came to take her home, she would observe, in the phraseology of the magazines, "the story to be continued in our next."

Between the age of six and seven she entered upon a course of English grammar, geography, history, and rhetoric, still under the direction and superintendence of her mother; but such was her ardour and application, that it was necessary to keep her in check, lest a too intense pursuit of knowledge should impair her delicate constitution. She was not required to commit her lessons to memory, but to give the substance of them in her own language, and to explain their purport; thus she learnt nothing by rote, but every thing understandingly, and soon acquired a knowledge of the rudiments of English education. The morning lessons completed, the rest of the day was devoted to recreation; occasionally sporting and gathering wild flowers on the banks of the Saranac; though the extreme delicacy of her constitution prevented her taking as much exercise as her mother could have wished.

In 1830 an English gentleman, who had been strongly interested and affected by the perusal of the biography and writings of Lucretia Davidson, visited Plattsburgh, in the course of a journey from Quebec to New York, to see the place where she was born and had been buried. While there, he sought an interview with Mrs. Davidson, and his appearance and deportment were such as at once to inspire respect and confidence. He had much to ask about the object of his literary pilgrimage, but his inquiries were managed with the most considerate delicacy. While he was thus conversing with Mrs. Davidson, the little Margaret, then about seven years of age, came tripping into the room, with a book in one hand and a pencil in the other. He was charmed with her bright intellectual countenance, but still more with finding that the volume in her hand was a copy of Thomson's Seasons, in which she had been marking with a pencil the passages which most pleased her. He drew her to him; his frank, winning manner soon banished her timidity; he engaged her in conversation, and found, to his astonishment, a counterpart of Lucretia Davidson before him. His visit was necessarily brief; but his manners, appearance, and conversation, and, above all, the extraordinary interest with which he had regarded her, sank deep in the affectionate heart of the child, and inspired a friendship that remained one of her strongest attachments through the residue of her transient existence.

The delicate state of her health this summer rendered it advisable to take her to the Saratoga Springs, the waters of which appeared to have a beneficial effect. After remaining here some time, she accompanied her parents to New York. It was her first visit to the city, and of course fruitful of wonder and excitement; a new world seemed to open before her; new scenes, new friends, new occupations, new sources of instruction and enjoyment; her young heart was overflowing, and her head giddy with delight. To complete her happiness, she again met with her English friend, whom she greeted with as much eagerness and joy as if he had been a campanion of her own age. He manifested the same interest in her that he had shown at Plattsburgh, and took great pleasure in accompanying her to many of the exhibitions and places of intellectual gratification of the metropolis, and marking their effects upon her fresh, unhackneyed feelings and intelligent mind. In company with him she, for the first and only time in her life, visited the theatre. It was a scene of magic to her, or rather, as she said, like a "brilliant dream." She often recurred to it with vivid recollection, and the effect of it upon her imagination was subsequently apparent in the dramatic nature of some of her writings.

One of her greatest subjects of regret on leaving New York, was the parting with her intellectual English friend; but she was consoled by his promising to pay Plattsburgh another visit, and to pass a few days there previous to his departure for England. Soon after returning to Plattsburgh, however, Mrs. Davidson received a letter from him saying that he was unexpectedly summoned home, and would have to defer his promised visit until his return to the United States.

It was a severe disappointment to Margaret, who had conceived for him an enthusiastic friendship remarkable in such a child. His letter was accompanied by presents of books and various tasteful remembrances, but the sight of them only augmented her affliction. She wrapped them all carefully in paper, and treasured them up in a particular drawer, where they were daily visited, and many a tear shed over them.

The excursions to Saratoga and New York had improved her health, and given a fresh impulse to her mind. She resumed her studies with great eagerness; her spirits rose with mental exercise; she soon was in one of her veins of intellectual excitement. She read, she wrote, she danced, she sang, and was for the time the happiest of the happy. In the freshness of early morning, and towards sunset, when the heat of the day was over, she would stroll on the banks of the Saranac, following its course to where it pours itself into the beautiful Bay of Cumberland in Lake Champlain. There the rich variety of scenery which bursts upon the eye; the islands, scattered, like so many gems, on the broad bosom of the lake; the Green Mountains of Vermont beyond, clothed in the atmospherical charms of our magnificent climate; all these would inspire a degree of poetic rapture in her mind, mingled with a sacred melancholy; for these were scenes which had often awakened the enthusiasm of her deceased sister Lucretia.

Her mother, in her memoranda, gives a picture of her in one of these excited moods.

"After an evening's stroll along the river bank, we seated ourselves by a window to observe the effect of the full moon rising over the waters. A holy calm seemed to pervade all nature. With her head resting on my bosom, and her eyes fixed on the firmament, she pointed to a particularly bright star, and said:

> " 'Behold that bright and sparkling star
> Which setteth as a queen afar:
> Over the blue and spangled heaven
> It sheds its glory in the even!

Our Jesus made that sparkling star
Which shines and twinkles from afar.
Oh! 'twas that bright and glorious gem
Which shone o'er ancient Bethlehem!'

"The summer passed swiftly away," continues her mother, "yet her intellectual advances seemed to outstrip the wings of time. As the autumn approached, however, I could plainly perceive that her health was again declining. The chilly winds from the lake were too keen for her weak lungs. My own health too was failing; it was determined, therefore, that we should pass the winter with my eldest daughter, Mrs. T——, who resided in Canada, in the same latitude, it is true, but in an inland situation. This arrangement was very gratifying to Margaret; and, had my health improved by the change, as her own did. she would have been perfectly happy. During this period she attended to a regular course of study, under my direction; for, though confined wholly to my bed, and suffering extremely from pain and debility, Heaven, in mercy, preserved my mental faculties from the wreck that disease had made of my physical powers." The same plan as heretofore was pursued. Nothing was learnt by rote, and the lessons were varied to prevent fatigue and distaste, though study was always with her a pleasing duty rather than an arduous task. After she had studied her lessons by herself she would discuss them in conversation with her mother. Her reading was under the same guidance. "I selected her books," says Mrs. Davidson, "with much care, and to my surprise found that, notwithstanding her poetical temperament, she had a high relish for history, and that she would read with as much apparent interest an abstruse treatise that called forth the reflecting powers, as she did poetry or works of the imagination. In polite literature Addison was her favourite author, but Shakspeare she dwelt upon with enthusiasm. She was restricted, however, to certain marked portions of this inimitable writer; and having been told that it was not proper for her to read the whole, such was her innate delicacy and her sense of duty, that she never overstepped the prescribed boundaries."

In the intervals of study she amused herself with drawing, for which she had a natural talent, and soon began to sketch with considerable skill. As her health had improved since her removal to Canada, she frequently partook of the favourite winter recreation of a drive in a traineau or sleigh, in company with her sister and her brother-in-law, and completely enveloped in furs and buffalo-robes; and nothing put her in a finer flow of spirits, than thus skimming along, in bright January weather, on the sparkling snow, to the merry music of the jingling sleigh-bells. The winter passed away without any improvement in the health of Mrs.

Davidson; indeed she continued a helpless invalid, confined to her bed, for eighteen months; during all which time little Margaret was her almost constant companion and attendant.

"Her tender solicitude," writes Mrs. Davidson, "endeared her to me beyond any other earthly thing; although under the roof of a beloved and affectionate daughter, and having constantly with me an experienced and judicious nurse, yet the soft and gentle voice of my little darling was more than medicine to my worn-out frame. If her delicate hand smoothed my pillow, it was soft to my aching temples, and her sweet smile would cheer me in the lowest depths of despondency. She would draw for me—read to me—and often, when writing at her little table, would surprise me by some tribute of love, which never failed to operate as a cordial to my heart. At a time when my life was despaired of, she wrote the following lines while sitting at my bed—

> " 'I'll to thy arms in rapture fly,
> And wipe the tear that dims thine eye;
> Thy pleasure will be my delight,
> Till thy pure spirit takes its flight.
>
> When left alone—when thou art gone,
> Yet still I will not feel alone:
> Thy spirit still will hover near,
> And guard thy orphan daughter dear!' "

In this trying moment, when Mrs. Davidson herself had given up all hope of recovery, one of the most touching sights was to see this affectionate and sensitive child tasking herself to achieve a likeness of her mother, that it might remain with her as a memento. "How often would she set by my bed," says Mrs. Davidson, "striving to sketch features that had been vainly attempted by more than one finished artist; and when she found that she had failed, and that the likeness could not be recognised, she would put her arms around my neck and weep, and say, 'Oh dear mamma, I shall lose you, and not even a sketch of your features will be left me! and if I live to be a woman, perhaps I shall even forget how you looked!' This idea gave her great distress, sweet lamb! I then little thought this bosom would have been her dying pillow!"

After being reduced to the very verge of the grave, Mrs. Davidson began slowly to recover, but a long time elapsed before she was restored to her usual degree of health. Margaret in the mean time increased in strength and stature; she still looked fragile and delicate, but she was always cheerful and buoyant. To relieve the monotony of her life, which had been passed too much in a sick chamber, and to preserve her spirits fresh and elastic, little excursions were devised for her about the country, to Missisque Bay, St. Johns, Alburgh, Champlain, &c. The following lines, addressed to her mother on one of these occasional separations, will serve as a specimen of her compositions in this the eighth year of her age, and of the affectionate current of her feelings.

"Farewell, dear mother; for a while
I must resign thy plaintive smile;
May angels watch thy couch of wo,
And joys unceasing round thee flow.

May the Almighty Father spread
His sheltering wings above thy head;
It is not long that we must part,
Then cheer thy downcast, drooping heart.

Remember, oh remember me,
Unceasing is my love for thee;
When death shall sever earthly ties,
When thy loved form all senseless lies,

Oh that my soul with thine could flee,
And roam through wide enternity;
Could tread with thee the courts of heaven,
And count the brilliant stars of even!

Farewell, dear mother; for a while
I must resign thy plaintive smile;
May angels watch thy couch of wo,
And joys unceasing round thee flow."

In the month of January, 1833, while still in Canada, she was brought very low by an attack of scarlet fever, under which she lingered many weeks, but had so far recovered by the middle of April as to take the air in a carriage. Her mother, too, having regained sufficient strength to travel, it was thought advisable, for both their healths, to try the effect of a journey to New York. They accordingly departed about the beginning of May, accompanied by a family party. Of this journey, and a sojourn of several months in New York, she kept a journal, which evinces considerable habits of observation, but still more that kindling of the imagination which, in the poetic mind, gives to commonplace realities the witchery of romance. She was deeply interested by visits to the "School for the Blind," and the "Deaf and Dumb Asylum;" and makes a minute of a visit of a very different nature—to Black Hawk and his fellow-chiefs, prisoners of war, who, by command of government, were taken about through various of our cities, that they might carry back to their brethren in the wilderness, a cautionary idea of the overwhelming power of the white man.

"On the 25th June I saw and shook hands with the famous Black Hawk, the Indian chief, the enemy of our nation, who has massacred our patriots, murdered our women and helpless children! Why is he treated with so much attention by those whom he has injured? It cannot surely arise from benevolence. It must be *policy*. Be it what it may, I cannot understand it. His son, the Prophet, and others who accompanied him, interested *me* more than the chief himself. His son is no doubt a fine specimen of Indian beauty. He has a high brow, piercing black eyes, long black hair, which hangs down his back, and, upon the whole, is well suited to captivate an Indian maiden. The Prophet we found surveying himself in a looking-glass, undoubtedly wishing to show himself off to the best advantage in the fair assembly before him. The rest were dozing on a sofa, but they were awakened sufficiently to shake hands with us, and others who had the courage to approach so near them. I remember I dreamed of them the following night."

During this visit to New York she was the life and delight of the relatives with whom she resided, and they still retain a lively recollection of the intellectual nature of her sports among her youthful companions, and of the surprising aptness and fertile invention displayed by her in contriving new sources of amusement. She had a number of playmates, nearly of her own age, and one of her projects was to get up a dramatic entertainment for the gratification of themselves and their friends. The proposal was readily agreed to provided she would write the play. This she readily undertook, and indeed devised and directed the whole arrangements, though she had never been but once to a theatre, and that on her previous visit to New York. Her little companions were now all busily employed, under her direction, preparing dresses and equipments; robes with trains were fitted out for the female characters, and quantities of paper and tinsel were consumed in making caps, helmets, spears, and sandals.

After four or five days had been spent in these preparations, Margaret was called upon to produce the play. "Oh!" she replied, "I have not written it yet."—"But how is this! Do you make the dresses first, and then write the play to suit them?"—"Oh!" replied she gaily, "the writing of the play is the easiest part of the preparation; it will be ready before the dresses." And, in fact, in two days she produced her drama, "The

Tragedy of Alethia." It was not very voluminous, to be sure, but it contained within it sufficient of high character and astounding and bloody
incident to furnish out a drama of five times its size. A king and queen
of England resolutely bent upon marrying their daughter, the Princess
Alethia, to the Duke of Ormond. The princess most perversely and
dolorously in love with a mysterious cavalier, who figures at her father's
court under the name of Sir Percy Lennox, but who, in private truth, is
the Spanish king, Rodrigo, thus obliged to maintain an incognito on
account of certain hostilities between Spain and England. The odious
nuptials of the princess with the Duke of Ormond proceed: she is led,
a submissive victim, to the altar; is on the point of pledging her irrev-
ocable word; when the priest throws off his sacred robe, discovers
himself to be Rodrigo, and plunges a daggar into the bosom of the
king. Alethia instantly plucks the daggar from her father's bosom,
throws herself into Rodrigo's arms, and kills herself. Rodrigo flies to a
cavern, renounces England, Spain, and his royal throne, and devotes
himself to eternal remorse. The queen ends the play by a passionate
apostrophe to the spirit of her daughter, and sinks dead on the floor.

The little drama lies before us, a curious specimen of the prompt talent
of this most ingenious child, and by no means more incongruous in its
incidents than many current dramas by veteran and experienced playwrights.

The parts were now distributed and soon learnt; Margaret drew out
a play-bill, in theatrical style, containing a list of the dramatis per-
sonæ, and issued regular tickets of admission. The piece went off with
universal applause; Margaret figuring, in a long train, as the princess,
and killing herself in a style that would not have disgraced an experienced stage heroine.

In these, and similar amusements, her time passed happily in New
York, for it was the study of the intelligent and amiable relatives, with
whom she sojourned, to render her residence among them as agreeable
and profitable as possible. Her visit, however, was protracted much
beyond what was originally intended. As the summer advanced, the
heat and restraint of the city became oppressive; her heart yearned
after her native home on the Saranac; and the following lines, written
at the time, express the state of her feelings—

HOME.

I would fly from the city, would fly from its care,
To my own native plants and my flowrets so fair;
To the cool grassy shade, and the rivulet bright,
Which reflects the pale moon on its bosom of light.

Again would I view the old mansion so dear,
Where I sported a babe, without sorrow or fear;
I would leave this great city so brilliant and gay,
For a peep at my home on this fine summer day.
I have friends whom I love and would leave with regret,
But the love of my home, oh, 'tis tenderer yet!
There a sister reposes unconscious in death—
'Twas there she first drew and there yielded her breath—
A father I love is away from me now—
Oh could I but print a sweet kiss on his brow,
Or smooth the gray locks, to my fond heart so dear,
How quickly would vanish each trace of a tear!
Attentive I listen to pleasure's gay call,
But my own darling home, it is dearer than all.

At length, late in the month of October, the travellers turned their faces homewards; but it was not the "darling home" for which Margaret had been longing: her native cottage on the beautiful banks of the Saranac. The wintry winds from Lake Champlain had been pronounced too severe for her constitution, and the family residence had been reluctantly changed to the village of Ballston. Margaret felt this change most deeply. We have already shown the tender as well as poetical associations that linked her heart to the beautiful home of her childhood; a presentiment seemed to come over her mind that she would never see it more; a presentiment unfortunately prophetic. She was now accustomed to give prompt utterance to her emotions in rhyme, and the following lines, written at the time, remain a touching record of her feelings—

MY NATIVE LAKE.

Thy verdant banks, thy lucid stream,
Lit by the sun's resplendent beam,
Reflect each bending tree so light
Upon thy bounding bosom bright.
Could I but see thee once again,
My own, my beautiful Champlain!

The little isles that deck thy breast,
And calmly on thy bosom rest,
How often, in my childish glee,
I've sported round them, bright and free!
Could I but see thee once again,
My own, my beautiful Champlain!

How oft I've watch'd the fresh'ning shower
Bending the summer tree and flower,
And felt my little heart beat high
As the bright rainbow graced the sky.
Could I but see thee once again,
My own, my beautiful Champlain!

And shall I never see thee more,
My native lake, my much-loved shore?
And must I bid a long adieu,
My dear, my infant home, to you?
Shall I not see thee once again,
My own, my beautiful Champlain?

Still, though disappointed at not returning to the Saranac, she soon made herself contented at Ballston. She was at home, in the bosom of her own family, and reunited to her two youngest brothers, from whom she had long been separated. A thousand little plans were devised by her, and some few of them put in execution, for their mutual pleasure and improvement. One of the most characteristic of these was a "weekly paper," issued by her in manuscript, and entitled "The Juvenile Aspirant." All their domestic occupations and amusements were of an intellectual kind. Their mornings were spent in study; the evenings enlivened by conversation, or by the work of some favourite author, read aloud for the benefit of the family circle.

As the powers of this excitable and imaginative little being developed themselves, Mrs. Davidson felt more and more conscious of the responsibility of undertaking to cultivate and direct them; yet to whom could she confide her that would so well understand her character and constitution? To place her in a boarding-school would subject her to increased excitement, caused by emulation, and her mind was already too excitable for her fragile frame. Her peculiar temperament required peculiar culture; it must neither be stimulated nor checked; and while her imagination was left to its free soarings, care must be taken to strengthen her judgment, improve her mind, establish her principles, and inculcate habits of self-examination and self-control. All this, it was thought, might best be accomplished under a mother's eye; it was resolved, therefore, that her education should, as before, be conducted entirely at home. "Thus she continued," to use her mother's words, "to live in the bosom of affection, where every thought and feeling was reciprocated. I strove to draw out the powers of her mind by conversation and familiar remarks upon subjects of daily study and reflection, and taught her the necessity of bringing all her thoughts, desires and feelings under the dominion of reason; to understand the importance of self-control, when she found her inclinations were at war with its dictates. To fulfil all her duties from a conviction of right, because they were duties; and to find her happiness in the consciousness of her own integrity, and the approbation of God. How delightful was the task of instructing a mind like hers! She seized with avidity upon every new idea, for the instruction proceeded from lips of love. Often would she exclaim, 'Oh mamma! how glad I am that you are not too ill to teach me! Surely I am the happiest girl in the world!' She had read much for a child of little more than ten years of age. She was well versed in both ancient and modern history, (that is to say, in the courses generally prescribed for the use of schools,) Blair, Kaimes, and Paley had formed part of her studies. She was familiar with most of the British poets. Her command of the English language was remarkable, both in conversation and writing. She had learned the rudiments of French, and was anxious to become perfect in the language; but I had so neglected my duty in this respect after I left school, that I was not qualified to instruct her. A friend, however, who understood French, called occasionally and gave her lessons for his own amusement; she soon translated well, and such was her talent for the acquisition of languages, and such her desire to read every thing in the original, that every obstacle vanished before her perseverance. She made some advances in Latin, also, in company with her brother, who was attended by a private teacher; and they were engaged upon the early books of Virgil, when her health again gave way, and she was confined to her room by severe illness. These frequent attacks upon a frame so delicate awakened all our fears. Her illness spread a gloom throughout our habitation, for fears were entertained that it would end in a pulmonary consumption." After a confinement of two months, however, she regained her usual, though at all times fragile, state of health. In the following spring, when she had just entered upon the eleventh year of her age, intelligence arrived of the death of her sister, Mrs. T., who had been resident in Canada. The blow had been apprehended from previous accounts of her extreme illness, but it was a severe shock. She had looked up to this sister as to a second mother, and as to one who, from the precarious health of her natural parent, might be called upon to fulfil that tender office. She was one, also, calculated to inspire affection; lovely in person, refined and intelligent in mind, still young in years; and with all this, her only remaining sister! In the following lines, poured out in the fulness of her grief, she touchingly alludes to the previous loss of her sister Lucretia, so often the subject of her poetic regrets, and of the consolation she had always felt in still having a sister to love and cherish her.

ON THE DEATH OF MY SISTER ANNA ELIZA.

While weeping o'er our sister's tomb,
  And heaving many a heartfelt sigh,
And while in youth's bewitching bloom,
  I thought not that thou too couldst die.

When gazing on that little mound,
  Spread o'er with turf, and flowers, and mould,
I thought not that thy lovely form
  Could be as motionless and cold.

When her light, airy form was lost
  To fond affection's weeping eye;
I thought not we should mourn for thee,
  I thought not that thou too couldst die.

Yes, sparkling gem! when thou wert here,
  From death's encircling mantle free,
Our mourning parents wiped each tear,
  And cried, "Why weep? we still have thee."

Each tender thought on thee they turn'd,
  Each hope of joy to thee was given,
And, dwelling on each matchless charm,
  They half forgot the saint in heaven.

But thou art gone, for ever gone!
  Sweet wanderer in a world of wo!
Now, unrestrain'd our grief must pour!
  Uncheck'd our mourning tears must flow.

How oft I've press'd my glowing lip
  In rapture to thy snowy brow,
And gazed upon that angel eye,
  Closed in death's chilling slumber now.

While tottering on the verge of life,
  Thine every nerve with pain unstrung,
That beaming eye was raised to heaven,
  That heart to God for safety clung.

And when the awful moment came,
  Replete with trembling hope and fear,

Though anguish shook thy slender frame,
    Thy thoughts were in a brighter sphere.

The wreath of light, which round thee play'd,
    Bore thy pure spirit to the skies;
With thee we lost our brightest gem,
    But heaven has gain'd a glorious prize.

Oh may the bud of promise left,
    Follow the brilliant path she trod,
And of her fostering care bereft,
    Still seek and find his mother's God.

But he, the partner of her life,
    Who shared her joy and soothed her wo,
How can I heal his broken heart?
    How bid his sorrow cease to flow?

It's only time those wounds can heal;
    Time, from whose piercing pangs alone,
The poignancy of grief can steal,
    And hush the heart's convulsive moan.

To parry the effect of this most afflicting blow, Margaret was sent on a visit to New York, where she passed a couple of months in the society of affectionate and intelligent friends, and returned home in June, recruited in health and spirits. The sight of her mother, however, though habituated to sorrow and suffering, yet bowed down by her recent bereavement, called forth her tenderest sympathies; and we consider it as illustrating the progress of the intellect and the history of the heart of this most interesting child, to insert another effusion called forth by this domestic calamity:

TO MY MOTHER OPPRESSED WITH SORROW.

Weep, oh my mother! I will bid thee weep!
For grief like thine requires the aid of tears;
But oh, I would not see thy bosom thus
Bow'd down to earth, with anguish so severe!
I would not see thine ardent feelings crush'd,
Deaden'd to all save sorrow's thrilling tone,
Like the pale flower, which hangs its drooping head
Beneath the chilling blasts of stern Æolus!

Oh I have seen that brow with pleasure flush'd,
The lightening smile around it brightly playing,
And the dark eyelids trembling with delight—
But now how changed!—thy downcast eye is bent,
With heavy, thoughtful glances, on the ground,
And oh how quickly starts the tear-drop there!
It is not age which dims its wonted fire,
Or plants his lilies on thy pallid cheek,
But sorrow, keenest, darkest, biting sorrow!
When love would seek to lead thy heart from grief,
And fondly pleads one cheering look to view,
A sad, a faint sad smile one instant gleams
Athwart the brow where sorrow sits enshrined,
Brooding o'er ruins of what once was fair;
But like departing sunset, as it throws
One farewell shadow o'er the sleeping earth,
(So soon in sombre twilight to be wrapt,)
Thus, thus it fades! and sorrow more profound
Dwells on each feature where a smile, so cold,
It scarcely might be called the mockery
Of cheerful peace, but just before had been.
Long years of suffering, brighten'd not by joy,
Death and disease, fell harbinger of wo,
Must leave their impress on the human face,
And dim the fire of youth, the glow of pride;
But oh my mother! mourn not thus for *her*,
The rose, just blown, transplanted to its home,
Nor weep that her angelic soul has found
A resting-place with God.
Oh let the eye of heaven-born faith disperse
The dark'ning mists of earthly grief, and pierce
The clouds which shadow dull mortality!
Gaze on the heaven of glory crown'd with light,
Where rests thine own sweet child with radiant brow,
In the same voice which charm'd her father's halls,
Chanting sweet anthems to her Maker's praise;
And watching with delight the gentle buds
Which she had lived to mourn; watching thine own,
My mother! the soft unfolding blossoms,
Which, ere the breath of earthly sin could taint,
Departed to their Saviour; there to wait
For thy fond spirit in the home of bliss!
The angel babes have found a second mother;

But when thy soul shall pass from earth away,
The little cherubs then shall cling to thee,
And their sweet guardian welcome thee with joy,
Protector of their helpless infancy,
Who taught them how to reach that happy home.
Oh think of this, and let one heartfelt smile
Illume the face so long estranged from joy;
But may it rest not on thy brow alone,
But shed a cheering influence o'er thy heart,
Too sweet to be forgotten! Though thy loved
And beautiful are fled from earth away,
Still there are those who love thee—who would live
With thee alone—who weep or smile with thee.
Think of thy noble sons, and think of her
Who prays thee to be happy in the hope
Of meeting those in heaven who loved thee here,
And training those on earth, that they may live
A band of saints with thee in Paradise.

The regular studies of Margaret were now resumed, and her mother found, in attending to her instruction, a relief from the poignancy of her afflictions. Margaret always enjoyed the country, and in fine weather indulged in long rambles in the woods, accompanied by some friend, or attended by a faithful servant woman. When in the house, the versatility of her talents, her constitutional vivacity, and an aptness at coining occupation and amusement out of the most trifling incident, perpetually relieved the monotony of domestic life; while the faint gleam of health that occasionally flitted across her cheek, beguiled the anxious foreboding that had been indulged concerning her. "A strong hope was rising in my heart," says her mother, "that our frail, delicate blossom would continue to flourish, and that it was possible I might live to behold the perfection of its beauty! Alas! how uncertain is every earthly prospect! Even then the canker was concealed within the bright bud, which was eventually to destroy its loveliness! About the last of December she was again seized with a liver complaint, which, by sympathy, affected her lungs, and again awakened all our fears. She was confined to her bed, and it was not until March that she was able to set up and walk about her room. The confinement then became irksome, but her kind and skilful physician had declared that she must not be permitted to venture out until mild weather in April." During this fit of illness her mind had remained in an unusual state of inactivity; but with the opening of spring and the faint return of health, it broke forth with a brilliancy and a restless excitability that astonished and alarmed. "In conversation," says her mother, "her sallies of wit were dazzling. She composed and wrote incessantly, or rather would have done so, had I not interposed my authority to prevent this unceasing tax upon both her mental and physical strength. Fugitive pieces were produced every day, such as 'The Shunamite,' 'Belshazzar's Feast,' 'The Nature of Mind,' 'Boabdil el Chico,' &c. She seemed to exist only in the regions of poetry." We cannot help thinking that these moments of intense poetical exaltation sometimes approached to delirium, for we are told by her mother that "the image of her departed sister Lucretia mingled in all her aspirations; the holy elevation of Lucretia's character had taken deep hold of her imagination, and in her moments of enthusiasm she felt that she held close and intimate communion with her beatified spirit."

This intense mental excitement continued after she was permitted to leave her room, and her application to her books and papers was so eager and almost impassioned, that it was found expedient again to send her on an excursion. A visit to some relatives, and a sojourn among the beautiful scenery on the Mohawk river, had a salutary effect; but on returning home she was again attacked with alarming indisposition, which confined her to her bed.

"The struggle between nature and disease," says her mother, "was for a time doubtful; she was, however, at length restored to us. With returning health, her mental labours were resumed. I reasoned and entreated, but at last became convinced that my only way was to let matters take their course. If restrained in her favourite pursuits, she was unhappy. To acquire useful knowledge was a motive sufficient to induce her to surmount all obstacles. I could only select for her a course of calm and quiet reading, which, while it furnished real food for the mind, would compose rather than excite the imagination. She read much and wrote a great deal. As for myself, I lived in a state of constant anxiety lest these labours should prematurely destroy this delicate bud."

In the autumn of 1835, Dr. Davidson made arrangements to remove his family to a rural residence near New York, pleasantly situated on the banks of the Sound, or East River, as it is commonly called. The following extract of a letter from Margaret to Moss Kent, Esq.,* will show her anticipations and plans on this occasion.

* This gentleman was an early and valued friend of the Davidson family, and is honourably mentioned by Mr. Morse for the interest he took in the education of Lucretia. The notice of Mr. Morse, however, leaves it to be supposed that Mr. Kent's acquaintance with Dr. and Mrs. Davidson was brought about by his admiration of their daughter's talents, and commenced with overtures for her instruction. The following extract of a letter from Mrs. Davidson will place this

"September 20, 1835.

"We shall soon leave Ballston for New York. We are to reside in a beautiful spot upon the East River, near the Shot Tower, four miles from town, romantically called Ruremont. Will it not be delightful? Reunited to father and brothers, we must, we will be happy! We shall keep a horse and a little pleasure waggon, to transport us to and from town. But I intend my time shall be constantly employed in my studies, which I hope I shall continue to pursue at home. I wish (and mamma concurs in the opinion that it is best,) to devote this winter to the study of the Latin and French languages, while music and dancing will unbend my mind after close application to those studies, and give me that recreation which mother deems requisite for me. If father can procure private teachers for me, I shall be saved the dreadful alternative of a boarding-school. Mother could never endure the thought of one for me, and my own aversion is equally strong. Oh! my dear uncle, you must come and see us. Come soon and stay long. Try to be with us at Christmas. Mother's health is not as good as when you was here. I hope she will be benefited by a residence in her native city—in the neighbourhood of those friends she best loves. The state of her mind has an astonishing effect upon her health."

The following letter to the same gentleman, is dated October 18, 1835. "We are now at Ruremont, and a more delightful place I never saw. The house is large, pleasant, and commodious, and the old-fashioned

---

matter in a proper light, and show that these offers on the part of Mr. Kent, and the partial acceptance of them by Dr. and Mrs. Davidson, were warranted by the terms of intimacy which before existed between them. "I had the pleasure," says Mrs. Davidson, "to know Mr. Kent before my marriage, after which he frequently called at our house when visiting his sister, with whom I was on terms of intimacy. On one of those occasions he saw Lucretia. He had often seen her when a child, but she had changed much. Her uncommon personal beauty, graceful manners, and superior intellectual endowments made a strong impression on him. He conversed with her, and examined her on the different branches which she was studying, and pronounced her a good English scholar. He also found her well read, and possessing a fund of general information. He warmly expressed his admiration of her talents, and urged me to consent that he should adopt her as his daughter, and complete her education on the most liberal plan. I so far acceded to his proposition as to permit him to place her with Mrs. Willard, and assured him I would take his generous offer into consideration. Had she lived, we should have complied with his wishes, and Lucretia would have been the child of his adoption. The pure and disinterested friendship of this excellent man continued until the day of his death. For Margaret he manifested the affection of a father, and the attachment was returned by her with all the warmth of a young and grateful heart. She always addressed him as her dear uncle Kent."

style of every thing around it, transports the mind to days long gone
by, and my imagination is constantly upon the rack to burden the
past with scenes transacted on this very spot. In the rear of the mansion
a lawn, spangled with beautiful flowers, and shaded by spreading
trees, slopes gently down to the river side, where vessels of every description are constantly spreading their white sails to the wind. In front,
a long shady avenue leads to the door, and a large extent of beautiful
undulating ground is spread with fruit-trees of every description. In
and about the house there are so many little nooks and byplaces, that
sometimes I fancy it has been the resort of smugglers; and who knows
but I shall yet find their hidden treasures somewhere? Do come and see
us, my dear uncle; but you must come soon, if you would enjoy any
of the beauties of the place. The trees have already doffed their robe
of green, and assumed the red and yellow of autumn, and the paths
are strewed with fallen leaves. But there is loveliness even in the
decay of nature. But do, do come soon, or the branches will be leafless,
and the cold winds will prevent the pleasant rambles we now enjoy.
Dear mother has twice accompanied me a short distance about the
grounds, and indeed I think her health has improved since we removed
to New York, though she is still very feeble. Her mind is much relieved,
having her little family gathered once more around her. You well know
how great an effect her spirits have upon her health. Oh! if my dear
mother is only in comfortable health, and you will come, I think I
shall spend a delightful winter prosecuting my studies at home."

"For a short time," writes Mrs. Davidson, "she seemed to luxuriate
upon the beauties of this lovely place. She selected her own room, and
adjusted all her little tasteful ornaments. Her books and drawing
implements were transported to this chosen spot. Still she hovered
around me like my shadow. Mother's room was still her resting-place;
mother's bosom her sanctuary. She sketched a plan for one or two
poems which were never finished. But her enjoyment was soon interrupted. She was again attacked by her old enemy, and though her
confinement to her room was of short duration, she did not get rid of
the cough. A change now came over her mind. Hitherto she had
always delighted in serious conversation on heaven; the pure and
elevated occupations of saints and angels in a future state had proved
a delightful source of contemplation; and she would become so animated that it seemed sometimes as if she would fly to realize her hopes
and joys!—Now her young heart appeared to cling to life and its
enjoyments, and more closely than I had ever known it. 'She was never
ill.'—When asked the question, 'Margaret, how are you?' 'Well, quite
well,' was her reply, when it was obvious to me, who watched her

every look, that she had scarcely strength to sustain her weak frame. She saw herself the last daughter of her idolizing parents—the only sister of her devoted brothers! Life had acquired new charms; though she had always been a happy, light-hearted child."

The following lines, written about this time, show the elasticity of her spirit, and the bounding vivacity of her imagination, that seemed to escape, as in a dream, from the frail tenement of clay in which they were encased:

STANZAS.

Oh for the pinions of a bird,
  To bear me far away,
Where songs of other lands are heard,
  And other waters play!

For some aerial car, to fly
  On through the realms of light,
To regions rife with poesy,
  And teeming with delight.

O'er many a wild and classic stream
  In ecstasy I'd bend,
And hail each ivy-cover'd tower,
  As though it were a friend.

O'er piles where many a wintry blast
  Is swept in mournful tones,
And fraught with scenes long glided past,
  It shrieks, and sighs, and moans.

Through many a shadowy grove, and round
  Full many a cloister'd hall,
And corridors, where every step
  With echoing peal doth fall.

Enchanted with the dreariness,
  And awe-struck with the gloom,
I would wander, like a spectre,
  'Mid the regions of the tomb.

And memory her enchanting veil
  Around my soul should twine,

And superstition, wildly pale,
 Should woo me to her shrine;

I'd cherish still her witching gloom,
 Half shrinking in my dread,
But, powerless to dissolve the spell,
 Pursue her fearful tread.

Oh what unmingled pleasure then
 My youthful heart would feel,
As o'er its thrilling cords each thought
 Of former days would steal.

Of centuries in oblivion wrapt,
 Of forms which long were cold,
And all of terror, all of wo,
 That history's page has told.

How fondly in my bosom
 Would its monarch, Fancy, reign,
And spurn earth's meaner offices
 With glorious disdain.

Amid the scenes of past delight,
 Or misery, I'd roam,
Where ruthless tyrants sway'd in might,
 Where princes found a home.

Where heroes have enwreathed their brows
 With chivalric renown,
Where beauty's hand, as valour's meed,
 Hath twined the laurel crown.

I'd stand where proudest kings have stood,
 Or kneel where slaves have knelt,
Til wrapt in magic solitude,
 I feel what they have felt.

Oh for the pinions of a bird,
 To waft me far away,
Where songs of other lands are heard,
 And other waters play.

About this time Mrs. Davidson received a letter from the English gentleman for whom Margaret, when quite a child, had conceived such a friendship, her dear elder brother, as she used to call him. The letter bore testimony to his undiminished regard. He was in good health; married to a very estimable and lovely woman; was the father of a fine little girl, and was at Havana with his family, where he kindly entreated Mrs. Davidson and Margaret to join them; being sure that a winter passed in that mild climate would have the happiest effect upon their healths. His doors, his heart, he added, were open to receive them, and his amiable consort impatient to bid them welcome. "Margaret," says Mrs. Davidson, "was overcome by the perusal of this letter. She laughed and wept alternately. One moment urged me to go, 'she was herself well, but she was sure it would cure me;' the next moment felt as though she could not leave the friends to whom she had so recently been reunited. Oh! had I gone at that time, perhaps my child might still have lived to bless me!"

During the first weeks of Margaret's residence at Ruremont, the character and situation of the place seized powerfully upon her imagination. "The curious structure of this old-fashioned house," says Mrs. Davidson, "its picturesque appearance, the varied and beautiful grounds which surrounded it, called up a thousand poetic images and romantic ideas. A long gallery, a winding staircase, a dark, narrow passage, a trap-door, large apartments with massive doors, and heavy iron bars and bolts, all set her mind teeming with recollections of what she had read and imagined of old castles, banditti, smugglers, &c. She roamed over the place in perfect ecstasy, peopling every part with images of her own imagination, and fancying it the scene of some foregone event of dark and thrilling interest." There was, in fact, some palpable material for all this spinning and weaving of the fancy. The writer of this memoir visited Ruremont at the time it was occupied by the Davidson family. It was a spacious, and somewhat crazy and poetical-looking mansion, with large waste apartments. The grounds were rather wild and overgrown, but so much the more picturesque. It stood on the banks of the Sound, the waters of which rushed, with whirling and impetuous tides, below, hurrying on to the dangerous strait of Hell Gate. Nor was this neighbourhood without its legendary tales. These wild and lonely shores had, in former times, been the resort of smugglers and pirates. Hard by this very place stood the country retreat of Ready Money Prevost, of dubious and smuggling memory, with his haunted tomb, in which he was said to conceal his contraband riches; and scarce a secret spot about these shores but had some tradition connected with it of Kidd the pirate and his buried treasures. All these circumstances were enough to breed thick-coming fancies in so imaginative a brain, and the result was a drama in six acts, entitled "The Smuggler," the scene of which was laid at Ruremont in the old time of the province. The play was written with great rapidity, and, considering she was little more than twelve years of age, and had never visited a theatre but once in her life, evinced great aptness and dramatic talent. It was to form a domestic entertainment for Christmas holidays; the spacious back parlour was to be fitted up for the theatre. In planning and making arrangements for the performance, she seemed perfectly happy, and her step resumed its wonted elasticity, though her anxious mother often detected a suppressed cough, and remarked a hectic flush upon her cheek. "We now found," says Mrs. Davidson, "that private teachers were not to be procured at Ruremont, and I feared to have her enter upon a course of study which had been talked of, before we came to this place. I thought she was too feeble for close mental application, while *she* was striving, by the energies of her mind and bodily exertion, (which only increased the morbid excitement of her system,) to overcome disease, that she feared was about to fasten itself upon her. She was the more anxious, therefore, to enter upon her studies; and when she saw solicitude in my countenance and manner, she would fix her sweet sad eyes upon my face, as if she would read my very soul, yet dreaded to know what she might find written there. I knew and could understand her feelings; she also understood mine; and there seemed to be a tacit compact between us that this subject, at *present*, was forbidden ground. Her father and brothers were lulled into security by her cheerful manner and constant assertion that she was well, and considered her cough the effect of a recent cold. My opinion to the contrary was regarded as the result of extreme maternal anxiety."

She accordingly went to town three times a week, to take lessons in French, music, and dancing. Her progress in French was rapid, and the correctness and elegance of her translations surprised her teachers. Her friends in the city, seeing her look so well and appear so sprightly, encouraged her to believe that air and exercise would prove more beneficial than confinement to the house. She went to town in the morning and returned in the evening in an open carriage, with her father and one of her elder brothers, each of whom was confined to his respective office until night. In this way she was exposed to the rigours of an unusually cold season; yet she heeded them not, but returned home full of animation to join her little brothers in preparations for their holiday fête. Their anticipations of a joyous Christmas were doomed to sad disappointment. As the time approached, two of her brothers were taken ill. One of these, a beautiful boy about nine years of age, had been the favourite companion of her recreations, and she had taken great interest in his mental improvement. "Towards the close of 1835," says her mother, "he began to droop; his cheek grew pale, his step languid, and his bright eye heavy. Instead of rolling the hoop, and bounding across the lawn to meet his sister on her return from the city, he drooped by the side of his feeble mother, and could not bear to be parted from her; at length he was taken to his bed, and, after lingering four months, he died. This was Margaret's first acquaintance with death. She witnessed his gradual decay almost unconsciously, but still persuaded herself 'he will, he must get well!' She saw her sweet little playfellow reclining upon my bosom during his last agonies; she witnessed the bright glow which flashed upon his long-faded cheek; she beheld the unearthly light of his beautiful eye, as he pressed his dying lips to mine and exclaimed, 'Mother! dear mother! the last hour has come!' Oh! it was indeed an hour of anguish never to be forgotten. Its effect upon her youthful mind was as lasting as her life. The sudden change from life and animation to the still unconsciousness of death, for the time almost paralysed her. She shed no tear, but stood like a statue upon the scene of death. But when her eldest brother tenderly led her from the room, her tears gushed forth—it was near midnight, and the first thing that aroused her to a sense of what was going on around her, was the thought of my bereavement, and a conviction that it was her province to console me."

We subjoin a record, from her own pen, of her feelings on this lamentable occasion.

ON THE CORPSE OF MY LITTLE BROTHER KENT.

Beauteous form of soulless clay!
  Image of what once was life!
Hush'd is thy pulse's feeble play,
  And ceased the pangs of mortal strife.

Oh! I have heard thy dying groan,
  Have seen thy last of earthly pain;
And while I weep that thou art gone,
  I cannot wish thee here again.

For ah! the calm and peaceful smile
  Upon that clay-cold brow of thine,
Speaks of a spirit freed from sin,
  A spirit joyful and divine.

But thou are gone! and this cold clay
  Is all that now remains of thee;

For thy freed soul hath wing'd its way
To blessed immortality.

That dying smile, that dying groan,
I never, never can forget,
Till death's cold hand hath clasp'd my own,
His impress on my brow has set.

Those low, and sweet, and plaintive tones,
Which o'er my heart like music swept,
And the deep, deathlike, chilling moans
Which from thy heaving bosom crept.

Oh! thou wert beautiful and fair,
Our loveliest and our dearest one!
No more thy pains or joys we share,
No more—my brother, thou art gone.

Thou'rt gone! What agony, what wo
In that brief sentence is express'd!
Oh that the burning tears could flow,
And draw this mountain from my breast!

The anguish of the mother was still more intense, as she saw her bright and beautiful but perishable offspring thus, one by one, snatched away from her. "My own weak frame," says she, "was unable longer to sustain the effects of long watching and deep grief. I had not only lost my lovely boy, but I felt a strong conviction that I must soon resign my Margaret; or rather, that she would soon follow me to a premature grave. Although she still persisted in the belief that she was well, the irritating cough, the hectic flush, (so often mistaken for the bloom of health,) the hurried beating of the heart, and the drenching night perspirations confirmed me in this belief, and I sank under this accumulated load of affliction. For three weeks I hovered upon the borders of the grave, and when I arose from this bed of pain—so feeble that I could not sustain my own weight, it was to witness the rupture of a blood-vessel in her lungs, caused by exertions to suppress a cough. Oh! it was agony to see her thus! I was compelled to conceal every appearance of alarm, lest the agitation of her mind should produce fatal consequences. As I seated myself by her, she raised her speaking eyes to mine with a mournful, inquiring gaze, and as she read the anguish which I could not conceal, she turned away with a look of despair. She spoke not a word, but silence, still, deathlike silence, pervaded the apartment." The best of medical aid was called in, but the physicians gave no hope; they considered it a deep-seated case of pulmonary consumption. All that could be done was to alleviate the symptoms, and protract life as long as possible by lessening the excitement of the system. When Mrs. Davidson returned to the bedside, after an interview with the physicians, she was regarded with an anxious, searching look by the lovely little sufferer, but not a question was made. Margaret seemed fearful of receiving a discouraging reply, and "lay, all pale and still, (except when agitated by the cough,) striving to calm the tumult of her thoughts," while her mother seated herself by her pillow, trembling with weakness and sorrow. Long and anxious were the days and nights spent in watching over her. Every sudden movement or emotion excited the hemorrhage. "Not a murmur escaped her lips," says her mother, "during her protracted sufferings. 'How are you, love? how have you rested during the night?' 'Well, dear mamma; I have slept sweetly.' I have been night after night beside her restless couch, wiped the cold dew from her brow, and kissed her faded cheek in all the agony of grief, while she unconsciously slept on; or if she did awake, her calm sweet smile, which seemed to emanate from heaven, has, spite of my *reason*, lighted my heart with hope. Except when very ill, she was ever a bright dreamer. Her visions were usually of an unearthly cast: about heaven and angels. She was wandering among the stars; her sainted sisters were her pioneers; her cherub brother walked hand in hand with her through the gardens of paradise! I was always an early riser, but after Margaret began to decline I never disturbed her until time to rise for breakfast, a season of social intercourse in which she delighted to unite, and from which she was never willing to be absent. Often when I have spoken to her she would exclaim, 'Mother, you have disturbed the brightest visions that ever mortal was blessed with! I was in the midst of such scenes of delight! Cannot I have time to finish my dream?' And when I told her how long it was until breakfast, 'It will do,' she would say, and again lose herself in her bright imaginings; for I considered these as moments of inspiration rather than sleep. She told me it was not sleep. I never knew but one, except Margaret, who enjoyed this delightful and mysterious source of happiness, that one was her departed sister Lucretia. When awaking from these reveries, an almost ethereal light played about her eye, which seemed to irradiate her whole face. A holy calm pervaded her manner, and in truth she looked more like an angel who had been communing with kindred spirits in the world of light, than any thing of a grosser nature."

How truly does this correspond with Milton's exquisite description of the heavenly influences that minister to virgin innocence—

"A thousand liv'ried angels lackey her,
Driving far off each thing of sin and guilt;
And in clear dream and solemn vision,
Tell her of things that no gross ear can hear;
Till oft converse with heavenly habitants
Begin to cast a beam on the outward shape,
The unpolluted temple of the mind,
And turn it by degrees to the soul's essence,
Till all be made immortal."

Of the images and speculations that floated in her mind during these
half dreams, half reveries, we may form an idea from the following lines,
written on one occasion after what her mother used to term her "descent
into the world of reality."

THE JOYS OF HEAVEN.

Oh who can tell the joy and peace
    Which souls redeem'd shall know,
When all their earthly sorrows cease,
    Their pride, and pain, and wo!
Who may describe the matchless love
Which reigneth with the saints above?

What earthly tongue can ever tell
    The pure, unclouded joy
Which in each gentle soul doth swell,
    Unmingled with alloy,
As, bending to the Lord Most High,
They sound his praises through the sky?

Through the high regions of the air,
    On angel wings, they glide,
And gaze in wondering silence there
    On scenes to us denied;
Their minds expanding every hour,
And opening like the summer flower.

Though not like them to fade away,
    To die, and bloom no more;
Beyond the reach of fell decay,
    They stand in light and power;
But pure, eternal, free from care,
They join in endless praises there!

When first they leave this world of wo
  For fair, immortal scenes of light,
Angels attend them from below,
  And upward wing their joyful flight;
Where, fired with heavenly rapture's flame,
They raise on high Jehovah's name.

O'er the broad arch of heaven it peals,
  While shouts of praise unnumber'd flow;
The full, sweet notes sublimely swell,
  And prostrate angels humbly bow;
Each harp is tuned to joy above,
Its theme, a Saviour's matchless love.

The dulcet voice, which here below
  Charm'd with delight each listening ear,
Mix'd with no lingering tone of wo,
  Swelling harmonious, soft and clear,
Will sweetly fill the courts above,
In strains of heavenly peace and love.

The brilliant genius, which on earth
  Is struggling with disease and pain,
Will there unfold in power and light,
  Nought its bright current to restrain;
And as each brilliant day rolls on,
'Twill find some grace, till then unknown.

And as the countless years flit by,
  Their minds progressing still,
The more they know, these saints on high
  Praise more His sovereign will;
No breath from sorrow's whirlwind blast
Around their footsteps cast.

From their high throne they gaze abroad
  On vast creation's wondrous plan,
And own the power, the might of God,
  In each resplendent work they scan;
Though sun and moon to nought return,
Like stars these souls redeem'd shall burn.

Oh! who would wish to stay below,
  If sure of such a home as this,

> Where streams of love serenely flow,
>   And every heart is filled with bliss?
> They praise, and worship, and adore
> The Lord of heaven for ever more.

During this dangerous illness she became acquainted with Miss Sedgwick. The first visit of that most excellent and justly distinguished person, was when Margaret was in a state of extreme debility. It laid the foundation of an attachment on the part of the latter, which continued until her death. The visit was repeated; a correspondence afterwards took place, and the friendship of Miss Sedgwick became to the little enthusiast a source of the worthiest pride and purest enjoyment throughout the remainder of her brief existence.

At length the violence of her malady gave way to skilful remedies and the most tender and unremitting assiduity. When enabled to leave her chamber, she rallied her spirits, made great exertions to be cheerful, and strove to persuade herself that all might yet be well with her. Even her parents, with that singular self-delusion inseparable from this cruelly flattering malady, began to indulge a trembling hope that she might still be spared to them.

In the month of July, her health being sufficiently re-established to bear the fatigues of travelling, she was taken by her mother and eldest brother on a tour to Dutchess County and the western part of New York. On leaving home, she wrote the following lines, expressive of the feelings called forth by the events of the few preceding months, and of a foreboding that she should never return:

FAREWELL TO RUREMONT.

> Oh! sadly I gaze on this beautiful landscape,
>   And silent and slow do the big tear-drops swell;
> And I haste to my task, while the deep sigh is breaking,
>   To bid thee, sweet Ruremont, a lasting farewell.

> Oh! soft are the breezes which play round thy valley,
>   And warm are the sunbeams which gild thee with light,
> All clear and serenely the deep waves are rolling,
>   The sky in its radiance is dazzlingly bright.

> Oh! gayly the birds 'mid thy dark vines are sporting,
>   And, heaven-taught, pouring their gladness in song;
> While the rose and the lily their fair heads are bending
>   To hear the soft anthems float gently along.

Full many an hour have I bent o'er thy waters,
  Or watch'd the light clouds with a joy-beaming eye,
Till, delighted, I long'd for the eagle's swift pinions,
  To pierce the full depths of that beautiful sky.

Though wild were the fancies which dwelt in my bosom,
  Though endless the visions which swept o'er my soul,
Indulging those dreams was my dearest enjoyment—
  Enjoyment unmingled, unchain'd by control!

But each garden of earth has a something of sorrow,
  A thorn in its rose, or a blight in its breeze,
Though blooming as Eden, a shadow hangs o'er thee,
  The spirit of darkness, of pain, of disease!

Yes, Ruremont! thy brow, in its loveliness deck'd,
  Is entwined with a fatal but beautiful wreath,
For thy green leaves have shrunk at the mourner's cold touch,
  And thy pale flowers have wept in the presence of death.

Yon violets, which bloom in their delicate freshness,
  Were strew'd o'er the grave of our fairest and best;
Yon roses, which charm by their richness and fragrance,
  Have wither'd and died on his icy-cold breast.

The soft voice of spring had just breathed o'er the valley,
  The sweet birds just caroll'd their song in her bower,
When the angel of death in his terror swept o'er us,
  And placed in his bosom our fragile young flower.

Thus, Ruremont, we mourn not thy beauties alone,
  Thy flowers in their freshness, thy stream in its pride,
But we leave the loved scene of our mourning and tears,
  We leave the dear spot where our cherish'd one died.

The mantle of beauty thrown gracefully o'er thee
  Must touch a soft chord in each delicate heart;
But the tie is more sacred which bids us deplore thee,
  Endear'd by affliction, 'tis harder to part.

The scene of enjoyment is ever most lovely,
  Where blissful young spirits dance mirthful and glad;
But when sorrow has mingled her tears with our pleasure,
  Our love is more tender, our parting more sad.

How mild is the wing of this delicate zephyr,
  Which fans in its coolness my feverish brow!
But that light wing is laden with breezes that wither,
  And check the warm current of life in its flow.

Why blight such an Eden, oh spirit of terror!
  Which sweepest thy thousands each hour to the tomb?
Why, why shouldst thou roam o'er this beautiful valley,
  And mingle thy breath with the rose's perfume?

The sun rises bright o'er the clear dancing waters,
  And tinges with gold every light, waving tree,
And the young birds are singing their welcome to morning—
  Alas! they will sing it no longer for me!

The young buds of summer their soft eyes are opening,
  The wild flowers are bending the pure ripples o'er;
But I bid them farewell, and my heart is nigh breaking
  To think I shall see them and tend them no more.

I mark yonder path, where so often I've wander'd,
  Yon moss-covered rock, with its sheltering tree,
And a sigh of deep sadness bursts forth to remember
  That no more its soft verdure shall blossom for me.

How often my thoughts, to these loved scenes returning,
  Shall brood o'er the past with its joy and its pain;
Till waking at last from the long, pleasing slumber,
  I sigh to behold thee, thus blooming, again.

The little party was absent on its western tour about two months.
"Margaret," says her mother, "appeared to enjoy the scenery, and every
thing during the journey interested her. But there was a sadness in her
countenance, a pensiveness in her manner, unless excited by external
circumstances, which deeply affected me. She watched every variation
in my countenance; marked every little attention directed to herself,
such as an alteration in her diet, dress, exposure to the changes of
weather, yet still discovered an unwillingness to speak of her declining
health, and laboured to conceal every unfavourable symptom or change
for the worse. This, of course, imposed upon me the most painful
restraint. How heart-breaking to find that she considered my tongue
as the herald of mournful tidings, and my face as the mirror of evil
to come. How true that self-deception seems to be an almost invariable
symptom attending this deadful complaint! Margaret, all unconscious
of the rapid strides of the destroyer, taught herself to believe that the
alarming symptoms of her case existed only in the imagination of her

too anxious mother. Yet knowing my experience in these matters, she still doubted and trembled and feared to ask, lest a confirmation of her vague apprehensions should be the result. She avoided the slightest allusion to the subject of her disease in any way; and in the morbid excitement of her mind it appeared to her almost like accusing her of something wrong to say she was not well."

The following letter was written by her to Miss Sedgwick, after her arrival in Dutchess County.

"Lithgow, Dutchess County.

"Happy as I am, my dear madam, in the privilege of writing to you, I cannot permit another day to pass ere I inform you of our safe arrival at one of the most lovely spots in this beautiful and healthy country. Our passage up the river was rather tedious, being debarred the pleasure of remaining upon deck, but this privation was counterbalanced by the pleasure of a few moments' conversation with dear brother, who was permitted to meet us when the boat stopped at West Point. Arrived at Poughkeepsie, brother M. procured a private carriage, which was to convey us to the end of our journey, a distance of twenty miles. The drive was delightful! The scenery ever changing, ever beautiful! We arrived at Lithgow without much fatigue, where a hearty welcome, that sweetest of cordials, was awaiting us. Oh! it is a lovely spot! I thought Ruremont the perfection of beauty! but here I find the flowers as blooming, the birds as gay, the air as sweet, and the prospect far more varied and extensive; 'tis true we have lost the beautiful East River, with its crowd of vessels sweeping gracefully along, but here are hills crowned with the richest foliage, valleys sprinkled with flowers, and watered with winding rivulets; and here, what we prize more than all, a mild, salubrious air, which seems, in the words of the divine poet, 'to bear healing in its wings.' Dear mother bore the fatigue of our journey better than we anticipated; and although I do not think she is permanently better, she certainly breathes more freely, and seems altogether more comfortable than when in the city. Oh! how sincerely I hope that a change of air and scene may raise her spirits and renovate her strength. She is now in the midst of friends whom she has known and loved for many years; and surrounded by scenes connected with many of her earliest remembrances. Farewell, my dear madam! Please give my love to your dear little nieces; and should you have the leisure and inclination to answer this, believe me your letter will be a source of much gratification to your

Highly obliged little friend,
M. M. DAVIDSON.

Miss CATHERINE SEDGWICK.
    August, 1836."

The travellers returned to Ruremont in September. The tour had been of service to Margaret, and she endeavoured to persuade herself that she was quite well. If asked about her health, her reply was, that "if her friends did not tell her she was ill, she should not, from her own feelings, suspect it." That she was, notwithstanding, dubious on this subject, was evident from her avoiding to speak about it, and from the uneasiness she manifested when it was alluded to. It was still more evident from the change that took place in her habits and pursuits; she tacitly adopted the course of conduct that had repeatedly and anxiously, but too often vainly, been urged by her mother, as calculated to allay the morbid irritability of her system. She gave up her studies, rarely indulged in writing or drawing, and contented herself with light reading, with playing a few simple airs on the piano, and with any other trivial mode of passing away the time. The want of her favourite occupations, however, soon made the hours move heavily with her. Above all things, she missed the exciting exercise of the pen, against which she had been especially warned. Her mother observed the listlessness and melancholy that were stealing over her, and hoped a change of scene might banish them. The airs from the river, too, had been pronounced unfavourable to her health; the family, therefore, removed to town. The change of residence, however, did not produce the desired effect. She became more and more dissatisfied with herself, and with the life of idleness, as she considered it, that she was leading; but still she had resolved to give the prescribed system a thorough trial. A new source of solicitude was now awakened in the bosom of her anxious mother, who read in her mournfully quiet manner and submissive silence, the painful effects of compliance with her advice. There was not a murmur, however, from the lips of Margaret, to give rise to this solicitude; on the contrary, whenever she caught her mother's eye fixed anxiously and inquiringly on her, she would turn away and assume an air of cheerfulness.

Six months had passed in this inactive manner. "She was seated one day by my side," says Mrs. Davidson, "weary and restless, and scarcely knowing what to do with herself, when, marking the traces of grief upon my face, she threw her arms about my neck, and, kissing me, exclaimed, 'My dear, dear mother!' 'What is it affects you now, my child?' 'Oh! I know you are longing for something from my pen!' I saw the secret craving of the spirit that gave rise to the suggestion. 'I do indeed, my dear, delight in the effusions from your pen, but the exertion will injure you.' 'Mamma, I *must write*! I can hold out no longer! I will return to my pen, my pencil, and my books, and shall again be happy!' I pressed her to my bosom, and cautioned her to remember she was feeble. 'Mother,' exclaimed she, 'I am well! I wish you were only as well as I am!'"

The heart of the mother was not proof against these appeals: indeed she had almost as much need of self-denial on this subject as her child, so much did she delight in these early blossomings of her talent. Margaret was again left to her own impulses. All the frivolous expedients for what is usually termed *killing time* were discarded by her with contempt; her studies were resumed; in the sacred writings and in the pages of history she sought fitting aliment for her mind, half famished by its long abstinence; her poetical vein again burst forth, and the following lines, written at the time, show the excitement and elevation of her feelings:

EARTH.

Earth! thou has nought to satisfy
  The cravings of immortal mind!
Earth! thou has nothing pure and high,
  The soaring, struggling soul to bind.

Impatient of its long delay,
  The pinion'd spirit fain would roam,
And leave this crumbling house of clay,
  To seek above, its own bright home!

The spirit, 'tis a spark of light
  Struck from our God's eternal throne,
Which pierces through these clouds of night,
  And longs to shine where once it shone!

Earth! there will come an awful day,
  When thou shalt crumble into nought;
When thou shalt melt beneath that ray
  From whence thy splendours first were caught.

Quench'd in the glories of its God,
  Yon burning lamp shall then expire;
And flames, from heaven's own altar sent,
  Shall light the great funereal pyre.

Yes, thou must die! and yon pure depths
  Back from thy darken'd brow shall roll;
But never can the tyrant death
  Arrest this feeble, trusting soul.

When that great voice, which form'd thee first,
   Shall tell, surrounding world, thy doom,
Then the pure soul, enchain'd by thee,
   Shall rise triumphant o'er thy tomb.

Then on, still on, the unfetter'd mind
   Through realms of endless space shall fly;
No earth to dim, no chain to bind,
   Too pure to sin, too great to die.

Earth! thou hast nought to satisfy
   The cravings of immortal mind!
Earth! thou has nothing pure or high,
   The soaring, struggling soul to bind.

Yet is this never-dying ray
   Caught in thy cold, delusive snares,
Cased in a cell of mouldering clay,
   And bow'd by woes, and pain, and cares!

Oh! how mysterious is the bond
   Which blends the earthly with the pure,
And mingles that which death may blight
   With that which ever must endure!

Arise, my soul, from all below,
   And gaze upon thy destined home,
The heaven of heavens, the throne of God,
   Where sin and care can never come.

Prepare thee for a state of bliss,
   Unclouded by this mortal veil,
Where thou shalt see thy Maker's face,
   And dews from heaven's own air inhale.

How sadly do the sins of earth
   Deface thy purity and light,
That thus, while gazing at thyself,
   Thou shrink'st in horror at the sight.

Compound of weakness and of strength,
   Mighty, yet ignorant of thy power!

Loftier than earth, or air, or sea,
    Yet meaner than the lowliest flower!

Soaring towards heaven, yet clinging still
    To earth, by many a purer tie!
Longing to breathe a tender air,
    Yet fearing, trembling thus to die!

She was soon all cheerfulness and enjoyment. Her pen and her pencil
were frequently in her hand; she occupied herself also with her needle
in embroidery on canvass, and other fancy work. Hope brightened
with the exhilaration of her spirits. "I now walk and ride, eat and
sleep as usual," she observes in a letter to a young friend, "and although
not well, have strong hopes that the opening spring, which renovates
the flowers, and fields, and streams, will revive my enfeebled frame,
and restore me to my wonted health." In these moods she was the life
of the domestic circle, and these moods were frequent and long. And
here we should observe, that though these memoirs, which are furnished principally from the recollections of an afflicted mother, may
too often represent this gifted little being as a feeble invalid struggling
with mortality, yet in truth her life, though brief, was a bright and happy
one. At times she was full of playful and innocent gaiety; at others of
intense mental exaltation; and it was the very intensity of her enjoyment that made her so often indulge in those poetic paroxysms, if we
may be allowed the expression, which filled her mother with alarm.
A few weeks of this intellectual excitement was followed by another
rupture of a blood-vessel in the lungs, and a long interval of extreme
debility. The succeeding winter was one of vicissitude. She had several
attacks of bleeding at the lungs, which evidently alarmed her at the
time, though she said nothing, and endeavoured to repress all manifesta-
tion of her feelings. If taken suddenly, she instantly resorted to the sofa,
and, by a strong effort, strove to suppress every emotion. With her
eyes closed, her lips compressed, and her thin pale hand resting in
that of her anxious mother, she seemed to be waiting the issue. Not
a murmur would escape her lips, nor did she ever complain of pain.
She would often say, by way of consolation, to her mother, "Mamma,
I am highly favoured. I hardly know what is meant by pain. I am sure
I never, to my recollection, have felt it." The moment she was able to
sit up, after one of these alarming attacks, every vestige of a sick
chamber must be removed. No medicine, no cap, no bed-gown, no loose
wrapper must be in sight. Her beautiful dark hair must be parted on her
broad, high forehead, her dress arranged with the same care and neat-
ness as when in perfect health; indeed she studied to banish from her

appearance all that might remind her friends that her health was impaired, and, if possible, to drive the idea from her own thoughts. Her reply to every inquiry about her health was, "Well, quite well; or at least *I* feel so, though mother continues to treat me as an invalid. True I have a cold, attended by a cough, that is not willing to leave me; but when the spring returns, with its mild air and sweet blossoms, I think this cough, which alarms mother so much, will leave me."

She had, indeed, a strong desire to live; and the cause of that desire is indicative of her character. With all her retiring modesty, she had an ardent desire for literary distinction. The example of her sister Lucretia was incessantly before her; she was her leading star, and her whole soul was but to emulate her soarings into the pure regions of poetry. Her apprehensions were that she might be cut off in the immaturity of her powers. A simple, but most touching ejaculation, betrayed this feeling, as, when lying on a sofa, in one of those alarming paroxysms of her malady, she turned her eyes, full of mournful sweetness, upon her mother, and, in a low, subdued voice, exclaimed, "Oh! my dear, dear mother! *I am so young!*"

We have said that the example of her sister Lucretia was incessantly before her, and no better proof can be given of it than in the following lines, written at this time, which breathe the heavenly aspirations of her pure young spirit, in strains, to us, quite unearthly. We may have read poetry more artificially perfect in its structure, but never any more truly divine in its inspiration.

TO MY SISTER LUCRETIA.

My sister! With that thrilling word
   What thoughts unnumber'd wildly spring!
What echoes in my heart are stirr'd,
   While thus I touch the trembling string!

My sister! ere this youthful mind
   Could feel the value of thine own;
Ere this infantine heart could bind,
   In its deep cell, one look, one tone,

To glide along on memory's stream,
   And bring back thrilling thoughts of thee;
Ere I knew aught but childhood's dream,
   Thy soul had struggled and was free!

My sister! with this mortal eye,
   I ne'er shall see thy form again;

And never shall this mortal ear
  Drink in the sweetness of thy strain!

Yet fancy wild and glowing love
  Reveal thee to my spirit's view,
Enwreath'd with graces from above,
  And deck'd in heaven's own fadeless hue.

Thy glance of pure seraphic light
  Sheds o'er my heart its soft'ning ray;
Thy pinions guard my couch by night,
  And hover o'er my path by day.

I cannot weep that thou art fled,—
  For ever blends my soul with thine;
Each thought, by purer impulse led,
  Is soaring on to realms divine.

Thy glance unfolds my heart of hearts,
  And lays its inmost recess bare;
Thy voice a heavenly calm imparts,
  And soothes each wilder passion there.

I hear thee in the summer breeze,
  See thee in all that's pure or fair;
Thy whisper in the murmuring trees,
  Thy breath, thy spirit every where.

Thine eyes, which watch when mortals sleep,
  Cast o'er my dreams a radiant hue;
Thy tears, "such tears as angels weep,"
  Fall nightly with the glistening dew.

Thy fingers wake my youthful lyre,
  And teach its softer strains to flow;
Thy spirit checks each vain desire,
  And gilds the low'ring brow of wo.

When fancy wings her upward flight
  On through the viewless realms of air,
Clothed in its robe of matchless light,
  I view thy ransom'd spirit there!

Far from her wild delusive dreams,
　　It leads my raptured soul away,
Where the pure fount of glory streams,
　　And saints live on through endless day.

When the dim lamp of future years
　　Sheds o'er my path its glimmering faint,
First in the view thy form appears,
　　My sister, and my guardian saint!

Thou gem of light! my leading star!
　　What thou hast been, I strive to be;
When from the path I wander far,
　　Oh turn thy guiding beam on me.

Teach me to fill thy place below,
　　That I may dwell with thee above;
To soothe, like thee, a mother's wo,
　　And prove, like thine, a sister's love.

Thou wert unfit to dwell with clay,
　　For sin too pure, for earth too bright!
And death, who call'd thee hence away,
　　Placed on his brow a gem of light!

A gem, whose brilliant glow is shed
　　Beyond the ocean's swelling wave,
Which gilds the memory of the dead,
　　And pours its radiance on thy grave.

When day hath left his glowing car,
　　And evening spreads her robe of love;
When worlds, like travellers from afar,
　　Meet in the azure fields above;

When all is still, and fancy's realm
　　Is opening to the eager view,
Mine eye full oft, in search of thee,
　　Roams o'er that vast expanse of blue.

I know that here thy harp is mute,
　　And quench'd the bright poetic fire,
Yet still I bend my ear, to catch
　　The hymnings of thy seraph lyre.

Oh! if this partial converse now
　　So joyous to my heart can be,
How must the streams of rapture flow
　　When both are chainless, both are free!

When borne from earth for evermore,
　　Our souls in sacred joy unite,
At God's almighty throne adore,
　　And bathe in beams of endless light!

Away, away, ecstatic dream!
　　I must not, dare not dwell on thee;
My soul, immersed in life's dark stream,
　　Is far too earthly to be free.

Though heaven's bright portal were unclosed,
　　And angels wooed me from on high,
Too much I fear my shrinking soul
　　Would cast on earth its longing eye.

Teach me to fill thy place below,
　　That I may dwell with thee above;
To soothe, like thee, a mother's wo,
　　And prove, like thee, a sister's love.

It was probably this trembling solicitude about the duration of her existence, that made her so anxious, about this time, to employ every interval of her precarious health in the cultivation of her mental powers. Certain it is, during the winter, chequered as it was with repeated fits of indisposition, she applied herself to historical and other studies with an ardour that often made her mother tremble for the consequences.

The following letters to a young female friend were written during one of these intervals.

"New York, February 26, 1837.

"Notwithstanding all the dangers which might have befallen your letter, my dear Henrietta, it arrived safely at its resting-place, and is now lying open before me, as I am quietly sitting, this chill February morning, to inform you of its safe arrival. I find I was not mistaken in believing you too kind to be displeased at my remissness; and I now hope that through our continued intercourse neither will have cause to complain of the other's negligence.

"For my own part, I am always willing to assign every reason but that of forgetfulness for a friend's silence. Knowing how often I am obliged to claim this indulgence for myself, and how often ill health prevents me from writing to those I love, I am the more ready to frame apologies for others; indeed I think this spirit of *charity* (if so I may call it) is necessary to the happiness of correspondents, and as I am sure you possess it, I trust we shall both glide quietly along without any of those little *jars* which so often interrupt the purest friendships. And now that my dissertation on letter-writing is at an end, I must proceed to inform you of what I fear will be a disappointment, as it breaks away all those sweet anticipations expressed in your affectionate letter. Father has concluded that we shall not return to Plattsburgh next spring, as he had once intended; he fears the effects of the cold winds of Lake Champlain upon mother and myself, who are both delicate; and as we have so many dear friends in and about the city, a nearer location would be pleasanter to us and to them. We now think seriously of returning to Ballston, that beautiful little village where we have already spent two delightful years; and though in this case I must relinquish the idea of visiting my dear '*old home*' and my dear *young friend*, hope points to the hour when *you* may become *my* guest, and where the charms of novelty will in some degree repay us for the delightful associations and remembrances we had hoped to enjoy. But I cannot help now and then casting a backward glance upon the beautiful scenes you describe, and wishing myself with you. A philosopher would say, 'Since you cannot enjoy what you desire, turn to the pleasures you may possess, and seek in them consolation for what you have lost;' but I am no philosopher.

❀   ❀   ❀   ❀   ❀   ❀   ❀

"I will endeavour to answer your question about Mrs. Hemans. I have read several lives of this distinguished poetess, by different authors, and in all of them find something new to admire in her character and venerate in her genius! She was a woman of deep feeling, lively fancy, and acute sensibilities; so acute, indeed, as to have formed her chief unhappiness through life. She mingles her own feelings with her poems so well, that in reading *them* you read *her* character. But there is one thing I have often remarked: the mind soon wearies in perusing many of her pieces at *once*. She expresses those sweet sentiments so often, and introduces the same stream of beautiful ideas so constantly, that they sometimes degenerate into monotony. I know of no higher treat than to read a few of her best productions, and comment upon and feel their beauties; but perusing her *volume* is to me like listening to a strain of sweet music repeated over and over again, until it becomes so familiar to the ear, that it loses the charm of variety.

"Now, dear H., is not this presumption in me, to criticise so exquisite an author? But you desired my opinion, and I have given it to you without reserve.

"You desire me to send you an *original poem* for yourself. Now, my dear Hetty, this is something I am not at present able to do for any of my friends, writing being supposed quite injurious to persons with weak lungs. And I have still another reason. You say the effect of conveying feelings from the heart and recording them upon paper, seems to deprive them of half their warmth and ardour! Now, my dear friend, would not the effect of forming them into verse seem to render them still *less* sincere? Is not plain prose, as it slides rapidly from the pen, more apt to speak the feelings of the heart, than when an hour or two is spent in giving them rhyme and measure, and all the attributes of poetry?" * * * * * * *

TO THE SAME.

"New York, April 2d, 1837.

"About an hour since, my dear Henrietta, I received your token of remembrance, and commence my answer with an act of obedience to your sovereign will; but I fear you will repent when too late, and while nodding over the closely written sheet, and peering impatiently into each crowded corner, you will secretly wish you had allowed my pen to commence its operations at a more respectful distance from the top of the page. However, the request was your own; I obey like an obedient friend, and you must abide the consequences of your rash demand. Should the first glance at my well-filled sheet be followed by a *yawn*, or its last word be welcomed with a smile, you must blame your own imprudence in bringing down upon your luckless head the accumulated nothings of a scribbler like myself. It is indeed true that we shall not return to Plattsburgh; and much as I long to revisit the home of my infancy, and the friends of my earliest remembrance, I shall be obliged to relinquish the pleasure in reality, though fancy, unshackled by earth, shall direct her pinions to the north, and linger, delighted, on the beautiful banks of the Champlain! Methinks I hear you exclaim, with impatience, 'Fancy! what is it? I long for something more substantial.' So do I, *ma chere*, but since I cannot hope to behold my dear native village and its dear inhabitants, with *other* eyes than those of fancy, I will e'er employ them to the best of my ability. You may be sure we do not prefer the confined and murky atmosphere of the city to the pure and health-giving breezes of the country; far from it— we are already preparing to remove, as soon as the mild influence of spring has prevailed over the chilling blasts which we still hear whistling around us; and gladly shall we welcome the day that will release us from our bondage. But there is some drawback to every pleasure— some bitter drop in almost every cup of enjoyment; and we shall taste this most keenly when we bid farewell to the delightful circle of friends who have cheered us during the solitude and confinement of this dreary winter. The New York air, so far from agreeing with us, has deprived us of every enjoyment beyond the boundaries of our own walls, and it will be hard to leave those friends who have taught us to forget the privations of ill health in the pleasure of their society. We have chosen Ballston for our temporary home, from the hope of seeing them oftener *there* than we could in a secluded town, and because pure air, medicinal waters, and good society have all combined to render it a delightful country residence; yet with all these advantages, it can never possess half the charms of my dear old home!

> That dear old home, where pass'd my childish years,
> When fond affection wiped my infant tears!
> Where first I learn'd from whence my blessings came,
> And lisp'd, in faltering tones, a *mother's* name!
>
> That *dear* old *home*, where memory fondly clings,
> Where eager fancy spreads her soaring wings;
> Around whose scenes my thoughts delight to stray,
> And pass the hours in pleasing dreams away!
>
> Oh, shall I ne'er behold thy waves again,
> My native lake, my beautiful Champlain?
> Shall I no more above thy ripples bend
> In sweet communion with my childhood's friend?
>
> Shall I no more behold thy rolling wave,
> The patriot's cradle, and the warrior's grave?
> Thy mountains, tinged with daylight's parting glow?
> Thy islets, mirror'd in the stream below?
>
> Back! back!—thou *present*, robed in shadows lie,
> And rise, thou *past*, before my raptured eye!
> Fancy shall gild the frowning lapse between,
> And memory's hand shall paint the glowing scene!
>
> Lo! how the view beneath her pencil grows!
> The flow'ret blooms, the winding streamlet flows;
> With former friends I trace my footsteps o'er,
> And muse, delighted, on my own green shore!

Alas! it fades—the fairy dream is past!
Dissolved the veil by sportive fancy cast.
Oh why should thus our brightest dreams depart,
And scenes illusive cheat the longing heart?

Where'er through future life my steps may roam,
I ne'er shall find a spot like thee, my home;
With all my joys the thought of *thee* shall blend,
And, join'd with *thee,* shall rise my childhood's friend.

"Mother is most truly alive to all these feelings. During our first year in New York, we were living a few miles from the city, at one of the loveliest situations in the world! I think I have seldom seen a sweeter spot; but all its beauties could not divert her thoughts from our own dear *home,* and despite the superior advantages we there enjoyed, she wept to enjoy it again. But enough of this; if I suffer my fancy to dwell longer upon these loved scenes, I shall scribble over my whole sheet, and, leaving out what I most wish to say, fill it with nothing but 'Home, home, sweet, sweet home!' as the song goes.   *   *   *   *
June, 1837.

"Now for the mighty theme upon which I scarcely dare to dwell: my visit to Plattsburgh! Yes, my dear H., I do think, or rather I do *hope,* that such a time may come when I can at least spend a week with you. I dare not hope for a longer time, for I know I shall be disappointed. About the middle of this month brother graduates, and will leave West Point for home. He intends to visit Plattsburgh, and it will take much to wean me from my favourite plan of accompanying him. However, all is uncertain—I must not think of it too much—but if I do come, it will be with the hope of gaining a still greater pleasure. We are now delightfully situated. Can you not return with me, and make me a visit? What joy is like the joy of anticipation? What pleasure like those we look forward to, through a long lapse of time, and dwell upon as some bright land that we shall inhabit when the *present* shall have become the *past?* I have heard it observed that it was foolish to anticipate—that it was only increasing the pangs of disappointment. Not so: do we not, in our most sanguine hopes, acknowledge to ourselves a fear, a doubt, an expectation of disappointment? Shall we lose the enjoyment of the present, because evil may come in future? No, no—if anticipation was not meant for a solace, an alleviation of the sorrows of life, would it have been so strongly implanted in our hearts by the great Director of all our passions? No—it is too precious! I would give up half the *reality* of joy for the sweet anticipation. Stop—I have gone too far—for indeed

I could *not* resign my visit to you, though I might hope and anticipate for years!

"Just as I had written the above, father interrupted me with an invitation to ride. We have just returned from a long, delightful drive. Though Ballston cannot compare with Plattsburgh for its rich and varied scenery, still there are romantic woods and shady paths which cannot fail to delight the true lover of nature. * * * * * * * *

"So you do have the *blues,* eh? I had almost said I was glad of it; but that would be too cruel—I will only say, one does not like to be alone, or in any thing singular, and I too, once in a while, receive a visit from these provoking imps—are they not? You should not have blamed Scott only, (excuse me,) but yourself, for selecting such a book to chase away melancholy.

"You ask me if I remember those *story-telling* days? Indeed I do, and nothing affords me more pleasure than the recollection of those happy hours! If my memory could only retain the particulars of my last story, gladly would I resume and continue it when I meet you again. I will ease *your* heart of its fear for *mine*—your scolding did not break it. My dear H., it is not made of such brittle materials as to crack for a trifle. No, no! It would be far more prudent to save it entire for some greater occasion, and then make the crash as loud as possible—don't you think so? Oh nonsensical nonsense! Well,

> 'The greatest and the wisest men
> Will fool a little now and then.'

But I believe I will not add another word, lest my pen should slide off into some new absurdity."

On the 1st of May, 1837, the family left New York for Ballston. They had scarce reached there when Mrs. Davidson had an attack of inflammatory rheumatism, which confined her to her bed, and rendered her helpless as an infant. It was Margaret's turn now to play the nurse, which she did with the most tender assiduity. The paroxysms of her mother's complaint were at first really alarming, as may be seen by the following extract of a letter from Margaret to Miss Sedgwick, written a short time afterwards:

"We at first thought she would never revive. It was indeed a dreadful hour, my dear madam—a sad trial for poor father and myself, to watch, as we supposed, the last agonies of one so beloved as my dear mother! But the cloud has passed by, and my heart, relieved from its burden, is filled, almost to overflowing, with gratitude and joy. After a few hours of dreadful suspense, reaction took place, and since then she has been slowly and steadily improving. In a few days, I hope, she will be able to ride, and breathe some of this delightful air, which cannot fail to invigorate and restore her. My own health has improved astonishingly since my coming here. I walk, and ride, and exercise as much as possible in the open air, and find it of great service to me. Oh how much I hope to see you here!   *   *   *   *   Do, if possible, try the Ballston air once more. It has been useful to you once, it might be still more so now. You will find warm hearts to welcome you, and we will do all in our power to make your visit pleasant to you. The country does indeed look beautiful! The woods are teeming with wild flowers, and the air is full of melody. The soft, wild warbling of the birds is far more sweet to me than the most laboured performances of art; *they* may weary by repetition, but what heart can resist the influence of a lovely day ushered in by the morning song of those sweet carollers! and even to sleep, as it were, by their melodious evening strain. How I wish you could be here to enjoy it with me."

The summer of 1837 was one of the happiest of her fleeting existence. For some time after the family removed to Ballston she was very much confined to the house by the illness of her mother, and the want of a proper female companion to accompany her abroad. At length, a Mr. and Mrs. H., estimable and intimate friends, of a highly intellectual character, came to the village. Their society was an invaluable acquisition to Margaret. In company with them she was enabled to enjoy the healthful recreations of the country; to ramble in the woods; to take exercise on horseback, of which she was extremely fond, and to make excursions about the neighbourhood; while they exerted a guardian care to prevent her, in her enthusiastic love for rural scenery, from exposing herself to any thing detrimental to her health and strength. She gave herself up, for a time, to these exhilarating exercises, abstaining from her usual propensity to overtask her intellect, for she had imbibed the idea that active habits, cheerful recreations, and a holiday frame of mind would effectually re-establish her health. As usual, in her excited moods, she occasionally carried these really healthful practices to excess, and would often, says her mother, engage, with a palpitating heart, and a pulse beating at the rate of one hundred and thirty in a minute, in all the exercises usually prescribed to *preserve* health in those who are in full possession of the blessing. She was admonished of her danger by several attacks upon her lungs during the summer, but as they were of short duration, she still flattered herself that she was getting well. There seemed to be almost an infatuation in her case. The exhilaration of her spirits was at times so great as almost to overpower her. Often would she stand by the window admiring a glorious sunset, until she would be raised into a kind of ecstasy; her eye would kindle;

a crimson glow would mount into her cheek, and she would indulge in
some of her reveries about the glories of heaven, and the spirits of her
deceased sisters, partly uttering her fancies aloud, until turning and
catching her mother's eye fixed painfully upon her, she would throw her
arms round her neck, kiss away the tears, and sink exhausted on her
bosom. The excitement over, she would resume her calmness, and converse on general topics. Among her writings are fragments hastily
scrawled down at this time, showing the vague aspirations of her spirit,
and her vain attempts to grasp those shadowy images that sometimes
flit across the poetic mind.

> Oh for a something more than this,
>   To fill the void within my breast;
> A sweet reality of bliss,
>   A something bright, but unexpress'd.
>
> My spirit longs for something higher
>   Than life's dull stream can e'er supply;
> Something to feed this inward fire,
>   This spark, which never more can die.
>
> I'd hold companionship with all
>   Of pure, of noble, or divine;
> With glowing heart adoring fall,
>   And kneel at nature's sylvan shrine.
>
> My soul is like a broken lyre,
>   Whose loudest, sweetest chord is gone;
> A note, half trembling on the wire—
>   A heart that wants an echoing tone.
>
> When shall I find this shadowy bliss,
>   This shapeless phantom of the mind?
> This something words can ne'er express,
>   So vague, so faint, so undefined?
>
> Language! thou never canst portray
>   The fancies floating o'er my soul!
> Thou ne'er canst chase the clouds away
>   Which o'er my changing visions roll!

And again—

> Oh I have gazed on forms of light,
>   Till life seem'd ebbing in a tear—

Till in that fleeting space of sight
  Were merged the feelings of a year.

And I have heard the voice of song,
  Till my full heart gush'd wild and free,
And my rapt soul would float along
  As if on waves of melody.

But while I glow'd at beauty's glance,
  I long'd to feel a deeper thrill:
And while I heard that dying strain,
  I sigh'd for something sweeter still.

I have been happy, and my soul
  Free from each sorrow, care, regret;
Yet even in these hours of bliss
  I long'd to find them happier yet.

Oft o'er the darkness of my mind
  Some meteor thought has glanced at will;
'Twas bright—but ever have I sigh'd
  To find a fancy brighter still.

Why are these restless, vain desires,
  Which always grasp at something more
To feed the spirit's hidden fires,
  Which burn unseen—unnoticed soar?

Well might the heathen sage have known
  That earth must fail the soul to bind;
That life, and life's tame joys, alone
  Could never chain the ethereal mind.

The above, as we have before observed, are mere fragments, unfinished and uncorrected, and some of the verses have a vagueness incident to the mood of mind in which they were conceived, and the haste with which they were penned; but in these lofty, indefinite aspirations of a young, half-schooled, and inexperienced mind, we see the early and impatient flutterings of a poetical genius, which, if spared, might have soared to the highest regions.

In a letter written to Miss Sedgwick during the autumn, she speaks of her health as having rapidly improved. "I am no longer afflicted by the cough, and mother feels it unnecessary now to speak to me as being ill; though my health is, and probably always will be, very delicate."—"And she really did appear better," observes her mother, "and even I, who had ever been nervously alive to every symptom of her disease, was deluded by those favourable appearances, and began to entertain a hope that she might yet recover, when another sudden attack of bleeding at the lungs convinced us of the fallacy of our hopes, and warned us to take every measure to ward off the severity of the climate in the coming winter. A consultation was held between her father and our favourite physician, and the result was that she was to keep within doors. This was indeed sad, but, after an evident struggle with her own mind, she submitted, with her accustomed good sense, to the decree. All that affection could suggest, was done, to prevent the effects of this seclusion on her spirits." A cheerful room was allotted to her, commanding an agreeable prospect, and communicating, by folding doors, to a commodious parlour; the temperature of the whole apartment was regulated by a thermometer. Hither her books, writing-table, drawing implements, and fancy work were transported. When once established in these winter quarters, she became contented and cheerful. "She read and wrote," says her mother, "and amused herself with drawing and needle-work. After spending as much time as I dare permit in the more serious studies in which she was engaged, she would unbend her mind with one of Scott's delightful novels, or play with her kitten; and at evening we were usually joined by our interesting friends Mr. and Mrs. H. It is now a melancholy satisfaction to me to believe that she could not, in her state of health, be happier, or more pleasantly situated. She was always charmed with the conversation of Mr. H., and followed him through all the mazes of philosophy with the greatest delight. She read Cousin with a high zest, and produced an abstract from it which gave a convincing proof that she understood the principles there laid down; after which she gave a complete analysis of the Introduction to the History of Philosophy, by the same author. Her mind must have been deeply engrossed by these studies, yet it was not visible from her manner. During this short winter she accomplished what to many would have been the labour of years, yet there was no haste, no flurry; she pursued quietly her round of occupations, always cheerful. The hours flew swiftly by; not a moment lagged. I think she never spent a more happy winter than this, with all its varied employments."

The following extract from a letter to one of her young friends, gives an idea of her course of reading during this winter; and how, in her precocious mind, the playfulness of the child mingled with the thoughtfulness of the woman.

"You ask me what I am reading. Alas! bookworm as I am, it makes me draw a long breath to contemplate the books I have laid out for perusal. In the first place, I am reading Condillac's Ancient History, in French, twenty-four volumes; Gibbon's Decline and Fall of the Roman Empire, in four large volumes. I have not quite finished Josephus. In my moments of recreation I am poring over Scott's bewitching *novels*. I wish we could give them some other name instead of *novels*, for they certainly should not bear the same title with the thousand and one productions of that class daily swarming from the press. Do you think they ought? So pure, so pathetic, so historical, and, above all, so true to human nature. How beautifully he mingles the sad with the grotesque, in such a manner that the opposite feelings they excite harmonize perfectly with each other. His works can be read over and over again, and every time with a growing sense of their beauties. Do you read French? If so, I wish we could read the same works together. It would be a great pleasure to me at least, and our mutual remarks might benefit each other. Supposing you will be pleased to hear of my amusements, however trifling, I will venture to name one, at the risk of lowering any great opinion you may have formed of my wisdom! A pet kitten!!! Yes, my dear Henrietta, a sweet little creature, with a graceful shape, playful temper, white breast, and dear little innocent eyes, which completely belie the reputed disposition of a *cat*. He is neither deceitful, ferocious, nor ungrateful, but is certainly the most rational being for an irrational one, I ever saw. He is now snugly lying in my lap, watching every movement of my pen with a quiet purr of contentment. Have you such a pet? I wish you had, that we might both play with them at the same time, sunset, for instance, and while so far distant, feel that we were enjoying ourselves in the selfsame way. You ask what I think of animal magnetism? My dear Hetty, I have not troubled my head about it. I hear of it from every quarter, and mentioned so often with contempt, that I have thought of it only as an absurdity. If I understand it rightly, the leading principle is the influence of one mind upon another; there is undoubtedly such an influence, to a reasonable degree, but as to throwing one into a magnetic sleep—presenting visions before their eyes of scenes passing afar off, it seems almost too ridiculous! Still it may all be *true!* A hundred years since, what would have been our feelings to see what is now here so common, a *steam engine*, breathing fire and smoke, gliding along with the rapidity of thought, and carrying at its *black heels* a train which a hundred men would fail to move. We know not but this apparent absurdity, this magnetism may be a great and mysterious secret, which the course of time will reveal and adapt to important purposes.   *   *   *   *   *

What are you studying? Do you play? Do you draw? Please tell me every thing. I wish I could form some picture of you in my mind's eye. It is so tormenting to correspond with a dear friend, and have no likeness of them in our fancy. I remember every thing as it used to be, but time makes great changes! Now here comes my saucy kitten, and springs upon the table before me as if he had a perfect right there. 'What do you mean, little puss? Come, sit for your portrait.' I hope, dear H., you will fully appreciate this painting, which I consider as my chef-d'œuvre, and preserve it as a faithful likeness of my inimitable cat. But do forgive me so much nonsense! But I feel that to you I can rattle off any thing that comes uppermost. It is near night, and the sun is setting so beautifully after the long storm, that I could not sit here much longer, even if I had a whole page to fill. How splendid the moon must look on the bright waters of the Champlain this night! Good bye, good bye—love to all from all, and believe me, now as ever,

Your sincere friend,
MARGARET."

The following passages from her mother's memorandums, touch upon matters of more solemn interest, which occasionally occupied her young mind:

"During the whole of the preceding summer her mind had dwelt much upon the subject of religion. Much of her time was devoted to serious reflection, self-examination, and prayer. But she evidently shunned all conversation upon the subject. It was a theme she had always conversed upon with pleasure until *now*. This not only surprised but pained me. I was a silent but close and anxious observer of the operations of her mind, and saw that, with all her apparent cheerfulness, she was ill at ease; perfect silence was however maintained on both sides until the winter commenced, and brought us more closely together. Then her young heart again reposed itself, in confiding love, upon the bosom that heretofore had shared its every thought, and the subject became one of daily discussion. I found her mind perplexed and her ideas confused by points of doctrine which she could neither understand nor reconcile with her views of the justice and benevolence of God, as exhibited in the Scriptures. Her views of the Divine character and attributes had ever been of that elevated cast, which, while they raised her mind above all grosser things, sublimated and purified her feelings and desires, and prepared her for that bright and holy communion without which she could enjoy nothing. Her faith was of that character 'which casteth out fear.' It was sweet and soothing to depend upon Jesus for salvation. It was delightful to behold, in the all-imposing majesty of God, a kind and tender father, who pitied her infirmities, and on whose justice and benevolence she could rest for time and eternity. She had, during the summer, heard much disputation on doctrinal points, which she had silently and carefully examined, and had been shocked at the position which many professing Christians had taken; she saw much inconsistency, much bitterness of spirit, on points which she had been taught to consider not essential to salvation; she saw that the spirit of persecution and uncharitableness which pervaded many classes of Christians, had almost totally destroyed that bond of brotherhood which ought firmly to unite the followers of the humble Saviour; and she could not reconcile these feelings with her ideas of the Christian character. Her meekness and humility led her sometimes to doubt her own state. She felt that her religious duties were but too feebly performed, and that without divine assistance all her resolutions to be more faithful were vain. She often said, 'Mamma, I am far from right. I resolve and re-resolve, and yet remain the same.' I had shunned every thing that savoured of controversy, knowing her enthusiasm and extreme sensibility on the subject of religion; I dreaded the excitement it might create. But I now more fully explained, as well as I was able, the simple and divine truths of the Gospel, and held up to her view the beauty and benevolence of the Father's character, and the unbounded love which could have devised the atoning sacrifice; and advised her at present to avoid controversial writings, and make a more thorough examination of the Scriptures, that she might found her principles upon the evidences to be deduced from that groundwork of our faith, unbiassed by the opinions and prejudices of *any man*. I represented to her, that, young as she was, while in feeble health, researches into those knotty and disputed subjects would only confuse her mind; that there was enough of plain practical religion to be gathered from the Bible; and urged the importance of frequent and earnest prayer, which, with God's blessing, would compose the agitation of her mind, which I considered as essential to her inward peace."

On one occasion, while perusing Lockhart's Life of Scott with great interest, her mother ventured to sound her feelings upon the subject of literary fame, and asked her whether she had no ambition to have her name go down to posterity. She took her mother's hand with enthusiasm, kissed her cheek, and, retiring to the other room, in less than an hour returned with the following lines:

TO DIE AND BE FORGOTTEN.

A few short years will roll along,
   With mingled joy and pain,
Then shall I pass—a broken tone!
   An echo of a strain!

Then shall I fade away from life,
　Like cloud-tints from the sky,
When the breeze sweeps their surface o'er,
　And they are lost for aye.

The world will laugh, and weep, and sing,
　As gaily as before,
But cold and silent I shall be—
　As I have been no more.

The haunts I loved, the flowers I nursed
　Will bloom as sweetly still,
But other hearts and other hands
　My vacant place shall fill.

And even mighty love must fail
　To bind my memory here—
Like fragrance round the faded rose,
　'Twill perish with the year.

The soul may look, with fervent hope,
　To worlds of future bliss;
But oh how saddening to the heart
　To be forgot in this!

How many a noble mind hath shrunk
　From death without a name;
Hath look'd beyond his shadowy realm,
　And lived and died for fame.

Could we not view the darksome grave
　With calmer, steadier eye,
If conscious that a world's regret
　Would seek us where we lie?

Faith points, with mild, confiding glance,
　To realms of bliss above,
Where peace, and joy, and justice reign,
　And never-dying love;

But still our earthly feelings cling
　Around this bounded spot;—
There is a something burns within
　Which will not be forgot.

It cares not for a gorgeous hearse,
   For waving torch and plume;
For pealing hymn, funereal verse,
   Or richly sculptured tomb;

But it would live undimm'd and fresh,
   When flickering life departs;
Would find a pure and honour'd grave,
   Embalm'd in kindred hearts.

Who would not brave a life of tears
   To win an honour'd name?
One sweet and heart-awakening tone
   From the silver trump of fame?

To be, when countless years have past,
   The good man's glowing theme?
To be—but I—what right have I
   To this bewildering dream?

Oh it is vain, and worse than vain,
   To dwell on thoughts like these;
I a frail child, whose feeble frame
   Already knows disease!

Who, ere another spring may dawn,
   Another summer bloom,
May, like the flowers of autumn, lie,
   A tenant of the tomb.

Away, away, presumptuous thought!
   I will not dwell on thee!
For what, alas! am I to fame,
   And what is fame to me?

Let all these wild and longing thoughts
   With the dying year expire,
And I will nurse within my breast
   A purer, holier fire!

Yes, I will seek my mind to win
   From all these dreams of strife,
And toil to write my name within
   The glorious book of life.

> Then shall old time who, rolling on,
> Impels me towards the tomb,
> Prepare for me a glorious crown,
> Through endless years to bloom.

December, 1837.

The confinement to the house, in a graduated temperature, the round of cheerful occupations, and the unremitting care taken of her, produced a visible melioration of her symptoms. Her cough gradually subsided, the morbid irritability of her system, producing often an unnatural flow of spirits, was quieted; as usual, she looked forward to spring as the genial and delightful season that was to restore her to perfect health and freedom.

Christmas was approaching, which had ever been a time of social enjoyment in the family; as it drew near, however, the remembrance of those lost from the fireside circle was painfully felt by Mrs. Davidson. Margaret saw the gloom on her mother's brow, and, kissing her, exclaimed, "Dear mother, do not let us waste our present happiness in useless repining. You see I am well, and you are more comfortable, and dear father is in good health and spirits. Let us enjoy the present hour, and banish vain regrets!" Having given this wholesome advice, she tripped off with a light step to prepare Christmas presents for the servants, which were to be distributed by St. Nicholas or Santa Claus, in the old traditional way. Every animated being, rational or irrational, must share her liberality on that day of festivity and joy. Her Jenny, a little bay pony on which she had taken many healthful and delightful rides, must have a gayer blanket, and an extra allowance of oats. "On Christmas morning," says her mother, "she woke with the first sound of the old house clock striking the hour of five, and twining her arms round my neck (for during this winter she shared my bed,) and kissing me again and again, exclaimed—

> 'Wake, mother, wake to youthful glee,
> The golden sun is dawning;'

then slipping a piece of paper into my hand, she sprang out of bed, and danced about the carpet, her kitten in her arms, with all the sportive glee of childhood. When I gazed upon her young face, so bright, so animated, and beautiful, beaming with innocence and love, and thought that perhaps this was the last anniversary of her Saviour's birth she might spend on earth, I could not suppress my emotions: I caught her to my bosom in an agony of tenderness, while she, all unconscious of

the nature of my feelings, returned my caresses with playful fondness."
The following verses were contained in the above-mentioned paper:

TO MY MOTHER AT CHRISTMAS.

Wake, mother, wake to hope and glee,
    The golden sun is dawning!
Wake, mother, wake, and hail with me
    This happy Christmas morning!

Each eye is bright with pleasure's glow,
    Each lip is laughing merrily;
A smile hath past o'er winter's brow,
    And the very snow looks cheerily.

Hark to the voice of the awaken'd day,
    To the sleigh-bells gaily ringing,
While a thousand, thousand happy hearts
    Their Christmas lays are singing.

'Tis a joyous hour of mirth and love,
    And my heart is overflowing!
Come, let us raise our thoughts above,
    While pure, and fresh, and glowing.

'Tis the happiest day of the rolling year,
    But it comes in a robe of mourning,
Nor light, nor life, nor bloom is here
    Its icy shroud adorning.

It comes when all around is dark,
    'Tis meet it so should be,
For its joy is the joy of the happy heart,
    The spirit's jubilee.

It does not need the bloom of spring,
    Or summer's light and gladness,
For love has spread her beaming wing
    O'er winter's brow of sadness.

'Twas thus he came, beneath a cloud
    His spirit's light concealing,
No crown of earth, no kingly robe
    His heavenly power revealing.

His soul was pure, his mission love,
   His aim a world's redeeming;
To raise the darken'd soul above
   Its wild and sinful dreaming.

With all his Father's power and love,
   The cords of guilt to sever;
To ope a sacred fount of light,
   Which flows, shall flow for ever.

Then we shall hail the glorious day,
   The spirit's new creation,
And pour our grateful feelings forth,
   A pure and warm libation.

Wake, mother, wake to chasten'd joy,
   The golden sun is dawning!
Wake, mother, wake, and hail with me
   This happy Christmas morning.

"The last day of the year 1837 arrived. 'Mamma,' said she, 'will you sit up with me to-night until after twelve?' I looked inquiringly. She replied, 'I wish to bid farewell to the present, and to welcome the coming year.' After the family retired, and we had seated ourselves by a cheerful fire to spend the hours which would intervene until the year 1838 should dawn upon us, she was serious, but not sad, and as if she had nothing more than usual upon her mind, took some light sewing in her hand, and so interested me by her conversation, that I scarcely noticed the flight of time. At half past eleven she handed me a book, pointing to some interesting article to amuse me, then took her seat at the writing-table, and composed the piece on the departure of the old year 1837, and the commencement of the new one 1838. When she had finished the Farewell, except the last verse, it wanted a few minutes of twelve. She rested her arms in silence upon the table, apparently absorbed in meditation. The clock struck—a sort of deep thought passed over her expressive face—she remained solemn and silent until the last tone had ceased to vibrate, when she again resumed her pen and wrote, 'The bell! it hath ceased.' When the clock struck, I arose from my seat and stood leaning over the back of her chair, with a mind deeply solemnized by a scene so new and interesting. The words flowed rapidly from her pen, without haste or confusion, and at one o'clock we were quietly in bed."

We again subjoin the poem alluded to, trusting that these effusions, which are so intimately connected with her personal history, will be read with greater interest, when given in conjunction with the scenes and circumstances which prompted them.

ON THE DEPARTURE OF THE YEAR 1837, AND THE COMMENCEMENT OF 1838.

HARK to the house clock's measured chime,
    As it cries to the startled ear,
"A dirge for the soul of departing time,
    A requiem for the year."

Thou art passing away to the mighty past,
    Where thy countless brethren sleep,
Till the great Archangel's trumpet blast,
    Shall waken land and deep.

Oh the lovely and beautiful things that lie
    On thy cold and motionless breast!
Oh the tears, the rejoicings, the smiles, the sighs,
    Departing with thee to their rest.

Thou wert usher'd to life amid darkness and gloom,
    But the cold icy cloud passed away,
And spring, in her verdure and freshness and bloom,
    Touched with glory thy mantle of gray.

The flow'rets burst forth, in their beauty—the trees
    In their exquisite robes were array'd,
But thou glidest along, and the flower and the leaf,
    At the sound of thy footsteps, decay'd.

And fairer young blossoms were blooming alone,
    And they died at the glance of thine eye,
But a life was within which should rise o'er their own,
    And a spirit thou could'st not destroy.

Thou hast folded thy pinions, thy race is complete,
    And fulfill'd the Creator's behest,
Then, adieu to thee, year of our sorrows and joys,
    And peaceful and long be thy rest.

Farewell! for thy truth written record is full,
    And the page weeps, for sorrow and crime,

Farewell! for the leaf hath shut down on the past,
And conceal'd the dark annals of time.

The bell! it hath ceas'd with its iron tongue
To ring on the startled ear,
The dirge o'er the grave of the lost one is rung,
All hail to the new-born year!

All hail to the new-born year,
To the child of hope and fear!
He comes on his car of state,
And weaves our web of fate,
And he opens his robe to receive us all,
And we live or die, and we rise or fall,
In the arms of the new-born year!

Hope! spread thy soaring wings!
Look forth on the boundless sea,
And trace thy bright and beautiful things,
On the veil of the great To Be.

Build palaces broad as the sky,
And store them with treasures of light,
Let exquisite visions bewilder the eye,
And illumine the darkness of night.

We are gliding fast from the buried year,
And the present is no more,
But, hope, we will borrow thy sparkling gear,
And shroud the future o'er.

Our tears and sighs shall sleep,
In the grave of the silent past,
We will raise up flowers—nor weep—
That the air hues may not last.

We will dream our dreams of joy,
Ah! fear! why darken the scene?
Why sprinkle that ominous tear,
My beautiful visions between.

Hath not sorrow swift wings of her own,
That thou must assist in her flight?

Is not daylight too rapidly gone,
    That thou must urge onward the night.

Ah! leave me to fancy, to hope,
    For grief will too quickly be here,
Ah! leave me to shadow forth figures of light,
    In the mystical robe of the year.

'Tis true, they may never assume
    The substance of pleasure—the real—
But believe me our purest of joy,
    Consists in the vague—the ideal.

Then away to the darksome cave,
    With thy sisters, the sigh and the tear,
We will drink, in the crystal wave,
    The health of the new-born year.

"She had been for some time thinking of a subject for a poem, and the next day, which was the first of January, came to me in great perplexity and asked my advice. I had long desired that she would direct her attention to the beautiful and sublime narratives of the Old Testament, and now proposed that she should take the Bible and examine it with that view. After an hour or two spent in research she remarked that there were many, very many subjects of deep and thrilling interest; but, if she now should make a failure, her discouragement would be such as to prevent her from ever making another attempt. 'I am now,' she said, 'trying my wings, I will take a lighter subject at first: if I succeed, I will then write a more perfect poem, founded upon Sacred History.'"

She accordingly took as a theme a prose tale, in a current work of the day, and wrote several pages with a flowing pen, but soon threw them by dissatisfied. It was irksome to employ the thoughts and fancies of another and to have to adapt her own to the plan of the author. She wanted something original. "After some farther effort," says Mrs. Davidson, "she came to me out of spirits and in tears. 'Mother,' said she, 'I must give it up after all.' I asked the reason, and then remarked that as she had already so many labors upon her hands, and was still feeble, it might be the wisest course. 'Oh mother,' said she, 'that is not the reason; my head and my heart are full: poetic images are crowding upon my brain, but every subject has been monopolised: "there is nothing new under the sun."' I said 'my daughter, that others have written upon a subject is not an objection. The most eminent writers do not always choose what is new.' 'Mother, dear mother, what can I say upon a theme which has been touched by the greatest men of this or some other age? I, a mere child; it is absurd in me to think of it.' She dropped beside me on the sofa, laid her head upon my bosom and sobbed violently. I wiped the tears from her face, while my own were fast flowing and strove to soothe the tumult of her mind.   *   *   *   When we were both more calm, I said, 'Margaret, I had hoped that during this winter you would not have commenced or applied yourself to any important work; but, if you feel in that way, I will not urge you to resign an occupation which gives you such exquisite enjoyment.'"

Mrs. Davidson then went on to show to her that, notwithstanding the number of poets that had written, the themes and materials for poetry are inexhaustible. By degrees Margaret became composed; took up a book and read. The words of her mother dwelt in her mind. In a few days she brought her mother the introduction to a projected poem to be called Lenore. Mrs. Davidson was touched at finding the remarks she had made for the purpose of soothing the agitation of her daughter, had served to kindle her imagination; and were poured forth with eloquence in those verses. The excitement continued and the poem of Lenore was completed, corrected and copied into her book by the first of March; having written her plan in prose at full length, containing about the same number of lines as the poem. "During its progress," says Mrs. Davidson, "when fatigued with writing, she would take her kitten and recline on the sofa, asking me to relate to her some of the scenes of the last war. Accordingly I would wile away our solitude by repeating anecdotes of that period; and before Lenore was completed she had advanced several pages in a prose tale, the scene of which was laid upon lake Champlain during the last war. She at the same time, executed faces and figures in crayon which would not have disgraced the pencil of an artist. Her labors were truly immense. Yet a stranger coming occasionally to the house would hardly observe that she had any pressing avocations."

The following are extracts from a rough draught of a letter written to Miss Sedgwick about this time.

"My Dear Madam:—

"I wish I could express to you my pleasure on receiving your kind and affectionate letter. So far from considering myself neglected by your silence, I felt it a great privilege to be permitted to write to you, and knew that I ought not to expect a regular answer to every letter, even while I was longing, day after day, to receive this gratifying token of remembrance. Unless you had witnessed, I fear you would hardly believe my extravagant delight on reading the dear little folded paper, so expressive of your kind recollection. I positively danced for joy; bestowed a thousand caresses upon every body and every thing I loved, dreamed of you all night, and arose next morning (with a heart full,) to answer your letter, but was prevented by indisposition, and have not been able until now to perform a most pleasing duty by acknowledging its receipt. My health during the past winter has been much better than we had anticipated. It is true I have been with dear mother, entirely confined to the house, but being able to read, write and perform all my usual employments, I feel that I have much more reason to be thankful for the blessings continued to me, than to repine because a few have been denied. But spring is now here in name, if not in reality, and I can assure you my heart bounds at the thought of once more escaping from my confinement, and breathing the pure air of Heaven, without fearing a blight or a consumption in every breeze. Spring! What pleasure does that magic syllable convey to the heart of an invalid, laden with sweet promises, and bringing before his mind visions of liberty, which those who are always free cannot enjoy. Thus do I dream of summer, I may never see, and make myself happy for hours in anticipating pleasures I may never share. It is an idle employment, and little calculated to sweeten disappointment. But it has opened to me many sources of delight otherwise unknown; and when out of humor with the present, I have only to send fancy flower gathering in the future, and I find myself fully repaid. Dear mother's health has also been much better than we had feared, and her ill turns less frequent and severe. She sits up most of the day, walks around the lower part of the house, and enjoys her book and her pen as much as ever. * * * * * * You speak of your intercourse with Mrs. Jameson. It must indeed be an exquisite pleasure to be intimately associated with a mind like hers. I have never seen anything but extracts from her writings but must obtain and read them. I suppose the world is anxiously looking for her next volume. * * * We have been reading Lockhart's Life of Scott. Is it not a deeply interesting work? In what a beautiful light it represents the character of that great and good man. No one can read his life or his works without loving and venerating him. As to 'the waters of Helicon' we have but a few niggardly streams in this, our matter of fact village; and father in his medical capacity has forbidden my partaking of them as freely as I could wish. But no matter, they have been frozen up, and will flow in 'streams more salubrious' beneath the milder sky of spring."

In all her letters we find a solicitude about her mother's health, rather than about her own, and indeed it was difficult to say which was most precarious.

The following extract from a poem written about this time to "Her mother on her fiftieth Birth-day" presents a beautiful portrait, and does honor to the filial hand that drew it.

> Yes, mother, fifty years have fled,
> With rapid foot-steps, o'er thy head:
> Have past with all their motley train,
> And left thee on thy couch of pain!
> How many smiles and sighs and tears,
> How many hopes and doubts and fears
> Have vanish'd with that lapse of years.
>
> Oh that we all could look, like thee,
> Back on that dark and tideless sea,
> And 'mid its varied records find
> A heart at ease with all mankind,
> A firm and self-approving mind.
> Grief that had broken hearts less fine
> Hath only served to strengthen thine—
>
> Time that doth chill the fancy's play
> Hath kindled thine with purer ray:
> And stern disease, whose icy dart
> Hath power to chill the breaking heart,
> Hath left thine warm with love and truth
> As in the halcyon days of youth.

The following letter was written on the 26th of March, to a female cousin resident in New York.

"DEAR KATE: This day I am fifteen, and you can, you will readily pardon and account for the absurd flights of my pen, by supposing that my tutelary spirits, nonsense and folly, have assembled around the being of their creation, and claimed the day as exclusively their own; then I pray you to lay to their account, all that I have already scribbled, and believe that, uninfluenced by these grinning deities, I can think and feel, and love, as I love you with all warmth and sincerity of heart. Do you remember how we used to look forward to sweet fifteen, as the pinnacle of human happiness, the golden age of existence? You have but lately passed that milestone in the highway of life; I have just reached it, but I find myself no better satisfied to stand still than before, and look forward to the continuance of my journey, with the same ardent longing I felt at fourteen.

"Ah, Kate, here we are, two young travellers starting forth upon our long pilgrimage, and knowing not whither it may conduct us! *You* some months my superior in age, and many years in acquaintance with society, in external attractions, and all those accomplishments necessary to form an elegant woman. *I*, knowing nothing of life but from books, and a small circle of friends, who love me as I love them, looking upon the *past* as a faded dream, which I shall have time enough to study, and expound, when old age and sorrow come on—upon the *present* as a nurseling—a preparative for the *future*, and upon that future, as what? a mighty whirlpool, of hopes and fears of bright anticipations and bitter disappointments into which I shall soon plunge, and find there, in common with the rest of the world, my happiness or misery." ❋ ❋ ❋ ❋ ❋

The following to a young friend, was also written on the 26th of March.

MY DEAR H.: You must know that winter has come, and gone, and neither mother nor myself have felt a single breeze which could not force its way through the thick walls of our little dwelling. Do you not think I am looking gladly forward to April and May, as the lovely sisters who are to unlock the doors of our prison house, and give us once more to the free enjoyment of nature, without fearing a blight or a consumption in every breath? And now for another, and even more delightful anticipation—your visit! Are you indeed coming? And when are you coming? Do answer the first that I may for once have the pleasure of framing delightful visions without finding them dashed to the ground by the iron hand of reality, and the last, that I may not expect you too soon, and thus subject myself to all the bitterness of "hope deferred." Come, for I have so much to say to you, that I cannot possibly contain it until summer; and come quickly, unless you are willing to account for my wasted time as well as your own, for I shall do little else but dream of you and your visit until the time of your arrival. You cannot imagine how those few words in your little *good for nothing* letter have completely upset my wonted gravity. Do not disappoint me. It is true, mother and I are both feeble and unable to go out with you and show you the lions of our little village, but if warm welcomes can atone for the want of ceremony, you shall have them in abundance, but it seems to me that I shall want to pin you down in a chair and do nothing but look at you from morning till night. As to coming to Plattsburgh, I think if we cannot do so in the spring, (which is doubtful,) we certainly shall in the course of the summer. Brother M. wrote to me yesterday, saying that he would spend the month of August in the country, and if nothing occurred to prevent, we would take our delightful trip by the way of Lake George. Oh it will be so pleasant! but my anticipations are now all bent upon a nearer object. Do not allow a slight impediment to destroy them. We expect in May to move to Saratoga. We shall then have a more convenient house, better society, and the benefit of a school in which I can practise music and drawing, without being obliged to attend regularly. We shall then be a few miles nearer to you, and at present even that seems something desirable to me. I have read and own three volumes of Scott's life, and was much disappointed to find that it was not finished in these three, but concluded the remainder had not yet come out. Are the five volumes all? It is indeed a deeply interesting work. I am very fond of biography, for surely there can be nothing more delightful or instructive than to trace in the infancy and youth of every noble mind the germs of its future greatness. Have you read a work called Letters from Palmyra, by Mr. Ware of New York? I have not yet seen it, but intend to do so soon. It is written in the character of a citizen of Rome at that early period, and it is said to be a lively picture of the manners and customs of the imperial city, and still more of the magnificence of Palmyra, and its splendid queen Zenobia. It also contains a beautiful story. I have lately been reperusing many of Scott's novels, and intend to finish them. Was ever any thing half so fascinating? Oh how I long to have you here and tell you all these little things in person. Do write to me immediately, and tell me when we may expect you, I shall open your next with a beating heart. Do excuse all the blunders and scrawls of this hasty letter. You must receive it as a proof of friendship, for to a stranger, or one who I thought would look upon it with a cold and critical eye, I certainly should not send it. I believe you and I have entered into a tacit agreement to forgive any little mistakes, which the other may chance to commit.

Croyez moi ma chère amie votre.

MARGUERITE.

The spirits of this most sensitive little being became more and more excited with the opening of spring. "She watched," says her mother, "the putting forth of the tender grass and the young blossoms as the period which was to liberate her from captivity. She was pleased with every body and every thing. She loved every thing in nature, both animate and inanimate, with a warmth of affection which displayed the benevolence of her own heart. She felt that she was well, and oh! the bright dreams and imaginings, the cloudless future, presented to her ardent mind—all was sunny and gay."

The following letter is highly expressive of the state of her feelings at that period.

"A few days since, my dearest cousin, I received your affectionate letter, and if my heart smote me at the sight of the well known superscription, you may imagine how unmercifully it thumped on reading a letter so full of affection, and so entirely devoid of reproach for my unkindly negligence. I can assure you, my dear coz., you could have found no better way of striking home to my heart the conviction of my error; and I resolved that hour, that moment, to lay my confessions at your feet, and sue for forgiveness: I knew you were too gentle to refuse. But alas! for human resolves! We were that afternoon expecting brother M. Dear brother! And how could I collect my floating thoughts and curl myself up into a corner with pen, ink and paper before me, when my heart was flying away over the sand hills of this un-romantic region to meet and embrace and welcome home the wanderer. If it can interest you, picture to yourself the little scene; mother and I breathless with expectation, gazing from the window, in mute suspense, and listening to the 'phiz, phiz' of the great steam engine. Then when we caught a rapid glance of his trim little figure, how we bounded away over chairs, sofas, and kittens, to bestow in reality, the greeting fancy had so often given him. Oh! what is so delightful as to welcome a friend! Well, three days have passed like a dream, and he is gone again. I am seated at my little table by the fire. Mother is sewing beside me. Puss is slumbering on the hearth, and nothing external remains to convince us of the truth of that bright sun-beam which had suddenly broken upon our quiet retreat, and departed like a vision as suddenly. When shall we have the pleasure of welcoming *you* thus, my beloved cousin? Your flying call of last summer was but an aggravation. Oh! may all good angels watch over you and all you love; shake the dew of health from their balmy wings upon your smiling home, and waft you hither, cheerful and happy, to sojourn awhile with the friends who love you so dearly! All hail to spring, the bright, the blooming, the renovating spring! Oh! I am so happy—I feel a lightness at my heart, and a vigor in my frame that I have rarely felt. If I speak, my voice forms itself into a laugh. If I look forward, every thing seems bright before me. If I look back, memory calls up what is pleasant, and my greatest desire is that my pen could fling a ray of sunshine over this scribbled page and infuse into your heart some of the cheerfulness of my own. I have been confined to the house all winter, as it was thought the best and only way of restoring my health. Now my symptoms are all better, and I am looking forward to next month and its blue skies with the most childish impatience. By the way, I am not to be called a child any more; for yesterday I was *fifteen*, what say you to that? I feel quite like an old woman, and think of putting on caps and spectacles next month."

It was during the same exuberance of happy feeling, with the delusive idea of confirmed health and the anticipation of bright enjoyments, that she broke forth like a bird into the following strain of melody.

Oh, my bosom is throbbing with joy,
   With a rapture too full to express;
From within and without I am blest,
   And the world, like myself, I would bless.

All nature looks fair to my eye,
   From beneath and around and above,
Hope smiles in the clear azure sky,
   And the broad earth is glowing with love.

I stand on the threshold of life,
   On the shore of its wide rolling sea,
I have heard of its storms and its strife
   But all things are tranquil to me.

There's a veil o'er the future—'tis bright
   As the wing of a spirit of air,
And each form of enchantment and light
   Is trembling in Iris hues there.

I turn to the world of affection,
   And warm, glowing treasures are mine;
To the past, and my fond recollection
   Gathers roses from memory's shrine.

But oh, there's a fountain of joy
   More rich than a kingdom beside,
It is holy—death cannot destroy
   The flow of its heavenly tide.

'Tis the love that is gushing within,
   It would bathe the whole world in its light;
The cold stream of time shall not quench it,
   The dark frown of wo shall not blight.

These visions of pleasure may vanish,
   These bright dreams of youth disappear,
Disappointment each air hue may banish,
   And drown each frail joy in a tear.

I may plunge in the billows of life,
    I may taste of its dark cup of wo,
I may weep, and the sad drops of grief
    May blend with the waves as they flow.

I may dream, till reality's shadow
    O'er the light form of fancy is cast;
I may hope, until hope, too, despairing
    Has crept—to the grave of the past.

But though the wild waters surround me,
    Misfortune, temptation and sin,
Though fear be about and beyond me
    And sorrow's dark shadow within.

Though age, with an icy cold finger,
    May stamp his pale seal on my brow—
Still, still in my bosom shall linger
    The glow that is warming it now.

Youth will vanish, and pleasure—gay charmer,
    May depart on the wings of to-day,
But that spot in my heart shall grow warmer,
    As year after year rolls away.

"While her spirits were thus light and gay," says Mrs. Davidson, "from the prospect of returning health, my more mature judgment told me that those appearances might be deceptive—that even now the destroyer might be making sure his work of destruction; but she really seemed better, the cough had subsided, her step was buoyant, her face glowed with animation, her eye was bright, and love, boundless, universal love seemed to fill her young heart. Every symptom of her disease assumed a more favorable cast. Oh how my heart swelled with the mingled emotions of hope, doubt and gratitude. Our hopes of her ultimate recovery seemed to be founded upon reason, yet her father still doubted the propriety of our return to lake Champlain; and as Saratoga held out many more advantages than Ballston as a temporary residence, he decided to spend the ensuing year or two there; and then we might perhaps, without much risk, return to our much loved and long deserted home on the banks of the Saranac. Accordingly a house was taken and every preparation made for our removal to Saratoga on the first of May. Margaret was pleased with the arrangement."

The following playful extract of a letter to her brother in New York, exhibits her feelings on the prospect of their change of residence.

"I now most humbly avail myself of your most gracious permission to scribble you a few lines in token of my everlasting love. 'This is to inform you I am very well, hoping these few lines will find you in possession of the same blessing'—notwithstanding the blue streaks that flitted over your pathway a few days after you left us. Perhaps it was occasioned by remorse, at the cruelty of your parting speech, perhaps it was the reflection of a bright blue eye, upon the deep waters of your soul, but let the cause be what it may, 'black spirits or white—blue spirits or grey,' I hope the effect has entirely disappeared, and you are no longer tinged with its most doleful shadow. A blue sky, a blue eye, or the blue dye of the violet, are all undeniably beautiful, but this tint when transferred from the works of nature to the brow of man, or the stockings of woman, becomes a thing to ridicule or weep at. May your spirits henceforth, my dear brother, be preserved from this ill-omened influence, and may your feet and ankles never be graced with garments of a hue so repulsive. Oh, brother, we are all in the heat of moving; we—I say, you will account for the use of that personal pronoun on the authority of the old proverb, 'What a dust we flies raise,' for, to be frank with you, I have little or nothing to do with it, but poor mother is over head and ears in boxes, bed-clothes, carpets, straw and discussions. Our hall is already filled with the fruits of her labours and perseverance, in the shape of certain blue chests, carpet cases, trunks, boxes, &c., all ready for a move, Dear mother is head, hands and feet for the whole machine; our *two helps* being nothing but cranks, which turn when you touch them, and cease their rotary movement when the force is withdrawn. Heigho. We miss our good C——, with her quick invention and helpful hand. *   *   *   *   *
Oh my dear brother, I am anticipating so much pleasure next summer, I hope it will not all prove a dream. It will be so delightful when you come up in August and bring cousin K—— with you; tell her I am calculating upon this pleasure with all my powers of fore-enjoyment—tell her also, that I am waiting most impatiently for that annihilating letter of hers, and if it does not come soon, I shall send her another cannonade, ere she has recovered the stunning effects of the first. Oh dear! I have written you a most dis-understandable letter, and now you must excuse me, as I have declared war against M——, and after mending my pen, must collect all my scattered ideas into a fleet, and launch them for a combat upon a whole sea of ink."

"The exuberance of her spirit," says her mother, "as the spring advanced, and she was enabled once more to take exercise in the open air, displayed itself in every thing. Her heart was overflowing with

thankfulness and love. Every fine day in the latter part of April, she
either rode on horseback or drove out in a carriage. All nature looked
lovely to her, not a tree or shrub but conveyed some poetical image or
moral lesson to her mind. The moment, however, that she began to
take daily exercise in the open air, I again heard with agony the
prophetic cough. I felt that all was over! She thought that she had
taken cold, and our friends were of the same opinion. 'It was a slight
cold which would vanish beneath the mild influence of spring.' I, however, feared that her father's hopes might have blinded his judgment,
and upon my own responsibility consulted a skillful physician, who
had on many former occasions attended her. She was not aware of
my present alarm, or that the physician was now consulted. He managed in a playful manner to feel her pulse, without her suspicions.
After he had left the room, 'Madam,' said he, 'it is useless to hold out
any false hopes, your daughter has a seated consumption, which is, I
fear, beyond the reach of medical skill. There is no hope in the case,
make her as happy and as comfortable as you can; let her enjoy riding
in pleasant weather, but her walks must be given up; walking is too
great an exertion for her.' With an aching heart I returned to the lovely
unconscious victim, and found her tying on her hat for a ramble. I
gently tried to dissuade her from going. She caught my eye, and read
there a tale of grief, which she could not understand, and I could not
explain. As soon as I dared trust my voice, I said 'my dear Margaret,
nothing has happened, only I have just been speaking with Dr. ————,
respecting you, and he advises that you give up walking altogether.
Knowing how much you enjoy it, I am pained to mention this, for I
know that it will be a preat privation.' 'Why, mamma,' she exclaimed,
'this cold is wearing off, may I not walk then?' 'The Doctor thinks
you should make no exertion of that kind, but riding in fine weather
may have a happy effect.' She stood and gazed upon my face long
and earnestly; then untied her hat and sat down, apparently ruminating
upon what had past; she asked no questions, but an expression of
thoughtfulness clouded her brow during the rest of the day. It was
settled that she was to ride out in fine weather, but not to walk out
at all, and in a day or two she seemed to have forgotten the circumstance altogether. The return of the cough, and profuse night perspirations, too plainly told me her doom, but I still clung to the hope, that,
as she suffered no pain, she might, by tender judicious treatment,
continue yet for years. I urged her to remit her labours; she saw how
much my heart was in the request, and promised to comply with my
wishes. On the first of May we removed to Saratoga. One short half hour
in the railroad car completed the journey, and she arrived fresh, cheerful

and blooming, in her appearance, such an effect had the excitement of pleasure upon her lovely face.

"On the day we left Ballston she wrote a 'Parting Word' to Mrs. H., who had been one of our most intimate and affectionate visitors throughout the winter, and whose husband had assisted her much in her studies of moral philosophy, as well as delighted her by his varied and instructive conversation.

A PARTING WORD TO MY DEAR MRS. H.

BALLSTON SPA, *April* 30, 1838.

At length the awful morn hath come,
    The parting hour is nigh,
And I sit down 'mid dust and gloom,
    To bid you brief "good bye."

Each voice to fancy's listening ear,
    Repeats the doleful cry,
And the bare walls and sanded floor,
    Re-echo back "good bye."

So must it be! but many a thought
    Comes crowding on my mind,
Of the dear friends, the happy hours,
    The joys we leave behind.

How we shall miss your cheerful face,
    Forever bright and smiling,
And your sweet voice so often heard,
    Our weary hours beguiling!

How shall we miss the kindly hearts,
    Which none can know unloving,
Whose thoughts and feelings none can read,
    Nor find his own improving!

And he, whose converse, hour by hour,
    Hath lent old Time new pinions,
Whose hand hath drawn the shadowy veil
    From wisdom's broad dominions.

Whose voice hath poured forth priceless gems,
    Scarce conscious that he taught,

Whose mind of broad, of loftiest reach,
Hath showered down thought on thought.

True we may meet with many a dear
And cherished friend, but yet
Oft shall we cast a backward glance
Of wistful—vain regret.

When evening spreads her sombre veil,
To fold the slumbering earth,
When our small circle closes round
The humble, social hearth—

Oft shall we dream of hours gone by,
And con these moments o'er,
'Till we half bend our ears to catch
Your footsteps at the door.
And then turn back and sigh to think
We hear those steps no more!

But tho' these dismal thoughts arise,
Hope makes me happy still,
There is a drop of comfort lurks,
In every draught of ill!

By pain and care each joy of earth
More exquisite is made,
And when we meet the parting grief
Shall doubly be o'erpaid.

In disappointments deep too quick
Our fairest prospects drown,
Let not this hope, which blooms so bright,
Be wither'd at his frown!

Come, and a mother's pallid cheek
Shall brighten at your smile,
And her poor frame so faint and weak,
Forget its pains the while.

Come, and a glad and happy heart,
Shall give the welcome kiss,
And puss shall purr, and frisk and mew,
In token of her bliss.

Come! and behold how I improve,
  In dusting—cleaning—sweeping,
And I will hear, with patient ear,
  Your lectures on house-keeping.

And now, may all good Angels guard,
  Your path where'er it lie,
May peace reign monarch in your breast,
  And gladness in your eye.

And may the dews of health descend,
  On him you cherish best,
To his worn frame their influence lend,
  And calm each nerve to rest!

And may we meet again! nor feel
  The parting hour so nigh,
Peace, love and happiness to all,
  Once more—once more, "good bye!"

"She interested herself," continued Mrs. Davidson, "more than I had anticipated in the arrangement of our new habitation and in forming plans of future enjoyment with our friends, when they should visit us; I exerted myself to please her taste in everything, although she was prohibited from making the slightest physical exertion herself. The house settled, then came the flower garden, in which she spent more time than I thought prudent: but she was so happy while thus engaged and the weather being fine, and the gardener disposed to gratify her and carry all her little plans into effect; I, like a weak mother, wanted resolution to interfere, and have always reproached myself for it although not conscious that it was an injury at the time. Her brother had invited her to return to New York with him when he came to visit us in June, and she was now impatiently counting the days until his arrival. Her feelings are portrayed in a letter to her young friend H."

"SARATOGA, *June* 1, 1838.

"June is at last with us, my dear cousin, and the blue-eyed goddess could not have looked upon the green bosom of her mother earth, attired in a lovelier or more enchanting robe. I am seated by an open window, and the breeze laden with the perfumes of the blossoms and opening leaves just lifts the edge of my sheet—and steals with the gentlest footsteps imaginable to fan my cheek and forehead. The grass tinged with the deepest and freshest green is waving beneath its influence; the birds are singing their sweetest songs; and as I look into the depths of the clear blue sky the rich tints appear to flit higher and higher as I gaze, till my eye seems searching into immeasurable distance. Oh! such a day as this, it is a luxury to breathe. I feel as if I could frisk and gambol like my kitten from the mere consciousness of life. Yet with all the loveliness around me I reperuse your letter, and long for wings to fly from it all to the dull atmosphere and crowded highways of the city. Yes! I could then look into your eyes and I should forget the blue sky; and your smile, and your voice would doubly compensate me for the loss of green trees and singing birds. There are green trees in the heart which shed a softer perfume, and birds which sing more sweetly. 'Nonsense, Mag is growing sentimental;' I knew you would say so, but the streak came across me and you have it at full length. In plainer terms, how delighted, how more than delighted I shall be when I do come! when I do come, Kate! oh! oh! oh! what would our language be without interjections, those expressive parts of speech which say so much in so small a compass. Now I am sure you can understand from these three syllables all the pleasure, the rapture I anticipate; the meeting, the parting, all the component parts of that great whole which I denominate a visit to New York! No not to New York! but to the few dear friends whose society will afford me all the enjoyment I expect or desire, and who, in fact constitute all my New York.

June 2d. I had written thus far, dear Kate, when I was most agreeably interrupted by a proposal for a ride on horseback; my sheet slid of itself into the open drawer, my hat and dress flew on as if by instinct, and in ten minutes I was galloping full speed through the streets of our little village with father by my side. I rode till nearly tea time and came home tired, tired, tired: Oh I ache to think of it. My poor letter slept all night as soundly as its writer, but now that another day has dawned the very opposite of its predecessor, damp, dark and rainy, I have drawn it forth from its receptacle, and seek to dissipate all outward gloom, by communing with one the thought of whom conveys to my mind any thing but melancholy. Oh, Kate, Kate, in spite of your disinterested and sober advice to the contrary, I shall come, I shall soon come, just as soon as M. can and will run up for me. Yet perhaps, in the end I shall be disappointed. My happy anticipations resemble the cloudless sky of yesterday and who knows but a stormy to-morrow may erase the brilliant tints of hope as well as those of nature. * * * * * Do write quickly and tell me if I am to prepare, if you continue to feel as when you last wrote and still advise me not to come—I shall dispose of your advice in the most approved manner, throw it to the winds, and embark armed and equipped for your city to make my destined visit, and fulfil its conditions by fair means or foul and bring you home in triumph. Oh! we shall have fine times. Oh dear, I blush, to look back upon my sheet and see so many I's in it."

"The time of her brother's coming drew near. He would be with us at nine in the morning. At eleven they were to start. I prepared all for her departure with my own hand, lest, should I trust it to a domestic to make the arrangements, she would make some exertion herself. She sat by me whilst thus engaged, relating playful anecdotes until I urged her to retire for the night. On going into her room an hour or two afterwards, I was alarmed to find her in a high fever. About midnight she was taken with bleeding at the lungs. I flew to her father, and in a few minutes a vein was opened in her arm. To describe our feelings at this juncture is impossible. We stood, gazing at each other in mute despair. After that shock had subsided her father retired, and I seated myself by the bedside to watch her slumbers, and the rising sun found me still at my post. She awoke, pale, feeble and exhausted by the debilitating perspiration which attended her sleep. She was surprised to find that I had not been in bed; but when she attempted to speak I laid my finger upon her lips and desired her to be silent. She understood my motive, and when I bent my head to kiss her, I saw a tear upon her cheek. I told her the necessity of perfect quiet, and the danger which would result from agitation. Before her brother came she desired to rise. I assisted her to do so, and he found her quietly seated in her easy chair, perfectly composed in manner, and determined not to increase her difficulties by giving way to feelings which must at that time, have oppressed her heart. My son was greatly shocked to find her in this state. I met him and urged the importance of perfect self-possession on his part, as any sudden agitation might in her present alarming state be fatal. Poor fellow! he subdued his feelings and met her with a cheerful smile which concealed a heart almost bursting with sorrow. The propriety of her taking this jaunt had been discussed by her father and myself for a number of weeks. We both thought her too ill to leave home, but her strong desire to go, the impression she had imbibed that travelling would greatly benefit her health, and the pleading of friends in her behalf, on the ground that disappointment would have a more unfavorable effect than the journey possibly could have, all had their effect in leading us to consent. It was possible it might be of use to her, although it was at best an experiment of a doubtful nature. But this attack was decisive; yet caution must be used in breaking the matter to her in her present weak state. Her brother stayed a day or

two with us, and then returned, telling her that when she was able
to perform the journey, he would come again and take her with him.
After he left us, she soon regained her usual strength, and in a fortnight
her brother returned and took her to New York."

The anxiety of Mrs. Davidson was intense until she received her first
letter. It was written from New York, and in a cheerful vein, speaking
encouragingly of her health, but showing more solicitude about the
health and well being of her mother than of her own. She continued to
write frequently, giving animated accounts of scenes and persons.

The following extract relates to an excursion, in company with two
of her brothers, into West Chester county, one of the pleasantest, and,
until recently, the least fashionably known, regions on the banks of
the Hudson.

"At three o'clock, we were in the Singsing steamer, with the water
sparkling below, and the sun broiling over head. In the course of our
sail a huge thunder cloud arose, and I retreated, quite terrified to the
cabin. But it proved a refreshing shower. Oh! how sweet, how delightful
the air was. When we landed at the dock, every thing looked so fresh
and green. We mounted into a real country vehicle, and rattled up
the hill to the village inn, a quiet, pleasant little house. I was immediately shown to my room, where I stayed until tea-time, enjoying
the prospect of a splendid sunset upon the mountains, and resting
after the fatigues of the day. At seven, we drank tea, a meal strongly
contrasted with the fashionable meagre unsocial city tea. The table
was crowded with every thing good, in the most bountiful style, and
served with the greatest attention by the landlord's pretty daughter.
I retired soon after tea, and slept soundly until day break. After breakfast, we sent for a carriage to take us along the course of the Croton,
to see the famous water works, but, to our disappointment, every
carriage was engaged, and we could not go. In the afternoon, a party
was made up to go in a boat across the river, and ascend a mountain
to a singular lake upon its summit, where all the implements of fishing
were provided, and a collation was prepared. In short, it was a pic-nic.
To this we were invited, but on learning they would not return until
nine or ten in the evening, that scheme also was abandoned. Towards
night we walked around the village, looked at the tunnel, and visited
the ice-cream man, and in spite of my various disappointments, I retired
quite happy and pleased with my visit. The next day was Sunday, and
we proposed going to the little Dutch church, a few miles distant, and
hearing the service performed in Dutch; but lo! on drawing aside my
curtains in the morning it rained, and we were obliged to content ourselves as well as we could until the rain was over. After dinner the
sun again peeped out, as if for our especial gratification, and in a few

minutes a huge country waggon, with a leathern top and two sleek horses drew up to the door. We mounted into it and away we rattled over the most beautiful country I ever saw. Oh! it was magnificent! Every now and then the view of the broad Hudson, with its distant hills, and the clouds resting on their summits, burst upon our view. Now we would ascend a lofty hill, clothed with forests, and verdure of the most brilliant hues; now dash down into a deep ravine, with a stream winding and gurgling along its bed, with its tiny waves rushing over the wheel of some rustic mill, embosomed in its shade and solitude. Every now and then the gable end of some low dutch building would present itself before us, smiling in its peaceful stillness, and conveying to the mind a perfect picture of rural simplicity and comfort, although, perhaps, of ignorance. At length we paused upon the summit of a gentle hill, and judge of my delight when I beheld below me, the old Dutch church, the quiet, secluded, beautiful little church yard, the running stream, the path, and the rustic bridge, the ever memorable scene of Ichabod's adventure with the *headless horseman*. There, thought I, rushed the poor pedagogue, his knees cramped up to his saddle-bow with fear, his hands grasping his horse's mane, with convulsive energy, in the hope that the rising stream might arrest the progress of his fearful pursuer, and allow him to pass in safety. Vain hope! Scarce had he reached the bridge when he heard, rattling behind him, the hoofs of his fiendish companion. The church seemed in a blaze to his bewildered eyes, and urging on, on, he turned to look once more, when, horror of horrors! the head, the fearful head, was in the act of descending upon his devoted shoulders. Ha! ha! ha! I never laughed so in my life. Well we rode on through the scene of poor Andre's capture, and dashed along the classic valleys of Sleepy Hollow. After a long and delightful drive, we returned in time for tea. After tea we were invited into Mrs. F.'s parlor, where, after a short time, were collected quite a party of ladies and gentlemen. At nine we were served with ice-cream, wine, &c. I retired very much pleased and very much fatigued. Early in the morning we rose with a most brilliant sun, breakfasted, mounted once more into the waggon, and rattled off to the dock. Oh! that I could describe to you how fresh and sweet the air was. I felt as if I wanted to open my mouth wide and inhale it. We gave M. our parting kisses, and soon found ourselves once more, after this charming episode, approaching the mighty city. We had a delightful sail of two or three hours, and again rode up to dear aunt M.'s, where all seemed glad at my return. I spent the remainder of the day in resting and reading."

"In these artless epistles," continues Mrs. Davidson, "there is much of character, for who could imagine this constant cheerfulness, this almost forgetfulness of self, these affectionate endeavors, by her sweetly playful account of all her employments while absent, to dispel the grief, which she knew was preying upon my mind on account of her illness. Who could conceive the pains she took to conceal from me the ravages, which disease was daily making upon her form. She was never heard to complain, and in her letters to me, she hardly alludes to her illness. The friends to whom I had entrusted her, during her short period of absence, sometimes feared that she would never be able to reach home again. Her brother told me, but not until long after her return, that on her way home she really fainted several times from debility—and that he took her from the boat to the carriage, as he would have done an infant.

"On the sixth of July, I once more folded to my heart this cherished object of my solicitude, but oh, the change which three short weeks had wrought in her appearance, struck me forcibly. I was so wholly unprepared for it, that I nearly fainted. After the excitement of the meeting, (which she had evidently summoned all her fortitude to bear with composure) was over, she sat down by me, and passing her thin arm around my waist, said, 'Oh, my dear mamma, I am home again at last, I now feel as if I never wanted to leave you again; I have had a delightful visit, my friends were all glad to see me, and have watched over me with all the kindness and care, which affection could dictate, but oh, there is no place like home, and no care like a mother's care; there is something in the very air of home, and in the sound of your voice, mother, which makes me happier just now, than all the scenes which I have passed through in my little jaunt; oh, after all, home is the only place for a person as much out of health as I am.' I strove to support my emotions, while I marked her pale cheek and altered countenance. She fixed her penetrating eyes upon my face, kissed me, and drawing back to take a more full survey of the effects which pain and anxiety had wrought in me, kissed me again and again, saying, 'she knew I had deeply felt the want of her society, and now once more at home, she should so prize its comforts, as to be in no haste to leave it again.' She was much wasted, and could hardly walk from one room to another; her cough was very distressing, she had no pain, but a languor and a depression of spirits, foreign to her nature. She struggled against this debility, and called up all the energies of her mind to overcome it, her constant reply to inquiries about her health, by the friends who called, was the same as formerly, "Well, quite well—mother calls me an invalid, but I feel well." Yet, to me, when alone, she talked more freely of her symptoms, and I thought I could discern from her manner, that she had apprehensions as to the result. I had often endeavored to acquire firmness sufficient to tell her what was her situation, but she seemed so studiously to avoid the disclosure, that my resolution had hitherto, been unequal to the task. But I was much surprised one day, not long after her return from New York, by her asking me to tell her without reserve, my opinion of her state; the question wrung my very heart. I was wholly unprepared for it, and it was put in so solemn a manner, that I could not evade it, were I disposed to do so. I knew with what strong affection she clung to life, and the objects and friends which endeared it to her; I knew how bright the world upon which she was just entering appeared to her young fancy, what glowing pictures she had drawn of future usefulness and happiness. I was now called upon at one blow, to crush these hopes, to destroy the delightful visions, which had hovered around her from her cradle until this very period; it would be cruel and wrong to deceive her; in vain I attempted a reply to her direct and solemn appeal, and my voice grew husky; several times I essayed to speak, but the words died away on my lips; I could only fold her to my heart in silence, imprint a kiss upon her forehead, and leave the room to avoid agitating her with feelings I had no power to repress.

"The following extract from a letter to her brother in New York, dated a short time after this incident occurred, and which I never saw until after her departure, will best portray her own feelings at this period.

" 'As to my health at present, I feel as well as when you were here, and the cough is much abated, but it is evident to me, that mother thinks me not so well as before I left home; I do not myself believe that I have gained any thing from the visit, and in a case like mine, standing still is certainly loss, but I feel no worse. However, I have learned, that feelings are no criterion of disease. Now, brother, I want to know, what Dr. M—— discovered, or thought he discovered in his examination of my lungs; father says nothing—mother, when I ask, cannot tell me, and looks so sad! Now, I ask you, hoping to be answered. If you have not heard the doctor say, I wish you would ask him, and write to me. If it is more unfavorable than I anticipate, it is best I should know now; if it is the contrary, how much pain and restlessness and suspicion will be spared me, by the knowledge. As to myself, I feel and know that my health is in a most precarious state, that the disease we dread, has perhaps fastened upon me, but I have an impression, that if I make use of the proper remedies and exercise, I may yet recover a tolerable degree of health. I do not feel that my case is incurable; I wish to know if I am wrong. I have rode on horseback twice since you left me; dear, dear brother, what a long egotistic letter I have written you; do forgive me, my heart was full, and I felt that I must unburden it. I wish you would write me a long letter. Do not let dear mother know at present, the questions I have asked you.' ✻ ✻ ✻ ✻ ✻ ✻ ✻ ✻ ✻

"From this period, she grew more thoughtful. There was even a solemnity in her manner, which I never before observed. Her mind, as I mentioned before, had been much perplexed by some doctrinal points. To solve these doubts, I asked if I should not send for some clergyman. She said no. She had heard many discussions on these subjects, and they had always served rather to confuse than to convince her. 'I would rather converse with you alone, mother.' She then asked me if I thought it essential to salvation that she should adopt any particular creed. I felt that I was an inefficient, perhaps a blind guide, yet it was my duty not only to impart consolation, but to explain to her my own views of the truth. I replied that I considered faith and repentance only, to be essential to salvation: that it was very desirable that her mind should be settled upon some particular mode of faith; but that I did not think it absolutely necessary that she should adopt the tenets of any established church, and again recommended an attentive perusal of the New Testament. She expressed her firm belief in the divinity of Christ. The perfections of his character, its beauty and holiness excited her admiration, while the benevolence which prompted the sacrifice of himself to save a lost world, filled her with the most enthusiastic gratitude. It was a source of regret that so much of her time had been spent in light reading, and that her writings had not been of a more decidedly religious character. She lamented that she had not chosen Scriptural subjects for the exercise of her poetical talent, and said, 'Mamma, should God spare my life, my time and talents shall for the future, be devoted to a higher and holier end.' She felt that she had trifled with the gifts of Providence, and her self condemnation and grief were truly affecting. 'And must I die so young? My career of usefulness hardly commenced? Oh! mother, how sadly have I trifled with the gifts of Heaven! What have I done which can benefit one human being?' I folded her to my heart, and endeavored to soothe the tumult of her feelings, bade her remember her dutiful conduct as a daughter, her affectionate bearing as a sister and friend, and the consolation which she had afforded me through years of suffering! 'Oh my mother,' said she, 'I have been reflecting much of late, upon this sad waste of intellect, and had marked out for myself a course of usefulness which, should God spare my life ———.' Here her emotions became too powerful to proceed. At times she suffered much anxiety with regard to her eternal welfare, and deeply lamented her want of faithfulness in the performance of her religious duties: complained of coldness and formality in her devotional exercises, and entreated me to pray with and for her. At other times, her hope of Heaven would be bright, her faith unwavering and her devotion fervent.

Yet it was evident to me, that she still cherished the hope that her life might be prolonged. Her mother had lingered for years in a state equally hopeless, and during that period had been enabled to attend to the moral and religious culture of her little family. Might not the same kind Providence prolong *her life*. It would be vain to attempt a description of those seasons of deep and thrilling interest. God alone knows in what way my own weak frame was sustained. I felt that she had been renovated and purified by Divine Grace, and to see her thus distrest when I thought that all the consolations of the Gospel ought to be hers, gave my heart a severe pang. Many of our friends now were of opinion that a change of climate might benefit, perhaps restore her. Heretofore, when the suggestion had been made, she shrunk from the idea of leaving her home for a distant clime. Now her anxiety to try the effect of a change was great, I felt that it would be vain, although I was desirous that nothing should be left untried. Feeble as she now was, the idea of her resigning the comforts of home and being subject to the fatigues of travelling in public conveyances was a dreadful one, yet if there was a rational prospect of prolonging her life by these means, I was anxious to give them a trial. Dr. Davidson after much deliberation on the subject, called counsel. Dr. ———— came, and when after half an hour's pleasant and playful conversation with Margaret, he joined us in the parlor, Oh! how my poor heart trembled. I hung upon the motions of his lips as if my own life depended on what they might utter. At length he spoke, and I felt as if an ice-bolt had passed through my heart. He had never thought, although he had known her many years, that a change of climate would benefit her. She had lived beyond his expectations many months, even years; and now he was convinced, were we to attempt to take her to a Southern climate, that she would die on the passage. Make it as pleasant as possible for her at home, was his advice. He thought that a few months must terminate her life. She knew that we had confidence in the opinion of this, her favorite physician. When I had gained firmness enough to answer her questions, I again entered the room and found her composed, although she had evidently been strongly agitated, and had not brought her mind to hear her doom. Never, oh! never to the latest hour of my life, shall I forget the look she gave me when I met her. What a heart-rending task was mine! I performed it as gently as possible. I said the Doctor thought her strength unequal to the fatigue of the journey; that he was not so great an advocate for change of climate as many persons; that he had known many cases in which he thought it injurious, and his best advice was that we should again ward off the severity of the winter by creating an atmosphere within our house. She mildly acquiesced, and the subject was dropped altogether. She sometimes read, and frequently from mere habit, held a book in her hand when unable to digest its contents, and within the book, there usually rested a piece of paper, upon which she occasionally marked the reflections which arose in her mind, either in poetry or prose."

We here interrupt the narrative of Mrs. Davidson, to insert a copy of verses addressed by Margaret to her brother, a young officer in the army, and stationed at a frontier post in the far west. They were written in September, about two months before her death, and are characterized throughout by her usual beauty of thought and tenderness of feeling; but the last verse, which alludes to the fading verdure, and falling leaf, and gathering melancholy, and lifeless quiet of the season, as typical of her own blighted youth and approaching dissolution, has something in it peculiarly solemn and affecting.

TO MY SOLDIER BROTHER IN THE FAR WEST.*

'Tis an autumn eve, and the tints of day
    From the west are slowly stealing,
And the clouds round the couch of the setting sun
    Are gently and silently wheeling.
'Tis the scene and the hour for the soul to bathe
    In its own deep springs of feeling,
And my thoughts, from their galling bonds set free,
Have fled to the "far, far west" to thee!

And perchance, 'mid the toils of thy varied life,
    Thou also art pausing awhile,
To behold how beautiful all things look
    In the sunlight's passing smile;
And perchance recollections of kindred and home
    Thy cares for a moment beguile;
Thy thoughts have met *mine* in their passage to thee,
And though distant, far distant, our spirits are free!

I know thou art dreaming of home,
    And the dear ones sheltered there;
Of thy mother, pale with the pain of years
    And thy sire with his silvered hair;
And with *them* blend thoughts of thy boyish years,
    When the world looked all so fair,

* This copy of verses has come to hand since the publication of the first edition of this memoir.

When thy cheek flushed high at the voice of praise,
  And thy breast was unknown to care;
And while memory burns her torch for thee,
I know that these thoughts and these dreams will be!

But when, in the shade of the autumn wood,
  Thy wandering footsteps stray,
When yellow leaves and perishing buds
  Are scattered in thy way;
When all around thee breathes of rest
  And sadness and decay—
With the drooping flower, and the falling tree,
Oh! brother, blend thy thoughts of me!

"The following fragments," continues Mrs. Davidson, "appear to be the very breathings of her soul during the last few weeks of her life— written in pencil, in a hand so weak and tremulous that I could with difficulty decipher them word by word with the aid of a strong magnifying glass.

"Consumption! child of wo, thy blighting breath
Marks all that's fair and lovely for thine own,
And, sweeping o'er the silver chords of life,
Blends all their music in one death-like tone."

1838.

"What strange, what mystic things we are,
With spirits longing to outlive the stars.
* * * * * * * * but even in decay
Hasting to meet our brethren in the dust.
As one small dew-drop runs, another drops
To sink unnoticed in the world of waves.

"O it is sad to feel that when a few short years
Of life are past, we shall lie down, unpitied
And unknown, amid a careless world;
That youth and age and revelry and grief
Above our heads shall pass, and we alone
Shall sleep! alone shall be as we have been,
No more.   *   *   *   *   *

"These are unfinished fragments, a part of which I could not decipher at all. I insert them to give an idea of the daily operations of her mind during the whole of this long summer of suffering. Her gentle spirit

never breathed a murmur or complaint. I think she was rarely heard
to express even a feeling of weariness. But here are a few more of
those outpourings of the heart. I copy these little effusions with all
their errors; there is a sacredness about them which forbids the
change even of a single letter. The first of the fragments which follow
was written on a Sabbath evening in autumn, not many weeks before
her death.

It is autumn, the season of rapid decay,
When the flow'rets of summer are hasting away
   From the breath of the wintry blast,
And the buds which oped to the gazer's eye,
And the glowing tints of the gorgeous sky,
And the forests robed in their emerald dye,
   With their loveliest blossoms have past.
'Tis eve, and the brilliant sunset hue
Is replaced by a sky of the coldest blue,
   Untouched by a floating cloud.
And all nature is silent, calm and serene,
As though sorrow and suffering never had been
   On this beautiful earth abroad.
'Tis a Sabbath eve, and the longing soul
Is charm'd by its quiet and gentle control
   From each wayward and wandering thought,
And it longs from each meaner affection to move,
And it soareth the troubles of earth above
To bathe in that fountain of light and love,
   Whence our purest enjoyments are caught.

                     1838.

But winter, O what shall thy greeting be
   From our waters, our earth and our sky;
What welcoming strain shall arise for thee
   As thy chariot wheels draw nigh?
Alas! the fresh flowers of the spirit decay
   As thy cold, cold steps advance,
And even young Fancy is shrinking away
   From the chill of thy terrible glance;
And Hope with her mantle of rainbow hue
   Hath flew from thy freezing eye,
And her bright train of visions are melting in air
   As thy shivering blasts sweep by.
Thy   *   *   *   *   *   *

                  Oct. 1838.

THE NATURE OF THE SOUL.

The spirit, what is it? Mysterious, sublime,
    Undying, unchanging, forever the same,
It bounds lightly athwart the dark billows of time,
    And moves on unscorched by its heavenly flame.

Man owns thee and feels thee, and knows thee divine;
    He feels thou art his, and thou never canst die;
He believes thee a gem from the Maker's pure shrine,
    A portion of purity holy and high.

'Tis around him, within him the source of his life,
    Yet too weak to contemplate its glory and might;
He trembling shrinks back to dull earth's humble strife,
    And leaves the pure atmosphere glowing with light.

Thou spark from the Deity's radiant throne,
    I know thee, yet shrink from thy greatness and power;
Thou art mine in thy splendor, I feel thee my own,
    Yet behold me as frail as the light summer flower.

I strive in my weakness to gaze on thy might,
    To trace out thy wanderings through ages to come,
Till like birds on the sea, all exhausted, at length
    I flutter back weary to earth as my home.

Like a diamond when laid in a rough case of clay,
    Which may crumble and wear from the pure gem enclos'd,
But which ne'er can be lit by one tremulous ray
    From the glory-crown'd star in its dark case reposed.

"As the cool weather advanced, her decline became more visible, and she devoted more and more of her time to searching the Scriptures, self-examination and subjects for reflection, and questions which were to be solved by evidences deduced from the Bible. I found them but a few days before her death, in the sacred volume which lay upon the table, at which she usually sat during her hours of retirement. She had been searching the holy book, and overcome by the exertion, rang the bell which summoned me to her side, for no person but myself was admitted during the time set apart for her devotional exercises.

Subjects for reflection.

1st. The uniform usefulness of Christ's miracles.

2d. The manner in which he overthrows all the exalted hopes which the Jews entertain of a temporal kingdom, and strives to explain to them the entire spirituality of the one he has come to erect.

3d. The deep and unchangeable love for man, which must have impelled Christ to resist so many temptations and endure so many sufferings, even death, that truth might enlighten the world, and heaven and immortality become realities instead of dreams.

4th. The general thoughtlessness of man with regard to his greatest, his only interest.

5th. Christ's constant submission to the will of his father, and the necessity of our imitating the meek and calm and gentle qualities of his character, together with that firmness of purpose and confidence in God which sustained him to the end.

6th. The necessity of so living, that we need not fear to think each day our last.

7th. The necessity of religion to soothe and support the mind on the bed of sickness.

8th. Self-examination.

9th. Is Christ mentioned expressly in Scripture as equal with God and a part?

10th. Is there sufficient ground for the doctine of the Trinity?

11th. Did Christ come as a prophet and reformer of the world, or as a sacrifice for our sins, to appease the wrath of his father.

12th. Is any thing said of infant baptism?

Written in November 1838.

"About three weeks before her departure, I one morning found her in the parlor, where, as I before observed, she spent a portion of her time in retirement, I saw that she had been much agitated, and seemed weary. I seated myself by her and rested her head on my bosom, while I gently pressed my hand upon her throbbing temples to soothe the agitation of her nerves. She kissed me again and again, and seemed as if she feared to trust her voice to speak lest her feelings should overcome her. As I returned her caresses, she silently put a folded paper in my hand. I began to open it, when she gently laid her hand on mine, and said in a low tremulous tone, 'Not now, dear mother!' I then led her back to her room, placed her upon the sofa, and retired to examine the paper. It contained the following lines.

TO MY MOTHER.

Oh Mother, would the power were mine,
To wake the strain thou lov'st to hear,

And breathe each trembling new-born thought,
  Within thy fondly listening ear.
As when in days of health and glee,
My hopes and fancies wander'd free.

But, mother, now a shade has past,
  Athwart my brightest visions here,
A cloud of darkest gloom has wrapt,
  The remnant of my brief career!
No song, no echo can I win,
The sparkling fount has died within.

The torch of earthly hope burns dim,
  And fancy spreads her wings no more.
And oh, how vain and trivial seem,
  The pleasures that I prized before.
My soul with trembling steps and slow,
  Is struggling on through doubt and strife,
Oh! may it prove as time rolls on,
  The pathway to eternal life;—
Then, when my cares and fears are o'er,
I'll sing thee as in days of yore.

I said that hope had pass'd from earth,
  'Twas but to fold her wings in Heaven,
To whisper of the soul's new birth,
  Of sinners sav'd and sins forgiven.
When mine are wash'd in tears away,
Then shall my spirit swell my lay.

When God shall guide my soul above,
By the soft cords of heavenly love,
When the vain cares of earth depart,
And tuneful voices swell my heart,
Then shall each word, each note I raise,
Burst forth in pealing hymns of praise,
And all not offered at His shrine,
Dear mother, I will place on thine.

  "It was long before I could regain sufficient composure to return to
her. When I did so, I found her sweetly calm, and she greeted me
with a smile so full of affection, that I shall cherish the recollection
of its brightness until my latest breath. It was the last piece she ever

wrote, except a paraphrase of four lines of the hymn, 'I would not live always,' which was written within the last week of her life.

"I would not live always, thus fettered by sin,
    Temptation without, and corruption within,
    With the soul ever dimm'd by its hopes and its fears,
    And the heart's holy flame ever struggling through tears."

Thus far, in preparing this memoir, we have availed ourselves almost entirely of copious memoranda, furnished us, at our request, by Mrs. Davidson; but when the narrator approached the closing scene of this most affecting story, the heart of the mother gave out, and she found herself totally inadequate to the task. Fortunately, Dr. Davidson had retained a copy of a letter, written by her in the midst of her affliction, to Miss Sedgwick, in reply to an epistle from that lady, expressive of the kindest sympathy, and making some injuiries relative to the melancholy event. We subjoin that letter entire, for never have we read any thing of the kind more truly eloquent or deeply affecting.

"SARATOGA SPRINGS.

"Yes, my dear Miss Sedgwick: she is an angel now; calmly and sweetly she sunk to her everlasting rest, as a babe gently slumbers on its mother's bosom. I thank my Father in heaven that I was permitted to watch over her, and I trust administer to her comfort during her illness. I know, my friend, you will not expect either a very minute or connected detail of the circumstances preceding her change, from me at this time, for I am indeed bowed down with sorrow. I feel that I am truly desolate, how desolate I will not attempt to describe. Yet in the depth of grief I have consolations of the purest, most soothing and exalted nature. I would not, indeed I could not murmur, but rather bless my God that he has in the plenitude of his goodness made me, even for a brief space on earth, the honored mother of such an angel. Oh my dear Miss Sedgwick, I wish you could have seen her during the last two months of her brief sojourn with us. Her meekness and patience, and her even cheerful bearing were unexampled. But when she was assured that all the tender and endearing ties which bound her to earth were about to be severed, when she saw that life and all its bright visions were fading from her eyes—that she was standing at the entrance of the dark valley which must be traversed in her way to the eternal world, the struggle was great, but brief—she caught the hem of her Saviour's robe and meekly bowed to the mandate of her God. Since the beginning of August, I have watched this tender blossom with intense anxiety, and marked her decline with a breaking heart; and although from that time until the period of her departure, I never spent a whole night in bed, my excitement was so strong that I was unconscious of the want of sleep. Oh, my dear madam, the whole course of her decline was so unlike any other death-bed scene I ever witnessed; there was nothing of the gloom of a sick chamber; a charm was in and around her; a holy light seemed to pervade everything belonging to her. There was a sacredness, if I may so express it, which seemed to tell the presence of the Divinity. Strangers felt it, all acknowledged it. Very few were admitted to her sick room, but those few left it with an elevation of heart new, solemn, and delightful. She continued to ride out as long as the weather was mild, and even after she became too weak to walk she frequently desired to be taken into the parlor, and when there, with all her little implements of drawing and writing, her books, and even her little work box and basket beside her: she seemed to think that by these little attempts at her usual employments, she could conceal from me, for she saw my heart was breaking, the ravages of disease and her consequent debility. The New Testament was her daily study, and a portion of every day was spent in private, in self-examination and prayer. My dear Miss Sedgwick, how I have felt my own littleness, my total unworthiness, when compared with this pure, this high-souled, intellectual, yet timid, humble child; bending at the altar of her God, and pleading for pardon and acceptance in his sight, and grace to assist her in preparing for eternity. As her strength wasted, she often desired me to share her hours of retirement and converse with her, and read to her, when unable to read herself. Oh! how sad, how delightful, how agonising is the memory of the sweet and holy communion we then enjoyed. Forgive me, my friend, for thus mingling my own feelings with the circumstances you wished to know; and, oh! continue to pray that God will give me submission under this desolating stroke. She was my darling, my almost idolized child: truly, truly, you have said, the charm of my existence. Her symptoms were extremely distressing, although she suffered no pain. A week before her departure, she desired that the sacrament of the Lord's Supper might be administered to her. 'Mother,' said she 'I do not desire it because I feel worthy to receive it, I feel myself a sinner, but I desire to manifest my faith in Christ by receiving an ordinance instituted by himself but a short time before his crucifixion.' The Holy Sacrament was administered by Mr. Babcock. The solemnity of the scene can be better felt than described. I cannot attempt it. After it was over, a holy calm seemed to pervade her mind, and she looked almost like a beatified spirit. The evening following, she said to me, 'mother I have made a solemn surrender of myself to God; if it is his

will, I would desire to live long enough to prove the sincerity of my
profession, but his will be done; living or dying I am henceforth
devoted to God.' After this, some doubt seemed to intrude, her spirit
was troubled. I asked her if there was any thing she desired to have
done, any little arrangements to be made, any thing to say which she
had left unsaid, and assured her that her wishes should be sacred to
me. She turned her eyes upon me with an expression so sad, so
mournfully sweet: 'Mother, "When I can read my title clear, to mansions
in the skies," then I will think of other matters.' Her hair, which when
a little child had been often cut to improve its growth, was now very
beautiful; and she usually took much pains with it. During the whole
course of her sickness I had taken care of it. One day, not long before
her death, she said, evidently making a great effort to speak with
composure, 'Mother, if you are willing I will have my hair cut off; it
is troublesome; I should like it better short.' I understood her at once,
she did not like to have the idea of death associated with those beautiful
tresses which I had loved to braid. She would have them taken off while
living. I mournfully gave my consent, and she said, 'I will not ask you,
my dear mother, to do it, my friend, Mrs. F—— will be with me to
night, and she will do it for me.' The dark rich locks were severed at
midnight; never shall I forget the expression of her young faded face
as I entered the room. 'Do not be agitated, dear mamma, I am more
comfortable now. Lay it away if you please, and to-morrow I will
arrange and dispose of it. Do you know that I view my hair as something sacred? It is a part of myself, which will be re-united to my
body at the resurrection.' She had sat in an easy-chair or reclined
upon a sofa for several weeks.

"On Friday the 22d of November, at my urgent entreaty, she consented to be laid upon the bed. She found it a relief, and sunk into a
deep sleep, from which she was only awoke when I aroused her to take
some refreshment. When she awoke, she looked and spoke like an
angel, but soon dropped asleep as before. Oh! how my poor heart
trembled, for I felt that it was but the precursor to her long last rest,
although many of our friends thought she might yet linger some weeks.
A total loss of appetite, and a difficulty in swallowing, prevented her
from taking any nourishment throughout the day, and when we placed
her in the easy chair, at night, in order to arrange her bed, I offered
her some nice food, which I had prepared, and found she could not
take it. My feelings amounted almost to agony. She said 'do not be
distressed. I will take it bye and bye.' I seated myself beside her, and
she said, 'Surely, my dear mother, you have many consolations. You
are gathering a little family in heaven to welcome you.' My heart
was full, when I could speak, I said, 'Yes my love, I feel I am indeed

gathering a little family in heaven to bid me welcome, but when they are all assembled there how dreadful to doubt whether I may ever be permitted to join the circle.' 'Oh hush, dear, dear mother, do not indulge such sad thoughts; the fact of your having trained this little band to inhabit that holy place, is sufficient evidence to me that you will not fail to join us there.' I was with her myself that night, and a friend in the neighborhood sat up also. On Saturday morning, after I had taken half an hour's sleep, I found her quiet as a sleeping infant. I prepared her some food, and when I awoke her to take it, she said 'dear mother, I will try if it is only to please you.' I fed her, as I would have fed a babe. She smiled sweetly and said, 'Mother, I am again an infant.' I asked if I should read to her; she said yes, she would like to have me read a part of the gospel of John. I did so, and then said 'my dear Margaret, you look sweetly composed this morning. I trust all is peace within your heart.' 'Yes mother, all is peace, sweet peace. I feel that I can do nothing for myself. I have cast my burden upon Christ.' I asked if she could rest her hopes there in perfect confidence. 'Yes,' she replied, 'Jesus will not fail me. I can trust him.' She then sank into a deep sleep, as on the preceding day. In the afternoon, Mr. and Mrs. H. came from Ballston, they were much affected by the change a few days had made in her appearance. I awoke her, fearing she might sleep too long; and said her friends had come. She extended her arms to them both, and kissed them, saying to Mr. H. that he found her a late riser, and then sank to sleep again. Mrs. H. remained with us that night. About sunset I spoke to her. She awoke and answered me cheerfully, but observing that I was unusually depressed, she said, 'Dear mother, I am wearing you out.' I replied, 'My child, my beloved child, it is not that, the thought of our separation fills me with anguish.' I never shall forget the expression of her sweet face, as she replied, 'Mother, my own dear mother, do not grieve. Our parting will not be long, in life we were inseperable, and I feel that you cannot live without me. You will soon join me, and we shall part no more.' I kissed her pale cheek, as I bent over her, and finding my agitation too strong to repress, I left the room. She soon after desired to get up; she said she must have a coughing fit, and she could bear it better in the chair. When there she began to cough, and her distress was beyond description; her strength was soon exhausted, and we again carried her to the bed. She coughed from six until half past ten. I then prevailed on her to take some nutritious drink, and she fell asleep. My husband and Mrs. H. were both of them anxious that I should retire and get some rest, but I did not feel the want of it, and impressed as I was with the idea that this was the last night she would pass on earth, I could not go to bed. But others saw not the change, and to satisfy them, I went at twelve to my room, which opened into hers. There I sat listening to every sound. All seemed quiet, I twice opened the door, and Mrs. H. said she slept, and had taken her drink as often as directed, and again urged me to go to bed. A little after two I put on my night dress, and laid down. Between three and four Mrs. H. came in haste for ether. I pointed to the bottle, and sprang up. She said, 'I entreat, my dear Mrs. Davidson, that you do not rise; there is no sensible change, only a turn of oppression.' She closed the door, and I hastened to rise, when Mrs. H. came again, and said 'Margaret has asked for her mother.' I flew—she held the bottle of ether in her own hand, and pointed to her breast. I poured it on her head and chest. She revived. 'I am better now,' said she. 'Mother you tremble, you are cold; put on your clothes.' I stepped to the fire, and threw on a wrapper, when she stretched out both her arms, and exclaimed, 'Mother take me in your arms.' I raised her, and seating myself on the bed, passed my arms around her waist; her head dropped upon my bosom, and her expressive eyes were raised to mine. That look I shall never forget; it said, 'Tell me, mother, is this death.' I answered the appeal as if she had spoken. I laid my hand upon her white brow, a cold dew had gathered there, I spoke, 'Yes, my beloved, it is almost finished; you will soon be with Jesus.' She gave one more look, two or three short fluttering breaths, and all was over—her spirit was with its God—not a struggle or groan preceded her departure. Her father just came in time to witness her last breath. For a long half hour, I remained in the same position with the precious form of my lifeless child upon my bosom. I closed those beautiful eyes with my own hand. I was calm. I felt that I had laid my angel from my own breast, upon the bosom of her God. Her father and myself were alone. Her Sabbath commenced in heaven. Ours was opened in deep, deep anguish. Our sons, who had been sent for, had not arrived, and four days and nights did Ellen, (our young nurse, whom Margaret dearly loved,) and I, watch over the sacred clay. I could not resign this mournful duty to strangers. Although no son or relative was with us in this sad and solemn hour, never did sorrowing strangers meet with more sympathy, than we received in this hour of affliction, from the respected inhabitants of Saratoga. We shall carry with us through life, the grateful remembrance of their kindness. And now, my dear madam, let me thank you for your kind consoling letter, it has given me consolation. My Margaret, my now angel child, loved you tenderly. She recognised in yours, a kindred mind, and I feel that her pure spirit will behold with delight your efforts to console her bereaved mother."

She departed this life on the 25th of November, 1838, aged fifteen years and eight months; her earthly remains repose in the grave yard of the village of Saratoga.

"A few days after her departure," observes Mrs. Davidson in a memorandum, "I was searching the library in the hope of finding some further memento of my lost darling, when a packet folded in the form of a letter, met my eye. It was confined with a needle and thread, instead of a seal, and secured more firmly by white sewing silk, which was passed several times around it; the superscription was, 'For my Mother, Private.' Upon opening these papers, I found they contained the results of self examination, from a very early period of her life, until within a few days of its close. These results were noted and composed at different periods. They are some of the most interesting relics she has left, but they are of too sacred a nature to meet the public eye. They display a degree of self knowledge and humility, and a depth of contrition, which could only emanate from a heart chastened and subdued by the power of divine grace."

We here conclude this memoir, which, for the most part, as the reader will perceive, is a mere transcript of the records furnished by a mother's heart. We shall not pretend to comment on these records; they need no comment, and they admit no heightening. Indeed, the farther we have proceeded with our subject, the more has the intellectual beauty and the seraphic purity of the little being we have endeavoured to commemorate broken upon us; and the more have we shrunk at our own unworthiness for such a task. To use one of her own exquisite expressions, she was "A spirit of Heaven fettered by the strong affections of earth;" and the whole of her brief sojourn here, seems to have been a struggle to regain her native skies. We may apply to her a passage from one of her own tender apostrophies, to the memory of her sister Lucretia.

> —One who came from Heaven awhile
>   To bless the mourners here,
> Their joys to hallow with her smile,
>   Their sorrow with her tear.
>
> Who joined to all the charms of earth
>   The noblest gifts of heaven,
> To whom the muses at her birth
>   Their sweetest smiles had given.
>
> Whose eye beamed forth with fancy's ray,
>   And genius pure and high;

Whose very soul had seemed to bathe
In streams of melody.

   ❋   ❋   ❋   ❋   ❋   ❋

The cheek which once so sweetly beamed,
  Grew pallid with decay,
The burning fire within consumed
  Its tenement of clay.

Death, as if fearing to destroy,
  Paused o'er her couch awhile;
She gave a tear for those she loved,
  Then met him with a smile.

END OF THE MEMOIR

EDITORIAL APPENDIX

Textual Commentary,
Discussions, and Lists by
Elsie Lee West

OLIVER GOLDSMITH:
A BIOGRAPHY

LIST OF ABBREVIATIONS

The following symbols have been used in the editorial apparatus to designate the manuscript and previously published texts of *Oliver Goldsmith*.

	1825P	*The Miscellaneous Works of Oliver Goldsmith with an Account of His Life and Writings....* Edited by Washington Irving, Esq. (Paris: A. and W. Galignani and Jules Didot, 1825)
Pre-copy Texts	1825	*The Miscellaneous Works of Oliver Goldsmith, with an account of his Life and Writings,* stereotyped from the Paris edition (Philadelphia: Crissy & Markley, 1849)
	1840	"Biography of Oliver Goldsmith," in *The Life of Oliver Goldsmith, with selections from his writings.* By Washington Irving.... (New York, 1840)
MS		512-page manuscript (New York Public Library, Seligman Collection)
	MSh	Handwritten portions of MS
	MSp	Printed portions of MS
Pr.		Proof sheet
	Prh	Handwritten additions on proof sheet
	Prp	Printed portions of proof sheet
ARE		*Oliver Goldsmith: A Biography* (New York, 1849); Author's Revised Edition (49 through 60, as listed below)
49		First American Impression (Putnam, 1849)
	49a	Earlier state of variant sheets within 49
	49b	Later states of variant sheets within 49
	49c	Illustrated edition of 49
		53 Reimpression of 49c
	50 51 54 55	Reimpressions of ARE

59	Reimpression of ARE, except that pages 138, 284, and 381–382 are reset
60	Reimpression of 59, without further alterations
E	English impression (Murray, 1849) printed from duplicate 49 plates except for Murray alterations
T	Twayne edition
Letters	*The Collected Letters of Oliver Goldsmith*, ed. Katharine C. Balderston (Cambridge, 1928)
Works	*Collected Works of Oliver Goldsmith*, 5 vols., ed. Arthur Friedman (Oxford, 1966)
Boswell	*The Life of Samuel Johnson, LL.D. including a Journal of a Tour to the Hebrides*, 5 vols., ed. John Wilson Croker (London, 1831)
Forster	John Forster, *The Life and Adventures of Oliver Goldsmith* (London, 1848)
Percy	*The Miscellaneous Works of Oliver Goldsmith, M. B. ... To Which Is Prefixed, Some Account of His Life and Writings.* vol. 1. (London, 1801)
Prior	James Prior, *The Life of Oliver Goldsmith*, 2 vols. (London, 1837)

EXPLANATORY NOTES

The numbers before all notes indicate page and line respectively. Chapter numbers, chapter or section titles, epigraphs, author's chapter or section summaries, text quotations, and footnotes are included in the line count. Only running heads and rules added by the printer to separate the running head from the text are omitted from the count. The quotation from the text, to the left of the bracket, is the matter under discussion. A key to identifying symbols used in referring to the manuscript and editions of *Oliver Goldsmith*, as well as to Irving's sources, is given on pages 347–48.

3.2 revised edition] On July 26, 1848, George P. Putnam contracted with Irving to publish a uniform edition of his works to include several new books, one of which was this life of Goldsmith.

3.3 biographical sketch] The second version of Irving's life of Goldsmith, which was prefixed to *The Life of Oliver Goldsmith with Selections from His Writings,* 2 vols. (New York: Harper & Brothers, 1840).

3.7 Prior,] James Prior, *The Life of Oliver Goldsmith, M. B. from a Variety of Original Sources,* 2 vols. (London: John Murray, 1837).

3.14 Forster,] John Forster, *The Life and Adventures of Oliver Goldsmith. A Biography: in Four Books* (London: Bradbury & Evans, 1848).

3.28–29 at my heels,] On the proof sheet for MS pp. 219–20 is written: "Please send, if practicable, several chapters together. One chapter is hardly enough for 2 men for a day.—Printer." Above this request Irving wrote, "I cannot furnish copy faster than I do—the press is too close upon my heels."

3.37 'labor of love'] In 1840 Irving wrote in a footnote (p. 10): "In the present article the author has undertaken, as a 'labour of love,' to collect from various sources materials for a tribute to the memory of one whose writings were the delight of his childhood, and have been a source of enjoyment to him throughout life."

4.2 to Virgil] *Inferno,* canto I, 85–87. As translated by John D. Sinclair, "Thou art my master and my author. Thou art he from whom alone I took the style whose beauty has brought me honour."

5.9 with their writings] In the first of the three versions of the life, published as a preface to *The Miscellaneous Works of Oliver Goldsmith* (Paris, 1825), Irving wrote (p. 27) in connection with Gold-

smith's "The Traveller": "In this poem, we may particularly remark a
quality which distinguishes the writings of Goldsmith; it perpetually
presents the author to our minds. He is one of the few writers who are
inseparably identified with their works. We think of him in every page;
we grow intimate with him as a man, and learn to love him as we read."
5.33 of his reader.]   The 1840 version contains the same two introductory
paragraphs with only minor variations. In 1825 Irving wrote: "There
are few writers for whom the reader feels such personal kindness as
for Oliver Goldsmith. The fascinating ease and simplicity of his style;
the benevolence that beams through every page; the whimsical yet
amiable views of human life and human nature; the mellow unforced
humour, blended so happily with good feeling and good sense, throughout his writings; win their way irresistibly to the affections and carry
the author with them. While writers of greater pretensions and more
sounding names are suffered to lie upon our shelves, the works of
Goldsmith are cherished and laid in our bosoms. We do not quote them
with ostentation, but they mingle with our minds; they sweeten our
tempers and harmonize our thoughts; they put us in good humour with
ourselves and with the world, and in so doing make us happier and
better men.

"We have been curious therefore in gathering together all the hetero-
geneous particulars concerning poor Goldsmith that still exist; and
seldom have we met with an author's life more illustrative of his
works, or works more faithfully illustrative of the author's life. His
rambling biography displays him the same kind, artless, good-
humoured, excursive, sensible, whimsical, intelligent being that he
appears in his writings. Scarcely an adventure or a character is
given in his page that may not be traced to his own parti-coloured
story. Many of his most ludicrous scenes and ridiculous incidents have
been drawn from his own blunders and mischances, and he seems
really to have been buffeted into almost every maxim imparted by him
for the instruction of his readers."
5.34 10th of November, 1728,]   In 1825 Irving's major source was the
biographical memoir attributed to Bishop Thomas Percy, in *The Miscellaneous Works of Oliver Goldsmith, M.B.* (London, 1801). Following Percy, Irving gave the date of Goldsmith's birth as November 29,
1728. In 1840, following Prior (I, 10), he changed it to November 10,
1728, the date also given by Forster (p. 1).
5.35 Ireland]   The Goldsmith country is in central Ireland. See Prior
(I, 9-10).
6.2 what they ought."]   Irving slightly alters the quotation from Prior
(I, 101), which represents a composite of what various members of
"the Goldsmith race" told him.

6.3 ways of the world."]   Irving slightly alters the quotations as it appears in Prior (I, 101–2). This paragraph was added in 1840 (10–11).

6.12 pounds a year.]   Goldsmith's "The Deserted Village," in *Collected Works of Oliver Goldsmith,* ed. Arthur Friedman (Oxford, 1966), IV, 293 (cited hereafter as *Works*). The quotation and the preceding sentence do not appear in 1840; the rest of the paragraph does (p. 11).

6.32 Lissoy]   A variant form is Lishoy. See Prior (I, 15).

7.6 Man in Black]   A character in Goldsmith's *The Citizen of the World; or Letters from a Chinese Philosopher, Residing in London, to His Friends in the East.* The following quotation is from Letter XXVII (*Works*, II, 113–14). Irving added it and the preceding two paragraphs in 1840 (12–13). In 1825 (8) Irving commented on the tendency to identify the Man in Black with Goldsmith's father and brother and added: "It is difficult, however, to assign with precision the originals of a writer's characters. They are generally composed of scattered, though accordant traits, observed in various individuals, which have been seized upon with the discriminating tact of genius and combined into one harmonious whole. Still, it is a fact, as evident as it is delightful, that Goldsmith has poured out the genuine feelings of his heart in his works; and has had continually before him, in his delineations of simple worth and domestic virtue, the objects of his filial and fraternal affection."

8.5 charity began.]   "The Deserted Village," lines 149–62. See *Works* (IV, 293). This and the next paragraph were added in 1840 (13–14).

8.19 Elizabeth Delap,]   According to Prior (I, 22), "she was a relative, resident in the family," who "died about 1787." This and the preceding paragraph were added in 1840 (14–15).

8.30 Byrne,]   The schoolmaster's name, which appears in Prior (I, 23) but not in the Percy *Memoir,* was added in 1840 (15).

8.31–32 the wars of Queen Anne's time,]   Queen Anne (1665–1714); War of the Spanish Succession (1701–1714).

9.20 all he knew.]   "The Deserted Village," lines 193–216 (*Works*, IV, 295). This paragraph was added in 1840 (15).

10.16 Roscommon]   A county about seventeen miles northwest of the county of Longford.

10.22–23 of his genius.]   This and the preceding three paragraphs were added in 1840 (16–17).

10.25 Cummings]   Prior (I, 28) says, "a youth named Cumming." In 1825 (8) Irving followed Percy in referring to him merely as "a fiddler."

10.29 Æsop]   A Greek fabulist, sixth century B.C., whose ugliness and buffoonery were traditional. This paragraph was added in 1840 (17–18). Compare 1825 (8): "The scraper of catgut, struck with the oddity of the boy's appearance, thought to display his waggery, by likening him to Aesop dancing. This comparison, according to his notions, being uncommonly happy, he continued to harp on it for a considerable time, when suddenly the laugh of the company was turned against himself, by Oliver sarcastically remarking. . . ."

10.39 the expense.] To this point the paragraph was added in 1840 (18), in which version the paragraph continues: "One of the foremost of them was his uncle, the Rev. Thomas Contarine, who had married a sister of his father, and who continued through life one of Goldsmith's most active, uniform, and generous friends." Compare 1825 (9).

10.40 Contarine] In a long footnote Percy (17–18) traced Contarine's ancestry to the Contarini family of Venice. Thomas Campbell, *Specimens of the British Poets; with Biographical and Critical Notices, and an Essay on English Poetry in Seven Volumes* (London, 1819), VI, 251–52, included this material. In 1825 (16, n.) Irving borrowed a quotation from Campbell's version. Prior (I, 50–51) paraphrased Percy's account, but in 1840 (18) Irving omitted the material altogether.

10.41 Bishop Berkeley] George Berkeley (1685–1753), Irish philosopher and divine, was the Bishop of Cloyne. For an article on Berkeley attributed to Goldsmith, see *Works* (III, 34–40).

10.42 Carrick-on-Shannon] Capital of the county of Leitrim, a suburb of which is in the county of Roscommon.

11.5 early playmate] Prior (I, 55) says that Jane Contarine was "a few years older than the poet." She married a man named Lawder in 1735. See *The Collected Letters of Oliver Goldsmith,* ed. Katharine C. Balderston (Cambridge, 1928), xii, n. 4 (hereafter cited as *Letters*). Percy (18 n.) included a lurid account of the murder of Lawder and the wounding of his wife some years after the death of Goldsmith. Prior (I, 130 n.) included the story, but it does not appear in 1825 or 1840.

11.8 considerate relative] The sentence to this point was added in 1849.

11.11 Edgeworthstown] A small town seven miles southeast of Longford.

11.17 Ovid and Horace] Publius Ovidius Naso (43 B.C.–17 A.D.), Roman poet; Quintus Horatius Flaccus (65–8 B.C.), Roman poet and satirist.

11.17 Livy] Titus Livius (59 B.C.–17 A.D.), Roman historian.

11.18 Tacitus] Publius (or Gaius) Cornelius Tacitus (ca. 55–120), Roman historian. This paragraph was added in 1840.

11.35 Ballymahon] A town about a mile and a half from Pallas, where Goldsmith was born.

11.40–41 deer-stealing colleagues] Prior (I, 44–45) wrote: "This story, although it may seem like a different version of the deer-stealing of

Shakespeare, I had no reason to disbelieve. . . ." This and the preceding paragraph were added in 1840.

12.22 in his inn,"] Shakespeare's *Henry IV, Part I*, III, iii, 91: "Shall I not take mine ease in mine inn?" This paragraph was added in 1840.

12.30 of his bent,"] Shakespeare's *Hamlet*, III, ii, 408: "They fool me to the top of my bent."

12.42 of a Night."] In 1825 (9) Irving paraphrased Percy's account of this famous incident (6–7). In 1840 (20–22) he added details from Prior (I, 45–47). In 1849 he used the 1840 version without change.

13.23 Hodson] Daniel Hodson was one of the "men of education and independent character," whom Goldsmith loved and esteemed, the others being his brother Henry and Thomas Contarine. See *Letters* (ix–x).

13.24–25 of wealthy parentage] Prior (I, 48) says that Hodson was "the son of a gentleman of good property, residing at St. John's, near Athlone." This and the preceding paragraph were added in 1840 (21–22).

14.8 11th June, 1745, when seventeen] The date of Goldsmith's entrance into Trinity College has been a matter of confusion and dispute. In 1825, following Percy (14), Irving wrote, "On the 11th of June, 1744, Goldsmith, then fifteen . . . " (vii). Prior (I, 58) said that 1744 was in error, and he established June 11, 1745, as the correct date. Irving's 1840 (23) reads, "11 June, 1747." Forster (16) follows Prior in adopting "11th of June, 1745," but Irving's MSp reads 1747; and this date is used in all impressions studied up to 1860, where 1745 is restored.

14.14 window frame] Prior (I, 62) said that the window pane "is still to be seen." In 1860 George Lloyd inquired in *Notes and Queries*, 2d ser. 9 (January–June, 1860), 11, about the present location of the pane. In response (91), an anonymous writer said that it had been "inclosed in a frame and deposited in the Manuscript Room of the College Library, where it is still to be seen." In response to an inquiry made by the present editor, Mr. M. Pollard, Rare Books Librarian of the Trinity College library, wrote on July 26, 1967: "the glass on which Goldsmith scratched his name is still in this library, though it is not at the moment deposited in the MS Room. The glass is in several pieces but is firmly anchored together and the signature etc. is present though the tops of some letters have suffered." The last sentence of the paragraph was added in 1849.

14.41 menial hands] This paragraph appears in 1840 (24). Compare Prior (I, 59–60).

15.7 except your own."] The quotation is from Goldsmith's letter from London to his brother Henry, dated January 13, 1759. See *Letters* (59).

The entire letter, including this passage, appears 68.5–71.21. It is also included in 1825 and 1840.

15.9 Theaker Wilder] According to Prior (I, 65), Wilder was "the youngest son of a gentleman living within a few miles of the Rev. Mr. Goldsmith."

15.12–16 by harsh means . . . personal violence.] Added in 1849. Compare Forster (22).

15.24 my childhood."] The quotation, added in 1849, is from Goldsmith's essay "A Description of Various Clubs" (*Works*, III, 7).

15.37 always muddy."] In 1840 (25–26) Irving added this quotation, which is from Goldsmith's *An Enquiry into the Present State of Polite Learning* (*Works*, I, 308). Compare Prior (I, 70).

16.5 Beatty] Prior (I, 62) identifies him as the Rev. John Beatty, Goldsmith's schoolmate at Edgeworthstown and roommate for a while at Trinity College. Compare Forster (17).

16.6 Bryanton] Prior (I, 115) identifies Robert Bryanton as Goldsmith's "companion in school and in college." Balderston (*Letters*, 8 n. 2) identifies him as Goldsmith's cousin. Compare Forster (18). This detail was added in 1849.

16.17 each received] The paragraph was added in 1840 (26). The phrase "a knack at hoping" is from *The Vicar of Wakefield* (*Works*, IV, 107). Compare Prior (I, 74).

16.18 Edmund Burke] Edmund Burke (1729–1797), statesman and philosopher, was later, like Goldsmith, to become a member of the Johnson circle. The paragraph was added in 1840 (26–27).

17.7 unlucky Goldsmith] This and the preceding two paragraphs appear essentially the same in 1840 (27–28). Compare Prior (I, 76–86).

17.11 collegiate career] Percy (15–16) says, "on June 15th, 1747, he was elected one of the exhibitioners on the foundation of Erasmus Smyth." In 1825 Irving did not include this statement, but he added a curious footnote (10): "During his studies at the university, he was a contemporary with Burke; and it has been said that neither of them gave much promise of future celebrity. Goldsmith, however, got a premium at a Christmas examination; and a premium obtained at such an examination is more honourable than any other, because it ascertains the person who receives it to be the first in literary merit. At the other examinations, the person thus distinguished may be only the second in merit; he who has previously obtained the same honorary reward, sometimes receiving a written certificate that *he* was the best answerer; it being a rule, that not more than one premium could be adjudged to the same person in one year." This note is a composite of four sentences, partly paraphrased and partly quoted, from James Boswell's *The Life of Samuel Johnson. LL.D. Including a Journal of a Tour to the Hebrides,* ed. John Wilson Croker (London, 1831), I, 420–21 (cited hereafter as *Boswell*). Compare Prior (I, 90). In 1840 (28) Irving omitted the footnote and added this paragraph. Compare Prior (I, 86–87).

18.15–16 a college intimate] This was Edward Mills, Goldsmith's cousin. See *Letters* (32, n. 2). The paragraph was added in 1840. Compare Prior (I, 94–96).

18.30 O. S.,] Old Style. The Gregorian calendar was adopted in England by act of Parliament in 1752.

18.31 of the University] In 1825 (10), following Percy (17), Irving wrote: "He was not, however, admitted to the degree of Bachelor of Arts till February 27, 1742, O.S. two years after the regular time." In 1840 (30), following Prior (I, 98), he wrote the sentence as it appears in 1849.

18.35 tyranny of Wilder] The balance of the paragraph was added in 1849. Compare Forster (26).

19.13 Citizen of the World] The quotation that follows (*Works,* II, 114–15) was added in 1840 (31–32). Compare Prior (I, 100).

19.32 his father's death] The paragraph to this point appears in 1840 (32) with quotation marks around "This kind . . . obliterated." This is a quotation from Prior (I, 54); in fact, the next clause is almost verbatim from Prior.

20.2 rejected the proposal."] The quotation (*Works,* II, 115–16) appears in 1840 (34). Compare Prior (I, 111).

20.5–6 unsettled life] This sentence in 1840 (32) reads: "For about two years Goldsmith led a loitering, unsettled life among his friends, undetermined how to shape his course, and waiting with the vague hope, common to reckless and improvident men, that 'something or other would turn up.'" The rest of the paragraph is the same in 1840 (32–33).

20.19–20 "The Traveller:"] The following lines are 1–2, 7–22. See *Works* (IV, 248–49). They were added in 1840 (33).

21.1–2 to the imagination.] The rest of this paragraph and the next one were considerably revised from the 1840 (33–34) version, though the details are essentially the same. Compare Prior (I, 114–16).

21.2 the river Inny] According to Prior (I, 9–10), "a stream which in passing Ballymahon in its course to the Shannon, assumes a very picturesque appearance."

21.13 strength went round] lines 15–18, 21–22 (*Works,* IV, 287–88). Added in 1849.

21.16 Ballymulvey House] "Ballymulvey, an agreeable house and grounds in the vicinity and afterwards the residence for some years of his friend Bryanton, was a frequent resort" (Prior, I, 116).

21.24 and his associates]   Tony Lumpkin is a character in *She Stoops to Conquer* (*Works*, V, 87–217). The rest of the paragraph was added in 1849.

21.26 the pewter platter."]   *She Stoops to Conquer*, act 1 (*Works*, V, 110).

21.37 Toroddle, toroddle, toroll]   This is the last of the three stanzas of Tony's drinking song (*Works*, V, 117).

22.2 at Ballymahon]   The rest of this paragraph was added in 1849.

23.19–20 fundmental objection]   In 1825 (10) Irving wrote: "... it is thought he was more pleased than disappointed when rejected by his lordship, on account of his youth." Compare 1840 (35): "He was rejected by the bishop; some say for want of sufficient studious preparation; others from accounts which had reached the bishop of his irregularities at college; but others shrewdly suspect that the scarlet breeches was the fundamental objection." Compare Prior (I, 110); Forster (32).

23.23 good natured."]   See *Works* (II, 116).

23.27 Mr. Flinn]   In 1825 (10), following Percy (9), Irving referred to him as "a neighbouring gentleman." Although Prior (I, 117) mentioned the name Flinn, Irving did not use it until 1849. Compare Forster (32).

23.34 situation as tutor]   In 1825, paraphrasing Percy (9), Irving wrote: "But finding the employment much more disagreeable than he had been taught to believe it, and the necessary confinement painfully irksome, he suddenly gave up his charge. ..." Prior (I, 118) pointed out that Goldsmith's leaving the Flinn family was due to "an altercation with one of the family, in consequence of sitting down to cards on the receipt of his salary, and by a train of ill luck, or as he did not hesitate to say by unfair play, losing the sum that had been paid him." In 1840 (35) Irving wrote: "The situation was not to his taste: there was a dependance, and a degree of servility in it that his spirit could not brook; add to this, he had received his salary, had more money in his pocket than he had ever earned before, and now his wandering propensity and his desire to see the world got the upper hand. Whatever was the real motive, he suddenly relinquished his charge. ..." Compare Forster (32–33).

24.1 hero of La Mancha]   Don Quixote, the hero of *The Ingenious Gentleman, Don Quixote de la Mancha* by Miguel de Cervantes Saavedra.

24.16 whimsical narrative]   In 1840 (36) the paragraph is the same to this point. It concludes: "which he drew up of his adventures." Compare 1825 (10): "As this singular unpremeditated step had been taken without consulting any of his friends, and as no intelligence could be obtained either of himself or the motives which had prompted his departure, his family became much alarmed for his safety, and were justly offended at his conduct. Week after week passed away, and no tidings of the fugitive. At last, when all hope of his return had been given up, and when they concluded he must have left the country altogether, the family were astonished by his sudden reappearance at his mother's house; safe and sound, to be sure, but not exactly in such good trim as when he had left them. His horse was metamorphosed into a shabby little pony, not worth twenty shillings; and instead of thirty pounds in his pocket, he was without a penny. On this occasion the indignation of his mother was strongly expressed; but his brothers and sisters, who were all tenderly attached to him, interfered, and soon effected a reconciliation."

24.18 "My dear mother,]   In 1825 (10–12) Irving paraphrased Catherine Hodson's account of the incident in Percy (9–13). In 1840 (36–41), following Prior (I, 119–25), he included the letter. For a discussion of this letter see *Letters* (xxiii–xxix).

27.23 future essayist]   Balderston (*Letters,* xxix) writes: "It seems safe to conclude that the surprising story of Fiddleback was Goldsmith's first fiction. . . ." Compare Prior (I, 125).

28.14 Fiddle-back]   This and the next paragraph are substantially the same in 1840 (41–42). Compare 1825 (12): "He fell by accident into the company of a sharper in Dublin, and being tempted to engage in play, was soon plundered of all his money, and again left to find his way home without a shilling in his pocket." Compare Prior (I, 128); Forster (35).

28.34 but juvenile]   This paragraph and the following poem were added in 1849. The poem appears in Prior (I, 132). Compare Forster (36).

29.21 to a Mr. Lawder]   See 11.5.

29.25 Dean Goldsmith of Cloyne]   The Reverend Isaac Goldsmith was Dean of Cloyne (1736–1769). See 10.41.

29.34 uncle Contarine]   This paragraph was added in 1849. Compare Forster (36).

30.2 as a guide]   This incident, told in Percy's *Memoir* (19), appears paraphrased in 1825 (12). In 1840 (42–43) Irving rewrote the paragraph essentially as it is here. Compare Prior (I, 134).

30.8 a whole week]   The paragraph to this point in 1825 (13) reads: "His first landlady, he used to say, nearly starved him out of his lodgings; and the second, though somewhat more liberal, was still a wonderful adept in the art of saving. When permitted to put forth all her talents in this way, she would perform surprising feats. A single loin of mutton would sometimes be made to serve our poet and two fellow-students a whole week. . . ." The following quoted passage is not in quotation marks. In 1849 Irving seems to be quoting his own 1825 passage. The entire paragraph was added in 1840 (43). Compare Percy (19); Prior (I, 134–35).

30.41 to raise the money."] This and the preceding paragraph, which were added in 1840, are a paraphrase of Prior (I, 136–37).

31.13 was present] This paragraph was added in 1849.

31.19 "MY DEAR BOB,] The letter was added in 1849. Percy (22–26) included it from a contemporary copy of the original. Irving followed Prior (I, 139–45), who used a copy which Balderston rejected because it had been corrected. See *Letters* (8, n. 2).

32.30–31 honour of Ceres] Ovid, in the story of Cinyras and Myrrha, *Metamorphoses*, Book X.

33.6–7 Duchess of Hamilton] Elizabeth Gunning (1734–1790) was one of two beautiful sisters who lived near Roscommon and whose mother took them to London in search of matrimonial fortune. Elizabeth married the Duke of Hamilton in 1752, and a year after his death in 1758 she married the future Duke of Argyll.

33.31 John Binley] The name is Binely in Prior (I, 145) and Bindley in (I, 244); in Forster (38) it is Bincly. See *Letters* (14).

33.40 *William Maclellan] The footnote is taken verbatim from Prior (I, 142). Compare *Letters* (12, n. 2).

34.4 of superior merit] In 1825 (12), paraphrasing Percy (21), Irving wrote: "About this period, his contemporaries have reported, that he sometimes also sacrificed to the Muses, but of these early effusions no specimen seems to have been preserved." Compare Prior (I, 137–38). Irving's 1840 version (44–45) of the statement was retained in 1849. The balance of the paragraph was added in 1849.

34.9 as his master."] The quotation is from a postscript to Goldsmith's letter to his uncle Contarine, dated May 8, 1753. Prior (I, 145–48) included the entire letter. See *Letters* (7–8).

34.15–16 as a physician."] The quotation, which was added in 1840 (44–45), is from a letter to his uncle Contarine, first published by Prior (I, 155–57). See *Letters* (17). For a discussion of the theories concerning Goldsmith's position in the household of the Duke of Hamilton, see *Letters* (18, n. 3).

34.32 harm in me."] *Citizen of the World*, Letter XXVII (*Works*, II, 116). Compare *The Vicar of Wakefield*, Chapter XX (*Works*, IV, 112). Irving added the quotation in 1849.

34.35 in a letter] The same letter mentioned in note 34.15–16.

34.36–37 Farheim, Petit, and Du Hammel de Monceau] Dr. Balderston (*Letters*, 15) identifies Antoine F. Ferrein (1693–1769) as a professor of medicine and surgery in the Royal College in Paris from 1742 to 1768, and Henri-Louis Duhamel du Monceau (1700–1782) as a famous botanist. Jean Louis Petit, who lectured in Paris on anatomy and surgery, died in 1750.

34.40 are so] At this point a passage was omitted from Goldsmith's letter. Prior (I, 155–56) did not omit it.

34.42 The great Albinus] Bernard-Siegfried Albinus (1697–1770) was professor of anatomy at Leyden.

35.10 cousin Jenny] Jane Contarine Lawder.

35.11–12 Jack Goldsmith] Goldsmith's youngest brother. See *Letters* (4, n. 3).

35.23 moral purpose] In 1840 (45) Irving wrote: "Medical instruction was the ostensible motive for his expedition, but the real one was doubtless his long-cherished desire to see foreign parts." Compare Prior (I, 148). The rest of the paragraph was added in 1849.

35.28 only a vagabond."] *Citizen of the World,* Letter VII (*Works,* II, 41).

35.31 will suffice."] From Goldsmith's letter to Thomas Contarine of December, 1753. See *Letters* (17).

35.36 half pasteboard] See *Don Quixote,* Chapter I.

35.38 all things] Compare 1 Cor. 14:7.

35.42 'sweet Lissoy'] Possibly a paraphrase of "Sweet Auburn" in the first line of "The Deserted Village."

36.17 of the voyage."] Irving is treating loosely a passage in Goldsmith's letter to Contarine from Leyden, first published by Percy (27–32). In 1825, following Percy (27), he wrote, "We all went ashore to refresh us, after the fatigues of our voyage." In 1840 (45) he wrote: "Of course Goldsmith and his fellow-voyagers went on shore to 'refresh themselves after the fatigues of their voyage.'" See *Letters* (19–21).

36.34 of the Hollanders] Compare Irving's descriptions of the Dutch in the *History of New York by Diedrich Knickerbocker.* This and the following two paragraphs are quotations from the letter mentioned in note 36.17. See *Letters* (22–25).

36.38 Louis XIV] King of France (1638–1715).

37.5 on two petticoats] Irving follows Percy (29), who omitted the following passage because he thought it indelicate: "...is it not surprizing how things shoud ever come close enough to make it a match. When I spoke of love I was to be understood not in a—in short I was not to be understood at all, a Dutch Lady...." Both Prior (I, 159–64) and Forster (41) excised the passage. See *Letters* (22); 1825 (13); 1840 (46).

37.9 Strephon] The conventional lover, derived from the name of a character in Sir Philip Sidney's *Arcadia.*

37.12 a dirty close] "The narrow streets or lanes in Edinburgh are called closes" Percy (31, n.).

37.21 usefully employed."]   This quotation precedes the previous paragraph in the letter. See *Letters* (24).

37.22 "The Traveller:"]   lines 281–96 (*Works*, IV, 260–61).

37.40 Gaubius]   In 1825 (14) Irving wrote: "While resident in Leyden,
he attended the lectures of Gaubius on chemistry, and those of
Albinus on anatomy. In the letters of Goldsmith to his uncle, Gaubius is
the only professor of whose talents he gives a favourable opinion." To
this statement he added the following footnote: "Gaubius died in
1780, at the age of 75, leaving a splendid reputation. He was the
favourite pupil of Boerhaave and wrote several learned and ingenious
works." This statement is a paraphrase of Percy (32), who recorded
the name as "Gambius"; but the footnote is not in Percy. In 1840
(47–48) the sentence is essentially the same as in 1849, but the footnote does not appear. Compare Prior (I, 168–69). According to
Balderston (*Letters*, 25, n. 3), Jérôme-David Gaubius (1705–1780) was
professor of chemistry at Leyden. He succeeded Boërhaave in 1729.

38.5 named Ellis]   Percy (33) referred to "The late Dr. Ellis, clerk of
the Irish House of Commons." Ellis gave Percy the anecdotes about
Goldsmith in Leyden. In 1825 (14–15) Irving paraphrased part of
Percy's account and converted part of it into a direct quotation. In
1840 (48) he reduced his long passage to: "A generous friend, who
had often counselled him in vain against his unfortunate propensity,
now stepped in to his relief, but on condition of his quitting the sphere
of danger." Compare Prior (I, 169–70); Forster (42–43).

38.11 of a scholar."]   The quotation was added in 1849. Compare Prior
(I, 170); Forster (42).

38.14 smattering of the French]   Compare 34.36–37.

38.16 Vicar of Wakefield]   *Works*, IV, 116.

38.31 tulip mania]   In 1825 (15) Irving wrote in a footnote: "It was the
celebrated tulip mania. For a tulip root, known by the name of Sem-
per Augustus, 550 £. sterling was given; and for other tulip
roots less rare, various prices were given, from one hundred to four
hundred guineas. This madness raged in Holland for many years, till
at length the State interfered, and a law was enacted which put a
stop to the trade." This note, which he did not find in Percy, was
omitted in 1840.

39.2 single guinea]   Compare 1825 (15): "for it has often been asserted,
that after his magnificent speculation in tulip roots he actually set
out upon his travels with only one clean shirt, and without a shilling
in his pocket." Compare 1840 (49): "and it is said that he actually
set off on a tour of the Continent with but one spare shirt, and without a shilling in his pocket."

39.6 innumerable privations."]   This quotation is not in Percy. It appears in 1825 (15) without quotation marks and with the following concluding clause: "and neither poverty, fatigue, nor hardship, seems to have dampened his ardour, or interrupted his progress." In 1840 (49) Irving wrote the passage as it appears in 1849. Possibly he was quoting from his own 1825 essay.

39.18 to please them."] The quotation is in *Works* (IV, 117–18). In both 1825 (15) and 1840 (49) Irving paraphrased the first two sentences. The third sentence in all three versions conforms to *Works* up to the phrase "the next day;" (39.15), but the balance of Goldsmith's sentence reads: "next day. I once or twice attempted to play for people of fashion; but they always thought my performance odious, and never rewarded me even with a trifle." This is the version used in Percy (34), Prior (I, 179), and Forster (46). Irving's version is found in the *Annual Register* 17 (1774), 30.

39.19 Rouelle] Guillaume-François Rouelle (1703–1770) was a famous French chemist. The rest of the sentence was added in 1849. Compare *Works* (I, 300); Forster (49).

39.22 Mademoiselle Clairon] Claire Josèphe Hippolyte Léris de la Tudi Clairon (1723–1803), French actress, made her début at the Comédie-Française in 1743 in the title role of Racine's *Phédre*. She was a great favorite of Voltaire, in many of whose plays she appeared. Goldsmith described her mode of acting in an essay, "On our Theatres" (*Works*, I, 389).

39.29 of the people."] Although Irving was probably following Forster (49) here, the quotation is also in Prior (I, 183), who cites Goldsmith's " 'Animated Nature,' vol. v. p. 207." Irving did not include it in 1840.

39.38 be free."] *Citizen of the World*, Letter LVI (*Works*, II, 235). The entire paragraph, with the exception of the first sentence, was added in 1849. Compare Forster (49–50).

39.41 Voltaire] François Marie Arouet de Voltaire (1694–1778), French author and philosopher. In 1840 (50), following Prior (I, 181), Irving wrote that Goldsmith "became acquainted with Voltaire," in Paris. In 1849 Irving ignored Forster's statement (50) that at the time Goldsmith was in Paris Voltaire was in exile, but that there was little doubt "the meeting actually took place," possibly in Geneva. According to Friedman (*Works*, III, 247, n. 2) "there is no satisfactory way of reconciling Goldsmith's statements [that is, that he had met Voltaire] with the facts. Unless, then, the anecdote is pure invention, Goldsmith must have borrowed it from his source."

39.41 a memoir] *Memoirs of M. de Voltaire*. The following quotation is from the *Memoir* (*Works*, III, 247–48). It appears in Prior (I, 182–83) but not in Irving's 1840 version.

40.8 Fontenelle]   Bernard le Bovier, Sieur de Fontenelle (1657–1757), French author.

40.11 Diderot]   Denis Diderot (1713–1784), French writer and critic.

40.28 the "Traveller."]   This sentence appears substantially the same in 1840 (50). In 1825 (16) Irving wrote: "To Goldsmith's close and familiar intercourse with the scenes and natives of the different countries through which he passed, the world is indebted for his 'Traveller.' For although that poem was afterwards 'slowly and painfully elaborated,' still the nice and accurate discrimination of national character displayed could only be acquired by actual examination. In the progress of his journey, he seems to have treasured his facts and observations, with a view to the formation of this delightful poem. The first sketch of it is said to have been written after his arrival in Switzerland, and was transmitted from that country to his brother Henry in Ireland." Compare Percy (35).

40.34 he and Goldsmith]   Percy (35–36) told this story as it had been "related by former Biographers," but added that it had been "doubted by his intimate friends, whether this connection has not rather been imagined from the adventure in the novel, than really experienced by himself." In 1825 (16) Irving wrote: "Here he appears to have found friends, or formed acquaintances; for we find him recommended at this place as tutor to a young gentleman on his travels." Prior (I, 188–89) discussed the earlier tendency to discount this story but concluded: "That some such connection was formed appears probable, from consideration of all the circumstances:—. . . ." The paragraph to this point appears in 1840 (50) but with an added sentence, which in 1849 was revised and shifted to 41.12–14. See note for 41.12–14.

40.36 Philosophic Vagabond]   For the quotation that follows see *Works* (IV, 120). Compare Forster (48–49), who drastically edits the passage. In 1840 Irving, following Prior (I, 190–91), included this quotation with two additional sentences from the Goldsmith text.

41.12–14 They had . . . glad to separate]   This is the sentence, mentioned in note 40.34, which was shifted. The rest of the paragraph was added in 1849.

41.27 for one night."]   *Works* (IV, 121). In 1825 (16) Irving, like Percy (34–35), paraphrased this passage. In 1840 (52) Irving, following Prior (I, 195–96), quoted the passage with an additional sentence from the Goldsmith text. In 1849 he omitted the added sentence at this point but shifted it in paraphrased form (despite the quotation marks) to 42.6–8. Compare Forster (56-57).

41.31 *my circumstances."*]   Irving's italics. In taking this sentence from an earlier passage in *The Vicar of Wakefield* (*Works*, IV, 116–17), Irving used it out of context and distorted its meaning. The passage in the *Vicar* reads: "This scheme thus blown up, I had some thoughts of fairly shipping back to England again; but happening into company with an Irish student, who was returning from Louvain, our conversation turning upon topics of literature, (for by the way it may be observed, that I always forgot the meanness of my circumstances when I could converse upon such subjects) from him I learned that there were not two men in his whole university who understood Greek." Irving's misuse of this sentence occurs in all three versions of the *Life*: 1825 (16); 1840 (52).

41.33 his medical degree]   Whether or not Goldsmith was ever awarded a medical degree has never been verified. See Percy (36); Prior (I, 171, 178, 193); Forster (56); and *Letters* (21, n. 1).

41.34 illness of his uncle]   1825 (16), 1840 (52), and 1849 read "death of his uncle." Contarine was still alive in August, 1758, when Goldsmith mentioned him, then in a state of imbecility, in a letter to Jane Contarine. See 59.3–5; 60.42–61.6. The error was originally Goldsmith's. See Katharine C. Balderston, *The History & Sources of Percy's Memoir of Goldsmith* (Cambridge, 1926), p. 15. See also *Letters* (xiii). Percy (36) included the error. The remainder of the paragraph was added in 1849.

42.8 of the picture."]   See note 41.27.

42.24 of three-score]   "The Traveller," lines 241–54 (*Works*, IV, 259).

43.8 losing content,"]   The title of Chapter XX of *The Vicar of Wakefield* is "The history of a philosophic vagabond, pursuing novelty, but losing content." The sentence appears in 1840 (52). Compare Prior (I, 197).

43.9–10 illness of his uncle]   1849 reads "death of his uncle." See note 41.34.

43.26 combat the other."]   The quotation is from the first paragraph of a letter to Daniel Hodson, dated December 27, 1757. Percy (40–45) included the entire letter. In 1825 (17) Irving quoted the phrase "without friend, recommendation, money, or impudence;" from the first paragraph of the letter and later included the entire letter (18–19). Prior (I, 210) quoted and paraphrased the first paragraph and then included the entire letter (246–51). In 1840 (53) Irving quoted the phrase and (60–64) the entire letter. See 54.4–55.22 where Irving includes the letter but omits the first paragraph. See *Letters* (26–32).

43.32 Philosophic Vagabond]   See *Works* (IV, 106).

43.33 Strolling Player]   See *Works* (III, 133–42). The substance of this paragraph appears in 1840 (52–53). Compare Prior (I, 202); Forster (57).

44.4 his own experience]   The following quotation is from "A City Night-Piece" (*Works*, II, 452). Irving took great liberties in quoting the passage. "The clock . . . two," (44.5) begins the essay; "what a gloom . . ." begins the third paragraph. After "watch-dog" (44.6) the rest of the paragraph and three following paragraphs are omitted, and there are other lesser excisions. Irving added the italics in 44.14–16. The quotation was added in 1849.

44.26 Sir Joshua Reynolds's] Sir Joshua Reynolds (1723–1792), portrait painter, was the first president of the Royal Academy of Art.

44.28 beggars of Axe Lane."] This sentence was added in 1849. See Prior (I, 210); Forster (59).

44.33 difficulty,] In MSh there is a period after "difficulty." Irving apparently intended at first to end his sentence here and then had second thoughts, but what follows the word "difficulty" seems confused. In 1840 (53) he wrote: "What was to be done to gain the immediate means of subsistence? With some difficulty, and after referring for a character to his friends in the University of Dublin, he at length obtained the situation of usher to a school." Compare 1825 (17): "There was not a moment to be lost, therefore, in seeking for a situation that might afford him the means of immediate subsistence. His first attempt was to get admission as an assistant to a boarding-school or academy, but, for want of a recommendation, even that poor and painful situation was found difficult to be obtained. This difficulty appears also to have been nothing lessened by his stooping to make use of a feigned name." See Prior (I, 205); Forster (58).

45.2 by the boys."] From *The Vicar of Wakefield* (*Works*, IV, 107–8). In 1825 (17) and 1840 (53–54) the quotation is accurate. Here the paragraph begins with the last two sentences of the source, and two parts of sentences have been omitted.

45.10 all the family."] From Goldsmith's "On Education" (*Works*, I, 458). This quotation was added in 1840 (54). Compare Prior (I, 207).

45.14 on the bolster."] The quotation in Percy (37–38), which according to him expresses what Goldsmith said in conversation, reads: "After all the fatigues of the day, the poor usher of an academy is obliged to sleep in the same bed with a Frenchman, a teacher of that language to the boys; who disturbs him every night an hour perhaps in papering and filleting his hair, and stinks worse than a carrion, with his rancid pomatums when he lays his head beside him on his bolster." In 1825 (17) Irving quotes the passage with several slight variations. In 1840 (54), instead of the quotation, Irving wrote: "That this was a picture of poor Goldsmith himself, we may presume from the facts of his having an awkward, clumsy person, a pock-marked face; of his being at times odd in his dress, eccentric in his manners, and his having an Irish brogue." Prior (I, 207) quotes this passage.

45.17 Dr. Sleigh] Dr. Joseph Fenn Sleigh, according to Prior (I, 148–

49), was "an amiable and intelligent Quaker, the schoolfellow of Burke at Ballitore, the first friend of Barry the painter, and who died prematurely in 1771, an eminent physician in Cork." See *Letters* (20 n. 2). In 1825 (18) Irving included the following footnote: "This gentleman subsequently settled in Cork, his native city, and was rapidly rising into eminence in his profession, when he was cut off in the flower of his age by an inflammatory fever, which deprived the world of a fine scholar, a skilful physician, and an honest man." This was taken from "Table Talk," *The European Magazine and London Review* 24 (August, 1793), 91. The anecdotes about Goldsmith in this periodical were attributed to William Cooke by Forster in his revised edition in four volumes ([New York, 1900], III, 120).

45.23 in London."] The quotation, which is from the "Table Talk" article cited in note 45.17, appears thus in 1840 (54–55) and with some variation in 1825 (17–18).

45.25 Bankside, Southwark] A district in London on the south bank of the Thames.

45.30–31 a fortnight's wear] Prior (I, 214–15) received this information and the quotation in the next paragraph from Beatty's son, the Rev. Thomas Beatty, "Rector of Moira in Ireland." Prior (I, 215–16) recounted a "ludicrous story" which appears in the present volume on 46.30–38. In 1840 (56–57) Irving telescoped the two stories.

45.38 introducing him] Irving also made this statement in 1825 (18) and 1840 (55). Compare Percy (39); Prior (I, 211).

45.43 Samuel Richardson] Samuel Richardson (1689–1761), English novelist.

46.5 in Salisbury Court] Compare Prior (I, 211–12). The passage was added in 1849. Compare Forster (61).

46.8–9 Dr. Young] Edward Young (1683–1765), English clergyman and poet. His *Night Thoughts* was published in 1742–1744.

46.13 Dr. Farr] Prior (I, 153) identifies him as "Mr. (afterwards Dr.) William Farr, a Fellow of the Royal Society, who having entered into the medical service of the navy about 1760, for a long term of years filled the office of physician to the great Naval Hospitals of Haslar and Plymouth." According to Balderston (*History & Sources*, 48), Farr was the father-in-law of Samuel Rose, who edited Percy's *Memoir*.

46.20 Garrick's farce of Lethe] David Garrick (1717–1779), English actor, manager, and dramatist. *Lethe*, his first play, was presented at Drury Lane, April 15, 1740. It was published in 1749.

46.29 on the performance."] Percy (39) referred to this account as "from another respectable physician, to whom he was much attached when he was at college in Edinburgh." In 1825 (19) in a footnote Irving wrote: "It is presumed that Dr. Sleigh is meant." In 1840 (55) he attributed the quotation to Dr. Farr, and he omitted a sentence at this point. In 1849 he omitted the first sentence of the 1840 quotation and shifted the last three sentences to 46.39–47.3, where they are paraphrased and quoted in part.

46.36 medical visits] This story is said to have been told by Mary Horneck on the authority of Reynolds. See Sir Joshua Reynolds, *Portraits*, ed. Frederick W. Hilles (New York, 1952), p. 35.

46.38 to his heart] See note 45.30–31. For the paragraph that follows see note 46.29.

46.42 the *written mountains*] Scholars of Goldsmith's time thought the inscriptions found in the Sinai peninsula would prove significant to students of the Bible.

48.7 Dr. Milner] According to Prior (I, 216), Dr. John Milner. Balderston (*Letters*, 68, n. 2) gives 1758 as the year of his death.

48.26–33 Once indeed . . . in his mind.] This passage was added in 1849. Compare Prior (I, 218–19); Forster (65–66).

49.1–2 good humored reply] The anecdote was added in 1849. Compare Prior (I, 217–18); Forster (63–64).

49.5 Griffiths] Ralph Griffiths (1720–1803), a bookseller in Paternoster Row, founded the *Monthly Review* in 1749 and was its editor until his death.

49.10 Smollett] Tobias Smollett (1721–1771), Scottish novelist.

49.18 small fixed salary] In 1825 (23), following Percy (60), Irving wrote "a handsome salary." Prior (I, 220) said, "an adequate salary"; whereupon in 1840 (57) Irving changed the phrase to "a fixed salary." Forster (67) wrote "a small regular salary."

49.23 "Vicar of Wakefield."] The following quotation (*Works*, IV, 108–109) was added in 1849. See Forster (67–68).

49.33–34 the *antiqua mater* of Grub Street] Irving's italics.

49.35 Dryden and Otway] John Dryden (1631–1700), English poet and dramatist; Thomas Otway (1652–1685), English dramatist.

50.15 by old women!"] Added in 1849. Compare Prior (I, 223, n.); Forster (79–80, 99).

50.25 with each other] In 1840 (57–58) Irving wrote: "He soon found the diurnal drudgery of this task insupportable. He had to write daily from nine o'clock until two, and often the whole day, and was treated as a mere literary hack by both Griffiths and his wife. But what was worse than all, his writings were liable to be altered and retouched by both those personages, for Mrs. Griffiths was a literary lady, and assisted her husband in the Review. At the end of six or seven months this arrangement was broken off by mutual consent." See Prior (I, 220–22); Forster (99–100).

50.33 Johnson] Samuel Johnson (1709–1784), English critic, essayist, poet, and conversationalist, was regarded as the foremost literary man of his day. Johnson said, "Goldsmith was a plant that flowered late" (Boswell, IV, 16). Irving added this paragraph in 1849.

51.7 John Newbery] John Newbery (1713–1767), English publisher and bookseller, was one of the first to exploit successfully the field of children's literature. See Prior (I, 339–40).

51.14 Vicar of Wakefield] *Works* (IV, 94–95). Irving added the following quotation in 1840 (58). See Prior (I, 342); Forster (356).

51.19–20 Mr. Thomas Trip] Charles Welsh, *A Bookseller of the Last Century, Being some Account of the Life of John Newbery, and of the Books he published, with a Notice of the later Newberys* (London and New York, 1885), p. 291, lists as one of the children's books Newbery published *A Pretty Book of Pictures for little Masters and Misses; or, Tommy Trip's History of Birds and Beasts* . . . .

51.32 of the place] The paragraph to this point appears with slight variations in 1840 (58–59). Compare Prior (I, 236–37).

51.40 and pay visits] Irving is paraphrasing either Boswell (I, 74) or Forster (189–90). Added in 1849.

52.6 names of notoriety] The paragraph was adapted from 1840 (59).

52.9 years afterwards] The *Enquiry* was published in 1759.

52.19 in her lap."] *Works* (I, 314–16). This and the next two paragraphs were added in 1849.

52.28–29 on their forefathers] *Works* (I, 311). The balance of the paragraph is from *Works* (I, 314).

53.12 insensibly away."] *Works* (I, 315).

53.20–21 and fine linen] Compare Luke 16:19.

53.23 brother Charles] Charles Goldsmith was born August 16, 1737. See *Letters* (xv–xix).

53.32 Addison] Joseph Addison (1672–1719), English essayist.

53.33 poem of the Campaign] "The Campaign" celebrates Marlborough's victory at the Battle of Blenheim.

53.35 second story."] All of this paragraph except the first clause ("While poor . . . an author,") appears in 1840 (59–60). Compare Prior (I, 244–45); Forster (101–3).

53.41 England] This paragraph appears in 1840 (64). Compare Prior (I, 245).

53.42 wrote a letter] See note 43.26.

54.32 the Padareen Mare] A race horse. See *Notes and Queries*, 8th ser. 9 (June 13, 1896), 461–62.

54.33 time of Usher] James Usher, or Ussher, (1581–1656), Irish clergyman, Archbishop of Armagh, scholar, and fellow of Trinity College, Dublin.

54.40 Signora Columba]   Signora Columba Mattei, a singer of Italian opera. See *Works* (I, 507).

54.41–42 Johnny Armstrong's 'Last Good-night']   Johnny Armstrong was a Scottish outlaw. See *The English and Scottish Popular Ballads*, ed. Francis James Child (New York, 1965), III, 363–67. This was one of Goldsmith's favorite ballads.

54.42 Peggy Golden]   In "Happiness, In a great Measure, Dependant on Constitution," *Works* (I, 385) Goldsmith wrote: "The music of the finest singer is dissonance to what I felt when our old dairy-maid sung me into tears with Johnny Armstrong's Last Good Night, or the Cruelty of Barbara Allen." Peggy Golden may have been this dairymaid.

55.11 to the brown]   Compare *Vicar* (*Works*, IV, 18).

55.15 Mohammed]   Mohammed or Mahomet (Western forms of the Arabic Muhammad), (570–632), prophet and founder of Islam, the Mohammedan religion. Irving wrote a life of the prophet: *Mahomet and His Successors*, ed. Henry A. Pochmann and E. N. Feltskog (Madison, Wisc., 1970).

56.18 of their author]   With the exception of the first sentence, this paragraph was added in 1849. Compare 1840 (64); Prior (I, 258); Forster (105–6).

56.19 the "Bee,"]   *The Bee*, published by "J. Wilkie, at the Bible, in St. Paul's Church-yard," appeared eight times in 1759. See *Works* (I, 345–48).

56.33 from ridicule."]   Irving added the quotation in 1849. See Forster (109); *Works* (I, 415–16).

56.38 East India director]   In 1825 (20), following Percy (45), Irving named the director as Mr. Jones. In 1840 (64), following Prior (I, 258), he omitted the name. Compare Forster (127).

56.39 appointment in India]   In 1825 (20), following Percy (45), Irving placed this incident at the time of Goldsmith's first employment at the school. In 1840 (64), following Prior (I, 258), he shifted it to the time of Goldsmith's second stint at the school. Compare Forster (110).

57.11 union]   The Act of Union on January 1, 1801, united Ireland with Great Britain.

57.21–22 writes Goldsmith]   Following Percy (50–53), Irving included this letter in 1825 (21). Although Prior (I, 259–62) also included it, Irving omitted it in 1840. See *Letters* (32–36).

57.25 to expect success]   Here Irving omitted a sentence from his source. It was not omitted in 1825 (21) nor in Prior (I, 259) and Forster (114–15).

58.13 to Robert Bryanton,]   The following letter, which is dated August 14, 1758, was first published by Prior (I, 264–67). Irving did not include it in 1840. See Forster (117–20).

58.38 as if on a whirligig."]   In Prior (I, 265) and *Letters* (38) the phrase reads: "disagreeably round like an wh⸺ in a whirligig." Forster (118) reads: "disagreeably round like a whore in a whirligig...."

59.5 soon released him]   See note for 41.34.

59.10 full of character]   The following letter to Mrs. Lawder, dated August 15, 1758, was first published by Prior (I, 268–73). Irving did not include it in 1840. See Forster (123–26); *Letters* (41–48).

60.41 Butler]   Samuel Butler (1612–1680), English satirist, is known today principally for his *Hudibras*.

60.43 once knew him.]   See note for 41.34.

60.43 Newton and Swift]   Sir Isaac Newton (1642–1727), English scientist and mathematician; Jonathan Swift (1667–1745), Irish clergyman, Dean of St. Patrick's, Dublin, and satirist.

62.10 Coromandel]   A district on the southeast coast of India.

62.17 before him]   In 1825 (20) Irving wrote: "This appointment seems, for a while, to have filled the vivid imagination of our author with splendid dreams of futurity. The princely fortunes acquired by some individuals in the Indies flattered him with the hope of success; and accordingly we find him bending his whole soul to the accomplishment of this new undertaking." There is no comparable passage in Percy. In 1840 (64–65) lines 9–16 appear and are followed by: "The only difficulty was how to raise funds for his outfit, which would be expensive; but, fortunately he was at that moment preparing for the press a treatise upon 'the Present State of Polite Literature in Europe,' the profits of which, he felt assured, would be sufficient to carry him to India. He accordingly drew up proposals to publish the work by subscription, and claimed the assistance of his friends to give them a wide circulation." Compare Prior (I, 274–75); Forster (110–11, 113).

62.33 the Old Bailey]   Another name for Newgate, a criminal court. This paragraph was added in 1849. Compare Forster (131–32).

62.40 to ascertain]   In 1825 (23) Irving wrote: "From what particular motive this expedition was given up, has never been accurately explained, but most likely it was owing to the immediate impracticability of raising an adequate sum for his equipment. Perhaps, however, a better reason may be found in the rapid change that took place in our author's circumstances about this time, in consequence of the increased patronage he began to receive from the booksellers." Compare Percy (60). This passage does not appear in 1840 (66) in which, after discussing Goldsmith's failure to pass his medical examination and his giving up the idea of going to India, Irving writes: "It is only recently that the true cause has been traced, by the indefatigable research of one of his biographers, to this rejection at Surgeons' Hall." See Prior (I, 281–82). Balderston (*Letters*, xxx–xxxiii) points out that the real cause was the French siege of Madras, news of which did not reach London until March, 1759. Compare her statement that Goldsmith's "literary fortunes were looking up" by the time the seige had been lifted by the English with Irving's speculation in 1825.

63.13 College of Physicians] The Royal College of Physicians, founded in 1518, issued licenses to those wishing to practice medicine in London.

63.26 from the tailor] This paragraph is an expansion of one in 1840 (65–66). Compare Prior (I, 284–85); Forster (138–39).

63.27 College of Surgeons] The Royal College of Surgeons evolved from the Barber-Surgeons' Company, instituted in 1540. It has power similar to that of the College of Physicians.

63.36 of his friends] The paragraph appears in 1840 (66). Compare Prior (I, 280–81).

64.8 from prison] This anecdote was added in 1849. Compare Forster (141–42).

64.21 and a prison] Compare 1840 (66–67). See Prior (I, 283–86; 327–28).

64.24 to despondency] The following letter, received by Griffiths in January, 1759, was first published by Prior (I, 266–88). It appears in 1840 (67–68). Compare Forster (142–44).

65.10 Mr. Dodsley] The *Enquiry* was published by "R. & J. Dodsley." When Robert Dodsley (1703–1764) retired in 1759, the year the firm published the *Enquiry,* he turned the business over to his brother James (1724–1797). See Elizabeth Eaton Kent, *Goldsmith and His Booksellers* (Ithaca, N.Y., 1933), pp. 33–50.

65.22 a short compilation] *The Life of Voltaire.* See 71.22. Compare Forster (147).

65.25 Monthly Review.] This paragraph appears in 1840 (68–69). See Prior (I, 292, 304).

65.32 with it,"] See 64.40–41.

65.37 these lodgings] See 62.31–33.

65.40 old woman] It was Prior who met this woman. See Prior (I, 326).

66.22 it was finished] This anecdote was added in 1840 (70–71). See Prior (I, 328–29).

66.26 and other works] The Reverend Thomas Percy (1729–1811) became bishop of Dromore in 1782. His *Reliques of Ancient English Poetry* was published in 1765. In the *Memoir* (60) Percy referred to himself as "a friend of his." In 1825 (24) Irving changed this to "one of his literary friends," and converted Percy's narrative (61) into a first-person anecdote, the same that appears in the 1840 version (71) and here in 1849.

66.27 by Grainger] James Grainger (1721–1766), Scottish physician and poet, introduced Goldsmith to Percy in 1758. See Prior (I, 237–43).

66.30 writing his 'Inquiry,'] Prior (I, 325) called attention to Percy's error. Since the *Enquiry* was published on April 3, 1759, Goldsmith must have been reading proof.

66.39 Beau Tibbs] A character in Goldsmith's *The Citizen of the World*.

67.18 a secret.' "*] In the original the passages here quoted are italicized. There are other variations, particularly in punctuation and capitalization. See *Works* (II, 230–31). The quoted passage appears in 1840 (71–72).

67.24 another publication] "The Club of Queer Fellows," in *Tales of a Traveller*.

67.39 general concert."†] This and the preceding paragraph were added in 1840 (72–73). Irving altered the first sentence of the quotation to adapt it to the new context. Forster (135–36), speaking of the state of the houses in Green Arbour Court in his own day said: "But Mr. Washington Irving saw them first, and with reverence had described them for Goldsmith's sake."

68.3 following letter] Balderston (*Letters*, 56) dates it about January 13, 1759. Compare 1825 (21–23); 1840 (73–79).

69.10 your son] Henry Goldsmith, Jr., then about three years old, later served in America as a lieutenant in the British army in 1775. He married a girl from Rhode Island and settled in Nova Scotia. See *Notes and Queries*, 12th ser. 4 (June–July, 1918), 177–78.

69.18 but your own] See note 15.7.

70.9 splenetic habit] On Goldsmith's relations with his mother, see *Letters* (xi–xii).

70.41 less fortunate] The footnote is taken verbatim from Prior (I, 301).

71.12 thus began," &c.*] Goldsmith included these lines in *The Citizen of the World*, Letter XXX (*Works*, II, 129). Compare "The Deserted Village," lines 217–36 (*Works*, IV, 295–96).

71.14 of Montaign's] Michel Eyquem de Montaigne (1533–1592), French essayist.

71.22 Life of Voltaire,] See 65.22.

71.24–25 Ned Purdon,] According to Prior (I, 62), Charles and Edward Purdon were "intimate associates" of Goldsmith at Trinity College, Dublin. After serving in the army as a private, Ned Purdon went to London to become a professional writer. See also Prior (I, 306–308). *The Henriade*, a poem by Voltaire on the subject of Henri IV of France, was published surreptitiously in Rouen in 1723 under the title *La Ligue ou Henri le grand*. During his stay in England (1726–1729) Voltaire dedicated the poem to Queen Caroline.

71.34 to come back] Friedman includes this epitaph in *Works* (IV,

414) in the section of "Poems of Doubtful Authenticity." Prior (I, 308) refers to the epitaph but does not include it. The entire paragraph was added in 1849. Compare Forster (154, 422).

72.16 all the day!] This and the preceding paragraph were added in 1849. See *Works* (II, 128–29); Forster (153).

73.16–17 its views] The paragraph to this point and the preceding paragraph appear in 1840 (79–80). In 1840 the paragraph continues: "and being the most important production that had yet come from his pen, and possessing his peculiar charm of style, it had a profitable sale, and added to his reputation.

"In fact, he had now grown into sufficient literary importance to become an object of hostility to the underlings of the press." (The balance of this paragraph conforms to the 1849 version.) Compare Prior (I, 309–13).

73.31 of the pillory."] The quotations, extracted from a longer passage in Prior (I, 289–90), are from the *Monthly Review* 21 (November, 1759), 389.

74.8 Kenrick] William Kenrick (1725?–1779) holds the dubious distinction of having been regarded by his contemporaries as a scurrilous libeler. According to Prior (I, 226, 294), Kenrick succeeded Goldsmith on the *Monthly Review*. See Boswell (I, 516–17) for Kenrick's attack on Dr. Johnson. Garrick brought a libel suit against Kenrick in King's Bench court. See Prior (I, 293–94).

74.18 themselves *known*."] See Boswell (I, 516–17). This paragraph was added in 1840 (80–81). Compare Prior (I, 295); Forster (491).

74.22 Ishmaelites of the press] Forster (492) called him "this Ishmael of criticism." See Gen 16:12.

74.28 Shirley] James Shirley (1596–1666) was an English dramatist, poet, and teacher.

74.39 till its stinks] Prior (I, 295–96) attributed these verses to Cuthbert Shaw, who wrote "The Race" under the pseudonym of Mercurius Spur. This paragraph was added in 1840 (81–82).

74.41 Gentleman's Magazine] The *Gentleman's Magazine* was founded in 1731 by Edward Cave (1691–1754), its publisher.

75.2–3 Johnson's Rambler] *The Rambler* was published twice a week (1750–1752), the 208 numbers devoted chiefly to matters of wisdom or piety.

75.4 Adventurer and Idler] *The Adventurer* (1752–1754) was a periodical produced by John Hawkesworth (1715?–1773), a friend of Dr. Johnson. *The Idler* (1758–1760) was a series of 103 essays which appeared weekly in *The Universal Chronicle*.

75.8 escaped oblivion] Irving added this paragraph in 1849. Compare Prior (I, 342–43).

75.9–10 Bee, the Busy Body, and the Lady's Magazine] *The Bee* was published weekly in October and November, 1759, by "Bookseller Wilkie, of the Bible in St. Paul's Churchyard . . ." (Forster, 192). According to Prior (I, 332), Goldsmith "furnished all the papers of value" to it. *The Busy Body* was published three times a week by I. Pottinger from October 9 to November 3, 1759. Goldsmith edited *The Lady's Magazine; Or, Polite Companion for the Fair Sex* (1759–1763) under the name of the Honourable Mrs. Caroline Stanhope. See Prior (I, 336).

75.18 British literature] This paragraph shows slight modification of the one added in 1840 (82).

75.23 Walpole] Horace Walpole (1717–1797), youngest son of the statesman Sir Robert Walpole, was a dilettante in literature, criticism, architecture, and gardening.

75.27 the *Provoked Husband*] A comedy begun as *A Journey to London* by Sir John Vanbrugh (1664–1726) and completed with the present title in 1728 by Colley Cibber (1671–1757).

75.27 at school."] The quotation from Walpole was added in 1849. Compare Forster (206).

75.34 before the public."] Irving followed Forster (208). Compare *Works* (I, 232).

75.43 called a conjuror."] Irving followed Forster (209). Compare *Works* (I, 328).

76.9 real characters."] Irving followed Forster (211) even to combining the first two sentences of this paragraph, which come from *Works* (I, 328) and the second two sentences from I, 329 with no indication of the long omission in between. These quotations from the *Enquiry* were added in 1849.

76.12–13 Society of Arts] The Society for the Encouragement of Arts, Manufactures, and Commerce, established in 1754, was the forerunner of the Royal Academy, established in 1768.

76.25 never forgotten] This paragraph is an adaptation of one in 1840 (115), derived from Prior (I, 378).

76.27 the British Magazine] *The British Magazine, or Monthly Repository for Gentlemen and Ladies* began publication in January, 1760. Prior (I, 342) said that "there is reason to believe Newbery had a share" in this publication.

76.31 Hume] David Hume (1711–1776), Scottish philosopher and historian.

76.32 for Riches] In his essay "A Resverie" [*sic*] (*Works*, I, 443–50). In 1825 (24) Irving wrote: "At this time also, Goldsmith wrote occasionally for the British Magazine and Critical Review, conducted by Dr. Smollett. To that celebrated writer he was originally introduced in consequence of the taste and accuracy with which he had criticised a despicable translation of Ovid's Fasti, by a pedantic schoolmaster; though the intercourse between them does not appear to have been kept up for any considerable time, yet Goldsmith is said to have derived important advantages from the connexion. It is well known that the liberal soul of Smollett made him the friend of every author in distress; and it is generally understood that, for some time, he warmly interested himself in Goldsmith's success. He not only recommended him to the patronage of the most eminent booksellers, but introduced him to the notice of the first literary characters." No comparable passage is found in the Percy *Memoir*. Irving's 1849 paragraph also appears in 1840 (82).

76.35 Public Ledger]   According to Prior (I, 356), Griffith Jones was said to have been the editor.

77.2 Fleet Street]   This and the previous paragraph were added in 1840 (82–83). Compare Prior (I, 355–61, 367–68).

77.7 kind to her."]   This paragraph was added in 1849. The quotation is from Forster (237).

77.15–16 Samuel Derrick]   Samuel Derrick (1724–1769), according to Frederick A. Pottle, was "a dingy fifth-rate man of letters . . ." (*James Boswell: The Earlier Years, 1740–1769* [New York, 1966], p. 47). In 1763 he was Master of the Ceremonies at Bath. (See *Boswell's London Journal, 1762–1763*, ed. Frederick A. Pottle [New York, 1950], p. 228.)

77.20 was a *baker*]   This paragraph, adapted from Prior (I, 419–21), was added in 1849. Compare Forster (251–52).

78.7–8 Guthrie, Murphy, Christopher Smart, and Bickerstaffe]   William Guthrie (1708–1770), Scottish writer; Arthur Murphy (1727–1805), Irish lawyer and playwright; Christopher Smart (1722–1771), English poet and essayist; Isaac Bickerstaffe (ca. 1735–ca. 1812), Irish playwright. Prior (I, 368-69) mentions other members of the group of lesser note. The paragraph with slight differences appears in 1840 (83).

78.12 one Pilkington]   According to Prior (I, 369), Pilkington was the "son of the Rev. Mathew and Mrs. Letitia Pilkington of Dublin, unhappily known by their quarrels and writings." There was a Pilkington at Trinity College in 1748. Percy (99) refers to him as "the noted John Cartaret Pilkington."

78.29 the white mice]   The paragraph to this point and the preceding paragraph appear in 1840 (83–84). The paragraph in 1840 (84) concludes thus: "Goldsmith used often to relate, with great humour, this story of his credulous generosity; he was in some degree indemnified by its suggesting to him the amusing little story of Prince Bonbennin and the White Mouse in 'the Citizen of the World.'" Compare Prior (I, 371–72); Forster (232).

78.36 Citizen of the World] Letters XLVIII and XLIX (*Works*, II, 201–10).

79.16 all authority."] The quotation is from Boswell (I, 43); the italics are Irving's. This paragraph was added in 1849.

79.39 "We rode and tied,"] A method of traveling when two people have only one horse. For an explanation of how it works, see Henry Fielding's *Joseph Andrews* (Book II, Chapter II). The anecdote that follows is in Boswell (I, 71, n. 1). This and the two preceding paragraphs were added in 1849.

80.6 his wit;"] Irving paraphrases 79.15.

80.8 Savage] Richard Savage (1697?–1743), English poet, spent years trying to establish his claim to being the illegitimate son of Earl Rivers and the Countess of Macclesfield. He and Samuel Johnson were close friends in 1738–1739 soon after the latter's arrival in London.

80.11 cave] See note 74.41.

80.13 behind a screen] See Boswell (I, 139, n. 1). The paragraph was added in 1849.

80.17 his wit."] Irving again paraphrases 79.15.

80.19 individual labor] Johnson's *Dictionary of the English Language*, begun in 1746, was published in 1755. Although Johnson had six copyists, the *Dictionary* is said to have been "essentially a one-man book" (E. L. McAdam, Jr. and George Milne, *Johnson's Dictionary: A Modern Selection* [New York, 1963], p. viii).

80.24–25 "The Great Cham of Literature."] Smollett used this phrase in a letter to John Wilkes. See Boswell (I, 338). This paragraph was added in 1849. Compare Forster (190).

80.31–32 Bee and the Chinese Letters] See *Works* (I, 447–48; II, 171).

80.38 a better example."] The substance of this paragraph and the quotation appeared in Percy (62–63) and in 1825 (24–25). In 1840 (84–85) Irving revised the paragraph, and there are further slight revisions in 1849. Compare Prior (I, 376–77); Forster (239).

80.40 shop of Davies] Thomas Davies (1712?–1785), actor turned bookseller, was the one who effected the meeting of Johnson and Boswell in 1763. See Boswell (I, 400–404).

81.4 Churchill in the Rosciad] Charles Churchill (1731–1764), clergyman who became a satirist and man about town. *The Rosciad*, published anonymously in 1761, was a satire on theatrical people.

81.6 *mouth a bone*.] *The Rosciad*, lines 321–22. Irving's italics. Boswell (IV, 78) includes only the second line of the couplet. Forster (248) refers to the poem but does not quote it.

81.14 pretty wife.] *The Rosciad*, lines 319–20. Only the second line of the couplet appears in Boswell (I, 496); it reads: "That Davies has a very pretty wife, ————" Compare Forster (248). This and the previous paragraph were added in 1849.

81.17 Ursa Major] Boswell's father coined this name for Johnson. See Boswell (III, 79).

81.23 Bennet Langton, George Steevens] Bennet Langton (1737?–1801) was a young gentleman from Lincolnshire. See 91–92. George Steevens (1736–1800) was a commentator on Shakespeare.

81.24 Warburton] Bishop William Warburton (1698–1779), English clergyman and writer on religious subjects, championed Alexander Pope's work and served as his literary executor.

81.28 Foote, the Aristophanes] Samuel Foote (1720–1777), English actor and playwright, was noted for caricaturing his contemporaries on the stage. He was nicknamed "The English Aristophanes" because of his "keen eye for character ... and brilliant sketches of contemporary manners." See *The Oxford Companion to the Theatre*, ed. Phyllis Hartnoll, 2d ed. (London, 1957), pp. 270–71.

82.2 with impunity."] See Boswell (III, 175); Forster (251).

82.5 essayist] The last four paragraphs were added in 1849.

83.17 to silver."] The quotation is from the *Citizen of the World*, Letter CVIII (*Works*, II, 418–19). This paragraph in a slightly varied form was added in 1840 (85). Compare Prior (I, 383).

83.29 at danger."] This and the preceding paragraph were added in 1840 (85–86). See *Works* (II, 421); Prior (I, 383–86).

83.30 Lord Bute] John Stuart, third Earl of Bute (1713–1792), was Prime Minister from 1761 to 1763.

83.31 George the Third] George III (1738–1820) succeeded his grandfather, George II, as king of Great Britain and Ireland in 1760.

83.35 Public Ledger] This and the following paragraph, in substance, appear in 1825 (28) as a paraphrase of Percy (64–66). The passage, revised in 1840 (86), is the same as in 1849. Compare Prior (I, 385–86).

84.8–9 wonderful improvement."] Compare Boswell (IV, 354); Prior (I, 383–84); Forster (254).

84.11 Cock-lane Ghost?] *The Mystery Revealed; Containing a Series of Transactions and Authentic Testimonials, Respecting the Supposed Cock-Lane Ghost; Which have hitherto Been concealed from the Public* was published in pamphlet form in 1762. See *Works* (IV, 417–41). See also Boswell (I, 414–15); Prior (I, 387–88).

84.12 Beau Nash] Richard Nash (1674–1762), English dandy, became Master of the Ceremonies at Bath in 1704. Newbery paid Goldsmith fourteen guineas for *The Life of Richard Nash, Esq.*, which was published on October 14, 1762. See *Works* (III, 281–398).

84.14 Chinese Letters] Goldsmith contributed a series of 119 letters to the *Public Ledger* in 1760–1761; they were collected as *The Citizen of the World* and published in 1762. See *Works* (II, ix–xiv).

84.21 pencil of a master."] In 1825 (25–26) the quotation appears without quotation marks. The final sentence, not included here, reads: "They have ever maintained their currency and reputation, and are ranked among the classical productions of the British muse." Compare Percy (64). The paragraph as it appears in 1849 was added in 1840 (87). Irving seems to have quoted from his own 1825 essay. Compare Prior (I, 396–98).

84.25 one of his writings] See Goldsmith's *A History of the Earth and Animated Nature* (Philadelphia, 1825), I, 345. A group of Cherokee Indians, headed by the warrior Outacity, visited London in 1761 and was received by King George III. Compare Prior (I, 417–19). This and the following paragraph appear in 1840 (87–88). Compare Prior (I, 458).

84.30 "merry Islington,"] See William Cowper's "The Diverting History of John Gilpin" (lines 133–36). Islington was a famous spa during the last decade of the seventeenth century, but it went out of fashion until 1733 when the daughters of George II patronized it. See Warwick Wroth, *The London Pleasure Gardens of the Eighteenth Century* (London, 1896), pp. 15–23.

84.34 Canonbury House] In "The Poor Devil Author," *Tales of a Traveller*, Irving wrote of a visit to "Canonbury Castle. It is an ancient brick tower, hard by 'merry Islington'; the remains of a hunting-seat of Queen Elizabeth, where she took the pleasure of the country when the neighborhood was all woodland." See John Nichols, *Islington: A Poem, Addressed to Mr. Benjamin Stapp. To Which are Subjoined Several Other Poetical Essays by the same Author* (London, 1763), p. 2. Compare Forster (260).

84.36 "White Conduit House,"] The White Conduit House according to Wroth (131–32), was originally a small alehouse in the seventeenth century. By 1745 it was a garden with arbors and a fishpond, and it became a popular place for refreshments and for playing cricket. It gradually became more elaborate, having boxes decorated with Flemish paintings for tea drinkers; and it continued popular throughout the eighteenth century.

85.8 with flying colors] The anecdote was added in 1840 (87–88). According to Prior (I, 372–73), it was told by Kenrick and was, therefore, apocryphal. Compare Forster (232–33).

85.11 "the History of England] See *Works* (V, 290, n. 1) for details of this work.

85.12–13 Rapin, Carte, and Kennet] Paul de Rapin (1661–1725), French historian, published *Histoire d'Angleterre* in 1724. Thomas

Carte (1686–1754), English historian, published *History of England to 1654*, 4 vols. (1747–1755). White Kennett (1660–1728), English clergyman, wrote the third volume of *A Compleat History of England* (1706), a three-volume work begun by a group of booksellers in 1705.

85.21 Lord Chesterfield] Philip Dormer Stanhope, fourth earl of Chesterfield (1694-1773), English statesman and man of letters, was famous for a series of letters he wrote to his natural son, Philip Stanhope, on the proper behavior of a gentleman; and for Dr. Johnson's famous letter to him declining the honor of his patronage. See Boswell (I, 244–50).

85.21–22 Lord Orrery] John Boyle, fifth earl of Cork and of Orrery (1707–1762), was an Irish writer and friend of Dr. Johnson. Percy (63) said that the book had been "attributed to Lord Lyttelton, the Earl of Orrery, and other noble authors...." Since the book was published in 1764, two years after the death of Lord Orrery, Percy's memory must have been at fault. See Forster (263, 417); Prior (I, 497).

85.22 Lord Lyttelton] George, Lord Lyttelton (1709–1773), poet, essayist, and politician, was a friend of Pope and Fielding.

85.27 to be written."] The quotation is from Prior (I, 495). The paragraph was added in 1840 (91–92). In 1825 (35–36) Irving wrote: "Here he began and finished one of his most pleasing and successful compilations, a 'History of England, in a series of Letters from a Nobleman to his Son.' This little work was at first published anonymously, and was very generally ascribed to the pen of Lord Lyttelton. That nobleman then held some rank in the world of letters, and as the chief feature in the performance was an easy elegance of language, without much depth of thought, or investigation, the public were the more easily betrayed into a belief that it was the work of his lordship. It had likewise the honour to be ascribed to the Earl of Orrery, and some other noble authors of that period. That it was really the production of Goldsmith, however, was soon afterwards generally known; a circumstance which in all probability, greatly enhanced its value in the estimation of the world." Compare Percy (63); Prior (I, 492–500).

85.37 nothing about it."] The paragraph was added in 1840 (92). In 1825 (26), following Percy (19–20), Irving included the anecdote in a group of stories about Goldsmith's desire for fame. Compare Boswell (IV, 107).

85.38 Boswell] James Boswell (1740–1795), Scottish advocate and man of letters. For Prior's evaluation of Boswell see (I, 428–57).

86.1 of the metropolis] The paragraph to this point appears in 1840 (88–89), followed by "Their first meeting was at the table of Mr.

Thomas Davies, bookseller, in Russell-street, Covent Garden." Compare Prior (I, 427). The remainder of the paragraph was added in 1849. See Boswell (I, 421–22); Forster (256–57).

86.14 poetry of the day] Dodsley's *Collection of Poems, by Several Hands* was published in 1748 in three volumes. Between 1748 and 1782 it was expanded into six volumes and was reprinted eleven times. This sentence in 1840 (89) reads: "Mr. Robert Dodsley, compiler of the well-known collection of modern poetry was present. In the course of conversation, the merits of the current poetry of the day were discussed." The rest of the 1840 paragraph conforms to the 1849. Compare Prior (I, 427–28); Forster (256).

86.22 of this conversation] Irving was in error. See Boswell (III, 402).

86.28 introduction to Johnson] The meeting occurred on May 16, 1763. See Boswell (I, 400–402); Forster (287–88).

86.31 Magnus Apollo] Dr. Johnson.

86.36 a smaller scale."] See Boswell (I, 421).

86.40 great master."] See Boswell (I, 429–30). The quotations in this paragraph were added in 1849. In 1840 (89) Irving wrote: "Boswell, as yet, had not met with Dr. Johnson, the great luminary of the day; an intimacy with whom he had made the crowning object of his aspiring and somewhat ludicrous ambition. In the mean time, he was probably glad to make the acquaintance of Goldsmith, though as yet a star of lesser magnitude. Subsequently, however, when he had effected his purpose, and become the constant satellite of Johnson, he affected to undervalue Goldsmith, whose merits, in fact, were of a kind little calculated to strike his coarse perceptions."

86.43 a Mr. Levett] Robert Levet was "an obscure practiser in physick amongst the lower people, his fees being sometimes very small sums, sometimes whatever provisions his patients could afford him..." (Boswell, I, 226). Johnson met him about 1746; and for years before Boswell met Johnson, Levet had an apartment in Johnson's house.

87.3 enough to Johnson."] This paragraph was added in 1849. See Boswell (I, 430); Prior (I, 474); Forster (259).

87.6 protection of Johnson."] The paragraph was added in 1849. See Boswell (I, 430); Prior (I, 474); Forster (259–60).

87.13 by Dr. Johnson] In 1840 (89) this sentence reads: "The lurking hostility to Goldsmith discernible throughout Boswell's writings, has been attributed by some to a silly spirit of jealousy of the superior esteem evinced for the poet by Dr. Johnson." The rest of the paragraph is the same in 1840. Compare Prior (I, 429–35).

87.19–20 Miss Williams] Mrs. Anna Williams, twice married, was a widow when she went to live with the Johnsons. She died in 1783. See Boswell (I, 220).

87.28–29 mark of distinction."] The paragraph was added in 1840 (89–90). See Boswell (I, 433–34); Prior (I, 431).

87.35 Sancho Panza] Don Quixote's squire.

87.41–42 faculty of sticking."] Though Prior (I, 436) told this story, Irving did not add it until 1849. Forster (291) acknowledged Prior as his source.

88.7 Hogarth the painter] William Hogarth (1697–1764), English painter and engraver.

88.8 Public Ledger] There are no references to Hogarth in the essays published in the *Public Ledger* which are included in *Works* (III, 158–79). There is one in the *Enquiry* (*Works*, I, 318). This and the next paragraph were added in 1849.

88.28 at him again!"] Compare Forster (264–65).

88.30 'Goldsmith's Hostess.'] Compare Forster (266). This and the following sentence were added in 1849. The balance of the paragraph in 1840 (91) is placed at the end of the next paragraph, where it applies to Reynolds.

88.34 painters and poets] Irving numbered many painters among his friends, including Washington Allston, Charles Leslie, Gilbert Stuart Newton, and David Wilkie. See Prior (I, 481).

88.40 Sir Joshua Reynolds] Sir Joshua Reynolds (1723–1792), English portrait painter, was knighted in 1769. The following sentence was added in 1849. The rest of the paragraph appears in 1840 (91). See note 88.30. Compare Forster (267–70).

89.21 Miss Reynolds] Frances Reynolds (1729–1807), the youngest sister of Sir Joshua Reynolds, kept house for him for many years.

89.25 a lady] The lady was Mrs. Cholmondeley, the sister of Margaret ("Peg") Woffington, the Irish actress who for some years was Garrick's mistress. Mrs. Cholmondeley was the wife of "the Hon. and Rev. George Cholmondeley." (Boswell, II, 472, n. 1). Although Prior (II, 56) included this incident, Irving did not add it until 1849. Compare Forster (321); Boswell (V, 386).

89.28–29 Courtenay to Sir James Mackintosh] John Courtenay (1738–1815), born in Ireland, was for many years a member of Parliament for Tamworth. Sir James Mackintosh (1765–1832) was a Scottish writer. Courtenay wrote a "Poetical Review of the Literary and Moral Character of the late Samuel Johnson, LL.D." which Croker included in his edition of Boswell's *Johnson* (V, 445–61) as an appendix along with a biographical sketch of Courtenay written by Mackintosh. This paragragh was added in 1849. Compare Forster (523–24); Boswell (III, 444).

90.19 Turk's Head] A coffee house patronized by Johnson. The Club met there until 1783.

90.21 year 1764]   In 1825 (30) Irving wrote: "This literary association
is said by Mr. Boswell to have been founded in 1764, but Dr. Percy
is of opinion that its institution was not so early." See Percy (71). In
1840 (98) Irving wrote that the meetings "took a regular form about
the year 1764. . . ." Prior (I, 483–84) discussed the disagreement and
concluded that 1763 was "probably the true date." Forster (270) said
that 1763 as "the year of its foundation, is unquestionable."

90.22 years afterwards]   In 1825 (30ff.) Irving, following Percy (69–
73), included at this point a history of The Club. In 1840 (98–99)
he reduced the long passage to a paragraph. The following paragraphs
on the original members of The Club were added in 1849.

90.23 Dr. Nugent]   Christopher Nugent (d. 1775) was an Irish Catholic
doctor practicing at Bath, whose daughter Jane married Edmund
Burke in 1757. In 1825 (30) Irving in a footnote, paraphrasing one in
Percy (70–71), wrote: "This gentleman was a physician, father of Mr.
Burke's wife; not the Dr. Nugent who published some volumes of
travels, and several philosophical works, for whom he had been sometimes mistaken. The above Dr. Nugent was a very amiable man, and
highly respected by his contemporaries." The footnote was omitted
in 1840.

90.24 Topham Beauclerc]   The Hon. Topham Beauclerk (1739–1780),
English dandy, is said to have been a descendant of Charles II and
Nell Gwynn.

90.24 Chamier, Hawkins]   Anthony Chamier (1725–1780) was a member of Parliament for Tamworth. Sir John Hawkins (1719–1789),
English musicologist, attorney, and magistrate, was knighted in 1772.
He was Johnson's literary executor and published his *Life of Johnson*
in 1787–1789.

90.27–28 Hamilton]   William Gerard Hamilton (1729–1796), English
politician and Member of Parliament for Petersfield, was known as
"Single-Speech" Hamilton because after a brilliant maiden speech
he rarely spoke in Parliament.

90.42 Dr. Burney]   Charles Burney (1726–1814) was an English musicologist.

91.5 rudeness to Burke]   Compare Boswell (I, 492); Forster (275).

91.6 war office]   Chamier was a secretary in the War Office in 1770;
from 1775 until his death he served as under secretary of state.

91.17 of this family."]   See Boswell (I, 232).

91.21 Boswell gives us]   See Boswell (I, 231–32).

92.4 were companions."]   See Boswell (I, 233).

92.20 frisk with you!"]   See Boswell (I, 234–35).

92.25–26 Lord Lansdowne's drinking song]   George Granville, Baron

Lansdowne (1667–1735) was a poet, wit, and statesman. The following verses are in Boswell (I, 235, n. 2). Compare Forster (281–82).

92.40 the Rake's Progress]   A series of eight engravings by Hogarth
(1733–1735) depicting the degeneration of a rich young man.

93.2 not *let* him!"]   See Boswell (I, 235–36). Compare Forster (282).

93.6 in Greek]   A reviewer of Irving's *Life of Goldsmith* in *The Gentleman's Magazine*, n.s. 32 (December, 1849), 617–18, said that he had
heard "from one of the very first and foremost Greek scholars of that
period, who knew Bennet Langton, that his knowledge of the language
for which he is here celebrated was by no means accurate or profound. . . ."

93.9 her Memoirs]   See *Gossip About Dr. Johnson and Others, Being
Chapters from the Memoirs of Miss Laetitia Matilda Hawkins*, ed.
Francis Henry Skrine (London, 1926), pp. 109–10. Irving's quotation
differs from this source. Compare Forster (282).

93.15 on one leg]   See Henry Best, *Personal and Literary Memorials, by
The Author of "Four Years in France," "Italy As It is," &c.* (London,
1829), p. 62; compare Forster (282–83). The "Cartoons" of the Italian
Renaissance painter Raphael (1483–1520) were executed for Pope Leo
X in 1515–1516.

93.17 George Selwyn]   George Selwyn (1719–1791) was an English
wit and Member of Parliament. Compare Forster (283).

93.28 Pope]   Alexander Pope (1688–1744), English poet.

93.29 says the other."]   Irving is here paraphrasing Boswell (I, 233–34).

93.37 like a gentleman."]   Compare Shakespeare's *Henry IV, Part I*,
(V, iv, 169–70): "for I'll purge, and leave sack, and live cleanly as a
nobleman should do." Compare Boswell (I, 234); Forster (283).

93.43 seeing your intention."]   Compare Boswell (I, 233); Forster
(284).

94.6 of poetical composition."]   See Sir John Hawkins, *The Life of
Samuel Johnson, LL.D.* (London, 1787), p. 420. Compare Forster
(273).

95.12 plunging him]   A corresponding paragraph, which has no model
in the Percy *Memoir,* appears in 1825 (25): "The connexion betwixt
our author and Johnson was henceforth more closely cemented by
daily association. Mutual communication of thought begot mutual
esteem, and as their intercourse increased, their friendship improved.
Nothing could have been more fortunate for Goldsmith. A man of
his open improvident disposition was apt to stand in need of the
assistance of a friend. The years, wisdom and experience of Johnson,
rendered his advice of the highest value, and from the kindness and
promptitude with which he undertook and performed good offices, he
might always be securely relied on in cases of difficulty or distress. It

was not long before the improvidence of our author produced embarrassment in his circumstances, and we find the illustrious moralist the prompt and affectionate Mentor of his imprudent friend. The sums which he was now receiving as a writer, might naturally be supposed to have been at least equal to his wants, and more than sufficient to have kept him out of debt. But Goldsmith's affections were so social and generous, that when he had money he gave it most liberally away. It is not to be wondered at, therefore, if we find him soon after this period in distress for money, and even under arrest for his rent. He had just put the finishing stroke to his Vicar of Wakefield when the arrest took place, and was obliged to send for his friend Johnson to raise money by a sale of the manuscript.

"Our author's situation, on this occasion, having been mis-stated, it may be proper to give an authentic detail of it as narrated by Johnson himself."

Here follows the quotation in the next paragraph, for which see Boswell (I, 427–28; V, 409, n. 2). In 1840 (92–93) Irving revised the passage as it appears in 1849. Compare Prior (II, 14–15).

95.29 Francis Newbery] Francis Newbery was the nephew of John Newbery. This paragraph appears with slight variation in 1840 (93). A similar passage appears in 1825 (25). Compare Percy (61).

95.35–36 "The Captivity,"] For a discussion of this oratorio see *Works* (IV, 209–13). The paragraph was added in 1840 (93–94) but without the following stanzas. Compare Prior (II, 1–5).

96.4 Bids expectation rise] This stanza is a variant of the standard one. See *Works* (IV, 222). Since both Prior (II, 5) and Forster (299) used the standard version, Irving must have been following his edition of Goldsmith's works.

96.14 acquire it."] The passage, which also appears in 1825 (26) and 1840 (94), is from Boswell (III, 233), where it is not a direct quotation. Compare Forster (322).

96.20 narrow circle."] From Goldsmith's dedicatory letter in "The Traveller" to his brother. See Friedman's textual note (*Works*, IV, 245–46). The quotation was included in 1825 (26) and 1840 (94). In 1825 Irving added the following sentence: "A short time, however, proved to our author how fallacious were his fears. In less than a year the publication of his 'Traveller,' placed him at the head of the poets of his time."

96.22 already been observed,] See 40.26–28. This paragraph was added in 1840 (94–95). The 1825 version (26–27) is much different.

96.30–31 a few lines] See Boswell (II, 6–7).

97.2 satisfy the child] lines 153–54 (*Works*, IV, 255). The anecdote was added in 1840 (95). Compare Prior (II, 33).

97.6 December, 1764,] In 1825 (26) Irving wrote "came out early in 1765." Compare Percy (63). This paragraph was added in 1840 (95–96). Compare Prior (I, 32–33); Forster (322).

97.12 solicitous to know."] See *Works* (IV, 247).

97.16 Critical Review] Prior (I, 34) said that it appeared in the December, 1764, issue. See Boswell (I, 494). In 1825 (27) Irving wrote: "When the 'Traveller' was published, Dr. Johnson wrote a review of it for one of the journals, and pronounced it the finest poem that had appeared since the time of Pope. This was no cold praise, for the versification of Pope was at that time the model for imitation; his rules were the standard of criticism, and the 'Essay on Man' was placed at the head of didactic poetry. The fame of Goldsmith was now firmly established; and he had the satisfaction to find, that it did not merely rest on the authority of the million, for the learned and the great now deemed themselves honoured by his acquaintance."

97.25 given by Hawkins] Hawkins's *Life of Johnson* (420). Irving is here following Forster (317–18). Compare 1840 (96).

97.35 a great deal."] For this quotation of Chamier and those in the following paragraph, see Boswell (IV, 107–8). Both Prior (II, 41) and Forster (318) included the incident. Irving added it in 1849.

98.8 in the poem] This sentence is slightly different from the 1840 version (96), which replaced a longer passage in 1825 (27–28) drawn from Boswell (II, 6–7). Compare Prior (II, 36–37); Forster (318–19).

98.14 Dr. Goldsmith ugly!"] See Boswell (V, 386). Both Prior (II, 55–56) and Forster (320) included the anecdote, which Irving added in 1849.

98.18 Charles Fox] Charles James Fox (1749–1806), English liberal statesman.

98.22 diminish it."] This conversation was included in 1825 (27) in dialogue form (compare Boswell, IV, 107); it was omitted in 1840. Both Prior (II, 36) and Forster (321–32) included it. The conversation occurred in 1778.

98.25–26 with his idol] Boswell returned to London in February, 1766. The following dialogue occurred in 1773. See Boswell (II, 203). Irving added this paragraph in 1849. Compare Prior (II, 40); Forster (320).

98.34–35 author's pen] Compare 97.18–21.

98.37 twenty guineas!] This sentence was added in 1849. Compare Forster (323).

99.14 the Spectator] *The Spectator*, begun on March 1, 1711, and appearing daily until December 6, 1712, was written by Joseph Addison and Sir Richard Steele (1672–1729), English essayist, dramatist, and politician.

99.27 Nil te quæsiveris extra"—] Seek for nothing outside yourself.

99.30 expenses accordingly] This paragraph underwent considerable revision from 1825 (29–30) and 1840 (96–97). Compare Percy (61); Prior (II, 136–37); Forster (295); Boswell (IV, 359).

99.32 of Northumberland] Sir Hugh Smithson (1715–1786) became second earl of Northumberland and Baron Warkworth in 1750 and duke of Northumberland in 1766. His natural son, James Macie Smithson, was the founder of the Smithsonian Institution in Washington, D.C.

99.38 relative Dr. Percy] Percy believed himself to be "the heir male of the ancient Percies,"; and Boswell, having examined the documentary proof, said, "and both as a lawyer accustomed to the consideration of evidence, and as a genealogist versed in the study of pedigrees, I am fully satisfied." See Boswell (IV, 127, n. 2). Later scholars regard Percy's claim as invalid.

100.16 I had committed."] The quotation appears in 1825 (29) and 1840 (104–105). Compare Percy (66), who gives the incident in indirect discourse. Irving's source was probably "Anecdotes of the late Dr. Goldsmith," *Annual Register* 17 (1774), 32.

100.38 to assist him."] This paragraph appears in 1840 (105–106) and with variations in 1825 (28–29). Compare Percy (66–67); Prior (II, 68–69); Forster (327–29). The original source is Hawkins (418–19).

101.6 heir male] See note 99.38.

101.11 lively talents."] See Boswell (IV, 127–28, n. 2). Boswell said that he had received help from Elizabeth, duchess of Northumberland, when he was studying Bishop Percy's genealogy. She was Lady Elizabeth Seymour before her marriage to Smithson in 1740.

101.14 "Edwin and Angelina."] The poem was included in Chapter VIII of *The Vicar of Wakefield* with the title "A Ballad." See *Works* (IV, 47). The source of the entire paragraph is Percy (74–76). Compare 1825 (34–35) and 1840 (106); see Prior (II, 73–83).

101.26–27 familiar in it] Paragraph added in 1849. Compare Forster (327).

101.28 the seat] Irving originally wrote "the noble seat." After a reviewer in *The Gentleman's Magazine*, n.s. 32 (December, 1849), 618, criticized him for using the word *noble* to describe a seat which was "situated in a small paddock," the word was deleted from later editions. Forster (331) said that Nugent "obtained one of the finest domains in Essex and the mansion of Gosfield Hall. . . ."

101.29 Robert Nugent] Robert Nugent (1702–1788), of the Nugent family of Carlanstown, county of Westmeath, Ireland, was created Viscount Clare in 1766 and Earl Nugent in 1776. This paragraph was added in 1849. Compare Forster (330–32, 424); Prior II (65–66).

101.42–43 Squire Gawkey] Forster (558) refers to "the Squire Gawkey of the libels of the day. . . ."

102.15 Ghost in Cock-Lane]   See note 84.11.

102.15 Siege of Ticonderoga]   "The siege of Ticanderago," *Works* (III, 1). The French Fort Carillon in Ticonderoga in northeastern New York was captured by Jeffrey Amherst in 1759 and renamed Fort Ticonderoga. This paragraph, which also appears in 1840 (107), is a revision of 1825 (26).

102.25 and Philanthropos]   Lover of self, lover of truth, lover of freedom, lover of man. At this point Irving omits a sentence from his source, in which "It is time..." begins a new paragraph. Irving also omitted the final sentence of the source. The paragraph is the same in 1840 (107–108), but the complete quotation appears in 1825 (26). See *Works* (III, 1–2).

102.32 British classics]   This paragraph was added in 1840 (108); in 1825 (26) Irving concludes the preceding paragraph thus: "The rapidity with which the first impression of this little volume was disposed of, greatly surpassed the expectations of its author. Since that time, few books have gone through a greater variety of editions." See Prior (II, 98–99).

102.34–35 as to expense]   In 1840 (108) the balance of the sentence reads: "his facility at being imposed upon, and a spontaneous and irresistible habit of giving to whoever asked." The next three sentences were added in 1849.

103.2 necessities of others."]   The quotation appears in 1840 (131). Prior (II, 184) identified it as "said to be written" by Glover, who published a *Life of Dr. Oliver Goldsmith* (Swan, 1774). According to Forster (420) Glover, an Irishman, was a protégé of Garrick.

103.13 "Goody Two Shoes,"]   There is no specific proof that Goldsmith wrote this. See Percy Muir, *English Children's Books: 1600 to 1900* (New York, 1954), p. 61. This and the following two paragraphs appear with slight variations in 1840 (108–109). Compare Prior (II, 100–101).

103.31–32 beneath their dignity]   This statement is reminiscent of Irving's unwillingness to acknowledge the plays he wrote in collaboration with John Howard Payne in 1823. See Thatcher T. Payne Luquer, ed., "Correspondence of Washington Irving and John Howard Payne," *Scribner's Magazine* 48 (October, 1910), 461–82, passim.

103.35 and Tom Thumb]   See Cornelia Meigs et al., *A Critical History of Children's Literature: A Survey of Children's Books in English from Earliest Times to the Present, Prepared in Four Parts under the Editorship of Cornelia Meigs* (New York, 1953), pp. 61–62, for an account of chapbook editions of these children's stories, three volumes of which Boswell had published by Dicey, Bow Churchyard. See Boswell's *London Journal*, p. 299.

104.3 of the times] This paragraph was added in 1840 (109–10). Compare Prior (II, 103–104).

104.11 lady patients] This paragraph was added in 1849. Compare Forster (342).

104.29 your enemies."] This and the next paragraph were added in 1840 (110). Compare Prior (II, 105); Forster (342–43).

105.29 *no mean price.*"] This paragraph appears in very different forms in all three versions. See 1825 (34) and 1840 (110–11). Compare Percy (61); Prior (II, 109–10); Forster (355–56). For Johnson's comments see Boswell (IV, 180–81). For a discussion of the composition and publication of the *Vicar*, see *Works* (IV, 3–11).

105.36 Rogers] Samuel Rogers (1763–1855), English banker, poet, and man of caustic wit, was a friend of Irving. In 1837, at a New York booksellers' entertainment of American authors at City Hall, Irving made a speech in which he referred to Rogers as the "friend of American genius." See "Recollections of Washington Irving by His Publisher," *The Atlantic Monthly* 6 (November, 1860), 602–603). When William Wordsworth died in 1850, Rogers was offered the laureateship but declined it.

106.3 undiminished] In MS Irving put a quotation mark after this word but failed to open the quotation. Irving may have been quoting from one of Rogers's works, or he may have been recalling a conversation with him. The quotation, if it be one, has not been identified.

106.6 Goethe] Johann Wolfgang von Goethe (1749–1832), German poet, dramatist, and government official of the court of Weimar. Compare Forster (367–69).

106.22 head and heart] Although Percy (61–62) includes no commentary on the *Vicar*, Irving in 1825 (34) wrote a long critical passage. In 1840 (111), he wrote a short paragraph which approximates the 1849 paragraph to this point. The balance of the paragraph was added in 1849. Compare Prior (II, 111–12); Forster (357–58).

107.16 is to die."] See *Works* (IV, 136). This and the preceding paragraph were added in 1849.

107.24 of the day] This paragraph appears in variant forms in 1825 (34–35) and 1840 (111). The following letter was added in 1840 (112–13). Compare Prior (II, 84–85).

108.19 Kenrick] See note 74.8. The following letter was added in 1840 (113–14). See Prior (II, 86–87).

109.6 not the author] On the financial returns of the *Vicar* see Welsh (61–63) and, as a corrective, *Works* (IV, 11, n. 1).

109.20 previous labours."] The paragraph was added in 1840 (114). Compare Prior (II, 130).

109.22 yet attempted] The corresponding sentence in 1840 (114–15) reads: "At that time, however, Goldsmith was preparing to try his fortune in quite a different walk of literature. He had become acquainted with Barry, Woodward, Quick, Mr. and Mrs. Yates, and other popular actors, and, being a frequent visiter at the theatres, was at length tempted to write for the stage." The following quotations, which were added in 1849, are from Goldsmith's "An Essay on the Theatre; or, A Comparison between Laughing and Sentimental Comedy" (*Works*, III, 212–13). Compare Forster (376–77).

110.9 Colman] George Colman (1732–1794), playwright and manager, was one of three who purchased Covent Garden Theater in 1767. He sold his share in 1774 and then in 1776 bought the Haymarket Theater from Samuel Foote. *The Clandestine Marriage* (1766) is a comedy of manners.

110.16–17 calculated to excel] The paragraph to this point was added in 1849. The remaining sentence compares with the balance of the 1840 (115) paragraph quoted in note 109.23: "He accordingly commenced his comedy of 'the Good-natured Man,' and wrought at it during the latter part of the year, whenever his hurried occupation in 'book building' would give him leisure. By the spring of 1767 it was ready for representation; but now came the great difficulty with a dramatic writer, that of getting his piece acted." Compare Forster (377).

111.15 his blunders,"] From his letter to Dan Hodson of December 27, 1757. See 54.21. Prior (I, 105) uses this phrase without quotation marks.

111.24 his brother] The Reverend Henry Goldsmith. The letter is dated by Balderston as ca. January 13, 1759. See *Letters* (57); Prior (I, 297–303).

112.4 or genius."*] See Forster (437). This and the next paragraph were added in 1849.

112.23 vigour and skill] See Boswell (IV, 484). For the next sentence see Boswell (I, 179). This and the next two paragraphs were added in 1849.

112.33 a new colouring."] See Boswell (IV, 142). According to John Nichols, *Literary Anecdotes of the Eighteenth Century* (London, 1812), III, 499, Robert Orme (d. 1801) was a native of Tilly Cherry, East Indies. In 1763 he published the first volume of his *History of the Military Transactions of the British Nation in India*.

112.36–37 distinct and clear."] Both Boswell (IV, 177) and Forster (279) read "distinct and bold."

113.10 talk about it] Irving discusses Goldsmith as a conversationalist in 1825 (12–13, 54–55) and in 1840 (99–104). Compare Percy (20–21, 118); Prior (II, 472–82); Forster (440–41, 515, 530–31).

113.13 when he has."] Johnson's comment appears in 1825 (54). Compare Boswell (IV, 361); Percy (118).

113.25–26 knowledge to himself."] Johnson's remark appears in 1825 (12) and 1840 (100). See Boswell (II, 188).

113.30–31 is made of."] This remark was added in 1840 (100). Compare Boswell (II, 502).

113.42 miserably vexed."] This quotation appears in 1825 (12–13) and 1840 (100). Compare Boswell (II, 219); Percy (20–21).

114.1 this vexation] In 1825 (24) Irving wrote: "Goldsmith, it is true, seemed sometimes, as it were, to *look up* to the great moralist, but it was rather with affection than with dread, more with the spirit of emulation than the despair of equal excellence."

114.5 Dr. Johnson's company."] This paragraph was added in 1849. Compare Boswell (V, 386–87).

114.12 robust sophistry;"] See Boswell (IV, 483). The following quotation, which is from Boswell (V, 172), appears in 1840 (101). The italics are Irving's.

114.29 like whales."] See Boswell (II, 220). This and the preceding paragraph appear in 1840 (101). Compare Prior (II, 479–80); Forster (532).

114.32 his benevolence] In 1840 (101–102) Irving wrote: "Johnson, in fact, was spoiled by being the oracle of the circle in which he moved. He talked as he wrote, for effect; and, being devoutly listened to, talked long and large, 'orated' on the most petty subjects, and was impatient of interruption or contradiction. Goldsmith had a proper reverence for his talents and his virtues, but not such blind bigotry as some of those around him. He felt that the oracle could sometimes err and often prose." Irving continues with the anecdote which appears in the present volume on pp. 215–17.

114.33 Dr. Shebbeare] John Shebbeare (1709–1788) was a political writer. As a result of a series of pamphlets attacking the ministry, he was tried for libel in 1758 and sentenced to three years in prison. Upon his release he changed sides and was in 1764 granted a pension of £200 a year (*DNB*). The following anecdote from Boswell (II, 68; IV, 485 n. 1), was added in 1849. Compare Prior (II, 479); Forster (247–48, 533).

114.42 Scotch tune.'"] See Boswell (IV, 483).

115.2–3 these occasions] In 1840 (103) Irving wrote: "He shone most when he least thought of shining; when he gave way to his natural impulses, and talked carelessly and at random. Even Boswell spoke favourably of him in that respect." The rest of the paragraph is substantially the same. The quotation is from Boswell (II, 179). Irving added the italics.

116.12 "rare Ben Jonson"] Ben Jonson (1572–1637) was an English dramatist and actor. "O rare Ben Jonson!" is Sir John Young's inscription on Jonson's tomb in Westminster Abbey.

116.33 for the evening] This paragraph was added in 1849. Compare Prior (II, 141–42); Forster (418–19).

116.39 'tun of man,'] See Shakespeare's *Henry IV, Part I*, II, iv, 493.

117.4 Tom King] Tom King (1730–1804), a comedian in Garrick's Drury Lane Company, became famous as Lord Ogleby in *The Clandestine Marriage*, a role originally written for Garrick, who declined to play it. The paragraph was added in 1849. Compare Forster (422).

117.7 Hugh Kelly] Hugh Kelly (1739–1777) was a playwright known today for his *False Delicacy* (1768). See Prior (II, 176); Forster (419–22).

117.21 in the room."] See Boswell (V, 321, n. 1). The paragraph was added in 1849.

117.24 name of Glover] See note 103.2. The "Anecdotes of the late Dr. Goldsmith," which appeared in the *Annual Register* 17 (1774), 29–34, signed "G," were attributed to Glover by Forster (420).

117.37–38 Colman, Sterne] For Colman, see note 110.10. Laurence Sterne (1713–1768), English clergyman and novelist, was not popular with the Johnson circle. See Boswell (II, 210).

117.40–41 by his humors] The paragraph to this point and the previous paragraph were taken with slight variations from 1840 (130). Compare Prior (II, 183–89).

118.15 the right way."] The anecdote was added in 1849. Compare Forster (467–68).

118.23 "Every Man in his Humour."] *Every Man in his Humour* is a comedy by Ben Jonson. There is a tradition that Shakespeare was a member of the cast when it was first acted in 1598.

118.27–28 making us melancholy."] *Citizen of the World*, Letter XV. See *Works* (II, 232).

118.29 his misfortune."] See Forster (423).

118.36 in a roar] Speaking of James Kenney (1780–1849), a British author, Pierre M. Irving in *The Life and Letters of Washington Irving* (New York, 1869), I, 394, said that he "was the personage alluded to in his [Irving's] 'Life of Goldsmith,' as the author whom he had seen with his back to a tree and his foot to a stone, trying to bother out a scene in a farce which he could not manage to his satisfaction." This and the preceding two paragraphs were added in 1849.

119.10 the prologue] In 1840 (117) Irving wrote: "The comedy of the 'Good-natured Man' had been read in manuscript and applauded by Burke, Reynolds, and other men of eminent talents: Johnson pronounced it the best comedy that had been written since the Provoked

Husband, and engaged to write the prologue. Colman, the manager of Covent Garden theatre, therefore, gladly undertook to produce it on his stage, where it was represented for the first time on the 29th January, 1768." Compare Prior (II, 149, 164); Forster (393).

120.26 to Dr. Johnson] The incident related in this and the preceding three paragraphs was added in 1849. Compare Boswell (II, 34–41); Forster (393–97).

120.30 death of Rich] John Rich (ca. 1682–1761) pioneered in producing pantomime in London, he himself playing the role of Harlequin. He also introduced the Irish actress Peg Woffington to London audiences in 1740. When Rich died in 1761, his son-in-law, John Beard, succeeded him as manager of Covent Garden.

120.30 Drury Lane] The Theatre Royal, Drury Lane, had a complicated history dating from 1674. John Rich's father, Christopher, bought the patent in 1690 but lost it in 1709. It was during Macklin's management that Garrick made his first appearance at Drury Lane on May 11, 1742. In 1743 Garrick and James Lacy became joint-managers of the theater (*Oxford Companion to the Theatre*, p. 201).

120.34 Society of Arts] See 76.10–25.

121.21 of his sincerity."] Thomas Davies, *Memoirs of the Life of David Garrick, Esq.* (London, 1780), II, 147. Compare Prior (II, 151–52); Forster (397–98).

121.31 passed away] This paragraph in abbreviated form appears in 1840 (115–16). Compare Prior (II, 151–54); Forster (397–400).

121.39 Whitehead, the laureate] William Whitehead (1715–1785) became the laureate in 1757. Irving added this paragraph in 1849. Compare Forster (402–403).

122.21 their anxieties."] Irving added this letter in 1849. Compare Forster (409–11).

122.32 OLIVER GOLDSMITH."] This paragraph was added in 1849. Compare Forster (412).

122.43 D. GARRICK."] Added in 1849. Compare Forster (412–13).

123.12 to his nephew] This paragraph was added in 1849. Compare Forster (416–17).

123.15 history of Rome] *The Roman History, From the Foundation of the City of Rome, To the Destruction of the Western Empire* was published in 1769. See *Works* (V, 332). Compare Prior (II, 159); Forster (417–18).

123.18–27 As usual . . . literary order.*] This passage, with slight variations, appears in 1840 (116). Compare Prior (II, 155–56).

123.41 for *babes*] Irving found the poem in Prior (II, 155–56), who did not identify it. It is quoted in Welsh (46) and Kent (65). Kent says, "The lines are by one Fox, about whom Welsh gives no information." Irving added it in 1849. Compare Forster (423–24).

124.1 Canonbury Castle]   See note 84.34.

124.15 in the Park."]   See *Works* (I, 399, textual n. 18). This paragraph in a slightly different form appears in 1840 (116–17). Compare Forster (324).

124.18–19 North's administration]   Frederick, eighth Lord North and third earl of Guilford (1732–1792), became prime minister in 1770.

124.21 Junius]   A series of letters critical of the North ministry, many of which were signed "Junius," appeared in the *Public Advertiser* from January, 1769, to the end of 1771. Suspicion rested upon many famous men, including Edmund Burke, John Wilkes, Benjamin Franklin, Tom Paine, and General Charles Lee. Although the identity of the author has never been positively determined, many modern scholars believe it was Sir Philip Francis (1740–1818), who was employed at the War Office from 1762 to 1772.

124.21 Wilkes]   John Wilkes (1727–1797), English politician, supported Pitt and attacked Lord Bute's ministry in the *North Briton* (1762–1763), which he founded.

124.33 Parson Scott]   James Scott (1733–1814), in the employ of John Montagu, fourth earl of Sandwich (1718–1792), wrote a series of papers against Lord Bute, which were published in the *Public Advertiser*. They were written "under a variety of signatures, particularly Anti-Sejanus, Panurge, and others..." (Prior, II, 277). Compare Forster (432–33).

125.1 in his garret!"]   The paragraph to this point is an expanded version of one in 1840 (139–40). Compare Prior (II, 277–78). The final sentences in the 1840 paragraph read: "Who does not admire the independent spirit of Goldsmith? Who does not smile at the astonishment of the political hireling?" Compare Forster (434–35).

125.14 the generous]   Irving added this paragraph in 1849. See Welsh (79) and Kent (75) for comments on Irving's "inexplicable antagonism" to Newbery.

126.22 brought forward]   This paragraph was added in 1849. Compare Forster (452–53).

126.37 Ned Shuter]   Edward Shuter (1728–1776), English actor, began his acting career in 1744. His final performance, in the role of Falstaff, occurred at Covent Garden in 1776.

126.38 Miss Walford]   According to Forster (458), "Goldsmith always remembered ... the praise proffered him by a pretty actress (Miss Wilford, just become Mrs. Bulkley)...." Mrs. Bulkley was one of the company at Covent Garden when Colman the elder and his con-

freres bought it. See *Oxford Companion to the Theatre,* p. 165. This
and the preceding paragraph were added in 1849.

127.13 £8 2s. 7d."] Prior (I, 377–78) said that he got the story from
John Filby, son of William, whom Boswell misnamed John. See Boswell (II, 85). Compare Forster (341–42). The following sentence is
adapted from one in 1840 (117), which serves as the first sentence
of the following paragraph.

127.17 Bensley] Robert Bensley (ca. 1738–1817), an English actor,
came to the stage after a career in the marines. After serving an
apprenticeship in the provinces he made his London debut at Drury
Lane in 1765. He retired from the stage in 1796. See *Oxford Companion to the Theatre,* p. 74.

127.27 of the audience] All but the first sentence of this paragraph
(mentioned in note 127.13) appears with slight variations in 1840 (117).
In 1825 (36) Irving mentioned the date of the opening performance
and added: "Contrary to the expectations of the author and his
friends, it did not meet with unqualified applause; and though it kept
possession of the stage nine nights, it was finally withdrawn. The
peculiar genius of its author was apparent in the ease and elegance of
the dialogue, and throughout the whole there were many keen remarks on men and manners; but the piece was deficient in stage-effect.
The Bailiff scene, in particular, was generally reprobated, though
the characters were well drawn. This scene was afterwards greatly
abridged. Whatever were the faults of the piece as a whole, it was
admitted that many of the parts possessed great comic effect, and
there were highly applauded." There follows a discussion of Shuter
in the role of Croaker, which is similar to the 1849 version. The
1825 passage is much more detailed than the corresponding passage
in Percy (77). Compare Prior (II, 163–65).

128.6 as the moon....] See *The Oxford Dictionary of Nursery Rhymes,*
ed. Iona and Peter Opie (Oxford, 1952), pp. 34–35, 433–34.

128.17–18 for the world."] This anecdote appears with only slight variations in 1840 (118–19). See Prior (II, 166–68). The next two sentences
were added in 1849. Compare Forster (461–62).

128.27 conceal them."] See *Works* (I, 394). For contemporary comments on this passage see *The Gentleman's Magazine* n.s. 32 (December, 1849), 618–19; *Notes and Queries* 1 (December 8, 1849), 83. This
paragraph was added in 1849. See Forster (195).

128.34 on the stage] For a comparable statement in 1825 see note
127.27. In 1840 (119) Irving wrote: "'The Good-natured Man' was
performed ten nights in succession, and then occasionally; but it has
always pleased more in the closet than on the stage. The profit of

the author from the theatre and publisher was about £500." Compare Prior (II, 165–66).

129.5 were discussed] Irving revised the comparable passage in 1840 (119). In 1825 (37) he wrote a similar passage, which concludes as follows: "These circumstances so wrought upon the irritable feelings of Goldsmith, in whose disposition, warm and generous as it was, envy had an unhappy predominance, that he renounced the friendship of Kelly, and could with difficulty be brought to forgive him this temporary success. Our author, though in the chief features of his character the original of his own 'Good-natured Man,' was yet strangely jealous of the success of others, and particularly in whatever regarded literary fame. Compare Prior (II, 173–74); Boswell (II, 49).

129.9 his feelings] In 1840 (120) Irving wrote: "Goldsmith's old enemy, Kenrick, was among the 'vipers of the press,' as Cumberland called them, who endeavoured on this, as on many other occasions, to detract from his well-earned fame. Poor Goldsmith was excessively sensitive to these attacks, and had not the art and self-command to conceal his feelings." Compare Prior (II, 178).

129.25 positive proof] The passage in 1840 (119–20) is substantially the same with the exception of the final sentence: ". . . but the jealousy and envy awakened in Kelly lasted through the life of his competitor, and found a vent in anonymous attacks in the newspapers, the basest resource of dastardly and malignant spirits." Both Prior (II, 174–75) and Forster (469–71) stress the end of their speaking acquaintance.

130.8–9 his publisher] Compare note 128.34.

130.27 gold buttons."] Irving added these details in 1849. Compare Prior (II, 231–34); Forster (471).

130.34 Blackstone] Sir William Blackstone (1723–1780) was an English jurist whose *Commentaries on the Laws of England* was published in 1765–1769. See Prior (II, 138); Forster (466).

130.40 "shoemaker's holyday."] In 1840 (128–29) Irving wrote: "When circumstances prevented Goldsmith from taking summer lodgings in the country, the rural feeling, which was strong within him throughout life, called from time to time for practical gratification. His great delight on such occasions was to make up a rural party of four or five of his intimate friends, to enjoy what he humorously called 'a tradesman's holyday.'" The next four sentences are substantially the same in 1840. The last two sentences of the paragraph were added in 1849. Compare Prior (II, 182–83); Forster (476). A reviewer in *The Gentleman's Magazine* n.s. 32 (December, 1849), ridiculed Irving's list of destinations: "This enumeration of places shews little knowledge of *suburban localities,* Chelsea being one mile from town and Hampton Court *fourteen;* and a morning's walk to Goldsmith of fifteen miles at least would not, we should think, fit him for 'an evening *stroll* back to town' of the same distance." Prior (I, 182) wrote, "Blackheath, Wandsworth, Fulham, Chelsea, Hampstead, Highgate, Highbury, and others. . . ."

131.29 the difference] In 1840 (129–30) Irving wrote: "These were the scenes and associates suited to the tastes and habits of Goldsmith. On these occasions he was in all his glory, the 'king of good fellows;' quite a different being from what he was when among the higher learned and literary circles of the metropolis. Here, too, he had his humble retainers and hangers-on, who sponged upon his generosity; for, however poor he might be, Goldsmith had always the luck of finding some one poorer than himself, to drain his scanty but ever-open purse. One of these humble companions. . . ." The balance of the paragraph contains minor revisions. Compare Prior (II, 183).

131.33 Wednesday Club] See 116–17.

132.30 of Goldsmith] This and the previous two paragraphs appear verbatim in 1840 (131–33). Prior (II, 186) thought the story "improbable."

132.40 General Oglethorpe] James Edward Oglethorpe (1698?–1785), English general, was involved in founding the colony of Georgia in America. See 174.4–175.15 for Irving's biographical sketch of him.

133.12 him afterwards."] The anecdote is told in *European Magazine* 24 (October, 1793), 260, where the unwelcome guest is identified as Pilkington. The passage was added in 1849. See Forster (493). Irving took Forster's page bodily as his manuscript page.

134.12 ruinous to him] Compare 1840 (97) "With his usual want of forethought, he obtained advances from booksellers and loans from private friends to enable him to furnish them [that is, the apartment in Brick Court] expensively, and thus burdened himself with debts which continued to harass him for the remainder of his days. One of the friends who assisted him with his purse on this occasion was Mr. Edmund Bott, a barrister and man of letters, with whom he lived on the most intimate and cordial terms, and who had rooms immediately opposite, on the same floor."

134.22 at home] Compare 1840 (127–28) where the paragraph to this point appears with slight modifications but concludes: "In some of the choicest and sweetest moments thus snatched from his coarser labours, and spent among the beautifully rural scenes which abound in the vicinity of London, he sketched off some of the first picturings of his 'Deserted Village.'" For the rest of the paragraph compare 1840 (128): "One of his country retreats was a little cottage with a garden, pleasantly situated about eight miles from town, on the Edgeware Road, which he took in conjunction with Mr. Botts, who had chambers adjacent to his own in the Temple." Prior (II, 138) identifies Mr. Edmund Bott as "a barrister, author of a work on the Poor Laws, said to be revised in its style and arrangement by Goldsmith. . . ." According to Prior, at Goldsmith's death Bott "became as his chief creditor, the possessor of his papers."

135.2 Edgeware Road] This paragraph, in substance, appears in 1840 (128). Compare 1825 (35): "About this period, or perhaps a little earlier, Goldsmith, in addition to the apartments he occupied in the Temple, took a countryhouse on the Edgeware-road, in conjunction with a Mr. Bott, one of his literary friends, for the benefit of good air, and the convenience of retirement. To this little mansion he gave the jocular appellation of *Shoemaker's Paradise,* the architecture being in a fantastic style, after the taste of its original possessor, who was one of the craft." Compare *The European Magazine* 24 (August, 1793), 94.

135.25 in the accusation] The paragraph is somewhat expanded from the 1840 (120–21) version. Compare Prior (II, 179–80); Forster (480).

135.29 we are told] Walter Scott in his essay on Goldsmith (*The Miscellaneous Prose Works* [Edinburgh, 1854], I, 292–93) quoted a passage on the composition of "The Deserted Village" from *The European Magazine* 24 (September, 1793), 172, which he attributed to Lee Lewes, the actor. Forster (474–75) pointed out that Goldsmith had not yet met Lewes at the time he wrote this poem and that the author of the anecdotes was Cooke. Irving's paragraph was added in 1849. Compare Forster (473–76). In 1825 (40–42) Irving included a very long discussion of "The Deserted Village," which in 1840 (136–39) he reduced to two short paragraphs and a long footnote.

136.2 his place] lines 143–44 (*Works,* IV, 293).

136.23 *led the way*] lines 177–88, 167–70 (*Works,* IV, 294).

137.10 Paul Hiffernan] Paul Hiffernan (1719–1777) was an Irish doctor and hackwriter who came to London about 1753. In the margin of MS at this point Irving wrote, "see prior." See Prior (II, 313–14).

137.26 his own works."] The paragraph was added in 1849. Compare Forster (488–90).

137.35 foster brother] This paragraph was added in 1849. Compare Forster (488).

138.3 both ends."] Both Irving and Forster (491–92) took Boswell's passage out of context. Compare Boswell (III, 95): "Sir John [Dalrymple] having affected to complain of the attacks made upon his 'Memoirs,' Dr. Johnson said, 'Nay, sir, do not complain. It is advantageous to an authour, that his book should be attacked as well as praised. Fame is a shuttlecock. . . .'"

138.4 Bickerstaffe] See note 78.7–8.

138.12 greater distance."] The anecdote, which was added in 1849, was told by Hester Lynch Piozzi in *Anecdotes of the Late Samuel Johnson, LL.D. During the Last Twenty Years of His Life*, 2d ed. (London, 1786), p. 168. Compare Forster (490–91).

138.14 polite society] Compare 1840 (140–41). "The slovenliness of dress for which Johnson, on his first interview with Goldsmith, had given him a practical reproof, was by no means to be laid to his charge since he had become elevated into polite society. On the contrary, if we may judge from certain anecdotes concerning him, and from some of his tailors' bills extant, he was prone to be expensive, if not tasteful in his attire, and at times, with great self-complacency, to sport his ungainly figure in the sunshine in Temple Gardens, arrayed with a finery that provoked the merriment of his friends." Compare Prior (II, 231–32).

138.15 one of his contemporaries] Judge Day, Irish jurist, wrote his reminiscences of Goldsmith in a letter to Prior dated February 20, 1831. This quotation appears in 1840 (127). See Prior (II, 357–62).

138.38 a colour.' "] The anecdote appears in Boswell (II, 85). Compare 1840 (141): "Boswell has rendered his peach-coloured dress famous. Goldsmith, with Johnson, Reynolds, Garrick, and others, were invited to dine with him, and they were awaiting the arrival of another guest. 'Goldsmith,' says Boswell, 'to divert the tedious minutes, strutted about....' " Compare Prior (II, 229–31).

138.40–41 from strangers] This sentence was added in 1849. The following anecdote, which in somewhat altered form appears in 1840 (127), was mentioned in Judge Day's letter (see note 138.15). See Prior (II, 359); Forster (571).

139.23 his ugliness] This paragraph was added in 1849.

139.29 Captain Kane Horneck] Edmund Burke and his cousin were trustees named in the will of Kane Horneck to administer his estate. See Sir Henry Bunbury, ed., *The Correspondence of Sir Thomas Hanmer, Bart., Speaker of the House of Commons with a Memoir of his Life, To Which Are Added Other Relicks of a Gentleman's Family* (London, 1838), p. 400.

139.35 William Henry Bunbury] Henry William Bunbury (1750–1811), the second son of Sir William Bunbury, was an amateur artist and caricaturist. The elder brother, Charles, succeeded to the title in 1764, and Henry's son, Henry Edward, assumed the title in 1821. Henry William was a first cousin of Charles Lee, the American general. Irving mentions the relationship in his *Life of George Washington*, Volume I, Chapter XXXVI. See Prior (II, 536). The name is used correctly in 171.8–9.

140.6 not repulsive.] Compare 1840 (143–44): "One of the most agreeable additions to Goldsmith's circle of intimacy was the family of a captain Horneck, with whom he had become acquainted at the house of Sir Joshua Reynolds. Mrs. Horneck and her two daughters were elegant and accomplished women, and the young ladies were remarkable for great beauty; their society, therefore, was much sought by several distinguished men of the day. Their attention had first been attracted to Goldsmith as a man of genius, their kind regard had subsequently been won by his honest simplicity and buoyant good-humour, and an intimacy ensued that continued uninterrupted for the remainder of his life." The rest of the paragraph and the verses were added in 1849. For the verses see *Works* (IV, 384–85); Forster (500–501).

140.9 Dr. Baker] According to Forster (501), "Doctor (afterwards Sir George) Baker" was Sir Joshua Reynolds's physician.

140.10 Angelica Kauffman] Angelica Kauffman (1741–1807), Swiss landscape and portrait painter, was brought to London in 1766 by Lady Wentworth, wife of the English ambassador.

140.31 *The following lines] This footnote, which does not appear in Forster (502), was added in 49a. Of the poem itself Prior (II, 209) wrote: "It will be found in the Works, and the reader is indebted for it to Major-General Sir Henry Bunbury, Bart." Irving had in his library a copy of Bunbury's *Correspondence of Hanmer*, to which Prior refers. See *Works* (IV, 385).

141.1 younger sister] Forster (501) said that Mary "exerted a strange fascination over Goldsmith. Heaven knows what impossible dreams may at times have visited the awkward, unattractive man of letters!" In his revised edition (III, 151) Forster added in a footnote: "This hint was first thrown out by me; but Mr. Washington Irving, who has done me the honor to copy it and many other things from the first edition of this biography, goes somewhat too far in accepting the suggestion as if it were an ascertained fact, and proceeding to install the 'Jessamy Bride' in all the honors of a complete conquest of Gold-smith.... In Mr. Irving's little book, the 'Jessamy Bride' becomes the very centre of all Goldsmith's hopes and thoughts in latter life.... This is running down a suggestion indeed!—and, with whatever success for romance-loving readers, less pleasantly, it must be admitted, for sober seekers after truth." See Introduction, pp. xxx–xxxi.

141.8 bloom color] Compare 1840 (141–42): "According to his tailors' bills, he had sometimes four and five full suits in the course of a year, besides separate articles of dress. Among the items we find a green half-trimmed frock and breeches, lined with silk; queen's-blue dress-suit; half-dress suit of ratteen, lined with satin; Tyrian bloom satin grain and garter-blue silk breeches, &c. Honest John Filby, as he used to term him, was his tailor for many years, and was always punctually paid."

142.11 Grattan] Henry Grattan (1746–1820), Irish statesman, was, according to Forster (568), nineteen years old when Goldsmith befriended him in 1771.

142.11–12 by the poet] The following quotation is from Judge Day's letter mentioned in note 138.15.

142.14 Roman histories] The letter in Prior (II, 359) reads: "Just arrived as I then was from College...." The rest of the quotation constitutes in Prior (II, 358–59) a separate paragraph, which precedes the first sentence in this quotation. In 1840 (125–27) Irving quoted all of Day's letter except the last four paragraphs, which appear in Prior (II, 360–61).

142.32 faithless fortune.'"] This quotation is another excerpt from Judge Day's letter mentioned in note 138.15. Compare Prior (II, 357–58). Actually lines 142.23–27 ("He frequented... hospitality") are a poor paraphrase of the corresponding passage in Prior (II, 357). According to "Spectator Paper No. 9" (March 10, 1711), "A Christian Name has likewise been often used as a Badge of Distinction, and made the Occasion of a Club. That of the *George's*, which used to meet at the Sign of the *George*, on *St. George's* Day, and swear *Before George*, is still fresh in every one's Memory."

142.37 Ranelagh, Vauxhall] Both Ranelagh and Vauxhall were pleasure resorts. Irving (187.22–25) describes Ranelagh; see also *Works* (V, 149, n. 1). For Vauxhall see *Citizen of the World*, Letter LXXI (*Works*, II, 293–98).

142.38 and amusement] At this point Irving omits the balance of the paragraph and the following paragraph from Day's Letter. Compare Prior (II, 359). The rest of the quotation constitutes in Prior (II, 360) a separate paragraph.

143.14 young and old] This paragraph, in substance, appears in 1840 (121). Compare Prior (II, 202–203).

143.18 of the latter] Compare 1840 (121): "It drew forth, a few years after its appearance, a most copious eulogy from Dr. Johnson, in the course of a conversation with Boswell." The quotation from Boswell (II, 224–25) follows in 1840 (121–22). See also 1825 (32).

143.25 Robertson] William Robertson (1721–1793), Scottish clergyman and historian, was appointed the King's historiographer in 1764. His *History of Scotland* was published in 1759 and his *History of America* in 1777.

143.25 Dalrymple] Sir David Dalrymple, Lord Hailes (1726–1792), Scottish historian, is best known for his *Annals of Scotland* (1776–1779).

144.3 Lucius Florus or Eutropius] Lulius, or Lucius Annaeus Florus, wrote an abridgment of Livy, probably during the reign of Hadrian, which served as a textbook during the Middle Ages. Eutropius (d. 370), Latin historian and secretary to the Emperor Constantine, wrote *Breviarum Historiae Romanae.*

144.4 Vertot] Abbé René Aubert de Vertot d'Auboeuf (1655–1735), French historian, published *Histoire des révolutions de la république romaine* (1719).

144.9–10 History of Animated Nature] *An History of the Earth, and Animated Nature: by Oliver Goldsmith.* See *Works* (V, 349, n. 1).

144.10 in 1769] The sentence to this point appears in 1840 (122–23). The rest of the paragraph was added in 1849. Griffin was William Griffin, "bookseller in Catherine Street in the Strand." See *Letters* (136, n. 5) for Griffin's transfer of the copyright to John Nourse. See also Prior II (198–201).

144.17–18 Brookes's Natural History] Richard Brookes, physician and author, published *A System of Natural History* in six volumes in 1763.

144.19 Pliny] Pliny (Gaius Plinius Secundus) the Elder (23–79 A.D.) was a Roman historian.

144.19–20 Buffon's work] Georges Louis Leclerc, Comte de Buffon 1707–1788), French naturalist, wrote *Histoire Naturelle* (1749–1767).

144.22 Cumberland] Richard Cumberland (1732–1811), politician turned playwright, is best known for his sentimental comedy *The West Indian*, produced successfully by Garrick in 1771. The quotation that follows is from *Memoirs of Richard Cumberland. Written by Himself. Containing an Account of His Life and Writings, Interspersed with Anecdotes and Characters of Several of the Most Distinguished Persons of His Time, with Whom He Has Had Intercourse and Connexion* (London, 1807), I, 352–53. In 1825 (36) Irving included an even longer quotation from Cumberland. See Introduction (pp. xxi–xxii). In 1840 (123) he shortened the quotation as it appears in 1849.

144.28 Pidcock's showman] Compare *The Bestiary: The Book of Beasts...*, ed. T. H. White (London, 1955), p. 105, n. 2: "Your vulgar writer is always the most vulgar the higher his subject, as the man who shewed the menagerie at Pidcock's was wont to say,—'This, gentlemen, is the *eagle* of the *sun*, from Archangel in Russia; the *otterer* it is the *igherer* he flies. Byron, 1821.' "

145.10 every particular."] This paragraph appears verbatim in 1840 (121–22). The anecdote is from Boswell (II, 221). Compare Prior (II, 452–53).

145.20 of animals] The paragraph to this point appears in 1840 (124–25), where the passage ends thus: "He was often a minute and shrewd observer, as his watching of the policy of rooks from his window overlooking the Temple Garden, and his admirable paper in the Bee on the habits of the spider, sufficiently testify." This is a revision of a similar passage in 1825 (39–40). Compare Percy (83).

145.35 fairly commenced."] In 1840 (97–98) the sentence introducing the quotation reads: "The pleasant situation of Goldsmith's chambers may be gathered from his remarks in his 'Animated Nature' on the habitudes of rooks." Compare Prior (II, 137), who cites "Animated Nature, vol. v. p. 232, 8vo. 1774."

145.37 The Bee] The long quotation in the next seven paragraphs was added in 1849. See *Works* (I, 423–24, 425–27).

148.6 Royal Academy of Arts] One of the original functions of the Royal Academy of Arts was to offer instruction to art students. For this purpose rooms in Pall Mall were opened on January 2, 1768. The first exhibit was held the following April 26.

148.22 of the arts] Compare 1840 (133): "In the latter part of 1768 the Royal Academy of Arts was instituted, to be under the patronage of the sovereign, and the direction of forty artists of the first rank in their several professions. In December of the following year, Dr. Johnson was appointed Professor of Ancient Iiterature, and Dr. Goldsmith Professor of History to the institution, mere honorary titles without any emolument." A similar paragraph appears in 1825 (43): "About this period, the Royal Academy of painting was established, and Sir Joshua seized the opportunity it afforded him of testifying his regard and partiality for Goldsmith, by procuring for him the appointment of Professor of Ancient History. Though unattended with either emolument or trouble, it conferred some respectability, and entitled him to a seat at the occasional meetings of the academicians, as well as at their annual dinner. He himself properly considered it a mere complimentary distinction, and from a passage in the following letter to his brother Maurice, it is evident he would have prized his new office much more highly had it been coupled with that unpoetical accompaniment, a salary." Compare Percy (86).

148.26 *Maurice Goldsmith*] For Goldsmith's relations with Maurice see *Letters* (xix–xxiii). The following letter appears in Percy (86–89). Following closely a footnote in Percy, Irving in 1825 (43–44) wrote in continuation of the passage quoted in note 148.22: "Maurice was the poet's youngest brother. Not having been bred to any business, he, upon some occasion, complained to Oliver, that he found it difficult to live like a gentlemen. On which the poet begged he would without delay quit so unprofitable pursuit, and betake himself to a trade. Maurice wisely took the hint, and bound himself apprentice to a cabinet-maker. He had a shop in Dublin when the Duke of Rutland was Lord Lieutenant; and his grace, at the instance of Mr. Orde (afterwards Lord Bolton,) made him an inspector of the licenses in

that city, out of regard for his brother's memory. He was also appointed mace-bearer on the erection of the Royal Irish Academy; both
of them places very compatible with his business. In the former, he
gave proofs of his integrity, by detecting several frauds in the revenue
in his department, by which he himself might have profited, if he had
not been a man of principle. He died without issue." In 1840 (133)
Irving omitted this passage. He continued the passage quoted in
148.22: "About the same time Goldsmith received notice that a small
legacy had been left him by his excellent and affectionate uncle
Contarine.

"These circumstances called forth the following letter, containing
domestic allusions of a moving nature...." The letter follows (133–
35). See *Letters* (83–87).

149.28 George Faulkner's]   According to Balderston (*Letters*, 86, n. 1),
George Faulkner was a "celebrated printer."

150.25–26 have effected]   Paragraph added in 1849. Compare Forster
(519–20).

151.15 without having it."]   The anecdote is told in Prior (I, 218–20).
Prior heard the story from "the Rev. H. Bishop, Chaplain to the Archbishop of Dublin," who was the son of "Master Bishop." This entire
paragraph was added in 1849. Compare Forster (66–67).

151.25 Forsitan et nostrum nomen miscebitur istis]   Ovid, *Ars Ama-
toria*, I, iii, 339. "Perhaps even our names will be mingled with these."
This translation was supplied to the editor by Morris Diamond of
Riverhead, New York.

151.30 miscebitur *istis*]   Irving included the anecdote in 1825 (33)
but omitted it in 1840. See Boswell (II, 226); Prior (II, 480); Forster
(494–95).

152.14 paid for."]   This paragraph appears with slight variations in
1840 (135–36). Both anecdotes are included in 1825 (40). In Prior
(II, 276–77) and Forster (545) there is a single anecdote, which is
a composite of the two in Irving. In his revised edition (III, 215–16)
Forster attributed the anecdote to the *Life* prefixed to Bewick's edition
of the *Poems* (1809), p. 11.

152.19 the public]   Compare 1840 (136): "Still, however, as has been
before observed, he found golden moments to steal away from his
prosaic labours and indulge the poetic vein, and, on the 26th May,
1770, was enabled to bring his 'Deserted Village' before the public."
Compare Prior (II, 240–41). Compare 1825 (40): "Although Goldsmith
thus toiled for a livelihood in the drudgery of compilation, we do not
find that he had become negligent of fame. His leisure hours were
still devoted to his Muse; and the next voluntary production of his

pen was the highly-finished poem of 'The Deserted Village' " See Percy (85).

152.27 greatest favorite] The paragraph to this point appears in 1840 (136), in which the word *favourite* is followed by an asterisk indicating the footnote which appears in the present volume as "NOTE" on 154.6–156.21. The balance of the paragraph in 1840 forms a separate paragraph.

152.41 inconsiderate generosity] Compare 1825 (40); 1840 (137–39). Of this anecdote Percy (85) wrote: " . . . although this would have been perfectly in character, the doctor was not quite so ignorant of the value of his own time and labour. . . ." Prior (II, 280) questioned its authenticity. Compare Forster (545).

153.3 of this poem] In 1825 (40–42) Irving's discussion of "The Deserted Village" includes the footnote which appears at 154.6–156.21. With the exception of the footnote this material was omitted in 1840 (136–39).

153.23 home at last] "Deserted Village," lines 83–96 (*Works*, IV, 290–91).

154.5 world be past] *Ibid.*, lines 97–112 (*Works*, IV, 291–92).

154.7 London periodical] "Modern Pilgrimages—Auburn," *New Monthly Magazine and Literary Journal* 2 (1821), 449–53. The quotation that follows is from pp. 451–53. The article is signed "R." See notes 152.27 and 153.3.

154.11 Captain Hogan.] John Hogan, who, according to Prior (I, 21, n.), succeeded to an estate in the vicinity of Auburn, "used all his influence to preserve from the ravages of time and passing depredators, such objects and localities as serve to make allusions in the poem."

154.16 General Napier] Prior (II, 259) said that the story of General Robert Napier's dispossessing tenants "must be taken with certain allowances for heat and misrepresentation; . . . if not wholly untrue it is highly exaggerated."

154.24 a year.'] "Deserted Village," line 142 (*Works*, IV, 293).

154.26 by oats] See Discussions of Adopted Readings.

154.35 neighbouring hill.'] "Deserted Village," line 12 (*Works*, IV, 287).

155.2 grows wild.'] *Ibid.*, lines 137–38 (*Works*, IV, 292).

155.6 'hawthorn-tree,'] *Ibid.*, line 13 (*Works*, IV, 287).

155.17 game of goose.'] *Ibid.*, lines 227–32 (*Works*, IV, 296).

155.25 to rule.'] *Ibid.*, line 195 (*Works*, IV, 295).

155.27 unprofitably gay.'] *Ibid.*, line 194 (*Works*, IV, 295).

155.33–34 in Gay's] A volume of poems of John Gay (1685–1732), said to have been found in a secret drawer in Gay's desk, was published by Henry Lee in 1820 under the title *Gay's Chair*. The volume was later exposed as a fraud. See William Henry Irving, *John Gay: Favorite of the Wits* (Durham, N.C., 1940), pp. 303–304.

156.1 "The controversy] See *Works* (IV, 273–77).

156.8 had made;'] "Deserted Village," line 124 (*Works*, IV, 292).

156.14 Pandemonium?'] Compare *Paradise Lost* (Book I, lines 700–757).

156.18 men decay.'] "Deserted Village," lines 51–52 (*Works*, IV, 289).

156.22 Davis] John Davis (1774–1854) was a bookseller and novelist. The following quotation is from his *Travels of Four Years and a Half in the United States of America during 1798, 1799, 1800, 1801, and 1802. With an introduction and notes by A. J. Morrison* (New York, 1909), p. 123. This book, dedicated to Thomas Jefferson when he was president, was originally published in 1803. The paragraph was added in 1849. See Prior (I, 17). Best was possibly the Reverend Henry Best, Fellow of St. Mary Magdalen College, Oxford, who wrote *Personal and Literary Memorials* (London, 1829). See note 93.15.

157.17 in the Temple] This and the previous paragraph were added in 1849. Compare Forster (569–70). For Judge Day, see note 138.15.

157.36 female society] This paragraph was added in 1849.

158.5 good qualities."] In 1840 (154–57) Irving quoted from Prior (II, 377–80) a long passage of which this quotation forms a part. Prior (II, 377) said that he had received his information "from one of the party, who entertains great regard for his memory. . . ." The rest of the paragraph was added in 1849. Compare Forster (590–91).

158.15 beautiful daughters] Compare 1825 (43): "Soon after the publication of 'The Deserted Village,' Goldsmith found leisure to accompany a party of ladies on an excursion to Paris." Compare 1840 (144): "In the latter part of July, 1770, Goldsmith made a six weeks' excursion to Paris in company with these ladies." The rest of the paragraph was added in 1849. Compare Forster (549).

158.19 works of Parnell] The poet Thomas Parnell (1679–1718) was born in Dublin. Goldsmith's *The Life of Thomas Parnell, D.D.* was prefixed to an edition of Parnell's *Poems on Several Occasions* (1770). See *Works* (III, 401–402). The following verses are from Parnell's "A Fairy Tale," lines 10–15. Irving added them in 1849. They do not appear in Prior (II, 284–87) or in Forster (557).

158.31 on the subject] This paragraph was added in 1849.

159.21 a new one."] This letter, which Balderston (*Letters*, 91) dates ca. July 27, 1770, is included in 1825 (43) and 1840 (144–45). Compare Percy (90–91); Prior (II, 288–89); Forster (549–51).

159.40 fixed upon him] The paragraph to this point and the preceding two paragraphs appear in 1840 (145–46). Compare 1825 (37): "When accompanying two beautiful young ladies, with their mother, on a

tour in France, he was amusingly angry that more attention was paid
to them than to him." Compare Boswell (I, 422–23), which reads
"seriously angry." The sentence in 1825 is part of a long discussion of
Goldsmith's envy, which at that time Irving accepted. See Introduction,
p. xxv.

160.3 for earnest."] Compare 1840 (156): "They accused him of envy,
but it certainly was not envy in the usual sense of that word; he was
jealous, perhaps, of giving praise where he thought praise was not
due; but I am sure that, on many occasions, from the peculiar manner
of his humour and assumed frown of countenance, what was often
uttered in jest was mistaken by those that did not know him for
earnest." See Prior (II, 290–91).

160.6 following letter] The letter appears in 1840 (146–49). See Prior
(II, 292–95); Forster (553–55).

160.31 Dyer] Samuel Dyer (1725–1772) was, according to Prior (I,
428), "a man of general erudition, a friend of the Burkes, and
formerly a commissary in the army." In 1825 (30) Irving included
a long footnote on Dyer, which he took verbatim from Percy (70–71).
In 1840 (98) he omitted Dyer's name from the list of members of The
Club and the footnote. See Boswell (II, 4, n. 1).

162.8 Bill Tibbs] Beau Tibbs, a character in *The Citizen of the World*,
refers to himself (*Works*, II, 227) as Ned. Bill Tibbs is the soldier who
"has lost both his legs, and an eye to boot" (*Works*, II, 460, textual
note 6). For the following quotations see *Works* (II, 296). The entire
paragraph was added in 1849.

162.25–26 of the ladies] The paragraph to this point is a revised version
of one in 1840 (149). The last sentence of the paragraph appears in
substance in 1840 (150) as does the quotation in the following paragraph. Compare Prior (295–97); Forster (555).

162.35 unlucky exploit?] This sentence was added in 1849.

162.37 "The Retaliation."] See *Works* (IV, 358). The following verses
were added in 1840 (149). Compare Prior (II, 295).

163.19 continual schooling."] This and the previous paragraph appear
in 1840 (149–50). The quotation is from a footnote in Prior (II, 297).

163.26 term comfort."] This and the following paragraph appear in
1840 (150–51). See Prior (II, 297).

164.15 feeling want] This paragraph with slight variations was added
in 1840 (151). See Prior (II, 298–99). For Goldsmith's relationship
with his mother see *Letters* (xi–xii).

164.23 the essay] This paragraph, in essence, and the quotation in the
following paragraph appear in 1840 (140). The quotation is from
Goldsmith's *Life of Parnell* (*Works*, III, 408–409). Compare Prior (II,
284). In 1825 (44) Irving wrote: "The lives of Lord Bolingbroke and

Dr. Parnell, undertaken for the booksellers, were the next productions that came from his pen. They were prefixed to the respective works of these writers, published about 1770–1771. Both performances are executed with his wonted taste and felicity of expression; and, in his memoir of Parnell, the poverty of incident peculiar to the life of a scholar is ingeniously supplied by the author's own reflections. When Dr. Johnson afterwards undertook to write the 'Lives of the Poets,' he concluded the series with that of Parnell, and seized the opportunity it afforded him of paying an elegant compliment to the memory of his deceased friend." Here Irving quotes from Johnson's *Life of Parnell*. See Samuel Johnson, *Lives of the English Poets*, ed. George Birkbeck Hill (Oxford, 1905), II, 49.

164.32–33 *meridian splendour.*"] Irving's italics.

164.34–35 an abridgment] In 1825 (38–39) Irving included in a footnote the contract between Goldsmith and Davies for this abridgment, which he found in Percy (78–79). In the text he merely mentioned the abridgment in a list of histories Goldsmith was engaged in compiling. In 1840 (122) the abridgment is mentioned in a quotation from Boswell (II, 224–25). See T 143–44.

164.37 Lord Bolingbroke's] Henry St. John, Viscount Bolingbroke (1678–1751) was an English statesman. Originally his *Dissertation on Parties*, a series of letters critical of Walpole, was published in the *Craftsman*. See note 164.23. See also *Works* (III, 431–33).

165.4 seat of Gosfield] See note 101.28.

165.6 Capua] During the Second Punic War (216 B.C.) Hannibal wintered at Capua, where his soldiers indulged in riotous living.

165.8–9 Lord Bolingbroke."] The quotation is from a letter of Thomas Davies to the Reverend James Grainger (October 27, 1770). Irving probably took the quotation from Forster (557–58).

165.20 lasting contention."] Irving took great liberties with this quotation, which is from the first paragraph of Goldsmith's *The Life of Henry Lord Viscount Bolingbroke*. See *Works* (III, 437). The entire paragraph was added in 1849.

165.25 Lord Camden] Charles Pratt (1714–1794), a Whig, was knighted in 1761 and raised to the peerage as Baron Camden in 1765. He was sympathic to the American cause. When he sought membership in The Club, he was blackballed (*DNB*).

165.36 neglected him."] The anecdote, which is told in Boswell (IV, 168), was added in 1849. In 1825 (55) Irving wrote: "Vanity was another of the weaknesses of Goldsmith; but it was rather amusing than offensive in its operation. He was vain of his literary consequence, as was strongly discovered in the complaint he once made with regard to Lord Camden.—'I met him,' said he, 'at Lord Clare's house in the country, and he took no more notice of me than if I had been an ordinary man.'" See Prior (II, 446–47); Forster (559).

166.17 *wanting a shirt*]   The verses are from "The Haunch of Venison. A Poetical Epistle to Lord Clare," lines 1–12; 31–34 (*Works*, IV, 313–14). The paragraph was added in 1849. Compare Forster (560–64).

166.20 in Bath]   Compare 1840 (152): "In the spring of this year he paid a visit to Lord Clare at Bath, in the course of which a whimsical blunder occurred. Lord Clare and the Duke of Northumberland had houses. . . ." The anecdote follows as in the next paragraph but with a few minor variations. According to Prior (II, 135), the duchess of Northumberland told this story to Percy. Irving followed Percy (68–69) closely in 1825 (35).

166.40 Northumberland House]   This sentence was added in 1849.

167.6 St. George's day]   April 23. St. George has been honored in England since the eighth century.

167.15 Chatterton]   Thomas Chatterton (1752–1770), called "the marvellous boy," became for the Romantics a symbol of neglected genius. He wrote a number of poems which he claimed were the work of an imaginary fifteenth-century poet named Thomas Rowley.

167.26 of Rowley]   This and the next five paragraphs are an expansion of the following paragraph in 1840 (151–52): "About this time, the friendship that had so long subsisted between Goldsmith and Dr. Percy was suddenly interrupted and almost destroyed by a dispute as to the authenticity of Rowley's poems. Percy maintained that they were entirely the productions of Chatterton, while Goldsmith, considering the merit of the poetry, the acquaintance with life and the human heart displayed in them, the antique quaintness of the language, and the familiar knowledge of historical events of their supposed day, was of opinion that they could not be the works of a boy of sixteen, of narrow education, and confined to the duties of an attorney's office; but must be the genuine productions of Rowley. So firmly was Goldsmith persuaded of this fact, that on one occasion, when dining at the Royal Academy, he spoke with rapture of them as a treasure of old English poetry wonderfully brought to light. Johnson, who was present, laughed at his enthusiasm, and Horace Walpole assured him he had for some time known of the treasure and its discoverer, and might have had the honour of ushering them to the learned world; 'but, though Goldsmith's credulity diverted me,' says he, 'my mirth was soon dashed; for, on asking about Chatterton, he told me he had been in London and had destroyed himself.'" Compare Prior (II, 219–20; 307–309); Forster (565–68).

167.28 Ossian]   Ossian (or Oisin) was a legendary fourth-century Celtic poet whose poems James Macpherson (1736–1796) claimed to have found. He published *Fragments of Ancient Poetry collected in the Highlands of Scotland, and translated from the Gaelic or Erse language* in 1760. Dr. Johnson challenged the authenticity of the poems. See Boswell (III, 170–78).

167.34 learned world."] The quotation appears in both Prior (II, 308–309) and Forster (566–67).

167.40 Gray and Mason] Thomas Gray (1716–1771) and William Mason (1725–1797) were English poets. Mason, who was Gray's executor, published his *Memoirs of Gray* in 1775.

168.6 inspired idiot;"] See Boswell (I, 422, n. 3).

168.10 destroyed himself."] See Prior (II, 308–309); Forster (567).

168.16 his death."] See Forster (567).

168.30–31 *such things.*"] See Boswell (III, 416). The italics are Irving's.

168.43–169.1 deliberate reasoner."] See *Works* (IV, 338–39); see also note 85.12–13. This sentence was added in 1849. Compare Forster (586).

169.18 *but mum!*"] See Forster (586–87). Compare 1840 (152).

169.22 kept its ground"] Irving appears to be quoting from his 1840 essay (152). Compare Prior (II, 322–30).

169.26 Countess Dowager of Rothes] See Boswell (II, 123, n. 2).

169.26 following letter] The letter appears in 1825 (45). Compare Percy (92–94). In 1840 (153–54) Irving omitted "I am . . . chemistry and physics" (169.34–170.2) and a number of other phrases and clauses. In 1849 Irving took the letter bodily from Forster (588–89) and used it as a manuscript page. Compare Prior (II, 328–30).

170.1 second Boyle] Robert Boyle (1627–1691) was an Irish physicist and chemist.

170.3 Doctor Taylor] The Reverend John Taylor, prebendary of Westminster and rector of Bosworth, lived in Derbyshire. See *Letters* (104, n. 4).

170.3 Mrs. Thrale's] Mrs. Hester Lynch Thrale (1741–1821) and her husband Henry, a wealthy brewer, were patrons of Dr. Johnson. When after Thrale's death in 1781 Mrs. Thrale married Gabriel Piozzi, an Italian musician (1784), she and Johnson became estranged.

171.8–9 Henry William Bunbury, Esq.] See note 139.35.

171.27 Horneck herself] Compare 1840 (154): "We have some farther traditional anecdotes of Goldsmith and his doings during the same year. In August, Miss Catherine Horneck, one of his beautiful fellow-travellers, was married to Henry William Bunbury, Esq., celebrated for the humorous productions of his pencil. Goldsmith shortly afterward made a visit to the newly-married couple, at their seat at Barton, in Suffolk, and the following particulars related by one of the inmates of the mansion, present him in all the amiable and whimsical peculiarities of his character." Compare Prior (II, 376–78). The balance of the paragraph, which appears in 1840 (154–55), was taken verbatim from Prior (II, 377–78), who does not use quotation marks.

172.2 their names."] In 1840 (157) and Prior (II, 380) this paragraph concludes the long passage on the visit to Barton.

172.22 a general smile."] Compare 1840 (155); Prior (II, 378).

172.30 present occasion] The paragraph to this point and the preceding paragraph were added in 1849. The balance of the paragraph appears in 1840 (155–56). Compare Prior (II, 379).

172.43 quoted elsewhere] See 157.37–158.5 and note 158.5. This and the following paragraph were added in 1849. Compare Forster (590–92).

174.4 General Oglethorpe] See note 132.40. This entire chapter was added in 1849. Compare Forster (494).

174.6 Prince Eugene] François Eugène de Savoie Carignan (1663–1736), Austrian soldier, entered the service of the Emperor Leopold against the Turks in 1683 and distinguished himself at the siege of Vienna. See Prior (II, 421–22).

174.19 pole to pole] Alexander Pope's imitation of "The Second Epistle of the Second Book of Horace," lines 276–77. Compare Boswell (III, 225, n. 2): "Or, driven by strong benevolence of soul, / Will fly like Oglethorpe from pole to pole." Prior's version (II, 422) is the same as Boswell's except that the word *Will* was changed to *Shall.*

174.26 more interesting."] See Boswell (III, 227).

174.29 has to say."] See Boswell (III, 422).

174.31 Boswell gives us] See Boswell (II, 176). Compare Forster (600).

175.7 drawcansir] Name of a braggart in *The Rehearsal* (1671) by George Villiers, second duke of Buckingham.

175.15 in good part] See Boswell (II, 175–76). Neither Prior nor Forster included this story, probably because it does not concern Goldsmith.

175.35 fight a duel."] See Boswell (II, 174–75). Compare Prior (II, 371–72); Forster (599–600).

176.5 could do it."] See Boswell (II, 176); Forster (600).

176.10 upon ghosts] See Boswell (II, 177–79).

176.11 Duke of Marlborough's] John Churchill, first duke of Marlborough (1650–1722), was the son of Sir Winston Churchill. The Battle of Malplaquet was fought on September 11, 1709.

176.20 Sir John Friend] Sir John Friend, a brewer, was knighted by James II in 1685. He was convicted of high treason for failure to reveal the identity of those in the plot against the life of William III, and was executed at Tyburn on April 3, 1696.

176.23 Colonel Cecil]   According to Croker (Boswell, II, 178, n. 2) Sir Henry Hardinge, secretary at war, was unable to identify Colonel Cecil. Croker doubted the truth of this anecdote.

176.35 shadowy being."]   See Boswell (II, 173).

177.5 Joseph Cradock]   Joseph Cradock (1742–1826) was a wealthy young man interested in literature and music. Compare Prior (II, 336); Forster (595). See *Letters* (106, n. 2).

177.13 Yates]   Richard Yates (1706–1796), English comedian, and his second wife, Mary Ann Graham (1728–1787), a tragic actress, were members of the Drury Lane company at this time.

177.18 Threnodia Augustalis]   See *Works* (IV, 323–40).

177.22 Mrs. Cornelys' rooms]   Theresa Cornelys (1723–1797), a native of Venice, came to England in 1759. She bought Carlisle House in Soho Square in 1760 and opened it for public entertainment. By 1770 she was enjoying a great vogue, but she later fell into disrepute and died in Fleet Prison. See E. Beresford Chancellor, *The XVIIIth Century in London: An Account of its Social Life and Arts* (London, 1920), 110–15. This paragraph was added in 1849. Compare Prior (II, 336–40); Forster (595–97).

177.37 every month!"]   Compare Forster (446).

178.3 baited by curs!"]   In 1840 (163) this quotation appears in a long passage attributed to Dr. M'Veagh M'Donnell, mentioned in the next paragraph. Compare Prior (II, 349).

178.7–8 in after years]   Compare 1840 (158–59): "We cannot refrain from subjoining the following testimonial to the benevolence of Goldsmith, and his disposition, though poor himself, to help those who were still poorer. It is from one Dr. M'Veagh M'Donnell, a man of classical attainments, who afterward rose to some degree of prosperity." The following quotations are from Prior (II, 346–47), who noted M'Donnell's recollections "in his presence and as far as relates to him are given as nearly as possible in his own words" (II, 344).

178.18 Boileau]   Nicolas Boileau (1636–1711), French critic.

178.25 rusticantur.']   "These studies spend the night with us, go abroad with us, go to the country with us." The quotation is from Cicero's speech for Aulus Licinius Archias. Several errors in the quotation in the first edition were pointed out by the reviewer in the *Gentleman's Magazine* (n.s. 32 [December, 1849], 619), who wrote: "Perhaps in his next edition Mr. Irving will do us the favour of reading *per*noctant and *per*egrinantur, for so, we believe, Cicero wrote." The corrections were made in the 1850 impression. Compare 1840 (159) where "pernoctant" is spelled correctly but the error "per*i*grinantur" appears.

179.3 Natural History."]   Irving here omits the following paragraph from 1840 (160): " 'I think it was generally believed by his acquaintance,' continues Dr. M'Donnell, 'that he graduated at Louvain; that is my impression. Perhaps it may have been at Padua, for that university had Irish professors; so had Louvain; also Manheim; and likewise the College of Maria Theresa at Brussells." See note 41.33.

179.9 he bore them] This and the preceding paragraph were added in 1849.

179.23–24 had little value."] Compare 1840 (160–61); Prior (II, 346–47).

179.30 *Spectator*] The allusion is to *Spectator*, no. 12 (March 14, 1711). Compare Boswell (II, 177); Prior (II, 331); Forster (587).

179.32 with Mickle] William Julius Mickle (1735–1788), Scottish poet, published his version of Camoens' *Lusiad* in 1771–1775. Prior (II, 95) said that both Johnson and Goldsmith contemplated translating this epic.

179.35 pencil] The paragraph is a paraphrase of Boswell (II, 177). In 1840 (157–58) Irving probably quoted the passage from Prior (II, 331). Compare 1825 (45–46).

179.40 flight of stairs] This paragraph was added in 1840 (158). Compare Prior (II, 332); Forster (587).

180.2 in his room] Compare 1840 (158): "Goldsmith spent most of his time in his room writing, where his meals were generally sent to him." The rest of the paragraph was added in 1849. Compare Forster (587).

180.16 for the poor] Compare 1840 (158): "Sometimes he strolled about the fields, or was seen loitering, and reading, and musing under the hedges. He read much at night, being subject to fits of wakefulness. He was noted here, as everywhere else, for his charitable feelings. No beggar applied to him in vain, and he evinced on all occasions great commiseration for the poor." Compare Prior (II, 332–33); Forster (587).

180.18 Hugh Boyd] Hugh Boyd (1746–1794) was an Irish essayist (*DNB*).

180.19 Sir William Chambers] Sir William Chambers (1726–1796) was an architect and writer of books on architecture. This and the next paragraph were added in 1840 (158). Compare Prior (II, 334–35).

180.31 always welcome] Compare 1840 (142): "Goldsmith had of course been brought into a higher sphere of society than he had originally been accustomed to, but he always preferred those easy domestic circles where there was little of the etiquette of polished life, and where he could indulge his playful and occasionally grotesque humour. One of his social resorts was the family of a Mr. Seguin, an Irish merchant of literary tastes, who had country lodgings near his rural retreat at Edgeware." Prior (II, 192) said that Goldsmith was godfather to two of the Seguin children.

180.33 game of romps] Compare 1840 (142): "In the bosom of this family he would completely unbend and play the boy. He was ready for anything that was going forward: conversation, music, or a game of romps." The rest of the paragraph is the same as in 1849. Compare Prior (II, 193).

181.4 Roubillac] Louis François Roubillac (1702 or 1705–1762), French sculptor, settled in London before 1738. Hawkins told the story in his life of Johnson (416–17). According to Austin Dobson (*Eighteenth Century Vignettes*, 2d ser. [Oxford, 1950], 78), "its authenticity is not above suspicion." Irving added the anecdote in 1849. Compare Prior (I, 425); Forster (233–34).

181.9 reach of art!] Alexander Pope, *An Essay on Criticism*, I, line 153. Compare Prior (I, 232). This paragraph was added in 1849.

181.13 on his fingers."] Compare Forster (414).

181.16–17 Burn the Bellows] Compare Forster (416).

181.18 George Colman] George Colman, "the Younger," (1762–1836) acted as manager of the Haymarket during his father's illness; and the patent was transformed to him in 1749 upon his father's death. The quotation was added in 1840 (142–43). Compare Prior (II, 194–95).

181.39 man's smile;'] "The Deserted Village." See *Works* (IV, 294).

182.3 Lord Clare] See note 101.29.

182.6 Italian Fantoccini] See the entry on puppets in *The Oxford Companion to the Theatre*, p. 646.

182.15 the puppets."] In 1825 (37) Irving used this passage from Boswell (I, 423), without quotation marks, as an example of Goldsmith's envy. See note 159.40. It was omitted in 1840. Compare Prior (I, 442); Forster (608–609).

182.24–25 *The Handsome Chambermaid*] Compare 196.26–27 where the title appears as the *Handsome Housemaid*, which is the correct title according to Samuel N. Bogorad and Robert Gale Noyes. See *Theatre Survey* 14 (Fall, 1973). This entire issue is devoted to the play.

182.30 *than Garrick*."] Compare Forster (623). The paragraph was added in 1849.

183.7 tied himself to the mast] An allusion to Homer's *Odyssey*, Book XII.

183.15 Mrs. Vesey's and Mrs. Montagu's] Elizabeth Vesey (1715?–1791) was the wife of Agmondesham Vesey, who was elected to The Club in 1773. The Vesey home was in Ireland, but Mrs. Vesey spent much time in London, where she was a popular hostess at her biweekly literary salon (*DNB*). Elizabeth Montagu (1720–1800), another "blue-stocking," was a wealthy society leader and patron of the arts. Writers and artists, as well as the nobility, attended her salon. Compare Forster (614).

183.28 of its success."] Compare Forster (628). This and the next paragraph were added in 1849.

183.31 the constable"] See 161.4.

183.38 James's powders] Dr. Robert James (1705–1776), a physician of Lichfield, patented his powder in 1746.

184.19 and talent] Compare Forster (529); Prior (II, 485–86). This and the preceding paragraph were added in 1849.

184.31 of a hotel] To this point in the paragraph Irving is paraphrasing Boswell (I, 423, n. 2). In the rest of the paragraph, which is from the same note, Irving took liberties in quoting his source. This and the preceding paragraph were added in 1849. Compare Forster (527–29).

185.12 a fool of himself] Boswell appeared in Corsican dress, which he described in detail in "A Letter from James Boswell, Esq; on Shakespeare's Jubilee at Stratford-upon-Avon." *The London Magazine* 38 (September, 1769), 451–56. Compare Forster (509–10).

185.14 the Beaux' Stratagem] *The Beaux' Stratagem* (1707) is a comedy by George Farquhar (1677?–1707), Irish actor and playwright. Scrub is a valet. The anecdote, which was added in 1849, appears in Prior (II, 369); Forster (612–13).

185.30 left the table."] This anecdote appears in Prior (II, 483–84) and Forster (525).

185.33 Lord Shelburne] Sir William Petty, second earl of Shelburne (1737–1805), became secretary of state in 1766 in Chatham's second administration.

185.34 Malagrida] Gabriel Malagrida (1689–1761), Italian Jesuit missionary, was convicted of heresy and burned at the stake.

185.38 Lord Charlemont] James Caulfield (1728–1799), fourth viscount and first earl of Charlemont, was an Irish statesman.

186.2 term of reproach."] This anecdote appears in 1825 (35). Compare Prior (II, 482–83); Forster (668–69); Boswell (V, 54).

186.3 Rogers the poet] See note 105.38.

186.10 *a fool, sir*."] Forster (479) said that it was Cooke to whom Rogers spoke and (475) that Cooke was "the young law student so often referred to as Goldsmith's countryman and near neighbour in the Temple. . . ." A reviewer (*Gentleman's Magazine*, n.s. 32 [December, 1849], 619) said that the person "was one of much literary knowledge and talent, called 'Conversation Cooke.' He collected and edited 'Additions to Pope's Works,' 2 vols." The reviewer recommended that "the story . . . be told in the next edition in better taste, especially as the contemptuous term 'old wiseacre' is much misapplied." Irving did not heed this advice in later impressions of the book.

186.21 before he is filled."] The clause reads: "before he fills his belly," in *The European Magazine* (24 [October, 1793], 262); Prior (II, 481); Forster (615).

186.41 of his heart] Prior (II, 381) paraphrased the anecdote, which appears in *The European Magazine* (24 [October, 1793], 261).

187.1 Baretti] Guiseppe Marc Antonio Baretti (1719–1789), an Italian critic, came to London in 1751 to teach Italian. He was one of the young men who assisted Johnson with the *Dictionary*. For Goldsmith's attitude toward Baretti, see Prior (II, 235–36).

187.10 sent her away."] Compare Prior (II, 420–21); Forster (664–65). The anecdote is found in *The European Magazine* 55 (June, 1809), 443.

187.13 Man in Black] *Citizen of the World* (*Works*, II, 111–12).

187.22 Ranelagh] Ranelagh House and gardens, built by Richard, Viscount of Ranelagh about 1690, opened as a place of public amusement in 1742. A rotunda, built by the architect William Jones, was compared to the Pantheon at Rome. See Boswell (II, 163–64); Wroth 199–218); Forster (572–73).

187.27 from vice."*] See Boswell (II, 164). Compare Forster (573).

187.43 home and think."] See Boswell (IV, 52).

188.7 vacant mind."] "The Deserted Village," line 122 (*Works*, IV, 292).

188.22 the Pantheon] The Pantheon, an indoor Ranelagh, built in 1772, was popular for balls and masquerades. See Wroth, 25.

188.29 Virtue's cause?] At this point in the printed passage of MS Irving crossed out the following two lines of the poem: "Would'st thou like Sterne, resolv'd at length to thrive; / Turn pimp, and die cockbawd at sixty-five?"

188.33 less than man.] Kenrick's verses appear in Prior (II, 351).

189.14 out in exercise] Compare Prior (II, 353); Forster (573).

190.12 playing Loo] Loo was a game of cards. See *Letters* (131, n. 2).

190.38 Goldsmith's reply] Irving took the letter bodily from Forster and used Forster's three pages (592–94) as manuscript. *Letters* (128) dates both this letter to Mrs. Bunbury and the letter to Garrick, which appears in 226.25–32, December 25, 1773. Irving's reference (226.6–7) to a second invitation to Barton for Christmas may be an error caused by Forster's having included the Bunbury letter in his section dealing with 1771 and the letter to Garrick under a section dealing with 1773 (674). In the latter case, however, Forster does not mention another Christmas invitation.

192.36 before Fielding] Sir John Fielding, justice of the peace for

Westminster, was the half-brother and successor in this office to Henry Fielding, the novelist.

193.12 Sir Charles] Sir Charles Bunbury was Henry Bunbury's elder brother.

193.36 lord of misrule] In medieval times noblemen appointed a lord of misrule to conduct their Christmas festivities. See E. K. Chambers, *English Literature at the Close of the Middle Ages* (New York, 1961), p. 84.

194.11 those perplexities] The paragraph to this point was added in 1849. The rest of the paragraph was adapted from 1840 (163–64). Compare Prior (II, 382–86). See 1825 (46); Percy (100).

194.23 following letter] The letter was added in 1840 (164–65). Compare Prior (II. 386); Forster (621).

195.11 on the subject] This paragraph was adapted from 1840 (163–64). Irving took the following letter bodily from Forster (622) and used it as manuscript copy.

195.28 kind of force,"] The quotation from Boswell (IV, 180) appears in Prior (II, 385) and Forster (622). It was added in 1849.

195.32 of a candle."] The quotation appears in 1840 (165). Compare Pror (II, 388).

195.34 Woodward and Gentleman Smith] Harry Woodward (1717–1777), English comedian, has been called "perhaps the last of the great Harlequins" (*Oxford Companion to the Theatre*, p. 846). William Smith (1730–1819) was an English actor known as "Gentleman Smith." In 1840 (165) Irving did not name these actors. Compare Prior (II, 387–88); Forster (624).

195.40 good acting."] The quotaton was added in 1840 (165). Compare Prior (II, 388); Forster (624).

195.41 Quick] John Quick (1748–1831) is said to have been "the favorite actor of George III" (*Oxford Companion to the Theatre*, p. 653).

195.41–196.1 Lee Lewes] Charles Lee Lewes (1740–1803), English actor, was the grandfather of George Henry Lewes, English philosopher and dramatic critic. This paragraph was added in 1849. Compare Forster (624–25).

196.12–13 Goldy's play."] Compare Boswell (II, 242); Prior (II, 389–90); Forster (627).

196.19 Mrs. Cowley] Hannah Cowley (1743–1809) was one of the first women playwrights in England.

196.23 Duke of Gloucester] Prince William Henry, duke of Gloucester (1743–1805), was George III's brother. Compare Prior (II, 384).

196.36 may have contributed] This paragraph was added in 1849. Compare Forster (623–24).

196.42 in his memoirs]   This paragraph was adapted from 1840 (165) and 1825 (46). The following quotation from Cumberland's memoirs was included in 1825 (46–47) and 1840 (165–67). Percy did not use it. Scott (293, n. 2) recommended Cumberland's memoir but did not include the passage. Croker included a long passage from the memoir, including this material, in the appendix of his edition of Boswell's *Life of Johnson* (V, 398–404).

197.5–6 Fitzherbert, Caleb Whitefoord]   According to Boswell (II, 471, n. 2), William Fitzherbert "sat in parliament from 1761 to his death, in 1772. In 1765 he was made a lord of Trade." Both Prior (II, 397) and Forster (629) said that Fitzherbert had died a year before this supposed event. Caleb Whitefoord (1734–1810), a friend of Benjamin Franklin, wrote newspaper pieces under the name of Papyrius Cursor (*DNB*).

197.7 Major Mills]   This person has not been identified.

197.18 Adam Drummond]   This person has not been identified.

197.21 son of Hystaspes]   Hystaspes, satrap of Parthia and heir to the Persian throne, had a son named Darius who in 521 B.C. conspired with a group of nobles, killed the usurping king, and seized the throne himself.

197.25 a flapper]   An allusion to Jonathan Swift's *Gulliver's Travels*, Book III, Chapter II.

198.8 greatest acclamations."]   This paragraph was added in 1849. Compare Prior (II, 396–400); Forster (628–30).

198.26 ill timed sally]   This paragraph in 1825 (47) is closer to *The European Magazine* (24 [September, 1793], 173) than to Percy (100–101). In 1840 (167–68) the passage was shortened. Prior (II, 389) included only the dialogue between Colman and Goldsmith, and placed it at a rehearsal of the play. Compare Forster (630–32).

198.36 of the comedy]   This paragraph in 1840 (168) is followed by another: "Neither did Goldsmith escape those sneers and jeers of the press usually levelled by the underlings of literature at successful authors; but he was amply indemnified by the award of all true critics." In 1825 (48), expanding a passage in Percy (102), Irving wrote: "The good fortune which attended this drama was productive of its usual concomitants—a mixed portion of applause and censure, with instances of fulsome flattery and furious detraction. While from less fortunate bards, whose poverty induced them to solicit his bounty, he received the incense of adulation in a torrent of congratulatory addresses; from others, more independent, who were jealous of his reputation, and envied his success, he experienced all the virulence of malignant criticism and scurrilous invective. A single instance of each may gratify the curiosity of our readers." He included a poem entitled "On Dr. Goldsmith's Comedy," found in Percy (102). For the quotation from Colman's letter, see *Letters* (xlix–l).

199.5 Wapping Wall] Wapping is a district along the Thames in southeast London.

199.6 Rag Fair] Rag-fair is an old-clothes market in Houndsditch, London (*OED*).

199.14 in *his name.*] The squib, which was added in 1849, appears in Prior (II, 405).

199.17–18 Ossian Macpherson] See note 167.30.

199.25 *Ride, si sapis*] "Laugh if you are wise." The epigram, which appears in Prior (II, 398), was added in 1849.

199.31 *Pair of Stays!*] This is one of two stanzas included in Prior (II, 404). It was added in 1849.

199.33 following letter] Irving took the letter bodily from Forster (626–27) and used it as a manuscript page. Prior (II, 391–92) also included the letter.

200.6 Miss Catley] Anne Catley (1745–1789), a singer, did not in fact play the role of Miss Neville. See *Letters* (119, n. 3).

200.7 Mrs. Bulkley] See note 126.4

200.19 a loser] According to Prior (II, 392–93) Goldsmith realized between £400 and £500. In 1840 (175) Irving wrote: "The profits of Goldsmith on the performance and publication of 'She Stoops to Conquer,' amounted to upward of eight hundred pounds." 1825 (50) reads: "He cleared, by this performance alone, upwards of eight hundred pounds."

200.28 audience merry."] The quotation appears in 1825 (48) and 1840 (168). See Boswell (II, 222); Prior (II, 400).

200.33 Northcote's] James Northcote (1746–1831) was a portrait and landscape painter. This paragraph in substance was added in 1840 (168). Compare Prior (II, 400–401).

201.1 unaffected piety."] Irving took the quotation bodily from Forster (634) and made it part of his manuscript page. See Boswell (II, 203, n. 4); *Works* (V, 101). This and the next paragraph were added in 1849.

201.9 felicitous composition] Compare 1840 (175) the passage which follows the sentence quoted in note 200.19: "They were soon absorbed, however, by his heedless expenses, his open-handed and profuse charities, his gaming propensities, and his accumulating debts. Indeed, he was generally in advance of his pen, and had received from the booksellers the price of his works before they were completed. An amount of debt for moneys borrowed from booksellers, and for purchases of various kinds, was going on increasing unknown to his friends, who had no idea of his embarrassments, and of the anxiety of mind

that kept him tasking his pen, while it impaired that ease and freedom of spirit necessary to felicitous composition." Compare 1825 (50).

202.9 equal equanimity]   Compare 1840 (169); 1825 (48). The following letter also appears in 1825 (48–49) and 1840 (169–70). Irving's
original source was Percy (103–105).

202.12 *par vanité*]   "You are drowning in vanity."

203.17–18 Home's tragedy of 'Alonso.']   John Home (1722–1808) was
a Scottish clergyman and playwright. His tragedy *Alonzo* was produced by Garrick at Drury Lane on January 27, 1773.

203.22 cache la vérité]   "Smash the false mirror that conceals the truth
from you."

203.24 It would be difficult]   The paragraph in 1840 (171) reads:
"Goldsmith might have suffered those parts of the letter to pass un-
heeded which related merely to himself and his authorship; but
the allusion to the lovely H——k, and to his being an unsuccessful
admirer, appears to have stung him to the quick. We presume the
lady in question was one of his beautiful fellow-travellers, the Miss
Hornecks, and it is possible the sly innuendo may not have been
entirely unfounded. The paragraph in question was first pointed out
to him by an officious friend, an Irishman, who very sagely told him
he was in honour bound to resent it. Goldsmith took fire in an
instant, and, accompanied by his sagacious adviser, called upon Evans,
the publisher, in Paternoster Row. Entering the shop and announc-
ing himself, 'I have called. . . .'" Compare 1825 (49): "Indignant at
the wanton scurrility of this letter, which was pointed out to him
by the officious kindness of a friend, and enraged at the indelicacy of
introducing the name of a lady with whom he was acquainted, Goldsmith, accompanied by one of his countrymen, waited on Mr.
Evans. . . ."

203.34 Captain Higgins]   Note in 1840 (161–62) in a quotation from
Dr. M'Veagh M'Donnell: "Captain Higgins, who had been an officer of marines, and is mentioned in the Haunch of Venison, and
who, I believe, was Goldsmith's companion when he beat Evans the
bookseller. . . ." See Prior (II, 347, 408–10). For the opinion that Goldsmith's companion on this occasion was Charles Horneck, see Prior
(II, 411); Forster (635). Compare 1825 (49).

203.35 Evans the publisher]   Thomas Evans who, according to Forster
(635–36), "must not be confounded with the worthy bookseller of the
same name, who first collected Goldsmith's writings."

203.40 be sported with."]   The quotation was added in 1840 (171).
Compare Prior (II, 411).

204.9 for a constable]   Compare 1840 (172) "A shopman ran off for a
constable, and Goldsmith's gunpowder friend, seeing matters grow-

ing serious, abandoned him to his fate, and fled the battle-ground. The author was nearly overpowered by the stout Welshman, when Dr. Kenrick...." The rest of the paragraph varies in minor details in 1840. The 1825 version (49) is similar to the 1840.

204.16 to compromise] Joseph Cradock (*Literary and Miscellaneous Memoirs* [London, 1828], I, 232–33) claimed to have been the mediator in this affair. This and the following paragraph appear in 1840 (172). Compare 1825 (49): "This ridiculous quarrel afforded considerable sport for the newspapers before it was finally made up. An action was threatened by Evans for the assault, but it was at length compromised. Many paragraphs appeared, however, reflecting severely on the impropriety of Goldsmith's attempting to beat a person in his own house; and to these he conceived it incumbent on him to make a reply. Accordingly the following justificatory address appeared in 'The Daily Advertiser' of Wednesday, March 31, 1773." The letter appears in 1840 (172–74) and 1825 (49). Irving's original source was Percy 107–108).

205.19 undeceived them] Compare 1840 (174): "This vindication, it was affirmed, had been written for the poet by Dr. Johnson, and Boswell intimated to the latter his suspicions that such was the fact." Compare 1825 (49): "The composition of this address is so much in the style of Dr. Johnson, that it was at first generally believed to be the production of his pen. Johnson, however, always disclaimed any participation in it; and his disavowal has since been recorded in the volumes of Mr. Boswell." The rest of the paragraph shows minor variations in 1840, but in 1825 (49–50) Irving quotes the entire passage from Boswell (II, 197–98). Compare Percy (109–10).

206.12 Miss Burney] Frances Burney (1752–1840), daughter of the musicologist Charles Burney, was a diarist and novelist, her best known novel being *Evelina*. She married General d'Arblay, a French emigre, in 1793. The quotation, which is from her *Memoirs of Doctor Burney* ([London, 1832], II, 191), was added in 1849.

206.19 from the priest."] See Boswell (II, 202). This and the next paragraph were added in 1849. Compare Forster (639).

207.2 lady's finger."] See Boswell (II, 368–69). Compare Forster (597). This and the next paragraph were added in 1849.

207.13–14 intellectual display] See Boswell (II, 205–207).

207.17 "Humours of Ballamaguery"] Croker (Boswell, II, 207, n. 1) wrote: "Mr. Moore has endeavoured to bring it back into good company; it is to be found in the ninth number of his Irish Melodies, p. 48." This was Thomas Moore (1779–1852), the Irish poet who was a close friend of Irving. Compare Prior (II, 380). This paragraph was added in 1849.

207.30 than to endear] The paragraph to this point was added in 1840. Compare Prior (II, 474–76); Forster (440–41, 529–30).

207.34 more *liked."*] See Boswell (II, 224). The anecdote was included in 1825 (32) but not in 1840.

207.36 General Paoli] Pasquale de Paoli (1725–1807), the Corsican patriot, was an early hero of Boswell.

207.37 Martinelli] Vincenzio Martinelli (1702–1785), Italian writer, came to England in 1748. See Boswell (II, 208, n. 1).

208.23–24 shield of truth."] The paragraph was added in 1849. See Boswell (II, 209–10); Prior (II, 448–49). Irving took a page from his source and used it as part of manuscript page 428. The source was either Boswell or Prior.

208.39 arts a friend.'"] The couplet is from John Dryden's *Absalom and Achitophel,* lines 872–73. The anecdote to this point was added in 1840 (174–75). Compare Boswell (II, 212); Prior (II, 449–50). The rest of the paragraph was added in 1849.

209.8 passage in the play] See Boswell (II, 212–13); *Works* (V, 141). This and the next paragraph were added in 1849. Compare Prior (II, 393–94, 450–51); Forster (643–44).

209.20 Mr. Harris] James Harris (1709–1780) was an English scholar whose *Hermes* (1751), a treatise on universal grammar, earned for him the nickname of "Hermes Harris." In 1849 Irving wrote "of a Mr. Harris." This provoked the reviewer of *The Gentleman's Magazine,* n.s. 32 (December, 1849), 619, to comment: "And is this the transatlantic manner of mentioning the English Plato, the learned author of *Hermes,* and of the Philosophical Essays, and the three beautiful Dialogues? A Mr. Harris! a gentleman of family and fortune —a scholar of the highest rank—a man known and esteemed as well abroad as at home for his unblemished character—his studious, unobstructive life—his rare acquirements—and his profound and elegant illustrations of the philosophy of the schools of Greece! We have read letters to him from the greatest scholars of his time, expressive of the highest admiration and respect,—and it all ends in these days with— 'a Mr. Harris!' " In the 1850 impression Irving omitted the word *a.* This and the next paragraph were added in 1849. See Boswell (II, 213–14; III, 73–74); Forster (642).

209.25 Giardini] Felice de' Giardini (1716–1796) was an Italian violinist and composer.

210.22 death itself] This paragraph was added in 1849. Compare Boswell (II, 217–18); Forster (644–45).

211.8 rising risibility] The incidents in this and the preceding two paragraphs are found in Madame d'Arblay's *Memoirs of Dr. Burney,*

II, 194–96. They were added in 1849. Compare Forster (597–98). See Introduction, p. xxv.

211.18 be so *ill.*"] See Boswell (IV, 123–24); Forster (597–98).

211.19 sick of both."] See Boswell (III, 423); Forster (598). This paragraph was added in 1849.

211.29 an acaadamy,"] Croker (Boswell, III, 78, n. 1) included this anecdote, which he attributed to Scott, in a footnote. Irving took the anecdote bodily from Forster (510) and used it as a manuscript page.

212.13 such language,'"] In 1825 (31) Irving included not only this anecdote but also Boswell's comments on Sir John Hawkins's inaccuracy in reporting the incident. See Boswell (I, 492–93). Irving omitted the incident in 1840. Compare Forster (339–40).

212.15 his buffoonery."] See 1825 (30–31); Boswell (I, 492).

212.22 pimp, or player.'"] This paragraph was added in 1849. See Boswell (I, 493); Forster (340).

212.28–29 Lady Diana Spencer] Diana Spencer (1734–1808) was the eldest daughter of the second duke of Marlborough. See Boswell (II, 230–31); George Birkbeck Hill, *Dr. Johnson, His Friends and His Critics* (London, 1878), pp. 289–95.

212.31 been augmented] Compare 1825 (30): "About the beginning of 1768, the attending of efficient members were reduced to eight; first by the secession of Mr. Beauclerk, who became estranged by the gayer attractions of more fashionable clubs; and next by the retirement of Sir John Hawkins." This was omitted in 1840. The rest of the paragraph is a revision of 1840 (99). See 1825 (31). Compare Forster (496–97); Boswell (V, 62).

213.6 Sir William Jones] Sir William Jones, lawyer and orientalist, was knighted in 1783. Jones is mentioned in 1825 (30) as having been elected to the Club, but his name does not appear in 1840. Compare Forster (649–50).

213.18 Bishop of St. Asaph] Dr. Jonathan Shipley (1714–1788), Bishop of St. Asaph, was elected to the Club in November, 1780. For the quotation see Forster (272).

213.31 social qualities] In 1825 (30) Boswell's election is merely mentioned. In 1840 (99) Boswell "was admitted into it some few years after its institution...." This paragraph was added in 1849. Compare Forster (650–51). See Introduction, p. xxvii.

213.33 the Adelphi] The Adelphi was a housing project on the north bank of the Thames, built by the Adam brothers in 1769.

214.8 Johnson himself] Compare 1825 (32). See Boswell (II, 223–24, 227–28); Forster (652–53).

214.9 quiet humor,"] Boswell (I, 318) speaks of *The Idler* as showing "admirable instances of grave humour, of which he had an uncommon share."

214.18–19 of the lexicographer]   Compare 1825 (33). See Boswell (II, 228); Forster (653).

214.22 Launcelot Gobbo]   Launcelot Gobbo is the clown in Shakespeare's *The Merchant of Venice*. Irving probably meant Launce, the clown in *Two Gentlemen of Verona*, who soliloquizes on his dog Crab (II, iii and IV, iv).

215.8 at the Dillys]   Charles Dilly (1739–1807) and Edward Dilly (1732–1779) were publishers; a third brother, John (1731–1806), was not directly connected with his brothers' business. The Dillys dealt liberally with authors. The Poultry, originally a street for poulterers, extended from Cheapside to Cornhill.

215.12 of this work."]   See Boswell (II, 229). Compare Prior (II, 363).

215.23 others do not."]   The incident is recorded in Boswell (II, 232–33). This and the next paragraph were added in 1849. Compare Prior (II, 453–54).

215.37 Mr. Toplady]   Augustus Montague Toplady (1740–1778), a clergyman of the Church of England, wrote the hymn "Rock of Ages."

216.30-31 another engagement]   The anecdote appears in 1825 (37) and 1840 (102–103). Compare Boswell (II, 233–41); Prior (II, 454–58).

216.43 empty purse."]   This paragraph was added in 1849. See Boswell (II, 241).

217.12 take ill!"]   In 1840 (102–103) the paragraph ends at this point. In 1825 (37) the paragraph continues the Boswell passage: "And so at once the difference was over; they were on as easy terms as ever, and Goldsmith rattled away as usual."

217.22 a republic."]   This quotation appears in 1825 (37–38) but not in 1840. See Boswell (II, 241–42); Prior (II, 460); Forster (531).

217.25 George Michael Moser]   George Michael Moser (1704–1783), goldchaser, medalist, and enameller, was the first keeper of the Royal Academy. Following Boswell (II, 242) in 1825 (38), Irving calls Moser "a German"; following Prior (II, 459) in 1840 (103), he refers to him as "a Swiss."

217.29 what he says?"]   This final question, which appears in 1840 (103), was omitted in 1825 (38) as it is in Boswell (II, 242). Prior (II, 459–60) attributes the final question to a second similar incident. Forster (531) indicates that Miss Reynolds's recollection of the incident included the final question.

218.2 commit suicide."]   This anecdote, which was added in 1849, is from Boswell's *Tour to the Hebrides*. See Boswell (II, 330). Compare Forster (442).

218.11 and Hebrides."] This anecdote was added in 1849. See Boswell (II, 244–45). Compare Forster (659).

218.15 Dr. Wolcot] John Wolcot (1738–1819), both a medical doctor and a clergyman, wrote satires under the pseudonym of Peter Pindar. The following verses are from his "A Poetical and Congratulatory Epistle to James Boswell, Esq. on His Journal of a Tour to the Hebrides," lines 1–6, 233–40.

219.6 money gone] Compare 183.20–21.

219.24 of his style] Compare 1840 (175–76) and 1825 (51). See Percy (112–13); Prior (II, 427–29); Forster (661–62).

219.27–28 are remarkable] This sentence, without reference to Bishop Percy, appears in 1840 (176). The following sentence was added in 1849. Compare 1825 (51): "So much had he this project at heart,—so sanguine was he of its success,—and so little doubt did he entertain of encouragement from the booksellers, that without previous concert with any one of the trade, he actually printed and published the *Prospectus* at his own expense." Compare Percy (112–13); Prior (II, 429–30); Forster (662).

219.38 been acquainted."] Compare 1840 (176): "Unfortunately, the booksellers, intimidated by the amount of capital required and the length of time that must expire before the work could be prepared for publication, shrunk from engaging in the undertaking, distrusting, perhaps, his steadfast application, and doubting his capacity for a work which required extent and accuracy of knowledge rather than fertility of genius." Compare 1825 (51): "These gentlemen, however, were not, at that time, disposed to enter upon so heavy an undertaking, and of course received his proposals so coldly, that he found himself obliged to abandon the design. It is supposed that he had fondly promised himself relief from his pecuniary difficulties by this scheme, and consequently his chagrin at the disappointment was the more keenly felt. He frequently lamented the circumstance to his friends; and there is little doubt that it contributed, with other vexations, to aggravate the disease which ended in his dissolution." Compare Prior (II, 430–31); Forster (671).

220.20 their own share] This anecdote, which was added in 1849, is found in Cradock's *Memoirs* (IV, 285–86). Percy (83, 111) does not mention the incident. Compare Prior (II, 437–38); Forster (662).

220.22–23 some literary ladies] This anecdote, which was added in 1849, is found in Prior (II, 437–38).

220.27 Gibbon] Edward Gibbon (1734–1794), English historian, wrote *The Decline and Fall of the Roman Empire* (1776–1788).

220.33 name, Porus] Alexander the Great (356–323 B.C.), king of Macedonia, defeated Porus, king of India, at Hydaspes (ca. 331 B.C.).

Montezuma II (1466–1520) was the last Mexican emperor. The anecdote, which was added in 1849, was told by Prior (II, 434–35), who
said that he had received it from Dawson Turner. Prior points out that
Gibbon did not appear publicly as a historian until after Goldsmith's
death. Compare Forster (603–604).

221.9 to remain]   Compare 1840 (176) "The failure of this project, on
which he had built such spacious hopes, sank deep in the heart of
Goldsmith; he was still farther grieved and mortified by the fruitless
result of an effort made by some of his friends to secure him a provision from government; with flagging spirits, therefore, he returned
to his irksome toil of 'book-building. . . .' " Compare Prior (II, 442–43);
Forster (665).

221.10 Dr. Beattie]   James Beattie (1735–1803) was a Scottish poet and
essayist. His "Essay on Truth" was published in 1770. This paragraph
was added in 1849. Compare Prior (II, 470–71); Forster (665–66).

221.27–28 to be resisted]   This anecdote, which was added in 1849,
appears in Mrs. Piozzi's Anecdotes of Johnson, p. 179.

221.32 ill-natured."]   This paragraph was added in 1849. Compare
Forster (666).

221.38 portrait of Beattie]   The picture, "Dr. Beattie Triumphing over
Infidelity," was exhibited in 1774. See Prior (II, 470).

222.9 of their intercourse]   This paragraph was added in 1849. See
James Northcote, The Life of Sir Joshua Reynolds, LL D. F.R.S. F.S.A.
&c. Late President of the Royal Academy, Comprising Original Anec-
dotes of Many Distinguished Persons, His Contemporaries; and a Brief
Analysis of His Discourses, 2d ed., 2 vols. (London, 1818), I, 300.
Compare Prior (II, 470–71); Forster (666–68).

223.11 original composition]   Compare 1840 (176–77). The balance of
the paragraph is the same in 1840 (177).

223.28 the players."]   This anecdote was added in 1849. Compare
Forster (527).

224.1–2 of the gardeners]   This paragraph was added in 1849. Compare Prior (II, 368–69); Forster (591).

224.7 story of Ugolino]   The story is told in Dante's Inferno, Canto
xxxiii. In 1825 (43) a quotation from Cumberland includes the statement: "From Goldsmith he caught the subject of his famous Ugolino.
. . ." This paragraph was added in 1849. Compare Forster (667).

224.22 extacy of admiration."°]   See Works (II, 294). Irving added
this paragraph in 1849. Compare Forster (674–76).

225.6 arts and sciences.' "]   This and the preceding two paragraphs
were added in 1849. Compare Prior (II, 443–45); Forster (676).

225.38 broken spirited poet]   This and the preceding four paragraphs
were added in 1849. Compare Prior (II, 444–45); Forster (676–77).

225.40 Mrs. Yates] See note 177.15.

226.4 brilliant audience] This paragraph was added in 1849. Compare Prior (II, 488–90); Forster (669–70).

226.6–7 Christmas invitation] See note 190.38.

226.21–22 own acceptance] This paragraph was added in 1849. Compare Forster (672–73).

226.23 reply of Goldsmith] Balderston (*Letters*, 127) dates this letter December 25, 1773. This and the next paragraph were added in 1849. Compare Prior (II, 439–40); Forster (674).

227.18 Scarron] Paul Scarron (1610–1660), French writer, published his *Le Roman comique* in 1651–1657.

227.19 heart faint] The paragraph to this point is a revision of 1840 (176–77). Compare Prior (II, 487); Forster (681–82).

227.25 light in comparison."] The quotation is from Scott's biographical essay "Charlotte Smith," *Biographical Memoirs* (*The Miscellaneous Prose Works of Sir Walter Scott, Bart.* [Edinburgh, 1827], IV, 61–62).

227.29 have no time."] This quotation appears in 1840 (180). Compare Prior (II, 510); Forster (572). The rest of the paragraph was added in 1849. Compare Forster (676).

228.1–2 intended rebuke] This paragraph was added in 1840 (180). Compare Prior (II, 511); Forster (682).

228.13 in a blaze] This paragraph was adapted from 1840 (180–81). Compare Prior (II, 512–13).

228.23 like poor poll.] Compare 1840 (177–78), which contains slight variations. In 1825 (50–51) Irving quoted a long passage from Cumberland's *Memoirs* (I, 369–71). Forster (677) labels Cumberland's version as "pure romance." See also Prior (II, 490–93).

228.29 good humored raillery] Compare 1825 (51); 1840 (178), which has slight variations. The rest of the paragraph was added in 1849. Compare Forster (678–79).

229.9 than caustic] The paragraph, with slight revisions, and the following verses appear in 1840 (178–79).

229.32 Woodfalls] Henry Sampson Woodfall (1739–1805), English printer and journalist, was the publisher of the Junius letters. His brother William (1746–1803) and his son George (1767–1844) were associated with him in business.

229.35 be-Rosciused] Quintus Roscius Gallus (d. 623 B.C.) was a popular actor in Rome.

229.41 Beaumonts and Bens] Sir Francis Beaumont (ca. 1584–1616), an English playwright, was a friend of Ben Jonson, one of the outstanding playwrights of his day.

230.21 sport here.] The verses and the preceding three lines appear in

1840 (179). Compare Prior (II, 498). See *Works* (IV, 358, lines 137–46).

231.5 was the case."]   This paragraph was added in 1849. The quotation is from Prior (II, 356), who attributes it to "a surviving friend." In 1825 Irving makes a good deal of Goldsmith's gambling. For example: "It happened, unfortunately for Goldsmith, that one of his most dangerous propensities met with too much encouragement during his stay in Holland. The people of that country are much addicted to games of chance. Gaming tables are to be met with in every tavern, and at every place of amusement. Goldsmith, unable to resist the contagion of example, with his usual facility sailed with the stream; and fortune, according to custom, alternately greeted him with smiles and frowns" (14). Prior (II, 354–57) included a lengthy defense of Goldsmith against the accusation and points out that Boswell, Johnson, or Reynolds never made such a charge. Compare Forster (445, 573–75).

231.20 Corregios]   Antonio Allegri da Correggio (ca. 1494–1534) was an Italian painter.

231.21 shifted his trumpet]   Sir Joshua used an ear trumpet for his deafness. See *Works* (IV, 359, n. 1). These verses were added in 1849. Compare Forster (681).

231.24 a local complaint]   Compare 1825 (51): "Goldsmith had been, for some years, occasionally afflicted with a strangury." See Percy (113). In 1840 (180–81) Irving wrote: "... the recurrence of a painful disease...." These words are verbatim from Prior (II, 513). For Forster (683) the disease was "a local disorder."

231.30 Sir Charles Bunbury]   See note 139.35.

232.7 of his age]   The paragraph is an expanded version of one in 1840 (180–81). In 1825 (51–52) Irving devoted five paragraphs to Goldsmith's illness and death. Compare Percy (113–15); Prior (II, 513–18); Forster (683–88).

232.13 family distress]   See 1840 (181). Compare Prior (II, 518–19); Forster (688–89).

232.17 feeling of despondency."]   The quotation from M'Donnell appears in 1840 (161). See Prior (II, 347).

232.23–24 so trusted before?"]   The quotation from Boswell (III, 122) appears in 1825 (52) and 1840 (181), but not in Percy.

232.29 every farthing."]   Compare Prior (II, 232–35).

232.35 when he can."]   Compare Prior (II, 521–22). The paragraph was added in 1849.

232.39 with poverty]   This paragraph was added in 1849. Compare Forster (689).

233.4 thus cherished!]   Irving added this paragraph in 1849. Compare Prior (II, 520–21); Forster (689–90).

233.6 Hazlitt] William Hazlitt (1778–1830) was an English critic and essayist.

233.20 Ninon de l'Enclos' people] Ninon de Lenclos or Anne de Lanclos (1620–1705) was a celebrated French courtesan who entertained people of the highest society and of the literary world. She is said to have shown interest in the child Voltaire, whose father was her lawyer.

233.21–22 with complacency."] This quotation, which was added in 1849, seems to have been taken directly from William Hazlitt, *Conversations of James Northcote Esq. R. A.* (London, 1949), pp. 61–62. Irving's version shows a few slight variations. Forster (501) paraphrased the account.

233.26 grace to each."] Hazlitt (62). The balance of the paragraph reflects Irving's own thinking. In his revised edition Forster (III, 151–52) was critical of these remarks. Compare note 140.31.

234.6 Lord Lowth] In 1825 (52), presumably following *The European Magazine* 24 (October, 1793), 258, Irving spelled the name Louth. In 1840 (182) it is spelled Lowth as it is in Prior (II, 520) and Forster (690). According to *DNB*, Robert Lowth or Louth (1710–1787) was appointed professor of poetry at Oxford in 1741. In 1777 he became bishop of London.

234.14–15 Dean of Cashel] This sentence was added in 1849. Compare Forster (690). The balance of the paragraph and the following verses were added in 1840 (182). Compare Prior (II, 520). For the verses see *The European Magazine* 24 (October, 1793), 258.

235.5 for the man] This and the preceding paragraph were added in 1840. Compare Prior (II, 532). See also 1825 (52).

235.8 Nollekens] Joseph Nollekens, R.A. (1737–1823) was an English sculptor who also did busts of Garrick and Sterne.

235.11 of Gay and the Duke of Argyll] John Gay (1685–1732), English poet. John Campbell, second duke of Argyll and duke of Greenwich (1678–1743). In 1968 the present editor found that John Gay's memorial had been moved to the triforum and that a bust of Sir Walter Scott was placed between the Goldsmith and the Argyll plaques.

235.19 so lasting an ornament."] According to Prior (II, 529), this passage is from the committee's request to Johnson, which was dictated by Edmund Burke and written by Sir William Forbes. Compare 1840 (183) and 1825 (53).

235.29 Joe Warton] Joseph Warton (1722–1800) was an English critic. This entire paragraph was added in 1849. Compare Forster (691–93).

236.18 embalmed to perpetuity] The paragraph to this point was added in 1840 (184–85).

236.21; 237.1 father to the man,"] Compare William Wordsworth's

"My Heart Leaps up" (line 7). See also Boswell (I, 22), who said of Johnson: "In short, he is a memorable instance of what has been often observed, that the boy is the man in miniature. . . ." This paragraph and the next fifteen were added in 1849.

236.22 of Boswell's Johnson] This is the translation in Forster (704). In 1840 (184) this line reads: "The following translation to the above is from Prior's life of Goldsmith." See Prior (II, 527–28). The two translations differ. In 1825 (53) Irving did not include a translation.

238.27 attended his gate."] This and the following quotation are from Goldsmith's *The Life of Richard Nash.* See *Works* (III, 391, 320).

239.2 touch of vulgarity?"] In a review of Forster's *The Life and Adventures of Oliver Goldsmith* in the *Edinburgh Review* 88 (July, 1848), 207. The review was written by Edward Bulwer, Lord Lytton. See his *Miscellaneous Prose Works* (London, 1868), I, 51–94.

239.36 worthy to do it."] See Prior (II, 296).

240.28 atmosphere of home."] From the review (211) mentioned in note 239.2.

240.42 a former occasion] Irving refers to the 1825 essay (56): "Such is the amount of information which we have procured concerning Goldsmith; and we have given it almost precisely in the words in which we found it. From the general tenor of his biography, it is evident that Goldsmith was one whose faults were at the worst but negative, not positive vices, while his merits were great and decided. He was no one's enemy but his own, his errors inflicted evil on none but himself, and were so blended with humorous, and even affecting circumstances, as to disarm anger and conciliate kindness. Where eminent talent is united to spotless virtue, we are awed and dazzled into admiration, but our admiration is apt to be cold; while there is something in the harmless infirmities of poor human nature that pleads touchingly to the feelings, and the heart yearns towards the object of our admiration, when we find that, like ourselves, he is mortal, and is frail." The balance of the paragraph is the same as in 1849. The 1840 conclusion (185–86) conforms to the 1849.

TEXTUAL COMMENTARY

In the effort to arrive at a critical text of *Oliver Goldsmith* that will come as near as possible to reproducing Irving's intention, the editor adopts W. W. Greg's theory of copy-text[1] as a useful device on the basis of which to construct a rationale for making editorial decisions on both substantives and accidentals.[2] Ideally, the manuscript that was used as printer's copy (or author-corrected proof sheets, if they survive) provides copy-text; when neither is extant, the printed version nearest the author's manuscript is chosen. Since in the case of *Oliver Goldsmith* the manuscript, twenty-eight author-corrected proof sheets, and a letter from the author to the publisher requesting ten corrections in the first edition survive, it might be supposed that the manuscript could unqualifiedly be regarded as copy-text. However, because of the haste with which Irving wrote *Goldsmith,* he did not produce fair-copy manuscript but rather what must be regarded as a next-to-final stage in composition. His known habit of altering his text right up to the last minute on proof sheets requires that, on pages for which proof sheets have not survived, every substantive variation between manuscript and first edition be judged on its merits. Furthermore, although theoretically the earliest text, being closest to the author's hand, will come nearest to the author's intention in accidentals, the rough state of the manuscript, which contains many careless errors and many omissions of needed punctuation marks, requires that weight be given to the first edition (49a) in this respect.

PRECOPY TEXTS

Before writing *Oliver Goldsmith* in 1849, Irving had published two earlier essays on the same subject. The first, a 128-page introduction to a four-volume edition of Goldsmith's works, was published in Paris by

1. The theory is explained in "The Rationale of Copy-Text," *Studies in Bibliography* 3 (1950–1951), 19–36, and is applied to editions of nineteenth-century American authors by the *Statement of Editorial Principles* . . . prepared by the Center for Editions of American Authors, Modern Language Association of America, July, 1967. The terminology used is Fredson Bowers' as set forth in his *Principles of Bibliographical Description* (Princeton, 1949).

2. Here and in the sequel, textual variants are classified as substantives when they affect meaning (i.e., word change) and as accidentals when they affect form (e.g., spelling and punctuation).

Galignani in 1825. There is no extant manuscript for this essay. Although Irving used it as the basis of a greatly revised and enlarged second essay in 1840, it has no textual significance for the 1849 biography. It has, however, proved invaluable for tracing the historical development of the final work; and many passages from this 1825 essay have been quoted in the Explanatory Notes to illustrate the development.

The second precopy essay was prepared as an introduction to a two-volume edition of Goldsmith's works, published by the Harper Brothers in New York in 1840. There is no extant manuscript for this 186-page essay. Using the 1825 version as a basis for the second essay, Irving altered it substantially by adding material from James Prior's recently published *The Life of Oliver Goldsmith, M. B. from a Variety of Original Sources.*[3] Again the 1840 essay contributes to an understanding of the historical development of the final biography, and many passages have been reproduced in the Explanatory Notes to illustrate changes. The textual significance of the second essay lies only in the fact that, when Irving prepared his final 1849 biography, he cut out large passages from his 1840 work and transferred them bodily to the new manuscript. Thus, when he incorporated them into the new manuscript, they became an integral part of it and ceased to belong to the earlier essay.

THE MANUSCRIPT

The manuscript[4] which became Irving's full-scale biography of Oliver Goldsmith fills two folio volumes bound in gold-tooled brown morocco. The sheets of manuscript measure 4 3/8 x 7 inches of rag paper, and are laid in pages measuring 8 1/2 x 11 inches. The text, covering both recto and verso of the pages, consists of holograph in ink mingled with portions of the earlier printed essay Irving published in 1840 and other printed passages taken from several sources.

The inside front cover of the first volume has mounted the small leather bookplate of Robert Hoe bearing a gold shield in the heart of an adorned machine, apparently a printing press, the decorative flourishes as well as the words "EX LIBRIS ROBERT HOE" printed in gold. The pages are numbered in the two volumes through 513. There are five additional leaves of a "preface," all in holograph. Volume I contains a frontispiece engraving of Irving by J. Sartain from a portrait by Gilbert

3. London: John Murray, 1837
4. Because the manuscript consists of both printed and handwritten passages, in most references to it a distinction has been made between them by the use of the following symbols: MSh for handwritten portions and MSp for printed portions. A key to identifying symbols used in referring to the manuscript and editions of *Oliver Goldsmith*, as well as to Irving's sources, is given on pages 347-48.

Stuart Newton, and pages i–v, 1–262. Volume II contains a frontispiece engraving of Goldsmith by Abm. [Abraham] Wivell from a portrait by Sir Joshua Reynolds, and pages 263–513.

In describing the manuscript William R. Langfeld said that the two volumes "contain 512 pages, of which approximately 175 are partially or entirely in type. Apparently in preparing the work, Irving inserted in his manuscript the printed portions of the earlier life which he retained, and supplied the additions and revisions in script."[5] Although this is essentially correct, the printed portions which Irving used in the manuscript are not all from the 1840 *Life*. At least twelve passages, ranging in length from a single paragraph to four or five pages, were taken bodily from John Forster's *The Life and Adventures of Oliver Goldsmith*. These passages are excerpts from Goldsmith's works and letters, and several anecdotes about Goldsmith which Forster took from other sources.[6] Several other passages, not traced in Forster and not included in the earlier essay, may have been taken from other original sources: notably MS, p. 428, which contains an extract from Boswell's *Life of Johnson*; MS, pp. 300–302, which contain a passage from Goldsmith's *Animated Nature*; and MS, p. 411, containing a squib traced to Prior (II, 405).

The eclectic nature of the printed parts of the manuscript creates the first of a number of problems for the textual editor. They represent several different house styles, which are not consistent with each other. There are even inconsistencies in the Forster passages, some of which, for example, place a quotation mark at the beginning of each line of a quotation (e.g., MS 60, 138, 272), and some of which do not (e.g., MS 105, 371). Irving seldom made changes in the printed texts, though next to one of the Forster passages (MS 352), which contains a number of italicized phrases, he wrote, "Not to be printed in italics." In general, English spelling is maintained in MSp, though one finds occasional double usages, such as "abridgment / abridgement." The passages in MSp are much more highly pointed than those in MSh.

Approximately two-thirds of the manuscript is in Irving's handwriting, and in this portion there is not always consistency within itself and very little with the various printed passages. Irving typically wrote a small crabbed hand, often close to unreadable or open to several alternate readings. His *Goldsmith* manuscript contains innumerable instances of these difficulties. The vowels are particularly difficult to decipher, since

5. William R. Langfeld, comp., *Washington Irving: A Bibliography* (New York: The New York Public Library, 1933), p. 39.

6. London, 1848. See, e.g., MS, pp. 60, 105–8, 138, 272, 351–52, 397–99, 403, 413, 415, 436.

in many passages all of them look alike. Did Irving, for example, write "on time" or "in time" in MSh 339? His habit of lifting his pen before reaching the end of a word causes a problem for his reader in determining whether words like "newspaper" and "fireworks" were intended to be one or two words. In forming the letter *d* he brought his pen up to make the stem of the letter and then drew back and over the letter itself, and this technique required him to lift his pen before continuing, as in "headquarters" and "landlady." Also difficult to interpret are letters whose capital and lowercase forms are similar except in size—e.g., *a, c, m, n*, etc.—but Irving compounded the problem sometimes by simply enlarging a lowercase letter (e.g., *g*) and making it do for a capital. Yet the size of a letter is not always a clear index, for he often wrote initial letters in a larger script without intending the uppercase form. He rarely used hyphens and apostrophes; and there appears to be no rationale for his use of capitalization, though here again it is often difficult to determine his intention from his handwriting. In words like "own" and "awkward" he usually wrote what looks like a *u* instead of a *w*; words ending with *ll* (e.g., "tell," "will") usually carry the second *l* at lower height. Such are the hazards resting in Irving's holograph for a present-day reader and editor.

In addition to Irving's peculiarities of handwriting MSh is marked by other factors that create problems for the editor. Although Irving was by this time committed to American spelling, the force of habit allowed many English spellings to creep in (e.g., "centre" and "connexion"); and sometimes he used two forms interchangeably (e.g., "endeavor / endeavour"). Certain words he consistently misspelled (e.g., "perceive" and "recollection"). Indeed, a linguist might find his spelling often instructive of his pronunciation. He wrote "sarface" for "surface," "Hempstead" for "Hampstead," "vartues" for "virtues," and "desarted" for "deserted." Although his punctuation tends to be chaotic in some respects, it shows a surprisingly high degree of consistency in others.

Such is the manuscript that was submitted piecemeal to the publisher. Irving knew that the first Putnam edition (1849) was designed as a volume to be included in the Author's Revised Edition. As such, it was set in conformity to Putnam's house style in general and to the entire edition of Irving's works then in process of publication. Although American spelling forms were adopted, in a few instances both the English and American forms were used. Irving's spelling errors were corrected and his omitted punctuation marks supplied. The most radical changes appeared in punctuation, the first edition being much more highly pointed than the handwritten parts of the manuscript and sometimes differently pointed from the printed parts.

The surviving galley sheets give evidence that Irving read proof for this volume. Following are the manuscript pages covered by the galleys (with corresponding pages in the Twayne edition in parentheses): 1–4 (Preface) (3–4); 35 (21–22); 39 (27); 40 (28); 52 (35); 53 (35); 54 (36); 67 (43); 79 (47); 87 (51); 88 (51–52); 147 (two sheets, one a regular proof sheet, the other a handwritten addition) (81); 148–50 (81–82); 219–20 (112–13); 226–28 (116–17); 270–72 (132–33); 279 (135–36); 357 (172–73); 366 (177); 389 (187); 391 (188); 395 (190–91); 426–27 (207); 428–30 (207–209); 442–43 (213–14); 478–81 (227–28); 490–92 (233). These proof sheets were bound in with the illustrated 53 impression. Copies of all but two of them (those for MS, pp. 35, 279) were also preserved with the manuscript. These two have not been located elsewhere.

The revisions which Irving made on the proof sheets are instructive. Six of the proofs represent the first page of chapters, for two of which he supplied only chapter headings and for the other four both chapter headings and revisions. The majority of the changes he requested represent additions of, or changes in, words, phrases, or longer passages. He corrected several typographical errors, changed one comma and two capital letters to lowercase, and crossed out quotation marks around the title of a play. Aside from these, he indicated no changes in accidentals.

One of the galleys contains a comment that may throw light on Irving's method of proofreading. This comment is, in fact, a gloss on the word "restlessness" (136.4). In the proof sheet the word appears as "worldliness." Irving crossed it out and wrote in the margin: "look at the MS. the word cannot be worldliness it may be restlessness." If this instance can be regarded as typical, he corrected proofs without reading them against copy, relied on his memory to correct obvious errors, and made other changes to polish his work.

With only twenty-eight proof sheets to judge from, one cannot be certain of the number and kinds of revisions Irving requested for the remaining pages of the volume. Yet the few changes in accidentals indicated on the extant proofs suggest that he was much more preoccupied with substantives. Of the many printed pages in MS only one contains a change in punctuation—a semicolon added in ink (MS, p. 133). Irving's apparent willingness to accept the accidentals in the extant galley sheets, excepting the half dozen changes mentioned, and the fact that revisions effected after the first impression were almost all substantive in nature imply that he was satisfied with the printer's accidentals.

Nevertheless, one must be wary about coming to such a conclusion. Early in his career as a writer Irving indicated his awareness that his manuscripts were not easy to read. In a letter to his friend Henry Brevoort, dated March 3, 1819, concerning the first section of *The Sketch*

Book, he wrote: "If the work is printed in N York will you correct
the proof sheets, as I fear the Mss: will be obscure & occasionally incorrect, & you are well acquainted with my handwriting."[7] Despite his
lack of self-confidence, Irving at this time had a clear idea of what he
thought punctuation ought to be, for on July 28 of the same year
after he had seen the first number in print, he again wrote to Brevoort:
"I would observe that the work appears to be a little too *highly* pointed.
I don't know whether my manuscript was so, or whether it is the scrupulous precision of the printer—high pointing is apt to injure the fluency
of the style if the reader attends to all the stops."[8] As a stylist, he was
concerned with the flow of his sentences, which too much pointing
would impede.

A study of the handwritten portions of the *Goldsmith* manuscript
reveals that Irving was actually ahead of his time in minimizing punctuation. It is true that he too often carelessly omitted such marks as
end punctuation, the period after abbreviations, and one of a pair of
commas; on the other hand, he rarely punctuated such constructions as
parallel elements, prepositional phrases, or restrictive modifiers. Though
thirty years had passed since he expressed his views on the subject to
Brevoort, this manuscript shows clearly that he still preferred under-
pointing.

Why then did Irving allow Putnam's excessive use of punctuation to
go unchallenged? Perhaps his extreme diffidence prevented him from
bucking the establishment; yet, as Henry A. Pochmann pointed out,
his failure to challenge accidentals in proofs does not necessarily
mean that he "approved every detail of the Putnam house style or that,
if he had been required to present perfect copy, he would have used
precisely the forms adopted by the printers."[9] He seems to have followed
the line of least resistance as long as the printer honored his choice of
substantives. In the case of *Goldsmith,* moreover, he wrote the book
much too fast to concern himself with such matters.

In the Twayne edition MS has, in general, been followed in accidentals.
However, where Irving omits needful punctuation and where his omissions or use of punctuation creates awkwardness or misreading, 49a
has been preferred. In spelling, errors have been corrected and American forms adopted as they were in 49a. A special situation exists in the
many direct quotations which Irving included from his sources, most of
them published in England. Often the printer indiscriminately changed

7. *The Letters of Washington Irving to Henry Brevoort,* ed. George S. Hellman
(New York, 1915), II, 87.

8. *Ibid.,* II, 101.

9. In *Mahomet and His Successors,* ed. Henry A. Pochmann and E. N. Feltskog
(Madison, Wisc., 1970), p. 572.

the quotations to conform to the Putnam house style. Where Irving copied his source correctly but Putnam changed it, MS reading has been adopted. Where Irving did not copy his source correctly but the Putnam change conforms to the source, the latter form has been adopted. Where neither MS nor the first edition conforms to the source, MS reading has been followed.

The question of substantives also poses serious problems for the editor. Probably one reason for the many variations between MS and 49a is the speed with which Irving wrote the book. Within two months from the day he conceived the idea of enlarging his 1840 essay, he was turning in copy to the publisher; and he complained of the pressures being put upon him by the printer to supply copy faster than he was able to do.[10] Such demands on the part of the printer would have left him little chance to revise his manuscript as carefully as he might have done had he been able to prepare it in more leisurely fashion, and thus it required more than his usual amount of "re-dressing" in the proof-sheet stage. As Dr. Pochmann succinctly explained: "Almost from the beginning of Irving's long literary career he held to the practice of making last-minute alterations in the proofs. This is what he called correcting the proof sheets, including what he also called re-dressing, that is, more than merely substituting the single word, which he said had sometimes great effect, however 'hard to hit' it might be, but altering and inserting new matter."[11]

The problem for the editor is to decide which variations are valid and which are not. The sheaf of available proof sheets indicates that many revisions were made, eleven of the twenty-eight galleys containing corrections or additions in varying degrees. Whether the many other variations represent last-minute authorial revisions on the missing proof sheets or whether they are printer's errors or alterations can be determined only after a consideration of each one individually from several points of view: the legibility of the handwriting in the manuscript, the context in which the variation occurs, the degree of revision, and the likelihood that the change was made by the author.

THE TEXT[12]

Putnam's first impression of 2,500 copies was set and stereotyped by John F. Trow ("Printer and Stereotyper, 49 Ann-street, New-York"), a

10. See Explanatory Notes, 3.28–29.
11. *Mahomet and His Successors*, p. 595.
12. A key to identifying symbols used in referring to the manuscript and editions of *Oliver Goldsmith*, as well as to Irving's sources, is given on pages 347–48.

duplicate set of plates presumably being made at the same time and shipped to John Murray and printed for Murray by Clowes. Murray paid £52.13.8 to Putnam for the set and later £–.13.6 for Clowes to correct some plates. According to Ben Harris McClary, it appeared "as both a hard-back issue and a title in Murray's Home and Colonial Library."[13]

Murray made four changes in the plates: "lest the book / lest the work" (169.11); "but in late years / only of late years" (190.39); "through more difficulties / through greater difficulties" (196.25); "New actors / Now actors" (199.5). He corrected ten errors, which were also corrected in later American impressions, but missed a number of others.

On August 25, 1849, Irving wrote a letter to Putnam requesting ten corrections be made.[14] By September 19, according to Pierre M. Irving, the first impression of 2,500 copies (49a) had been sold, and a second of 2,000 was being prepared (49b).[15] In 49b nine of the indicated errors were corrected: "cicumstantial" / "circumstantial" (3.33); "most" / "almost" (97.25); "Foster's" / "Forster's" (112.42); "love all" / "love of all" (173.2); "1722" / "1772" (174.31); "idem volle" / "idem nolle" (175.39); "Augustales" / "Augustalis" (177.27); "made wrong" / "made weary" (227.19); "features" / "pictures" (239.10). The tenth change that Irving requested was not really an error but rather a poorly inked letter. This appears at 200.9–10 in the phrase "thought of," the final *f* appearing to be an *r* in 49a. In later impressions the form is correct. Besides these requested changes three others were made: *"un-ideal"* / *"un-idea'd"* (92.34); "Shannon" / "Channel" (150.35); "conversational" / "conventional" (186.5). These variations, for which no written authorization has been found, are dealt with in the Discussions of Adopted Readings.

49c is an illustrated edition, only the table of contents having been reset to make room for pen drawings by W. Roberts. All changes noted in 49b also appear in 49c with the exception of the word "conversational" (186.5), which remains. In addition, nine variations occurred in the reset table of contents, eight of them being in accidentals and the ninth a reduction of the four lines under Chapter V (ix.22–26) to "Tour in Holland.—Sojourn in Paris."

In 50, twenty-two new variations occurred, fourteen of which were corrections of misspellings and other errors and the supplying of missing words. For the other changes there is indirect evidence of authorial sanction, for they were probably made as the result of criticisms in a

---

13. *Washington Irving and the House of Murray: Geoffrey Crayon Charms the British, 1817–1856*, ed. Ben Harris McClary (Knoxville, Tenn., 1969), p. 190.

14. The original is in the possession of Sleepy Hollow Restorations.

15. Pierre M. Irving, *The Life and Letters of Washington Irving* (New York, 1869), III, 165.

review published in *The Gentleman's Magazine*.[16] They are as follows: "solitary" / "melancholly" (97.39); "Gosford" / "Gosfield" (101.28); "the noble seat" / "the seat" (101.28); "his noble seat" / "his seat" (165.4); "Gosford" / "Gosfield" (165.4); "a Mr. Harris" / "Mr. Harris" (209.20); "pronoctant" / "pernoctant" (178.25); "perigrinantur" / "peregrinantur" (178.25).

Like 49c, 53 is an illustrated edition with pen drawings by W. Roberts. Eighteen new variations appear, four of which are substantive: "outset" / "onset" (ix.17); "Reduced again to" / "reduced to" (xi.14); "Grief of his" / "grief–his" (xii.37); "time was" / "time had" (23.5).

In 59, which is a reimpression of ARE except that pages 138, 284, and 381–82 are reset, one important substantive variation appears: "death" / "illness" (43.9). There is no evidence that Irving requested this change, but it corrects an error not heretofore noticed. In 60, which is a reimpression of 59, four new substantive variations occurred: "1747" / "1745" (14.8); "1775" / "1755" (39.1); "women" / "woman" (161.21); "of his" / "of her" (183.25). These later variations are dealt with in the Discussions of Adopted Readings.

The manuscript and all authorized editions (Putnam and Murray) published during Irving's lifetime were collated according to the following pattern:

1. Two sight collations of MS with the first Putnam impression (49a)
2. One machine collation of 49a with E, the first (and only) Murray impression
3. Two sight collations of 49a with 49b
4. One machine collation of 49a with another 49a (Peabody)
5. One machine collation and one sight collation of 49a with 49c
6. One machine collation of 49a with 50
7. One sight collation of 49a with 51 (NYPL)
8. One machine collation of 50 with 51 (Duke)
9. Two sight collations of 49a with 53
10. One machine collation of 50 with 54
11. One sight collation of cruces only of 49a with 55
12. One machine collation of 49a with 59
13. One machine collation of 49a with 60 (Haverford)
14. Two sight collations of 49a with 60 (Columbia)[17]

16. N.s. 32 (December, 1849), 617–20.

17. Copies for these collations are recorded by library name and call number, or name of the present owner, together with whatever identifying marks can be noted: (1) MS (NYPL) *vs.* Elsie Lee West's copy of Putnam's first impression of 1849, uncataloged, with a printed bookplate bearing the legend, "The property of William Crowninshield Endicott" on the verso of the cover and the name "Wm. C. Endicott" written in ink on the recto of the first flyleaf; (2) West copy *vs.* Univer-

TREATMENT OF SUBSTANTIVES

To determine the authenticity of the many variations in substantives between manuscript and first edition, the editor has only one piece of evidence in documentary form: the twenty-eight surviving proof sheets. These account for only a miniscule number in comparison to the total: about fifteen variations of single words and phrases, and a dozen longer passages added in handwriting to the printed proofs.

A detailed analysis of the first proof sheet, which covers MS, pp. 1–5 and constitutes the Preface, will serve to illustrate the various kinds of changes Irving made. The printer omitted the phrase "to a selection" (3.4); Irving inserted a caret after the word "introductory" and wrote the phrase in the margin. Also omitted was the phrase "in a form" (3.9). In the margin Irving wrote, "in a ⟨manne⟩ ↑form↓." In MS he wrote "manner in which I had to do this . . ." (3.27). On the proof sheet he put a caret after "I" and wrote in the margin "h/." In MS he wrote, "has prevented ⟨my handling⟩ ↑giving↓ some parts of my subject" (3.29).

---

sity of Texas (uncataloged) copy of Murray 1849: 8° (6⅞ x 4½): ⟨A⟩⁸ B–I⁸ K–U⁸ X–Z⁸ 2A⁸, 192 leaves ⟨signed regularly on 1 and 2, 2 with added 2⟩; pp. ⟨i half-title⟩ ⟨ii blank⟩ ⟨iii title⟩ ⟨iv printer⟩ ⟨v preface⟩ vi ⟨vii contents⟩ viii–xv ⟨xvi blank⟩ ⟨17 text⟩ 18–382 ⟨383–384 blank⟩; (3) West copy *vs.* Columbia University 824/G57/BI/1849/v.xi; (4) West copy *vs.* Peabody 928.2/G6241/1849; (5) West copy *vs.* Yale University Im/G574/W84 O he/ 1849; (6) West copy *vs.* Ralph M. Aderman's (uncataloged) 1850 impression: 12° (7¼ x 4⅞): ⟨1⟩¹² 2–16¹² [leaves 1 and 5 signed regularly, 5 with added asterisk] 192 leaves; pp ⟨i series title⟩ ⟨ii blank⟩ ⟨iii title⟩ ⟨iv copyright and printer⟩ ⟨v contents⟩ vi–xiii ⟨xiv blank⟩ ⟨xv–xvi preface⟩ ⟨17 text⟩ 18–382 ⟨383 publisher's ad⟩ ⟨384 blank⟩; (7) West copy *vs.* NYPL 1851 An (Goldsmith,O)/ 1851, v. XI; (8) Aderman (uncataloged) 1850 *vs.* Duke University 823.64/G624Zk/ 1851.

(9) West copy *vs.* NYPL (Seligman Collection) 1853. On the verso of the cover is a small book plate, black with gold design and in gold lettering "Ex libris Robert Hoe." Two loose cards are found in the book. One reads "Irving, Washington/ Oliver Goldsmith, 1853, 4to, green morocco tooled in fillets, gilt top, uncut pages, by William Matthews./ Irving's original manuscript corrections and revisions for the edition printed by G. P. Putnam and company in 1853, bound in with the printed volume." The second card reads: "Irving's own copy of the book, with very numerous autograph corrections and editions. Full morocco. From the collection of Robert Hoe."

(10) Aderman (uncataloged) 1850 *vs.* 1854–University of Michigan 828/G6240/ 17/1854; (11) West copy *vs.* Margaret Brown's (uncataloged) 1855; (12) West copy *vs.* 1859–University of Texas IR/8As/v.11/1859: 12° (7⁹⁄₁₆ x 5) ⟨1⟩¹² 2–16¹² ⟨signed regularly on 1 and 5, 5 with added asterisk, 192 leaves⟩; pp. ⟨a series title⟩ ⟨b blank⟩ ⟨i title⟩ ⟨ii copyright⟩ ⟨iii preface⟩ ⟨iv⟩ ⟨v contents⟩ vi-xiii ⟨xiv blank⟩ ⟨17 text⟩ 18–382 ⟨383–384 blank⟩. Following ⟨b blank⟩ 2 unpaged leaves, containing 2 engravings, are tipped in; (13) West copy *vs.* 1860 Haverford PR/3493/17/1860; (14) West copy *vs.* 1860 Columbia University 812Ir8/I2/1860.

Where the proof sheet reads "has prevented giving some parts of my subject" Irving put a caret after "prevented" and a line through "my"; in the margin he wrote "me from / the." In MS he wrote, "would do well to refer them selves to ⟨the⟩ ⟨circumstantial pages⟩ ↑ ⟨Mr Forsters elaborate⟩ and ↓ ⟨of⟩ Mr Priors ⟨and the⟩ circumstantial volumes or the eloquent and discursive pages of Mr Forster." The proof sheet reads: "would do well to refer themselves to Mr. Prior's cicumstantial volumes, or the elegant and discursive pages of Mr. Forster." Irving inserted a caret after the word "or," but gave no indication of the word to be substituted. He apparently did not notice the misspelled word or the substitution of "elegant" for "eloquent." In 49a (3.32–34) the phrase reads the same as in proof with the exception of the word "to" inserted after "or." The question is: Did Irving notice "elegant" and approve the substitution? Since he did not notice the misspelling nearby, the implication is that he did not see the substitution either. Here the decision has been to restore MS reading. In MS Irving wrote (3.36): "a 'labor of love'; a tribute of gratitude." The printer omitted the single quotation marks. On the proof Irving inserted a caret after the semicolon and wrote in the margin, "for it is." He showed no awareness of the omitted quotation marks (see p. 449). The typesetter had trouble with the three lines of Dante (4.3–5), and on the proof Irving made eight corrections. One error ("du" / "da," line 4) he missed, but it was corrected in 49a.[18] Here on one page of proof, then, are demonstrated the various kinds of problems the editor faces: the typesetter's omissions, substitutions, and mistakes, some of which Irving noticed and some of which he did not; the typesetter's difficulties with the handwriting; Irving's last-minute changes and insertions; and his insertion of a caret without including the word to be added.

The changes which Putnam made to correct outright errors in MS have been adopted. These include repetitions of words or phrases (e.g., "had had" [75.1]; "He could not stifle He could not stifle [238.23]), omitted words (e.g., "some years the time" / "some years after the time" [71.28–29]), and careless errors probably due to hasty writing (e.g., "they person" / "thy person" [141.6]). Several changes necessitated by Irving's careless revising have been adopted, such as the following: "The Colonel and Burke were walking one ⟨and Burke, walking one⟩ day" / "The Colonel and Burke, walking one day" (184.27).

Some of Putnam's changes have been adopted for various other reasons. For example, MS reading "on a rough" has been rejected in

18. Compared with the passage in the John D. Sinclair edition of *The Divine Comedy* (New York, 1958), I, 26, Irving's quotation contains several errors; the comma in each midline is incorrect, and the word "stile" in line 5 should be "stilo."

favor of 49a "in a rough" (6.14) because of the context in which it appears. Some variations may be due merely to poorly formed letters, and for that reason 49a "track" (49.39) has been adopted in preference to MS "truck." The reading in 49a "Covent Garden" (121.43–122.1) has been adopted because it corrects a factual error in MS—"Drury lane." In another instance "fondness for" in 49a (109.23) has been adopted in preference to MS "fondness of," which appears to be an idiosyncratic use of the preposition.

On the other hand, a number of readings adopted in 49a have been rejected for various reasons. One is that the printer probably misread the handwriting as at 98.16, where MS reading "Reynolds Bennet Langton" was changed in 49a to "Reynolds's board, Langton." MS is here restored with the erroneous possessive corrected and the missing comma added. When Irving quotes his sources correctly but 49a alters them, MS reading is restored as at 64.28, where MS "prevent somewhat more" was changed to "prevent something more." In recording these instances in the List of Emendations the editor has included the probable source reference. When a change in 49a results in outright error, it has been rejected. Such is the case at 124.25, where MS "Ministers were" was changed to "ministry were." The word "ministry," implying a body of ministers acting together, would require a singular verb (compare Forster [332]: "The ministry . . . was"). When a change in 49a destroys Irving's style, it is rejected as at 117.10, where MS "apprentice to a stay maker" was changed to "apprenticed to a staymaker." Irving's "apprentice" is parallel in structure to "writer" and "hack" at 117.10–17; 49a destroys the parallelism. When no rationale for a change can be discovered, it has been rejected. At 110.14–15 "The new comedy" was changed to "The comedy." Irving is writing here about both a new comedy and a new kind of comedy. No question of repetition is involved. This may have been an accidental omission of the typesetter, unnoticed by Irving in proofreading. Occasionally a 49a variation changes the meaning of the original sentence. An example occurs at 210.25, where 49a omitted the "or" from MS "others, or when." The MS reading has been restored.

Decisions whether or not to adopt individual substantive variations in 49a rest largely upon the rule of thumb stated by Dr. Pochmann: "that whereas a compositor or house editor may be expected to correct misspellings or errors of fact, because he is more cost-conscious than the author he is not as likely as the author to make stylistic changes that may involve costly resetting."[19] This is paricularly true of a literary stylist like Irving. When a word, clearly readable in the manuscript, was

19. *Mahomet and His Successors*, p. 597.

changed in 49a, the editor is aware of Irving's tendency to search for a more telling word. Thus 49a "clothing" (23.10) has been adopted in preference to MS "arraying," and 49a "baneful" (172.29) rather than MS "fatal." Similarly, since an experienced writer often eliminates ineffectual words, 49a readings have been adopted in such instances as "an old second hand suit" / "a secondhand suit" (45.30) and "very aristocratic" / "aristocratic" (91.11).

Words, phrases, and longer passages added in 49a which are not likely to have been the work of a printer without authorization have in general been adopted. Examples of such emendations are "to Maurice" / "to his brother Maurice" (148.2); and "flute was" / "flute—his magic flute!—was" (42.9). An entire sentence ("His perfect . . . played off" [172.3–4]), which is not in the manuscript, has been adopted. The same can be said of major revisions as at 66.19–20, where the 49a reading—"It was probably his old task-master Griffiths, whose press might have been waiting"—has been adopted in preference to MS—"It was supposed to be some impatient publisher, whose press was waiting. . . ."

Some of the changes in 49a appear to have been stylistic in intention. At 16.32, for example, "for a riot" was changed to "for riot." The context ("aptness at mischief and fondness for riot") suggests that the deletion of "a" was effected to secure parallelism. The 49a reading has been adopted.

Several passages, erroneously omitted from 49a, have been restored. One example is the sentence at 131.8–10 ("Sometimes . . . the waiter"), which appears in the MS. Next to it is written, "left out of Book." Another instance occurs at 189.8–9 ("Goldsmith's taste for masquerades and given rise to the following incident. Sir Joshua" / "Goldsmith's taste for masquerades. Sir Joshua") where the omitted words represent a line of handwriting. The printer's eye apparently skipped a line.

One puzzling passage which appears in MSh, p. 62 but not in 49a reads: "Nothing can more truly depict the affectionate tenderness of his nature, and ⟨perpetual⟩ ↑the fond↓ yearning after a quiet home which incessantly battled with his wandering propensities, than his opening address to that brother." This sentence is bracketed, and in the margin is written, "See p. 76 This belongs elsewhere." It obviously does not belong at 46, which corresponds with MS, p. 76. The only place it might be inserted is at 97.9, but the sentence in lines 9–10 seems to be a substitute for it. Irving also speaks of Goldsmith's love for Henry at 135.10–15 but the sentence would not fit there either. It has been omitted.

One other omitted passage is of particular interest. The anecdote at 186.29–41 ("Among the many . . . of his heart") is given in a slightly different form on MS, p. 427 but is not included at 207 where it would normally belong. The MS paragraph reads:

Goldsmith had in fact a good voice and correct ear and sang with expression. He was one evening in a drawing room with a party of ladies when a ballad singer ↑under the window↓ struck up his favorite song of Sally Salisbury. "How miserably this woman sings," exclaimed he. This as usual was instantly attributed to vanity and envy. "Pray Doctor" said the lady of the house, "⟨can⟩ ↑could↓ you do it better?" "Yes, Madam, and the Company shall be judges." The Company of course prepared for something absurd, but Goldsmith acquitted himself with a skill and pathos that drew universal applause. ⟨Course [?] gossips [?] however appear⟩ He was evidently fond of pathetic ballads, and there were some like "Johnny Armstrongs last good night," associated with the reccollections of his childhood that were always sure to touch the springs of his heart.

Lines 1–12 of the proof sheet for (207.9–20) are visible. Covering the balance of the page is a sheet of paper on which Irving wrote the paragraph that constitutes lines 21–34. The added slip reveals just enough of the original line 21 to show that the above passage was actually set in print. Presumably Irving realized that he had repeated the anecdote and, consequently, wrote the new paragraph as a substitute.

With the exception of Irving's letter to Putnam of August 25, 1849,[20] there is no documentary evidence to support the validity of variations in substantives that cropped up in later impressions. These have been judged on the same basis as variations in 49a for which there is no tangible authorization. Thus, for example, at 150.34–35 the phrase "over the Shannon," which appeared in MS, 49a, and E, is found as "over the Channel," in 49b and all later impressions examined. Since Irving was repeating a phrase in Goldsmith's letter (see 149.30), the change has been rejected. Also rejected is a new variant appearing in 60 ("women" / "woman" [161.21]). While Goldsmith was traveling on the continent with Mrs. Horneck and her two daughters, he wrote a letter to Sir Joshua Reynolds, in which he said: "if any thing could make France pleasant, the very good women with whom I am at present would certainly do it." The change of "women" to "woman" is particularly interesting because of the criticism leveled at Irving for making too much of Goldsmith's relationship with Mary Horneck.[21] There is no evidence that Irving ever reverted to the subject after 1849. If there was design in the change to "woman," it was probably someone else's. Quite possibly, however, the change represents a chance error. Whatever the explanation, the variant has been rejected because Irving had originally quoted his source correctly.

20. See p. 436 and note 14.
21. See Introduction, pp. xxx–xxxi.

The editor has also made a half dozen emendations to correct mistakes not hitherto noticed. For example, Irving wrote (41.33–34): "It is probable he was brought to a pause in this city by the death of his uncle Contarine. . . ." Actually, Contarine was still alive at this time.[22] The mistake was corrected in 59, which reads "by the illness." The same error occurred in 49a (49.9–10) where Irving again referred to "The death of his uncle Contarine," but this was never corrected in any impression examined to 1860 or, in fact, in several editions published after that year. Therefore, it has been emended to read "The illness of his uncle Contarine. . . ." On the other hand, the temptation to change "oats" to "goats" (154.26) has been resisted. The sense of the sentence suggests that "goats" was the word intended, but not only the source but also all impressions to 1860 examined read "oats." Two undated editions, one published in Boston by DeWolfe, Fiske & Co., the other in Albany by James B. Lyon & Co., changed the word to "goats."[23] Other editorial emendations are explained in the Discussions of Adopted Readings.[24]

All substantive variations from MS which have been adopted in the Twayne edition have been included in the List of Emendations, and many of them have been explained in the Discussions of Adopted Readings.

TREATMENT OF ACCIDENTALS

The choice of accidentals is an even more complicated matter than that of substantives. Whether MSh, MSp, or 49a were chosen as model, there would be little consistency in the end result. In deciding to follow manuscript wherever possible, the editor recognizes that there will be unevenness, especially in punctuation, because MSp and quotations from sources in MSh will be more highly pointed than the rest of the work. Nevertheless, the total impression, it is hoped, will reflect Irving's preferences obvious in the handwritten parts of the manuscript.

Irving's erratic spelling has often been the subject of comment,[25] but the fact is that many of his errors are the very ones found today among college students and, indeed, even some professors. He had particu-

---

22. See Explanatory Notes, 41.34.

23. The source is "Modern Pilgrimages—Auburn," *New Monthly Magazine and Literary Journal* 2 (1821), 451.

24. See, e.g., x.33 ("Gosford" / "Gosfield"); x.3 ("Wells" / "Mills"); 202.1 ("Chapter XXXVII" / "XXXVIII"); 134.25 ("Bott" / "Botts"); 190.7 ("Burton" / "Barton").

25. For a detailed discussion of Irving's spelling habits and his attitude toward Americanized spelling, see *Mahomet and His Successors*, pp. 607–11.

lar difficulty with *ei* words (e.g., "conceive") and with the doubling of consonants (e.g., "reconcile," "afraid"). He confused pairs of words (e.g., "affect" / "effect"), used "*en*" / "*em*" prefixes in such words as "increasing" and "imprisonment," and misspelled many other words that still plague people today (e.g., "harass," "mischievous," "tragedy"). These errors have been corrected in T as they were in 49a.

Irving's inconsistencies in spelling have been retained except where a word has been used frequently enough to demonstrate a predominant form. For example, nineteen instances of "practice" / "practise" were noted, of which twelve are spelled with the *s* (three in MSh; nine in MSp) and seven with *c* (all in MSp). In 49a nine are spelled with the *s* and ten with *c*. Webster (1806) lists only "practice." With the almost equal division between the two forms one surmises that this word was in a transitional state in the 1840's. The decision made, therefore, has been to follow MS, despite the inconsistencies, to show this transitional state. On the other hand, the word "gayety" / "gayeties" appears seven times and "gaiety" twice in MSh. 49a consistently uses the *y* spelling, which has been adopted in T as Irving's preferred form.

The case is slightly altered in the matter of inconsistencies of English-American spelling. Since Putnam adopted American spelling for the Author's Revised Edition of Irving's works, of which *Goldsmith* formed a volume, American spelling has been adopted in T even when MSh fluctuates between the two forms. A good example is the word "favor" and its derivatives, which are used many times. Irving writes the English form as often as the American. MSp consistently uses "favour"; 49a as consistently reads "favor," the form adopted in T. Two exceptions must be noted. In the first, one instance of English spelling—"theatre"—has been adopted in T because MSh and 49a consistently use it. The second exception is that English spelling appearing in quotations from sources is retained if either MS or 49a quotes the source correctly.[26]

Rarely does Irving use the sign of possession in MSh. Although fourteen instances were noted in which a mark may or may not be an apostrophe, in only one of them was the sign as used acceptable to the printer, and that in a double genitive ("a protégé of Garrick's" [186.17]). Twice, however, the printer changed what would probably be acceptable today: "Mrs Mills' bedchamber" / "Mills's" (57.32); "Ninon de l'Enclos' people" / "l'Enclos's" (233.20). Both of these changes have been rejected in favor of MS because Irving followed his sources accurately. In several instances what looks like the sign of possession is placed over an *s* in which the possessive does not apply (e.g., "deck'd his brows"). Such errors have been corrected in T as they were in 49a, and apostrophes

---

26. See pp. 434–35.

have also been added where omitted in MS. Several of the printer's attempts to supply missing signs of possession were unsuccessful and have been corrected. For example, at 183.13–15 Irving originally wrote (MSh p. 379): "he is a guest with Johnson at the Thrales and an object of Mrs Thrales lively sallys; he is a lion at Mrs Veseys and Mrs Montagus. . . ." In 49a (293.14–15) the passage reads: "he is a guest with Johnson at the Thrales, and an object of Mrs. Thrale's lively sallies—he is a lion at Mrs. Vesey's and Mrs. Montagu's. . . ." Thus, of the four erroneous possessives only three were corrected. The fourth—"at the Thrales"—should have been changed to "at the Thrales'. . . ." This error was never corrected until after 1860; it has been corrected in T.

Several of Irving's misspellings found their way into 49a and were never subsequently corrected. One example is "Pidcock's" (144.28). In 1825 he correctly used the quotation from Cumberland in which this word appears. The erroneous "Pidock's" first occurred in 1840 and has never before been corrected. In another instance Irving wrote both "Squire Gawky" (101.42–43) and "Squire Gawkey" (124.28), the latter being the correct spelling according to Forster (p. 558—"the Squire Gawkey of the libels of the day"). The misspelling at 101.42–43 has been eliminated. Other words misspelled in both MS and 49a but corrected in T are "sibylline" (10.2) and "panelled" (124.4).

Both Irving and the printer had difficulty with a number of men's names. One example will suffice. Isaac Bickerstaffe's name appears nine times in the text. The first usage (78.10), which is in a printed passage of the manuscript taken from the 1840 essay, is spelled "Bickerstaffe"; but over the final *e* is written an *f* in what appears to be the same black ink that was used in adding chapter headings to the same page. Presumably Irving made the alteration. In four other usages he wrote "Bickerstaffe" and in another the faulty possessive form "Bickerstaffes." Once he wrote "Bickerstaff" and twice "Bickerstuff," though the *u*'s may be simply ill-formed *a*'s. In 49a the word is consistently spelled "Bickerstaff." Goldsmith spelled the name "Bickerstaff" three times (*Works* I, 14; *Letters*, 96, 111) as did Forster (452, 466); and Boswell (II, 84) in his single reference to the man also spelled it without the *e*, though in a footnote by Croker it appears with the *e*. The correct spelling is "Bickerstaffe."[27] Irving may have been only inadvertently correct in the five out of nine usages, but he *was* correct. Consequently, in those five instances MS spelling has been restored. The other four usages have been corrected on the ground that, since 49a was consistent in its spelling of the name, it is not improper to make it consistently correct in T.

27. See *Letters*, p. 96, n. 2; Chambers's *Biographical Dictionary*, ed. J. O. Thorne (New York, 1962).

In his treatment of compounds and possible compounds Irving differed radically from that of 49a and even MSp. He preferred either the two-word or single-word form to the hyphenated word as is obvious from the fact that he rarely hyphenated in MSh. In seven particular instances in which he did, three are found in quotations from sources ("*clean-shirt-day*" [51.39]; "draggle-tailed" [152.12]; and "free-warren" [91.15]), and two were probably taken from sources which he was paraphrasing ("appointment-warrant" [62.24–25]; "foot-ball" [189.11]). Of the other two, one ("quiet-seeking" [99.17]) was also hyphenated in 49a; the other ("black-lead pencil" [179.35]) was not.

In multiple uses of compounds and possible compounds there is, indeed, a great deal more consistency in MSh than in 49a. For example, Irving wrote "county seat(s)" twice; 49a hyphenated once and omitted the hyphen once. So with "box ticket," used twice in MSh but hyphenated only once in 49a. This is all the more noticeable in larger groups, such as words compounded with "half." In MSh twenty-three such combinations were noted (e.g., "half cloistered," "half concealed"), in only one of which Irving used a hyphen ("half-pence" [44.30]). In MSp twelve such combinations were noted, and only one is hyphenated ("half-cocked" [36.40]). Of the total of thirty-five "half" words, 49a hyphenates thirteen and writes two as single words ("halfpence," "half-penny"). In two other usages of "half-pence" 49a hyphenates. In the matter of numbers, both cardinal and ordinal, Irving clearly preferred the two-word form. Of sixteen instances noted, four in MSp are hyphenated; the other twelve in MSh are not. Also in MSh are many words used only once, which Irving does not hyphenate but which 49a does: "blue stocking," "burying ground," "cold hearted," to mention but a few.

In some instances Irving shows a preference for the one-word form rather than two words, with or without hyphens. Examples are "black-ball," "bookcases," and "flowergarden." Because of his habit of lifting his pen midword, it is not always easy to tell whether he intended one or two words, since the space between syllables varies considerably in size. For example, "childhood" appears in MSh four times and "child hood" twice. In the latter two instances the space between syllables is so slight that one can assume his intention was to write one word. In all six instances 49a uses the one-word form. Another example is his one usage of "common place," in which the two syllables are close together. The word appears as "commonplace" in 49a, the form sanctioned by Webster (1806). On the other hand, some spaces between syllables are wide enough to suggest Irving's intention to write two words. Examples are "ále house," "bed chamber," and "death bed."

In T, then, Irving's preference for the two-word or single-word form is honored rather than the hyphenated form in 49a. His inconsistencies have been adopted except, as in the "half" combinations already mentioned, where there is a clearly predominant form used in MSh. Furthermore, Irving's clear preferences have prevailed even in MSp in passages not quoted from sources. For example, in MSh he used compounds with "ill" six times, always in two-word form. Of six instances in MSp two are not hyphenated; four are. Of the latter four three appear in quoted passages, one in Irving's own prose. This one has been changed to the two-word form—"ill will" (129.21)—to conform to Irving's predominant form in MSh. When a hyphenated form appears in MSp in a quoted passage, it is adopted if either MS or 49a follows the source regardless of Irving's preference in other usages of the word.

The large number of variations in capitalization between MSh and 49a presents an especially difficult problem for the editor. In many instances it is impossible to determine what Irving's intention was, especially in letters that are similarly written in capital and lowercase form. The *c* is a case in point. When one finds capitals on such ordinary words as "competent," "cards," and "chamber," one supposes that careless handwriting is involved. On the other hand, when such words as "cavalier," "clergyman," and "colony" (of Georgia) are capitalized, one wonders whether Irving thought of them as proper nouns. All of these words, and many others, were changed to lowercase in 49a. Because of the almost insurmountable difficulty of determining Irving's intention in capitalization from his handwriting, this is one area in accidentals in which the editor has placed heavy reliance on 49a in making decisions.

Actually there is very little consistency in capitalization in either MSh or 49a. Consider the following examples: "deserts of Arabia" / "Deserts of Arabia" (43.40); "Irish Channel" / "Irish channel" (57.13); "Northumberland house" / "Northumberland House" (100.6); "Northumberland House" / "Northumberland house" (101.24–25); "wilton Carpets" / "Wilton carpets" (130.23). Despite the many *c*'s that look like capitals, Irving distinctly writes "christmas" (six times), "canonbury," "charles"; in all of these 49a capitalizes. In such instances the editor has had to rely on common sense to resolve the confusion.

Occasionally, however, it is possible to detect in MSh a consistency in capitalization. For instance, at least fourteen times Irving wrote of "the Club," meaning the famous club of the Johnsonian group; in all of these usages 49a reduces the *C* to lowercase. On three other occasions, however, when Irving wrote "the Literary club," 49a reads "the Literary Club." In such instances MSh has been followed rather than 49a.

Although there has been no attempt to impose consistency in capitalization on the entire work, in several instances it seemed desirable to do so. Such a one is street names, which normally appear in MS as, for example, "Fleet Street" and in 49a as "Fleet-street." Nevertheless,

"Drury Lane" is so spelled in both MS and 49a twice, but it also appears as "Drury Lane" / "Drury-Lane" and "Drury lane" / "Drury-lane." Irving's preference for capitalizing "Street" and using the two-word form has been followed in T even when he departs from custom in MSh. Another area of confusion is book titles. There are at least seven combinations of variations between MS and 49a in the title *The Good Natured Man*: the Good natured man / "The Good-natured Man" (seven times); the Good natured man / the Good-natured Man (once); The Good Natured Man / "The Good-natured Man" (once); the Good Natured Man / "The Good-natured Man" (three); the Good Natured man / "The Good-natured Man" (four); the Good Natured Man / "the 'Good-natured Man' " (once); the Good Natured Man / the Good-Natured Man (once). The form adopted in T is "The Good Natured Man."[28]

In no aspect of accidentals are there more variations between MS and 49a than in punctuation. Wherever possible, MS punctuation has been retained, but in the interest of providing a literate and readable text—surely a desideratum with Irving—omissions have been supplied and outright errors corrected as they were in 49a. Irving rarely inserted end punctuation, the period after abbreviations like "Mr." or "Dr." or the sign of contraction in words like "won't." He often failed to insert one of a pair of commas as in the following example: "he attended the chemical lectures of Rouelle, then in great vogue where..." (39.19–20). 49a normally supplied the second comma, but see Discussions of Adopted Readings, 134.35, for an instance in which the printer did not do so and in which Irving's single comma has been omitted from T. He also failed on occasion to alter punctuation when he revised copy. An example is found on the proof sheet for 22. The paragraph originally ended with the word "life" (line 7). When he added to the sentence on the proof, he failed to change the original end punctuation.

Certain constructions Irving rarely punctuated, such as initial prepositional phrases as well as those elsewhere in the sentence. He did not usually punctuate restrictive clauses such as "Johnson was so delighted with his friend's elevation that he..." (148.10–11), nor did he usually place a comma between subject and verb or between verb and object. He tended not to punctuate parallel structures such as "he joined ... and became" (21.4); "in the wide but improvident" (29.25–26); "to have looked ... but to have read" (39.23–24). Although in all of these instances 49a supplied punctuation, MS reading has been adopted in T.

Nevertheless there are times when both MS and 49a are inconsistent and erratic in punctuation. A good case in point is that of the absolute construction. Sometimes when MSh does not punctuate at all, 49a adds

28. See Discussions of Adopted Readings, 118.32.

a comma as in the following example: "His purse thus slenderly replenished Goldsmith paid" / "replenished, Goldsmith" (62.30). At other times when MS uses a semicolon, 49a changes it to a comma as in this passage: "His name appearing in the newspapers ... amusements; his old enemy" / "amusements, his old enemy" (188.10–11). Again when MS uses a comma, 49a changes it to a semicolon: "authenticity, they have been pronounced" / "authenticity; they" (167.18–19). MS readings have been retained except where they cause confusion or ambiguity.

One cannot deduce any rule of thumb for the uses of colons and semicolons in either MS or 49a. Irving, for instance, punctuates a word preceding a quotation in many different ways: "Virgil–" (4.2); "fireside." (7.34); "associates," (21.24); "Smithfield" (71.30); "song;" (92.26); "Dryden.-" (208.34); "subject:-" (208.37). In all of these instances 49a uses a colon, but in another (76.1) where Irving uses no punctuation, 49a uses a period. Colons have been used in T to punctuate a word introducing a quotation. There is even less consistency in the punctuation of compound sentences: "infancy,-" / "infancy;" (11.4); "money:" / "money;" (29.33); "kinds;" / "kinds:" (75.2); "metropolis: an" / "metropolis. An" (86.1); "equipages; the" / "equipages–the" (196.30). The fact is that some punctuation marks in MSh are not at all clear; indeed, in some instances what appears to be a punctuation mark may be a slip of the pen or a random mark.[29] Irving's punctuation of compound sentences is adopted except where his mark seems irrational or where he omits any mark at all.

Irving normally used commas in a series but omitted the comma before the "and" of the last element. Both MS and 49a use an occasional semicolon in one element of a series, but they do not always agree when to use it. For instance, Irving writes: "He mingled in their Sports, told them droll stories; played on the flute for their amusement, and spent his money ..." (48.20–22). Compare 49a: "sports; ... stories; ... amusements, and." Conversely, Irving writes: "comprizes a world of beauty of imagery, tenderness of feeling; delicacy and refinement of thought, and matchless purity of style ..." (106.33–34). Here 49a removes the semicolon and replaces it with a comma. In one last example Irving writes: "Goldsmith paid for his warrant, wiped off the Score of his Milk maid, abandoned his garret and Moved into ..." (62.30–32). Here 49a changes the first two commas to semicolons. MS is followed in the punctuation except where its usage would cause confusion.

Other inconsistencies can be mentioned. More often than not Irving did not punctuate parenthetic expressions ("however," "of course,"). His inconsistencies have been permitted to remain in T. He seldom punctu-

29. *Ibid.*, 58.40.

ated appositives, whether restrictive or nonrestrictive; 49a punctuated both indiscriminately. In T, MS has been followed in restrictive appositives, but commas have been added in the case of nonrestrictive ones. Irving did not normally place a comma between subject and verb, but 49a sometimes did, especially when a phrase or clause separates them as in "A boon companion in...amusements, was" (21.14). In several similar situations in which Irving did punctuate, 49a removed the comma, as in "indiscretion attended" (36.7). Again MS punctuation has been adopted.

Nowhere, undoubtedly, was the printer's patience tried more than in the use, misuse, and omission of quotation marks in MSh. Many times Irving opened a quotation but failed to close it, especially in quotations interrupted by explanatory words; for example, "I have Spent" says he in one of his letters more than a fortnight..." (34.12–13). Sometimes he began a passage, included explanatory words, but used no quotation marks until the very end as in the following example: Beauclerc he would say using a quotation from Pope, has a love of folly...the other" (93.27–29). Although the printer struggled manfully to supply quotation marks in the proper places, he sometimes missed the mark. Such is the case at 235.24–25 (He was willing he said to) where Irving was paraphrasing his source. In the use of quotation marks MS has been followed except where Irving obviously erred.

Several times the printer enclosed names of characters in quotation marks: e.g., the "Man in Black" (34.17). These have been rejected, since in a similar instance Irving crossed out the quotation marks on the proof sheet corresponding to 51.13–14. Here the phrase reads, "in his novel of the Vicar of Wakefield." Irving makes it quite obvious in this instance that the Vicar of Wakefield represents the character rather than the title of the novel.

Conversely, in a number of places Irving used quotation marks, usually single rather than double, around a phrase; but 49a omitted them. One example is 'a labor of love' (3.36). The phrase appeared originally in 1840 with double quotation marks. Presumably Irving was either recalling the biblical expression (1 Thess. 1:3) or thinking of it as a well-known phrase. Even though he did not restore the quotation marks to the proof sheet, MS reading has been adopted. Sometimes the phrase had appeared in an earlier passage as in 'robust sophistry' (114.39), which is found previously at 114.12. At 181.9 ('snatched a grace...of art') he was quoting Pope's *Essay on Criticism* (part I, line 153). In both of these instances MS has been followed.

In approximately forty passages of quoted poetry noted, more than half in MSh are not enclosed in quotation marks; the remainder in MSp are. In all but two instances 49a uses quotation marks. Irving's preference for not enclosing poetry in quotation marks has been honored in T.

One unique situation concerns a set of pages taken bodily from Forster and included in the manuscript as copy. These pages (191–193) contain Goldsmith's letter and verses to the Horneck girls. Over and over again Forster used dots as in "name .. but" (191.10). In 49a the dots were usually changed to dashes ("name—but"); in a number of lines, however, the printer allowed the dots to remain.[30] To the modern reader dots are a sign of omission, but no omissions were made in the text. Therefore, in T these dots have been consistently changed to dashes.

In the last analysis the editor has had to tread a fine line between a hastily written manuscript replete with many passages in illegible handwriting, many careless omissions, and often chaotic accidentals, but with an obvious preference for conservative pointing; and a first edition highly pointed and sometimes even perverse in the revisions it imposed. No claim can be made that every single editorial decision is one that Irving would have approved, but at least every decision has been made with Irving's demonstrated preferences and intentions in mind. Every variation in accidentals from MS adopted in T has been included in the List of Emendations, and many of them have been explained in the Discussions of Adopted Readings. No silent changes have been made.

30. Compare *Letters*, p. 130—"name, but."

DISCUSSIONS OF ADOPTED READINGS

The adopted readings discussed in this list are those which are preceded by an asterisk in the List of Emendations. The editor's decisions to emend or not to emend are based on her acceptance or rejection of the variant reading as Irving's.

The page and line figures are keyed in each case to a word or words in the text to which the discussion or comment refers. A bracket separates the key word or words from the comment that follows.

A key to identifying symbols used in referring to the manuscript and editions of *Oliver Goldsmith*, as well as to Irving's sources, is given on pages 347–48.

ix.1 Contents.] The table of contents is set in conformity with the style adopted for the Twayne edition. Not included in MS, it was probably set from chapter headings in MS. When the table of contents was reset for the illustrated edition (49c, 53), a number of variations crept in, the most drastic one being the reduction of the notes for Chapter V to "Tour in Holland.—Sojourn in Paris." This may have been caused by the fact that the chapter headings were not included on MS, p. 54 but were later supplied on a proof sheet. The variations in the table of contents which are unique to 49c and 53 and which were never adopted in the standard impressions have been rejected in favor of 49a readings.

ix.9 studies—School] Compare 5.6.

ix.17 outset] Only 53 reads "onset," which seems to reflect an aberration of the typesetter.

ix.20–21 toadyism] "Toryism" in 49a was probably a misreading of Irving's misspelled "Todyism" in the headnotes to Chapter IV, which were added in handwriting to the proof sheet for the first page of that chapter.

ix.22 fellow passengers] See explanation for 36.2.

ix.23 way side] See explanation for 36.3.

ix.30 secondhand] See 43.5.

ix.34 picture book memory] See 51.2.

x.3 Mills] On three other occasions Irving wrote of Edward Mills, and in each instance the compositor misread the name as "Wells" (56.4; 57.20; 58.10). These errors were never corrected in any impression examined. The other three errors have been corrected on the

452

authority of MS; this one has been silently corrected. Irving also wrote of Mrs. Mills, and this is the only usage of the name which appears correctly in 49a (99.26). Amusingly enough, the correct name in this instance was changed to "Wells" in 50 and all later impressions except E.

x.8 Green Arbour]   See 77.2.

x.15 Hangers on]   See 78.2.

x.26 Club]   See Textual Commentary, p. 447.

x.33 Gosfield]   In four other references to Gosfield, Irving erroneously wrote "Gosford." In 50 the mistake was corrected in all but this and one other instance (99.4). These two errors have been corrected in T.

x.35 Two Shoes]   See 99.6.

x.38 Goethe]   Compare 105.3 and 106.6, where the umlaut is not used in either MS or 49a.

x.39 Book building]   See 134.2.

x.40 position]   Compare 111.1.

xi.7 manoeuvring]   Compare 126.2.

xi.8 "The Good Natured Man"]   See 118.32.

xi.11 holyday]   Compare 130.3.

xi.15 paradise]   Compare 134.2–3.

xi.17 Bickerstaffe's]   See Textual Commentary, p. 445.

xi.19 bloom colored]   See 137.3.

xi.35–36 The Haunch of Venison]   See 164.3–4.

xii.6 widow]   Compare 183.2.

xii.8 ballad singers]   See 186.31; compare 183.4.

xii.9 spring velvet]   See 190.2.

xii.10 Loo]   See 190.12.

xii.14 Puppet-Shew]   See 182.24.

xii.18 Holy Week]   See 206.2.

xii.18 Oglethorpe's—Ballad singing—Dinner]   See 206.2–3.

xii.22 objections]   Compare 212.2.

xii.26 Man worship]   Compare 00.0

xii.30 high minded]   See 92.8.

xii.31 green room]   See 129.4.

xii.31 poet]   Compare 223.2.

xii.39 remarks]   See 234.2.

3.4 introductory to a selection from]   For a detailed discussion of the proof sheet for the Preface, see Textual Commentary, pp. 438–39.

3.33 circumstantial]   Irving called Putnam's attention to the misspelling of this word in 49a in his letter of August 25, 1849. The error also appears in 50, 51, 54, and 59; it was corrected in 49b, 49c, 53, 55, 60, and E.

3.36 a 'labor of love';]   See Textual Commentary, p. 450.

4.6 W. I.] The initials and the following place and date do not appear in MS or Pr. They are accepted as probably the author's additions.

5.1 *CHAPTER I*] Irving was inconsistent about putting a period after the chapter number. Here in T the periods are omitted in keeping with the style for the Twayne edition.

5.4 *schoolmistress*] Of eleven compounds with "school" in MSh Irving wrote the one-word form twice: "schoolboy" and "schoolmate." In six instances the two syllables are so close together that one word seems to have been intended: "school boy" (twice), "school boys," "school mate" (twice), and "school master." In the other three instances the space between the two syllables being wider, the two-word form may have been intended: "school boy" (twice) and "school mistress." In MSp there are six "school" compounds in one-word form. Since Irving's predominant usage appears to be the one-word form, that is adopted in T. It is also the form sanctioned by Webster (1806).

5.12 humor,] The word "humor" and its derivatives are used many times. In MSp English spelling is consistently used, but Irving writes both the "or" and "our" forms in MSh. 49a consistently follows the American form, which is also adopted in T except where Irving is correctly quoting English spelling from his source.

5.13 blended] MS reading is adopted because the word is parallel with "dashed" in the next line. Irving was usually so attentive to such stylistic devices that the change in 49a does not ring true to his general custom.

5.22 good humor] Twenty-six usages of "good humor (humour)" and its derivatives were noted in MSh, only one of which is hyphenated ("good-humoured" [228.29]). In thirteen instances in MSp all but one are hyphenated. 49a is inconsistent. Irving's predominant usage, the two-word form, has been adopted in T except when he properly quotes a hyphenated form from a source.

5.35 Pallas, or Pallasmore, county] Added phrases are not likely to be the work of a printer. This is accepted as a probable last-minute authorial revision.

6.1 any thing] In MSh "any thing" appears twelve times; in MSp "anything" appears thirteen times. 49a consistently reads "any thing," the form which is adopted in T because it reflects Irving's obvious preference.

6.14 in a rough,] The Putnam choice of preposition is idiomatically correct.

6.22 were in vain;] This is accepted as a probable last-minute revision, since it more accurately expresses the probable intended meaning of the sentence.

6.24 jackboots,] Even though MSp uses the hyphenated form, one cannot determine whether in 49a the word is hyphenated because the first syllable comes at the end of a line. Since Webster (1806) lists "jackboots," that is the form adopted in T.

6.33 of that pretty little village.] In MSp Irving changed the word "the" to "that" by writing *a* over *e* and adding *t*. Without touching the period he wrote after "village" the words "pretty little village."

7.6 the Man in Black,] See Textual Commentary, p. 450.

7.34 fireside:] This word appears thus once again in MSh but also as "fire side(s)" twice. In MSp "fireside" is used three times and "fire-side" once. 49a consistently reads "fireside." Since in MSh no dominant usage is indicated and since 49a is consistent in using the one-word form, which Webster (1806) sanctions, that is the form used in T.

7.35 His house] See Textual Commentary, pp. 450–51.

9.14 gauge:] The word, which was misspelled in all impressions examined, is spelled correctly in *Works* (IV, 293).

9.35 Every thing,] MSh and 49a consistently use the two-word form, which is adopted in T; MSp usually reads "everything."

10.2 sibylline] This word, which was misspelled in all impressions examined, was not corrected until after 1860.

10.14 throughout] The question here is whether the printer accidentally omitted the second syllable or whether Irving made a last-minute revision. Either form would be satisfactory in the context, but "through-out" better fits the rhythm of the sentence. MS reading is, therefore, retained.

10.21 favorite,] The word "favor" and its derivatives are used many times. Irving writes the English form as often as the American. MSp consistently uses "favour"; 49a as consistently reads "favor." The American spelling is adopted in T.

10.42 Carrick-on-Shannon.] The hyphenated form appears once in MSp, in Prior (I, 12), and in Forster (16).

11.4 holydays;] Irving wrote "holy days" twice more, in both instances the syllables being close together, "holyday" four times, and "holy days" once where the first syllable comes at the end of a line and no hyphen appears. His clear preference for "holyday," a form sanctioned by Webster (1806), is honored in T.

11.13–14 have been brilliant.] This is accepted as a probable last-minute revision. Eliminating the ineffectual "very" suggests Irving's concern with improving style.

11.30 easily] The word is defective in MSp: only the *ly* and the dot of the preceding *i* are visible.

11.34 man, Jack] Irving did not eliminate the word "one" in two other similar usages: "one Dr. Goldsmith" (86.8, quoting Boswell); "one Hugh Kelly" (117.7). Here, however, he may well have crossed the word out on the proof sheet to avoid repetition with the word "one" following "Fitzimmons." The 49a version is, therefore, accepted.

11.42 connections] The word "connexion" appears four times in MSh and once again in MSp. 49a consistently reads "connection," which is the preferred spelling in Webster (1806) and is, therefore, adopted in T.

12.28–29 this intruding guest] This is adopted as a probable last-minute revision made to avoid repetition of "his" earlier in the sentence.

13.13 and thence] In MS there is a very light line drawn through the word "from." Compare 6.34, where the MS reads "world ⟨from⟩ whence."

14.8 1745, when seventeen] See Explanatory Notes.

14.13 building, numbered 35,] Without the commas the phrase seems to modify building, but the remainder of the sentence makes clear that the number belongs to the room. The punctuation is, therefore, adopted to avoid ambiguity.

14.30 base mind baser.] The inserted word has been accepted as a probable authorial revision made to improve style.

15.24 childhood."] MSh reads "childhood" six times and "child hood" twice, but in the latter two instances the two syllables are so close as to suggest that one word was intended. Two instances of "child-hood" were noted in MSp, the form that 49a consistently uses. Irving's clear preference for the one-word form is honored in T.

15.42 to leave] Irving's perfect infinitive was grammatically incorrect.

16.9 sank] Webster (1806) lists "sank" as the preterite and "sunk" as both preterite and past participle of "sink." Either form would thus be acceptable; however, the number of substantive variations in these immediate pages strongly suggests the author's hand at work. "Sank" is accepted as a probable Irving revision.

16.14–15 told that he would stroll] MS reading is adopted here for the following reason: as the sentence in 49a is punctuated, the part follow-ing the comma is extremely awkward because the "we are told" seems to be the subject and verb of a new clause. If it were punctuated—"and, we are told,"—the sense would be clear. Irving's habit of constantly changing words and phrases up to the last minute was in the interest of improved style and easily flowing sentences. Here he seems to have nodded while proofreading; otherwise he would not have per-mitted this awkward sentence to remain.

16.22 fellow students] See 36.2.

16.32 for riot.] The context ("aptness at mischief and fondness for riot") suggests that Irving removed the "a" in order to secure par-allelism.

16.38–39 Newgate, or the Black Dog, as the prison was called, and effect] This is the kind of addition a printer is not likely to make without the author's sanction. It is, therefore, accepted as Irving's probable revision.

17.23–24 chastisement received] Compared with the variation in 16.14–15, which was rejected, this one is perfectly clear and is not awkward. It is accepted as a probable Irving revision.

17.30 walls the very next day, intending] The added words are not likely to have been the work of a printer. They are accepted as a probable Irving revision.

17.36 the clothes from his back,] This change is accepted because it is the kind of stylistic change typical of Irving.

18.14 eccentric, yet endearing] The reversal of words reflects a search for a more exact expression, which is the sort of improvement Irving tried to achieve.

19.27 "This] Irving used quotation marks in this passage through "obliterated" in line 30 advisedly because he was quoting from Prior (I, 54). The quotation is exact except for the comma after "mature," which in Prior is a semicolon. In fact, the first ten words of the following sentence are also verbatim from Prior.

20.3 overruled,] At least twenty compounds with "over" were noted. In ten of them Irving clearly wrote one word. In eight others the two syllables are so close as to suggest his intention of writing one word, and in two other instances in which the space between the syllables seems to indicate that two words were intended, the end of the *r* is extended toward the second syllable. Since Irving's dominant usage is the one-word form, it is adopted in T.

21.13 round.] In MSh Irving used a quotation mark here, but he did not open the quotation before "How" (21.8).

21.25 horse doctor,] The comparable passage in *Works* (V, 110) reads: "There's Dick Muggins the exciseman, Jack Slang the horse doctor, Little Aminadab that grinds the music box, and Tom Twist that spins the pewter platter."

22.7 few] In MSh the word "few" looks very much like "free." In a proof sheet for this page the word appeared as "free." Irving crossed it out but did not insert a substitute.

22.7 life;] Irving failed to change the period in the proof sheet when he added the balance of the paragraph in handwriting.

22.7–9 and though he ... THREE JOLLY PIGEONS.] These lines, which do not appear in MS, were added by hand to a proof sheet as follows: "and though he rose eventually to and though he ultimately rose to associate with birds of a finer feather, his heart would still yearn in Secret after the THREE JOLLY PIGEONS." Irving apparently meant to cross out the first six words but failed to do so.

23.5 time was now arrived] The change in 53 to "had now arrived" is rejected as unauthorized. Compare 89.34, where "guests were arrived" has the sanction of Boswell (III, 445).

23.10 clothing]   This is the kind of word change that Irving was in the habit of making on proof sheets. It is accepted as probably his.

23.15–16 club at Ballymahon, having been much in the way]   This was apparently one of Irving's last-minute changes. Notice that at the end of the last chapter he drew the analogy of the club at Ballymahon with the fictional club at the Three Jolly Pigeons. In the proof sheet he added three lines to the end of the chapter, in which he again mentioned the Three Jolly Pigeons and emphasized it by placing it at the end of the sentence and, hence, the end of the chapter. There is no extant proof sheet for this page, but Irving probably changed this passage to eliminate repetition and to take the fictional inn out of a nonfictional context.

23.37 ascendency.]   Webster (1806) lists this spelling.

27.27 bitterness.]   This paragraph ("We cannot . . . bitterness") is not in MS. It was added to the Pr. in handwriting.

28.4 Hocus-pocus]   The word also appears once in MSp as "hocus-pocus" [one word]. 49a hyphenates in both usages. Since Irving's preference cannot be determined from a single instance and since the hyphenated form is sanctioned by Webster (1806), it is adopted in T.

28.4 boarding house]   In MSp "boarding-houses" occurs once, and 49a again hyphenates. This word is not listed in Webster (1806). In MSh there is one instance of "boarding school," correctly quoted from *Works* (IV, 107) and thus printed in 49a. Webster (1806) lists "boardingschool." In all three of these instances the two-word form has been adopted in T.

28.5 mock ghost]   In MSh Irving wrote five other expressions with "mock," all in two-word form. There is also one such unhyphenated combination in MSp. The two-word form is adopted in T because it represents Irving's predominant usage.

28.13 gambling house,]   The two-word form is adopted here by analogy with "gambling tables" and "gaming table" in MSh (38.19; 93.18).

29.37 Having taken lodgings]   MS is in error.

29.37 haphazard.]   MSh reads "hap/-hazard." Irving also spelled this word "hap hazard" (113.20), the two parts being close together, and "haphazard" (150.15). In the first two instances in 49a "hap-" comes at the end of a line. In the third 49a hyphenates. The word is listed as "haphazard" in Webster (1806), the form adopted in T.

29.41 himself with the name either]   The shift of the word "either" reflects Irving's habit of polishing his sentences to achieve better effects.

30.5 boarding houses] See 28.4.

30.23 lay chiefly] At this point MSp has defective letters, which look like "iay emeny."

33.8 chariot;] There is no footnote on the MS page to correspond with the dagger symbol which follows the semicolon.

34.17 autobiography,] In MS the two parts of the word are written close together.

35.15–16 Mrs. Lawder."] In Pr. Irving put a line through the *u* and the *o* of "Laudor." and wrote "Mrs Lawder," in the margin.

35.17 Mrs. Lawder was Jane, his] In the margin of Pr. Irving wrote, "Mrs. Lawder ⟨*Illegible word or syllable*⟩ was Jane-his."

35.17–18 the object of his valentine—his first poetical inspiration. She had been] In the margin of Pr. Irving wrote: "⟨his valentine⟩—the object of his Valentine—his first poetical inspiration. She had been."

35.35–42 and almost . . . and Ballymahon.] This passage, which is not in MS, was added to Pr. in handwriting. It replaces the following MS passage: "he made this his final sally forth upon the world, whence he was never to return to the friends of his infancy or his early haunts at Lishoy and Bally mahon."

35.41 friends] The printer possibly changed "friends" to "friend" with the thought that the word refers to Contarine, but more likely Irving was referring to Goldsmith's friends in Ballymahon. There is, in fact, a series here: little thinking that he will never see his uncle again, that he will never return to his friends, and that he will never revisit his old haunts. For this reason the MS reading has been retained.

35.42 'sweet Lissoy'] Lishoy is an alternate form of Lissoy, the latter being used most often by other writers on Goldsmith. Irving's quotation marks suggest that he may have been paraphrasing "Sweet Auburn" from the first line of Goldsmith's "Deserted Village."

36.2 *fellow passengers*] In MSh Irving used the word "fellow" in at least ten combinations ("fellow members," "fellow student," etc.), always observing the two-word form. In MSp are found "fellow proprietors" once and "fellow-student" eight times. 49a is inconsistent, half the time hyphenating and half the time not. Irving's obvious preference for the two-word form is honored in T.

36.3 *way side*] The headnotes to this chapter, which are not in MS, were supplied on the proof sheet. This is the only usage of the word except the one in the table of contents, which was apparently set from the chapter headings. In both instances in 49a the word is hyphenated because the first syllable comes at the end of a line. Since the word is not listed in Webster (1806), Irving's two-word form appears to be acceptable and is, therefore, adopted both here and in the table of contents.

36.17 voyage."]　In 1840 Irving put quotation marks around this phrase even though he was paraphrasing his source. See Explanatory Notes. In MS there is a quotation mark before the word "refresh" but not after "voyage." For a discussion of Irving's use of quotation marks, see Textual Commentary, pp. 450–51.

36.33 deviations to]　Since in MSh there is no comma after "proceeded," this one has been omitted. Irving usually did not set off prepositional phrases in commas.

37.12 well-dressed]　At least a dozen compounds of "well" appear as adjectives. Those in MSh are not hyphenated; those in MSp are. There is no consistency in 49a. Irving's practice of using the two-word form is adopted in T except, as here, where a source hyphenates.

38.8 life "that]　Although in MSh Irving closed the quotation after "scholar" (line 11), he did not open it. The error was never rectified. The quotation is opened at this point on the authority of Forster (42), where the first clause reads: "that it was a common subject of remark in the place, that. . . ."

38.12 undertook]　This is probably an instance of Irving's occasional failure to use a hyphen when dividing a word at the end of a line. He wrote "undergo," "undergone," "underwent," and "underrate"; in fact, this is the only instance in MSh in which he used a two-word form in a compound with "under." Webster (1806) lists "undertook."

39.1 Continent, in February, 1755, with]　In MSp Irving put a caret after "Continent," but he did not write in the insertion. The original date of 1775, which was not corrected until 60, was an obvious error. Goldsmith returned to England in 1756.

39.2 shirt, a flute and a single guinea.]　In MSp Irving, without crossing out the period after "shirt," added these words in handwriting.

39.3–4 "Blessed," . . . adventurous]　The shift in words has all the earmarks of a change effected by Irving in the interest of improved style.

39.30–38 "When]　The passage "When I. . . . be free" was taken bodily from Forster (50) and used as manuscript copy. Each line of the Forster material begins with a single quotation mark, which 49a eliminated.

39.39 During a brief]　In MSh Irving did not indicate a new paragraph at this point as did 49a; but, since he did begin a new subject, the paragraph has been allowed to stand.

40.8–9 Fontenelle, [then . . .old,] who]　Since the clause is not in the source which Irving was quoting (Prior, I, 182), he was correct in using the brackets.

40.28 "Traveller."]　Following this line in MSh is a passage not included in the book. For an explanation see Textual Commentary, p. 441.

41.11 pawnbroker,]　In MSh the two-word form appears in two other instances, in both of which the two syllables are so close together as to suggest the intention of writing one word. MSp has three instances of the one-word form, which is also sanctioned by Webster (1806). On the assumption that Irving's habit of lifting his pen between syllables was exerted in this word, the one-word form is adopted in T.

41.18 acquired, as has been shown, a] This addition probably represents another example of Irving's last-minute tinkering with his text and is, therefore, accepted.

41.34 by the illness] This is a legitimate correction. For an explanation of the error see Explanatory Notes.

41.37 brother in law, Hodson,] In MSh the unhyphenated word appears three more times, and Irving also wrote "father in law." His preference for the three-word form is honored in T.

42.2 spendthrift.] Irving's habit of extending the *d* back over the word forced him to start anew with the second syllable. The space between the syllables is small. The only other instance noted is in MSp, where the one-word form is used. This form is sanctioned by Webster (1806).

42.9 flute—his magic flute!—was] This sounds very much like an Irving addition and is accepted as such.

42.24 threescore.] Since Irving did not open the verses with a quotation mark and since it was not his general practice to use quotation marks when quoting poetry, this mark is here omitted.

43.5 *secondhand*] The word appears five times in MSh, and in each instance the formation of the final *d* of "second" forced Irving to begin anew with "hand." The space between the syllables varies in size. Since Webster (1806) lists "secondhand," the assumption here is that Irving intended the one-word form, which is adopted in T.

43.5–6 *A tragedy in embryo—Project of the written mountains*] The headnotes to this chapter are not in MS. All but these two segments were handwritten on the Pr. Irving added in parentheses: "The remainder of the table of contents will be furnished when I see the proof of the rest of the chapter." This note testifies to the speed with which he was having to produce copy in order to keep up with the printer.

43.9 illness] Although the same error in 41.34 was eventually corrected in 59, this one never was. It is here corrected for the first time. See Textual Commentary, p. 443.

43.15 penniless] This is the form listed in Webster (1806).

44.30 half pence] Irving used more than thirty expressions with "half." This is the one time in MSh that he hyphenated. In MSp only one is hyphenated ("half-cocked"). 49a observes no consistency. Irving's preference for the two-word form is honored in T.

44.33 difficulty,]   See Explanatory Notes.

44.40–41 school. I have]   Irving broke off at "school" in his source
(*Works*, IV, 108) and shifted back to the previous page (IV, 107).
The same character is speaking in both parts.

45.5–6 "He is generally," says he, "the laughing stock]   With the words
"He is" Irving came to the end of his MS page. In starting a new
sheet of paper he originally omitted the words "generally the." The
quotation marks were rightly added when the error was remedied.
The addition of "says he" is accepted as a probable Irving revision.

45.10 "He]   Concerning this quotation see Explanatory Notes, 45.14.

45.16 Fish Street Hill.]   See 117.11.

45.17 fellow student]   See 36.2.

45.30 a secondhand suit]   The deletion of the word "old" is accepted
as Irving's probable attempt to improve style. For "secondhand" see
43.5.

45.40 journeyman.]   In two other instances in MSh Irving wrote "journeyman" and the erroneous possessive form "journeymans." Webster
(1806) lists the one-word form, which is adopted here.

46.5 Court; an occupation]   Although the word "certainly" was not
actually crossed out in MS, it obviously modified the excised "was"
rather than the remaining appositive.

46.10 familiarity took place]   Since the altered verb involves a change
in meaning, it was probably Irving's rather than the printer's and is
accepted as such.

46.34 secondhand one]   See 43.5.

48.22 sweetmeats.]   Irving again wrote "sweet meats" (151.2), but in
both instances the two syllables are so close as to suggest his intention
of writing one word. One instance of "sweetmeats" occurs in MSp,
the form which is sanctioned by Webster (1806).

49.8 "Critical Review,"]   Irving used italics for emphasis, for foreign
phrases (e.g., *jeux d'esprit*), for nicknames (e.g., *Jessamy Bride*), and
in a dozen instances for titles of books, plays, etc. 49a normally followed MS in this respect. Why Irving used italics here, especially
since he did not italicize "Monthly Review" (line 4), is a question.
With the exception of 52.9, this is the only time 49a used both italics
and quotation marks. Since Irving's italics here seem to have been
the result of aberration rather than design, they are omitted.

49.12–13 books which fell]   At first glance the omission of "occasionally"
may seem like an unauthorized emendation because it creates the impression of a Goldsmith conversing as an equal at the table, of which
he 'has just been described as "a humble occupant." However, Irving
probably scratched the world to eliminate the repetition with "occasion" in the following sentence.

49.17 life and in April 1757] Irving rarely sets off a prepositional phrase in commas. Since here he inserted a comma after "and" but not after "1757," his comma is regarded as an aberration and is here omitted.

49.20 Dunciad, Paternoster Row.] Twice in MSh Irving wrote "Pater noster" with the two words so close as to suggest his intention of writing one word. The *r* of "Row" in both instances is an enlarged lowercase *r*.

49.21 semifictitious] The only other "semi" compound noted in MSh is "semibreves," which has the sanction of Webster (1806). Webster includes a large number of "semi" compounds, but "semifictitious" is not one of them. Since Irving inserted the prefix after having written the line and since there is the analogy with "semibreves," the one-word form is adopted in T rather than the hyphenated form in 49a.

49.38 voracity] Irving apparently started to write "voracity," the word called for by the context, but settled for "vivacity" when he had trouble spelling it. Either the typesetter caught the error, or Irving altered it on Pr.

49.39 track] Irving's *u* in "truck" may simply be an ill-formed *a*.

51.2 *picture book*] Irving again wrote the two-word form in 125.7.

51.9 picture books] See 51.2 and Textual Commentary, pp. 446–47.

51.9–10 kind hearted] Irving wrote the two-word form four times; MSp used the hyphenated form in one other passage. Irving's preference for the two-word form is honored in T.

51.13–14 in his novel of the Vicar of Wakefield.] Pr. originally read "in the 'Vicar of Wakefield.'" Irving put a caret after "in" and drew a line to the left-hand margin, where he wrote, "his novel of." He also crossed out the quotation marks. Then at the bottom of the proof page he wrote, "friendly manner in his novel of the Vicar of Wakefield." Irving here makes a clear distinction between title of novel and name of character.

51.22 Besides his literary job work Goldsmith] In MSp these six words were added in handwriting.

51.25 Fleet Street;] See 117.11.

51.31 calls; hence] The deletion of "from" is accepted as a probable Irving correction, since the word is redundant.

51.33 Thirty] The passage which begins here and ends with "in those days" (52.2–3) was written by hand on a separate proof sheet. The last six words were the clue that the passage was to be inserted after "of the place" (line 32). Since Irving was paraphrasing either Boswell (I, 74) or Forster (189–90), he was right not to use quotation marks. MS reading is thus retained.

51.36 coffee house] The word is thus spelled once again in MSh but also "coffeehouse" and "Coffee Houses." In addition, six instances of specific coffee houses appear in MSh, never hyphenated but inconsistent in capitalization: e.g., "Chapter coffee House," "Grecian Coffee House," etc. Irving's predominant usage—two-word form, lowercase for the general term, and capitals for specific coffee houses—is adopted in T.

51.39 six pence;] In MSh the word is so written five times; in only one instance are the two syllables close enough to suggest that one word was intended. Although "sixpence" is listed in Webster (1806), Irving's preference for the two-word form is honored in T.

52.1 leaf out of] Since this passage was added on a proof sheet, the change to "leaf from" in 49a would seem to have been made by the printer and is, therefore, rejected.

52.8 career? We] Whoever supplied the question mark to correct the comma-splice failed to capitalize "We," an error never before corrected.

52.9 *Enquiry into the State of polite learning*] Irving's single quotation mark preceding "Enquiry" appears to have been a slip of the pen. See 49.8. According to *Works* (I, x), the correct title is *An Enquiry into the Present State of Polite Learning in Europe*.

53.18 relatives] This is accepted as a probable last-minute authorial change.

55.22 assistance."] The necessary quotation mark was not supplied until after 1860.

56.32 self-approving] In thirteen instances of "self" words in MSh Irving never hyphenates. Three such combinations in MSp are hyphenated. Irving's preference for the two-word form is honored in T except, as here, where the 49a hyphenated form agrees with the source.

56.37 requital for] This is accepted as probably Irving's revision.

57.32 bedchamber,] Irving's formation of the letter *d* required him to start anew with "chamber." The two words are very close together as they are in another usage in MSh (91.26). In the present instance, whether Irving was following Prior (I, 260) or Forster (114), he would have found "bedchamber."

58.38 round as] See Explanatory Notes.

58.39 runs into] This is accepted as a probable Irving revision.

58.40 prospects, the] In MSh Irving's punctuation marks are often as difficult to decipher as the rest of his handwriting. Here what seems at first glance to be a period could very well be a comma. The sentence that follows is meaningless as it appears in 49a; but, if the period is read as a comma and if "the wonderful career of fame and fortune that awaits him," is read as an appositive of "prospects," meaning suddenly emerges. This is the reading adopted in T.

59.6 co-operation] In MSh there is a decided space after "co," but this is the only such instance noted. Since Webster (1806) lists "co-operation," the form used in 49a, it has been adopted here.

59.7 schoolboy] See 5.4.

59.11 he begins,] This line begins a three-and-a-half-page passage which Irving took bodily from Forster (123–26) and used as MS copy.

59.37 not–I own I could not–continue] See Textual Commentary, p. 451.

60.13–14 me, * * * * Is it] It does not seem probable that the printer would have censored this line without Irving's approval. Compare 58.38.

62.5 *Gayeties*] MSh reads "gayety / gayeties" seven times and "gaiety" in only one other instance. 49a consistently uses the *y* spelling, which is adopted in T as Irving's preferred form.

62.6 *Scroggen,*] See 72.8.

62.21 forthcoming] This is the only usage of the word noted. Although in MSh there is a considerable space after "forth," Irving also wrote "forth with" twice, in both instances the two words being so close together as to suggest his intention of writing one word. Webster (1806) lists both "forthcoming" and "forthwith." Since the two instances of the latter could very well be one word and since this is the only instance of "forth coming," the one-word form is adopted in all three.

62.38 enterprise] In MSh the *s* form is used twice, the *z* form four times; in MSp the *s* form appears twice. 49a consistently reads "enterprise," the spelling listed in Webster (1806) and adopted in T.

63.14 of hospital mate.] The deletion of *a* is accepted as probably Irving's revision.

63.25 bookseller,] Of the more than sixty usages of this word noted, in only one other does Irving seem to write two words. In both instances, however, the two words are so close together as to suggest his intention of writing one word. His predominant one-word form is adopted in T.

63.34 reexamination] Both here and in the next line Irving wrote, without doubt, "re examination." It is difficult to believe that he intended two words here any more than in "co operation" (59.6). Since Webster (1806) lists "reexamine," the decision here is to adopt "reexamination" on the ground that the size of the space is not necessarily an infallible proof of intention.

63.40 woman from whom] There is no proof sheet to indicate who changed the preposition; possibly the printer had in mind the well-known phrase "a laborer worthy of his hire." Since Irving's phraseology seems preferable, it has been retained.

65.28 outran] In MSh Irving wrote six compounds with "out." In two instances the one-word form is certain ("outrun"; "outright"); in two others the two syllables are written close together ("out vied"; "out ward"); and in the final two the space between syllables is sizeable ("out ran"; "out run"). All of these "out" compounds are in one-word form in both 49a and Webster (1806), the form adopted in T.

66.19–20 It was probably... been waiting,] This kind of major revision is not likely to have been made by a printer without the author's approval. It is accepted as probably authentic. Since both here and in 50.7 Irving distinctly wrote "task master," his preference for the two-word form is adopted in both instances even though Webster (1806) lists "taskmaster."

66.39 make shift] The two-word form is used twice in MSh and is, therefore, adopted here. It is not listed in Webster (1806).

67.37 swarms] The word "screams," which makes the sentence meaningless, must have been a printer's misreading of Irving's MS for the 1840 essay. "Swarms" is the word Irving used in "The Club of Queer Fellows," the essay from *Tales of a Traveller* from which he was quoting.

67.41 letter lv.] The error was not rectified in any impression examined.

71.28–29 years after the] The omission of "after" in MS was an obvious slip of the pen.

72.3 "heroi-comical poem" also] Irving correctly used quotation marks: he was quoting 70.29.

72.5 autobiography;] In MSh the space after "auto" being small, it is assumed that Irving intended one word.

72.8 Scroggen:] Both Forster (153), Irving's probable source, and *Works* (II, 128) read "Scroggen."

72.18 the author's other writings it might have abounded] The 49a reading is adopted as probably Irving's last-minute revision.

72.22 and have remained] The change to the perfect tense completes the parallel structure of the sentence.

73.8 expense] Compare 1826 (20): "The expense of his equipment...."

73.21 title page.] In MSh "title page" appears once again; in MSp there are two instances of "title-page." Webster (1806) lists "titlepage." Irving's preferred two-word form is adopted in T.

74.14 first rate] The two-word form appears in MSh (72.23). The word is not listed in Webster (1806).

75.10 the Busy Body] According to *Works* (III, 4), *Busy Body* is the correct spelling of this title.

75.25 fireworks,] In MSh the two syllables are very close together. Since the source reads "fireworks," the form listed in Webster (1806), it is adopted here.

75.27 the *Provoked Husband*,] What Irving meant by double underlining the two initial letters is unclear. Since he was using Forster here as his source, he may have meant that the title should be italicized as it is in Forster; and that is the assumption followed in T.

76.1 of Garrick was the following:] For an explanation of the colon see Textual Commentary, p. 449.

76.2–9 "I have . . . characters."] This passage was taken bodily from Forster (211) and made part of the MS. In Forster there is a single quotation mark at the beginning of each line of print. These marks have been omitted in T as they were in 49a.

76.8–9 it, they] The edition of Forster from which Irving cut this paragraph has a defective comma here.

76.16 conciliated. In] In MSh the capital *I* seems to have been superimposed on a lowercase *i*.

77.2 Wine Office Court,] Twice in MSh Irving wrote "Wine office Court" and once "wine office Court." One usage in MSp reads "Wine-office Court." Prior (I, 368) reads "Wine-Office Court" and Forster (237) "Wine Office Court." An analogy can be found in "Green Arbour Court," which Irving wrote twice, and "Green arbour Court" once. Both Prior (I, 367) and Forster (237) read "Green Arbour Court," the form which appears in MSp five times. There is no question of Irving's preference for the unhyphenated form, but there is a question of the lowercase *o* in "office." Since in general Irving was erratic in capitalization, the decision here is to follow sources and 49a in capitalizing "Office."

77.2 Fleet Street] See 117.11.

78.8 Bickerstaffe.] See Textual Commentary, p. 445.

78.9 hangers on,] On five occasions in MSh Irving wrote the two-word form. His clear preference is adopted in T.

78.30 scapegrace,] This is the only usage of the word noted. In MSh the two syllables are close together and may have been intended as one word.

79.20 himself] Both here and in "themselves" (3.32) the first syllable comes at the end of a line in MSh, and there is no hyphen. Irving often failed to hyphenate such divided words, even those of a noncompound nature (e.g., "exaggera / tion," MSh, p. 145). Often he put the hyphen at the beginning of the next line (e.g., "depend / -ant," MS p. 146), and just as often he put a hyphen at the end of the line and another at the beginning of the next line (e.g., "com- / -panion," MSh, p. 145).

79.36 a half written] See 44.30. Irving's single quotation mark is omitted because he did not close the quotation and because the source of the potential quotation has not been identified.

79.43 yes: I came] The problem here is that Irving omitted the word "when" preceding "I came" in line 41. Without the first "when" the second one is meaningless. The choice is either to insert the first "when" or omit the second, the latter being the solution adopted by 49a and T.

80.4 joint note to] The omission of "note" in MSh was an obvious slip of the pen.

80.11 Cave his bookseller's,] In a possessive noun of this nature, in which an appositive is involved, the sign of possession may be added either to the noun or its appositive. Since Irving was correct in his usage except for the misspelled possessive form, his wording has been retained and the error corrected. Compare 86.4.

80.20 the admiration of] This is accepted as a probable Irving revision.

80.23 fellow wayfarer] For "fellow" combinations see 36.2. In MSh the words "way" and "farer" are close together. Irving also wrote "way faring" with the two words close together. Webster (1806) lists both "wayfarer" and "wayfaring." The one-word form is adopted in T. See also "way side" (36.3).

80.39–41 into intimacy . . . Covent Garden] The 49a version is the same as T except for "Russell-street,".

81.9 somewhat] This word is so spelled many times in MSh. In four instances of "some what" the space between the syllables is small. In another, "some" comes at the end of the line with no hyphen added. In Webster (1806) "somewhat" is the form listed.

81.14 wife.] What is recorded here is a single quotation mark in MSh may be a random pen mark. Irving did not put such a mark at the beginning of the quoted verses.

81.36 sir?"] Boswell (III, 175) reads: "What was the common price of an oak stick?"

84.28 ecstasy] In MSh Irving wrote "extacy" three times. 49a consistently uses "ecstasy." Webster (1806) lists "ecstasy or ecstacy."

85.9 by him] The substitutions of the pronouns for nouns here and in 85.19 are accepted as probable authorial revisions designed to improve style.

86.5 but he was] This is accepted as probably Irving's revision.

87.33–34 in juxtaposition] This is accepted as a probable Irving revision designed to improve style.

88.16–17 the pervading amenity of those] In MSh there is a mark that looks like either a caret or a faulty *x* underneath the word "same." Whether or not the symbol indicates that the word was to be omitted is not clear, but in the context the word is superfluous. It is omitted in T.

88.32 landlady.] Three times in MSh Irving wrote the two-word form with the two parts close together. Once he succeeded in joining the two words despite his formation of the *d,* and he also wrote "land-lord." Both "landlady" and "landlord" appear more than a dozen times in MSp, the spelling sanctioned by Webster (1806).

89.34 were arrived] Compare 23.5.

90.12 meetings] In MS Irving's pen failed on the upstroke of the *s,* but the downstroke was successful. This defective *s* looks at first like a comma, but the printer ignored the mark altogether.

90.24 Beauclerc,] In MSh a *k* appears to have been superimposed upon an original final *c.*

91.8 Beauclerc until] In MSh the *c* was superimposed upon an original *k.*

91.11 and aristocratic] This is accepted as a probable Irving revision designed to improve style.

91.24–25 to find him "a decent,] The words "a decent" begin a quotation from Boswell (I, 232) that continues to the end of the paragraph. In MSh there is a single quotation mark after "preserved" (91.32), which was omitted in 49a.

91.26 down from his bedchamber] For "bedchamber" see 57.32.

92.5 in college chambers] This is accepted as a probable authorial revision.

92.5–6 when the youths came] Irving probably made this revision to avoid using a pronoun whose antecedent was not immediately obvious.

92.8 high born, high bred,] The word "high" is used in at least fourteen combinations in MSh, always in two-word form.

92.12 tavern,] Irving's comma after "Langton" indicates his intention of setting off the following participial phrase; but, as he often did, he failed to add the second of the pair of commas. Perversely the printer, who normally added the missing comma in such instances, chose here to omit Irving's comma. Since the phrase is nonrestrictive, the comma has been retained and its mate added.

92.21–22 Covent Garden; figured] The unhyphenated name appears four more times in MSh. In one usage Irving wrote "CoventGarden" (195.26).

92.28 For I'm] A dot above the *m* in MSh may have been intended as an apostrophe.

92.29 boat, rowed] Since there is no reference earlier in the anecdote to the men's having taken boat, the addition of "again" seems to be in error. MS reading is, therefore, accepted.

93.5 life.] In MSh this sentence appears at the bottom of the page following the words "standing on one leg" (line 15).

93.5–6 the mild, enthusiastic] In MSh the words "Langton, however, was still the" are part of the passage at the bottom of the page. See previous note.

93.8 "Oh!]   See Explanatory Notes, 93.9.

93.33 overcleanly]   See 20.3.

94.14 of all who knew him.]   This is accepted as probably Irving's revision.

95.37 ushered]   In MSh the word is clearly "tortured." Since the 49a reading could hardly be a printer's error, it is accepted as probably Irving's last-minute revision.

96.40 page were]   This is accepted as a probable authorial revision.

97.18–19 win, not to]   In MSp the *n* of "win" and the words "not to" are missing.

97.25–26 almost ludicrous.]   This is one of the corrections requested by Irving in his letter of August 25, 1849, to Putnam.

97.26 a "newspaper essayist"]   The word "newspaper" and its plural are used many times. In the eleven usages noted in MSh Irving lifted his pen after "news." In all but two instances the space after "news" is small. The one-word form, which was noted nine times in MSp, agrees with the Webster (1806) entry. It is adopted in T.

98.16 Reynolds's, Bennet Langton]   In MSh the word "Bennet" is so carelessly written that the printer's misreading is understandable, especially in light of Irving's erroneous possessive form of "Reynolds." The correction is made here in T for the first time.

99.4 *Gosfield*]   See x.33.

99.12 library stair case,]   Irving wrote "stair case" once again (130.19).

99.17 is to]   Twice in this sentence Irving omitted one of a pair of commas. The one added in 49a after "which" (line 15) is permitted to remain because of the length of the phrase ending with "metropolis" (line 17). Here the comma after "is" is omitted because Irving did not use one after "author."

99.35 The earl held]   In MSh in the word "Earl" a capital *E* was superimposed upon a lowercase *e*. According to Forster (328), "the earl was already Lord Lieutenant, and held that office till Grenville's ministry went out." The revision is accepted as probably Irving's.

100.6 House,]   49a follows the source, the *Annual Register* 17 (1774), 32. In both 1825 (29) and 1840 (104–105) Irving began a new sentence with "Taking" (line 9) as he did in MSh. 49a reads "appearance: taking." Percy (66), Irving's major source in 1825, paraphrased this anecdote.

101.7 kinswoman, the countess;]   In MSh there is a distinct space between "kins" and "woman." In MSp "kinsman" appears once. Webster (1806) lists the one-word form for both words.

101.28 Gosfield, the seat]   Presumably Irving deleted the word "noble" after a reviewer in the *Gentleman's Magazine* criticized him for thus describing a seat "situated in a small paddock." See Explanatory Notes.

101.29 Nugent, afterwards] Of twenty-four instances of "afterward(s)" noted in MSh this is the only one in which Irving wrote two words.

101.42 nickname] In MSh Irving distinctly wrote two words, but in another usage the two words are so close that one word seems intended. In MSp "nicknamed" appears twice. Since Webster (1806) lists the one-word form, that is adopted in T.

101.43 Gawkey] See Textual Commentary, p. 445.

102.42 countrymen,] In MSh "countryman / men" appears nine times, "country man / men" four times. In three of the latter instances the words are written close together. The one-word form is obviously Irving's preferred spelling.

104.1 small-clothes,] This is the only instance of the word noted. Since it is not listed in Webster (1806), the hyphenated form is permitted to remain.

105.22 brilliancy] This is the form listed in Webster (1806).

105.38 eminently] MSh reads "literature, ⟨whose Pleasures of Memory shew him a man emenently [*illegible word*] to appre- / -ciate a work of the kind declared that above⟩ ↑whose refined purity of taste and↓ exquisite mental organization, rendered him emenenlty calculated...."

105.39 kind, declared] Even though Rogers was still alive in 1849, a verb in the present tense here cannot be accepted unless the tenses of other verbs in the sentence ("rendered," "had seen," "had continued") are altered.

106.24–25 the most amiable picture] The word "tender" is perfectly clear in MSh. Irving probably changed the word to avoid repetition with "tender" in line 27.

106.30 seemed to mark him] The verb tenses are inconsistent in this paragraph. In reading proof Irving may well have sensed an awkwardness here and made the change to improve style. Since the end of the sentence reads more smoothly as it is in 49a, it is adopted in T.

106.41 honeysuckle] In MSh, 49a, and the source, the word is hyphenated because in each instance "honey" comes at the end of the line. Since Webster (1806) lists the one-word form, that is adopted here.

109.10 job work] Since the two-word form appears twice in MSh, it is adopted here.

110.14–15 The new comedy] See Textual Commentary, p. 440.

110.19 a comedy of the same class,] It seems unlikely that a printer would have inserted the phrase without authorization; therefore the 49a reading has been adopted.

112.42 *Forster's Goldsmith, p. 437.] Originally Irving put a star after the word "biographer" (111.36), but he crossed it and the footnote out. On the next MS page he put a star after the word "genius" (112.4) but failed to include the footnote at the bottom of the page. In his letter of August 25, 1809, Irving called Putnam's attention to the mis-spelled name.

112.10 surprise]   In MSh "surprize" appears in two other usages. In all other instances the *s* spelling is used as it is consistently in 49a.

112.10–11 he showed himself capable]   This is accepted as a probable authorial revision.

113.4 lexicographer]   This is an instance of Irving's frequent tendency to omit one of a pair of commas. The printer inserted the mate after "not." However, since Irving did not use commas in a similar construc-tion in the preceding sentence ("He had not like Johnson a . . ."), the single comma is omitted here.

113.10 company,]   Irving's failure to put the second of a pair of commas here was not, as usual, remedied by the printer. It is, therefore, added in T.

113.20 haphazard]   See 29.37.

114.11 downright]   In MSh the two parts of the word are written close together. In MSp the one-word form is used twice.

114.15 *of it.*"*]   In MSh the footnote indicated by the star appears at the end of the chapter on the page corresponding with 115.

114.19 good nature.]   MSh contains three instances of "good nature" and two of "good natured." MSp reads "good nature" twice, "good-nature" three times, and "good-natured" four times. 49a is inconsis-tent. Irving's preference for the two-word form is honored in T except where he correctly quotes a hyphenated form from a source.

114.32–33 to Dr. Johnson and Dr. Shebbeare]   Irving probably added "Dr." to achieve balance with "Dr. Shebbeare."

114.39 'robust sophistry':—]   Irving was correct in using quotation marks, since he was quoting from line 12 above.

116.29 counterfeit.]   In MSh "counter" comes at the end of the line; there is no hyphen. Since the one-word form is listed in Webster (1806), the assumption here is that Irving carelessly omitted the hyphen. Compare line 32 below.

116.38 sarcasm of the learned circle.]   In Pr. "learned club" is crossed out; a line is drawn to the bottom of the page, where "learned circle" is handwritten. The bracket before "sarcasm" in Pr. was put in by hand, but no closing bracket was inserted.

116.39 'tun of man,']   In Pr. the *T* of "Tun" is crossed out, and a lower-case *t* is written in the margin.

117.4 author, and here]   In Pr. the word "and" is written in the margin.

117.10 apprentice]   See Textual Commentary, p. 440.

117.10 staymaker]   In MSh the two words are fairly close together. In another instance (199.27) where Irving wrote "Stay making," the two words are not quite so close, but the one-word form is adopted by analogy with "staymaker." Webster (1806) lists "staymaker" but not "staymaking."

117.11 Grub Street] In MSh Irving distinctly wrote "Grub Street" four times. In two other instances the *s* of "street" could be either a capital or a lowercase letter. Twice (49.34, 56.31) he was quoting, probably from Forster, who in both instances wrote "Grub Street." This being Irving's predominant usage, it is adopted in T. Of fifteen other specific streets mentioned in MSh "Street" is capitalized in ten, the *s* is lowercase in two, and the *s* in each of the other three is indeterminate. All are unhyphenated. Irving's preference for capitalizing "Street" and using the two-word form is followed in T. See Textual Commentary, pp. 447–48.

117.35 He was a] In MSp in the margin next to the crossed-out words is written in handwriting, possibly not Irving's, "He was a."

118.4 pig butcher:] In three other instances in MSh Irving consistently used the two-word form.

118.4 cry,] The word looks clear enough in MS; but, because it and "say" have a similar conformation, the printer may have misread it.

118.28 melancholy." Often] The source (Forster, 423) reveals that Irving placed his quotation marks properly in this passage. The words "Often . . . abruptly" are paraphrased.

118.32 "The Good Natured Man."] The large number of variations between MS and 49a in this title was mentioned in the Textual Commentary (p. 448). Of the twelve usages noted in MSh, "Good Natured" is never hyphenated. Only once is the initial "The" capitalized, and the word "Natured" is capitalized in seven instances. Only once does Irving use quotation marks around the title (173.10–11), and the present instance is one of only two in which 49a does not. Irving's preference for the unhyphenated form is adopted in T as is the general tendency of 49a to capitalize "The" and to use quotation marks around the title.

118.35 writer—still, we hope, living—whom] This is not the kind of change a printer would be likely to make. It is accepted as Irving's change.

119.26 talk,' said he, 'and] The inserted words are accepted as authorial.

119.35 Louis the Fourteenth] "Lewis" was not changed to "Louis" until after 1860. Boswell (II, 40) reads "Louis XIV." Compare 36.38 ("Louis XIV").

120.1 any thing.] Irving apparently had Boswell (II, 36) open before him, and some of his phrases are verbatim (e.g., "writing any thing"; "he thought he had already done his part as a writer"). Irving's quotation "But did you make no reply . . ." is in indirect discourse in Boswell. The random quotation mark after "any thing" would require one before "writing." There is another after "so well" (line 3). The printer supplied its mate at "I should" (line 2), which is not in MS.

120.25 Goldsmith and] Since the change from "or" to "and" involved an alteration of meaning, it was probably Irving's revision and is so accepted.

120.34 secretaryship] Compare 76.12, where Irving wrote "Secretary-Ship." In the present instance "Secretary" comes at the end of a line, and there is no hyphen.

121.5 Davies in] Since Irving did not supply a comma after "Garrick" and since his predominant usage is not to punctuate prepositional phrases, this comma is omitted.

121.10–11 had been so long treated] MS reading agrees with Thomas Davies, *Memoirs of the Life of David Garrick, Esq. . . .* (London, 1780), II, 147.

121.36 the comedy] As Irving originally wrote it, "his" refers to Garrick. The change may well have been made to remove the ambiguity.

122.3 proprietor of Covent Garden,] Irving was in error in writing "Drury Lane." Garrick became joint-patentee of Drury Lane in 1747. Drury Lane and Covent Garden were the two patent theaters in London at this time. See Explanatory Notes, 120.30.

122.21 anxieties."] In MSh Irving wrote the following conclusion of the letter: *paragraph* "I am Dear Sir, with the greatest esteem your most obedient humble Servant / Oliver Goldsmith / To / George Colman Esq / Richmond-" It does not seem probable that the printer would have omitted this without authorization. Because it is a typical complimentary close, Irving probably wanted it omitted, especially since the final sentences of the next two letters are included (122.32; 122.42–43).

123.13 bibliopole,] In MSh the first *b* is superimposed on a capital *B*.

123.16–17 complete it in two years, if possible,] The revision is accepted as probably Irving's, since it achieves greater exactness of expression.

124.3 sitting room] This is the only instance of this word noted. Since it appears in MSp and since it is not listed in Webster (1806), Irving's general tendency not to hyphenate is observed here.

124.4 panelled] The misspelling was not corrected until after 1860.

124.15 disappear,] Irving originally wrote "disappears"; then he extended the tail of the *r* over the *s*.

124.22 Grub Street] See 117.11.

124.25 Ministers] See Textual Commentary, p. 440.

124.28 Gawkey,] See Textual Commentary, p. 445.

125.1 to me;'—and so] In MSh the dash is superimposed on a semicolon.

125.7–8 renown, closed his mortal career. The poet] The half-line left blank in MSh suggests that Irving meant to cross out what preceded but failed to do so.

126.20 pasteboard] Although in MSh the space between the two words is such that Irving's intention is difficult to determine, the one-word form is adopted because it is listed in Webster (1806).

126.20 other's hand] Irving's singular noun is correct. The expression is from card games.

127.7 unusual care.] This revision is accepted as probably Irving's.

127.8–9 wardrobe and toilet.] Here and in two other usages of "wardrobe" in MSh the two words are written close enough together to be regarded as one word in intention. In a fourth usage (140.33) in which the first syllable comes at the end of a line, Irving wrote "ward- / -robe."

127.18 gloom over] In MSh the word "over" is so carelessly written that on first glance it does look like "on."

127.35 childlike] Here and in two other usages the two syllables are written close enough together to be regarded as one word in intention. The one-word form is sanctioned by Webster (1806).

128.3 went, he said, to] In MSp a caret was inserted after "went," and the words "he said" were written in the margin.

128.35 entirely devoid] MSh is perfectly clear at this point. The revision is accepted as probably Irving's.

129.4 green rooms,] Here and in two other instances in MSh Irving appears to have written "Green Room," though in all three the capital G and R could be read as lowercase letters. His preference for the two-word form is honored in T. Compare 76.8 where "green-room" agrees with the source (Forster, 211). In this instance *Works* (I, 329) reads "Green Room."

129.15 deemed jealous] Since this is from a printed passage, it does not seem likely to have been a printer's error. It is accepted as Irving's change.

130.3 *Shoemaker's holyday*] In MSh Irving wrote "Shoe makers" once again but also "'shoemaker" five times, the latter being accepted as his preferred form. For "holyday" see 11.4.

130.33 blind man's] The two-word form appears again in MSp (180.38), in which instance 49a does not hyphenate.

130.35 below,] In MSh the punctuation after "below" is uncertain. It could be a colon or semicolon, or it could be a dot over the *i* of occupied" in the next line, followed by a comma.

130.36 overhead] See 20.3.

131.5 footpaths] In MSh the two syllables are close together. Webster (1806) lists "footpaths."

131.8–10 excursion. . . . waiter.] The sentence following the word "excursion" was omitted from 49a and all other impressions examined. In the margin of MSh next to this sentence is written, "left out in Book."

131.10 evening they]   In MSh the dot after "evening" is below the line and may be a random mark.

131.22 company. Peter]   This revision is accepted as probably Irving's.

131.39 tea table]   Compare 81.16.

132.3–4 eye on]   This is accepted as a probable authorial revision.

132.38 "Why, sir,]   In MSp the passage following these words to the end of the chapter constitutes a page taken bodily from Forster (493) and used as MS copy. At the beginning of each line of Forster's excerpt is a single quotation mark, which 49a omitted.

134.2 *book building*]   This expression appears four times in MSp. 49a followed MS twice and hyphenated twice. The two-word form has been adopted in T.

134.18 Roads,]   Of four instances of "Edgeware Road" in MSh the word "Road" in only one contains a standard capital *R*. In the other three the *r* is an enlarged lowercase letter. Just as Irving apparently preferred to capitalize "Street" in specifically named streets (see 117.11), so his intention seems to be to capitalize "Road." The word "Edgeware" is so written in all but two instances, in which it reads "Edge ware."

134.21 hedge rows,]   Both here and in one other instance in MSh two words seem intended. Since the word is not listed in Webster (1806), Irving's two-word form is apparently acceptable and is, therefore, adopted.

134.25 Mr. Edmund Bott,]   Both Forster (465, 480) and Prior (II, 138, 521) spell the name "Bott."

134.35 sometimes in]   Here the printer did not, as usual, remedy Irving's omission of one of a pair of commas by putting one after "labor." Since Irving did not usually set off a prepositional phrase, this single comma is omitted in T.

135.3 gayety]   See 62.5.

135.13 affliction at his]   Although in MSh the word is certainly "affliction," it could easily be misread.

135.28 heartfelt]   In MSh the two syllables are close together. Irving also wrote "heart sick" (227.33), and here again the two syllables are close. Webster (1806) lists both "heartfelt" and "heartsick."

136.4 restlessness,]   See Textual Commentary, p. 433.

137.3 bloom colored]   Irving wrote this two-word phrase once again (190.16–17), and it appears once hyphenated in MSp (138.33).

137.33 Bickerstaffe]   See Textual Commentary, p. 445.

137.37 of this kind.]   This is accepted as probably Irving's revision.

138.20 for ever]   Irving wrote "forever" twice more in MSh, in one instance (222.5) incorrectly quoting Forster (667), who used the two-word form; but he also wrote "for ever" twice, in both instances correctly quoting from sources. "For ever" appears twice in MSp, and 49a consistently uses this form. The word is not listed in Webster (1806).

139.9–10 others of Goldsmith's] The singular "other" is obviously in error in MSh.

139.13 defects,] This is accepted as a probable Irving revision, effected perhaps to avoid repetition with "ugliness" in line 23.

139.14 playmates, and which had been] Irving's false start indicates his original intention of maintaining the parallel structure. After crossing out the passage he probably forgot to restore the word "and." The printer's substituting "and" for "which" instead of inserting it destroys the style of the sentence.

139.28 of a Mrs.] Irving used the word "a" in this way at least a dozen times. See, however, 209.20.

139.37 byname] In MSh "bye" and "name" have a small space between them, but the *e* of "bye" is extended in the direction of the *n*. This could be regarded as one word. Since Webster (1806) does not list "byname" but does use it as a synonym for the word "nickname," the one-word form is adopted here. This is the only instance of the word noted.

139.38 prepared] Irving failed to include a comma after "sister" in the next line; 49a supplied one at that point. Both commas have been omitted in T, as Irving seldom punctuated prepositional phrases.

140.7 them remains] In MSh the mark after "them" may be a period, or it may be the end of the letter *m*. Irving rarely put a comma between subject and verb.

140.15 verses!] The verses that follow (lines 16–27) were taken bodily from Forster (502) and used as part of the MS page.

140.19 night—] For this and the previous item, see Textual Commentary, p. 451.

141.6 thy person,] MSh version is an obvious slip of the pen.

142.25 delighted too in collecting] The printer apparently regarded "to in" as an error, but the context suggests that Irving meant to write "too."

142.38 amusement. Whenever] See Explanatory Notes, 142.38.

144.18 Goldsmith's intention] The error in 49a was not corrected until after 1860.

144.28 Pidcock's] In 1825 the word is spelled correctly in a quotation from the *Memoirs of Richard Cumberland* (London, 1807), II, 352. The misspelling, which first occurred in 1840, was not corrected in any of the impressions examined.

148.2 *to his brother Maurice*] This revision is accepted as probably Irving's.

148.10 knighthood.*] In MS the footnote does not appear on the page but was added at the end of the chapter (MS, p. 313, which corresponds to 151).

148.34; 149.1 I believe I could get] It is difficult to account for the variation in 49a unless, while reading proof, Irving decided to change "believe" to "think" but failed to cross out "believe." The proof sheet for this page is not extant, but the MS reading agrees with Percy (87), Irving's original source, and *Letters,* p. 83.

150.14–15 forlorn, haphazard] For "haphazard" see 29.37.

150.31 fame, and] MS here is obviously in error.

150.32–33 mezzotinto] When Irving wrote this word again in line 37, the printer did not change it as he did here. Webster (1806) lists "mezzotinto."

150.34–35 over the Shannon] See Textual Commentary, p. 442.

151.2 sweetmeats] See 48.22.

152.36–37 as may well be supposed,] This is accepted as probably Irving's revision made to improve the style of the sentence.

153.5 for ever] See 138.20.

153.27 childlike] See 127.35.

154.6 NOTE] In MS preceding the note is the following in Irving's handwriting: "NB. The following is to follow the chapter as an illustration or note but to be set up in the same type with it." The source of the following quotation is "Modern Pilgrimages—Auburn," *New Monthly Magazine and Literary Journal* 2 (1821), 449.

155.8 post chaise] In the source and in MSp and 49a "post" comes at the end of the line and is hyphenated. In MSh (179.28) Irving wrote "post chaises" without the hyphen. Webster (1806) lists "postchaise."

155.26 It is] 49a agrees with source in omitting the quotation marks but erroneously indents for a new paragraph.

155.29 There is] 49a was correct in omitting the quotation mark in MS but erred in beginning a new paragraph. The source, which reads "Here is," does not paragraph at this point.

156.23 hawthorn-bush] The word appears twice more in this paragraph; in MSh Irving wrote "haw thorn bush" (line 28), the two syllables being close together, and "hawthorn / bush" (line 30). All three instances are hyphenated in Prior (I, 17, 18), the probable source.

157.8 himself] In MSh this is the only two-word form of this word noted. It is probably an instance of Irving's failure to add a hyphen at the end of the line.

157.38 appeared at] Irving's preposition seems to have been a slip of the pen.

158.20 Fairy Tale?—] See Textual Commentary, p. 449.

161.2 perform it;] In MSp the mark after "it" is probably a defective semicolon.

161.21 women] See Textual Commentary, p. 442.

162.5 high bred] The handwriting at this point in MS is so crabbed that what looks like "lived" could be "bred"; and the next word, which the printer read as "notions," is practically illegible. Irving used "high bred" three more times and "high life" once again, but there is no other instance of "high lived."

162.13 outrun] See 65.28.

163.23 rich,] the word "sick" in MSp and 49a is meaningless in the context. The printed passage of MS is from the 1840 essay, and it is easy to see how the printer may have misread Irving's handwriting in the 1840 MS.

164.3–4 *The Haunch of Venison*] Irving was right to capitalize, since this is the title of a poem by Goldsmith.

164.9 early follies] Irving wrote the word "follies" in the left-hand margin of MS.

164.34–35 abridgment] Twice in MSp the American spelling is found, and 49a consistently uses it.

165.4 a visit] The omission of "long" is accepted as probably Irving's revision.

165.4 seat of Gosfield,] See Explanatory Notes, 101.28.

165.20 received by the author] This is accepted as probably Irving's revision.

167.16 Rowley, discovered] This is accepted as a probable revision made by Irving to eliminate the ambiguity of the original "he."

168.2 coldness had dashed] This is accepted as a probable authorial revision designed to achieve parallelism with "had changed" in the preceding line.

168.18 end; nor have] Irving's singular verb was an obvious error.

168.23 raillery] Irving's handwriting is not absolutely clear at this point.

168.28 poor Chatterton] The addition of the word "poor" has the ring of an Irving revision. He often used this epithet for Goldsmith as an expression of sympathy, and the context here makes evident that he was also sympathetic to Chatterton.

168.41 Rapin, Carte, Smollett] Irving often failed to cross his *t*'s, and this happened in the case of "Carte." The printer's misreading is understandable. See Explanatory Note, 85.12–13.

169.30–170.23 "My dear Sir . . . Oliver Goldsmith] This letter was taken bodily from Forster (588–89) and used as MS copy.

169.41–42 We . . . you.]   This sentence is italicized in MSp (i.e., Forster, 588), but Irving wrote in the margin next to it, "not Italics."

170.7–8 There . . . countenance.]   In the margin next to this sentence in MSp is written, "not to be printed in Italics." The sentence in lines 9–11 ("God . . . circumstances") has a line marked next to it, but Irving did not repeat the instruction. Next to lines 16–18 ("God knows . . . would do no harm to nobody") there is a line and the word "idem" written in the margin, and the same direction is written next to lines 19–20 ("When . . . Whig").

171.3 *Barton—Aquatic misadventure*]   The fact that the table of contents contains the 49a reading rather than the MS suggests that it was compiled from galley sheets rather than MS. The medley letter, mentioned in MS headnotes, does not appear until Chapter XXXVI.

171.6 somewhat]   See 81.9.

171.27 Barton," she says,]   From here to the end of the paragraph is a quotation from Prior (II, 377–78), who was paraphrasing what Mary Horneck told him. Irving's use of quotation marks in the passage, especially the one at the end of the paragraph, created understandable confusion for the printer.

171.36 group."]   Irving's quotation mark is retained here for two reasons. First, this concludes the paraphrased passage from Prior, erroneously attributed to Mary Horneck (see preceding note). Secondly, six paragraphs in Prior were omitted between this and the following paragraph.

172.3–4 His perfect . . . played off.]   This sentence is not in MS. Since the next sentence is meaningless without it, Irving must have supplied it either on request of the printer or on noting the omission while reading proof.

172.8 ladylike]   Both here and in 190.14 Irving wrote the two-word form. From the space between the syllables it is difficult to determine his intention, but "ladylike" is adopted by analogy with "childlike" (see 127.35) and on the ground that this is the form listed in Webster (1806).

172.29 equally baneful]   There is no question here of the printer's having misread the MS, nor is this the kind of change a printer would make on his own. It is, therefore, accepted as probably Irving's revision.

172.43 elsewhere,]   The one-word form, which appears once in MSh and once in MSp, is listed in Webster (1806).

173.2 the love of all]   Irving mentioned this error in his letter of August 25, 1849, to Putnam.

173.3–19 Among the circumstances . . . Mr. Newbery!]   In MSh the paragraph originally read as follows: "While at Barton he read to the fair sisters some chapters of the tale which he was preparing for

Newbery; but which he never finished. The bookseller objected to it as a mere narrative version of 'the Good Natured Man,' which it probably was; having been written in a hurry ⟨to⟩ when pressed for pecuniary means. The loss of the manuscript is to be regretted as it could not fail to bear traces of his delightful Style." In the margin of MS is written very lightly, "See 3rd [? or 5 ?] paragraph p 307." MS, p. 307 corresponds with 149.28–150.6.

174.8 1745] The dot in MSh looks more like a random pen mark than a purposeful mark of punctuation.

174.19 Oglethorpe,] The verses in Prior (II, 422) read: "Or driven by strong benevolence of soul, / Shall fly like Oglethorpe from Pole to Pole." Since in MSh Irving put a comma after "fly," the printer's comma after "Oglethorpe" seems necessary.

174.31 1772,)] In MSh Irving seems first to have written "1722" and then put a 7 over the first 2. In his letter to Putnam of August 25, 1849, he called attention to the error in 49a.

174.33 Belgrade] It is difficult to know whether the period in MSh is a random pen mark or whether Irving closed his sentence and then added an afterthought. He seldom used a comma to set off a prepositional phrase at the end of a sentence.

175.24 replied he] Irving was correct in not using quotation marks here and at the end of the sentence. He should not have used them in line 15 either. In both passages he was paraphrasing Boswell (II, 174).

175.39 idem nolle–] This is one of the errors that Irving pointed out in his letter of August 25, 1849, to Putnam. In Boswell (II, 176) the Latin phrase is italicized.

176.6 that Goldsmith had the best] There is no evidence that Irving requested this change, but the original clause is a misstatement of what he obviously meant to say.

176.11 Colonel Prendergast] Boswell (II, 178) spells the name thus.

176.24 Prendergast] Both MSh and 49a are in error. See preceding note.

176.39 Cock-lane] The name appears in MSp as "Cock-lane" and "Cock-Lane." 49a uses "Cock-lane" twice and "Cock-Lane" once. The spelling in sources is even more varied: "Cock Lane" in Prior (I, 387) and Forster (240), and "Cock-lane" in Boswell (I, 415). In *Works* (IV, 415) "Cock-Lane" appears on the title page, "Cock-lane" in the body of the essay (417), and "Cock Lane" in Friedman's editorial comment (417). Regarding all of these usages, one must conclude that the hyphenated form was the most frequently used; and that is the form adopted in the present instance.

177.2 Mr.] The headnotes are not in MS; and only the first four items were added by hand to the proof sheet, at the bottom of which

Irving wrote, "NB. The table of contents is not complete—I forget what is in the residue of the chapter—"

177.23 enterprise]   See 62.38.

177.24 somewhat]   See 81.9.

179.27 summer]   In MS the passage "To escape . . . post chaises" (lines 25–28) is written at the bottom of the page following line 40.

179.28 Road]   See 134.18.

179.30 landlady]   See 88.32.

180.14 every where]   This two word form appears twice in MSh, in one instance (224.16) in a quotation from *Works* (II, 294), which also uses the same form.

180.29 Edgeware]   See 134.18.

181.7 eyes]   In illustrating this usage Webster's unabridged (1934) quotes Shakespeare: "How earnestly he cast his eyes upon me!"

181.9 'snatched]   Irving is here quoting from Pope's *Essay on Criticism* (pt. 1, line 153).

182.1 headquarters]   In MSh there is a space after "head," but this appears to be another instance of Irving's peculiar formation of the letter *d*, which forces him to begin anew with the rest of the word. It is interesting to note that Webster (1806) does not list this word but does include other "head" compounds, such as "headdress," "head-piece," and "headworkman."

182.10–11 When Burke, said he, praised]   Irving had either Boswell (I, 423) or Forster (608) open before him, probably the latter. Since, in either case, he was paraphrasing, the absence of quotation marks in MS is correct.

182.13 myself." "The]   Here the quotation marks added in 49a are necessary in light of those used by Irving in the passage. He was actually in error, since the quotation in both Boswell and Forster reads: "He went home with Mr. Burke to supper, and broke his shin. . . ."

182.16 surpasses]   The context suggests that MS is correct.

182.19 puppets]   MSh reads: "⟨to return to⟩ the *capital T superimposed on lowercase t* Panton Street puppets, ⟨they⟩ were. . . ." Irving failed to cross out the comma when he revised the sentence.

182.24 Puppet-Shew]   This is the form used in Samuel N. Bogorad and Robert Gale Noyes's critical edition of *Samuel Foote's Primitive Puppet-Shew Featuring Piety in Patterns* published in *Theatre Survey* 14 (Fall, 1973), the entire number being devoted to this edition of the play.

182.25 *Chambermaid*]   According to Bogorad and Noyes, *ibid.*, p. 68, the word should be *Housemaid*. Compare 196.27.

182.27 idea of a play] This is the third instance on this page of a word omitted in MS. It suggests the haste with which Irving was writing.

183.4 poet] Compare 99.2; 157.2.

183.14 Thrales'] See Textual Commentary, p. 445.

183.27 portfolio;] This is the only instance of the word noted. In MSh "port" comes at the end of a line. Since "portfolio" is listed in Webster (1806), one can regard this as another instance of Irving's failure to add a hyphen in such a situation.

183.31 "overrunning] See 20.3.

183.40 of a practical joke] This is another example of Irving's failure to complete a revision.

184.27 Burke, walking] MSh reads "Burke were walking one ⟨and Burke, walking one⟩ day." Irving appears to have crossed out the wrong words.

184.33–34 Burke received Goldsmith with unusual reserve] Irving's failure to cross out the word "affected" probably confused the typesetter.

185.25 (Turnham Green).] Neither Prior (II, 483) nor Forster (525) felt it necessary to clarify the point of the joke; therefore the place is not mentioned in either of the possible sources. Irving's general preference for unhyphenated place names, however, suggests the appropriateness of adopting his form here.

185.29 dead silence] The way Irving formed his letters in the word "silence," it is not impossible that the printer misread the word. "Silence" seems more appropriate in the context.

185.34 nickname Malagrida.] For "nickname" see 101.42.

186.17 Drury Lane] Of four usages in MSh this is the only instance of a lowercase *l*. 49a follows MS twice and hyphenates twice. Irving's preferred two-word form is adopted in T.

186.17 protégé] The accent marks were supplied by the editor.

186.26 finding himself caught] Irving's "him" was undoubtedly an error.

186.29–41 Among the many . . . of his heart.] See Textual Commentary, pp. 441–42.

187.13–14 wherein he describes "a woman] Irving was here quoting from *The Citizen of the World.* See *Works* (II, 111).

187.43 think."] Written vertically in the margin next to this footnote in MSh is the following: "*NB.* This to form a note at the bottom of the page."

188.1–2 him, would decry] In Prp Irving put a line through the letter *n* in the word "deny" and in the margin wrote, "cr /."

188.10 newspapers] See 97.26.

188.13 purport] In Pr. Irving inserted a caret after the word "purport" and wrote in the margin: "NB Separate the title from the letter press."

189.8–9 for masquerades . . . incident.]   The omitted passage represents a line of handwriting in MS. This suggests that the printer's eye skipped a line.

189.9 calling on the poet one morning,]   The comma, added in 49a, would seem to require another after "Reynolds" to set off the non-restrictive participial phrase. Notice, however, that Irving used only a single comma in a similar construction at 189.3.

190.2 *spring velvet*]   This adjective appears four times in MSh and four times in hyphenated form in MSp. Since *Works* (IV, 401) uses the two-word form, it is adopted in T.

190.2 *The haymaking*]   Twice "hay makers" appears in MSh. In all three instances the two words are so close together that one word seems to have been intended. Since "haymaker" is listed in Webster (1806), the one-word form is adopted in T.

190.7 Barton]   This error was not corrected in any impression examined up to 1860.

190.12 Loo]   Loo is the name of a game. Compare *Works* (IV, 401, 402), where both Mrs. Bunbury and Goldsmith capitalize. Three times in MSh Irving used a lowercase *l* and 49a followed him, but in MSp the word is properly capitalized. It has been consistently capitalized in T.

190.14 ladylike]   See 172.8.

190.23–25 The new wig . . . his sword.]   This paragraph is not in MS. Irving wrote it at the bottom of the proof sheet and drew an arrow to the place where it was to be inserted.

191.6 answer.–I]   See Textual Commentary, p. 451. Irving took this letter bodily from Forster (592–94) and used it as MS copy.

194.4 *Puppet Shew*]   See 182.24.

194.7 The gay life depicted in the two last chapters,]   A note on the previous MS page following the last line reads: "N. B. If this chapter is inserted the first line of the next chapter must be altered to read as follows   The gay life depicted in the two last chapters while it kept &c".

195.10 forthwith to Colman]   MSh reads: "to∧ ↑go forthwith,↓ ⟨had⟩ ⟨have a talk with Colman⟩ ⟨go immediately⟩ to Colman."

195.11 Goldsmith, therefore,]   MSh reads, "Goldsmith ⟨immediately⟩ ↑thereupon↓ penned." The 49a reading is accepted as probably Irving's revision.

195.22 entreat,]   Irving took this letter bodily from Forster (622) and used it as MS copy.

196.28 Haymarket]   In MSh the two words are written close together, but in another usage (223.25) they are farther apart. "Haymarket," which is the correct spelling, appears once in MSp and in all three instances in 49a.

199.27 staymaking:] See "staymaker" (117.10).

200.1–23 "My Dear Sir ... Mrs Cradock."] Irving took this letter bodily from Forster (626) and used it as MS copy.

200.9–10 thought of] This is one of the errors in 49a that Irving mentioned in his letter to Putnam of August 5, 1849.

200.31 Reynolds,] The printer was in error in supplying a semicolon here. A second comma is needed to set off the appositive.

200.39 "In inscribing] Irving took this quotation bodily from Forster (635) and used it as MS copy.

201.4 preengaged] In MSh Irving actually wrote "pre eng aged," both spaces being small. Webster (1806) lists "preengagement."

202.1 *CHAPTER XXXVIII*] Irving's mistake in numbering this chapter created a problem that continued for the rest of the MS. The printer noticed the incorrect numbering in Chapter XL, but Chapters XXXVIII and XXXIX remained in error and were not corrected until after 1860.

203.35 Paternoster Row] See 49.20.

204.6 stout, high blooded] For "high blooded" see 92.8.

204.7 overhead] See 20.3.

206.2 *Boswell in Holy Week*] Twice more on this page Irving wrote "Holy Week" (line 8) and "Holy week" (line 16). His preference for the two-word form is honored in T. The next topic, "Ballad singing," was omitted from 49a. The chapter having a long set of headnotes, Irving may have eliminated this topic because only a short paragraph is devoted to the subject. On the other hand, the printer may have missed it by accident.

206.14 thinking of and] The quotation has been corrected because Irving's omission of the word "of" makes the statement meaningless even with the printer's addition of a comma. The source is the *Memoirs of Doctor Burney* (London, 1832), II, 191.

206.15 some secondhand homilies] For "secondhand" see 43.5. The word "homilies" is accepted as a probable last-minute revision on the proof sheet, which has not survived.

206.20 this reply] In MSh the word "this" is written so carelessly that the printer could have misread it. MS reading is retained.

207.8 Soldiers on six pence a day] For "six pence" see 51.39.

207.11–14 The conversation ... display.] This sentence, which is not in MS, was added to the proof sheet by hand.

207.16 Lumpkin's song] On the proof sheet Irving crossed out the *s'* and wrote in the margin the symbol "tr."

207.21–34 It was . . . more *liked*.] This paragraph, which is not in MS, was added to the proof sheet by hand.

207.21 in these] In MSh the word "on" was probably a slip of the pen.

207.35 Oglethorpe's Goldsmith] Irving probably made this change to eliminate the ambiguous pronoun.

209.20 of Mr. Harris] See Explanatory Notes.

209.30 get," observed Johnson, "who does] The addition of "observed Johnson" is accepted as a probable authorial revision.

210.28 truth,] The comma appears in the source: *Memoirs of Doctor Burney* . . . (London, 1832), II, 194. This source has also been consulted in resolving other variations in this quotation and those in the next two paragraphs.

210.39 eavesdropping] In MSh the two words are close enough to suggest that one word was intended, the form listed in Webster (1806).

210.40–41 there, Sir?" cried he, turning round angrily and] *Memoirs of Doctor Burney,* II, 195, reads: "What do you do there, Sir?—Go to the table, Sir!"

211.16 pill garlic,] This is the only usage of the word noted. Webster (1806) lists "pillgarlic."

211.25 "There's] Irving took the following anecdote bodily from Forster (510) and used it as MS copy. Each of Forster's five lines begins with a single quotation mark, which was omitted in 49a.

211.25–26 mon," said he to a friend; "Jamie] Irving added "said he to a friend" in ink.

212.6 exclusiveness] Since this is not the sort of change a printer would make without authorization, it is accepted as probably Irving's.

212.17 admission, he would black-ball] In MSh the two words of "black ball" are written close together. In the next sentence Irving wrote "blackball," but there 49a's hyphenated form is adopted because it conforms to the source. Since Irving was using the same source in both instances, the hyphenated form is permitted to remain here too.

212.32 Goldsmith. It] Irving correctly used quotation marks in this passage except for "agreeable variety," which should have been quoted, since these are Boswell's words (V, 62).

214.4 suppose therefore] This is the only instance noted in MSh of "there fore," but the first syllable comes at the end of a line. It is probably another instance of Irving's failure to use a hyphen in such a situation.

214.7–22 of Doctor Johnson himself . . . his dog.] Irving rewrote from here to the end of the chapter on a separate piece of paper, which is among the surviving proof sheets. MSh reads: "At least we have a right to presume all this from the conduct of the great Lexicographer himself, who, with all his gravity, possessed a deep fund of quiet ⟨*illegible word⟩* humor. The moment Boswell entered he ⟨adv⟩ ⟨rose⟩ advanced, placed himself behind a ⟨desk⟩ chair on which he leaned as on a desk or pulpet, and ⟨delivered⟩ gave him a mock solemn charge, pointing out the Conduct expected from him as a good member of the Club. It is to be regretted that Boswell has never thought proper to ⟨Set.⟩ note down the particulars of this charge, in which it is probable were enumerated all ⟨the⟩ his petty prying gossipping questioning brabling habits which had so often grieved the spirit of the Lexicographer. In a word from the well knoun characters and humors of the parties, it might have formed a parallel to the noted charge of Launcelot Gobbo to his dog."

215.6 serio-comic] The hyphenated form appears once in MSp (18.19). It is not listed in Webster (1806).

215.18 the poet] This is accepted as a probable authorial revision.

218.21–31 to frighten . . . at his tail!] Only the first four lines of the poem are in MSh, but there is a note in the margin: "Want 10 Lines of Poem See p 386." This page number may refer to the source from which Irving took the verses.

219.4 *A high minded*] See 92.8.

219.20 whole.] In MSh the period seems to have been superimposed upon a comma.

219.29 always] Irving's "at" was either a slip of the pen or an intention to write "as."

219.35 importance,] Irving appears to have quoted this passage inexactly from Forster (671), whose account is in indirect discourse.

220.10–11 Temple, where they] This is accepted as probably Irving's revision.

221.23 sixpences you know] This conforms to the source: Hester Lynch Piozzi, *Anecdotes of the Late Samuel Johnson . . .*, 2d ed. (London, 1786), p. 179.

221.29 "Every body," exclaimed] Irving has been writing in the past tense; therefore this sudden switch to present tense is out of place. The revision is accepted as probably authorial.

221.35 extravagant,] In MSh the mark after the word is below the line and may be random marks rather than punctuation.

221.40–42 while Voltaire . . . utter darkness.] A revision of this magnitude is not likely to have been the printer's. It is accepted as probably Irving's.

222.5 for ever.] See 138.20.

223.2 *green room*] See 129.4.

224.3 wore] The revision of tense in this and the next verb is accepted as probably Irving's.

225.26–27 and a tart;] Irving's repetition of the word "fish" was obviously a slip of the pen.

226.7 country Christmas!] In MSh the exclamation point seems to have been superimposed on a semicolon.

226.8 fireside] See 7.34.

226.18–19 as Garrick] The omission of "Mr" is accepted as probably Irving's work.

226.36 circle and a Christmas fireside at Barton.] The revision is accepted as probably Irving's.

227.1 *CHAPTER XLIV*) In MSh the "3" seems superimposed on a "4."

227.18–19 drudging, depressing kind,] In the proof sheet the word "unexciting" is crossed out and a line drawn from the word to the margin, where no substitute is written.

227.19 made weary] In his letter of August 25, 1849, to Putnam, Irving called attention to the erroneous word "wrong" in 49a.

227.19 faint. "If] On the proof sheet the word "He" is crossed out, and a line is drawn to the bottom of the page and around a handwritten passage which constitutes lines 19–25 ("If there is . . . in comparison").

227.26 Goldsmith again] On the proof sheet the word "He" is crossed out. At the bottom of the page following the handwritten insertion, Irving began a new paragraph thus: "Goldsmith again makes an effort &c."

227.32–33 companion's heartsick] See 135.28.

228.7 serene quiet, and] Pr. reads "serene, quiet and." Irving marked in the proofreader's symbol, wrote "tr" in the margin, and drew a line to the bottom of the page where he wrote, "Serene quiet,".

228.29 good humored] In MSh following "good" but placed below the line is a mark that might be a colon or a dot with a dash below it. The lower mark might, on the other hand, be a dot belonging to the *i* of the word "its" in the line beneath it.

231.7–8 originally intended to be introduced,] The added phrase is accepted as probably Irving's revision.

231.23 friendly portrait] The revision is accepted as probably Irving's.

231.31 afternoon,] In MSh "after" comes at the end of the line, and Irving did not use a hyphen. The one-word form is listed in Webster (1806).

233.3 that such a memorial] Pr. reads, "that a simple memorial." Irving put a caret after "that," wrote the word "such" above, and crossed out "simple." Then he drew a line to the bottom of the page and wrote, "that such a memorial."

233.8 General Gwyn] The change from "Colonel" to "General" is not likely to have been made by a printer without authorization. It is accepted as probably Irving's revision.

233.11 "I don't know," said] Irving seems to have taken this passage directly from William Hazlitt's *Conversations of James Northcote Esq. R. A.* See edition edited by Frank Swinnerton (London, 1949), pp. 61–62. The source reads, "and he said, 'I don't know why she is so kind as to come, except that. . . .' "

233.14–15 life." "Not only so,"] The source reads, "life.' I said, Not only so, but. . . ."

234.1 *CHAPTER XLV*] In MSh the second "4" is written over a large but light "5."

234.2 *Concluding remarks*] Since the word "reflections" is clearly written in MSh, the revision is accepted as probably Irving's.

234.19 offences] In three usages of this word noted in MSh, two are spelled with an *s* and one with a *c*. MSp uses the *c* spelling once, the form consistently used in 49a. Webster (1806) lists "offense." Since the spelling of this word was apparently in a transitional state, the inconsistencies in MS are permitted to remain.

234.24 Hence] The first line of the poem as it appears in *The European Magazine* 24 (October, 1793), 258, reads, "Hence K——y, who years thro' *sans* honour or shame."

235.10 south door in Poets' Corner] Compare 151.23.

235.24–25 He was willing, he said, to] Irving used quotation marks correctly in this passage. Up to the word "*but*" in line 26, he was paraphrasing Boswell (III, 449).

235.26 pleased; "*but*] In MSh Irving placed a comma after the word "pleased" and then added what looks like a semicolon.

235.32 bust:] In MSh following this word is written in Irving's handwriting "(Insert the latin Epetaph)." In the margin is written in what appears to be someone else's handwriting, "Epitaph left out See 417."

235.33 "OLIVARII GOLDSMITH,] Neither the Latin epitaph nor the translation in the footnote appears in MS.

236.16 scope,] The passage beginning with "on his writings;" (line 13) and ending here is written in MSh in a handwriting not Irving's. The passage is signed with the symbol M ,.

237.12 wayward] In MSh the two syllables are close enough together to suggest that one word was intended.

237.13 throughout] In MSh the first syllable comes at the end of a line. Since "throughout" is listed in Webster (1806), the assumption is that Irving omitted the hyphen as he often did in this position.

237.16 feelings; they dispose] Because the change of "and" to "they" results in a better structured sentence, Irving's hand in the revision is suspected.

237.20 delusive gifts,] The revision is accepted as probably Irving's.

237.28 for the customary time,] The word "customary" is accepted as probably Irving's revision.

237.41 secondhand] See 43.5.

238.16 forerun] In MSh the first syllable comes at the end of the line, and there is no hyphen. This is the only usage of the word noted. In Webster (1806) the one-word form is listed.

238.20–21 without] In MSh the first syllable comes at the end of the line, and Irving failed to insert the hyphen.

238.23 "He could not stifle] In MSh the first phrase is at the end of the page. In turning to a fresh sheet, Irving merely repeated himself.

239.1 company,] The source of the quotation is the *Edinburgh Review* 88 (July, 1848), 207. See Explanatory Notes, 239.2. Where MSh and 49a differ in punctuation, this source has been consulted.

239.10 pictures of life] Irving pointed out this error in his letter of August 25, 1849, to Putnam.

239.32 village pastor,] Since the "village pastor" is a character rather than a title, the capitalization in 49a is rejected.

240.17 firesides,] See 7.34.

240.25–26 so affectionate, so confiding–] The source (see 239.1) reads, "so affectionate and so confiding–..."

240.29 are evident,] Irving's singular verb is an obvious error.

240.30 more significancy] This is accepted as probably Irving's revision.

240.37 associates] This is accepted as a probable authorial revision. Notice that Irving used the word "friends" in line 35.

240.42 general tone] This passage being from a printed part of MS, it seems unlikely that the printer misread the word. Since there are several other substantive revisions on this page, it is more probable that Irving changed the word himself.

241.8–9 and we turn more kindly] This is not the sort of change a printer would make without authorization. It is accepted as probably Irving's.

241.20 kind hearted] See 51.9–10.

LIST OF EMENDATIONS

These notes identify all emendations of the copy-text. The numbers before each note indicate the page and line. Epigraphs, author's chapter or section summaries, texts, quotations, and footnotes are included in the line count. Only running heads and rules added by the printer to separate running heads from the text are omitted from the count.

The reading to the left of the bracket is the portion of the text under consideration or discussion and represents an accepted reading that differs from the copy-text. The source of the reading is identified by symbol after the bracket. The reading after the semicolon is the rejected reading of the copy-text and any other text in which that reading occurs; if other alternatives are also available, they are recorded following that reading.

The swung (wavy) dash ~ represents the same word, words, or characters that appear before the bracket, and is used in recording punctuation variants; the caret ∧ indicates that a mark of punctuation is omitted. T signifies that a decision to emend or not to emend has been made on the authority of the editor of this edition. These decisions are based upon the editor's acceptance or rejection of the variant as Irving's. Some of these editorial decisions are explained in the Discussions of Adopted Readings, which include decisions to emend as well as some decisions not to emend. Discussion is identified by an asterisk *.

A key to identifying symbols used in referring to the manuscript and editions of *Oliver Goldsmith,* as well as to Irving's sources, is given on pages 347–48.

* ix.1	CONTENTS.] 49a
ix.7	Byrne,] 49a; ~∧ 53
ix.9	studies–School] T; studies and school 49a
ix.14	bishop] 49a; Bishop 49c, 53
ix.16	counsellor] 49a; Counsellor 49c, 53
* ix.17	outset] 49a, 49c; onset 53
ix.19	Transformations] 49a; transformations 49c, 53
* ix.20–21	toadyism] T; Toryism 49a
* ix.22	fellow passengers] T; ~-~ 49a
* ix.23	way side] T; wayside 49a
* ix.30	secondhand] T; second-hand 49a

ix.35   Newbery,] 49a; Newbury, 53
* ix.35   picture book memory] T; ~-~ ~ 49a; picture memory
                      49c, 53
* x.3   Mills] T; Wells 49a
* x.8   Green Arbour] T; Green-Arbor 49a
x.11   Griffiths'] 49a; Griffith's 49c, 53
* x.15   Hangers on] T; ~-~ 49a
* x.26   the Club] T; ~ club 49a
x.30   Club] T; club 49a
* x.33   Gosfield] 50, 51, 54, 59, 60; Gosford 49a, 49c
x.35   Hangers on] T; ~-~ 49a
x.35   Job writing] 49a; Job Writing 53
* x.35   Two Shoes] T; Two-shoes 49a
* x.38   Goethe] 49c, 53; Goëthe 49a
* x.39   Book building] 49c, 53; ~-~ 49a
* x.40   position] T; condition 49a
x.40   His] T; his 49a
xi.2   Reynolds's] 49a, 49c; Reynolds' 53
xi.3   Their] T; their 49a
* xi.7   manoeuvring] T; manoeuvering 49a
* xi.8   "The Good Natured Man"] T; "The Good-natured Man"
                      49a; the "Good-natured Man' 49c, 53
* xi.11   holyday] T; holiday 49a
xi.14   Reduced again to] 49a; Reduced to 53
xi.14   book building] T; ~-~ 49a
* xi.15   paradise] 49c, 53; Paradise 49a
* xi.17   Bickerstaffe's] T; Bickerstaff's 49a
xi.17   Hiffernan] 49a; Hifferman 49c
* xi.19   bloom colored] T; ~-~ 49a
xi.30   Description] T; description 49a
* xi.35–36   The Haunch of Venison] T; The haunch of venison 49a
xii.6   debts] 49a; debt 53
* xii.6   widow] 49c, 53; Widow 49a
* xii.8   ballad singers] 49c, 53; ~-~ 49a
xii.8   The poet] 49a; The Poet 49c, 53
* xii.9   spring velvet] 49c, 53; ~-~ 49a
* xii.10   Loo] T; loo 49a
* xii.14   Puppet-Shew,] T; Puppet Show, 49a; Puppet show, 49c
* xii.18   Holy Week] T; ~-~ 49a
* xii.18   Oglethorpe's—Ballad singing—Dinner] T; Oglethorpe's—
                      Dinner 49a
* xii.22   objections] T; objection 49a
* xii.26   Man worship] T; ~-~ 49a

*xii.30   high minded] T; ~-~ 49a
*xii.31   green room] T; ~-~ 49a
*xii.31   poet] T; Poet 49a
xii.34   Forced] T; forced 49a
xii.34   Retreat] T; retreat 49a
xii.36   poet] 49a; Poet 49c, 53
xii.36   Grief of his] 49a; grief ~ ~ 49c; grief—his 53
*xii.38   remarks] T; reflections 49a
3.3   Biographical sketch] Pr., 49a; biograph / ical Sketch MSh
3.3   Goldsmith,] Pr., 49a; ~ᴧ MSh
3.5   in it] Pr., 49a; of [at ?] it MSh
3.6–7   Mr. James Prior,] Pr., 49a; ~ᴧ ~ ~ᴧ MSh
3.8   poet's] Pr., 49a; poets MSh
3.9   thought, in a form too cumbrous] 49a; ~, ~ ~ ~ ~
        cum / brous MSh; thought, too cumbrous Pr.
3.10   uninteresting] Pr.; unin / teresting MSh
3.12   sketch,] Pr.; Sketch MSh
3.13   republication,] Pr.; ~ᴧ MSh
3.13   hands,] Pr.; ~ᴧ MSh
3.14   Mr. John Forster,] Pr.; ~ᴧ ~ ~ᴧ MSh
3.15   Prior,] Pr.; ~ᴧ MSh
3.16   biography] Pr.; biogra / phy MSh
3.21   meager] 49a; meagre MSh, Pr.
3.23   substituted.] Pr.; ~ᴧ MSh
3.24   subject, and gone] Pr.; ~, ~, ⟨giving [?]⟩ ↑gone↓ MSh
3.26   poet,] Pr.; ~ᴧ MSh
3.27   I have had] 49a; I had MSh; Iᴧ had Pr.
3.29   prevented me from giving some parts of the subject]
        49a; prevented, giving some parts of my subject MSh;
        prevented ᴧ giving some parts of ⟨my⟩ subject Pr.
3.30   wished.] Pr.; ~ᴧ MSh
3.32   themselves] Pr.; them / selves MSh
3.33   Mr. Prior's] Pr.; ~ᴧ Priors MSh
3.33   or to the eloquent] T; or the eloquent MSh; orᴧ the
        elegant Pr.; or to the elegant 49a
3.34   Mr. Forster.] Pr.; ~ᴧ ~ᴧ MSh
3.35   For my own part,] Pr.; ~ ~ oun ~ᴧ MSh
3.36   for it is a tribute] 49a; a tribute, MSh
3.37   childhood,] Pr.; ~ᴧ MSh
4.1   life;] Pr.; ~: MSh
4.2   apostrophe] Pr.; Apostrophe MSh
4.2   Virgil:] Pr.; Vergil— MSh
*4.6   W. I.] 49a

4.7   Sunnyside, Aug. 1, 1849.] 49a
*5.1   *CHAPTER I*] T; CHAPTER I. 49a; chap 1. MSh
5.2   *Birth and*] 49a; ~ & MSh
5.2   *Characteristics*] 49a; characteristics MSh
5.2   *Poetical*] 49a; poetical MSh
5.3   *boyhood*] 49a; boy hood MSh
5.3   *Picture*] 49a; picture MSh
5.4   *Goldsmith's*] 49a; Goldsmiths MSh
*5.4   *schoolmistress*] T; school mistress MSh, 49a
5.4   *Byrne,*] 49a; ~∧ MSh
5.4–5   *schoolmaster*] T; school- / master 49a; school master MSh
5.5   *Goldsmith's*] 49a; Goldsmiths MSh
*5.12   humor,] 49a; humour, MSp
*5.22   good humor] 49a; good humour MSp
5.27   good humored] T; good-humoured, MSp; good-humored
               49a
5.30   parti-colored] 49a; parti-coloured MSp
5.34   November, 1728,] 49a; ~∧ ~, MSp
*5.35   Pallas, or Pallasmore, county] 49a; Pallas, county MSp
*6.1   any thing] 49a; anything MSp
6.11   parish,] 49a; ~∧ MSh
*6.14   in a rough,] 49a; on ~ ~, MSp
6.17   neighboring] 49a; neighbouring MSp
*6.22   were in vain] 49a; were vain MSp
*6.24   jackboots,] T; jack-boots MSp; jack- / boots 49a
*6.33   of that pretty little village.] 49a; of the village. MSp
*7.6   the Man in Black,] T; the "Man in Black," MSp, 49a
*7.34   fireside:] 49a; ~. MSp
*7.35   His house] T; "~ ~ MSp, 49a
7.37   long-remembered] 49a; long-remember'd MSp; long re-
               membered *Works* (IV, 293)
8.4   woe;] 49a; ~. *Works* (IV, 293); wo; MSp
8.6   began.] T; ~." MSp, 49a
8.17   neighborhood] T; ~, 49a; neighbourhood∧ MSp
8.25   any thing] 49a; anything MSp
8.37   Beside] T; "~ MSp, 49a
*9.14   gauge:] T; guage: MSp, 49a
9.16   vanquished,] 49a, *Works* (IV, 295); vanquish'd, MSp
9.20   knew.] T; ~." MSp, 49a
9.35   Every thing,] 49a; Everything, MSp
9.36   savored] 49a; savoured MSp
9.40   preceptor, Byrne,] 49a; ~∧ ~∧ MSp
*10.2   sibylline] T; sybilline MSp, 49a

10.21	humor,] 49a; humour, MSp
*10.21	favorite,] 49a; favourite MSp
10.27	discolored] 49a; discoloured MSp
10.39	uncle,] 49a; ~∧ MSh
10.41	Berkeley,] 49a; Barkeley, MSh
10.41–42	means, holding] 49a; means ⟨as⟩ holding MSh
*10.42	Carrick-on-Shannon.] 49a; ~∧~∧~. MSh
11.1	Goldsmith's] 49a; Goldsmiths MSh
11.4	infancy;] 49a; ~.- MSh
*11.4	holydays;] T; holy days; MSh; holidays 49a
11.5	poet,] 49a; ~∧ MSh
11.8	Oliver] 49a; oliver MSh
*11.13–14	have been brilliant.] 49a; ~ ~ very ~. MSp
11.21	endeavor] 49a; endeavour MSp
11.25	honors] 49a; honours MSp
*11.30	easily] 49a
11.31	harbor] 49a; harbour MSp
*11.34	man, Jack] 49a; ~, one ~ MSp
*11.42	connections] 49a; connexions MSp
12.20	parlor,] 49a; parlour, MSp
12.25	pock-marked] 49a, Forster (5); pockmarked MSp
12.27	humor,] 49a; humour, MSp
*12.28–29	this intruding guest] 49a; his ~ ~ MSp
13.3	*Wilder,*] 49a; ~∧ MSh
13.3–4	*Pecuniary*] 49a; pecuniary MSh
*13.13	and thence] 49a; and ⟨from⟩ thence MSp
13.18	neighborhood,] 49a; neighbourhood, MSp
13.22	Catherine] 49a, *Letters* (x); Catharine MSp
13.34	neighborhood;] 49a; neighbourhood; MSp
14.5	honor.] 49a; honour. MSp
*14.8	1745, when seventeen] 60; 1747, when sixteen MSp, 49a
*14.13	building, numbered 35,] 49a; ~∧ ~ ~. MSh
*14.30	base mind baser.] 49a; base baser. MSp
15.12	favorite] 49a; favourite MSh
15.23	mirth, good humour,] T, *Works* (III, 7); ~∧ ~ ~∧ MSh; ~, good-humor, 49a
*15.24	childhood."] 49a; ~∧" MSh; ~.∧ *Works* (III, 7)
15.26	endeavored] 49a; endeavoured MSp
15.30	honors.] 49a; honours. MSp
15.33	years'] 49a, Prior (I, 70); ~∧ MSp
*15.42	to leave] 49a; to have left MSp
16.4	sums;] 49a; ~, MSh
16.5	Beatty;] 49a; ~, MSh

*16.9	sank] 49a; sunk MSp
*16.22	fellow students] T; ∼-∼ MSp, 49a
*16.32	for riot.] 49a; for a riot. MSp
*16.38–39	Newgate, or the Black Dog, as the prison was called, and effect] 49a; Newgate and effect MSp
17.22	fellow students] T; ∼-∼ MSp, 49a
*17.23–24	chastisement received] 49a; ∼ he had ∼ MSp
*17.30	walls the very next day, intending] 49a; walls, intending MSp
*17.36	the clothes from his back,] 49a; his ∼ ∼ ∼ ∼, MSp
*18.14	eccentric, yet endearing] 49a; endearing, yet eccentric MSp
19.2–3	Catherine.] 49a; Catharine. MSp
19.8	any thing] 49a; anything MSp
19.39	Black:"–"To] 49a; ∼:"–"to MSh
*20.3	overruled,] 49a; over ruled MSh
20.20	Traveller:"] 49a; ∼." MSp
20.21	Remote,] T; "∼, MSp, 49a
20.39	good.] T; ∼." MSp, 49a
21.1	every thing,] 49a; everything MSp
21.5	favorite] 49a; favourite MSh
21.6	Recollections] 49a; Reccollections MSh
21.7	sports"] 49a; ∼' MSh
21.7	"Deserted Village:"] 49a; deserted village, MSh
21.8	bless'd] 49a; bless∧d MSh; blest Works (II, 287)
21.11	their] 49a; thier MSh
21.12	o'er] 49a, Works (IV, 288); oer MSh
*21.13	round.] T; ∼." 49a; ∼∧" MSh; ∼.∧ Works (IV, 288)
21.15	crony, Robert Bryanton,] 49a; ∼∧ ∼ ∼∧ MSh
21.16	Ballymulvey] 49a; Bally mulvey MSh
21.18–19	Ballymahon,] 49a; Bally mahon; MSh
21.20	associates:] 49a; ∼, MSh
*21.25	horse doctor,] T, Works (V, 110); Horse Doctor, MSh; horse doctor; 49a
21.26	platter."] 49a; ∼∧∧ MSh
21.26	Nay,] 49a; ∼∧ MSh
21.27	Tony's drinking song] 49a; Tony∧s Drinking Song MSh
21.28	Ballymahon:] 49a; Bally mahon. MSh
21.30	clever,] 49a, Works (V, 117); ∼∧ MSh
21.31	stout,] 49a, Works (V, 117); ∼∧ MSh
21.32	Here's] 49a, Works (V, 117); Heres MSh
21.34	ducks,] 49a, Works (V, 117); ∼∧ MSh

21.34	widgeons;] T, *Works* (V, 117); widgions; MSh; widgeons, 49a
21.36	Here's] 49a, *Works* (V, 117); Heres MSh
21.36	Pigeons.] 49a, *Works* (V, 117); ~∧ MSh
22.2	Ballymahon.] 49a; ~, MSh
22.3	emerged however] T; ~ ~, MSh; ~, ~, 49a
22.5	checkered] 49a; checquered MSh
*22.7	few] 49a; few [?] MSh; ⟨free⟩ Pr.
*22.7	life;] 49a; ~. MSh
*22.7–9	and though he . . . THREE JOLLY PIGEONS.] Prh
23.7	life,] 49a; ~; MSh
*23.10	elothing] 49a; arraying MSh
23.10	sturdy but awkward] T; ~ ~ aukward MSh; ~, ~ awkward 49a
23.11	colors;] 49a; colours; MSh
23.12	gravity,] 49a; ~∧ MSh
*23.15–16	club at Ballymahon having been much in the way] T; ~ ~ ~, ~ ~ ~ ~ ~ ~ 49a; club of the "Three Jolly Pigeons having been very much in the way MSh
23.17	irregularities,] 49a; ~∧ MSh
23.21	representative, the "Man in Black"–"my friends] 49a; ~∧ ~∧ *Man* ~ ~∧–∧My ~ MSh
23.23	in him,] 49a, *Works* (II, 116); ~ ~∧ MSh
23.24	kindness,] 49a; ~∧ MSh
23.26	action,] 49a; ~∧ MSh
23.27	Mr.] 49a; ~∧ MSh
23.31	position,] 49a; ~∧ MSh
23.33	ensued,] 49a; ~∧ MSh
*23.37	ascendency.] 49a; ascendancy. MSh
24.16	brother's] 48a; brothers MSp
24.17–18	her:/ "My dear mother, if] 49a; ~, "my Dear Mother./ "If you MSp
24.29	every thing] 49a, Prior (I, 120); everything MSp
24.43	purse.'] 49a, Prior (I, 120); ~.∧ MSp
26.42	every thing] 49a, Prior (I, 124); everything MSp
27.21	poet-errant] Pr.; poet-errants MSh
27.25	humor,] 49a; humour, Prh
*27.27	bitterness.] 49a; ~∧ Prh
*28.4	Hocus-pocus] 49a; hocus pocus Prh
*28.4	boarding house] T; bourding ~ Prh; boarding-house 49a
*28.5	mock ghost] 49a; mockghost Prh
28.6	*toadyism*] 49a; Todyism Prh

28.6   A *poet's purse for a Continental tour*] 49a; ⟨plans for an⟩
              ↑a poets purse for a [? blurred]↓ continental tour, Prh
28.7   consultation] Pr.; consullation MSh
28.7   Goldsmith's] Pr.; Goldsmiths MSh
*28.13   gambling house,] T; ∼-∼, MSp, 49a
28.25   Goldsmith still received] 49a; goldsmith ∼ recieved MSh
28.30   formerly;] 49a; ∼, MSh
28.31   harpsichord,] 49a; ∼ᴧ MSh
28.33   which,] 49a; ∼ᴧ MSh
28.34   specimen,] 49a; ∼ᴧ MSh
28.34   juvenile:] 49a; ∼ᴧ-[?] MSh
29.20   tender] 49a; tendre MSh
29.21   Mr. Lawder.] 49a; ∼ᴧ Lauder. MSh
29.26   connection,] 49a; connexion, MSh
29.29   divinity] 49a; Divinity MSh
29.34   blessing,] 49a; ∼; MSh
29.33   money;] 49a; ∼: MSh
29.33   Goldsmith's] 49a; Goldsmiths MSh
29.34   (Mrs. Hodson)] 49a; (∼ᴧ ∼) MSh
*29.37   Having taken lodgings] 49a; Having lodgings MSh
*29.37   haphazard,] T; hap / -hazard, MSh; hap- / hazard, 49a
29.38   effects,] 49a; ∼ᴧ MSh, 60
29.40   confusion,] 49a; ∼ᴧ MSh
*29.41   himself with the name either] 49a; ∼ either with the
              name MSp
30.4   hocus-pocus] 49a; hocuspocus MSp
*30.5   boarding houses] T; ∼-∼ MSp, 49a
30.7–8   fellow students] T; ∼-∼ MSp, 49a
30.12   good humored] T; ∼-humoured MSp; ∼-humored 49a
*30.23   lay chiefly] 49a
30.25   favorite] 49a; favourite MSp
30.26   humor,] 49a; humour, MSp
30.31   play;] 49a; ∼, MSp
30.43   ghosts, some] 49a; ∼ᴧ ⟨and⟩ some MSh
31.9   performed,] 49a; ∼ᴧ MSh
31.14–15   Goldsmith's] 49a; Goldsmiths MSh
31.16   humor] 49a; humour MSh
31.16   writings.] 49a; ∼ᴧ MSh
31.18   "Robert] 49a; ᴧ∼ MSp
33.8   chariot;] 49a; chariot;† MSp; ∼; Prior (I, 143)
33.24   circumstances,] 49a, Prior (I, 144); ∼ᴧ MSp
34.4   month's] 49a; months MSh
34.5   foot,"] 49a; ∼ᴧ" MSh

34.6   Contarine,] 49a; ~ₐ MSh
34.6   ill-natured] 49a, Prior (I, 147); ~ₐ ~ MSh
34.9   master."] 49a; ~.ₐ MSh
34.11   quarter,] 49a; ~ₐ MSh
34.12   correctly.] 49a; ~ₐ MSh
34.12   spent,"] 49a; ~ₐ" MSh
34.13   letters, "more] 49a; ~ₐ ₐ~ MSh
34.13–14   Hamilton's;] 49a, Prior (I, 157); Hamiltons; MSh
34.15   an employment] 49a; an an ~ MSh
34.16   physician."] 49a; ~.ₐ MSh
*34.17   autobiography] T; ~, 49a; ⟨story⟩ auto biographyₐ MSh
34.18   "At first,"] 49a; ₐ~ ~,ₐ MSh
34.18   "I was] 49a; ₐ~ ~ MSh
34.19   man's] 49a; mans MSh
34.20   disagreeable;] 49a, Works (II, 116); ~ₐ MSh
34.23   soon, his] 49a; ~ₐ ~ MSh; soon, that his Works (II, 116)
34.24   myself, and] 49a; ~ₐ ~ MSh; ~; ~ Works (II, 116)
34.25   receiving] 49a, Works (II, 116); recieving MSh
34.25–26   submission:] 49a, Works (II, 116); ~; MSh
34.28   praise,] 49a, Works (II, 116); ~ₐ MSh
34.29   perceived] 49a, Works (II, 116); percieved MSh
34.32   in me."] 49a; ~ ~ₐ" MSh
34.38   French,] 49a, Prior (I, 155); ~ₐ MSh
34.40   language,] 49a, Prior (I, 155); ~ₐ MSh
34.41   Paris,] 49a, Prior (I, 155); ~ₐ MSh
35.14   you.**] Pr., 49a; you. X X X X MSh; you..... Prior
            (I, 155)
35.15   Mr.] Pr.; ~ₐ MSh
*35.15–16   Mrs. Lawder."] T; ~ₐ Lauder." MSh; ~ₐ Laudor." Pr.;
            ~. Lawder.ₐ 49a
*35.17   Mrs. Lawder was Jane, his] 49a; Jane his MSh; ~, ~ Pr.
*35.17–18   the object of his valentine—his first poetical inspiration.
            She had been] 49a; the object of his first poetical
            inspiration—had been MSh, Pr.
35.19   instruction,] Pr.; ~ₐ MSh
35.19   perceived,] Pr.; percievedₐ MSh
35.20   Continent,] Pr.; continentₐ MSh
35.22   reconcile] Pr.; recconcile MSh
35.27   country,] Pr., Works (II, 41); ~ₐ MSh
35.28   vagabond."] Pr.; ~ₐ" MSh
35.30–31   shirts, &c.,] Pr., Letters (17); ~ₐ &cₐ, MSh
35.34   money,] Pr.; ~ₐ MSh
35.34–35   experience,] Pr.; ~ₐ MSh

*35.35–42	and almost . . . and Ballymahon.] 49a
35.36	head piece] Prh; ~-~ 49a
35.36	half iron, half pasteboard,] 49a; ~ ~ₐ ~ ~, Pr.
35.38	checkered] 49a; checquered Prh
35.42	fondly remembered haunts] Prh; ~-~ ~ 49a; early haunts MSh
*35.42	'sweet Lissoy'] Prh; Lishoy MSh
*36.2	*fellow passengers*] Prh; ~-~ 49a
*36.3	*way side*] Prh; wayside 49a
36.4	*tulip*] 49a; Tulip Prh
36.5	*Voltaire*] 49a; voltaire Prh
36.8	enterprise.] Pr.; ~ₐ MSh
36.11	impulse; so,] Pr.; ~. So, MSh
36.12	Holland,] Pr.; ~ₐ MSh
36.13	continent.] Pr.; Continent. MSh
36.15	Newcastle-upon-Tyne.] Pr.; New Castle-upon-Tyne. MSh
*36.17	voyage."] Pr.; ~.ₐ MSh
36.19	open,] Pr.; ~ₐ MSh
36.19	serjeant] Pr.; sarjeant MSh
36.24	French army.] 49a; French Army. MSh
36.25	revellers] 49a; revallers MSh
36.25	prison,] 49a; ~ₐ MSh
36.26	fortnight. With] 49a; ~. with MSh
36.27	misadventures,] 49a; mis adventures, MSh
36.28	best. His imprisonment] 49a; best—His emprisonment MSh
36.28	life,] 49a; ~ₐ MSh
36.31	Goldsmith's] 49a; Goldsmiths MSh
36.31	direct,] 49a; ~ₐ MSh
*36.33	deviations to] T; ~, ~ MSp, 49a
36.35	every thing] 49a, Percy (29); everything MSp
*37.12	well-dressed] 49a, Percy (31); ~ₐ ~ MSh
37.22	Traveller:"] 49a; ~." **MSp**
37.23	To men] T; "~ ~ MSp, 49a
37.28	pride.] 49a, *Works* (IV, 261); ~, MSp
37.34	smile;] 49a; ~, MSp; ~. *Works* (IV, 261)
37.38	reign.] T; ~." MSp, 49a
37.40	chemistry] 49a; chymistry MSh
38.5	Ellis,] 49a; ~ₐ MSh
38.6	Goldsmith,] 49a; ~ₐ MSh
38.7	awkward] 49a; aukward MSh
*38.8	life "that] T, Forster (42); ~ ₐ~ MSh, 49a
38.9	Leyden,] 49a; Leydanₐ MSh; the place, Forster (42)

38.11	scholar."] 49a; ~ᴧ" MSh
*38.12	undertook] 49a; under took MSh
38.13	Dutch,] 49a; ~ᴧ MSh
38.15	embarrassment] 49a; embarrasment MSh
38.16	*philosophical*] 49a; *Philosophical* MSh
38.18	their own] 49a; ~ oun MSh
38.19	flush,] 49a; ~ᴧ MSh
38.19	gambling tables,] 49a; ~ ~; MSh
38.22	own punishment,] 49a; oun ~ᴧ MSh
38.23	shilling.] 49a; ~ᴧ MSh
38.24	Irishman's] 49a; Irishmans MSh
38.26	Irishman,] 49a; ~. MSh
*39.1	Continent, in February, 1755, with] 60; ~, ~ ~, 1775, ~ 49a; Continentᴧ with MSp
*39.2	shirt, his flute and a single guinea.] T; ~. his ~ ~ ~ ~ ~, MSh; ~, a ~, ~ ~ ~ ~. 49a
*39.3–4	"Blessed," says one of his biographers, "with a good constitution, an adventurous] 49a; "Blessed with a good constitution," says one of his biographers, "an adventurous MSp
39.9	music,] 49a, *Works* (IV, 117); ~ᴧ MSh
39.19	Paris] 49a; paris MSh
39.20	vogue,] 49a; ~ᴧ MSh
39.21	Versailles.] 49a; ~ᴧ MSh
39.22	Clairon,] 49a; ~. MSh
39.26	Paris] T; paris MSh; Paris, 49a
*39.30	"When] 49a; '~ MSp
39.38	free."]49a; ~.' MSp
*39.39	*Paragraph* During a brief] 49; *no paragraph* ~ ~ ~ MSh
39.40	honor] 49a; honour MSh
39.42	says he, "no] 49a; ~ ~ᴧ ᴧ~ MSh
39.43	conversation; which, however,] 49a, Prior (I, 182); ~: ~ᴧ ~ᴧ MSh
40.1	despised,] 49a, Prior (I, 182); ~ᴧ MSh
40.2	discourse,] 49a, Prior (I, 182); ~ᴧ MSh
40.4	hear him.] 49a, Prior (I, 182); ~ ~ᴧ MSh
40.6	he, "remembers] 49a; ~ᴧ ᴧ~ MSh
40.7	Paris,] 49a, Prior (I, 182); ~ᴧ MSh
40.8	learning.] 49a, Prior (I, 182); ~ᴧ MSh
*40.8–9	Fontenelle, [then . . . old,] who] T; ~ᴧ [~ ~ ~ᴧ] ~ MSh; ~, (~ ~ ~,) ~ 49a
40.9	party,] 49a; Prior (I, 182); ~. MSh

40.11	began] 49a; Prior (I, 182); begun MSh
40.14	perceived] 49a, Prior (I, 182); percieved MSh
40.25	dispute."] 49a; ∼∧" MSh
40.26	Goldsmith's] 49a; Goldsmiths MSh
40.28	sketch,] 49a; ∼∧ MSh
*40.28	"Traveller."] 49a; ∧∼·∧ MSh
41.2	any thing] 49a; any- / thing MSp
41.7	all this] 49a, Works (IV, 120); all ⟨this⟩ ↓⟨Such⟩↑ MSh, MSp
41.8	twenty-one."] 49a; ∼-∼·∧ MSp, Works (IV, 120)
41.10	gentleman,] 49a; ∼∧ MSh
*41.11	pawnbroker,] 49a; pawn broker, MSh
41.12	overlaying] 49a; over laying MSh
41.15	'bear leader,'] 49a; '∼ ∼∧' MSh
*41.18	acquired, as has been shown, a] 49a; acquired, however, a MSp
*41.34	by the illness] 59, 60; by the death MSh, 49a
*41.37	brother in law, Hodson,] T; ∼ ∼ ∼∧ ∼∧ MSh; brother-in-law, Hodson, 49a
41.40	relatives,] 49a; ∼∧ MSh
*42.2	spendthrift.] 49a; spend thrift. MSh
42.3	resources,] 49a; ∼∧ MSh
42.6	staff,] 49a; ∼∧ MSh
*42.9	flute—his magic flute!—was] 49a; flute was MSh
42.10	Traveller:] 49a; ∼. MSh
42.11	ease,] 49a, Works (IV, 259); ∼∧ MSh
42.12	please,] 49a, Works (IV, 259); ∼∧ MSh
42.17	tune,] 49a, Works (IV, 259); ∼∧ MSh
42.17	dancer's] 49a, Works (IV, 259), dancers MSh
*42.24	threescore.] T, Works (IV, 259); ∼." MSh; three-score." 49a
43.3	Theatricals] 49a; theatricals Prh
43.4	A doctor] 49a; a Doctor Prh
43.5	Poor] 49a; poor Prh
*43.5	secondhand] T; second hand Prh; second-hand 49a
*43.5–6	A tragedy in embryo—Project of the written mountains] 49a
43.7	"pursuing] Pr.; '∼ MSh
48.7–8	novelty," as he said, "and losing content,"] Pr.; ∼∧" ∼ ∼ ∼∧ "∼ ∼ ∼∧" MSh
*43.9	illness] T; death MSh, Pr., 49a
43.13	world.] Pr.; ∼∧ MSh
*43.15	penniless] 49a; pennyless MSh, Pr.

43.16	destitute?] 49a; ~. MSh, Pr.
43.19	night's] Pr.; nights MSh
43.21	brother in law,] T; ~ ~ ~∧ MSh; ~-~-~, Pr.
43.39	February,] 49a; ~∧ MSh
44.3	illustration? We] 49a; ~: we MSh
44.3	own] 49a; oun MSh
44.5	two;] 49a; ~∧ MSh
44.6	clock,] 49a, *Works* (II, 452); ~∧ MSh
44.6	watch-dog.] 49a, *Works* (II, 452); ~∧ ~. MSh
44.8	couch,] 49a, *Works* (II, 453); ~∧ MSh
44.10	wanderers,] 49a, *Works* (II, 453); ~∧ MSh
44.12	rags,] 49a, *Works* (II, 453); ~∧ MSh
44.18	curse,] 49a, *Works* (II, 454); ~∧ MSh
44.19	relieve them.] 49a, *Works* (II, 454); ~ ~, MSh
44.20	"Why,] 49a, *Works* (II, 454); ∧~, MSh
44.20	man,] 49a, *Works* (II, 454); ~∧ MSh
44.26–27	Reynolds's by humorously] 49a; Reynolds by humerously MSh
44.28	Axe Lane."] 49a; ~ ~∧" MSh
*44.30	half pence] T; ~-~ MSh, 49a
44.32	school,] 49a; ~∧ MSh
*44.33	difficulty,] 49a; ~. MSh
44.37	won't] 49a, *Works* (IV, 107); wont MSh
44.38	won't do] 49a, *Works* (IV, 107); wont do MSh
44.38	school. Can] 49a, *Works* (IV, 108); ~." "~ MSh
44.39	bed?" "No." "Then] 49a; ~?" "~." ∧~ MSh
44.40	stomach?"] 49a; ~.?" MSh
*44.40–41	school. I have] 49a; ~." ~ ~ MSh
44.42	necklace,] 49a, *Works* (IV, 107); ~∧ MSh
44.42	Newgate.] 49a, *Works* (IV, 107); New Gate∧ MSh
45.2	boys."] 49a; ~∧" MSh
45.3	situation,] 49a; ~∧ MSh
45.5	usher's] 49a; ushers MSh
*45.5–6	"He is generally," says he, "the laughing stock] T; He is laughing stock MSh; "He is generally," says he, "the laughing-stock 49a; they are generally the laughing stock *Works* (I, 458)
45.7	dress, or] 49a, *Works* (I, 458); ~∧ ~ MSh
45.7	language, is] 49a; ~∧ ~ MSh; language, are *Works* (I, 458)
*45.10	"He] 49a; '~ MSh
45.11	teacher,] 49a; ~∧ MSh
45.15	chemist] 49a; chymist MSp

*45.16   Fish Street Hill.] T; Fish-street ~. MSh, 49a
*45.17   fellow student] T; ~-~ MSp, 49a
45.25   way, in Bankside, Southwark,] 49a, Prior (I, 210); ~ᴧ
                ~ Bank sideᴧ South wark, MSh
45.29   university,] 49a; University, MSh
*45.30   a secondhand suit] T; an old second hand suit MSh;
                a second-hand suit 49a
45.31   fortnight's] 49a; fortnights MSh
45.32   endeavored] 49a; endeavoured MSh
45.33   said, "and] 49a; ~. "~ MSh
45.37   fellow student Dr. Sleigh] T; ~ ~ ~ᴧ ~ MSh;
                ~-~, ~. ~, 49a
45.38   booksellers,] 49a; ~ᴧ MSh
*45.40   journeyman] 49a; journey man MSh
45.42   perceived] 49a; percieved MSh
45.43   Mr. Samuel] 49a; ~ᴧ ~ MSh
46.2–3   journeyman's] 49a; journeymans MSh
*46.5   Court; an occupation] 49a; ~; ⟨It was⟩ ↑certainly↓ ⟨among
                the humblest of literary employments but it suited
                the learned [?] hopes and prospects of one whose only
                present ambition was [illegible word]⟩ an occupation
                MSh
46.7   Richardson's parlor,] 49a; Richardsons parlourᴧ MSh
46.8–9   Dr. Young,] 49a; ~ᴧ ~ᴧ MSh
*46.10   familiarity took place] 49a; ~ could have taken ~ MSh
46.11   Æsculapius] 49a; Esculapius MSh
46.13   teeming. Dr.] 49a; ~ᴧ ~ᴧ MSh
46.15   lectures,] 49a; ~ᴧ MSh
46.16   character.] 49a; ~ᴧ MSh
46.21   breakfast,] 49a, Percy (39); ~ᴧ MSp
46.29   performance."] 49a; ~.ᴧ MSp
46.30   Dr. Farr,] 49a; ~. ~ᴧ MSh
46.31   perceived] 49a; percieved MSh
46.33   indispensable to medical doctors] 49a; indispensible to
                medi / cal Doctors MSh
*46.34   secondhand one] T; second hand one MSh; second-hand
                one, 49a
46.40   Dr. Farr;] 49a; ~ᴧ ~; MSh
46.42   mountains,] 49a, Percy (40); ~ᴧ MSh
47.2   pounds," adds Dr. Farr, "which] 49a; ~,ᴧ ~ ~ᴧ ~,
                ᴧ~ MSh
47.3   temptation."] 49a; ~ᴧ" MSh
47.4   teem. On] 49a; ~ᴧ on MSh

47.6 well instructed judgment.] T; ~ ~ judgement. MSh;
  ~-~ judgment. 49a
47.7 wonders] 49a; unders [?] MSh
48.2 *Kindness*] 49a; kindness Prh
48.3 *Expensive*] 49a; expensive Prh
48.3 "Monthly Review"] 49a; ∧~ review∧ Prh
48.4 *Rupture*] 49a; rupture Prh
48.5 Goldsmith's] Pr.; Goldsmiths MSh
48.6–7 fellow students in Edinburgh.] T; ~ ~ ~ ~, ⟨and one
  proof of [*illegible word*]⟩ MSh; ~-~ ~ ~. Pr.
48.7–8 son of a Dr. Milner, a dissenting minister,] Pr.; Son
  of a ⟨Doctor⟩ ⟨Dr⟩ Dr∧ Milner a dissenting Minister
  MSh
48.9 Goldsmith's] Pr.; Goldsmiths MSh
48.12 ill,] Pr.; ~∧ MSh
48.19 Dr. Milner] Pr.; ~∧ ~ MSh
*48.22 sweetmeats] 49a; sweet meats MSh
48.23 schoolboy] 49a; school boy MSh
48.25–26 good humor.] 49a; ~ humour. MSh
48.29 gentleman,] 49a; ~∧ MSh
48.30 Goldsmith,] 49a; ~∧ MSh
48.31 awkwardness] 49a; aukwardness MSh
48.32 situation,] 49a; ~∧ MSh
48.34 Dr. Milner's employ,] 49a; ~∧ Milners ~∧ MSh
48.35 purse,] 49a; ~∧ MSh
48.38 better, Mr. Goldsmith,] 49a; ~∧ ~∧ Gold smith∧ MSh
48.39 money," said Mrs.] 49a; ~,∧ ~ ~∧ MSh
49.1 truth, madam,] 49a; ~∧ ~. MSh
49.3 Dr. Milner] 49a; ~∧ ~ MSh
49.4 "Monthly Review,"] 49a; ∧~ ~∧∧ MSh
49.5 Whig] 49a; whig MSh
49.6–7 years. Of] 49a; ~: of MSh
49.7 exceedingly,] 49a; ~∧ MSh
49.8 Tory] 49a; tory MSh
*49.8 "Critical Review,"] T; *Critical review*∧ MSh; "Critical
  Review," 49a
49.9 Hamilton,] 49a; ~∧ MSh
49.9 bookseller,] 49a; ~∧ MSh
49.10 Dr.] 49a; ~∧ MSh
49.12 Dr. Milner's] 49a; ~∧ Milners MSh
*49.12–13 books which fell] T; ~ ~ occasionally fell MSh; ~,
  which fell 49a
49.14 inclination and] 49a; ~ and and MSh

49.14	reviewer,] 49a; reviewor, MSh
*49.17	life and in April 1757] T; ~ ~, ~ ~ ~ MSh; ~, ~ ~ ~, ~, 49a
49.18	"Monthly Review"] T; ∧~ review∧ MSh; "~ Review," 49a
49.19	Mr. Griffiths] T; ~∧ ~ MSh; ~. ~, 49a
*49.20	Dunciad, Paternoster Row.] 49a; ~. Pater noster row. MSh
*49.21	his semifictitious] T; ~ ↑Semi↓ fictitious MSh; ~ semi-fictitious 49a
49.23	"Vicar of Wakefield."] 49a; ∧~ ~ ~.∧ MSh
49.24	George's] 49a; Georges MSh
49.25–26	books, no doubt,] 49a, *Works* (IV, 108); ~∧ ~ ~∧ MSh
49.30	shoes,] 49a, *Works* (IV, 108); ~∧ MSh
49.31	"Finding" (says George) "that] 49a; '~∧ (~ ~) ~ MSh; "Finding that *Works* (IV, 108)
49.35	me." Alas,] 49a; ~∧"–~∧ MSh
49.36	days; and Otway,] 49a; ~, ~ ~∧ MSh
49.38	bread,] 49a; ~∧ MSh
*49.38	voracity] 49a; ⟨voura⟩ vivacity MSh
49.38	man.] 49a; ~∧– MSh
49.39	Goldsmith's] 49a; Goldsmiths MSh
*49.39	track] 49a; truck MSh
49.40	shrewd,] 49a; ~∧ MSh
49.43	wife, who,] 49a; ~∧ ~∧ MSh
50.1	Smollett,] 49a; ~∧ MSh
50.2	'Review.'" Such] 49a; review–Such MSh
50.5	o'clock] 49a; oclock MSh
50.7	taste; in a word,] 49a; ~. ~ ~ ~∧ MSh
50.10	Griffiths,"] 49a; ~∧' MSh
50.12	'Review.'] 49a; review. MSh
50.12	heaven,"] 49a; ~∧∧ MSh
50.12	"the 'Critical Review'] 49a; ∧~ ∧~ ~∧ MSh
50.15	women!"] 49a; ~!∧ MSh
50.19	of the day; and of assuming] 49a; ~ ~ ~; ⟨of occasionally assuming⟩ ⟨and⟩ ⟨when the poor jaded hack replied to these⟩ of assuming MSh
50.21	him,] 49a; ~∧ MSh
50.24	rupture,] 49a; ~∧ MSh
50.28	"Review"] 49a; ∧review∧ MSh
50.32	sound, easy] 49a; ~∧ ~ MSh
50.33	genial] 49a; ginial MSh
50.33	Goldsmith's] 49a; Goldsmiths MSh

51.2	*Newbery,*] 49a; Newbury$_\wedge$ Prh
*51.2	*picture book*] Prh; ~-~ 49a
51.2	*How*] 49a; how Prh
51.3	*A poor*] 49a; a poor Prh
51.4	known] Pr.; knoun MSh
51.4	world,] Pr.; ~$_\wedge$ MSh
51.5	quarters;] Pr.; ~$_\wedge$ MSh
51.7	Newbery,] 49a; Newbury$_\wedge$ MSp, Pr.
51.9	Newbery] 49a; Newbury MSp, Pr.
*51.9	picture books] T; ~-~ MSp, Prp, 49a
*51.9–10	kind hearted] T; ~-~ MSp, 49a
51.12	labor] Pr.; labour MSh
*51.13–14	in his novel of the Vicar of Wakefield.] Pr.; in the "Vicar of Wakefield." MSp
*51.22	Besides his literary job work Goldsmith] T; ⟨Being now known in the publishing world, he found employment in other quarters; he⟩ ↑Beside his literary job work Goldsmith MSp; Besides his literary job work, Goldsmith 49a
*51.25	Fleet Street;] T; Fleet-street; MSp, 49a
51.30	Coffee House] T; Coffee-house MSp, 49a
*51.31	calls; hence] 49a; ~; from hence MSp
*51.33	Thirty] Prh; "~ 49a
51.33	year,] Prh; ~," 49a
51.33	painter,] 49a; ~$_\wedge$ Prh
51.34	shifting, is] Prh; ~, "~ 49a
*51.36	coffee house,] T; ~ ~$_\wedge$ Prh; ~-~, 49a
51.37	where] Prh; ~, 49a
51.37	threepence] Prh; ~, 49a
51.39	penny;] 49a; ~$_\wedge$ Prh
*51.39	six pence;] T; ~ ~, Prh; sixpence; 49a
51.40	visits.] Prh; visits." 49a
*52.1	leaf out of] Prh; leaf from 49a
52.1	devil's] 49a; devils Prh
52.1	manual] 49a; manuel Prh
52.2	coffee house] Prh; ~-~ 49a
52.2	Indeed, coffee houses] T; ~$_\wedge$ ~ ~ Prh; ~, ~-~ MSp, 49a
52.7	Goldsmith's] 49a; Goldsmiths MSh
*52.8	career? We] T; ~, we MSh; ~? we 49a
*52.9	*Enquiry into the State of polite learning*] T; 'Enquiry into the State of polite learning MSh; "Inquiry into the state of polite learning," 49a

52.10   "The author,] 49a; '∼ ∼∧ MSh; ∧∼ ∼, *Works* (I, 316)
52.10   Great,] T, *Works* (I, 316); ∼∧ MSh; great, 49a
52.11   cannot, perhaps, be] 49a; ∼∧ ∼∧ ∼ MSh; cannot be,
             perhaps, *Works* (I, 316)
52.13   possible;] 49a, *Works* (I, 316); ∼: MSh
52.17   sits down] 49a; ∼ doun MSh
52.20   Again.] 49a; ∼∧— MSh
52.21–22   conclude, perhaps,] 49a, *Works* (I, 311); ∼∧ ∼∧ MSh
52.26   jest, becomes] 49a, *Works* (I, 311); ∼∧ ∼ MSh
52.28   laugh,] 49a, *Works* (I, 311); ∼∧ MSh
52.29   * * * * The poet's] 49a, *Works* (I, 314); X X X X X X
             The poets. MSh
52.31   mankind,] 49a, *Works* (I, 314); ∼∧ MSh
52.32   poor,] 49a, *Works* (I, 314); ∼∧ MSh
52.36   the writer's fault?] T, *Works* (I, 314); ∼ writers ∼?
             MSh; a careless ∼? 49a
52.43   age,] 49a, *Works* (I, 314); ∼∧ MSh
52.43   redress." * * * *] 49a; ∼·∧ X X X X MSh
53.1   "If the] 49a; ∧∼ ∼ MSh
53.2   rent-charge] 49a, *Works* (I, 315); ∼∧ ∼ MSh
53.5   himself.] 49a, *Works* (I, 315); ∼! MSh
53.17   Lissoy] 49a; Lishoy MSp
*53.18   relatives] 49a; relations MSp
53.26   by-path] 49a; bye-path MSp
53.32   good humor;] T; ∼-humour; MSp; ∼-humor; 49a
53.42–43   brother in law, Daniel Hodson, Esq.,] T; ∼ ∼ ∼∧ ∼
             ∼∧ ∼∧, MSh; ∼-∼-∼, ∼ ∼, ∼., 49a
53.43–54.1   it was partly intended,] 49a; ∼ was was ∼ ∼∧ MSh
54.2–3   imagination of his friends in Ballymahon.] 49a; imag-
             inations of his ∧ ↑⟨indigent⟩↓ friends in Bally mahon.
             MSh
54.20   place,] 49a, Percy (42); ∼∧ MSp
54.21   any thing] 49a, Percy (42), 1825 (18); any- / thing MSp
54.26   perhaps? No.] 49a; ∼? no. MSp; ∼? No!— Percy (42)
54.27   Ireland? No.] 49a; ∼? no. MSp; ∼? No.— Percy (42)
*55.22   assistance."] T; ∼·∧ MSp, 49a
56.2   *Return*] 49a; return MSh
56.15   idleness: these] 49a; ∼: These MSh
56.19   "Bee,"] 49a; ∧∼∧∧ MSh
56.23   resolved,] 49a, Forster (109); ∼∧ MSh
56.25   reflection, however,] 49a; ∼∧ ∼, MSh; recollection, ∼,
             Forster (109)
56.25   what set] 49a, Forster (109); what a set MSh

56.26	rashness. The sun] T, Forster (109); ~∧ ~ ~∧ MSh; ~. ~ ~, 49a
56.30	spleen;] 49a, Forster (109); Spleen; MSh
*56.32	self-approving] 49a, Forster (109); ~∧ ~ MSh
56.35	Goldsmith's] 49a; Goldsmiths MSh
56.36	superintendence] 49a; superintendance MSh
56.37	Dr.] 49a; ~∧ MSh
*56.37	requital for] 49a; ~ of MSh
56.40	Dr.] 49a; ~∧ MSh
57.2	Indies?] 49a; ~. MSh
57.8	Present State of Polite] 49a; present state of polite MSh
57.16	Mr. Bradley,] 49a; ~∧ ~∧ MSh
57.20	intimate, Edward Mills,] T; ~∧ ~ ~∧ MSh; ~, ~ Wells, 49a
57.21	Roscommon.] 49a; ~∧ MSh
57.22	Goldsmith,] 49a; ~∧ MSh
57.22	pursue,] 49a, Prior (I, 259); ~∧ MSh
57.23	tranquillity.] 49a, Prior (I, 259); tranquility. MSh
57.25	success.] 49a, Prior (I, 260); ~∧ MSh
57.26	subject,] 49a, Prior (I, 260); ~∧ MSh
57.26	bench,] 49a, Prior (I, 260); ~∧ MSh
57.27	myself,] 49a, Prior (I, 260); ~∧ MSh
57.29	this, it seems] T, Prior (I, 260); ~∧ ~ ~ MSh; ~, ~ ~, 49a
57.31	own] 49a, Prior (I, 260); oun MSh
57.32	Mrs. Mills's] 49a, Prior (I, 260); ~∧ Mills' MSh
*57.32	bedchamber,] 49a, Prior (I, 260); bed chambre, MSh
57.34	life,] 49a, Prior (I, 260); ~∧ MSh
57.40	aside,] 49a, Prior (I, 260); ~∧ MSh
58.2–3	No, my dear Ned,] 49a, Prior (I, 261); ~∧ ~ Dear ~, MSh
58.4	request,] 49a, Prior (I, 261); ~∧ MSh
58.4	true,] 49a, Prior (I, 261); ~∧ MSh
58.5	petitioner,] 49a, Prior (I, 261); ~. MSh
58.7	London," &c.] 49a; ~∧∧ ~. MSh
58.10	Mr. Mills] T; ~∧ ~ MSh; ~. Wells, 49a
58.12	Dr. Goldsmith] T; ~∧ ~ MSh; ~. ~, 49a
58.12	celebrity.] 49a; ~∧ MSh
58.13	Goldsmith's] 49a; Goldsmiths MSh
58.13	Bryanton,] 49a; ~∧ MSh
58.14–15	believe," writes he, "that] 49a; ~∧" ~ ~∧ ∧~ MSh
58.18	can't] 49a, Forster (117); cant MSh
58.23	own. Indeed,] 49a, Forster (117); oun. ~∧ MSh

58.24	conceive] 49a, Forster (117); concieve MSh
58.25	pleasure,] 49a, Forster (117); ~∧ MSh
58.27	you, I] 49a, Forster (117); ~∧ ~ MSh
58.29	fireside] 49a, Forster (118); fire side MSh
58.30	college,] 49a, Forster (118); ~∧ MSh
58.32	you, though] 49a, Forster (118); ~∧ ~ MSh
58.36	fortune's] 49a, Forster (118); fortunes MSh
58.37	circumference,] 49a, Forster (118); ~∧ MSh
*58.39	runs into] 49a; ~ on ~ MSh
*58.40	prospects, the] T; ~, The MSh; ~. The 49a
58.41	him, and] 49a; ~∧ ~ MSh
58.41	gasconades concludes:] T; gasconads ~. MSh; gascon-ades, ~: 49a
58.42–43	and, as] 49a, Forster (119); ~∧ ~ MSh
58.43	down] 49a, Forster (119); doun MSh
59.1	down,] 49a, Forster (119); doun, MSh
59.4	Contarine,] 49a; ~∧ MSh
*59.6	co-operation] 49a; co∧operation MSh
59.6	uncle,] 49a; ~∧ MSh
*59.7	schoolboy] T; school boy MSh; school-boy 49a
59.8	Mr. Lawder.] 49a; ~∧ Laudor. MSh
*58.11	he begins,] 49a; ⟨it began,⟩ MSp; ↑he begins↓ MSh
*59.37	not—I own I could not—continue] 49a; not..I own I could not..continue MSp, Forster (124); I could not, I own, I could not continue Letters (43)
60.11	virtue in your breast.] 49a; ~ ~ ~ ~; Letters (44); ~ of ~ ~. MSp, Forster (124)
*60.13–14	me. * * * * Is it] 49a; me. God's curse, Madam! is it MSp, Forster (124–25); me. Gods curse, Madam, is it Letters (44)
60.42	names—my] 49a; names...my MSp, Forster (125); names My Letters (46)
61.6	hereafter. But] 49a; hereafter....But MSp, Forster (126); hereafter. Paragraph But Letters (47)
61.8	London a book] 49a; ~, ~ ~ MSp, Forster (126); London A Book Letters (47)
61.12	Lawder] 49a, Letters (47); Lauder MSp, Forster (126)
61.22	Mr. Lawder] 49a; ~∧ Lawder Letters (47); ~. Lauder MSp, Forster (126)
61.23	say—if] 49a; say..if MSp, Forster (126); ~∧~ Letters (48)
62.3	Surgeons—] 49a; Surjions MSh
62.3	Fresh] 49a; fresh MSh

62.4	*The*] 49a; the MSh
62.4	*Punishment*] 49a; punishment MSh
*62.5	*Gayeties*] 49a; gaieties MSh
62.5	*Green Arbour Court*] T; green arbour Court MSh; Green Arbor Court 49a
*62.6	*Scroggen,*] T; Scroggins∧ MSh; Scroggins, 49a
62.6	*mock heroic*] 49a; ∼ Heroic MSh
62.9	Dr.] 49a; ∼∧ MSh
62.9	effect,] 49a; ∼∧ MSh
62.10	surgeon] 49a; Surjion MSh
62.10	coast] 49a; Coast MSh
62.13	pounds,] 49a; ∼∧ MSh
62.13	physician,] 49a; ∼∧ MSh
62.16	per cent.;] 49a; ∼ ∼∧; MSh
62.17	him.] 49a; ∼.' MSh
*62.21	forthcoming] 49a; forth coming MSh
62.23	drudge, his muse,] 49a; ∼∧ ∼ ∼∧ MSh
62.26	unknown] 49a; unknoun MSh
62.27	Grub Street.] T; ∼ street. MSh; ∼-street. 49a
62.28	Hamilton,] 49a; ∼∧ MSh
62.28	"Critical Review,"] 49a; ∧∼ review,∧ MSh
62.30	replenished,] 49a; ∼∧ MSh
62.32	court] 49a; Court MSh
62.33	Old Bailey;] 49a; old ∼; MSh
62.36–37	despondency in London,] 49a; despondancy ∼ ∼∧ MSh
*62.38	enterprise] 49a; enterprize MSh
62.40	patron, Dr.] 49a; ∼∧ ∼∧ MSh
63.1	time,] 49a; ∼∧ MSh
63.3	own] 49a; oun MSh
63.3	indigence;] 49a; ∼, MSh
63.4	cause,] 49a; ∼∧ MSh
63.12	scheme,] 49a; ∼; MSh
62.13	College of Physicians] 49a; college of physicians MSh
*63.14	of hospital mate.] 49a; of a Hospital Mate. MSh
63.17–18	him, came] 49a; ∼∧ ∼ MSh
63.19	"Monthly Review,"] 49a; ∧∼ review,∧ MSh
63.21	occasion,] 49a; ∼∧ MSh
63.23	paid] 49a; payed MSh
*63.25	bookseller,] 49a; book seller∧ MSh
63.27	Surgeons] T; Surjeons MSh; Surgeons, 49a
63.28	Surgeons' Hall] T; Surjeons ∼ MSh; Surgeons' Halls, 49a
*63.34	reexamination] T; re examination MSh; re-examination 49a

63.35   reexamination] T; re examination MSh; re-examination
               49a
63.38   Surgeons,] 49a; Sarjeons, MSh
64.4   done?] 49a; ∼. MSh
64.6   Surgeons' Hall.] 49a; Surjeons ∼. MSh
64.7   pawnbroker's] T; paun brokers MSh; pawnbroker's, 49a
64.8   own debt] T; oun ∼ MSh; own debt, 49a
64.9   despondency] T; despondancy MSh; despondency, 49a
64.10   wants,] 49a; ∼∧ MSh
64.12   harassments] T; harrassments MSh; harassments, 49a
64.14   same. It] 49a; ∼∧–∼ MSh
64.15   pawnbroker's.] 49a; paun brokers. MSh
64.25   SIR,–"I know] 49a; "Sir, [paragraph] "I know MSh
65.26   detail,] 49a; ∼∧ MSh
65.27   Goldsmith's] 49a; Goldsmiths MSh
*65.28   outran] 49a; out ran MSh
65.28   forecast,] 49a; ∼; MSh
65.32   with it," resulted,] 49a; ∼ ∼∧" ∼∧ MSh
65.32   shown,] 49a; shoun MSh
66.3   good humored] T; good-humoured MSp; good-humored
               49a
66.9   humor.] 49a; humour. MSp
66.13   visitor] 49a; visiter MSp
66.18   visitor from a neighboring] 49a; visiter ∼ ∼ neighbouring
               MSp
66.19   good humor.] T; good-humour. MSp; good-humor. 49a
*66.19–20   It was probably his old task master Griffiths, whose
               press might have been waiting,] T; It was supposed
               to be some impatient publisher, whose press was wait-
               ing, MSp; It was probably his old task-master Griffiths,
               whose press might have been waiting, 49a
*66.39   make shift] T; ∼-∼ MSp, 49a
66.40   visitor] 49a; visiter MSp
67.32   popped] 49a, Tales of a Traveller; peeped MSp
67.33   clamor] 49a; clamour MSp
*67.37   swarms] T, Washington Irving's Tales of a Traveller,
               Knickerbocker Edition (New York, 1868), p. 150;
               screams MSp, 1840 (73), 49a
67.37   children] 49a, Tales of a Traveller; ∼, MSp
70.19   any thing] 49a, Prior (I, 301); anything MSp
70.34   "The] T, Prior (I, 302); "'∼ MSp, 49a
70.35   lay;] 49a, Prior (I, 302); ∼: MSp
71.6   board."] T, Prior (I, 302); ∼.'" MSp, 49a

71.9	"Not] T, Prior (I, 303); "'~ MSp, 49a
71.12	began,"] T, Prior (I, 303); ~,'" MSp, 49a
71.22	Voltaire,] 49a; ~∧ MSh
71.23	letter,] 49a; ~∧ MSh
71.25	Goldsmith's] 49a; Goldsmiths MSh
71.27	Goldsmith's] 49a; Goldsmiths MSh
*71.28–29	years after the] 49a; years the MSh
71.30	Smithfield:] 49a; ~∧ MSh
71.32	bookseller's] 49a; booksellers MSh
72.1	translation,] 49a; translution∧ MSh
72.1	volume,] 49a; ~∧ MSh
*72.3	"heroi-comical poem" also] T; '~-~ ~" ~ MSh; ∧~- ̇ ~ ~,∧ ~, 49a
72.4	embryo.] 49a; Embrio. MSh
*72.5	autobiography;] 49a; auto biography; MSh
72.6	own] 49a; oun MSh
*72.8	Scroggen:] T; ~∧ MSh; Scroggin: 49a
72.9	o'er] 49a, Forster (153), *Works* (II, 128); oer MSh
72.11	Calvert's] 49a, Forster (153); Calverts MSh
72.11	Parson's] 49a, Forster (153); Parsons MSh
72.14	stretch'd] 49a, Forster (153); stretched MSh
72.15	brows] 49a, Forster (153); brow's MSh
*72.18	the author's other writings it might have abounded] T; the ⟨othe [?]⟩ Authors other writing it would have abound MSh; the author's other writings, it might have abounded 49a
72.19	drawn] 49a; draun MSh
72.22	"Traveller" and "Deserted Village,"] 49a; ∧~∧ ~ ∧~ ~,∧ MSh
*72.22	and have remained] 49a; and remained MSh
73.2	*"The Inquiry"*] 49a; '~ ~' MSh
73.2	*Griffiths' Review*] 49a; Griffiths review MSh
73.2	*Kenrick,*] T; ~∧ MSh, 49a
73.3	*Goldsmith's essays*] 49a; Goldsmiths assays MSh
73.4	*manager*] 49a; Managor MSh
73.4	*Change*] 49a; change MSh
73.5	*The*] 49a; the MSh
73.20	Goldsmith's pen,] 49a; Goldsmiths ~∧ MSh
*73.21	title page.] T; ~ ~∧ MSh; ~-~. 49a
73.22	known] 49a; knoun MSh
73.22	letters,] 49a; ~∧ MSh
73.35	honor] 49a; honour MSp
*74.14	first rate] T; ~-~ MSp, 49a

74.26   Dreaming] T; "~ MSp, 49a
74.39   stinks.] T; ~." MSp, 49a
74.41   inhabitant," the Gentleman's] 49a; ~ˬ" ~ Gentlemans
             MSh
75.1   St. John's] 49a; S' Johns MSh
75.1   title page, had] T; ~ ~, had had MSh; ~-~, had 49a
75.2   kinds; Johnson's] T; ~; Johnsons MSh; ~: Johnson's 49a
75.4   Idler. Imitations] 49a; ~, ⟨and⟩ imitations MSh
75.7   outset,] 49a; ~ˬ MSh
75.10   the Busy Body, and the Lady's Magazine.) T; ~ ~ ~ˬ
             the Ladys ~. MSh; ~ ~-~, and the Lady's ~. 49a
75.10   essays,] 49a; ~ˬ MSh
75.12   humor,] 49a; humour, MSp
75.20   Garrick,] 49a; ~ˬ MSh
75.20   autocrat] 49a; Autocrat MSh
75.21   clamor] 49a; clamour MSh
75.24   "Garrick," said he, "is] 49a; "~ˬ" ~ ~ˬ ˬ~ MSh
75.25   scenes,] 49a, Forster (206); ~ˬ MSh
*75.25   fireworks,] T, Forster (206); fire worksˬ MSh; ~-~, 49a
*75.27   the *Provoked Husband*,] T, Forster (206); ~ provoked
             Husband, MSh; the Provoked Husband, 49a
75.27   school."] 49a; Schoolˬ" MSh; school.' Forster (206)
75.30   poet's] 49a, Forster (208); poets MSh
75.31   he, "must] 49a; ~ˬ "~ MSh
75.32   manager's] 49a, Forster (208); managers MSh
75.33   corrections,] 49a, Forster (209); ~ˬ MSh
75.34   public."] 49a; ~ˬ"— MSh
75.38–39   ancestors] 49a, Forster (209); Ancestors MSh
75.43   conjuror." But] T; ~."—But MSh; conjurer." But 49a;
             conjuror.' Forster (209)
*76.1   of Garrick was the following:] T; of ⟨the⟩ Garrick ⟨who
             carried the pride of the⟩ was the following (which
             smacked a little of per / sonality)ˬ MSh; of Garrick,
             was the following. 49a
*76.2   "I have] 49a; ˬ~ ~ MSp
*76.8–9   it, they] 49a, *Works* (I, 329); ~. ~ MSp, Forster (211)
76.9   characters."] 49a; ~.' MSp, Forster (211)
76.10–11   himself, and] 49a; ~⟨;⟩, ~ MSh
76.12   secretaryship] 49a; SecretaryShip MSh
76.13   Arts,] 49a; ~ˬ MSh
76.13   member.] 49a; Member. MSh
76.14   renown] 49a; renoun MSh

76.14   great and] T; great ⟨may have looked down upon Gold- / -smith as an author⟩ and MSh; great, and 49a
76.15   reputation,] 49a; ~₍ MSh
*76.16   conciliated. In] 49a; ~; In MSh
76.22   second] 49a; Second MSh
76.24   years,] 49a; ~; MSh
76.25   forgotten.] 49a; ~₍ MSh
76.29   good humored] T; good-humoured MSp; good-humored 49a
*77.2   Wine Office Court,] T; Wine-office Court, MSp; Wine-Office Court, 49a
*77.2   Fleet Street.] T; Fleet-street. MSh, 49a
77.6   own table,] 49a, Forster (237); oun ~₍ MSh
77.6–7   purpose to be kind] 49a, Forster (237); purpose [blank space] kind MSh
77.8   club,] 49a; ~₍ MSh
77.8–9   Robin Hood,] 49a; ~ ~₍ MSh
77.10   student,] 49a; Student, MSh
77.12   disputant,] 49a, Prior (I, 421); ~₍ MSh
77.13   society."] 49a; Society." MSh
77.14   social, jovial nature,] 49a; ~₍ ~ ~₍ MSh
77.15   club,] 49a; Club, MSh
77.15–16 Derrick,] 49a; ~₍ MSh
77.16   humor. On entering,] 49a; humour—On ~₍ MSh
77.18   "This," said he, "must] 49a; ₍~ₘₘ ~ ~₍ ₍~ MSh
77.19   least." "No, no," replied Derrick, "he's] 49a; least—No, no replied Derrick, he's MSh
77.19   rolls."—] 49a; ~₍"— MSh
78.2   lodgings] 49a; Lodgings MSh
78.2   Visits] 49a; visits MSh
78.3   white mouse] 49a; White Mouse MSh
78.3   Dr.] 49a; ~₍ MSh
78.4   Mrs.] 49a; ~₍ MSh
78.4   Criticism] 49a; criticism MSh
78.5   Wine Office Court] T; Wine office ~₍ MSh; Wine-Office ~, 49a
78.5   receive] 49a; recieve MSh
*78.8   Bickerstaffe.] 1840 (83); Bickerstaff⟨e⟩. MSp; Bickerstaff. 49a
*78.9   hangers on,] T; ~-~, MSp, 49a
78.28   neighboring] 49a; neighbouring MSp
78.29   white mice.] 49a; White Mice. MSh
*78.30   scapegrace,] 49a; scape grace₍ MSh

78.33	humor] 49a; humour MSh
78.36	World.] 49a; world. MSh
78.37	Dr.] 49a; $\sim_\wedge$ MSh
79.1	Goldsmith, buoyant,] 49a; $\sim_\wedge$ $\sim$, MSh
79.5	Johnson,] 49a; $\sim_\wedge$ MSh
79.12	college] T; College MSh; college, 49a
79.13	there, "Ah, sir!"] 49a; $\sim_\wedge$ "$\sim_\wedge$ Sir!$_\wedge$ MSh; "Ah, sir, Boswell (I, 43)
79.14	*poor,*] 49a; $\sim_\wedge$ MSh; poor, Boswell (I, 43)
79.17	Goldsmith's] 49a; Goldsmiths MSh
*79.20	himself] 49a; him self MSh
79.21	friends;] 49a; $\sim_\wedge$ MSh
79.22	retribution.] 49a; $\sim_\wedge$ MSh
79.23	master.] 49a; $\sim$, MSh
79.27	student,] 49a; $\sim_\wedge$ MSh
79.28–29	scholar. While Goldsmith's] 49a; Scholar, ⟨and from his insatiable love of reading⟩ ⟨The house which Goldsmiths happiness⟩ while Goldsmiths MSh
79.29	humors] 49a; humours MSh
79.30	Johnson's] 49a; Johnsons MSh
79.35	Johnson,] 49a; $\sim_\wedge$ MSh
79.36	age,] 49a; $\sim_\wedge$ MSh
*79.36	a half written] T; '$\sim$ $\sim$ $\sim$ MSh; $\sim$ $\sim$-$\sim$ 49a
79.36	pocket;] 49a; $\sim_\wedge$ MSh
79.37	junior,] 49a; $\sim_\wedge$ MSh
79.38	companion,] 49a; $\sim_\wedge$ MSh
79.38	penniless,] 49a; $\sim_\wedge$ MSh
79.39	tied,"] 49a; $\sim_\wedge$" MSh
79.41	London,"] 49a; $\sim_\wedge$" MSh
79.41	twopence halfpenny] 49a, Boswell (I, 71, n. 1); two pence half penny MSh
79.42	pocket."–"Eh, what's that you say?"] 49a; $\sim_\wedge$"–"Eh whats $\sim$ $\sim$ $\sim$?' MSh; "Eh? what do you say? Boswell (I, 71, n. 1)
79.42–43	Garrick, "with twopence halfpenny] 49a; $\sim_\wedge$ $_\wedge\sim$ two pence half penny MSh; with twopence halfpenny Boswell (I, 71, n. 1)
79.43	pocket?"] 49a, Boswell (I, 71, n. 1); $\sim$?"– MSh
*79.43	yes: I came] 49a; $\sim$; when I came MSh; $\sim$; when I came Boswell (I, 71, n. 1)
79.43	twopence halfpenny] 49a, Boswell (I, 71, n. 1); two pence half penny MSh

80.1   pocket, and thou, Davy,] 49a, Boswell (I, 71, n. 1);
           ∼∧ ∼ ∼∧ ∼, MSh
80.1   halfpence] 49a, Boswell (I, 71, n. 1); half pence MSh
*80.4   joint note to] 49a; joint to MSh
80.5   Many, many] 49a; ∼∧ ∼ MSh
80.5   London,] 49a; ∼∧ MSh
80.6   wit;"] 49a; ∼:" MSh
80.8   St. James's Square,] 49a; St∧ James ∼∧ MSh
80.9   night's lodging,] 49a; nights ∼∧ MSh
80.10   country; so] 49a; country [*dash superimposed on semi-
           colon*] So MSh
*80.11   Cave his bookseller's,] T; ∼ ∼ booksellers, MSh; Cave's,
           his bookseller, 49a
80.15   self dependent,] T; self dependant, MSh; ∼-∼, 49a
80.17   wit."] 49a; ∼∧" MSh
80.17   "Rambler" and "Idler"] 49a; ∧∼∧ ∼ ∧∼∧ MSh
80.19   Language,"] 49a; language∧" MSh
80.19   labor,] 49a; labour∧ MSh
*80.20   the admiration of] 49a; the wonder and admiration
           of MSh
80.22   autocrat] 49a; Autocrat MSh
*80.23   fellow wayfarer] T; ∼ way farer MSh; ∼-∼ 49a
80.24   stage,] 49a; ∼∧ MSh
80.24   Smollett, "The] 49a; ∼∧ '∼ MSh
80.25   Literature."] 49a; ∼.' MSh
80.26   Dr. Johnson when] T; ∼∧ ∼ ∼ MSh; ∼. ∼, ∼ 49a
80.26   the 31st of May, 1761,] 49a; the 31: ∼ ∼∧ ∼. MSh
80.28   Wine Office Court.] T; ∼ office ∼. MSh; ∼-Office ∼.
           49a
80.31   honorable] 49a; honourable MSh
80.31   Bee] 49a; ∼, MSh
80.39   commenced ripened] 49a; commenced soon ripened MSp,
           Pr.; commenced ⟨Soon⟩ ripened Prh 2
*80.39–41 into intimacy in the course of frequent meetings at
           the shop of Davies, the bookseller, in Russell Street,
           Covent Garden.] T; into an intimate friendship, which
           continued through life. ⟨For a time their meeetings
           were⟩ Johnson most probably first introduced Gold-
           smith into one of his literary haunts, the Shop of Mr∧
           Thomas Davies the Bookseller in Russell Street Covent
           Garden, ⟨the resort of many of the notorieties of the
           day.⟩ MSh, MSp; into∧ ⟨an intimate friendship, which
           continued through life. Johnson most probably first

introduced Goldsmith into one of his literary haunts, the shop of Mr. Thomas Davis, bookseller, in Russell-street, Covent Garden.⟩ Pr.; into ⟨infanc⟩ intimacy in the course of frequent meetings at the Shop of ⟨Mr Thomas⟩ Davies the bookseller on Russell Street Covent Garden. Prh 2

80.41   gossiping] 49a; gossipping Prh 2

80.42   circle] 49a; cercle Prh 2

80.42   presided,] 49a; ∼∧ Prh 2

80.43–81.2   Mr. Thomas Davies, . . . stage, and] 49a; Davies had originally been on the Stage and MSh; Davies had originally been on the stage, and Pr.; Mr∧ Thomas Davies, ⟨had originally been on the⟩ noted in after times as the biographer of Garrick, had originally been on the Stage and Prh 2

81.2   tragedy,] Pr.; tragady, MSh

81.3   size,] Pr.; ∼∧ MSh

81.4   Rosciad:] Pr.; ∼∧ MSh

81.6   *bone.*] T; *bone–* MSh; *bone."* Pr.

*81.9   somewhat] Pr.; some what MSh

81.10   stage] T; Stage∧ MSh; stage, Pr.

81.13   life,] Pr.; ∼∧ MSh

*81.14   wife.] T; ∼.' MSh; ∼." Pr.

81.15   Mrs.] Pr.; ∼∧ MSh

81.16–17   Her tea table . . . shop.] T; Her tea table ⟨was ad⟩ became almost as much a literary lounge as her husbands shop. Prh; Her tea-table . . . shop. 49a

81.17–20   She found favor . . . haunt. Others] 49a; She found favor even in the eyes of the Ursa Major of literature by her winning ways and is said to be one reason of his habitual resort to her husbands shop, ⟨and⟩ Others MSh. ⟨She found favor even in the eyes of the Ursa Major of literature by her winning ways∧ and is said to be one reason of his habitual resort to her husband's shop.⟩ Others Pr.; She found favor in the eyes of the Ursa Major of literature by her winning ways as she poured out for him c [blank space] ps without stint of his favorite bevera [blank space] . . , Indeed it is suggested that she was one ↑leading↓ cause of his habitual resort to this literary haunt. Prh

81.21   Johnson's] Pr.; Johnsons MSh

81.23   Steevens,] 50; Steevans, MSh; Stevens, Pr., 49a

81.23   Dr. Percy,] Pr.; Doctor Percy∧ MSh

81.24   ballads,] Pr.; ~∧ MSh
81.24   Warburton] Pr.; ~, MSh
81.25   state.] Pr.; State. MSh
81.26   authors] Pr.; Authors MSh
81.26   Mr. Davies's] Pr.; ~∧ Davies MSh
81.28   Foote,] Pr.; ~∧ MSh
81.28   day,] Pr.; ~∧ MSh
81.29   satirical] Pr.; satyrical MSh
81.32   Davies's] Pr.; Davies MSh
81.33   The Orators,] Pr.; the orators, MSh
81.34   show] Pr.; shew MSh
*81.36   sir?"] Pr.; ~," MSh
81.37   "Sixpence,"] Pr.; "Six pence." MSh; sixpence, Boswell
                    (III, 175)
81.37   sir,] Pr.; Sir, MSh; sir," Boswell (III, 175)
82.2   it with] Pr., Boswell (III, 175); ~, ~ MSh
82.4   The Orators] 49a; the ~ MSh, Pr.
83.2   jobs—The] T; Jobs—the MSh; jobs.—The 49a
83.4   Dinner] 49a; dinner MSh
83.4   Anecdotes] 49a; anecdotes MSh
83.28   fatigue,] 49a, Works (II, 421); ~∧ MSp
83.33   insure] 49a; ensure MSp
83.34   to the government] 49a; to government MSp
84.2   favorite] 49a; favourite MSp
84.10   connection] 49a; connexion MSp
84.12   famous] 49a; Famous MSp
84.15   World," a] 49a; ~." a MSp
*84.28   ecstasy] 49a; ecstacy MSp
84.35   neighborhood] 49a; neighbourhood MSp
85.8   colors.] 49a; colours. MSp
*85.9   by him] 49a; by Goldsmith MSp
85.20   by him] 49a; by Goldsmith MSp
85.36   any thing,] 49a, Boswell (IV, 107); anything MSp
85.38   Boswell,] 49a; ~∧ MSh
85.39   gossipings] 49a; gossippings MSh
86.1   Dr. Johnson,] 49a; ~∧ ~∧ MSh
86.2   day,] 49a; ~∧ MSh
*86.5   but he was] 49a; ~ Goldsmith ~ MSh
86.8   Dr.] 49a; ~∧ MSh
86.8–9   'An Inquiry into] 49a; "An ~ in to MSh; 'An Enquiry
                    into Boswell (I, 421)
86.9   Polite] 49a; ⟨Polit⟩ Polite MSh; polite Boswell (I, 421)

86.10   'The Citizen of the World,'] 49a; "The Citizen of the world" MSh

86.11   Chinese."] 49a; chinese." MSh

86.12   Mr.] 49a; ∼∧ MSh

86.14   poetry,] 49a; ∼∧ MSh

86.24   endeavored to console] 49a; endeavored ⟨to stay the Stomach of⟩ to console MSh

86.28   Johnson,] 49a; ∼∧ MSh

86.30   Goldsmith's] 49a; Goldsmiths MSh

86.31   Apollo.] 49a; Appollo. MSh

86.32   enough," says he,] 49a; ∼∧" ∼ ∼∧ MSh

86.35   indeed,] 49a, Boswell (I, 421); ∼∧ MSh

86.36   scale."] 49a; ∼∧" MSh; ∼·∧ Boswell (I, 421)

86.38   Johnson,"] 49a; ∼∧" MSh

86.41   garrulous] 49a; garrullous MSh

86.43   Mr. Levett,] 49a; ∼∧ ∼∧ MSh

86.43–87.1   Johnson's] 49a; Johnsons MSh

87.1   who, Boswell thought,] 49a; ∼∧ ∼ ∼∧ MSh

87.2   honest,"] 49a; ∼∧" MSh

87.3   Goldsmith,] 49a; ∼∧ MSh

87.3   recommendation] 49a; reccommendation MSh

87.3   to Johnson."] 49a; ∼ ∼∧" MSh; ∼ ∼:" Boswell (I, 430); for ∼.' Forster (259)

87.5   Johnson's kindness] 49a; Johnsons Kindness MSh

87.6   Johnson."] 49a; ∼∧" MSh

87.10   idolatry,] 49a; ∼∧ MSh

87.10   Goldsmith,] 49a; ∼∧ MSh

87.13   Dr.] 49a; ∼∧ MSh

87.15   resort,] 49a; ∼∧ MSh

87.15   Fleet Street.] T; Fleet-street MSp, 49a

*87.33–34   in juxtaposition] 49a; ∼ perpetual ∼ MSp

87.38   Johnson's] 49a; Johnsons MSh

87.39   companionship.] 49a; ∼∧ MSh

87.42   sticking."] 49a; ∼∧∧ MSh

88.2   his] 49a; His MSh

88.4   Club] 49a; club MSh

88.4   Johnson's] 49a; Johnsons MSh

88.5   the Club] T; ∼ ∼. MSh; ∼ club. 49a

88.10   stout, active,] 49a; ∼∧ ∼∧ MSh

88.10–11   sky blue coat,] T; Sky blue ∼; MSh; sky-∼ ∼, 49a

88.12   nature. He] 49a; ∼, He MSh

*88.16–17   the pervading amenity of those] 49a; the same pervading ⟨amenity with those of⟩ ↑amenity with those of↓ MSh

88.18   humors] 49a; humours MSh
88.19–20   precept,] 49a; ~. MSh
88.26   Hogarth's] 49a; ⟨Hog⟩ Hogarth MSh
88.26   Castle Street,] T; ~ ~ₐ MSh; ~-street, 49a
88.29   again! D— him,] 49a; ~! D— ~ₐ MSh
88.30   of him!] 49a; ~ ~; [?] MSh
88.32   oil, called 'Goldsmith's] 49a; ~ₐ ~ 'Goldsmiths MSh
*88.32   landlady.] 49a; land lady. MSh
89.4   coloring] 49a; colouring MSh
89.5   genius,] 49a; ~ₐ MSh
89.6   color is in painting;] 49a; colour ~ ~ ~, MSh
89.14   Reynolds's] 49a; Reynolds MSh
89.19   Dr.] 49a; ~ₐ MSh
89.21   appearance,] 49a; ~ₐ MSh
89.24   Dr.] 49a; ~ₐ MSh
89.27   Reynolds's] 49a; Reynolds MSh
89.28   Mr.] 49a; ~ₐ MSh
89.30   "There] 49a; ₐ~ MSh
89.30   singular,"] 49a; ~,' [or ~;] MSh
89.31   "in] 49a; ₐ~ MSh
89.31   Joshua's] 49a; Joshuas MSh
89.32   good-humour,] T; ~ₐ ~ₐ MSh; ~-~; Boswell (III,
            444); ~-humor, 49a
89.33–34   o'clock precisely dinner was served, whether] T, Boswell
            (III, 445); oclockₐ ↑precisely↓ ⟨illegible word⟩ was
            served whether was served whether MSh; o'clock pre-
            cisely, dinner was served, whether 49a
89.35   ill-bred] 49a, Boswell (III, 445); ~ₐ ~ MSh
89.36   title,] 49a, Boswell (III, 445); ~ₐ MSh
89.41   knives, forks, plates,] 49a, Boswell (III, 444); Knives,
            ~ₐ ~ₐ MSh
90.2   dinner,] 49a, Boswell (III, 444); ~ₐ MSh
90.7–8   recommended.] 49a, Boswell (III, 445); reccommended
            MSh
90.8   guests,] 49a, Boswell (III, 445); ~ₐ MSh
90.10   was eat or drank,] T; was eat or drunk, MSh; was ate
            or drank, 49a; was eat or drank Boswell (III, 445)
90.11   himself."] 49a; ~.ₐ MSh
90.14   statesmen renowned] T; ~ renouned MSh; ~, renowned
            49a
90.15   kind] T; Kind MSh; kind, 49a
90.16   Johnson,] 49a; ~ₐ MSh

90.19   week on Monday night] T; ∼ ∼ monday ∼ MSh;
              ∼, ∼ Monday ∼, 49a
90.19   Turk's Head] 49a; Turks Head MSh
90.20   Gerard Street, Soho,] T; ∼ street∧ ∼∧ MSh; ∼-Street,
              ∼, 49a
90.21   receive] 49a; recieve MSh
90.23   Dr. Nugent,] 49a; ∼∧ ∼. MSh
*90.24   Beauclerc,] 49a; Beauclerk, MSh
90.29   dawning] 49a; dauning MSh
90.29   Dr.] 49a; ∼∧ MSh
90.30–31   Mr. afterwards] 49a; ∼, ∼, MSh
90.32   member of] 49a; Member ⟨of th⟩ MSh
90.32   Johnson's Ivy Lane club.] 49a; Johnsons ⟨club⟩ Ivy
              lane club. ⟨He was a Dabbler in literature and music⟩
              MSh
90.33   law in consequence of] T; law ⟨on receiving⟩ ↑in conse-
              quence of↓ MSh; law, in consequence of 49a
90.34   wife,] 49a; ∼∧ MSh
90.36   music,] 49a; ∼∧ MSh
90.42–43   excused?" asked Dr. Burney of Johnson. "Oh yes,] 49a;
              excused, asked Dr∧ Burney of Johnson "Oh yes MSh
91.2   bottom,] 49a; ∼∧ MSh; ∼; Forster (275)
91.2   penurious,] 49a, Forster (275); ∼∧ MSh
91.3   owned] 49a; ouned MSh
91.3   savageness."] 49a; ∼."– MSh
91.5   Burke.] 49a; ∼∧ MSh
91.6   Mr. Anthony Chamier was Secretary in the war office]
              T; Mr∧ Anthony Chamier was ↑⟨illegible word⟩↓
              Secretary ⟨of⟩ ↑in↓ ⟨War⟩ ↑the War office↓ MSh; Mr.
              Anthony Chamier was Secretary in the war office, 49a
91.7   Beauclerc,] 49a; ∼∧ MSh
91.7   mention] 49a; Mention MSh
*91.8   Beauclerc until] 49a; ∼ ⟨to⟩ ∼ MSh
91.9   them. They] 49a; ∼; ⟨The intimacy of these two very
              young⟩ ⟨They were induced to join the⟩ They MSh
*91.11   and aristocratic] 49a; ∼ very ∼ MSh
91.11   men] 49a; ∼, MSh
91.13   family,] 49a; ∼∧ MSh
91.14   Lincolnshire, a] 49a; ∼. A MSh
91.15   sir,"] 49a; Sir," MSh; sir, Boswell (I, 232)
91.15   "has] 49a; ∧has MSh
91.16   John's] 49a; Johns MSh
91.19   Johnson's] 49a; Johnsons MSh

91.21   author.] 49a; Author. MSh
91.21   interview,] 49a; ~∧ MSh
91.23   preconceived] 49a; preconcieved MSh
91.24   Langton,] 49a; ~∧ MSh
91.24   Johnson,] 49a; ~∧ MSh
*91.24–25   to find him "a decent,] T; to ⟨see a⟩ ↑find him a↓ decent,
               MSh; to find him a decent, 49a
*91.26   down from his bedchamber] 49a; doun from his bed
               chamber MSh; down from his bed-chamber, Boswell
               (I, 232)
91.29   rich, so animated,] 49a, Boswell (I, 232); ~∧ ~ ~∧
               MSh
91.31   conceived] 49a, Boswell (I, 232); concieved MSh
91.32   preserved."] T; ~.' MSh; ~.∧ 49a
91.33   Trinity College, Oxford,] 49a; ~ ~∧ ~∧ MSh
91.42   St. Albans,] 49a; S' Albans, MSh
91.43–92.1   recommendations with Johnson,] 49a; reccommendations
               ⟨to⟩ ↑with↓ Johnson∧ MSh
92.3   time," says Boswell, "the] 49a; ~∧" ~ ~∧ ∧~ MSh
*92.5   in college chambers] 49a; in their college chambres
               [chambers?] MSh
*92.5–6   when the youths came] 49a; when they came MSh
92.6   uncouth, unwieldy] 49a; ~∧ ~ MSh
*92.8   high born, high bred,] T; ~ ~, ~ ~∧ MSh; ~-
               ~, ~-~, 49a
*92.12   tavern,] T; ~∧ MSh, 49a
92.12   o'clock] 49a; OClock MSh
92.15   head instead] T; ~ ⟨by⟩ ~ MSh; ~, ~ 49a
92.16   castle:] 49a; ~; MSh
92.17   Beau,] 49a; ~∧ MSh
92.17–18   them, presented] 49a; ~; ~ MSh
92.19   "What,] 49a; '~, MSh
92.19   you, ye dogs!"] T; ~∧ ye ~!' MSh; ~, ~ ~?" 49a;
               ~, you ~!∧ Boswell (I, 234–35)
92.19–20   "Faith, I'll] 49a; "~∧ ~ MSh; I'll Boswell (I, 235)
92.21   so done.] 49a; ~ ~∧– MSh
*92.21–22   Covent Garden; figured] T; ~ ~. ⟨Johnson⟩ Figured
               MSh; ~-~; figured 49a
92.22   women,] 49a; ~∧ MSh
92.23   tavern,] 49a; ~∧ MSh
92.24   bishop,] 49a; ~∧ MSh
92.25   anathematized] 49a; anathematised MSh
92.26   Lansdowne's] 49a; Lansdounes MSh

92.26	song:] 49a; ∼; MSh
92.27	reign,] 49a, Boswell (I, 235, n. 2); ∼∧ MSh
*92.28	For I'm] 49a; ⟨and⟩ For Im MSh
92.29	Billingsgate,] 49a; Billings / gate, MSh
92.30	"keep it up"] 49a; '∼ ∼ ∼' MSh
92.32	ladies;] 49a; ∼, MSh
92.34	*un-idea'd*] 49b, Boswell (I, 235), E; *un-idead* MSh; *un-ideal* 49a
92.35	sensation,] 49a; ∼∧ MSh
92.36	"I heard] 49a; ⟨"I shall have my old friend to bail out of the round house; youll⟩ "∼ ∼ MSh
92.37	t'other night,"] 49a; to'ther ∼∧" MSh
92.37	"you'll] 49a; '∼ MSh
92.37	Chronicle."] 49a; chronicle."– MSh
92.38	forebodings] 49a; forbodings MSh
92.39	round-house," said he.] 49a; ∼-∼'" Boswell (I, 233); ∼∧ ∼," ∼ ∼– MSh
92.40	Rake's Progress,] 49a; Rakes progress, MSh
93.2	"his] 49a; ∧His MSh
93.3	the Club,] T; ∼ ∼∧ MSh; the club, 49a
93.4	twenty two,] T; ∼ ∼∧ MSh; ∼-∼, 49a
*93.5	life.] 49a; ∼∧ MSh
*93.5–6	the mild, enthusiastic] 49a; ⟨a⟩ mild∧ ∼ MSh
93.6	Greek,] 49a; ∼∧ MSh
93.7–8	upwards of] 49a; upwards [*or* upward,] of MSh
*93.8	"Oh!] 49a; '∼! MSh
93.8	him,"] 49a; ∼,' MSh
93.9	Memoirs, "with] 49a; memoirs, ∧∼ MSh
93.13	weight] T; wieght MSh; weight, 49a
93.14	knee."] 49a; ∼∧"– MSh
93.15	Raphael's Cartoons,] 49a; Raphaels cartoons, MSh
93.15	leg.] 49a; ∼∧ MSh
93.16	"man upon town,"] 49a; '∼ ∼ ∼∧' MSh
93.16	St. James's] 49a; S' James MSh
93.21	self possession,] T; ∼ ∼∧ MSh; ∼-∼, 49a
93.27	talent. "Beauclerc,"] 49a; ∼, ∧∼∧∧ MSh
93.27	say,] 49a; ∼∧ MSh
93.28	"has] 49a; ∧∼ MSh
93.29	says the other."] 49a; ∼, ∼ ∼∧" MSh
93.32	Johnson,] 49a; ∼∧ MSh
*93.33	overcleanly] T; over cleanly MSh, 49a
93.33	receiving] 49a; recieving MSh
93.34	crown,] 49a; ∼∧ MSh

93.36	"he'd] 49a; $_\wedge\sim$ MSh
93.37	gentleman."] 49a; $\sim_\wedge$" MSh
93.37–38	good humor,] 49a; $\sim$ humour, MSh
93.39	Beauclerc's] 49a; Beauclercs MSh
93.39	vein] 49a; $\sim_\wedge$ MSh
93.39	side,] 49a; $\sim_\wedge$ MSh
93.40	"Sir,"] 49a; "$\sim_\wedge$" MSh
93.40	occasion,] 49a; $\sim_\wedge$ MSh
94.1	enroll] 49a; enrol MSh
94.2	association,] 49a; $\sim_\wedge$ MSh
94.3	booksellers,] 49a; Booksellers$_\wedge$ MSh
94.9	merits,] 49a; $\sim$; MSh
94.11	awkward] 49a; aukward MSh
94.12	society, and] 49a; society; ⟨he felt himself strange and out of place⟩ and MSh
94.13	humors] T; humours MSh; humor 49a
*94.14	of all who knew him.] 49a; of those who truly knew him. MSh
94.17	ease, the more awkward] 49a; $\sim_\wedge$ $\sim$ $\sim$ aukward MSh
95.2	*monitor*] 49a; Monitor MSh
95.3	*oratorio*] 49a; Oratoria MSh
95.3–4	*Poem of the*] 49a; poem of The MSh
95.5	*Observations*] 49a; observations MSh
95.6	Goldsmith's] 49a; Goldsmiths MSh
95.7	character,] 49a; $\sim_\wedge$ MSh
95.10	judgment] 49a; judgement MSh
95.22	me that he had] MSp, Boswell (I, 427); me he had 49a
95.37	muse] 49a; Muse MSh
*95.37	ushered] 49a; tortured MSh
96.1	part,] 49a, *Works* (IV, 222); $\sim_\wedge$ MSh
96.5	taper's] 49a; *Works* (IV, 222); tapers MSh
96.34	poem,] 49a; $\sim_\wedge$ MSp
96.35	ardor] 49a; ardour MSp
96.37	sit] 49a; set MSp
*96.40	page were] 49a; page before him were MSp
97.1	By sports] T; "$\sim$ $\sim$ MSp, 49a
97.2	child.] T; $\sim$." MSp, 49a
97.3	good humor,] T; $\sim$-humour, MSp; $\sim$-humor, 49a
97.8	well merited] T; $\sim$-$\sim$ MSp, 49a
97.15–16	favorable] 49a; favourable MSp
97.17	favor.] 49a; favour. MSp
*97.18–19	win, not to] 49a; wi MSp
97.19	favor;] 49a; favour; MSp

97.20   afterwards,] 49a; afterward, MSp
97.23   "The Traveller"] 49a; ₍the ～₍ MSh
97.23   Goldsmith's] 49a; Goldsmiths MSh
97.24   society;] 49a; Society; MSh
97.25   Hawkins,] 49a; Hawkens₍ MSh
°97.26–27   a "newspaper essayist" and "bookseller's drudge"] 49a;
                 a 'news paper ～' ～ 'booksellers ～' MSh
97.29   "rattling] 49a; '～ MSh
97.29   usual,"] 49a; ～.' MSh
97.30   grace, the] 49a; ～₍ ↑the↓ MSh
97.33   in general, says Johnson, "it] 49a; ⟨～ generul,⟩ ↑～
                 ～₍↓ ～ John/son₍ '～ MSh
97.34   hearing."] 49a; ～₍' MSh
97.34   Chamier, "I] 49a; ～, ₍～ MSh
97.35   deal."] 49a; ～₍" MSh
97.37   "Mr. Goldsmith," said he, "what] 49a; ～₍ ～ₐₐ ～ ～,
                 ₍～ MSh
97.39   melancholy,] T, *Works* (IV, 248), Forster (318); solitary,
                 MSh, 49a, 49b, 49c, E; melancholly, 50
97.39   "Yes,"] 49a; "～,' MSh
98.1   solitude,"–"Ah,"] 49a; ～₍"–"～₍" MSh
98.3   line, and a rumor became prevalent that] 49a; ～₍ ～
                 ⟨it was even asserted⟩ ↑a rumor ～ ～ ～↓ MSh
98.6   towards the conclusion,] 49a; toward, ～ ～₍ MSh
98.11   acquaintance.] 49a; ～₍ MSh
98.11–12   "The Traveller" Dr.] T; ₍the ～₍ ～₍ MSh; "～ ～," ～.
                 49a
98.13   "Well," exclaimed she,] 49a; –Well ⟨'said⟩ ↑exclaimed↓
                 She, MSh
98.13   "I] 49a; ₍～ MSh
98.14   Dr.] 49a; ～₍ MSh
98.15   "The Traveller"] 49a; ₍the ～₍ MSh
°98.16   Reynolds's, Bennet Langton] T; Reynolds Bennet Lang-
                 ton MSh; Reynolds's board, Langton 49a
98.17   Dryden's careless verses."] 49a; Drydens ～ ～.". MSh
98.17   glad,"] 49a; ～₍" MSh
98.18   Reynolds, "to] 49a; ～₍ ₍～ MSh
98.19   language." "Why] 49a; ～.' 'why MSh
98.19–20   was you glad?" rejoined Langton, "you] 49a; ～ ～ ～?'
                 ～ ～, '～ MSh; were you glad? Boswell (IV, 107)
98.20   before." "No,"] 49a; ～.' –"～₍ₐ MSh
98.21   merit] 49a, Boswell (IV, 107); merits MSh
98.21   'The Traveller'] 49a, Boswell (IV, 107); ₍the ～₍ MSh

98.21–22	Mr. Fox's] 49a; ~ₐ Fox; MSh
98.24	Goldsmith,] 49a; ~ₐ MSh
98.28	you, sir,"] 49a; you, Sir," MSh; you, 'sir,' Forster (320)
98.28–29	"Why no, sir,"] 49a; '~ ~, ~,' Forster (320); "~, ~, Sir," MSh
98.30	Goldy, sir, has great merit."] 49a; '~, ~, ~ ~ ~.' Forster (320); ~ₐ Sir, ~ ~ merit."– MSh
98.30	"But, sir, he] 49a; "~, Sir, "he MSh; '~ sir,' Forster (320)
98.31–32	estimation." "Why, sir,] 49a; ~."–'~, Sir, MSh; ~.' '~, sir, Forster (320)
98.34	received] 49a; recieved MSh
98.34–35	author's pen.] 49a; Authors ~. MSh
98.35	Mr.] 49a; ~ₐ MSh
99.2	*Johnson's compliment–*] T; ~ ~.– 49a; Johnsons complement– MSh
99.2	*A titled*] 49a; a ~ MSh
99.3	*His*] 49a; his MSh
99.3–4	*The Countess*] 49a; the ~ MSh
*99.4	*Gosfield*] T; Gosford MSh, 49a
99.5	*Publication*] 49a; publication MSh
99.5–6	*Hangers on–Job*] T; hangers on–job MSh; Hangers-on.– Job 49a
99.6	*Mrs.*] 49a; ~ₐ MSh
99.8	Goldsmith,] 49a; ~ₐ MSh
99.8	notoriety,] 49a; ~ₐ MSh
99.10	Wine Office Court] T; wine office ~ MSh; Wine-Office Court, 49a
*99.12	library stair case,] T; Library Stair case, MSh; library staircase, 49a
99.13	Jeffs,] 49a; ~ₐ MSh
99.13	society.] 49a; Society. MSh
99.15	which,] 49a; ~ₐ MSh
*99.17	is to] T; ~, ~ MSh, 49a
99.18	a desert. Johnson,] 49a; ~ ↑~ₐ↓ ~, MSh
99.18–19	who had become a] 49a; ~ ⟨was always⟩ ↑had become↓ a MSh
99.19	of the poet's] 49a; ~ ⟨Goldsmiths⟩ ↑the poets↓ MSh
99.20	had installed] 49a; ~ ⟨entered⟩ installed MSh
99.22	fidgeted] 49a; fidgetted MSh
99.25–26	Johnson,] 49a; ~ₐ MSh
99.26–27	"Nay, sir," said he, "never] 49a; "~ₐ Sir," ~ ~ₐ "~ MSh; '~, sir, never Boswell (IV, 359)

99.30	outward show.] 49a; ~. show∧" MSh
99.33	Goldsmith's writings,] 49a; Goldsmiths ~∧ MSh
99.35	good will.] 49a; ~ ~∧ MSh
°99.35	The earl held the office of Lord Lieutenant] 49a; ~ Earl was appointed Lord lieutenant MSh
99.40	fortune,] 49a; ~∧ MSh
100.3	House,] 49a; house∧ MSh
100.4	visit:—"I] 49a; Visit∧ [paragraph] I MSh
°100.6	House,] 49a; ~. MSh
100.7	duke,] 49a; ~∧ MSh
100.28	the Traveller,] 49a, Percy (67); "~ ~," MSh; the '~,' 1825 (29)
100.34	dependence] 49a, Percy (67), 1825 (29); dependance MSp
100.41	favors] 49a; favours MSp
101.6	Dr.] 49a; ~∧ MSh
101.6	ancient Percies,] 49a; Ancient ~∧ MSh
°101.7	kinswoman, the countess;] 49a; kins woman the Countess, MSh
101.8	earl,] 49a; Earl, MSh
101.8	own] 49a; oun MSh
101.8	House] 49a; house MSh
101.9	"She] 49a; ∧~ MSh
101.9	lady,"] 49a; ~,∧ MSh
101.9	"not] 49a; ∧~ MSh
101.11	talents."] 49a; ~.∧ MSh
101.11–12	Goldsmith's] 49a; Goldsmiths MSh
101.13	ballad] 49a; Ballad MSp
101.23	Goldsmith's] 49a; Goldsmiths MSh
101.24	circle] 49a; Circle MSh
101.25	House,] 49a; house, MSh
101.26	taste,] 49a; ~∧ MSh
°101.28	Gosfield, the seat] 50; Gosford the noble seat MSh; Gosford, the noble seat 49a
°101.29	Nugent, afterwards] 49a; ~∧ after wards MSh
101.31	town] 49a; toun MSh
101.33	Protestant religion] T; protestant reli / gion MSh; Protestant religion, 49a
101.33	fortunes; he] 49a; ~; He MSh
101.34	Irishman's inclination] 49a; Irishmans ~ MSh
101.34	Irishman's luck] 49a; Irishmans ~ MSh
101.39	showed] 49a; shewed MSh
101.40	House of Commons,] 49a; house ~ ~∧ MSh

101.42	awkward] 49a; aukward MSh
*101.42	nickname] 49a; nick name MSh
*101.43	Gawkey]T; Gawky, 49a; Gawky∧ MSh
102.3–4	"The Traveller,"] 49a; "the ∼," MSp
102.7	collected] 49a; ∼, MSp
102.9	appeared] 49a, *Works* (III, 1); ∼, MSp
102.9	times,] 49a, *Works* (III, 1); ∼∧ MSp
102.24	Philautos,] 49a, *Works* (III, 1); Philantos, MSp
102.33	risen,] 49a; ∼∧ MSh
102.39	counsel;] 49a; council; MSh
102.40	"Our Doctor,"] 49a; "our ∼∧" MSh; 'Our Doctor,' Forster (420)
*102.42	countrymen,] 49a, Forster (420); ∼∧ MSh
103.1–2	guinea, in order to] 49a, Forster (420); ∼∧ ∼ 'order' ∼ MSh
103.2	others."] 49a; ∼·∧ MSh; ∼.' Forster (420)
103.5	with Mr.] 49a; with with Mr∧ MSh
103.6	pounds,] 49a; ∼∧ MSh
103.8	effusions,] 49a; ∼∧ MSh
103.17	humor.] 49a; humour. MSp
103.24	Who,] T; "∼, MSp, 49a
103.27	six.] T; ∼." MSp, 49a
103.28	humor,] 49a; humour, MSp
*104.1	small-clothes,] 49a; smallclothes, MSp
104.7	sceptre, the cane,] 49a; ∼∧ ∼ ∼∧ MSh
104.9	at least,] 49a; ∼ ∼∧ MSh
104.10	chamber] 49a; chambre MSh
104.11	patients.] 49a; ∼∧ MSh
104.16	meetings,] 49a; ∼∧ MSh
104.18	acquaintance] 49a; '∼ MSh
104.19	phrase,] 49a; phraze∧ MSh
104.22–23	compounder of drugs. His] 49a; compounder of [*illegible word*] drugs, has MSh
104.24–25	Mrs. Sidebotham sided] 49a; ⟨even of his latin if he quoted it fell on an uninstructed ear⟩ Mrs∧ ∼ Sided MSh
104.25	mortar; and] 49a; ∼; ⟨took the medi / cine around⟩ and MSh
104.27	Beauclerc,] 49a; ∼∧ MSh
104.27	so,] 49a, Prior (II, 105); ∼∧ MSh
104.28	kill,] 49a, Prior (II, 105); ∼∧ MSh
104.30	Goldsmith's] 49a; Goldsmiths MSh
105.3	*Dr.*] 49a; ∼∧ MSh

105.3	*Exquisite*] 49a; exquisite MSh
105.4	*Project*] 49a; project MSh
105.6	"The Traveller"] T; ∧the ∼∧ MSh; "The ∼," 49a
105.8	"The Vicar of Wakefield"] 49a; ∧the ∼ ∼ ∼∧ MSh
105.10	Mr.] 49a; ∼∧ MSh
105.13	mistake;] 49a; ∼, MSh
105.15	purchaser.] 49a; ∼, MSh
105.18–19	"The Traveller"] 49a; ∧the ∼∧ MSh
105.20–21	undervalue, if not reject,] 49a; ∼∧ ∼ ∼ ∼∧ MSh
105.21	excellence,] 49a; ∼; MSh
°105.22	brilliancy] 49a; brilliance MSh
105.22	"effect."] 49a; '∼.' MSh
105.24	Dr. Johnson,] 49a; ∼∧ ∼∧ MSh
105.25	publication, observed, "I] 49a; ∼∧ ∼, ∧∼ MSh
105.27	'The Traveller'] T; ∧the ∼∧ MSh; "The ∼," 49a; his '∼,' Boswell (IV, 180)
105.28	'The Traveller,'] T, Boswell (III, 180); ∧the ∼∧ MSh; "The ∼," 49a
105.31	Dr.] 49a; ∼∧ MSh
105.34	March,] 49a; ∼∧ MSh
105.36	Rogers,] 49a; ∼∧ MSh
°105.38	eminently] 49a; emenenlty MSh
°105.39	kind, declared] 49a; ∼∧ declares MSh
106.3	undiminished.] 49a; ∼∧" MSh
106.5	language,] 49a; ∼∧ MSh
106.6–7	Germany, declared] 49a; ∼∧ ∼, MSh
106.17	author,] 49a; Author, MSh
106.22	colorings of his own] 49a; colourings of his oun MSh
°106.24–25	the most amiable picture] 49a; ∼ ∼ tender ∼ MSh
106.26	bachelor,] 49a; ∼∧ MSh
°106.30	seemed to mark him] 49a; ∼ ∼ have marked him MSh
106.33	comprises] 49a; comprizes MSh
106.33	feeling,] 49a; ∼; MSh
106.36	woman's] 49a; womans MSh
°106.41	honeysuckle] T; honey- / suckle MSh, 49a, *Works* (IV, 136)
107.5	'Do,] 49a; "∼, MSh
107.5	Olivia,'] 49a; ∼," MSh
107.6	'let] 49a; "∼ MSh
107.7	father.'] 49a; ∼∧" MSh
107.15	lover,] 49a, *Works* (IV, 136); ∼∧ MSh
107.16	die."] T; ∼.∧ MSh, *Works* (IV, 136); ∼.' " 49a
107.18	received] 49a; recieved MSh

107.19-20   newspapers.] 49a; news papers. MSh
107.21   Hermit,] 49a; ∼∧ MSh
107.24   day:] 49a; ∼. MSh
107.26   "Sɪʀ,–In] 49a; "Sir, / "In MSp
107.34   'No,] T, Prior (II, 84); " '∼, MSp, 49a
108.5   'And] T; 'And Prior (II, 85); " 'And MSp, 49a
108.16   "I am, sir, yours, &c.,] 49a; I am, sir, / "Yours, &c., MSp
108.20   "Sɪʀ,–As] 49a; "Sir, / "As MSp
109.10   dishonored.] 49a; dishonoured. MSp
*109.10   job work] T; ∼-∼ MSp, 49a
109.14   labor] 49a; labour MSp
109.23   his fondness for] 49a; ⟨His⟩ his fondness of MSh
109.24   though,] 49a; ∼∧ MSh
109.24   shown,] 49a; shewn, MSh
109.28   *Sentimental Comedy,*] MSh, *Works* (III, 212); *senti-
             mental comedy*, 49a
109.29   the vices] 49a; their vices MSh; the Vices *Works* (III,
             212)
109.40   this, however,] 49a, *Works* (III, 212); ∼∧ ∼∧ MSh
109.41   no ways solicitous,] 49a; ∼ ∼ ∼∧ MSh; noway ∼,
             Works (III, 212)
109.41-42   profits. * * * *] 49a; ∼. X X X X MSh
110.10   comedy] 49a; Comedy MSh
110.10   the *Clandestine Marriage,*] 49a; The ∼ ∼; MSh
110.11   Hogarth's] 49a; Hogarths MSh
110.11-12   *Marriage à la mode,*] T; ∼ a ∼ Mode, MSh; ∼ a ∼
             mode, 49a
110.12   town by storm,] 49a; toun ∼ ∼; MSh
110.14   Goldsmith's] 49a; Goldsmiths MSh
110.16   sentimental school;] 49a; Sentimental School; MSh
110.17   humor,] 49a; humour∧ MSh
*110.19   a comedy of the same class,] 49a; a comedy MSh
110.21   leisure.] 49a; leisure∧ MSh
111.3   *Anecdotes*] 49a; ⟨classification of their⟩ anecdotes MSh
111.4   social] 49a; Social MSh
111.14   Ireland,] 49a; ∼∧ MSh
111.15   blunders,"] 49a; ∼∧" MSh
111.16   travelled,] 49a; ∼∧ MSh
111.19   mind,] 49a; ∼; MSh
111.20   heart,] 49a; ∼∧ MSh
111.20   pictures,] 49a; ∼∧ MSh
111.23   humiliations.] 49a; ∼∧ MSh
111.23   conceive,"] 49a; concieve∧" MSh

111.24–25   disappointment, anguish,] 49a, Prior (I, 298); $\sim_\wedge\ \sim_\wedge$ MSh

111.25   down."] 49a; doun;" MSh; down.$_\wedge$ Prior (I, 298)

111.27   apothecary's] 49a; apothecarys MSh

111.28   bookseller's] 49a; booksellers MSh

111.31–32   poverty," to which,] 49a; $\sim_\wedge$" $\sim$ $\sim_\wedge$ MSh

111.35   The Traveller] T; the $\sim$ MSh; The $\sim$, 49a

111.38   years' conflict;] 49a, Forster (437); $\sim_\wedge\ \sim$; MSh

112.5   awkward] 49a; aukward MSh

112.9   part,] 49a; $\sim_\wedge$ MSh

*112.10   surprise] 49a; surprize MSh

*112.10–11   he showed himself capable,] 49a; he was capable, MSh

112.15   there,] 49a; $\sim_\wedge$ MSh

112.16   master.] 49a; $\sim_\wedge$ MSh

112.17   temperament,] 49a; $\sim_\wedge$ MSh

112.18   youth,] 49a; $\sim_\wedge$ MSh

112.21   "He] 49a; $_\wedge\sim$ MSh

112.21   life,"] 49a; $\sim,_\wedge$ MSh

112.22   Boswell, "habituated] 49a; $\sim$, $_\wedge$habituate MSh; habitu-ated Boswell (IV, 484)

112.23   disciplined] 49a; diciplined MSh

112.27   language."] 49a; $\sim._\wedge$ MSh

112.31   care,"] 49a; $\sim_\wedge$" MSh

112.34   Dr.] 49a; $\sim_\wedge$ MSh

112.35   Johnson,"] 49a; $\sim_\wedge$" MSh

112.35   said he,] T; $\sim\ \sim_\wedge$ MSh; says $\sim$, 49a

112.37   clear."] Pr.; $\sim._\wedge$ MSh

112.38   Goldsmith's] Pr.; Goldsmiths MSh

112.41; 113.1   in, was] Pr.; $\sim_\wedge\ \sim$ MSh

*112.42   *Forster's Goldsmith, p. 437.] T; ⟨*Forsters Goldsmith P 437⟩ MSh; *Foster's Goldsmith 49a; Forster's $\sim_\wedge$ 49b, E

*113.4   lexicographer] T; $\sim$, MSh, 49a

113.4   ideas,] Pr.; $\sim_\wedge$ MSh

113.6   confused,] Pr.; $\sim_\wedge$ MSh

113.8   say,] Pr.; $\sim$; MSh

*113.10   company,] T; $\sim_\wedge$ MSh, Pr., 49a

113.11   somewhat] 49a; some what MSh

113.12   man,"] Pr.; $\sim_\wedge$" MSh

113.13   has."] Pr.; $\sim_\wedge$" MSh

113.19   things,] Pr.; $\sim$; MSh

113.20   perceived] 49a; percieved MSh

*113.20   haphazard] T; hap hazard MSh; hap- /hazard 49a

113.21	"The misfortune] 49a; ∧~ ~ MSh
113.22	conversation,"] 49a; ~,∧ MSh
113.22	"is] 49a; ∧~ MSh
114.1	vexation.] 49a; ~∧ MSh
114.5	Dr. Johnson's company."] 49a; ~∧ Johnsons ~∧" MSh
114.7	lexicographer,] 49a; Lexicographer, MSh
114.10	thunder] 49a; thundre MSh
114.10	periods; and,] 49a; ~, ~∧ MSh
114.11	failed,] 49a; ~∧ MSh
*114.11	downright] 49a; doun right MSh
114.12	sophistry;"] 49a; ~∧" MSh
114.13–14	Johnson,"] 49a; ~∧" MSh
114.14	he, "*for, when*] 49a; ~∧ "~∧ ~ MSh; Johnson: for if Boswell (V, 172)
114.14	*fire, he*] 49a; ~∧ ~ MSh; fire, he Boswell (V, 172)
*114.15	*of it."*] 49a; ~ ~."∧ MSh; of it." Boswell (V, 172)
*114.19	good nature.] T; ~-~. MSp, 49a
114.23	fishes,] 49a, Boswell (II, 220); ~∧ MSp
*114.32–33	to Dr. Johnson and Dr. Shebbeare,] 49a; to Johnson and ~∧ ~∧ MSh
114.33	king] 49a, Boswell (IV, 485, n. 1); King MSh
114.34–35	replied, "Johnson,] 49a; ~∧ "~∧ MSh; well:–"Johnson, Boswell (II, 68)
*114.39	'robust sophistry':–] T; '~ ~'∧– MSh; ∧~ ~∧:– 49a
114.40	advantage,] 49a, Boswell (IV, 483); ~∧ MSh
114.41	let's] 49a, Boswell (IV, 483); lets MSh
114.42	tune.'"] 49a; ~.∧∧ MSh; ~.∧" Boswell (IV, 483)
115.2	impulses.] 49a; ~∧ MSh
115.2	perceive] 49a; percieve MSh
115.3	part,"] 49a; ~∧" MSh
115.7	good humor,] T; ~-humour, MSp; ~-humor, 49a
115.8	intimates;] 49a; ~: MSh, MSp
116.2	A *practical*] 49a; a ~ MSh
116.3	'*tun of man*'] 49a; 'Tun of Man' MSh
116.5	Goldsmith's] 49a; Goldsmiths MSh
116.10	shilling whist] 49a; Shilling Whist MSh
116.11–12	classic, we are told,] 49a; ~∧ ~ ~ ~∧ MSh
116.13	The company] 49a; The The ~ MSh
116.13	familiar,] 49a; ~∧ MSh
116.16	coach,] 49a; ~∧ MSh
116.18	down] 49a; doun MSh
116.18	likelihood, he said,] 49a; ~∧ ~ ~∧ MSh
116.22	surprise] 49a; surprize MSh

116.24   honesty,] Pr.; ~∧ MSh
116.25   increasing] 49a; encreasing MSh
116.26   own] Pr.; oun MSh
116.27   conduct.] Pr.; ~∧ MSh
116.27   chanting] Pr.; chaunting MSh
116.27   praises,] Pr.; ~∧ MSh
116.28–29   Goldsmith's] Pr.; Goldsmiths MSh
°116.29   counterfeit.] Pr.; counter fiet. MSh
116.31   showed] Pr.; shewed MSh
116.32   counterfeit] 49a; counterfiet MSh
116.32   disconcerted,] Pr.; ~∧ MSh
116.36   Pigeons: songs,] Pr.; Pigions: Songs, MSh
116.37   humor] T; humour MSh; humor, Pr.
°116.38   sarcasm of the learned circle.] 49a; ~ ~ ~ literary
              club. MSh; [sarcasm of the ⟨literary club.⟩ learned
              circle Pr.
°116.39   'tun of man,'] 49a; 'Tun of Man,' MSh; '⟨T⟩un of man,' Pr.
116.39   Gordon,] Pr.; ~∧ MSh
117.2   butcher,] 49a; ~∧ MSh
117.3   The Traveller,] Pr.; the traveller∧ MSh
°117.4   author, and here] 49a; Author. Here MSh; author/∧
              ⟨H⟩ere Pr.
117.4   King, the comedian,] Pr.; ~∧ ~ Comedian, MSh
117.6   new comedy] Pr.; New Comedy MSh
117.7   second rate] T; Second ~ MSh; second-rate Pr.
117.8   a kind of competitor] Pr.; a Kind of Competitor MSh
117.8   Goldsmith's,] Pr.; Goldsmiths MSh
117.9–10   age, originally] 49a; ~. Originally MSh
°117.10   staymaker] 49a; Stay maker MSh
°117.11   Grub Street] T; Grubstreet MSh; Grub-street 49a
117.11–12   newspapers.] 49a; news papers MSh
117.12   satirist,] 49a; Satirist, MSh
117.13   in emulation] 49a; an ~ MSh
117.13   Churchill's] 49a; Churchills MSh
117.13   harassed] 49a; harrassed MSh
117.17   vanity.] 49a; ~∧ MSh
117.18   Johnson;] 49a; ~, MSh
117.19   leave,] 49a; ~∧ MSh
117.20   sir,"] 49a; Sir∧' MSh; sir." Boswell (V, 321, n. 1)
117.20   surly moralist,] 49a; Surly Moralist, MSh
117.23   Goldsmith's] 49a; Goldsmiths MSh
117.24   hangers on] T; Hangars on MSh; hangers-on, 49a
117.26   Cork,] 49a; ~∧ MSh

117.27   malefactor,] 49a; ~_∧ MSh
*117.35   He was a] 49a; ⟨He was a⟩ MSp
117.41   humors.] 49a; humours. MSh
117.42   Club,] 49a; ~_∧ MSh
118.1   patron,] 49a; ~_∧ MSh
*118.4   pig butcher:] T; ~ ~_∧ MSh; ~-~: 49a
118.4   "Come, Noll,"] 49a; _∧~_∧ ~_{∧∧} MSh
118.5   "here's] 49a; "heres MSh
118.5   you, old] 49a; ~_∧ Old MSh
118.6   "should] 49a; _∧~ MSh
118.7   "you'll] 49a; "youll MSh
118.8   down." After a time] T; ~_∧" after ~ ~_∧ MSh; ~."
                  After ~ ~, 49a
118.9   "Mr. B.,] 49a; _∧~_∧ ~·_∧ MSh
118.9   Alas!] 49a; ~_∧ MSh
118.10   Goldsmith's forte:] 49a; Goldsmiths ~; MSh
118.11   "Thank'ee, thank'ee, Noll,"] 49a; "Thank_∧ee_∧ thankee_∧
                  Noll_∧" MSh
118.11   pig butcher,] T; ~-~, 49a; ~ ~_∧ MSh
118.12   don't] 49a; dont MSh
118.12   reproof,"] 49a; ~_∧" MSh
118.13   Glover.] 49a; ~_∧"— MSh
118.13   good humored] T; ~ humoured MSh; ~-humored 49a
118.14   shrug,] 49a; ~. MSh
118.14   known] 49a; knoun MSh
118.15   way."] 49a; ~_∧" MSh
118.17   circles,] 49a; ~; MSh
118.22   Jonson"] 49a; ~," MSh
118.23   Humour."] T; ~_∧" MSh; Humor." 49a
118.25   taste:] 49a; ~; MSh
118.25   merriment, he] 49a; ~. ~ MSh
118.26   company] 49a; Company MSh
118.26   fools,"] 49a; ~.' MSh
118.27   essays, "may] 49a; ~_∧ '~ MSh
*118.28   melancholy." Often] T; ~_∧" ~ MSh; ~." "~ 49a
118.29   "to go] T; '~ ~ MSh; _∧~ ~ 49a
118.29   misfortune."] 49a; ~.' MSh; misfortunes.' Forster (423)
*118.32   "The Good Natured Man."] T; the good natured Man.
                  MSh; "The Good-natured Man." 49a
118.32   humor] 49a; humour MSh
*118.35   writer—still, we hope, living—whom] 49a; writer, whom
                  MSh
119.2   *Great Cham*] 49a; great cham MSh

119.3   *Reynolds's*] 49a; Reynolds MSh
119.5   "The Good Natured Man"] T; ∧the ~ natured ~∧ MSh;
                 "The Good-natured Man" 49a
119.9   comedy] 49a; Comedy MSh
119.9–10   "The Provoked Husband,"] 49a; ∧the ~ ~,∧ MSh
119.11   Goldsmith,] 49a; ~∧ MSh
119.11   weight] 49a; wieght MSh
119.13   public;] 49a; ~, MSh
119.14   Johnson's] 49a; Johnsons MSh
119.15   Queen's] 49a; Queens MSh
119.16   books, in] 49a; ~∧ ↑in↓ MSh
119.17   librarian, Mr. Bernard,] 49a; ~∧ ~∧ ~∧ MSh
119.19   (George III.),] 49a; (George III). MSh
119.22   interview,"] 49a; ~∧" MSh
119.22   Boswell,] 49a; ~∧ MSh
119.23   respect,] 49a, Boswell (II, 40); ~∧ MSh
119.25   drawing room.] T; ~ ~∧ MSh; ~-~. 49a
119.25   'I found] 49a; "~ ~ MSh
119.25   majesty] 49a; Majesty MSh
*119.26   talk,' said he, 'and] 49a; talk and MSh
119.27   sovereign.] 49a, Boswell (II, 40); Sov reign. MSh
119.27   place,] 49a; ~∧ MSh
119.28   passion–.'"] 49a; ~–∧∧" MSh
119.28   Johnson's] 49a; Johnsons MSh
119.29   disputants,] 49a; ⟨antagonists⟩ ↑disputants∧↓ MSh
119.32   behavior. "Sir,"] 49a; behaviour, "Sir∧" MSh
119.33–34   seen."–"Sir,"] 49a; ~∧"–"~,∧ MSh
*119.35   Louis the Fourteenth] T; Lewis ~ ~ MSh, 49a; Louis
                 XIV Boswell (II, 40)
119.36   Second."] 49a; ~∧" MSh; Charles II." Boswell (II, **40**)
119.37   Johnson's] 49a; Johnsons MSh
119.37   royalty,] 49a; ~∧ MSh
119.38   group] 49a; groupe MSh
119.38   Reynolds's,] 49a; Reynolds, MSh
119.39   anxious] 49a; anxous MSh
*120.1   any thing.] 49a; ~ ~." MSh
120.2   "I] 49a; ∧~ MSh
120.2   too,"] 49a; ~∧∧ MSh
120.2   "if] 49a; ∧~ MSh
120.3   "No man," said Johnson,] 49a; ∧~ ~∧∧ ~ ~∧ MSh
120.4   "could] 49a; ∧~ MSh
120.4   compliment;] 49a; complement; MSh
120.5   decisive."–] 49a; decesive".–MSh

120.6	compliment?"] 49a; complement? MSh
120.6	company.] 49a; Company. MSh
120.6	"No, sir,"] 49a; "~∧ Sir." MSh
120.7	"when] 49a; "When MSh
120.8	sovereign."] 49a; Sovriegn." MSh
120.9	forth, Goldsmith,] 49a; ~∧ ~∧ MSh
120.10	present,] 49a; ~∧ MSh
120.11	sofa] 49a; Sofa MSh
120.12	recollecting himself,] 49a; reccollecting ~∧ MSh
120.12	up, and advancing, exclaimed,] 49a; ~∧ ~ ~∧ ~∧ MSh
120.13	simplicity,"] 49a; ~∧∧ MSh
120.18	excitement,] 49a; ~∧ MSh
120.21	Goldsmith's] 49a; Goldsmiths MSh
120.22	"that] 49a; '~ MSh
120.23	honour Dr.] T, Boswell (II, 41); ~ ~∧ MSh; honor Dr. 49a
120.24	to ascribe] 49a; too ~ MSh
*120.25	Goldsmith and] T; ~ or MSh; ~, and 49a
120.26	honor] 49a; honour MSh
120.26	Dr.] 49a; ~∧ MSh
120.27	"The Good Natured Man"] T; ∧~ ~ ~ ~∧ MSh; "The Good-natured ~" 49a
120.27	performance,] 49a; ~∧ MSh
120.28	stage.] 49a; Stage. MSh
120.30	Rich, the manager. Drury Lane] 49a; ~∧ The Manager. ~ lane MSh
120.30–31	management of Garrick,] 49a; Management ~ ~∧ MSh
120.31	feud,] 49a; ~∧ MSh
120.31	recollected,] 49a; reccollected∧ MSh
*120.34	secretaryship] 49a; Secretary Ship MSh
120.35	changed.] 49a; ~∧- MSh
120.36	unknown] 49a; unknoun MSh
120.36	society.] 49a; Society. MSh
120.37	lion;] 49a; ~, MSh
120.37	the Literary Club;] 49a; the ⟨Gerard⟩ ↑Literary↓ Street club; MSh
120.38	Johnson,] 49a; ~∧ MSh
120.39	word,] 49a; ~∧ MSh
120.41	author and actor,] 49a; Author and Actor, MSh
120.42	talents,] 49a; ~∧ MSh
120.43	other,] 49a; ~∧ MSh
121.1	worn out pique,] T; ~ ~ ~∧ MSh; ~-~ ~, 49a
121.2	Reynolds's] 49a; Reynolds MSh

121.2   Square.] 49a; ~∧ MSh
121.3   stage;] 49a; Stage; MSh
121.4   civil,] 49a; ~∧ MSh
*121.5   Davies in] T; ~, ~ MSh, 49a
121.5   "Life of Garrick"] T; ∧life ~ ~∧ MSh; "Life ~ ~," 49a
121.6   manager,"] 49a; ~∧" MSh
121.7   "was] 49a; ∧~ MSh
121.7   (Goldsmith's)] 49a; (Goldsmiths) MSh
121.9   was, on] 49a; ~∧ ~ MSh
121.10   own] 49a; oun MSh
121.10   Mr. Garrick,] 49a; ~∧ ~∧ MSh
121.12   actor,] 49a; ~∧ MSh
121.15   parties,] 49a; ~∧ MSh
121.15   Mr.] 49a; ~∧ MSh
121.21   sincerity."] 49a; ~∧" MSh
121.28   further] 49a; farther MSh
121.32   Goldsmith's] 49a; Goldsmiths MSh
121.32   supplied,] 49a; ~∧ MSh
*121.36   the comedy] 49a; his ~ MSh
121.39   Whitehead,] 49a; ~∧ MSh
121.39   laureate,] 49a; laureat, MSh
121.40   "reader"] 49a; '~' MSh
121.41   ensued,] 49a; ~∧ MSh
122.1   Colman] 49a; Coleman MSh
122.2   "The Clandestine Marriage,"] 49a; ∧~ ~ ~,∧ MSh
*122.3   proprietor of Covent Garden,] 49a; ~ ~ the ⟨rival
             theatre⟩ ↑Drury Lane↓, MSh
122.5   Colman;] 49a; Coleman; MSh
122.7   warm,] 49a; ~∧ MSh
122.9   Colman.] 49a; Coleman. MSh
122.9   "Dear Sir,"] T; ∧~ ~,∧ MSh, Forster (409); "~ sir," 49a
122.10   July 19th,] T; ~ ~. MSh; ~ ~∧ Forster (409), *Letters*
             (74); July 9th, 49a
122.10   "I] 49a; ∧~ MSh
*122.21   anxieties,"] 49a; ~.∧ MSh
122.22   Garrick,] 49a; ~- MSh
122.25   claimed, observing, "as I] 49a; ~: ⟨and that he had done
             so *illegible word*⟩∧ ↑observing,↓ "As I MSh
122.26   piece,] 49a, Forster (412); ~∧ MSh
122.26   * * * * * * * *] 49a; X X X X X MSh
122.28   judgment] 49a, Forster (412); judgement MSh
122.30   you, sir,] 49a, Forster (412); ~∧ Sir, MSh
122.32   GOLDSMITH."] 49a; ~.∧ MSh

122.33	observed,] 49a; ~. MSh
122.36	own] 49a; oun MSh
122.38	receiving] 49a; recieving MSh
122.39	will be,] 49a, Forster (413); ~ ~ₐ MSh
122.40	Dr.] 49a; ~ₐ MSh
122.43	well-wisher.] 49a, Forster (413); ~ₐ ~. MSh
122.43	D. GARRICK."] 49a; Dₐ Garrick.ₐ MSh; D. Garrick.' Forster (413)
123.2	*authorship*] 49a; Authorship MSh
123.3	*Pecuniary*] 49a; pecuniary MSh
123.5	Goldsmith's comedy] 49a; Goldsmiths Comedy MSh
123.5	performed,] 49a; ~ₐ MSh
123.6	Christmas;] 49a; christmasₐ MSh
123.8	sums,] 49a; ~ₐ MSh
123.9	pounds,] 49a; ~ₐ MSh
123.9	elder] 49a; Elder MSh
123.10	patronage,] 49a; ~ₐ MSh
123.10	products,] 49a; ~ₐ MSh
123.11	cease;] 49a; ~ₐ MSh
123.13	Davies,] 49a; ~ₐ MSh
123.13	Roscius,] 49a; ~ₐ MSh
*123.13	bibliopole,] 49a; ~ₐ MSh
123.14	Goldsmith's] 49a; Goldsmiths MSh
123.16	made.] 49a; ~: MSh
*123.16–17	complete it in two years, if possible,] 49a; ~ ~, if possible, in two years, MSh
123.17	guineas,] 49a; ~; MSh
123.19	labors] 49a; labours MSh
123.22	Mr. Newbery in] T; ~ₐ ~ ~ MSh; ~. ~, ~ 49a
123.22	Canonbury] 49a; Canon bury MSh
123.23	Castle,] 49a; ~ₐ MSh
123.24	Elizabeth,] 49a; ~ₐ MSh
123.25	Goldsmith's] 49a; Goldsmiths MSh
123.26	country] T; Country MSh; country, 49a
123.26	favorite] 49a; favourite MSh
123.27	authors,] 49a; Authorsₐ MSh
123.28	castle;] 49a; Castle; MSh
123.29	club,] 49a; ~ₐ MSh
123.29–30	Tavern, in] T; ~ₐ ~ MSh; ~ₐ on 49a; tavern, in Prior (II, 156)
123.31	company.] 49a; Company. MSh
123.33	Canonbury's] 49a; cannonbury's MSh

123.36   Thither, in latter days,] 49a, Prior (II, 155); ~$_\wedge$ ~
                ~ ~$_\wedge$ MSh
123.40   Chambers] 49a, Prior (II, 156); chambers MSh
123.41   And Newbery] 49a, Prior (II, 156); and ~ MSh
123.41   his A B C's] 49a, Prior (II, 156); his A, B, C's MSh
°124.3   sitting room] T; ~-~ MSp, 49a
°124.4   panelled] T, Forster (424); panneled MSp, 49a
124.9   Elysium,] 49a; elysium, MSh
124.11   gardens, where] 49a; ~. ⟨After his rise in the world,
                however, he found⟩ where MSh
°124.15   disappear,] T; ~$_\wedge$ MSh; disappears, 49a
124.15   stroll] 49a; Stroll MSh
124.15   Park."] 49a; ~$_\wedge$" MSh
124.17   pen,] 49a; ~$_\wedge$ MSh
124.18   North's] 49a; Norths MSh
°124.22   Grub Street] T; ~ street MSh; Grub-street 49a
124.24   activity,] 49a; ~$_\wedge$ MSh
124.24   pamphlets,] 49a; ~$_\wedge$ MSh
124.25   grossest kinds.] 49a; Grossest Kinds. MSh
124.27   countryman,] 49a; Countrymen$_\wedge$ MSh
124.28   known] 49a; knoun MSh
°124.28   Gawkey,] T; ~$_\wedge$ MSh; Gawky, 49a
124.29   colonial taxation,] T; Colonial ~, MSh; colonial ~; 49a
124.31   example,] 49a; ~$_\wedge$ MSh
124.33   pension?] 49a; ~. MSh
124.35   administration,] 49a; ~$_\wedge$ MSh
124.36   Dr.] 49a; ~$_\wedge$ MSh
124.38   livings,] 49a; ~$_\wedge$ MSh
124.40   chambers] 49a, Prior (II, 278); chambres MSh
124.42   'I can] 49a; $_\wedge$~ ~ MSh
°125.1   to me;'—and so] 49a; ~ ~$_\wedge$"–⟨"⟩ and so MSh
125.1   him in] 49a; him—in MSh
125.3   job,] 49a; ~$_\wedge$ MSh
125.4   divine,] 49a; ~$_\wedge$ MSh
125.4   *was*] 49a; was MSh
125.5   crown livings?] 49a; croun ~. MSh
125.6   Goldsmith's] 49a; Goldsmiths MSh
°125.7–8   renown, closed his mortal career. The poet] 49a; renown,
                22^d - of December 1767. It is customary to speak of
                him as [*half line left blank*] closed his mortal career.
                ⟨He died on the 22^d of December (1767)⟩ The poet
                MSh
125.11   drowning.] 49a; drouning. MSh

126.2   *manoeuvring*] 49a; manouvaring MSh
126.2   *The comedy of "False Delicacy"*] 49a; ↑the Comedy of↓
             ∧‿ ‿∧ MSh
126.3   *"The Good Natured Man"*] T; ∧the ‿ ‿ ‿∧ MSh; "The
             Good-natured Man" 49a
126.5   comedy of "The Good Natured Man"] T; Comedy ‿
             ∧the Good natured ‿∧ MSh; comedy of "The Good-
             natured Man" 49a
126.6   Garrick,] 49a; ‿∧ MSh
126.7   professions,] 49a; ‿∧ MSh
126.7   author] T; Author∧ MSh; author, 49a
126.8   enterprise.] 49a; enterprize. MSh
126.9–10   Goldsmith's boon companion] 49a; Goldsmiths ‿ Com-
             panion MSh
126.11   comedy] 49a; Comedy MSh
126.11   *False Delicacy,*] 49a; ‿ ‿∧ MSh
126.12   sentimental school.] 49a; Sentimental School. MSh
126.13   school] T; School MSh; school, 49a
126.13   comedy of "The] 49a; Comedy of ∧the MSh
126.14   Marriage"] 49a; ‿∧ MSh
126.14   it,] 49a; ‿: MSh
126.14   "False Delicacy"] 49a; ∧‿ ‿∧ MSh
126.15   skies] T; Skies MSh; skies, 49a
126.16   effect.] 49a; affect. MSh
126.18   colleague, Colman,] 49a; ‿∧ ‿∧ MSh
*126.20   pasteboard] T; paste board MSh; ‿- / ‿ 49a
126.20   equally prone] 49a; equally ⟨politic⟩ prone MSh
*126.20   other's hand] T; others ‿ MSh; other's hands 49a
126.21–22   Goldsmith's] 49a; Goldsmiths MSh
126.22   Kelly's] 49a; Kellys MSh
126.23   author,] 49a; Author, MSh
126.24   scenes,] 49a; Scenes; MSh
126.25   "False Delicacy"] 49a; ∧‿ ‿∧ MSh
126.26   (January 23, 1768)] 49a; (Jan 23, 1768) MSh
126.28   newspapers] 49a; news papers MSh
126.29   triumph.] 49a; ‿∧ MSh
126.30   "False Delicacy"] 49a; ∧‿ ‿∧ MSh
126.31   prosperity,] 49a; ‿∧ MSh
126.31   "The Good Natured Man"] T; ∧the ‿ ‿ man∧ MSh;
             "The Good-natured Man" 49a
126.33   author, manager and actors.] T; Author, Manager and
             Actors. MSh; author, manager, and actors. 49a
126.34   Colman's] 49a; Colmans MSh

126.35   proprietors,] 49a; ~∧ MSh
126.36   parts,] 49a; ~∧ MSh
126.37   Shuter,] 49a; ~∧ MSh
126.39   recollection.] 49a; reccollection. MSh
126.40   Goldsmith's] 49a; Goldsmiths MSh
127.3   rehearsals;] 49a; ~, MSh
127.5   counsel] T; council MSh; counsel, 49a
127.6   Inspirited] 49a; Enspirited MSh
127.6   sympathy,] 49a; ~∧ MSh
*127.7   unusual care.] 49a; uncommon ~. MSh
*127.8–9   wardrobe and toilet.] 49a; ward robe and toilette. MSh
127.11   tailor,] 49a; taylor∧ MSh
127.11   Mr.] T; Mr∧ MSh, 49a
127.11   Filby,] 49a; ~∧ MSh
127.12   suit] 49a; Suit MSh
127.12   bloom, satin grain,] 49a; ~∧ Satin ~∧ MSh
127.12–13   breeches, £8 2s. 7d."] 49a; ~. £8.2.7.∧ MSh
127.13   attired,] 49a; ~∧ MSh
127.16   Johnson's] 49a; Johnsons MSh
127.16   itself,] 49a; ~∧ MSh
127.17   Hamlet,] 49a; ~∧ MSh
127.19   applause,] 49a; ~∧ MSh
127.22   Shuter,] 49a; ~∧ MSh
127.25   scenes] T; Scenes MSh; scenes, 49a
127.28   author] 49a; Author MSh
127.31   endeavored] 49a; endeavoured MSp
*127.35   childlike] 49a; child like MSh
127.37   overrated] 49a; over rated MSh
*128.3   went, he said, to] 49a; ~∧ ~ ~∧ ~ MSh, MSp
128.5   favorite] 49a; favourite MSp
128.6   moon. . . .] 49a; Moon. . . MSp
128.7   while,"] 49a; ~,∧ MSp
128.7   "I] 49a; ∧~ MSp
128.14   childlike] 49a; child like MSh
128.14–15   self accusation] T; ~ ⟨confession⟩ ↑accusation↓ MSh;
                    self-accusation 49a
128.15   Goldsmith. When] 49a; ~; when MSh
128.15   pause,] 49a; ~: MSh
128.16   this, doctor,"] 49a; ~∧ Doctor," MSh
128.17   me,] 49a; ~; MSh
128.18   world."] 49a; ~."– MSh
128.18   secrets:] 49a; ~; MSh
128.19   surface;] 49a; sarface; MSh

128.23   Goldsmith,] 49a; ~ₐ MSh
128.24   himself,] 49a; ~ₐ MSh
128.27   speech] 49a; Speech MSh
128.27   them."] 49a; ~ₐ⁻" MSh
128.29   Talleyrand!] 49a; ~. MSh
128.30   "The Good Natured Man"] T; ₐ~ ~ natured ~ₐ MSh;
            "~ Good-natured ~" 49a
128.31   author's] 49a; authors MSh
128.32   majesties;] 49a; Majesties; MSh
128.34   stage.] 49a; Stageₐ MSh
128.35   As to Kelly's comedy,] 49a; As to ↑Kellys↓ Comedy
            ⟨of False Delicacy⟩, MSh
*128.35   entirely devoid] 49a; totally ~ MSh
128.36   character,] 49a; ~ₐ MSh
128.36   oblivion.] 49a; ~ₐ - MSh
128.39   "False Delicacy"] 49a; ₐ~ ~ₐ MSh
128.42   o'clock] 49a; oₐclock MSh
128.43   publication;] 49a; ~ₐ MSh
128.43   copies,] 49a; ~ₐ MSh
129.3   comparative] 49a; Comparative MSh
129.4   continual] T; continual⟨ly⟩ MSh; continually 49a
*129.4   green rooms,] T; Green Rooms, MSh; green-rooms, 49a
129.4   coffee houses,] T; ~ ~. MSh; ~-~, 49a
129.6   Goldsmith's old enemy,] 49a; Goldsmiths ~ ~ₐ MSh
129.6   press,"] 49a; ~ₐ" MSh
129.11   Goldsmith's] 49a; Goldsmiths MSh
129.12   elsewhere,] 49a; ~ₐ MSh
129.13   mischievous] 49a; mischevious MSh
*129.15   deemed jealous] 49a; termed ~ MSp
129.21   harbor] 49a; harbour MSp
129.21   ill will] T; ~-~ MSp, 49a
129.22   Kelly's] 49a; Kellys MSh
129.24   newspapers,] 49a; news papers, MSh
*130.3   Shoemaker's holyday] T; Shoe maker Holyday MSh;
            Shoemaker's holiday 49a
130.3–4   jolly pigeon] 49a; Jolly pigion MSh
130.4   Barlow,] 49a; ~ₐ MSh
130.4   Hampstead] 49a; Hempstead MSh
130.6   "The Good Natured Man"] T; ₐthe ~ ~ ~ₐ MSh; "The
            Good-natured Man" 49a
130.11   inexhaustible.] 49a; inexhaustable. MSh
130.13–14   "The Good Natured Man"] T; ₐthe ~ natured ~ₐ MSh;
            "The Good-natured Man" 49a

130.14	performed.] 49a; ~∧ MSh
130.15	Jeffs,] 49a; ~∧ MSh
130.16	Johnson's] 49a; Johnsons MSh
130.18	No. 2] 49a; No∧ 2 MSh
130.20	umbrageous] 49a; umbragious MSh
130.20	Temple garden.] 49a; ~ Garden. MSh
130.23	Wilton carpets] 49a; wilton Carpets MSh
130.23	awkward] 49a; aukward MSh
130.24–25	bloom, satin] 49a; ~∧ Satin MSh
130.26	Mr. Filby] T; ~∧ ~ MSh; ~. ~, 49a
130.27	arrayed,] 49a; ~∧ MSh
130.29	Johnson,] T; ~∧ MSh; John / son, 49a
130.30	Percy,] 49a; ~∧ MSh
130.31–32	cards, at] 49a; ~. at MSh
130.32	sport] 49a; Sport MSh
*130.33	blind man's] T; ~ mans MSh; ~-man's 49a
130.34	misrule. Blackstone,] 49a; Misrule. ~∧ MSh
*130.35	below,] 49a; ~∧ MSh
*130.36	overhead] 49a; over head MSh
130.39	"jolly pigeon"] 49a; "Jolly pigion" MSh
130.40	"shoemaker's holyday."] T; 'Shoemakers Holyday' MSh; "shoemaker's holiday." 49a
131.3	attendance.] 49a; ~∧ MSh
*131.5	footpaths] T; foot paths MSh; foot-paths 49a
131.8	crowned] 49a; crouned MSh
*131.10	evening they] 49a; ~. ~ MSh
131.16	crown] T; croun MSh; crown, 49a
131.17	shillings;] 49a; Shillings∧ MSh
131.18	entertainment,] 49a; ~: MSh
131.19	conversation,] 49a; ~∧ MSh
131.20	Goldsmith's] 49a; Goldsmiths MSh
131.21	amanuensis,] 49a; Amanuensis∧ MSh
*131.22	company. Peter] 49a; Company. He MSh
131.22	punctilious,] 49a; ~; MSh
131.27	"shoemaker's holydays."] T; "Shoemakers holy days;' ⟨but as⟩ MSh; "shoemaker's holidays." 49a
131.29	sum,] 49a; ~∧ MSh
131.29	difference.] 49a; ~∧ MSh
131.31	"pay the shot,"] 49a; '~ ~ Shot,∧ MSh
131.31	countryman, Glover,] 49a; ~∧ ~∧ MSh
131.36	Hampstead] 49a; Hempstead MSp
*131.39	tea table] T; ~-~ MSp, 49a
*132.3–4	eye on] 49a; ~ upon MSp

132.4	good natured] T; $\sim$-$\sim$ MSp, 49a
132.8	guests that] 49a; $\sim$, that MSp
132.29	embarrassment,] Pr.; $\sim_\wedge$ MSh
132.31–32	ruts; nor a man keep two] Prp, Prh; ruts; and it is almost as difficult for a man to keep two MSh
132.33	'jolly pigeon'] Pr.; 'Jolly Pigion' MSh
132.33	awkwardly] Pr.; aukwardly MSh
132.36	apartments] Pr.; appartments MSh
*132.38	"Why, sir,] Pr.; "$\sim_\wedge$ Sir$_\wedge$ MSh
133.5	'Here, my] 49a; "$\sim$,'" $\sim$ MSp
133.9	gratitude.' This,"] 49a; $\sim$." '$\sim$,' MSp
133.10	"was] 49a; '$\sim$ MSp
133.12	afterwards.'] 49a; $\sim$.' MSp
134.1	*CHAPTER XXIV*] T; CHAPTER XXIV. 49a; ch ⟨23.⟩ 24 MSh
*134.2	*book building*] T; Book $\sim$ MSh; book-building 49a
134.2	*Rural*] 49a; rural MSh
134.2	*Shoemaker's*] 49a; Shoemakers MSh
134.11	"The Good Natured Man"] T; $_\wedge$the $\sim$ $\sim$ $\sim_\wedge$ MSh; the "Good-natured Man" 49a
134.15	custom.] 49a; $\sim_\wedge$ MSh
134.15	shown,] 49a; shewn, MSh
*134.18	Roads,] T; $\sim_\wedge$ MSh; roads, 49a
*134.21	hedge rows,] T; $\sim$ $\sim_\wedge$ MSh; $\sim$-$\sim$, 49a
134.22	home.] 49a; $\sim_\wedge$ MSh
134.23	year, 1768,] 49a; $\sim_\wedge$ $\sim_\wedge$ MSh
134.24	Edgeware Road] 49a; Edge ware road MSh
*134.25	Mr. Edmund Bott,] T; $\sim_\wedge$ $\sim$ $\sim_\wedge$ MSh; $\sim$. $\sim$ Botts, 49a
134.26	Temple,] 49a; $\sim_\wedge$ MSh
134.27–28	intimates, and Bott] T; $\sim_\wedge$ $\sim$ $\sim$ MSh; $\sim$, $\sim$ Botts 49a
134.30–31	shoemaker of Piccadilly,] 49a; Shoemaker of Piccadilly$_\wedge$ MSh
134.32	jets,] 49a; $\sim_\wedge$ MSh
134.33–34	Shoemaker's Paradise.] 49a; Shoemakers $\sim_\wedge$- MSh
134.34	Mr. Bott] T; $\sim_\wedge$ Botts MSh; $\sim$. Botts 49a
134.35	town,] 49a; $\sim_\wedge$ MSh
*134.35	sometimes in] T; $\sim$, $\sim$ MSh, 49a
134.36	evening.] 49a; $\sim$.. MSh
134.37	table,] 49a; $\sim$; MSh
134.39	Bott] T; Botts MSh, 49a
135.3	Goldsmith's] 49a; Goldsmiths MSh
*135.3	gayety] 49a; gaiety MSh
135.6	youth,] 49a; $\sim_\wedge$ MSh

135.11	brother] 49a; Brother MSh
135.13	Christian virtues;] 49a; christian vartues; MSh
*135.13	affliction at his] T; ~ ~ hes MSh; affection at his 49a
135.15	affection.] 49a; ~∧ MSh
135.17	favor] 49a; favour MSh
135.23	friends, ignorant] 49a; ~∧ ignarunt MSh
135.26	recollections] 49a; reccollections MSh
135.27	childhood,] 49a; ~∧ MSh
*135.28	heartfelt] 49a; heart felt MSh
135.38	recollections] 49a; reccollections MSh
136.1	towns] 49a; touns MSh
136.2	e'er] 49a; ee'r MSh; ere *Works* (IV, 293)
*136.4	restlessness,] 49a; worldliness, MSh
136.6	practise:] 49a; ~∧ MSh
136.7	grace,] 49a, *Works* (IV, 294); ~∧ MSh
136.8	place;] 49a, *Works* (IV, 294); ~∧ MSh
136.19	* * * * * * *] 49a; X X X X X X X MSh
137.1	*CHAPTER XXV*] T; CHAPTER XXV. 49a; Ch ⟨24⟩ 25 MSh
137.2	*Bickerstaffe's*] T; Bickerstaffes MSh; Bickerstaff's 49a
137.2	*Kenrick's*] 49a; Kenricks MSh
137.3	*Johnson's*] 49a; Johnsons MSh
137.3	*Goldsmith's toilet*] 49a; Goldsmiths Toilette MSh
*137.3	*bloom colored*] T; ~ coloured MSh; ~-colored 49a
137.4	*A touch*] 49a; a ~ MSh
137.8	"Love in a Village," "Lionel] 49a; ∧~ ~ ~ ~,∧ ∧~ MSh
137.8	Clarissa"] T; ~∧ MSh; ~," 49a
137.10	Bickerstaffe] T; Bickerstuff MSh; Bickerstaff 49a
137.10	play.] 49a; ~∧ MSh
137.10	Hiffernan,] 49a; Hiffarnan MSh
137.13	Goldsmith,] 49a; ~∧ MSh
137.13	vagabond's] 49a; vagabonds MSh
137.15	Hiffernan] 49a; Haffernan MSh
137.16	emptiness] 49a; emptyness MSh
137.18	newspapers] T; news papers MSh; newspapers, 49a
137.18	critic,] 49a; ~∧ MSh
137.20	author] 49a; Author MSh
137.20	second] 49a; Second MSh
137.21	snored] 49a; Snored MSh
137.23	read,] 49a; ~∧ MSh
137.24	author came] 49a; Author Came MSh
137.24	Bick,] 49a; ~∧ MSh

137.25	on,"] 49a; ~,ᴧ MSh
137.26	own works."] 49a; oun ~ᴧ" MSh
137.27	Goldsmith's] 49a; Goldsmiths MSh
137.29	Bickerstaffe] T; Bickerstaff MSh, 49a
137.29	Homer.] 49a; ~ᴧ MSh
137.31	thorough-bred] 49a, Forster (488); ~ᴧ~ MSh
137.32	Griffin's shop,] 49a, Forster (488); Griffins Shop, MSh
*137.33	Bickerstaffe,] T; Bickerstaffᴧ MSh; Bickerstaff, 49a, Forster (488)
137.33	Kelly * * *] 49a; ~ X X X MSh; ~ . . . Forster (488)
137.35	brother.] 49a; ~ᴧ MSh
*137.37	of this kind.] 49a; of the Kind. MSh
137.37	sir,"] 49a, Forster (491); Sir," MSh
138.1	attacked. Fame, sir,] 49a, Forster (492); ~ᴧ ~ᴧ Sirᴧ MSh
138.1	shuttlecock;] 49a; ~: Forster (492); shuttle cock, MSh
138.2	room,] 49a, Forster (492); ~ᴧ MSh
138.3	up, it] 49a, Forster (492); ~ᴧ ~ MSh
138.3	ends."] 49a; ~ᴧ" MSh; ~.' Forster (492)
138.8	"Why, sir?"] 49a; "~ᴧ ~ᴧ" MSh
138.8	Thrale;] 49a; ~, MSh
138.10	brewer,] 49a; ~. MSh
138.11	ground,"] 49a; ~,ᴧ MSh
138.11	"dirt] 49a; ᴧ~ MSh
138.12	distance."] 49a; ~ᴧ" MSh
138.13	increased] 49a; encreased MSh
138.14	Goldsmith's wardrobe] 49a; Goldsmiths ward robe MSh
138.14	society.] 49a; Society. MSh
138.17	arrayed,] 49a; ~ᴧ MSh
138.18	Gardens,] 49a; ~ᴧ MSh
138.18	own] 49a; oun MSh
*138.20	for ever] 49a; forever MSh
138.21	16th] 49a; 16' MSh
138.21	year,] 49a; ~ᴧ MSh
138.22	Reynolds,] 49a; ~ᴧ MSh
138.22	Murphy, Bickerstaffe] T; ~ᴧ Bickerstaff MSh; ~, Bickerstaff, 49a
138.24	table,] 49a; ~ᴧ MSh
138.25	arrive,] 49a; ~ᴧ MSh
138.26	about,"] 49a; ~ᴧ" MSh
138.34	any body] 49a, Boswell (II, 85); anybody MSp
138.35	Water Lane."] 49a; ~ ~ᴧ"' MSp; ~-lane.'" Boswell (II, 85)

138.40	kind] 49a; Kind MSh
139.1	it."] 50, 51, 60; ~∧" MSh, 49a, 49b, 49c, 53, 54
139.1	Goldsmith's] 49a; Goldsmiths MSh
139.3	pickpockets"] 49a, Forster (571); pick pockets," MSh
139.4	joker,] 49a; ~∧ MSh
139.5	manner,] 49a; ~∧ MSh
139.8	spectators.] 49a; Spectators∧ MSh
°139.9–10	others of Goldsmith's] 49a; other of Goldsmiths MSh
139.11	arose,] 49a; ~∧ MSh
139.11	convinced,] 49a; ~∧ MSh
°139.13	defects,] 49a; ugliness, MSh
°139.14	playmates, and which had been] T; ~, ⟨and which had accompanied him throughout life⟩ which had been MSh; ~, and had been 49a
139.16	awkwardness] 49a; aukwardness MSh
139.18	society;] 49a; Society; MSh
139.20	phrase,] 49a; phraze, MSh
139.26	appearance.] 49a; ~∧ MSh
139.27	Devonshire,] 49a; Devon shire∧ MSh
°139.28	of a Mrs.] T; ~ ~ ~∧ MSh; of Mrs. 49a
139.29	daughters, seventeen] 49a; ~∧ Seventeen MSh
139.30	age,] 49a; ~∧ MSh
139.30	Charles,] 49a; charles, MSh
139.32	beautiful,] 49a ~∧ MSh
139.33	Catharine,] 49a; ~∧ MSh
139.33	eldest,] 49a; ~∧ MSh
139.34	*Little Comedy,*] 49a; *little Comedy*∧ MSh
139.35	Bunbury, second] 49a; ~∧ Second MSh
°139.37	byname] T; bye name MSh; by-name 49a
°139.38	prepared] T; ~, MSh, 49a
139.40	painter,] 49a; ~∧ MSh
139.41	shown,] 49a; shewn, MSh
139.42	The Traveller] 49a; the ~ MSh
140.2	benevolence,] 49a; ~∧ MSh
140.4	society] T; Society MSh; society, 49a
°140.7	them remains] T; ~. ~ MSh; ~, ~ 49a
140.8	verse,] 49a; ~∧ MSh
140.9	Dr. Baker,] 49a; ~∧ ~∧ MSh
140.10	mother's] 49a; mothers, MSh
140.12	Dr.] 49a; ~∧ MSh
140.12	liberty,] 49a; ~∧ MSh
140.15	scrawled,] 49a; Scrawled∧ MSh
°140.15	verses!] 49a; Verses! MSh

140.17	*Lace–*] 49a; ~... MSp, Forster (502)
*140.19	night–] 49a; ~... MSp, Forster (502)
140.29	Hornecks,] 49a; ~ₐ MSh
140.33	toilet.] 49a; toilette. MSh
140.34	tailor, Mr. William Filby,] 49a; taylorₐ ~ₐ ~ ~ₐ MSh
140.31	day's Advertiser] T; days advertiser MSh; day's Advertiser, 49a
140.32	the portrait] 60, E; a ~ MSh; the portraiₐ 49a, 49b, 49c, 50, 51, 53, 54, 59
140.33	Kauffman:–] 49a; ~. MSh
140.33	Angelica,] 49a; *Works* (III, 385); ~ₐ MSh
140.34	grace,] 49a; *Works* (IV, 385); ~ₐ MSh
140.34	Conway's lovely] T, *Works* (IV, 385); Conways ~ MSh; Conway's burly 49a
140.34	Stanhope's] 49a; Stanhopes MSh
141.7	silk;] 49a; ~. MSh
141.7	a queen's-blue] T; a Queens-blue MSh; a queen's blue 49a
141.7	ratteen] T; Ratteen MSh; ratteen, 49a
141.8	satin;] 49a; Satin; MSh
141.8	silk stocking breeches] T; Silk Stocking ~ₐ MSh; silk stocking breeches, 49a
141.8	color.] 49a; colour. MSh
141.9	dictated,] 49a; ~ₐ MSh
141.10	vanity, but] 49a; ~ₐ ~, MSh
*141.11	thy person,] 49a; they ~, MSh
142.2	*Labor*] 49a; labour MSh
142.3	*Publication*] 49a; publication MSh
142.3	*History*] 49a; history MSh
142.4	*Anecdotes of a spider*] 49a; anecdotes of a Spider MSh
142.6	Temple,] 49a; ~ₐ MSh
142.6	"building up"] 49a; '~ ~' MSh
142.6	History.] 49a; history. MSh
142.9	Bench,] 49a; bench; MSh
142.10	speak] 49a; Speak MSh
142.12	College,"] T; ~ₐₐ MSh; ~,ₐ Prior (II, 359); college," 49a
142.12	he, "full] 49a; ~ₐ "~ MSh; ~, ₐ~ Prior (II, 359)
142.13	Academic gleanings,] T, Prior (II, 359); ~ ~ₐ MSh; academic ~, 49a
142.13	receive] 49a, Prior (II, 359); recieve MSh
142.19	Court] T, Prior (II, 358); court, MSh; Court, 49a
142.22	judge] 49a; Judge MSh
142.22	Goldsmith's] 49a; Goldsmiths MSh

142.24	Coffee House,] T; ~ ~∧ MSh; ~-~, 49a
142.24	favorite] 49a; favourite MSh
*142.25	delighted too in collecting] T; ~ to ~ Collecting MSh; delighted in collecting 49a
142.27	"Occasionally,"] 49a; ∧~,∧ MSh
142.28	judge,] 49a; Judge, MSh
142.29	latter, but in] T, Prior (II, 358); ~; ~ ~ MSh; ~, ~, on 49a
142.29	money,] 49a, Prior (II, 358); ~∧ MSh
142.30	play,] 49a, Prior (II, 358); ~∧ MSh
142.32	fickle, faithless fortune.'"] 49a; ~∧ ~ ~∧∧" MSh; ~, ~, Fortune!' Prior (II, 358)
142.33	judge] 49a; Judge MSh
142.35	replenished,"] 49a; ~." MSh
142.37	Vauxhall,] 49a, Prior (II, 359); ~∧ MSh
*142.38	amusement. Whenever] 49a; ~; whenever MSh
143.7	window.] 49a; ~∧ MSh
143.10–11	schools and colleges; but,] 49a; Schools and Colleges; but∧ MSh
143.12	perspicuity,] 49a; ~∧ MSh
143.13	received] 49a; recieved MSh
143.13	critics,] 49a; ~. MSh
143.18	he, "as] 49a; ~∧ "as MSp
143.40	know;] 49a, Prior (II, 206); ~: MSp, Boswell (II, 225)
144.6	every thing] 49a, Prior (II, 206), Boswell (II, 225); everything MSp
144.10	Nature,"] 49a; ~∧" MSh
144.10	1769,] 49a; ~: MSh
144.11	Griffin,] 49a; ~∧ MSh
*144.28	Pidcock's] 1825; Pidock's 1840, MSp, 49a
144.37	walks] 49a, Boswell (II, 221); walked MSp
145.19	Goldsmith's] 49a; Goldsmiths MSp
145.21	them;] 49a; ~∧ MSh
145.28	"Animated Nature"] 49a; ∧~ ~∧ MSh
145.28	Rooks,] 49a; ~∧ MSh
145.29	myself," says he, "with] 49a; ~∧∧ ~ ~∧ ∧~ MSh
145.32	spring] 49a, Prior (II, 137); Spring MSh
145.35	commenced."] 49a; ~∧" MSh
145.38	"Of all] 49a; ∧~ ~ MSh
145.38	remarked, the spider] 49a, Works (I, 423); ~∧ ~ Spider MSh
145.40	them,] 49a, Works (I, 424); ~∧ MSh
145.40	belief. * * *] 49a; ~. X X X MSh

146.3	"In three] 49a; ∧∼ ∼ MSp
146.18	"Now,] 49a; ∧∼, MSp
146.28	"In this] 49a; ∧∼ ∼ MSp
146.39	"I had] 49a; ∧∼ ∼ MSp
147.5	"Of this] 49a; ∧∼ ∼ MSp
147.18	"The insect] 49a; ∧∼ ∼ MSp
147.18	years;] 49a, *Works* (I, 427); ∼: MSp
148.2	*Honors*] 49a; Honours MSh
*148.2	*to his brother Maurice*] 49a; to Maurice Goldsmith MSh
148.3	*miniature*] 49a; Miniature MSh
148.4	*Abbey*] 49a; abbey MSh
148.6	Arts,] 49a; ∼: MSh
148.8	Reynolds,] 49a; ∼∧ MSh
*148.10	knighthood.*] 49a; Knighthood.* MSh
148.10	friend's] 49a; friends MSh
148.12	wine,] 49a; ∼∧ MSh
148.16	December,] 49a; ∼∧ MSh
148.16–17	Ancient Literature] T; ∼ literature MSh; ∼ Literature, 49a
148.17	History.] 49a; history. MSh
148.22	arts.] 49a; Arts. MSh
148.29	"DEAR BROTHER,—I should] 49a; "Dear Brother, [*paragraph*] "I should MSp
149.24–25	good humour] T, Percy (87); ∼ ∼, Prior (II, 222); ∼-∼ MSp; ∼-humor 49a
149.30	myself,] 49a, Percy (88), 1825 (44); ∼∧ 1840 (135), MSp
150.5	"Yours, most] 49a; ∧yours, ∼ Percy (89), 1825 (44); "Yours∧ ∼ MSp, 1840 (135)
150.7	shifting,] 49a; Shifting∧ MSh
150.8	formerly;] 49a; ∼, MSh
150.8	family,"] 49a; ∼∧" MSh
150.8	other's back] 49a; others ∼, MSh
150.9	surface.] 49a; Sarface. MSh
150.13	rest, "what] 49a; ∼∧ "What MSh
150.14	live;] 49a; ∼, MSh
150.14	do;] 49a; ∼∧– MSh
*150.14–15	forlorn, haphazard] T; ∼∧ ∼ MSh; ∼, hap-hazard 49a
150.15	questions!] 49a; ∼∧- MSh
150.15	that, with] 49a; ∼∧ ∼ MSh
150.16	shown] 49a; sheun MSh
150.16	Goldsmith's] 49a; Goldsmiths MSh
150.17	there? Yet] 49a; ∼∧ - ∼ MSh

150.18	there. He] 49a; $\sim_\wedge$ - he MSh
150.19	him; he] 49a; $\sim_\wedge$ - $\sim$ MSh
150.20	miniature;] 49a; $\sim_\wedge$– MSh
150.20	offer;"] 49a; $\sim_\wedge$"– MSh
150.21	him,] 49a; $\sim_\wedge$ — MSh
150.22	does: in] 49a; $\sim_\wedge$– MSh
150.23	Contarine,] 49a; $\sim$; MSh
150.24	flute.] 49a; $\sim_\wedge$– MSh
150.26	effected.] 49a; affected. MSh
150.27	Goldsmith's relatives,] 49a; Goldsmiths $\sim_\wedge$ MSh
150.28	pounds,] 49a; $\sim_\wedge$ - MSh
150.28	give. His] 49a; $\sim$, his MSh
150.30	influence;] 49a; $\sim_\wedge$– MSh
*150.31	fame, and] 49a; $\sim$, and but MSh
150.31	them;] 49a; $\sim_\wedge$ MSh
150.32	professor, without pay;] 49a; $\sim_\wedge$ $\sim$ $\sim$, MSh
150.33	friends,] 49a; $\sim_\wedge$ MSh
150.33	Johnson,] 49a; $\sim_\wedge$ MSh
150.36	How] 49a; how MSh
150.37	writer!] 49a; $\sim_\wedge$ - MSh
150.37	By the by,] 49a; $\sim$ $\sim$ bye$_\wedge$ MSh
150.38–39	Goldsmith,] 49a; $\sim$: MSh
150.42	arm,] 49a; $\sim_\wedge$ MSh
151.1	Bishop,] 49a; $\sim_\wedge$ MSh
*151.2	sweetmeats] 49a; sweet meats MSh
151.2	Milner's] 49a; Milners MSh
151.3	revived,] 49a; $\sim_\wedge$ MSh
151.3–4	familiarity,] 49a; $\sim_\wedge$ MSh
151.5	personage,] 49a; $\sim_\wedge$ MSh
151.6	"Come, my boy,"] 49a; "$\sim_\wedge$ $\sim$ $\sim_\wedge$" MSh; '$\sim$, $\sim$ $\sim$,' Forster (66)
151.6	Goldsmith as] T; $\sim$ ⟨in the old tone and⟩ as MSh; Goldsmith, as 49a
151.7	to a schoolboy, "Come, Sam,] 49a; to ⟨his pupil⟩ ↑a school boy -↓ "Come$_\wedge$ Sam$_\wedge$ MSh
151.9	apples?"] 49a; $\sim$? ⟨Sam⟩ - MSh
151.9	woman's stall; then, recollecting] 49a; womans $\sim$." Then, reccollecting MSh
151.9–10	print shop window:] T; $\sim$ $\sim$ $\sim_\wedge$ MSh; $\sim$ - $\sim$ $\sim$: 49a
151.11	it, Sam?] 49a; $\sim_\wedge$ $\sim$? MSh
151.11	engraving?"] 49a; $\sim$?– MSh
151.12	caught; he equivocated;] 49a; $\sim_\wedge$–$\sim$ $\sim_\wedge$– MSh
151.13	fixed upon] 49a, Forster (67); fixed on MSh

151.14	"Ah, Sam!"] 49a; "~$_\wedge$ ~!$_\wedge$ MSh
151.14	reproachfully, "if] 49a; ~$_\wedge$ $_\wedge$~ MSh
151.15	published,] 49a; ~$_\wedge$ MSh
151.16	all, it] 49a; ~$_\wedge$ ~ MSh
151.16	vanity,] 49a; ~$_\wedge$ MSh
151.18	"hung] 49a; '~ MSh
151.18	history"] 49a; ~' MSh
151.19	friend,] 49a; ~$_\wedge$ MSh
151.19	moralist] 49a; Moralist MSh
151.21	monarchs,] 49a; Monarchs$_\wedge$ MSh
151.21–22	statesmen,] 49a; Statesmen$_\wedge$ MSh
151.22	mementos] 49a; mementoes MSh
151.23	·Poets' Corner.] T, Boswell (II, 226); Poets Corner. MSh; poets' corner. 49a
151.24	companion,] 49a; ~$_\wedge$ MSh
151.25	istis.] 49a; ~$_\wedge$ MSh
151.26	afterwards,] 49a; afterward$_\wedge$ MSh
151.27	Temple Bar,] T; Temple Bar$_\wedge$ MSh; Temple-bar, 49a
151.27	rebels,] 49a; ~$_\wedge$ MSh
151.28	treason,] 49a; ~$_\wedge$ MSh
151.29	grizzly mementos] T; grizly mementoes MSh; grizzly mementos, 49a
151.29	intimation,] 49a; ~$_\wedge$ MSh
152.3	elapsed] 49a; Elapsed MSh
152.3	The Traveller,] 49a; the ~$_\wedge$ MSh
152.5	attempts.] 49a; ~$_\wedge$ MSh
152.8	he, "by courting] 49a; ~$_\wedge$ $_\wedge$~ Courting MSh
152.8	starve,] 49a; ~$_\wedge$ MSh
152.11	pen,] 49a; ~; MSh
152.11	fellow,"] 49a; ~$_\wedge$" MSh
152.12	he good humoredly,] T; ~$_\wedge$ ~ humouredly, MSh; ~, good-humoredly, 49a
152.13	productions] 49a, 1825 (40); production MSh, 1840 (136)
152.15	shown,] 49a; shewn, MSh
152.18	26th of May, 1770,] 49a; 26' ~~$_\wedge$ ~$_\wedge$ MSh
152.20	The Traveller] 49a; the ~ MSh
152.21	poem,] 49a; ~$_\wedge$ MSh
152.25	critics] 49a; Critics MSh
152.27	the Deserted Village] 49a; ~ desarted ~ MSh
152.27	favorite.] 49a; favourite, MSh
152.29	one hundred guineas.] 49a; One ~ Guineas, MSh
*152.36–37	as may well be supposed,] 49a; as may be well supposed, MSh

152.37	acknowledgments] 49a; acknowledgements MSh
152.39	grounds;] 49a; ~, MSh
152.39	incompatible] 49a; incompatable MSh
152.40	Goldsmith,] 49a; ~; MSh
153.1	memoir] 49a; ~, MSh
153.2	Goldsmith's writings,] 49a; goldsmiths ~ₐ MSh
153.4	author's] 49a; authors MSh
*153.5	for ever] 49a; forever MSh
153.6	received] 49a; recieved MSh
153.9	lines:] 49a; ~. MSh
153.25	buffetings] 49a; buffettings MSh
153.26	worldly; which] T; ~: ~ₐ MSh; ~; ~, 49a
*153.27	childlike] 49a; child like MSh
153.27	which,] 49a; ~ₐ MSh
153.28	metropolis,] 49a; ~ₐ MSh
153.29	seclusion:] 49a; ~; MSh
153.32	blest] 49a, *Works* (IV, 291); bless'd MSp
153.32	these,] 49a, *Works* (IV, 291); ~ₐ MSp
*154.6	NOTE] T; NOTE. 49a
154.8	Lissoy;] T; Lissoy. 49a; Lishoy. MSp
*155.8	post chaise] T; ~-/~ MSp, 49a
155.10–11	every thing] 49a; everything MSp
155.17	goose.'] 49a; ~.ₐ MSp
*155.26	It is] T; "~ ~ MSp; *paragraph* ₐIt is 49a
*155.29	There is] T; *paragraph* ~ ~ 49a; "~ ~ MSp
156.19	But] 49a; "~ MSp
156.22	Best,] 49a; ~ₐ MSh
156.22	clergyman,] 49a; Clergymanₐ MSh
*156.23	hawthorn-bush] 49a, Prior (I, 17); Hawthorn bush MSh
156.24	"with Brady,] 49a; ₐ~ ~ₐ MSh
156.25	Me, 'Ma foy] 49a; ~ₐ "~ ~ MSh
156.25	overgrown] 49a; overgroun MSh
156.26	be cut down.'] 49a; ~ ~ doun,ₐ MSh
156.26	'what, sir!' replied I, 'cut] 49a; "~ₐ Sir," ~ ~ₐ ₐ~ MSh
156.27–28	"The Deserted Village?" '–'Ma foy!'] 49a; ₐthe ~ ~?"ₐ ₐ ₐ~ ~, ! " MSh
156.28	Bishop, 'is] T, Prior (I, 18); ~ , ₐ~ MSh; bishop, 'is 49a
156.28	hawthorn-bush?] 49a, Prior (I, 17); ~ₐ~? MSh
156.29	axe,] 49a, Prior (I, 18); ~ₐ MSh
156.30	branch.'"] 49a; ~.ₐ" MSh
156.30	hawthorn-bush,] 49a, Prior (I, 18); ~ₐ~, MSh

156.31	up, root and branch,] 49a; ~∧ ~ ~ ~∧ MSh
156.31	relics] 49a; reliques MSh
157.2	*description*] 49a; Description MSh
157.4	*Hickey, the special attorney*] 49a; ~∧ ~ Special Attorney MSh
157.7	author;] 49a; Author; MSh
157.8	ladies'] 49a; ~∧ MSh
*157.8	himself] 49a; him self MSh
157.9	society;] 49a; Society; MSh
157.9	society of] 49a; Society of MSh
157.10	circle,] 49a; Circle, MSh
157.13	ladies'] 49a; ~∧ MSh
157.15	caricature;] 49a; ~ , MSh
157.17	Temple.] 49a; ~∧ MSh
157.18	"In person," says the judge, "he] 49a; ∧~ ~,∧ ~ ~ Judge, ∧~ MSh
157.19	strong,] 49a, Prior (II, 358); ~∧ MSh
157.20	brown] 49a; broun MSh
157.22	perhaps] 49a, Prior (II, 358); ~, MSp
157.29	restraint,"] 49a; ~ .∧ MSp
157.30	recollected,] 49a; reccollected, MSh
157.31	coffee houses,] T; Coffee Houses; MSh; coffee-houses, 49a
157.32	students'] 49a; ~∧ MSh
157.32–33	poet's own chambers;] 49a; poets own Chambers; MSh
157.33	dress;] 49a; ~∧ MSh
157.37	him;] 49a; ~, MSh
157.37	fortunately,] 49a; ~∧ MSh
*157.38	appeared at] 49a; ~ to MSh
158.1	man,"] 49a; ~∧" MSh
158.1	say,] 49a; ~; MSh
158.1	so,] 49a, Prior (II, 379); ~∧ MSh
158.2	heart,] 49a, Prior (II, 379); ~∧ MSh
158.3	unquestionable,] 49a, Prior (II, 379); ~∧ MSh
158.5	qualities."] 49a; ~."– MSh
158.8	brow,] 49a; ~; MSh
158.9	attentions and] T; ~ and and MSh; ~, and 49a
158.14	weeks'] 49a; ~∧ MSh
158.15	Mrs.] 49a; ~∧ MSh
158.17	Mr.] 49a; ~∧ MSh
*158.20	Fairy Tale?–] T; ~ ~∧∧ MSh; ~ tale?– 49a
158.24	Edith's] 49a; Ediths MSh
158.34	Calais:] 49a; ~. MSh

158.37	sea-sick,] 49a, Prior (II, 288), 1825 (43), Percy (90); seasick, MSp, 1840 (144)
158.38–39	sea-sickness] 49a; Prior (II, 288), 1825 (43), Percy (90); seasickness MSp, 1840 (144)
159.34	humor] 49a; humour MSp
159.39	humor,] 49a; humour, MSp
160.1	"from] 49a; ∧∼ MSh
160.2	countenance,] 49a, Prior (II, 379); ∼∧ MSh
160.2	those who] 49a, Prior (II, 379); ∼ that MSh
160.5	humor.] 49a; humour; ⟨which⟩ MSh
160.9	"MY DEAR FRIEND,—I began] 49a; "My dear Friend, [paragraph] "I began MSp
160.18	at every thing] 49a, Prior (II, 292); ∼ everything MSp
160.19	praising every thing] 49a, Prior (II, 292); ∼ everything MSp
160.25	peas;] 49a; ∼, Prior (II, 293); pease; MSp
*161.2	perform it;] 49a, Prior (II, 294); ∼ it MSp
161.7	know of any thing] T, Prior (II, 294); ∼ ∼ anything MSp; know any thing 49a
161.8	any body] 49a, Prior (II, 294); any-/body MSp
161.15	any thing] 49a, Prior (II, 294); anything MSp
161.20	any thing] 49a, Prior (II, 294); anything MSp
161.25	say,] 49a, Prior (II, 295); ∼∧ MSp
161.31	letter:] 49a; ∼. MSh
161.33	twenty,] 49a; ∼∧ MSh
161.34	from town] 49a; ∼ toun MSh
161.35	country,] 49a; ∼∧ MSh
161.35	flute,] 49a; ∼∧ MSh
161.36	pleased,] 49a; ∼; MSh
161.37	down,] 49a; doun∧ MSh
161.39	wrong: he] 49a; ∼∧ - ∼ MSh
161.40	postillions,] 49a; ∼; MSh
161.40	landladies,] 49a; ∼∧ MSh
161.40	barns,] 49a; ∼∧ MSh
161.41	eaten,] 49a; ∼∧ MSh
161.41	peas!] 49a; ∼. MSh
161.42	secret:] ∼∧ MSh
162.1	seen."] 49a; ∼."— MSh
162.3	amusement.] 49a; ∼∧ - MSh
162.4	Goldsmith!] 49a; ∼∧ - MSh
162.5	say,] 49a; ∼∧ MSh
*162.5	high bred] T; high lived [?bred?] MSh; high-bred 49a
162.8	Tibbs,] 49a; ∼∧ MSh

162.10	Lady Crimps;"] T; ～ ～," MSh; Lady Crimp's;" 49a; lady Crimps; *Works* (II, 296)
162.10	grown] 49a; groun MSh
162.11	"smacks] 49a; ∧～ MSh
162.11	custard."] 49a; ～.∧ MSh
162.13	constable;"] 49a; ～." MSh
*162.13	outrun] 49a; out run MSh
162.18	Mr.] 49a; ～∧ MSh
162.18	attorney,] 49a; ～; MSh
162.23	perceived] 49a; percieved MSh
162.23	Goldsmith's] 49a; Goldsmiths MSh
162.24	broad] 49a; broat MSh
162.25	expense,] 49a; ～; MSh
162.27	Goldsmith's vanity:] 49a; Goldsmiths ～. MSh
162.29	present,] 49a, Prior (II, 296); ～∧ MSp
162.37	"The Retaliation."] 49a; "the Rataliation∧" MSh
162.38	Here] T; "～ MSp, 49a
163.7	attorney.] T; ～." MSp, 49a
163.17	any thing] 49a, Prior (II, 297, n.); anything MSp
*163.23	rich,] T, Prior (II, 297); sick∧ MSp; ～, 49a
164.2	*Goldsmith's*] 49a; Goldsmiths MSh
*164.3–4	*The Haunch of Venison*] T; ～ ～ ～ Venason MSh; The haunch of venison 49a
*164.9	early follies] 49a; ～ ⟨irregularities⟩ MSp
164.16	pen,] 49a; ～∧ MSh
164.17–18	a Life of Parnell,] 49a; ～ life ～ ～∧ MSh
164.18	Village. It was,] 49a; ～, ～ ～∧ MSh
164.19	job work,] T; ～ ～∧ MSh; ～ - ～, 49a
164.33	*splendour.*"] T; ～∧∧ MSh; splendour. *Works* (III, 409); *splendor.*" 49a
164.34	Davies,] 49a; ～∧ MSh
*164.34–35	abridgment] 49a; abridgement MSh
164.36	History] 49a; history MSh
164.37–38	Bolingbroke's *Dissertation on Parties,* which he conceived] 49a; Bolingbrokes *dissertation on Parties*∧ which he concieved MSh
164.41	prefatory] 49a; prefaratory MSh
165.1	Goldsmith's] 49a; Goldsmiths MSh
165.1	countryman] T; Countryman MSh; countryman, 49a
165.2	affliction,] 49a; ～∧ MSh
165.2	son,] 49a; ～∧ MSh
165.4	request,] 49a; ～∧ MSh
*165.4	a visit] 49a; a long visit MSh

*165.4   seat of Gosfield,] 50; noble seat of Gosford∧ MSh; noble seat of Gosford, 49a

165.5   him.] 49a; ∼∧ MSh

165.5   Gosfield] 50; Gosford MSh, 49a

165.6   lost. "Dr.] 49a; ∼∧ for '∼∧ MSh

165.7   friend, "has] 49a; ∼∧ ∧∼ MSh

165.7   country,] 49a; ∼∧ MSh

165.9   in time] 49a; on ∼ MSh

165.14   into a clear,] 49a; onto ∼ ∼∧ MSh

165.15   narrative,] 49a; ∼∧ MSh

165.15   who,] 49a; ∼∧ MSh

165.16   "seemed] 49a; ∧∼ MSh

165.18   own] 49a; oun MSh

165.18–19   politics,] 49a, *Works* (III, 437); ∼∧ MSh

165.19   combat, has] 49a; ∼∧ ∼ MSh; ∼, he has *Works* (III, 437)

165.20   contention."] 49a; ∼∧" MSh

*165.20   received by the author] 49a; Goldsmith received MSh

165.26–27   he, "at Lord Clare's] 49a; ∼∧ "∼ ∼ Clares MSh

165.27   country;] 49a; Country; MSh; country, Boswell (IV, 168)

165.28   man."] 49a; ∼∧" MSh

165.28–29   "The company," says Boswell, "laughed] 49a; ∧∼ Company,∧ ∼ ∼∧ ∧∼ MSh

165.29   'diverting simplicity.'" And] 49a; "∼ ∼, ∧" and MSh

165.31   however,] 49a; ∼∧ MSh

165.34   gentlemen,"] 49a; Gentlemen," MSh

165.34   "Dr."] 49a; ∧∼∧∧ MSh

165.37   Goldsmith's] 49a; Goldsmiths MSh

165.37–38   present of game,] 49a; ∼ of of ∼∧ MSh

165.39   the "Haunch of Venison."] 49a; The ∧∼ ∼ venison,∧ MSh

165.42   treat:] 49a; ∼. MSh

166.1   Thanks, my lord,] T, Forster (560); ∼ , ∼ Lord, MSh; "∼, ∼ lord, 49a

166.1   venison;] 49a; ∼, Forster (560); Venison; MSh

166.1   fatter] 49a, Forster (560); ∼, MSh

166.3   haunch] 49a, Forster (560); Haunch MSh

166.8   shown] 49a, Forster (560); shoun MSh

166.12   fry'd] 49a; *Works* (IV, 313); ⟨fry'd⟩ fry,'d MSh; fried Forster (560)

166.13   * * * * * * *] 49a; X X X X X MSh

166.18   Goldsmith's] 49a; Goldsmiths MSh

166.19   Clare's,] 49a; Clares, MSh

166.20	Bath.] 49a; ∼ₐ MSh
166.30	endeavored,] 49a; endeavoured, MSp
167.2	*controversy*] 49a; Controversy MSh
167.3	*Walpole's*] 49a; Walpoles MSh
167.3	*Redcliffe*] 49a; Red Cliffe MSh
167.3	*Church*] 49a; church MSh
167.4	*Goldsmith's*] 49a; Goldsmiths MSh
167.4	*Davies's*] 49a; Davies MSh
167.6	St. George's] 49a; ∼ₐ Georges MSh
167.7	room;] 49a; ∼, MSh
167.8	inspection.] 49a; ∼ₐ MSh
167.9	festival,] 49a; ∼ₐ MSh
167.10	Drs.] 49a; ∼ₐ MSh
167.11	academy;] 49a; Academy, MSh
167.11	academicians,] 49a; Academiciansₐ MSh
*167.16	Rowley, discovered] 49a; Rowley, which he had discovered MSh
167.16	Redcliffe] 49a; Red cliff MSh
167.19	Chatterton's.] 49a; Chattertons. MSh
167.20	considered, he said,] 49a; ∼ₐ ∼ ∼ₐ MSh
167.24	sixteen] T; Sixteen MSh; sixteen, 49a
167.25	attorney's] 49a; attorneys MSh
169.27	Johnson,] 49a; ∼ₐ MSh
167.29	Walpole,] 49a; ∼ₐ MSh
167.29	near by,] 49a; ∼ ∼ₐ MSh
167.30	"*trouvaille*,"] 49a; "∼ₐ" MSh
167.31	matter,] 49a; ∼ₐ MSh
167.32	Goldsmith,] 49a; ∼ₐ MSh
167.32	novelty] 49a; ∼, MSh
167.34	world."] 49a; ∼ₐ" MSh
167.37	spirit; and had been] 49a; ∼; had been MSh
167.39	unknown] 49a; unknoun MSh
167.40	circumstances,] 49a; ∼ₐ MSh
*168.2	coldness had dashed] 49a; coldness dashed MSh
168.4	society] 49a; Society MSh
168.5–6	Goldsmith,] 49a; ∼ₐ MSh
168.6	idiot;"] 49a; ∼;ₐ MSh
168.7	dashed,] 49a; ∼ₐ MSh
168.10	himself."] 49a; ∼ₐ" MSh
168.12	Walpole; a] 49a; ∼ₐ A MSh
168.13	present,"] 49a; ∼ₐ' MSh
168.16	death."] 49a; ∼ₐ" MSh
168.17	contributed to] 49a; ∼ to to MSh

168.18   towards] 49a; toward MSh

*168.18   end; nor have] 49a; ~: ~ has MSh

168.19   Walpole's] 49a; Walpoles MSh

168.19   admirers] 49a; admires MSh

168.21   credulity] 49a; credality MSh

*168.23   raillery] 49a; railling [or raillery?] MSh

168.23   Walpole?] 49a; ~. MSh

168.24   Rowley,] 49a; ~∧ MSh

168.27   Redcliffe] 49a; Red Cliffe MSh

168.28   shown the coffer] 49a; shewn the Coffer MSh

*168.28   poor Chatterton] 49a; Chatterton MSh

168.29   "This," said he,] 49a; "~∧" ~ ~∧ MSh

168.31   *things.*"] 49a; ~.∧ MSh

168.32   Goldsmith,] 49a; ~∧ MSh

168.33   Dr.] 49a; ~∧ MSh

168.34   generous,] 49a; ~∧ MSh

168.35   genius,] 49a; ~∧ MSh

168.36   one's self] 49a; one self MSh

168.37   sixteen.] 49a; Sixteen. MSh

168.39   England,] 49a; ~∧ MSh

168.40   preface,] 49a; ~∧ MSh

*168.41   Rapin, Carte, Smollett] T; ~∧ ~∧ ~ MSh; ~, ~,
              ~, 53, 55, 59, 60; ~, Carle, ~, 49a, 49b, 49c, E, 50,
              51, 54

168.41–42   Hume, each of whom, says he, "have their peculiar
              admirers,] T; Hume each of whom, says he, "have their
              peculiar admirers, MSh; 'They have each,' he says,
              speaking of Rapin, Carte, Smollett, and Hume, 'their
              peculiar admirers, Forster (586); Hume, "each of
              whom," says he, "have their admirers, 49a

169.1   reasoner."] 49a; ~∧" MSh

169.2   clear,] 49a; ~∧ MSh

169.2   style,] 49a; ~∧ MSh

169.4   research.] 49a; ~∧ MSh

169.6   Son"] 49a; ~' MSh

169.6   work,] 49a; ~∧ MSh

169.10   Davies,] 49a; ~∧ MSh

169.11   Russell Street,] T; ~ street, MSh; Russell-street, 49a

169.12   unsaleable,] 49a; ~∧ MSh

169.13   "The Public Advertiser."] 49a; ∧the public advertiser.∧
              MSh

169.16   "an impartial account of Goldsmith's History of Eng-
              land?] T; "~ ~ ~ ~ Goldsmiths ~ ~ ~.? MSh; '~

~ ~ ~ Goldsmith's *History of England?* Forster
(586); "'An Impartial Account of Goldsmith's ~ ~
~?' 49a

169.18	*but mum!*"] 49a; ~ ~!∧ MSh; *but Mum!*' Forster (587)
169.19	received;] 49a; recieved; MSh
169.20	critics] 49a; Critics MSh
169.20	history] 49a; History MSh
169.21	epitomized, "and,] 49a; ~∧ "~∧ MSh
169.24	Lincolnshire,] 49a; ~; MSh
169.26	Rothes. The] 49a; ~: the MSh
169.27	7th of September,] 49a; Seventh ~ ~∧ MSh
169.28	summer] 49a; Summer MSh
169.29	History of England:] 49a; history ~ ~. MSh
*169.30–31	"My dear Sir, [*paragraph*] "Since] 49a; "My dear Sir, Since MSp
*169.41–42	We . . . you.] 49a, Percy (92), 1825 (45); *We . . . you.* MSp, Forster (588)
*170.7–8	There . . . countenance.] 49a, Percy (93), 1825 (45); *There . . . countenance.* MSp, Forster (589)
170.9–11	God . . . circumstances.] 49a, Percy (93), 1825 (45); *God . . . circumstances.* MSp, Forster (589)
170.16–18	God knows . . . would do no harm to nobody.] T; *God knows . . . would do no harm to nobody.* MSp, Forster (589); God knows . . . *would do no harm to nobody.* 49a
170.19–20	When . . . Whig.] 49a; *When . . . Whig.* MSp, Forster (589)
170.22–23	humble servant, [*paragraph*] "Oliver Goldsmith."] 49a; humble servant, Oliver Goldsmith." MSp, Forster (589)
171.2	*Practical*] 49a; practical MSh
*171.3	*Barton—Aquatic misadventure*] T; ~.—~ ~. 49a; Barton—Medley ⟨letter⟩ ↑epistle↓ to Mrs∧ Bunbury MSh
171.6	quarter,] 49a; ~∧ MSh
*171.6	somewhat] 49a; some what MSh
171.7	Catherine Horneck,] 49a; Catharine ~∧ MSh
171.8	*Comedy*,] 49a; ~∧ MSh
171.10	Bunbury, Esq.,] 49a; ~∧ ~.∧ MSh
171.10	fortune,] 49a; ~∧ MSh
171.11	afterwards] 49a; afterward MSh
171.14	true,] 49a; ~∧ MSh
171.15–16	way. New] 49a; ~; new MSh
171.17	showed] 49a; shewed MSh
171.18	so,] 49a; ~∧ MSh

171.19   "by hook or by crook,"] 49a; '~ ~ ~ ~ ~,' MSh
171.25   circle.] 49a; ~ᴧ MSh
*171.27   Barton," she says,] 49a; ~ᴧ" ~ ~ᴧ MSh
171.29   mirth,] 49a, Prior (II, 377); ~ᴧ MSh
171.30   'Come now and let] T; "~ ~ ~ ~ MSh, Prior (II, 377);
              '~, ~, let ~ 49a
171.30   little.' At cards,] 49a Prior (II, 377); ~ᴧ" ~ Cards, MSh
171.31   game,] 49a, Prior (II, 378); ~; MSh
*172.3–4   His perfect . . . played off.] 49a
*172.8   ladylike] 49a; lady like MSh
172.8   "he] 49a; ᴧ~ MSp
172.11   probably by design,] 49a; ~ ~ ~ᴧ Prior (II, 378);
              probably design, MSp
172.16   head of Reynolds] 49a; ~ ~ ~, Prior (II, 378); ~ by
              ~ MSp
172.24–25   appearance,] 49a; ~ᴧ MSh
*172.29   equally baneful] 49a; ~ fatal MSh
172.31   "having] 49a; ᴧ~ MSh
172.41   herself;] 49a; ~, MSh
172.41–42   Goldsmith's eccentricities] T; Goldsmiths excentricitiesᴧ
              MSh; Goldsmith's eccentricities, Pr.
172.42   mischievous] Pr.; mischevious MSh
*172.43   elsewhere,] Pr., 49a; else where, MSh
*173.3–19   Among the circumstances . . . Mr. Newbery!] 49a
173.6   chapter,] 49a; ~ᴧ Prh
173.9   bookseller,] 49a; ~ᴧ Prh
173.9–10   manuscript,] 49a; ~ᴧ Prh
173.10–11   "The Good Natured Man."] T; ᴧ~ ~ ~ ~.ᴧ Prh; ᴧthe
              Good-Natured Man.ᴧ 49a
173.11   Goldsmith,] 49a; ~ᴧ Prh
173.11   conceit] 49a; conciet Prh
173.12   aside,] 49a; ~; Prh
173.13   years] 49a; ~, Prh
173.15   press,] 49a; press [undecipherable pen marks] Prh
173.18   Barton] Prh; ~, 49a
173.19   astute Mr. Newbery!] 49a; Astute ~ᴧ ~. Prh
174.2   Oglethorpe's] 49a; oglethorps MSh
174.4   Goldsmith's] 49a; Goldsmiths MSh
174.5   1698,] 49a; ~. MSh
174.7   military] 49a; Military MSh
174.8   major general] T; Major General [or general?] MSh;
              major general; 49a
*174.8   1745] T; ~. MSh; ~, 49a

174.9	tendencies,] 49a; $\sim_\wedge$ MSh
174.11	inquiry,] 49a; $\sim_\wedge$ MSh
174.11	language,] 49a; $\sim_\wedge$ MSh
174.13	learning,] 49a; $\sim_\wedge$ MSh
174.14	historical,] 49a; $\sim_\wedge$ MSh
174.15–16	settlement of the colony] 49a; Settlement of the Colony MSh
174.17	Pope's:] 49a; Popes$_\wedge$ MSh
°174.19	Oglethorpe,] 49a; $\sim_\wedge$ MSh
174.23	talent.] 49a; $\sim_\wedge$ MSh
174.24	"experiences."] 49a; "$\sim_\wedge$" MSh
174.25	life.] 49a; $\sim_\wedge$ MSh
174.25	man," said he, "whose] 40a; $\sim,_\wedge \sim \sim, _\wedge\sim$ MSh
174.26	interesting."] 49a; $\sim_{\wedge\wedge}$ MSh
174.26	general's] 49a; Generals, MSh
174.31	general's,] 49a; Generals, MSh
°174.31	1772,)] 49b, E; $\sim_\wedge$) MSh; 1722,) 49a
174.32	removed,] 49a; $\sim_\wedge$ MSh
174.33	Johnson's] 49a; Johnsons MSh
174.33	siege] 49a; Siege MSh
°174.33	Belgrade] T; $\sim$. MSh; $\sim$, 49a
174.34	style.] 49a; $\sim_\wedge$ MSh
174.34	table,] 49a; $\sim_\wedge$ MSh
174.36	forces.] 49a; $\sim$, MSh
174.36	Turks,"] 49a; $\sim_\wedge$" MSh
175.1	general] 49a; General MSh
175.3	Würtemberg,] T; Wortemberg, MSh; Wurtemberg, 49a; Wirtemberg, Boswell (II, 175)
175.4	Oglethorpe's face.] 49a; Oglethorpes $\sim$: MSh
175.6	officer?] 49a; $\sim$. MSh
175.6	seriously,] 49a; $\sim_\wedge$ MSh
175.8	notice,] 49a; $\sim_\wedge$ MSh
175.9	smiling, "that] 49a; $\sim_\wedge _\wedge\sim$ MSh
175.10	England."] 49a; $\sim._\wedge$ MSh
175.10	saying,] 49a; $\sim_\wedge$ MSh
175.11	prince's face.] 49a; princes $\sim_\wedge$ MSh
175.11	prince,"] 49a; $\sim_\wedge$" MSh
175.12	commencé."] 49a; $\sim_\wedge$" MSh
175.13	prince; you] 49a; $\sim$, You MSh
175.13	it.)] 49a; $\sim_\wedge$) MSh
175.14	Oglethorpe's] 49a; Oglethorpes MSh
175.14	in kind] 49a; $\sim$ Kind MSh
175.19	"Undoubtedly] 49a; $_\wedge$Undoubtedly MSh

175.21   Boswell's] 49a; Boswells MSh
175.25   question,"] 49a; ∼∧" MSh
175.25   Goldsmith.] 49a; ∼∧ MSh
175.25   "No, sir!"] 49a; "∼, ∼,∧ Boswell (II, 174); "No Sir! MSh
175.26   Johnson; "it] 49a; ∼. "It MSh
175.27   right."] 49a; ∼∧" MSh
175.27   show] 49a; shew MSh
175.30   duel.] 49a; ∼∧ MSh
175.30   he, "who] 49a; ∼∧ "∼ MSh
175.31–32   self-defence,] 49a; ∼-∼; Boswell (II, 175); ∼∧ ∼∧
                MSh
175.32   world,] 49a, Boswell (II, 175); ∼∧ MSh
175.38   not,] 49a; ∼-, MSh
175.39   aversions.] 49a, Boswell (II, 176); ∼∧– MSh
175.40   sir,"] 49a; ∼,∧ Boswell (II, 176); Sir," MSh
175.41   "when] 49a; ∧∼ MSh
175.43   story] 49a, Boswell (II, 176); Story MSh
175.43   Bluebeard:] T; ∼, MSh; ∼. Boswell (II, 176); Blue
                Beard: 49a
175.43   'You] T, Boswell (II, 176); "∼ MSh; 'you 49a
176.1   one.' But] T, Boswell (II, 176); ∼." ∼ MSh; ∼;' but 49a
176.3   voice, "I] 49a; ∼, ∧∼ MSh
*176.6   that Goldsmith had the best] 50; ∼ ∼ ∼ not ∼ ∼
                MSh, 49a, 49b, 49c, E
176.6   contest?] 49a; ∼. MSh
176.7   remark!] 49a; ∼, MSh
176.8   chamber!] 49a; ∼, MSh
176.9   argument!] 49a; ∼. MSh
*176.11   Colonel Prendergast,] 49a; colonel Pendergast MSh
176.11–12   Marlborough's army,] 49a; Marlboroughs ∼∧ MSh
176.13   colonel] 49a; Colonel MSh
176.16   he gravely;] T; ∼ ∼∧ MSh; ∼, ∼; 49a
176.17   true.] 49a; ∼∧ MSh
176.18   batteries,] 49a; ∼: MSh
176.19   colonel] 49a; Colonel MSh
176.23   battle).] 49a; ∼.) MSh
*176.24   Prendergast] T; Pendergast, MSh, 49a
176.25   Pope,] 49a; ∼∧ MSh
176.26   The story] T; ∼ Story MSh; This story, 49a
176.26   general] T; General MSh; general, 49a
176.27   credited,] 49a; ∼∧ MSh
176.27   Goldsmith,] 49a; ∼; MSh
176.28   Goldsmith's brother,] 49a; Goldsmiths ∼∧ MSh

176.29	confidence,] 49a; ~∧ MSh
176.30–31	Mr. Edward Cave, the printer] T, Boswell (II, 173); ~∧ ~ ~∧ ~ ~ MSh; Mr. Cave, the printer, 49a
176.31	St. John's Gate, "an] 49a; S' Johns ~, ∧~ MSh
176.31	man,"] 49a; ~,∧ MSh
176.32	ghost:] 49a; ~; MSh
176.33–34	"And pray, sir"] 49a; '~ ~∧ Sir,' MSh; "Pray, sir, Boswell (II, 173)
176.34	Boswell,] 49a; ~∧ MSh
176.34	appearance?"] 49a, Boswell (II, 173); ~.?∧–MSh
176.34	"Why, sir,] 49a, Boswell (II, 173); "~∧ Sir, MSh
176.37	recollects] 49a; reccollects MSh
*176.39	Cock-lane] 49a; ~∧~ MSh
176.39	Dr.] 49a; ~∧ MSh
*177.2	*Mr.*] 49a; ~∧ Prh
177.2	*An author's confidings*] 49a; an authors Confidings Prh
177.2	*An amanuensis*] 49a; an Amanuensis Prh
177.5	Mr.] Pr.; ~∧ MSh
177.9	Voltaire's] Pr.; Voltaires MSh
177.12	harass] Pr.; harrass MSh
177.13	Yates, the actor,] Pr.; ~∧ ~ Actor∧ MSh
177.14	Clare,] Pr.; ~∧ MSh
177.15–16	intimacy, especially as they found] 49a; ~; and they soon found MSh; ~, ⟨and⟩ they ⟨soon⟩ found Pr; [*added to margin of Pr. by hand*] especially as / ⸹
177.17	tragedy of Zobeide;] Pr.; Tragedy ~ ~∧ MSh
177.19	Princess Dowager] Pr.; ~ dowager MSh
177.22	Mrs. Cornelys'] 49a; ~∧ Cornely's MSh
177.23	Square,] 49a; ~; MSh
*177.23	enterprise] 49a; enterprize MSh
*177.24	somewhat] 49a; some what MSh
177.26	Cornelys."] 49a; ~∧" MSh
177.36	"Ah! Mr. Cradock,"] 49a; "~∧ ~∧ ~!" MSh
177.36	"think of me,] 49a, Forster (446); ∧~ ~ ~∧ MSh
177.37	attempts] 49a; attempt MSh
177.39	denomination,] 49a; ~∧ MSh
178.3	fulness] 49a; fullness MSh
178.3	heart, "I] 49a; ~, ∧~ MSh
178.3	curs!"] 49a; Curs.' MSh
178.4	acquaintance,] 49a; ~∧ MSh
178.6	recollections] 49a; reccollections MSh
178.8	years:] 49a; ~. MSh
178.9	he, "that] 49a; ~∧ ∧~ MSh

178.13   any thing,] 49a; ~ ~∧ Prior (II, 344); anything, MSp
178.25   peregrinantur] 50; perigrinantur MSp, 49a, 49b, 49c, E
179.4   Goldsmith's] 49a; Goldsmiths MSh
179.4   him, and] 49a; ~∧ ~ MSh
179.6   spoken of] 49a; Spoken ~, MSh
179.6   Mr.] 49a; ~∧ MSh
179.8   embarrassments] 49a; barrassments MSh
179.9   with which he bore them:] 49a; ~ which which ~ ~
          ~∧ MSh
179.10   "that] 49a; ∧~ MSh
179.11   for what] 49a, Prior (II, 346); ~, ~ MSp
179.16   dependent] 49a, Prior (II, 346); dependant MSp
*179.27   summer] 49a; Summer MSh
179.27   six-mile stone] 49a, Prior (II, 331); Six Mile Stone MSh
*179.28   Road] T; road MSh; ~∧ 49a
179.28   returned post chaises,] T, Prior (II, 331); ~ ~ ~∧ MSh;
          return ~-~. 49a
179.29   farmer's] 49a; farmers MSh
*179.30   landlady] 49a; land lady MSh
179.33   at home. Having] 49a; ~ ~∧ having MSh
179.34   apartment,] 49a; ~∧ MSh
179.35   scrawled] 49a; scrauled MSh
179.36   farm house] T; ~ ~, Prior (II, 331); farmhouse MSp;
          farm-house 49a
179.42   farmer,] 49a; ~∧ MSh
180.1   family,] 49a; ~∧ MSh
180.2   room,] 49a; ~∧ MSh
180.5   kitchen,] 49a; Kitchen, MSh
180.10   to read,] 49a; ~ ~∧ MSh
180.11   it, and] 49a; ~∧ ~ MSh
180.12   reach,] 49a; ~∧ MSh
180.13   grease.] 49a; ~∧ MSh
*180.14   every where] 49a; everywhere MSp
180.17   receive] 49a; recieve MSh
180.20   rarely,] 49a; ~∧ MSh
*180.29   Edgeware] T; Edge/ware MSh; Edgeware, 49a
180.29   Mr. Seguin,] 49a; ~∧ ~∧ MSh
180.30   tastes,] 49a; ~∧ MSh
180.32   humor,] 49a; humour, MSh
180.33   any thing—conversation,] 49a; ~ ~, ~, MSh
180.36   good humor.] T; good-humour. MSp; good-humor. 49a
180.43   skill] 49a; SKill MSh
181.4   Roubillac, the statuary,] 49a; ~∧ ~ ~∧ MSh

181.6	finished,] 49a; ~ₐ MSh
*181.7	eyes] 49a; eye MSh
181.11	humors.] 49a; humours. MSh
181.11	thought,"] 49a; ~ₐ" MSh
181.13	fingers."] 49a; ~ₐ" MSh
181.14	Mrs. Garrick,] 49a; ~ₐ ~ₐ MSh
181.14	told,] 49a; ~ₐ MSh
181.15	*Chimney Sweep*] 49a; *chimney sweep* MSh
181.18	Colman,] 49a; ~ₐ MSh
181.27	hand,] 49a, Prior (II, 194); ~ₐ MSp
181.36	conjurer,] 49a; Prior (II, 195); conjuror, MSp
*182.1	headquarters] 49a; head quarters MSh
182.2	summer,] 49a; Summerₐ MSh
182.3	Clare and Mr. Langton] T; ~ ~ ~ₐ ~ MSh; ~, ~ ~. ~, 49a
182.8	wires,] 49a; ~ₐ MSh
*182.10–11	When Burke, said he, praised] T; ~ ~, ~ ~ₐ ~ MSh; "~ ~," ~ ~, "~ 49a
182.12	pike, "Pshaw,"] T; ~ₐ "~ₐ" MSh; ~," '~,' 49a
182.12	*warmth,* "I] T; ~ₐ ₐ~ MSh; ~, '~ 49a
*182.13	myself." "The] T; ~.ₐ ₐ ~MSh; ~.' " "~ 49a
182.13	Boswell,] 49a; ~ₐ MSh
182.13	Burke's] 49a; Burkes MSh
182.16–17	Boswell's] 49a; Boswells MSh
*182.19	puppets] 49a; ~, MSh
182.20–21	autocrat of the stage.] 49a; Autocrat ~ ~ Stage MSh
182.21	Foote,] 49a; ~ₐ MSh
182.22	on the alert to] 49a; on the to MSh
182.23	Fantoccini,] 49a; fantoccini, MSh
*182.24	Puppet-Shew] T; ~ₐ~ MSh; Puppet-show 49a; puppet-show Forster (609)
182.24	at the Haymarket,] 49a; at Haymarketₐ MSh
*182.25	*Chambermaid,*] 49a; ~ₐ MSh
182.26	*sentimental comedy*] 49a; *Sentimental Comedy* MSh
*182.27	idea of a play] 49a; idea of play MSh
182.29	life, Mr.] 49a; ~ₐ ~ₐ MSh
182.29	"Oh, no,] 49a; "~ₐ ~, MSh
182.29	lady,"] T; ~,' MSh; ~;" 49a
182.30	Foote,] 49a; ~ₐ MSh
183.2	*debts*] 49a; Debts MSh
183.3	*jokes*] 49a; Jokes MSh
183.4	*ballad*] 49a; Ballad MSh
*183.4	*poet*] T; Poet MSh, 49a

183.5	autumn (1772)] T; Autumn ∼ MSh; autumn ∼, 49a
183.6	application,] 49a; ∼∧ MSh
183.9	summer.] 49a; Summer. MSh
183.10	siren] 49a; syren MSh
183.10	temptation which,] T; ∼∧ ∼∧ MSh; ∼, ∼, 49a
183.11	notoriety,] 49a; ∼∧ MSh
183.12	dissipation;] 49a; dissapation; MSh
183.13	clubs, at routs, at theatres;] 49a; Clubs, ∼ ∼; ∼ Theatres; MSh
*183.14	Thrales'] T; ∼∧ MSh; ∼∧, 49a
183.14	Mrs. Thrale's lively sallies;] 49a; ∼∧ Thrales ∼ sallys; MSh
183.15	Mrs. Vesey's and Mrs. Montagu's,] 49a; ∼∧ Veseys ∼ ∼∧ Montagus∧ MSh
183.16–17	peradventure,] 49a; ∼∧ MSh
183.17	Irishman."] 49a; ∼∧" MSh
183.19	harassment] 49a; harrassment MSh
183.20	Nature,] 49a; ∼∧ MSh
183.20	finished,] 49a; ∼∧ MSh
183.22	Newbery's note] T; Newberys ∼ MSh; Newbery's ∼, 49a
183.22	debt. The] 49a; ∼; ⟨Newbury⟩ The MSh
183.27	comedy] 49a; Comedy MSh
*183.27	portfolio;] 49a; port folio, MSh
183.28	Frank," said he,] 49a; ∼∧∧ ∼ ∼∧ MSh
183.28	success."] 49a; ∼∧" MSh
*183.31	"overrunning] 49a; "over running MSh
183.31	constable"] T; Constable" MSh; constable," 49a
183.27	system,] 49a; ∼∧ MSh
183.38	James's] 49a; James' MSh
*183.40	of a practical joke] T; of ⟨one of the⟩ ↑a↓ practical Jokes MSh; of practical jokes 49a
184.1	poor, simple hearted] T; ∼∧ ↑∼ ∼↓ MSh; ∼, ∼- ∼ 49a
184.3	authoress] T; Authoress MSh; authoress, 49a
184.8	own poems and] T; oun ∼ ∼ MSh; own ∼, ∼ 49a
184.8	own with] T; ∼ ⟨; with in⟩ with MSh; own, with 49a
184.15	compliments] 49a; complements MSh
184.17	company,] 49a; ∼∧ MSh
184.18	widow,] 49a; ∼∧ MSh
184.18	performed,] 49a; ∼∧ MSh
184.18–19	Mrs. Balfour,] 49a; ∼∧ ∼∧ MSh
184.19	connection,] 49a; connexion, MSh
184.20	alleged] 49a; alledged MSh

184.25	Goldsmith's] 49a; Goldsmiths MSh
184.25–26	was related] 49a; is ↑was↓ related MSh
184.26	O'Moore,] 49a, Boswell (I, 423); ⌒ᴧ MSh
184.26	Castle in Ireland,] T, Boswell (I, 423); ⌒ ⌒ ⌒; MSh; ⌒, ⌒ ⌒, 49a
*184.27	Burke, walking] 49a; Burke were walking MSh
184.28	Reynolds's,] 49a; Reynolds, MSh
184.31	Goldsmith,"] 49a; ⌒ᴧ" MSh
184.32	O'Moore,] 49a; ⌒ᴧ MSh
184.32–33	Sir Joshua's."] 49a; Sir Joshua ś." MSh
*184.33–34	Burke received Goldsmith with unusual reserve] T; Burke affected ⟨great⟩ ↑received Goldsmith with unusual↓ reserve MSh; Burke received Goldsmith with affected reserve 49a
184.35	reason, "Really," said he, "I] 49a; ⌒ᴧ ᴧreallyᴧᴧ ⌒ ⌒ᴧ ᴧ⌒ MSh
184.37	"Why,"] 49a; "⌒ᴧ" MSh
184.40	unnoticed?"] 49a, Boswell (I, 423, n. 2); ⌒." MSh
184.41	surely,] 49a, Boswell (I, 423, n. 2); ⌒ᴧ MSh
184.41	friend,"] 49a; ⌒ᴧ" MSh
184.41	alarm, "surely] 49a; ⌒ᴧ ᴧSurely MSh
184.42	"Nay,"] 49a, Boswell (I, 423, n. 2); '⌒ᴧ" MSh
184.43	"That's true,"] 49a, Boswell (I, 423, n. 2); "Thats ⌒ᴧᴧ MSh
185.1	*recollect that something*] 49a, Boswell (I, 423, n. 2); *reccolect that some thing* MSh
185.2	*uttered it."*] 49a, Boswell (I, 423, n. 2); *uttered it.'* MSh
185.7	latter and his guileless] T; ⌒ ⌒ ⌒ guiless MSh; ⌒, ⌒ ⌒ guileless 49a
185.8	associates;] 49a; ⌒.- MSh
185.9	watch to give] 49a; watch give MSh
185.11	jubilee] T; Jubilee MSh; jubilee, 49a
185.11	Shakespeare,] T; ⌒ᴧ MSh; Shakspeare, 49a
185.12	himself,] 49a; ⌒ᴧ MSh
185.12	every one's] 49a; ⌒ ones MSh
185.14	Beaux'] T; Beauxᴧ MSh, 49a
185.15	Literary Club.] 49a; ⌒ club. MSh
185.15	"Then,"] 49a; "⌒ᴧ" MSh
185.15	Goldsmith,] 49a; ⌒. MSh
185.17	character."] 49a; ⌒ᴧ" MSh
185.17	speech,] 49a; ⌒ᴧ MSh
185.18	comment,] 49a; ⌒ᴧ MSh
185.19	characteristic.] 49a; ⌒ᴧ MSh

185.22	Sir Joshua's] 49a; Sir Joshuas MSh
185.23	color.] 49a; colour. MSh
185.24	Hammersmith, as that was the way] 49a; Hammersmith as that was sent to Hammersmith as that was the way MSh
*185.25	(Turnham Green).] T; (∼ ∼.) MSh; (∼-∼). 49a
185.25	Goldsmith,] 49a; ∼ₐ MSh
185.26	pun,] 49a; ∼ₐ MSh
185.26	Burke's] 49a; Burkes MSh
185.27	"That] 49a; ₐ∼ MSh
185.27	green,"] 49a; ∼ₐ" MSh
185.27	he. No body] T; he–no body MSh; he. Nobody 49a
185.27–28	laughed. He perceived] 49a; ∼, he percieved MSh
185.28	turn 'em green." A] 49a; Turn em green⁼a MSh
185.29	"whereupon,"] 49a; ₐ∼ₐₐ MSh
185.29	"he] 49a; ₐ∼ MSh
185.30	table."] 49a; ∼.ₐ MSh
185.31	Beauclerc's] 49a; Beauclercs MSh
185.33	Lord Shelburne, the minister,] 49a; ∼ Shelₐ ∼ Ministerₐ MSh
*185.34	nickname Malagrida.] 49a; nick name ∼ₐ MSh
185.36	conceive] 49a; concieve MSh
185.36	you Malagrida,] 49a, Boswell (V, 54); ∼ ∼; MSh
185.40	compeer,] 49a; ∼ₐ MSh
185.41–42	Goldsmith's whole life."] 49a; Goldsmiths ∼ ∼ₐ" MSh
185.42	Dr. Johnson alone,] 49a; ∼ₐ ∼, ∼ₐ MSh
185.42	Goldsmith's] 49a; Goldsmiths MSh
185.43	blunder,] 49a; ∼ₐ MSh
185.43	defence: "Sir,"] 49a; ∼. "∼.' MSh
185.43	he, "it] 49a; ∼, ₐ∼ MSh
186.2	reproach."] 49a; ∼ₐ" MSh
186.2	Goldsmith! On] 49a; ∼ₐ– MSh
186.3	Rogers the poet,] T; ∼ ∼ ∼ₐ MSh; ∼, ∼ ∼, 49a
186.4	subsequent] 49a; ∼, MSh
186.4	days,] 49a; ∼ₐ MSh
186.7	"Sir,"] 49a; "∼ₐ" MSh
186.7	wiseacre,] 49a; ∼ₐ MSh
186.8	shilling, he'd say, Why it's] 49a; ∼ₐ ∼ ∼ₐ ∼ its MSh
186.10	sir,] 49a, Forster (479); Sir, MSh
186.10	*sir."] 49a; Sir." MSh; sir." Forster (479)
186.11	Goldsmith's] 49a; Goldsmiths MSh
186.13	others,] 49a; ∼-; MSh

186.16	a tavern in Dean Street,] T; ⟨at Jack's⟩ a Tavern in Dean Street∧ MSh; a tavern in Dean-street, 49a
186.17	Drury Lane] T; ∼ lane MSh; Drury-lane, 49a
°186.17	protégé] T; protege MSh; protegee 49a
186.19	kidneys,] 49a; Kidneys, MSh
186.20	"These," said he, "are] 49a; "∼∧' ∼ ∼∧ ∧∼ MSh
186.20	things;] 49a; ∼∧ MSh
186.21	filled."] 49a; ∼∧" MSh
186.22	them," asked] 49a, Prior (II, 481); them∧∧ 'asked MSh; them∧' asked Forster (615)
186.22–23	simplicity, "would] 49a; ∼∧–∧∼ MSh
186.23	moon?" "To the moon!] 49a; ∼?"–"∼ ∼ ∼? MSh; ∼?' '∼ ∼ ∼!' Forster (616)
186.23	Ah, sir,] 49a; ∼∧ Sir, MSh
186.23	that, I fear,] 49a; ∼∧ ∼ ∼∧ MSh
186.24	calculation."] 49a; ∼."– MSh
186.24	all, sir;] 49a; ∼, Sir, MSh
186.24	tell." "Pray, then, sir,] 49a; ∼."–"∼∧ ∼, Sir∧ MSh
186.25	hear." "Why, sir, one,] 49a; ∼."–why, Sir,–one- MSh
186.25	enough!"] 49a; ∼∧" MSh
°186.26	finding himself caught] 49a; ∼ him ∼ MSh
186.26–27	"Well, sir,"] 49a; "∼. Sir∧' MSh
186.28	question."] 49a; ∼∧" MSh
°186.29–41	Among the many . . . of his heart.] 49a
186.29	Goldsmith's] 49a; Goldsmiths MSh
186.32	struck] 49a; Struck MSh
186.33	sings!"] 49a; ∼∧" MSh
186.33	"Pray, doctor," said] 49a; "∼∧ Doctor∧" Said MSh
186.34	better?" "Yes, madam,] 49a; ∼?"–"∼∧ Madam, MSh
186.36	tears,] 49a; ∼. MSh
186.38	music,] 49a; ∼∧ MSh
186.39–40	ballads, associated] 49a; ∼-∼MSh
186.40	recollections] 49a; reccollections MSh
186.40	childhood,] 49a; ∼∧ MSh
186.43	Berners Street,] T; ∼ street, MSh; Berners-street, 49a
187.1	William, Lady Chambers] T; ∼∧ ∼ chambers MSh; ∼, ∼ Chambers, 49a
187.1	Baretti,] 49a; ∼∧ MSh
187.2	threw down] 49a; ∼ doun MSh
187.3	seat,] 49a; ∼∧ MSh
187.5	retreat,] 49a; ∼∧ MSh
187.6	Goldsmith;] 49a; ∼, MSh
187.7	street,] 49a; ∼∧ MSh

187.12	the reality] Prh; one [*written over another word, possibly "the"*] reality MSh
187.13	scene in the story of the Man in Black;] Prh; scene in the Man in Black: MSh
*187.13–14	wherein he describes "a woman] T; wherein he describes a woman Prh; 'A woman MSh
187.14	rags,] Prh, *Works* (II, 111); ∼∧ MSh
187.14–15	back, attempting] 49a; ∼∧ ∼ Prh; ∼, was ∼ MSh, *Works* (II, 111)
187.15	ballads,] 49a, *Works* (II, 111); ∼∧ MSh; ∼ &c Prh
187.16–17	A wretch," he adds, "who in the deepest distress] T; 'A wretch who in the deepest distress MSh; A wretch, he adds, who in the deepest distress &c Prh; "A wretch," he adds, "who, in the deepest distress, 49a
187.17	good humor,] 49a; ∼ ∼∧ MSh; good humour, *Works* (II, 112)
187.18	withstanding."] 49a; ∼∧"– MSh
187.19–20	matches; Goldsmith, it is probable,] T; ∼; ∼∧ ∼ ∼ ∼∧ MSh; ∼. Goldsmith, ∼ ∼ ∼, 49a
187.22	vogue] 49a; Vogue MSh
187.23	entertainment.] 49a; ∼∧ MSh
187.25	occasionally.] 49a; ∼∧ MSh
187.26	amusements,"] 49a; ∼∧" MSh
187.27	vice."*] 49a; ∼∧*" MSh
187.32	alone;] 49a; ∼∧ MSh
187.33	disguise,] 49a; ∼∧ MSh
187.36	*"Alas, sir!] 49a; *"∼∧ Sir∧" MSh
187.37	amusement; "alas, sir!] 49a; ∼∧ "Alas, Sir! MSh
187.43	afraid] 49a; affraid MSh
*187.43	think."] 49a; ∼∧" MSh
*188.1–2	him, would decry] 49a; ∼∧ ∼ ∼ MSh; ∼, ∼ deny Pr.
188.2	contemporaries;] Pr.; cotemporaries; MSh
188.5	teasing,] Pr.; ∼∧ MSh
188.5	supposed,] Pr.; ∼∧ MSh
*188.10	newspapers] Pr.; news papers MSh
188.11	amusements,] Pr.; ∼; MSh
188.11	enemy, Kenrick,] Pr.; ∼∧ ∼∧ MSh
*188.13–14	purport. [*paragraph*] To Dr. Goldsmith; on] 49a; ∼. To ∼∧ ∼, ∼ MSh; purport–To ∼. ∼; ∼ Pr.
188.15	masquerade:] Pr.; ∼. MSh
188.16	How] T; "∼ MSp, 49a
188.33	man.] T; ∼." MSp, 49a

188.34   kind,] 49a; ∼∧ MSh

188.35   Chapter Coffee House,] T; ∼ ∼ ∼∧ MSh; ∼ Coffee-house,) 49a

189.1   kind,] 49a; Kind, MSh

189.8   Goldsmith's] 49a; Goldsmiths MSh

*189.9   calling on the poet one morning,] 49a; ∼ ⟨on him⟩ ↑the poet↓ ∼ ∼∧ MSh

189.12   dress,] 49a; ∼∧ MSh

189.13   money,] 49a; ∼∧ MSh

*190.2   *spring velvet*] T; Spring Velvet MSh; spring-velvet 49a

*190.2   *The haymaking*] 49a; the hay making MSh

190.3   *The fair*] 49a; the ∼ MSh

190.6   country.] 49a; Country. MSh

190.7   Mrs.] 49a; ∼∧ MSh

*190.7   Barton] T; Burton MSh; Burton, 49a

190.8   Christmas holydays] T; christmas holy days. MSh; Christmas holidays. 49a

190.9   family.] 49a; ∼∧ MSh

190.10   spring velvet coat,"] T; Spring Velvet Coat," MSh; spring-velvet coat," 49a

190.11   haymakers] 49a; hay makers MSh

190.11   in, and] 49a; ∼∧ ∼ MSh

*190.12   Loo.] T; loo. MSh, 49a

190.13   Goldsmith's] 49a; Goldsmiths MSh

*190.14   ladylike] 49a; lady like MSh

190.14   him,] 49a; ∼∧ MSh

190.15   spring velvet] T; Spring ∼ MSh; spring-velvet 49a

190.16–17   bloom colored coat)] T; ∼ coloured ∼) MSh; bloom-colored ∼,) 49a

190.19   Mr.] 49a; ∼∧ MSh

190.19   tailor:] 49a; taylor∧ MSh

190.20   *suit,* £21 10s. 9d.] 49a; ∼∧ £21.10.9 MSh

190.20   Also] T; also MSh; Also, 49a

*190.23–25   The new wig . . . his sword.] Prh

190.23   bag wig] Prh; ∼-∼ 49a

190.23   still] 49a; Still Prh

190.26   haymakers,] Pr.; hay makers∧ MSh

190.30   Loo,] T; loo∧ MSh; loo, Pr.

190.31   doctor's] Pr.; Doctors MSh

190.33   ventures;] Pr.; ∼, MSh

190.33   cowardice;] Pr.; ∼∧ MSh

190.35   sisters'] Pr.; ∼∧ MSh

190.38   Goldsmith's] Pr.; Goldsmiths MSh

190.38	Mrs. Bunbury,] Pr.; ~∧ ~∧ MSh
190.39	off hand,] T; ~ ~∧ MSh; off-hand, Pr., 49a
*191.6	answer.—I] Pr.; ~∧ . . ~ MSp, Forster (592); reply. I *Letters* (129)
191.6	madam,] Pr.; Madam, MSp, Forster (592); madam∧ *Letters* (129)
191.10	name—but] Pr.; ~ . . ~ MSp, Forster (592); ~, ~ *Letters* (130)
191.10–11	for!)—I] Pr.; ~!) . . I MSp, Forster (592); ~∧) ∧~ *Letters* (130)
191.11	madam,] Pr., 49a; Madam, MSp, Forster (592); madam∧ *Letters* (130)
191.14	hope my] MSp, Forster (592), *Letters* (130); ~, ~ 49a
191.17	madam,] 49a; Madam, MSp, Forster (592); madam∧ *Letters* (130)
191.22	winter!—a] 49a; ~! . . a MSp, Forster (592); ~.∧ A *Letters* (130)
191.34	ancients] 49a, *Letters* (130); antients MSp, Forster (593)
192.2	to be Loo:] 49a, *Letters* (131); ~ ~, ~: MSp, Forster (593)
192.15	ass.] T, *Letters* (132); ~, . . MSp, Forster (593); ~, . . . 49a
192.16	Bunbury?'—] T; ~?' . . MSp, Forster (593), 49a; ~?∧ *Letters* (132)
192.17	do.'] T; ~,' . . MSp, Forster (593), 49a; ~.∧ *Letters* (132)
192.18	too.'] 49a; ~.∧ MSp, Forster (593), *Letters* (132)
192.24	own.—] T; ~∧ . . MSp, Forster (593); ~ . . . 49a; ~.∧ *Letters* (132)
192.26	rich.—ah!] T; ~, . . ~! MSp, Forster (593), 49a; ~.∧ Ah. *Letters* (133)
192.31	own.] T, *Letters* (133); ~. . . MSp, Forster (593), 49a
192.35	you're] 49a; your're MSp, Forster (593); youre *Letters* (133)
193.1	fennel,] 49a; fennell, MSp, Forster (594); Fennel∧ *Letters* (134)
193.4	buzz] 49a, *Letters* (134); buz MSp, Forster (594)
193.5	crimes?'—] T; ~?' . . MSp, Forster (594), 49a; Crimes?∧ *Letters* (134)
193.6	pilfer'd?'—] T; pilfer'd?' . . MSp, Forster (594), 49a; pilfered?∧ *Letters* (134)
193.8	same.'—] T; ~.' . . MSp, Forster (594), 49a; ~. ∧ ∧ *Letters* (134)

193.23	pounds.–I] 49a; ～, . . I MSp, Forster (594); ～·ᴧ I *Letters* (135)
193.23	them!'–] 49a; ～!' . . MSp, Forster (594); ～·ᴧᴧ *Letters* (135)
193.24	case,–it] T; ～, . . ～ MSp, Forster (594), 49a; ～·ᴧ It *Letters* (135)
193.25	kneel! Is] 49a; ～? ～ MSp, Forster (594); ～; is *Letters* (135)
193.26	moves:–so] T; ～: . . ～ MSp, Forster (594), 49a; ～, ～ *Letters* (135)
193.27	spent.'] 49a; ～·ᴧ MSp
193.29	and next–] 49a, *Letters* (136); ～ ～ . . MSp, Forster (594)
193.29	room–] 49a, *Letters* (136); ～ . . MSp, Forster (594)
193.31	week.–] 49a; ～. . . MSp, Forster (594); ～·ᴧ *Letters* (136)
193.31–32	you all! [*paragraph*] "O.G."] 49a; you all! O.G. MSp, Forster (594); you all. *Letters* (136)
193.33	Christmas] 49a; christmas MSh
193.37	Christmas] 49a; christmas MSh
193.39	spring velvet] T; Spring ～ MSh; spring-velvet 49a
194.1	*CHAPTER XXXVII*] T; CHAPTER XXXVII. 49a; ch ⟨36⟩ 37 MSh
194.2	*Letter*] 49a; letter MSh
194.3	*Naming*] 49a; naming MSh
194.4	*Foote's*] 49a; Footes MSh
*194.4	*Puppet Shew,*] T; puppet shew– [puppet Shew ? puppetshew ?] MSh; Puppetshow, 49a
194.5	*comedy*] 49a; Comedy MSh
194.5	*author*] 49a; Author MSh
194.5	*Colman*] 49a; colman MSh
*194.7	The gay life depicted in the two last chapters,] 49a; The feverish town life which we have just depicted; MSh
194.11	increasing] 49a; encreasing MSh
194.14	comedy,] 49a; Comedyᴧ MSh
194.15	stage.] 49a; Stage. MSh
194.23	decision.] 49a; ～ᴧ MSh
194.23	season] 49a; Season MSh
194.23–24	away, and Goldsmith's] 49a; ～ᴧ ～ Goldsmiths MSh
194.25	him. We] 49a; ～ᴧ-～ MSh
194.25	letter:] 49a; ～. MSh
195.1	Colman] 49a; Coleman MSh

195.5	friends,] 49a; ∼∧ MSh
195.5	trivial,] 49a; ∼∧ MSh
195.7	Colman's] 49a; Colmans MSh
195.8	Garrick;] 49a; ∼, MSh
*195.10	forthwith to Colman] T; ∼, ∼ ∼ MSh; ∼ ∼ ∼, 49a
*195.11	Goldsmith, therefore,] 49a; ∼∧ thereupon, MSp
195.12	Garrick:] 49a; ∼, MSh
195.13–14	"DEAR SIR, [*paragraph*] "I ask] 49a; "Dear Sir, I ask MSp
*195.22	entreat,] 49a, *Letters* (118); ∼∧ MSp, Forster (622)
195.23–24	time. [*paragraph*] "I am,] 49a; ∼. I am, MSp
195.24–25	servant, [*paragraph*] "Oliver Goldsmith."] 49a; ∼, Oliver Goldsmith." MSp
195.26	Covent Garden] T; CoventGarden MSh; Covent-Garden 49a
195.27	Colman, he says, "was] T; ∼∧ ∼ ∼∧ "∼ MSh; "∼," ∼ ∼, "∼ 49a; Colman, *who was* Forster (622)
195.27–28	last by much solicitation, nay,] T; ∼ ∼ ∼ ∼∧ ∼, MSh; *last by much solicitation, nay,* Forster (622); last, by much solicitation, nay, 49a
195.28	comedy.] 49a; Comedy. MSh
195.30–31	plot, he said,] 49a; ∼∧ ∼ ∼∧ MSh
195.31	sustained;] 49a; ∼∧ MSh
195.32	candle."] 49a; ∼∧" MSh
195.38–39	"No," said he, "I] 49a; "∼∧" ∼ ∼, ∧∼ MSh
196.3	Goldsmith's] 49a; Goldsmiths MSh
196.5	connection,] 49a; connexion, MSh
196.8	applause,] 49a; ∼; MSh
196.12–13	for Goldy's play,"] 49a; ∼ Goldys ∼∧' MSh; to Goldy's play." Boswell (II, 242)
196.13	who, as] 49a; ∼∧ ∼ MSh
196.14	Goldsmith's] 49a; Goldsmiths MSh
196.16	"The Belle's Stratagem,"] 49a; "∼ Belles ∼∧" MSh
196.17	comedy] 49a; Comedy MSh
196.18	hero,] 49a; ∼∧ MSh
196.19	Mrs.] 49a; ∼∧ MSh
196.19	"The Mistakes] 49a; ∧∼ "∼ MSh
196.23	servant] 49a; Sarvant MSh
196.23	Gloucester,] 49a; ∼∧ MSh
196.26	Foote's] 49a; Footes MSh
196.26	*Puppet Shew,*] T; ∼ ∼∧ MSh; *Puppetshow,* 49a
196.27	*Housemaid,*] 49a; ∼∧ MSh
*196.28	Haymarket] 49a; Hay market MSh
196.28	world,] 49a; ∼∧ MSh

196.29	unfashionable,] 49a; ~∧ MSh
196.29	crowded] 49a; crouded MSh
196.31	successful,] 49a; ~∧ MSh
196.31	sentimental comedy] 49a; Sentimental Comedy MSh
196.32	Garrick,] 49a; ~∧ MSh
196.33	down hill,] 49a; doun ~; MSh
196.34	school.] 49a; School. MSh
196.35	terms,] 49a; ~; MSh
196.36	circle] 49a; Circle MSh
196.37	comedy] 49a; Comedy MSh
197.19	and at] 49a, Cumberland (I, 368), 1825 (47); ~, ~ MSp
197.23	us that] 49a, Cumberland (I, 368); ~, ~ MSp, 1825 (47)
197.30	and when] 49a, Cumberland (I, 368), 1825 (47); ~, ~ MSp
197.37	but alas!] 49a; ~ ~, Cumberland (I, 369); ~, ~! MSp, 1825 (47)
197.39	every thing] 49a, Cumberland (I, 369), 1825 (47); everything MSp
198.2	Cumberland's memoirs] 49a; Cumberlands Memoirs MSh
198.3	romance,] 49a; ~∧ MSh
198.4	himself,] 49a; ~; MSh
198.6–7	accounts, public and private,] 49a; ~∧ ~ ~ ~∧ MSh
198.8	"received] 49a; "recieved MSh
198.8	acclamations."] 49a; ~∧" MSh
198.13	theatre,] 49a; ~∧ MSh
198.14	St. James's Park: there] 49a; S' James ~∧ There MSh
198.14	seven] 49a; Seven MSh
198.15	o'clock] T; oclock MSh; o'clock, 49a
198.15	down] 49a; doun MSh
198.15	spirit.] 49a; Spirit. MSh
198.16	theatre,] 49a; ~∧ MSh
198.19	Lumpkin's] 49a; Lumpkins MSh
198.20	mother] T; Mother MSh; mother, 49a
198.20–21	Crackskull] 49a; Crackscull MSh
198.22	"What's that? what's that!"] 49a; "Whats ~? Whats ~!∧ MSh
198.22	manager] T; Manager MSh; manager, 49a
198.23	sarcastically, "don't] 49a; ~∧ "dont MSh
198.25	nature,] 49a; ~∧ MSh
198.26	sally.] 49a; Sally MSh
198.38	manager:] 49a; ~∧ MSh
198.41	Come,] T; "~, MSp, 49a
199.2	damn'd.] 49a, Prior (II, 405); ~∧ MSp

199.14   *name.*] T; ~." MSp, 49a
199.16   newspaper] 49a; news paper MSh
199.16   himself,] 49a; ~∧ MSh
199.17–18   Macpherson,] 49a; ~∧ MSh
199.18   Goldsmith's] 49a; Goldsmiths MSh
199.19   rival, Kelly.] 49a; ~∧ ~∧ MSh
199.20   appeared:] 49a; ~∧ MSh
199.21   At Dr. Goldsmith's]; T; ~ ~∧ Goldsmiths MSh; "~ ~.
                Goldsmith's 49a
199.22   laugh,] 49a, Prior (II, 398); ~∧ MSh
199.23   deny,] 49a; ~∧ MSh
199.26   Another,] 49a; ~∧ MSh
199.26   Goldsmith,] 49a; ~∧ MSh
*199.27   staymaking:] T; stay making- MSh; stay-making: 49a
199.28   If] T; "~ MSp, 49a
199.30   surely,] 49a, Prior (II, 404); ~∧ MSp
199.31   *Stays!*] T; ~!" MSp, 49a
199.33   play;] 49a; ~, MSh
199.33   letter of Goldsmith to Craddock, written] T; letter fol-
                lowing letter of Goldsmith to Cradock written MSh;
                letter, written 49a
199.35   literature:] 49a; ~∧ MSh
*200.1–2   "MY DEAR SIR, [*paragraph*] "The play] 49a; "My Dear
                Sir, The play MSp, Forster (626)
200.3   which, however,] 49a, *Letters* (119); ~∧ ~∧ MSp,
                Forster (626)
200.8   "unless, according] 49a, *Letters* (119); "unlessaccording
                MSp, Forster (626)
200.8   theatre,] 49a, *Letters* (119); ~∧ MSp, Forster (626)
200.15   thing,] 49a, *Letters* (119); ~∧ MSp, Forster (626)
200.20–21   in agitation. [*paragraph*] "I am] 49a, *Letters* (120);
                ~ ~. I am, MSp, Forster (627)
200.21–23   servant, [*paragraph*] "OLIVER GOLDSMITH. [*paragraph*]
                "P. S. Present] 49a, *Letters* (120); ~, Oliver Gold-
                smith. P. S. Present MSp, Forster (627)
200.23   Craddock,"] T; ~."; 49a; ~.' MSp, Forster (627)
200.24   Johnson,] 49a; ~∧ MSh
200.25   "Goldy,"] 49a; "~∧" MSh
200.26   comedy] 49a, Boswell (II, 222); Comedy MSh
200.26   he, "that] 49a; ~∧ "~ MSh
200.27   audience;] 49a; ~, Boswell (II, 222); Audience; MSh
200.28   comedy–] 49a, Boswell (II, 222); Comedy– MSh

200.28	audience merry."] 49a, Boswell (II, 222); Audience $\sim_\wedge$" MSh
200.30	Northcote, the painter,] 49a; $\sim_\wedge \sim \sim_\wedge$ MSh
*200.31	Reynolds,] T; $\sim_\wedge$ MSh; $\sim$; 49a
200.31	Ralph, Sir Joshua's] 49a; $\sim_\wedge \sim$ Joshuas MSh
200.31	man,] 49a; $\sim_\wedge$ MSh
200.33	Northcote's] 49a; Northcotes MSh
200.34–35	laugh?" "Oh, exceedingly!"] 49a; $\sim$?"$-_\wedge\sim_\wedge \sim$!"– MSh; $\sim$?" "Exceedingly" Prior (II, 401)
200.35	require,"] 49a; $\sim_{\wedge\wedge}$ MSh
200.38	terms:] 49a; $\sim_\wedge$ MSh
*200.39	"In inscribing] 49a; '$\sim \sim$ MSp
201.1	piety."] 49a, Boswell (II, 203, n. 4); $\sim$.' MSp, Forster (635)
201.2	Mr. Newbery,] 49a; $\sim_\wedge \sim_\wedge$ MSh
201.2–3	agreement,] 49a; $\sim$; MSh
*201.4	preengaged] T; pre engaged MSh; pre-engaged 49a
201.6	friends,] 49a; $\sim_\wedge$ MSh
201.7	success,] 49a; $\sim_\wedge$ MSh
201.9	composition.] 49a; $\sim_\wedge$ MSh
*202.1	*CHAPTER XXXVIII*] T; ch 37 MSh; CHAPTER XXXVII. 49a
202.2	*Johnson's comments*] T; Johnsons $\sim$ MSh; Johnson's comment. 49a
202.5	authors.] 49a; Authors$_\wedge$ MSh
202.8	letter,] 49a; $\sim_\wedge$ MSh
202.9	equanimity:] 49a; $\sim_\wedge$ MSh
203.19	sort; and] 49a, Percy (105); $\sim$: $\sim$, 1825 (49); $\sim$, $\sim_\wedge$ MSp
203.22	vérité.] 49a; $\sim_\wedge$ MSh
203.23	"Tom Tickle."] 49a; "$\sim \sim_{\wedge\wedge}$ MSh
203.26	could have tolerated;] 49a; might have $\sim$, MSh
203.30	nature.] 49a; $\sim_\wedge$ MSh
203.30	paragraph, it is said,] 49a; $\sim_\wedge \sim \sim \sim_\wedge$ MSh
203.32	it;] 49a; $\sim$, MSh
203.33	excitement] 49a; excitment MSh
203.33	indignation. Accompanied] T; $\sim_\wedge$ Accompanied MSh; $\sim$, and accompanied 49a
203.33	friend,] 49a; $\sim_\wedge$ MSh
*203.35	Paternoster Row]; T; Pater noster row MSh; Paternoster-row, 49a
203.38	he, "in] 49a; $\sim_\wedge$ "$\sim$ MSh
203.40	with."] 49a; $\sim_{\wedge\wedge}$ MSh

204.1	editor.] 49a; Editor. MSh
204.2	Goldsmith's] 49a; Goldsmiths MSh
204.5–6	instant and,] T; ~ ~ₐ MSh; ~, ~, 49a
*204.6	stout, high blooded] T; ~ₐ ~ ~ MSh; ~, ~-~ 49a
*204.7	overhead] 49a; over head MSh
204.9	Dr. Kenrick,] 49a; ~ₐ ~ₐ MSh
204.10	room,] 49a; ~ₐ MSh
204.13	home,] 49a; ~ₐ MSh
204.13	commiseration,] 49a; commisseration; MSh
204.18	Newspapers] 49a; ⟨The⟩ newspapers MSp
205.15–16	newspaper] 49a; news paper MSh
205.16	Dr. Johnson's. The doctor] 49a; ~ₐ Johnson, The Doctor MSh
205.17	time,] 49a; ~ₐ MSh
205.17	Mrs. Williams,] 49a; ~ₐ ~ₐ MSh
205.19	lexicographer] 49a; Lexicographer MSh
205.19	undeceived] 49a; undecieved MSh
205.20	"Sir,"] 49a; '~,' MSh
205.20	"Goldsmith] 49a; ₐ~ MSh
205.21	him, than] 49a, Boswell (II, 198); ~ₐ ~ MSh
205.23	Sir,] 49a, Boswell (II, 198); ~ₐ MSh
205.24	well;] 49a, Boswell (II, 198); ~, MSh
205.25	done.] 49a, Boswell (II, 198); ~, MSh
205.26	comedy,] 49a, Boswell (II, 198); Comedyₐ MSh
205.27	public."] 49a; ~ₐ" MSh; publick." Boswell (II, 198)
206.1	CHAPTER XXXIX] T; Ch 38. ⟨or 39⟩ MSh; CHAPTER XXVIII. 49a
*206.2	Boswell in Holy Week] T; Boswells ⟨illegible word or syllable⟩ in Holy Week MSh; Boswell in Holy-Week 49a
206.3	Paoli's] 49a; Paolis MSh
206.4	Johnson's eulogium] 49a; Johnsons Eulogium MSh
206.5	Question about suicide] 49a; question about Suicide MSh
206.5	subserviency.] 49a; Subserviency. MSh
206.8	Holy Week.] T; ~ week. MSh; Holy-Week, 49a
206.8–9	Johnson was] 49a; ~, ↑⟨this guest [?]⟩↓ was MSh
206.10	Boswell,] 49a; ~ₐ MSh
206.10	every thing,] 49a; ~ ~ₐ MSh
206.11	"He had] 49a; ₐ~ ~ MSh
206.13	"which] 49a; ₐ~ MSh
*206.14	thinking of and] T; thinking and MSh; thinking, and 49a
206.14	Dr.] 49a; ~ₐ MSh

206.14   seem] 49a; seen MSh
*206.15   some secondhand homilies] T; Some Second Hand Ser-
                monizing ⟨to and⟩ MSh; some second-hand homilies,
                49a
206.16   Holy Week.] T; ∼ week. MSh; Holy-Week. 49a
206.18   "Sir,"] 49a; '∼ₐ' MSh
206.18   "as I take my shoes from the shoemaker,] 49a, Boswell
                (II, 202); 'as I take my Shoes from the Shoemakerₐ
                MSh
206.19   priest."] 49a, Boswell (II, 202); ∼.ₐ MSh
206.21   afterwards, the 9th of April,] 49a; afterward, the 9" April,
                MSh
206.22   Dr. Johnson] T; ∼ₐ ∼ MSh; ∼. ∼, 49a
206.27   talking."] 49a; ∼ₐ" MSh
206.29   nothing."] 49a; ∼ₐ" MSh
206.30   Boswell,] 49a; ∼ₐ MSh
206.31   journal.] 49a; Journal. MSh
206.34   increasing] 49a; encreasing MSh
206.37   "Why, sir," answered Johnson, his] 49a; "∼ₐ Sirₐ" ∼ ∼.
                ∼ MSh; "Why, sir, you Boswell (II, 368)
207.2   lady's finger."] 49a, Boswell (II, 369); ladys ∼ₐ" MSh
207.4   old General Oglethorpe] T; Old ∼ oglethorpeₐ MSh;
                old General Oglethorpe, 49a
*207.8   Soldiers on six pence a day] T; ∼ ∼ Six ∼ ∼ ∼ MSh;
                ∼, ∼ sixpence ∼ ∼, 49a
207.9   classes,] Pr.; ∼ₐ MSh
207.10   them,] Pr.; ∼ₐ MSh
*207.11–14   The conversation . . . display.] Prh
207.13   one,] 49a; ∼ₐ Prh
207.15   ladies,] Pr.; ∼ₐ MSh
*207.16   Lumpkin's song] 49a; Lumpkins Song Msh; Lumpkin⟨s'⟩
                song Pr.
207.16–17   "Three Jolly Pigeons,"] Pr.; ₐ∼ ∼ Pigions,ₐ MSh
207.17   "Humours of Ballamaguery"] T; '∼ ∼ ∼' MSh; "Humors
                ∼ ∼," Pr.
*207.21–34   It was . . . more liked] Prh
*207.21   in these] 49a; on these Prh
207.21   Goldsmith's] 49a; Goldsmiths Prh
207.25   own] 49a; oun Prh
207.26–27   ammunition] 49a; amunition Prh
207.27   tongue] 49a; ∼; Prh
207.28   thoughts,] 49a; ∼; Prh
207.30   amazing,"] 49a; ∼ₐ" Prh

207.33   else." "Yet,"] 49a; ~∧"–"~∧" Prh
207.34   *liked."*] 49a; ~∧" Prh; liked." Boswell (II, 224)
*207.35   Oglethorpe's Goldsmith] T; Oglethorpes he MSh; Ogle-
          thorpe's, Goldsmith 49a
207.36   Paoli,] 49a; ~∧ MSh
207.37   Martinelli of Florence,] T; ~∧ ~ ~∧ MSh; ~, ~
          ~, 49a
207.37   England,] 49a; ~∧ MSh
207.40   down] 49a; doun MSh
207.41   should,"] 49a; ~∧" MSh
207.41   "No, sir;" cried Johnson, "it] Pr.; '~, Sir; ~ ~∧ ∧~
          MSh
208.14   Goldsmith.] 49a, Boswell (II, 210); *paragraph* ~.– MSp
208.16   Surely,] Pr., Boswell (II, 210); ~∧ MSp
208.16–17 Johnson. "Why, sir,] T, Boswell (II, 210); ~. "~, Sir,
          MSp; ~.–"~, sir, Pr.
208.20–21 Johnson, "Yes, sir,] T, Boswell (II, 210); ~. "~, Sir,
          MSp; ~.–"~, sir, Pr.
208.25   Goldsmith's] Pr.; Goldsmiths MSh
208.26   favor.] Pr.; ~∧ MSh
208.27   "We talked,"] Pr.; ⟨"⟩ We talked, ⟨"⟩ MSh; ∧~ ~∧∧
          Boswell (II, 212)
208.27   "of the king's] 49a; ∧~ ~ ~ Boswell (II, 212); ⟨"⟩ of
          the Kings MSh; ∧~ ~ King's Pr.
208.27   Goldsmith's] Pr.; Goldsmiths Msh
208.28   play." "I] Pr.; ~.∧ '~ MSh; ~.–"~ Boswell (II, 212)
208.28   would,"] Pr.; ~∧' MSh
208.28   adding, however,] Pr., Boswell (II, 212); ~∧ ~∧ MSh
208.29   indifference,] Pr., Boswell (II, 212); ~∧ MSh
208.29   good."] Pr., Boswell (II, 212); ~∧" MSh
208.30   "Well, then, Sir,"] T; "~∧ ~, ~," MSh; "~, ~, sir,
          Boswell (II, 212); "~, ~," Pr.
208.30   Johnson laughing, "let] T; ~ ~∧ ∧~ MSh; ~, ~,
          "~ Pr.
208.31   sir,] Pr., Boswell (II, 212); Sir, MSh
208.32   ours,] Pr., Boswell (II, 212); ~∧ MSh
208.35   'And every] Pr., Boswell (II, 212); ∧~ ~ MSh
208.35   monarch's friend.'] T, Boswell (II, 212); monarchs
          ~.∧ MSh; monarch's ~,' Pr.
208.36   "Nay,"] Pr.; "~∧" MSh
208,36   Johnson, "there] Pr.; ~∧ ∧~ MSh
208.37   subject:] Pr., Boswell (II, 212); ~:- MSh
208.38   'For colleges] Pr., Boswell (II, 212); ∧~ Colleges MSh

208.38	kings] Pr., Boswell (II, 212); Kings MSh
208.39	friend,'"] Pr., Boswell (II, 212); ~.ₐ" MSh
209.1	"successful] Pr.; ₐ~ MSh
209.1–2	rebellions,"] Pr.; ~ₐ' MSh
209.2	phrase,"] Pr.; ~ₐₐ MSh
209.3	thing?"] Pr.; ~?ₐ MSh; *thing?*" Boswell (II, 212)
209.3	"Yes,"] Pr.; "~ₐ" MSh
209.4	constitution,] Pr., Boswell (II, 212); ~ₐ MSh
209.5	HAPPY REVOLUTION."] Pr., Boswell (II, 212); HAPPY REVOLUTION." MSh
209.6	Jacobitism,] Pr., Boswell (II, 212); ~ₐ MSh
209.9	distinction,] Pr.; ~ₐ MSh
209.11	king] 49a; King MSh
209.11	Boswell,] 49a; ~ₐ MSh
209.11	out,] 49a; ~ₐ MSh
209.13	general] 49a; General MSh
209.13	"Monsieur Goldsmith," said he, "est] 49a; ₐ~ ~,ₐ ~ ~ₐ ₐ~ₐ MSh; "*Monsieur Goldsmith est* Boswell (II, 213)
209.15	appercevoir." (Mr.] 49a; ~ₐₐ (~ₐ MSh
209.16	pearls] 49a; pearles MSh
209.16	perceiving it.)] 49a; percieving itₐ) MSh
209.17	"Tres-bien dit, et tres-élégamment,"] 49a; Tres-bien dit, et tres-élégamment- MSh; "*Très bien dit, et très élégamment.*" Boswell (II, 445)
*209.20	of Mr. Harris] T; of a Mrₐ Harris MSh; of a Mr. Harris, 49a, 49b, 49c, E; of Mr. Harris, 50
209.21–22	better,"] 49a; ~ₐ" MSh
209.22	worthy,] 49a, Boswell (II, 214); ~ₐ MSh
209.23	"Nay, sir,"] 49a; '~, Sir,' MSh; "~, sir, Boswell (II, 214)
209.25	Grecian."] 49a, Boswell (II, 214); ~ₐ" MSh
209.26	scrape and seized] T; ~ ~ siezed MSh; ~, ~ seized 49a
209.27	performers,"] 49a; ~ₐ" MSh
209.27	he, dextrously] 49a; ~ₐ ~ MSh
209.28	Giardini, I am told,] 49a, Boswell (II, 214); ~ₐ ~ ~ ~ₐ MSh
209.29	"That is] 49a, Boswell (II, 214); ₐ~ ~ MSh
*209.30	get," observed Johnson, "who does] 49a; get, who does MSh
209.32	shown] 49a; shoun MSh
209.36	fiddle stick,] T; ~ ~ₐ MSh; fiddlestick, 49a; fiddle-stick, Boswell (II, 214)
209.36	nothing."] 49a; ~ₐ" MSh

209.37   whole,] 49a; ∼ₐ MSh
209.39   heedless, often illogical,] 49a; ∼ₐ ∼ ∼ₐ MSh
209.43   Mr. Thrale's] 49a; ∼ₐ Thrales MSh
210.1   suicide.] 49a; ∼ₐ MSh
210.1   think, sir,"] 49a; ∼, ∼,ₐ Boswell (II, 217); ∼ₐ Sir," MSh
210.1   Boswell,] 49a; ∼ₐ MSh
210.2   mad?"] 49a, Boswell (II, 217); ∼!" MSh
210.2   "Sir,"] 49a; ₐ∼ₐ" MSh
210.2   Johnson, "they] 49a; ∼ₐ ₐ∼ MSh
210.5   thought," added he, "that] 49a; ∼ₐ" ∼ ∼ₐ ₐ∼ MSh
210.7   don't] 49a, Boswell (II, 217); dont MSh
210.8   "Nay, but my dear sir,"] 49a; "∼, ∼, ∼ ∼ ∼,ₐ Boswell (II, 217); "∼, ∼ ∼ ∼ Sir," MSh
210.8–9   Johnson, "why] 49a; ∼ₐ ₐ∼ MSh
210.10   Goldsmith,] 49a; ∼ₐ MSh
210.11   restrain him?"] 49a, Boswell (II, 217); ∼ ∼." MSh
210.12   Johnson, "that] 49a; ∼ₐ ₐ∼ MSh
210.14   conscience,] 49a, Boswell (II, 217); ∼ₐ MSh
210.26–27   *presence,"*] 49a; ∼·ₐ MSh
*210.28   truth,] 49a; ∼ₐ MSh
210.28   Dr. Johnson,] 49a; ∼ₐ ∼ₐ MSh
210.29   said,] 49a; ∼ₐ MSh
210.32   forth,] 49a; ∼ₐ MSh
210.33   Mr. Boswell] T; ∼ₐ ∼ MSh; ∼. ∼, 49a
210.35   nay,] 49a; ∼ₐ MSh
210.38   doctor] 49a; Doctor MSh
210.38   Boswell, or Bozzy] T; ∼ₐ ∼ ∼ MSh; ∼, ∼ ∼, 49a
*210.39   eavesdropping] 49a; eves dropping MSh
210.40   Thrale's] 49a; Thrales MSh
*210.40–41   there, Sir?" cried he, turning round angrily and] T; ∼ₐ Sir, turning round angrily and MSh; ∼, sir?" cried he, turning round angrily, and 49a
210.42   table, Sir."] T; ∼, Sirₐ" MSh; ∼, sir." 49a
211.1   face.] 49a; ∼, MSh
211.1   seat,] 49a; ∼ₐ MSh
211.2   Johnson,] 49a; ∼ₐ MSh
211.3   show him when the doctor] T; shew ∼ ∼ ∼ Doctor MSh; ∼ ∼, ∼ ∼ doctor 49a
211.4   authoritatively, "What] 49a; ∼ₐ ₐ∼ MSh
211.5–6   place, Sir;"–and] T; ∼ₐ Sirₐ"–∼ MSh; ∼, sir;"–and 49a
211.6   spaniel] 49a; Spaniel MSh
211.7   doctor,] 49a; Doctor, MSh

211.9	Johnson,] 49a; ~, MSh
211.10	man.] 49a; ~, MSh
211.10–11	questions,] 49a; ~, MSh
211.11	do, sir?] 49a; ~, Sir? MSh; ~, sir, Forster (597)
211.11	say, sir?] 49a; ~, Sir. MSh; *say sir,*' Forster (597)
211.13	*question!*" roared he. "Don't] 49a; ~." ~ ~." ,Dont MSh; *question.* 'Don't Forster (597)
211.13	sir,] 49a, Forster (597); Sir, MSh
211.14	gentleman?] 49a, Forster (587); gentleman, MSh
211.15	cow's] 49a, Forster (598); cows MSh
211.15	fox's tail bushy?"] 49a; ~ ~ ~?' Forster (598); foxes ~ ~, " MSh
211.16	"Why, sir,"] 49a; "~, Sir," MSh
*211.16	pill garlick,] T; ~ ~, MSh; pil-garlick, 49a
211.16	"you] 49a; ,~ MSh
211.17	"Sir," replied Johnson,] 49a; "~," ~ ~, MSh
211.18	sir;"] 49a; Sir;" MSh; sir,' Forster (598)
211.19	occasion, "yourself] 49a; ~. "Yourself MSh
211.20	Boswell's] 49a; Boswells MSh
211.21	father,] 49a; ~, MSh
211.21	Auchinleck (or Affleck.)] T; ~ (~ ~,) MSh; ~, (~ ~.) 49a
211.23	hero;] 49a; ~, MSh
211.23–24	Dr. Johnson,] 49a; ~, ~, MSh
211.24	pedagogue,] 49a; ~. MSh
*211.25	There's] 49a; '~ MSp
*211.25–26	mon," said he to a friend; "Jamie] 49a; ~., ↑~ ~ ~ ~ ~;↓ ,~ MSp
211.29	acaadamy."] 49a; ~.' MSp
211.30	show] 49a; shew MSh
211.30	Jamie's] 49a; Jamies MSh
211.31	unrewarded.] 49a; ~, MSh
212.1	*CHAPTER XL*] T; CHAPTER XL. 49a; ch 39- MSh
212.2	*Johnson's*] 49a; Johnsons MSh
212.4	Literary Club] 49a; ~ club MSh
*212.6	exclusiveness] T; exclusive character MSh; exclusiveness, 49a
212.9	David briskly;] T; ~ ~, MSh; ~, ~; 49a
212.9	"When Sir] 49a; , ~ ~ MSh
212.10	Dr. Johnson," says Boswell, "he] 49a; ~, ~., ~ ~, ,~ MSh
212.11	actor's conceit.] 49a; Actors Conciet, MSh
212.11	*'He'll be of us?*'] 49a; "~ ~ ~ ~?, MSh

212.11   'How does] 49a; ∧~ ~ MSh
212.12   duke] 49a, Boswell (I, 493); Duke MSh
212.13   language.'"] 49a; ~.∧∧ MSh; ~.∧" Boswell (I, 493)
212.14–15   Garrick's pretensions, "Sir,"] 49a; Garricks ~∧ "~∧" MSh
212.15   buffoonery."] 49a; ~∧" MSh
212.16   Mr. Thrale,] 49a; ~∧ ~∧ MSh
*212.17   admission, he would black-ball] 49a; ~∧ ~ ~ ~∧ ~ MSh
212.17   "Who, sir?"] 49a; "~, Sir?' MSh
212.18   surprise;] 49a; ~, MSh
212.18   "Mr. Garrick–] 49a; "~∧ ~, MSh
212.18   companion–black-ball] 49a, Boswell (I, 493); ~,– blackball MSh
212.19   sir,"] 49a; Sir,∧ MSh
212.20–21   society like ours,] 49a, Boswell (I, 493); Society ~ ~– MSh
212.22   'Unelbowed . . . player.'"] T; ∧~ . . . ~∧" MSh; "'~ . . . ~.'" 49a; 'Unelbow'd . . . ~.'" Boswell (I, 493)
212.23   Garrick,] 49a; ~∧ MSh
212.25   it–what] 49a; ~, ~ MSh
212.25   there–whether] 49a; ~, ~ MSh
212.26   rigor] 49a; rigour MSh
212.31   augmented.] 49a; ~∧ MSh
212.32   increase] 49a; encrease MSh
*212.32   Goldsmith. It] T; ~∧ ~ MSh; ~. "~ 49a
212.33   meetings; "for] T; ~∧ "~ MSh; ~; ∧~ 49a
212.34   among us," said he;] T; ~ ~∧" ~ ~, MSh; ~ ~: we Boswell (V, 62); amongst us," said he; 49a
212.34   each other's minds."] 49a; ~ others ~∧" MSh; one another's minds. Boswell (V, 62)
212.35   he,] 49a; ~∧ MSh
212.36   mind, I promise you."] 49a, Boswell (V, 62); ~∧ ~ ~ ~∧" MSh
212.36   Sir Joshua,] 49a; ~ ~∧ MSh
212.37   mind,] 49a; ~∧ MSh
213.1   Goldsmith's] 49a; Goldsmiths MSh
213.3   election,] 49a; ~∧ MSh
213.5   Beauclerc's friend Lord Charlemont; and] T; Beauclercs ~∧ ~ ~; And MSh; Beauclerc's ~, ~ ~; and 49a
213.6   Mr.,] 49a; ~∧∧ MSh
213.6   Orientalist,] 49a; orientalist∧ MSh
213.7   time a young] 49a; ~ a a ~ MSh
213.10   Goldsmith,] 49a; ~∧ MSh

213.10	23d] 49a; 23ᵈ MSh
213.12	Club,] T; club∧ MSh; club, 49a
213.12	place at] 49a; place on MSh
213.12	30th);] 49a; 30ʰ)∧ MSh
213.14	candidate.] 49a; Candidate. MSh
213.17	"The honor] 49a; ∧~ ~ MSh; ∧the honour Forster (272)
213.17	Turk's Head Club,"] 49a; Turks head club∧∧ MSh; Turk's Head Club∧∧ Forster (272)
213.18	"is not] 49a; ∧~ ~ MSh
213.19	Surrey." What] T; ~·∧ ~ MSh; ~:" what 49a
213.20	it?] 49a; ~. MSh
213.20	simple:] 49a; simple· MSh
213.22	lexicographer] 49a; Lexicographer MSh
213.24	candidate,] 49a; Candidate∧ MSh
213.25	own coining. He was *clubable*.] T; oun Coining. He was *Clubable*. MSh; own coining: he was *clubable*. 49a
213.27	made;] 49a; ~, MSh
213.29	pleased,] 49a; ~∧ MSh
213.30	satisfied. Beside,] T; ~. ~∧ MSh; ~: besides, 49a
213.30	faults,] 49a; ~; MSh
213.32	place,] 49a; ~∧ MSh
213.36	known.] 49a; knoun. MSh
213.40	dinner,] 49a; Dinner, MSh
213.40	Burke,] 49a; ~∧ MSh
213.41	Goldsmith and Mr.] T; ~ ~ ~∧ MSh; ~, ~ ~. 49a
213.43	"unbend . . . fool"] 49a; '~ . . . ~' MSh
214.3	"an old] 49a; '~ ~ MSh
214.3	blanket,"] 49a; ~,∧ MSh
*214.4	suppose therefore] T; ~ there fore MSh; ~, therefore, 49a
*214.7–8	of Doctor Johnson himself. [*paragraph*] With all his gravity he possessed a deep] 49a; of the Great Lexicographer himself, who, with all his gravity, possessed a deep MSh
214.9–12	quiet humor, . . . on them.] Prh, 49a; quiet humor. MSh
214.12	Rising,] 49a; ~∧ Prh
214.13	chair] Prh; ~, 49a
214.14	delivered *ex cathedra*] Prh; ~, ~ ~, 49a
214.14–15	mock solemn charge,] 49a; Mock Solemn charge; Prh
214.15	member] 49a; Member Prh
214.16	the Club;] Prh; ~ club; 49a
214.16	do and] Prh; ~, ~ 49a
214.17	latter no doubt] Prh; ~, ~ ~ ', 49a

214.18	habits which] 49a; ∼, ∼ Prh
214.20	down] 49a; doun Prh
214.20	known] 49a; knoun Prh
214.21	parties,] 49a; ∼ₐ Prh
215.1	*CHAPTER XLI*] 49a; ch 40 MSh
215.2	*Dilly's*] 49a; Dillys MSh
215.2	*Conversations on natural history*] 49a; conversations on Natural History MSh
215.2	*Intermeddling*] 49a; intermeddling MSh
215.3	*Dispute about toleration*] 49a; dispute about Toleration MSh
215.3	*Johnson's*] 49a; Johnsons MSh
215.4	*Man worship*] T; man ∼ MSh; Man-worship 49a
*215.6	serio-comic] 49a; ∼ₐ ∼ MSh
215.8	booksellers] T; Booksellers MSh; booksellers, 49a
215.8	Poultry,] 49a; ∼ₐ MSh
215.10	Dr. Johnson,] T; ∼ₐ ∼, MSh; ∼. ∼; 49a
215.12	work."] 49a; ∼ₐ" MSh
215.13	occasions,] 49a; ∼ₐ MSh
215.14	Goldsmith's] 49a; Goldsmith MSh
215.14	show] 49a; shew MSh
*215.18	the poet] T; Goldsmith MSh; the poet, 49a
215.21–22	swallows,] 49a; Swallows, MSh
215.22–23	ones," said he, "migrate,] 49a; ∼ₐ" ∼ ∼ₐ ∧∼, MSh
215.24	"Birds,"] 49a; "∼ₐ" MSh
215.26	ever build."] 49a; ∼ ∼ₐ" MSh
215.27	bird's] 49a; birds MSh
215.28	again."] 49a; ∼ₐ" MSh
215.28	Johnson, "that] 49a; ∼ₐ ∧∼ MSh
215.30	lay,] 49a, Boswell (II, 233); ∼ₐ MSh
215.32	history,] 49a, Boswell (II, 233); ∼ₐ MSh
215.33	in it."] 49a, Boswell (II, 233); ∼ ∼·ₐ MSh
215.34	placid,] 49a; ∼ₐ MSh
215.34	manner,] 49a; ∼ₐ MSh
215.36–37	clergymen; another, Mr. Toplady,] 49a; ∼, ∼ₐ ∼ₐ ∼ₐ MSh
215.38	zealous,] 49a; ∼ₐ MSh
215.40	company,] 49a; ∼ₐ MSh
216.2	debate."] 49a; ∼ₐ" MSh
216.4	Boswell's] 49a; Boswells MSh
216.11	misinterpretation,] 49a; ∼ₐ MSh
216.14	gamester,] 49a, Boswell (II, 238); ∼ₐ MSh
216.14	night,] 49a, Boswell (II, 238); ∼ₐ MSh

216.17 Johnson,] 49a; ~∧ MSh
216.18 perceive] 49a; percieve MSh
216.19 down,] 49a; doun, MSh
216.20 Johnson,] 49a; ~∧ MSh
216.20 tone,] 49a, Boswell (II, 238); ~∧ MSh
216.22 him, Goldsmith,] 49a; ~∧ ~, MSh
216.23 seized] 49a; siezed MSh
216.24 Johnson,] 49a; ~∧ MSh
216.26 him."] 49a; ~∧" MSh
216.26 lexicographer's] 49a; Lexicographers MSh
216.28 he sternly,] T; ~ ~∧ MSh; ~, ~, 49a
216.30 reply,] 49a, Boswell (II, 239); ~∧ MSh
216.33 club, he seized] 49a; Club∧ he siezed MSh
216.34–35 great lexicographer.] 49a; Great Lexicographer. MSh
216.35 pity," he said, "that] 49a; ~∧∧ ~ ~∧ ∧~ MSh
216.36 himself."] 49a; ~.∧ MSh
216.38 conversation;] 49a; ~, MSh
216.39 company, replied, "Madam,] 49a; ~∧ ~∧ '~, MSh
216.40 pounds."] T; ~.⟨"⟩ MSh; ~∧" 49a
216.42 sir,"] 49a; Sir," MSh; sir,∧ Boswell (II, 241)
216.43 purse."] 49a; ~∧" MSh; ~!" Boswell (II, 241)
217.2 subsided,] 49a; ~∧ MSh
217.4 "brooding,"] 49a; "~∧" MSh
217.5 received."] 49a; recieved." MSh
217.5 Johnson's] 49a; Johnsons MSh
217.6 towards him;] 49a; toward ~∧ MSh
217.6 nature, "I'll] 49a; ~∧ 'Ill MSh
217.7 me,"] 49a; ~,∧ MSh
217.7 voice, "Dr. Goldsmith,"] 49a; ~∧ "~∧ ~∧∧ MSh
217.8 to-day] 49a, Boswell (II, 241); ~∧ ~ MSh
217.8–9 *I ask your pardon."*] 49a; ~ ~ ~ ~!" MSh; I ask your
         pardon." Boswell (II, 241)
217.9 The ire] 49a; *paragraph* ~ ~ MSh
217.9 instant,] 49a; ~∧ MSh
217.11 heart.] 49a; ~∧- MSh
217.11 you, sir,"] 49a; ~∧ ~," MSh; ~, ~,∧ Boswell (II, 241)
217.11–12 he, "that] 49a; ~∧ ∧~ MSh
217.12 "And so," adds Boswell, "the] 49a; ∧ and ~,∧ ~ ~, ∧~
         MSh
217.13 ever,] 49a, Boswell (II, 241); ~∧ MSh
217.14 usual."] 49a; ~.∧ MSh, Boswell (II, 241)
217.14 poet's] 49a; poets MSh
217.15 Boswell.] 49a; ~∧ MSh

217.19   autocrat.] 49a; Autocrat. MSh
217.21   "Sir,] 49a; '~, MSh
217.22   republic."] 49a; ~ₐ" MSh; republick." Boswell (II, 242)
217.24   him, an] 49a; ~ₐ ⟨when⟩ an MSh
217.25   keeper] 49a; Keeper MSh
217.26   Perceiving Dr. Johnson] 49a; percieving ~ₐ ~- MSh
217.27   speak, exclaimed, "Stay, stay!] 49a; Speakₐ ~ₐ "~,
              Stay; MSh; him, saying, "Stay, stay - Boswell (II, 242)
217.27-28   something." "And] 49a; ~ₐₐ ₐ~ MSh
217.28   sir,"] 49a; Sir," MSh
217.28   Goldsmith sharply,] T; ~ Sharply, MSh; ~, sharply, 49a
217.30   rebuke,] 49a; ~ₐ MSh
217.31   perceive] 49a; percieve MSh
217.34   Graham,] 49a; ~ₐ MSh
217.34   who,] 49a; ~ₐ MSh
217.36   another." "Doctor,"] 49a; ~ₐ - " - Doctor," MSh
217.36   ecstasy] 49a; extacy MSh
217.38   "Eton."] 49a, Boswell (II, 330); "~."- MSh
217.38   you,"] 49a; ~ₐ" MSh
217.39   Goldsmith.] T; ~.⟨"⟩ MSh; ~." 49a
217.39   "No. no!"] 49a; "~ₐ - ~!" MSh
217.39   "'tis] 49a, Boswell (II, 330); "ₐ~ MSh
217.40   mean, Doctor] 49a; ~ₐ~ MSh; ~, Dr. Boswell (II, 330)
217.40   'tis] 49a, Boswell (II, 330); ₐ~ MSh
217.40   there." "You] 49a; ~ₐ" - ₐ~ MSh
217.40-41   conceive,"] 49a; concieveₐ" MSh
217.42   Goldsmith,] 49a; ~ₐ MSh
217.42   hornet."] 49a; ~ₐ" MSh
218.1   humor] 49a; humour MSh
218.1   bitterness:] 49a; ~ₐ MSh
218.1   Graham," said he,] 49a; ~ₐ" ~ ~ₐ MSh
218.2   suicide."] 49a; ~ₐ" MSh
218.6   Dilly's] T; Dillys MSh; Dilly's, 49a
218.8   Goldsmith,] 49a; ~ₐ MSh
218.12   Johnson,] 49a; ~ₐ MSh
218.15   (Dr. Wolcot)] 49a; (~ₐ ~) MSh
218.15   *jeux d'esprit*] 49a; *jeux d'Esprit* MSh
218.16   epistle] 49a; apestle[?] MSh
218.16   tour,] 49a; ~: MSh
218.19   forth,] 49a; ~ₐ MSh
*218.21-31   to frighten . . . at his tail!] 49a
219.1   *CHAPTER XLII*] T; CHAPTER XLII. 49a; ⟨ch 41⟩ ch 42
              MSh

219.3	*Beattie's*] 49a; Beatties MSh
*219.4	*A high minded*] T; a ∼ ∼ MSh; A high-minded 49a
219.7	future—for impending] 49a; ∼; ⟨to⟩ for ⟨the⟩ impending MSh
219.8	increasing.] 49a; encreasing. MSh
219.10	scale,] 49a; ∼ₐ MSh
219.13	ethics;] 49a; Ethics; MSh
219.14	Beautiful,] 49a; beautiful; MSh
219.14	system of philosophy,] 49a; System of Philosophyₐ MSh
219.15	political science;] 49a; Political Science; MSh
219.15	Reynolds an essay on painting;] T; ∼ ∼ Essay on Painting; MSh; ∼, ∼ essay on painting; 49a
219.17	Dr.] 49a; ∼ₐ MSh
219.19	science.] 49a; Science. MSh
*219.20	whole.] 49a; ∼.- MSh
219.23	judgment] 49a; judgement MSh
219.29	Goldsmith's] 49a; Goldsmiths MSh
*219.29	always] 49a; at always MSh
219.33	Russell Street,] T; ∼ ∼ₐ MSh; Russell-street, 49a
219.34	booksellers," said he,] 49a; Booksellersₐ" ∼ ∼ₐ MSh
*219.35	importance,] 49a, Forster (671); ∼ₐ MSh
219.36	undertaking,] 49a; ∼ₐ MSh
219.38	acquainted."] 49a; ∼". MSh
220.3	whole,] 49a; ∼ₐ MSh
220.6	occasion,] 49a; ∼ₐ MSh
220.7	Natural History,] 49a; ∼ historyₐ MSh
220.7	Dr.] 49a; ∼ₐ MSh
220.7	himself,] 49a; ∼ₐ MSh
220.9	urgent,] 49a; ∼; MSh
*220.10–11	Temple, where they] 49a; ∼. They MSh
220.13	open] 49a; ∼; MSh
220.15	off, related] 49a; ∼ₐ ∼ MSh
220.16	Dr. Percy smiling.] T; ∼ₐ ∼ ∼: MSh; ∼. ∼, ∼. 49a
220.16	atom," replied Cradock;] 49a; Atom," ∼ ∼, MSh
220.17	"Not I! I scarcely] 49a; "∼ ∼!" I carcely MSh
220.17	swan: however,] 49a; Swan. However, MSh; swan; however Prior (II, 438)
220.19	it, made] 49a; ∼ₐ ∼ MSh
220.20	own] 49a; oun MSh
220.21	Windsor,] 49a; ∼ₐ MSh
220.22	engagements,] 49a; ∼ₐMSh
220.23	current,] 49a; ∼ₐ MSh

220.27 volume, Gibbon, the historian,] 49a; ~∧ ~∧ ~ His-
     torian∧ MSh

220.28 "You] 49a; ∧~ MSh

220.28 see,"] 49a; ~,∧ MSh

220.30 king] 49a; King MSh

220.31 trouble?" "Montezuma,"] 49a; ~?" - "~∧" MSh

220.31 Gibbon sportively.] T; ~ Sportively. MSh; ~, sportively.
     49a

220.32 reflection,] 49a; ~; MSh

220.33 recollect] 49a; reccollect MSh

220.33 himself,] 49a; ~; MSh

220.33 name, Porus.] 49a; ~∧ ~.' MSh

220.36 booksellers] 49a; Booksellers MSh

220.41 scheme,] 49a; ~∧ MSh

220.41 hopes,] 49a; ~∧ MSh

220.42 Goldsmith's] 49a; Goldsmiths MSh

221.4 Goldsmith,] 49a; ~∧ MSh

221.5 them, they] 49a; ~∧ ~ MSh

221.7 by Parson Scott, the cabinet emissary.] 49a; by ⟨Dr∧
     Scott⟩ ↑Parson↓ Scott the cabinet emissary; ⟨and had
     preferred poverty ↑independ.↓ and his garret to⟩ MSh

221.8 "*his garret*,"] 49a; '~ ~∧' MSh

221.9 remain.] 49a; ~∧ MSh

221.10 Truth,] 49a; ~∧ MSh

221.11 ecstasy.] 49a; extacy. MSh

221.14–15 doctor of civil law] T; Doctor of Civil law MSh; doctor
     of civil law, 49a

221.15 king] 49a; King MSh

221.18 might without vanity] 49a; ~, ~ ~, MSh

221.19–20 feelings. "Here's] 49a; ~, "Heres MSh

221.20 stir,"] 49a; ~∧" MSh

221.20 Thrale's table,] 49a; Thrales ~∧ MSh

221.22 "Ah, Doctor!"] 49a; '~∧ ~," MSh

221.22 Johnson,] 49a; ~∧ MSh

°221.23 sixpences you know] T; six pences ~ ~ MSh; sixpences,
     you know, 49a

221.23 guinea."] 49a; ~∧" MSh

221.25 thing."] 49a; ~∧" MSh

221.27 Goldsmith;] 49a; ~∧ MSh

°221.29 "Every body," exclaimed] 49a; "~ ~∧" exclaims MSh

221.29 Mrs. Thrale, "loves] 49a; ~∧ ~∧ '~ MSh

221.29 Dr. Beattie] T; ~∧ ~ MSh; ~. ~, 49a; Doctor Beattie∧
     Forster (666)

221.32	ill-natured."] 49a; ~-~?' Forster (666); ~ₐ ~ₐ" MSh
*221.35	extravagant,] 49a; ~:[?] MSh
221.36	uncharitableness.] 49a; ~ₐ MSh
221.36	annoyance,] 49a; ~ₐ MSh
221.39	doctor's] 49a; doctors MSh
221.40	angel of truth] 49a; Angels of Truth MSh
*221.40–42	while Voltaire figures as one of the demons of infidelity, sophistry, and falsehood, driven into utter darkness.] 49a; while the demons of infidelity sophistry and falsehood; typified by Hume and Voltaire, were driven into outer darkness. MSh
221.43	known] 49a; knoun MSh
222.3	Joshua,] 49a; ~ₐ MSh
222.4–5	years, while Voltaire's] 49a, Forster (667); ~; ~ Voltaires MSh
*222.5	for ever.] 49a, Forster (667); forever. MSh
223.1	*CHAPTER XLIII*] T; Ch 4 ⟨2⟩ ↑3↓. MSh; CHAPTER XLIII. 49a
*223.2	*green room*] T; Green room MSh; green-room 49a
223.4	*an invitation*] 49a; An ~ MSh
223.10	application,] 49a; ~ₐ MSh
223.11	composition.] 49a; ~ₐ MSh
223.12	good humor] T; ~ humour MSh; good-humor, 49a
223.24	heavens, Mr. Foote,"] 49a; ~ₐ ~ₐ ~," MSh
223.25	Haymarket] 49a; Hay market MSh
223.25	theatre, "what] 49a; ~ₐ ₐ~ MSh
223.25	humdrum] 49a; hum drum MSh; *humdrum* Forster (527)
223.25	Dr.] 49a; ~ₐ MSh
223.26	green-room] 49a, Forster (527); ~ₐ ~ MSh
223.27	poetry!"] 49a, Forster (527); ~." MSh
223.27	that, madam,"] 49a; ~ₐ ~,' Forster (527); ~ₐ Madam," MSh
223.28	players."] 49a; ~ₐ" MSh
223.29	Beauclerc's] 49a; Beauclercs MSh
223.29	Charlemont,] 49a; ~ₐ MSh
223.30	Ireland,] 49a; ~ₐ MSh
223.32	he; "we] 49a; ~," ₐWe MSh
223.32	entertained, as usual,] 49a; ~ₐ ~ ~ₐ MSh
223.33	Goldsmith's] 49a; Goldsmiths MSh
223.34	threatens,] 49a; ~ₐ MSh
223.37	annoyance–Johnson] 49a; ~ₐ ~ MSh
223.37	books;] 49a; ~. MSh
223.38	*flowers;* and last,] 49a; ~ₐ ~, ~ₐ MSh

*224.3   wore] 49a; wears MSh

224.3   He had] 49a; He has MSh

224.5   Reynolds, who perceived] 49a; ∼∧ ∼ percieved MSh

224.5   mind,] 49a; ∼∧ MSh

224.12   oriental splendor] 49a; Oriental Splendor MSh

224.14–15   gardens," says the Chinese philosopher,] 49a; ∼∧" ∼ ∼ chinese ∼∧ MSh

224.17   full-bodied] 49a, *Works* (II, 294); ∼∧ ∼ MSh

224.18   grove,] 49a, Works (II, 294); ∼∧ MSh

224.19   gayly] 49a, *Works* (II, 294); gaily (MSh)

224.22   lawgiver,] 49a, *Works* (II, 294); ∼∧ MSh

224.30   skilful] 49a; skillful MSh

224.30–31   Goldsmith's] 49a; Goldsmiths MSh

224.31   him. "I] 49a; ∼. ∧∼ MSh

224.33   works;] 49a, Prior (II, 443); ∼, MSh

224.38   "Goldsmith," said he,] 49a; "∼∧" ∼ ∼∧ MSh

224.39   copies,] 49a, Prior (II, 444); ∼∧ MSh

224.39   them.'] 49a; ∼∧" MSh

224.41   proceedings.] 49a, Prior (II, 444); ∼." MSh

225.3   'Here] 49a; "∼ MSh

225.4   *midnight,*] 49a; ∼∧ MSh; midnight, Prior (II, 444)

225.4   them.' 'These,'] 49a; ∼." "∼∧" MSh

225.4–5   I, 'are] 49a; ∼∧ "∼ MSh

225.5   indeed.' 'They] 49a; ∼.' - '∼ MSh

225.6   arts and sciences,'"] 49a; ∼ ∼ ∼.' Prior (II, 444); Arts and Sciences." MSh

225.8–9   dictionary,] 49a; Dictionary∧ MSh

225.10   Philosophy."] 49a; ∼∧∧– MSh

225.11   nothing,] 49a; ∼∧ MSh

225.14   enterprises,] 49a; enterprize, MSh

225.15   Cradock's] 49a; Cradocks MSh

225.17   "The day] 49a; ∧∼ ∼ MSh

225.18   replied 'I will,] T, Prior (II, 444); ∼ ∧∼ ∼∧ MSh; ∼, '∼ ∼, 49a

225.19   'Nay,'] 49a, Prior (II, 444); '∼∧' MSh

225.21   'Well,'] 49a, Prior (II, 444); '∼∧' MSh

225.22   Mrs. Cradock] T, Prior (II, 444); ∼∧ ∼ MSh; ∼. ∼, 49a

225.23   you.'] 49a; ∼∧∧ MSh

225.24   "The Doctor] T, Prior (II, 444); '∼ ∼ MSh; "∼ doctor 49a

225.24   newspapers] 49a, Prior (II, 445); News papers MSh

225.24–25   pamphlets,] 49a, Prior (II, 445); ∼∧ MSh

225.26   fish,] 49a, Prior (II, 445); ∼∧ MSh

*225.26–27 and a tart;] 49a, Prior (II, 445); and some fish; MSh

225.29 while,] 49a, Prior (II, 445); $\sim_\wedge$ MSh

225.29 day's] 49a; days MSh

225.31 Mrs.] 49a; $\sim_\wedge$ MSh

225.34 gate."] 49a; $\sim_\wedge$" MSh

225.36 recollections] 49a; reccollections MSh

225.39 autumn.] 49a; Autumn. MSh

225.40 Mrs. Yates, an actress] 49a; $\sim_\wedge$ $\sim_\wedge$ $\sim$ Actress MSh

225.41 esteem,] 49a; $\sim_\wedge$ MSh

225.41 poetical exordium of his composition.] 49a; Poetical Exordium of his Composition. MSh

226.3 received] 49a; recieved MSh

226.6 another Christmas] 49a; $\sim$ christmas MSh

*226.7 country Christmas!] 49a; $\sim$ christmas! MSh

*226.8 fireside] 49a; fire side MSh

226.9 bachelor's] 49a; bachelors MSh

226.10 means?] 49a; $\sim$. MSh

226.12 resource,] 49a; $\sim_\wedge$ MSh

226.14 Newbery's note,] 49a; Newberys $\sim_\wedge$ MSh

226.14 security,] 49a; $\sim_\wedge$ MSh

226.16 insure] 49a; ensure MSh

226.16 payment,] 49a; $\sim_\wedge$ MSh

226.17 Newbery's] 49a; Newberys MSh

226.17 comedy] 49a; Comedy MSh

226.18 "The Good Natured Man"] T; the $\sim$ $\sim$ man$_\wedge$ MSh; $_\wedge$the Good-natured Man$_\wedge$ 49a

*226.18–19 as Garrick] 49a; as Mr$_\wedge$ Garrick MSh

226.20 comedy,] 49a; $\sim$; MSh

226.21 own] 49a; oun MSh

226.25 thank you.] 49a; $\sim$ $\sim_\wedge$ MSh; $\sim$ $\sim$! Forster (674)

226.28 refusal. * * * * I] 49a; $\sim$. – – – – $\sim$ MSh

226.29 sixty pounds and] T; Sixty $\sim$ $\sim$ MSh; sixty $\sim$, $\sim$ 49a; $\sim$ pound $\sim$ Forster (674)

226.31–32 Ever, / "Oliver Goldsmith."] 49a; $\sim$, $_\wedge\sim$ $\sim$–" MSh

*226.36 circle and a Christmas fireside at Barton.] 49a; $\sim$ at Barton. MSh

*227.1 *CHAPTER XLIV*] T; CHAPTER XLIV. 49a; ch 43. MSh

227.2 *Forced*] T; forced MSh, 49a

227.4 *poet*] T; Poet MSh, 49a

227.4 *Grief*] T; grief MSh, 49a

227.4 *A last*] 49a, Pr.; a last MSh

227.11 interrupted,] Pr.; $\sim_\wedge$ MSh

227.14 volume] T; Volume MSh; volume, Pr.

227.14   schools.] Pr.; Schools∧ MSh
227.15   receives] Pr.; recieves MSh
*227.18–19   drudging, depressing kind,] 49a; ∼, ⟨unexciting⟩ kind,
                Pr.; ∼, unexciting ∼, MSh
*227.19   faint. "If] 49a; ∼. ⟨It seems with him⟩ He MSh; faint.
                ⟨He⟩ Pr.
227.21   lacerates] 49a; lascerates Prh
227.23–24   author's task sickness,] 49a; authors ∼, ∼∧ Prh
*227.26   Goldsmith again] Prh; He again MSh; ⟨He⟩ again Pr.
227.27   society. "Our club,"] Pr.; ∼; ⟨a mode of dissipating care
                reccomended in his essays.⟩ "Our Club∧" MSh; "Our
                club," Prior (II, 510)
227.29   time."] Pr.; ∼∧" MSh
227.30   poet's] Pr.; poets MSh
*227.32–33   companion's heartsick] T; companions heart sick MSh;
                companion's heart-sick Pr.
227.34   chambers] Pr.; chambres MSh
227.35   Temple; the] Pr.; ∼∧ ⟨and at an expense⟩ the MSh
227.38   up, Johnson] Pr.; ∼∧ ∼ MSh
228.1   untasted.] Pr.; ∼: MSh
228.4   harassed] Pr.; harrassed MSh
*228.7   serene quiet, and] 49a; Serene ∼, and Pr.; serene ∼∧ ∼
                MSh
228.12   extinguished,] Pr.; ∼∧ MSh
228.15   occasionally] 49a; occasionly MSh
228.16   St. James's] 49a; S. James's MSh
228.16   At these dinners as usual] T; ∧↑at ∼ ∼↓ As ∼ MSh;
                ∼ ∼ ∼, ∼ ∼, 49a
228.18   usual,] 49a; ∼∧ MSh
228.18   seized] 49a; siezed MSh
228.19   Dr. Goldsmith,"] 49a; ∼∧ ∼∧" MSh
228.21   pungency:] 49a; ∼∧- MSh
228.22   Goldsmith,] 49a, Forster (678); ∼∧ MSh
228.25   not very] 49a; not–very MSh
228.25   repartee;] 49a; ∼∧ MSh
228.27   sketches,] 49a; Sketches, MSh
*228.29   good humored] T; ∼ humoured MSh; good-humored 49a
228.32   The Traveller,] 49a; the ∼; MSh
228.37   off, he] 49a; ∼∧ ∼ MSh
228.39   David's cavalier] 49a; Davids Cavalier MSh
229.1   familiarity,] 49a; ∼∧ MSh
229.2   superiority;] 49a; Superiority; MSh
229.3   expense,] 49a; ∼∧ MSh

229.6	rival,] 49a; $\sim_\wedge$ MSp
229.7	persecutor,] 49a; $\sim_\wedge$ MSp
229.9	caustic:] 49a; $\sim$. MSp
229.10	Here lies] T; "$\sim \sim$ MSp, 49a
229.41	above.] T; $\sim$." MSp, 49a
230.3	caricature:] 49a; $\sim$. MSp
230.4	Here, Hermes,] T; "$\sim$, $\sim$, MSp, 49a
230.21	here.] T; $\sim$." MSp, 49a
230.22	raking,] 49a; $\sim_\wedge$ MSh
230.23	sportive] 49a; Sportive MSh
230.24	Garrick's] 49a; Garricks MSh
230.24–25	course of Goldsmith's] 49a; Course of Goldsmiths MSh
230.27	kind.] 49a; Kind$_\wedge$ MSh
230.28	unskilful] 49a; unskillful MSh
230.34	clothes. He] T; $\sim$, He MSh; $\sim$; he 49a
230.34	thrown] 49a; throun MSh
230.34–35	players,] 49a; $\sim$; MSh
230.36–37	at Ballymahon could their half crowns. Being at all times magnificent in money matters, he] T; at Bally-mahon being at all times magnificent could their half crowns; ⟨Goldsmith, at all times heedless, may have occasionally⟩ ↑⟨and somewhat magnificent⟩↓ in money matters, he MSh; at Ballymahon could their half-crowns. Being at all times magnificent in money matters, he 49a
230.37–38	may have played with them in their own way without] T; ⟨and extremely apt to be⟩ may have ⟨occasionally caught their social [?] tone⟩, ↑played with them in their own way↓ without MSh; may have played with them in their own way, without 49a
230.38–39	to them to him] 49a; $\sim \sim$ - $\sim \sim$ MSh
230.40	kind incurred] T; Kind $\sim$ MSh; kind, $\sim$ 49a
230.40	inadvertently,] 49a; $\sim_\wedge$ MSh
231.1	gamester,"] 49a; $\sim$;" MSh
231.1	contemporaries;] 49a; $\sim$, MSh
231.4	any one,] 49a, Prior (II, 356); $\sim \sim_\wedge$ MSh
231.5	case."] 49a; $\sim_\wedge$" MSh
231.6	Retaliation,] 49a; $\sim_\wedge$ MSh
231.6	thrown] 49a; throun MSh
231.7	intervals,] 49a; $\sim_\wedge$ MSh
*231.7–8	originally intended to be introduced,] 49a; originally intended, MSh
231.8	unattempted;] 49a; $\sim$, MSh

231.9   sketched. Such] T; Sketched$_\wedge$ Such MSh; sketched—such
             49a
231.10   with a felicity] 49a; with with $\sim$ $\sim$ MSh
231.12   and to] 49a, *Works* (IV, 358); $\sim$, $\sim$ MSh
231.18   coxcombs] 49a, *Works* (IV, 358); Coxcombs MSh
231.21   snuff.] 49a, *Works* (IV, 359); $\sim$, MSh
*231.23   friendly portrait] 49a; $\sim$ picture MSh
231.23   easel; the] 49a; $\sim_\wedge$ $-$ $\sim$ MSh
231.24   complaint,] 49a; $\sim_\wedge$ MSh
231.25   health,] 49a; $\sim_\wedge$ MSh
231.30   connection,] T; connexion$_\wedge$ MSh; connection), 49a
*231.31   afternoon,] 49a; after noon, MSh
231.32   bed;] 49a; $\sim$, MSh
231.33   days,] 49a; $\sim_\wedge$ MSh
231.34   recovery,] 49a; $\sim_\wedge$ MSh
231.35   skilful] 49a; skillful MSh
231.38   him, but] 49a; $\sim_\wedge$ $\sim$ MSh
232.4   sleep,] 49a; $\sim_\wedge$MSh
232.6   o'clock] 49a; O'clock MSh
232.10   peculiarities,] 49a; $\sim_\wedge$ MSh
232.13   death," writes Dr.] 49a; $\sim_\wedge$" $\sim$ $\sim_\wedge$ MSh
232.15   amanuensis, "and] 49a; $\sim$; $_\wedge\sim$ MSh
232.16   relatives,] 49a, Prior (II, 347); $\sim_\wedge$ MSh
232.18   afterwards] 49a; afterward MSh
232.19   observed,] 49a; $\sim_\wedge$ MSh
232.19   Dr.] 49a; $\sim_\wedge$ MSh
232.21   afraid, more violent] 49a, Boswell (III, 122); affraid, $\sim$
             $\sim$, MSh
232.22   heavy,] 49a, Boswell (III, 122); $\sim_\wedge$ MSh
232.24   before?"] 49a; $\sim_\wedge$" MSh; $\sim?_\wedge$ Boswell (III, 122)
232.25–26   tailor, Mr. William Filby,] 49a; taylor, $\uparrow\sim_\wedge$ $\sim$ $\sim_\wedge\downarrow$ MSh
232.27   father,"] 49a; $\sim,_\wedge$ MSh
232.27   "though] 49a; $_\wedge\sim$ MSh
232.28   amount,] 49a, Prior (II, 235); $\sim_\wedge$ MSh
232.29   customer,] 49a; $\sim_\wedge$ MSh; $\sim$; Prior (II, 235)
232.29   lived,] 49a, Prior (II, 235); $\sim_\wedge$ MSh
232.30   integrity] T; tegrity MSh; integrity, 49a
232.31   sister milliners in Temple Lane,] 49a; Sister Milliners
             $\sim$ $\sim$ $\sim_\wedge$ MSh
232.32   him,] 49a; $\sim_\wedge$ MSh
232.33   "Oh Sir,"] T; "O Sir,$_\wedge$ Prior (II, 522); "Oh Sir$_{\wedge\wedge}$ MSh;
             "Oh, sir," 49a
232.34   Mr. Cradock, "sooner] 49a; $\sim_\wedge$ $\sim$, "Sooner MSh

232.37	charity,] 49a; ~∧ MSh
232.40	memory,] 49a; ~∧ MSh
232.41	foreseen,] 49a; ~∧ MSh
232.42	down,] 49a; ~∧ MSh
233.2	again,] 49a; ~∧ MSh
233.3	Goldsmith!] Pr.; ~: MSh
*233.3	that such a memorial] Prh; that a simple memorial MSh
233.5	lady,] Pr.; ~∧ MSh
233.6	ventured to advert.] 49a; ⟨had occasion⟩ ↑ventured↓ to advert. Pr.; had occasion to advert. MSh
233.6	Hazlitt] Pr.; Hazlett MSh
233.7	Northcote's] Pr.; Northcotts MSh
233.7	Mrs. Gwyn,] Pr.; ~∧ ~∧ MSh
*233.8	General Gwyn] 49a; Colonel ~ MSh, Pr.
233.8	army.] Pr.; Army. MSh
233.9	seventy years of age.] Pr.; Seventy ~ ~ Age. MSh
233.10	gone, Hazlitt] Pr.; ~∧ Hazlett MSh
*233.11	"I don't know," said] T; "~ dont ~," replied MSh; "~ do not know," said Prp, 49a
233.12	me, except] Pr.; ~∧ ~ MSh
233.13	Reynolds,] Pr.; ~∧ MSh
*233.14–15	life." "Not only so,"] Pr.; ~∧" ∧~ ~ ~,∧ MSh
233.21	room, looking] Pr.; ~∧ ~ MSh
233.26	each."] Pr.; ~∧" MSh
233.26	gayly] Pr.; gaily MSh
233.27	awkward] Pr.; aukward MSh
233.30–31	having been an object of his affectionate regard; it certainly rendered] 49a; being associated with his name; ⟨in after years⟩ his tender regard rendered MSh; having been an object of his ↑affectionate↓ regard, it certainly rendered Prp, Prh
*234.1	*CHAPTER XLV*] T; Ch 44 MSh; CHAPTER XLV. 49a
234.2	*The monument*] 49a; the Monument MSh
234.2	*The epitaph*] 49a; the Epitaph MSh
*234.2	*Concluding remarks*] 49a; confluding reflections MSh
234.4	honor] 49a; honour MSh
234.6	designated:] 49a; ~; MSh
234.6	Shelburne,] 49a; ~; MSh
234.7	Mr. Beauclerc, Mr.] 49a; ~∧ ~, ~∧ MSh
234.7	down,] 49a; ~∧ MSh
234.10	therefore,] 49a; ~∧ MSh
234.10	o'clock] 49a; oclock MSh
234.10	evening,] 49a; ~∧ MSh

234.10   April,] 49a; $\sim_\wedge$ MSh
234.11   Temple Church;] 49a; $\sim$ church; MSh
234.12   mourners,] 49a; $\sim_\wedge$ MSh
234.14   Reynolds's nephew] T; Reynolds $\sim$ MSh; Reynolds's $\sim$, 49a
234.16   occasion.] 49a; $\sim_\wedge$ MSh
234.18   said,] 49a; $\sim_\wedge$ MSh
234.18   newspapers.] 49a; $\sim_\wedge$ MSh
234.19   offences,] 49a; $\sim_\wedge$ MSh
*234.24   Hence] T; "$\sim$ MSp, 49a
234.29   state.] T; $\sim$." MSp, 49a
234.33   execration:] 49a; $\sim$. MSp
234.34   By his] T; "$\sim$ $\sim$ MSp, 49a
234.37   head.] T; $\sim$." MSp, 49a
235.6   subscription] T; Subscription MSh; subscription, 49a
235.8   Nollekens] T; $\sim$, 50; Nollekins$_\wedge$ MSh; $\sim$, 49a
*235.10   south door in Poets' Corner] T; south door in Poet's Corner, 49a; South door in Poets Corner MSh
235.12   Latin epitaph,] 49a; latin Epetaph$_\wedge$ MSh
235.12–13   Reynolds,] 49a; $\sim_\wedge$ MSh
235.14–15   composition,] 49a; $\sim_\wedge$ MSh
235.16   epitaph] 49a; epetaph MSh
235.21   Johnson,] 49a; $\sim_\wedge$ MSh
235.23   sailors] 49a; Sailors MSh
235.24   Round Robin.] 49a; round $\sim$. MSh
*235.24–25   He was willing, he said, to] T; $\sim$ $\sim$ $\sim$, $\sim$ $\sim_\wedge$ to MSh; "$\sim$ $\sim$ $\sim$," $\sim$ $\sim$, "$\sim$ 49a
235.25   epitaph] 49a; Epetaph MSh
*235.26   pleased; "*but*] T; $\sim$, "*but* MSh; $\sim$; $_\wedge\sim$ 49a
235.26   *disgrace*] 49a; *desgrace* MSh
235.27   *inscription.*"] 49a; $\sim$:$_\wedge$ MSh
235.28   Dr. Warton] 50; $\sim_\wedge$ Wharton MSh; $\sim$. Wharton 49a
235.29   Joe Warton,] 50; $\sim$ Wharton, MSh, 49a
235.31   sense."] 49a; $\sim_\wedge$" MSh
235.31   epitaph] 49a; Epetaph MSh
*235.32   bust:] 49a; $\sim$. MSh
*235.33   "OLIVARII GOLDSMITH,] 49a
*236.15   scope,] 49a; $\sim_\wedge$ ———— MSh
236.17   generations,] 49a; $\sim$; MSh
236.21   apothegm,] 49a; $\sim_\wedge$ MSh
237.1   man,"] 49a; $\sim_\wedge$" MSh
237.2   shy, awkward] T; $\sim_\wedge$ aukward MSh; $\sim$, awkward, 49a
237.3   companions, but] 49a; $\sim$.-but MSh

237.5	devourer of the] 49a; ⁓ of of ⁓ MSh
237.6	dunce,] 49a; ⁓∧ MSh
237.8	friends.] 49a; ⁓∧ MSh
*237.12	wayward] 49a; way ward MSh
*237.13	throughout] 49a; through out MSh
237.13	school,] 49a; School∧ MSh
237.14	science,] 49a; ⁓∧ MSh
*237.16	feelings; they dispose] 49a; ⁓, and dispose MSh
237.17	hedges, green] 49a; hedges .green MSh
237.19	gipsy] 49a; gypsy MSh
*237.20	delusive gifts,] 49a; inward ⁓∧ MSh
237.20–21	present nor] 49a; ⁓ or MSh
237.21	future,] 49a; ⁓; MSh
237.21–22	knowledge,] 49a; ⁓., MSh
237.22	plan,] 49a; ⁓; MSh
237.22	recommended] 49a; reccommended MSh
237.23	friends,] 49a; ⁓; MSh
237.23	ministry,] 49a; ⁓; MSh
237.24	Edinburgh,] 49a; ⁓∧ MSh
237.25	science,] 49a; ⁓; MSh
237.26	there,] 49a; ⁓; MSh
237.27	him;] 49a; ⁓, MSh
*237.28	for the customary time,] 49a; for a reasonable time∧ MSh
237.31	lectures] 49a; ⁓; MSh
237.33	studies] 49a; Studies MSh
237.33–34	surgeon's mate;] 49a; surgeons ⁓∧ MSh
237.34	medicine,] 49a; ⁓∧ MSh
237.35	pursuit,] 49a; ⁓∧ MSh
237.36	humbler] 49a; humble MSh
237.36	life,] 49a; ⁓∧ MSh
237.37	pen,] 49a; ⁓∧ MSh
237.39	pen: he] 49a; ⁓: He MSh
*237.41	secondhand] T; second hand MSh; second-hand 49a
237.42	seizes] 49a; siezes MSh
237.43	theme:] 49a; ⁓; MSh
238.3	gold,] 49a; ⁓; MSh
238.10	hand,] 49a; ⁓∧ MSh
238.11	competent] 49a; Competent MSh
238.12	Goldsmith's] 49a; Goldsmiths MSh
*238.16	forerun] 49a; fore run MSh
*238.20–21	without] 49a; with out MSh
*238.23	"He could not stifle] 49a; "He could not Stifle "He could not stifle MSh

238.25   borrow, he] 49a, *Works* (III, 391); $\sim_\wedge \sim$ MSh
238.26   to shed tears as] 49a; $\sim \sim \sim$, $\sim$ *Works* (III, 391);
              to shed as MSh
238.27   gate." * * * * *] 49a; $\sim$". X X X X X MSh
238.32   sincerity."*] 49a; $\sim$."ˣ MSh
238.39   critic,] 49a; $\sim_\wedge$ MSh
238.41   muse.] 49a; $\sim$, MSh
238.42   *Goldsmith's Life of Nashe.] 49a; Goldsmiths life of
              Nashe. MSh
*239.1   company,] 49a; $\sim_\wedge$ MSh
239.4   nature;] 49a; $\sim_\wedge$ MSh
239.6   poor,] 49a; $\sim_\wedge$ MSh
239.6   depraved.] 49a; $\sim_\wedge$ MSh
239.13   gentle,] 49a; $\sim_\wedge$ MSh
239.15   year,"] 49a; $\sim_\wedge$" MSh
239.17   uncle,] 49a; $\sim_\wedge$ MSh
239.26   life,] 49a; $\sim_\wedge$ MSh
239.28   recollections] 49a; reccollections MSh
239.29   infancy.] 49a; $\sim_\wedge$ MSh
239.32   Vicar of Wakefield,] 49a; vicar $\sim$ $\sim$; MSh
*239.32   village pastor,] T; Village pastor MSh; Village Pastor,
              49a
239.35   Church Service] 49a; church Sarvice MSh
239.36   Sunday,] 49a; $\sim_\wedge$ MSh
239.36   do it."] 49a; $\sim$ $\sim_\wedge$" MSh
239.39   functions?] 49a; $\sim_\wedge$ MSh
239.40   Boswell:] 49a; $\sim$; MSh
239.42   other;] 49a; $\sim$, MSh
239.42   Christian] 49a; christian MSh
240.6   neither] 49a; niether MSh
240.10   awkward] 49a; aukward MSh
240.15   circles,] 49a; $\sim_\wedge$ MSh
240.17   intercourse,] 49a; $\sim$; MSh
*240.17   firesides,] 49a; fire sides; MSh
240.20   critic] 49a; Critic MSh
240.20   quoted,] 49a; $\sim_\wedge$ MSh
240.22   foibles,] 49a; $\sim$; MSh
240.24   self-love] 49a; $\sim_\wedge\sim$ MSh
240.25   Goldsmith's] 49a; Goldsmiths, MSh
*240.25–26   so affectionate, so confiding–] 49a; $\sim$ $\sim_\wedge$ $\sim$ $\sim$– MSh
*240.29   are evident,] 49a; is evident MSh
240.29   think,] 49a; $\sim_\wedge$ MSh
*240.30   more significancy] 49a; $\sim$ instance MSh

240.32   detect,] 49a; ～ₐ MSh
240.35   kind—the] 49a; ～; ～ MSh
240.35   friends—might] 49a; ～, ～ MSh
*240.37   associates] T; friends MSh; associates, 49a
240.40   death.] 49a; ～ₐ MSh
240.42   occasion.] 49a; ～ₐ MSh
*240.42   general tone] 49a; ～ turn MSp
*241.8–9   and we turn more kindly] 49a; and the heart yearns
                  more kindly MSp
241.15   Johnson; "he] 49a; ～; "[*defective MS*] MSp
241.16   part, we] 49a; ～, [*defective MS*] MSp
241.16   "Let] 49a; "let MSp
241.17–18   since their tendency is to endear; and we question
                  whether he himself would not feel gratified in hear-
                  ing] 49a; for [*missing word*] question whether he him-
                  self would not feel gr [*missing letters*] fied in hearing
                  MSp
241.18–19   with admiration] 49a; with [*missing letters*] miration MSp
*241.20   kind hearted] T; ～-～ MSp, 49a

LIST OF REJECTED SUBSTANTIVES

This list provides a historical record of substantive variants in the authorized texts which appeared during Irving's lifetime but which were not adopted for the Twayne text.

The numbers before each entry indicate the page and line number. The reading to the left of the bracket is the word or words accepted from the manuscript. The source or sources of the reading are identified by the symbol after the bracket. The reading after the semicolon indicates the rejected form, the sources of which are identified by symbol.

A key to identifying symbols used in referring to the manuscript and editions of *Oliver Goldsmith*, as well as to Irving's sources, is given on pages 347–48.

°3.4   introductory to a selection from] MSh; introductory from his writings Pr.

5.5–6   *School studies–School sports*] MSh; School studies and school sports 49a

°5.13   blended] MSp; blending 49a

8.36   in the] MSp; ~ his 49a

°10.14   throughout] MSp; through 49a

°16.14–15   told that he would stroll] MSp; told would stroll 49a

°23.5   time was now arrived] MSh, 49a, 49b, 49c, 50, 51, 54, E; ~ had ~ ~ 53, 55, 59, 60

25.6–7   not to have given] MSp, Prior (I, 121); not have given 49a

25.19   loved on the earth,] MSp, Prior (I, 121); loved on earth 49a

26.6   "The lenten] MSp, Prior (I, 122); "This ~ 49a

26.38   my old hospitable] MSp, Prior (I, 124); my hospitable 49a

°35.41   friends] MSh, Prh; friend 49a

36.7   indiscretions] MSh; indiscretion, Pr.; ~$_\wedge$ 49a

37.34   beneath] MSp, *Works* (IV, 261); before 49a

40.20   elegance] MSh, *Works* (III, 248); defiance 49a

49.30   lives have only mended] MSh, *Works* (IV, 108); ~ only have ~ 49a

52.35   I dare hope,] MSh, *Works* (I, 314); ~ have ~$_\wedge$ 49a

58.28   Every day do I] MSh, Forster (118); ~ ~ or so I 49a

58.36   revolve never so fast,] MSh, Forster (118); ~ ever ~ ~, 49a

*58.38		round as] MSh; ∼, ∼ 49a; ∼_∧ like Forster (118)

*63.40		woman from whom] MSh; ∼ of ∼ 49a

64.28		prevent somewhat more] MSp, Prior (I, 286); ∼ something ∼ 49a

*67.41		letter lv.] MSp; ∼ iv. 49a

*73.8		expense] MSp; expenses 49a

*89.34		were arrived] MSh, 49a, Boswell (III, 445); had ∼ 50

*90.12		meetings] MSh; meeting 49a

91.27		huge uncouth figure,] MSh; ∼, ∼ ∼, Boswell (I, 232); large ∼ ∼, 49a

*92.29		boat, rowed] MSh; ∼ again, ∼ 49a

96.5		Illumes] MSh, 49a; Adorns *Works* (IV, 222)

*97.25–26		almost ludicrous.] MSh, 49b, E; most ∼. 49a

99.15		abodes] MSh; abode 49a

100.24		told him I was,] MSp, Percy (67), 1825 (29); told him that I was, 49a

107.6		papa] MSh; father 49a; pappa *Works* (IV, 136)

*110.14–15		The new comedy] MSh; The comedy 49a

*117.10		apprentice] MSh; Apprenticed 49a

*118.4		cry,] MSh; say, 49a

*121.10–11		had been so long treated] MSh; ∼ so long been ∼ 49a

122.20		dependent situation;] MSh, Forster (410); dreadful ∼; 49a

123.9		Newbery for a] MSh; ∼, ∼ an 49a

*124.25		Ministers] MSh; ministry 49a

124.39		sett] MSh; set Prior (II, 278); suit 49a

127.17		Bensley] MSh, *Works* (V, 15); Brinsley 49a

*127.18		gloom over] MSh; ∼ on 49a

130.17		apartment] MSh; apartments 49a

*131.8–10		excursion. Sometimes it was at Highbury Barn, where there was a very good ordinary of two dishes and pastry at ten pence a head, including a penny to the waiter.] MSh; excursion. 49a

140.7		terms on] MSh; terms in 49a

*144.18		Goldsmith's intention] MSp; Goldsmith ∼ 49a

145.42		her fatal broom] MSp, *Works* (I, 425); her broom 49a

*148.34; 149.1	I believe I could get] MSp, Percy (87), 1825 (44), 1840 (133); I believe I think I could get 49a

149.8		in a royal academy] MSp, 1840 (134); ∼ ∼ ∼ Academy Percy (87); ∼ ∼ Royal Academy 1825 (44); in the royal academy 49a

*150.32–33		mezzotinto] MSh; mezzotint, 49a

*150.34–35   over the Shannon,] MSh, 49a, E; over the Channel, 49b, 49c

155.26   of its identity] MSp; of identity 49a

159.3   landing two little trunks,] MSp, 1825 (43), Percy (90), 1840 (144), Prior (II, 289); landing, with two little trunks, 49a

160.15   and at forty] MSp, Prior (II, 292); and forty 49a

160.41   at table,] MSp, Prior (II, 294); at the table, 49a

*161.21   women] MSp, Prior (II, 295), 49a; woman 60

163.8   during this tour] MSp; ∼ his ∼ 49a

165.8   of his Life] MSh; ∼ ∼ Life Forster (558); ∼ the Life 49a

169.11   lest the book] MSh, 49a; ∼ ∼ work E

170.5   is a visiting] MSp, Percy (93), Forster (588); is visting 1825 (45), 49a

171.30   invitation by] MSh, Prior (II, 377); ∼ with 49a

*171.36   group."] MSh; ∼.∧ 49a

*173.2   the love of all] MSh, 49b, E; the love all Pr., 49a

*175.24   replied he] MSh; ∼, "∼ 49a

*175.39   idem nolle–] MSh, 49b, E; idem volle– 49a

178.10   brother when in London on our way to Ireland left] MSh; ∼ in London on our way to Ireland, left Prior (II, 344); ∼ – when in London, on my way to Ireland–left 49a

179.5   Five volumes] MSh; *Paragraph* ∼ ∼ 49a

181.2   had probably a] MSh; had a 49a

*181.9   'snatched] MSh; ∧∼ 49a

*182.16   surpasses] MSh; passes 49a

*185.29   dead silence] MSh; ∼ pause 49a

185.33–34   writers had thought] MSh; writer thought 49a

186.5   old conventional character] MSh, 49b, 50; ∼ conversational ∼ 49a, 49c, E

*189.8–9   for masquerades and given rise to the following incident.] MSh; for masquerades. 49a

190.39   but in late years] MSh, 49a; only of late years E

194.10   dissipations] MSh; dissipation 49a

196.25   through more difficulties.] MSh, 49a; ∼ greater ∼. E

199.5   New actors] MSp, 49a, Prior (II, 405); Now ∼ E

199.19   the epigrams] MSh; he ∼ 49a

*200.9–10   thought of] MSp, 49b; ∼ or 49a

*206.20   this reply] MSh; the ∼ 49a

206.39   find one who does what] MSh, Boswell (II, 368), Forster (597); find one to do what 49a

208.20   tell truth,] MSp, Boswell (II, 210); tell the truth, Pr.

210.9   else sees?"—"It] MSh; else does?" "It 49a; else sees? Goldsmith. "It Boswell (II, 217)

210.25   others, or when] MSh; ∼, when 49a

212.2   *objections*] MSh; objection 49a

224.2   gardeners.] MSh; gardener. 49a

*227.19   made weary] MSh, 49b, E; ∼ wrong Pr., 49a

231.4   sums.] MSh, Prior (II, 356); sum. 49a

233.25   life," said] MSh; ∼," says Pr.

*239.10   pictures of life] MSh; features ∼ ∼ 49a

239.21   toned it] MSh; tuned it 49a

LIST OF COMPOUND WORDS
HYPHENATED
AT END OF LINE

List I includes all compound and possible compound words that are hyphenated at the end of the line in the manuscript. In deciding whether to retain the hyphen or to print the word as a single-word compound (without the hyphen) or as two words without the hyphen, the editor has made her decision first on the use of each compound word elsewhere in the manuscript; or second, when the word appears in a quotation, on the usage in the source; or third, when the word does not appear elsewhere in the manuscript, on Irving's practice in other writings of the period (chiefly *A Tour on the Prairies*, 1835; *Biography of the Late Margaret Miller Davidson*, 1841; and *Mahomet*, 1849–1850); or finally, if the word does not appear in Irving's other writings of the period, on contemporary American usage, chiefly as reflected in Webster's dictionary of 1806. Each word is listed in its editorially accepted form after the page and line numbers of its appearance in the T text.

List II presents all compounds, or possible compounds, that are hyphenated or separated as two words at the end of the line in the T text. They are listed in the form in which they would have appeared in the T text had they come in mid-line.

LIST I

6.16	birthplace	29.26	throughout
7.4	fireside	31.40	forget
9.33	good-for-nothing	38.4	countryman
11.28	schoolmates	41.2	any thing
12.11	somewhat	44.30	half pence
12.36	breakfast	46.21	breakfast
12.38	gentleman	46.40	gentleman
14.39	outbreak	51.20–21	red-pimpled
18.14	throughout	51.30	Coffee House
19.7	goblin-house	52.42	under-rate
19.10	somewhat	53.32	by-and-by
21.17	sometimes	54.21	any thing

55.4	sometimes		145.6	without
61.9	booksellers		149.1	brother-in-law
67.28	washerwomen		155.8	post chaise
71.7	landlord		155.29	parsonage-house
84.13	however		161.8	any body
85.36	any thing		162.13	outrun
88.9	friendship		164.6	Notwithstanding
90.35	moreover		165.31	however
95.9	undervalue		166.25	breakfast
95.25	bookseller		166.34	free-and-easy
97.8	well merited		170.18	However
99.17	quiet-seeking		172.36	without
100.29	lord-lieutenant		178.6	befriended
102.27	cannot		185.6	countryman
105.28	bookseller		191.12	ill-natured
106.41	honeysuckle		197.40	mal-a-propos
108.20	newspaper		202.20	orang-outang's
108.24	bookseller		202.28	without
112.16–17	childhood		206.23	crossbuns
113.36	cannot		216.6	clergymen
114.31	overbearing		216.10	overbearing
131.39	tea table		216.28	gentleman
132.5	forthwith		219.40	undertakings
140.33	wardrobe		226.35	bachelorhood
141.2	queen's-blue		229.4	therefore
143.9	without			

LIST II

5.4–5	schoolmaster		36.16–17	themselves
8.27–28	schoolmaster		45.39–40	however
10.15–16	schoolmaster		46.2–3	journeyman's
11.38–39	however		48.26–27	schoolboy
11.40–41	deer-stealing		51.20–21	red-pimpled
12.26–27	however		62.24–25	appointment-warrant
12.31–32	schoolboy		74.21–22	became
14.17–18	himself		76.10–11	himself
18.41–42	henceforth		91.11–12	somewhat
19.1–2	childhood		95.17–18	landlady
23.3–4	Fiddle-back		102.30–31	however
28.17–18	however		103.3–4	undertake
30.11–12	landlady		103.40–41	man-servant
33.20–21	handsome		105.7–8	bookseller

107.19–20 newspapers
112.16–17 childhood
117.11–12 newspapers
119.10–11 became
130.19–20 overlooked
134.33–34 Shoemaker's
148.23–24 foregoing
151.21–22 statesmen
153.7–8   childhood
154.26–27 however
155.4–5   hollyhock
155.19–20 bookstall
158.38–39 sea-sickness
159.10–11 sixpence
175.31–32 self-defense
180.3–4   Sometimes
183.32–33 overtasked

196.34–35 however
197.36–37 without
198.10–11 overcome
199.26–27 apprenticeship
202.15–16 *humbug*
202.27–28 water-gruel
205.15–16 newspaper
206.14–15 undertook
209.41–42 sometimes
215.37–38 himself
217.27–28 something
227.39–40 understanding
232.4–5   however
240.29–30 throughout
241.9–10   ourselves
241.17–18 himself

BIOGRAPHY

OF

THE LATE

MARGARET MILLER DAVIDSON

LIST OF ABBREVIATIONS

The following symbols have been used in the editorial apparatus to designate the previously published texts of *Margaret Davidson*.

41   First American edition (Philadelphia: Lea and Blanchard, 1841)

41a   Second American edition (Philadelphia: Lea & Blanchard, 1841)

42   Third American edition (Philadelphia: Lea & Blanchard, 1842)

43   New Edition, revised (Philadelphia: Lea & Blanchard, 1843)

45 46 47 48	} Reimpressions of 43

51 52 54	} (New York: Clark, Austin and Co.); reimpressions of 43

43E   (London: Tilt and Bogue, 1843; reimpression, London: David Bogue, 1843)

T   Twayne edition

EXPLANATORY NOTES

The numbers before all notes indicate page and line respectively. Epigraphs, author's chapter or section summaries, text quotations, and footnotes are included in the line count. Only running heads and rules added by the printer to separate the running head from the text are omitted from the count. The quotation from the text, to the left of the bracket, is the matter under discussion. A key to identifying symbols used in referring to previously published editions of *Margaret Davidson* is given on page 611.

245.5 Lucretia Davidson] Lucretia Davidson (1808–1825), Margaret's sister, was also a child poet who died of tuberculosis. A volume of her poetry, *Amir Khan and Other Poems*, was published in 1829.

245.7–8 President Morse] Samuel Finley Breese Morse (1791–1872), an artist, was the first president of the National Academy of Design. His interest later turning to the study of electricity, he invented the electric telegraph, the practicality of which he demonstrated in 1844.

245.8 American Society of Arts] The American Academy of Fine Arts was founded in 1801 and revived in 1816 after a "dormant period." In 1825 out of dissatisfaction with the American Academy, a group of artists at the suggestion of Morse founded the New York Drawing Association, which in 1826 became the National Academy of Design with Morse as president. See Oral Sumner Coad, *William Dunlap: A Study of His Life and Works and of his Place in Contemporary Culture* (New York, 1962), pp. 97–98, 104–105.

245.9–10 Miss Sedgwick] Catharine Maria Sedgwick (1789–1867) was one of the first of a large number of women novelists in nineteenth-century America. Her best known novel is *Hope Leslie* (1827).

245.11 Robert Southey] Robert Southey (1774–1843), English poet and essayist, became poet laureate in 1813. His review of *Amir Khan* was the lead article in *The Quarterly Review* 41 (November, 1829), 289–301.

245.13 intimate acquaintance] In 1840 in a letter to his sister, Sarah Van Wart, Irving wrote: "You may recollect the family of Mrs. Davidson; she is one of a number of sisters—very beautiful girls—of the name of Miller, who, in your younger days, lived in Maiden Lane" (PMI, II, 373).

245.17 Mrs. Davidson] Margaret Miller Davidson (1787–1844) was the daughter of Dr. Matthias Burnet Miller of Utica, New York. According to Miss Sedgwick, *Poetical Remains of the Late Lucretia Maria Davidson* ... (Philadelphia, 1841), p. 33, Mrs. Davidson "received the best education her times afforded at the school of the celebrated Scottish lady, Isabella Graham, an institution in the city of New York, that had no rival in its day...."

245.18 a new edition] This was probably Miss Sedgwick's edition cited in the previous note. It was dedicated to Irving.

245.30 daughter Margaret] Margaret wrote her impressions of this visit: "On the 31st July the celebrated Washing [*sic*] Irving honored us with a call, I have seen this *great man*, the pride of his country, the ornament of Society, and the author of Knickerbocker, the Sketch Book, Alhambra, and the life of Columbus, imagination cannot paint my feelings at this moment, I have met, I have for a few short blissful moments breathed the same air with him; I felt a sensation of awe, reverence, and admiration, steal over my mind, as I gazed on the fine lineaments of his noble face, his piercing eye, his jet black hair his broad high brow excited feelings I am unable to describe; in every feature, I thought I could trace some amiable quality, or some trait of brilliant genius, the hair which clustered around his forehead seemed to my enraptured eyes, a wreath of laurel bound around it by the 'genius of America' some guardian Muse seemed hovering near to inspire his heart with poetic enthusiasm; my mind was strongly excited long after he bade us farewell, and the effect produced upon it, will never be erased—". From Margaret's holograph diary (pp. 24–25) in the possession of Rutgers University Library. See Walter Harding, ed., "Sentimental Journal: The Diary of Margaret Miller Davidson," *The Journal of The Rutgers University Library* 13 (December, 1949), 19–24. This article includes excerpts from the diary, including the above quotation.

246.12 rural retreat] Ruremont on the East River is the place where the Millers were living at this time. See 268.4.

246.23 a number of manuscripts] In his letter to Sarah Van Wart Irving wrote that the biography "is made up in a great degree from memorandums furnished by her mother, who is of almost as poetical a temperament as her children. The most affecting passages of the biography are quoted literally from her manuscript." He transferred the copyright to Mrs. Davidson but retained the right of republication. See PMI (II, 373).

246.33–34 to sunder them] Of this passage Edgar Allan Poe (*Complete Works*, ed. James A. Harrison [New York, 1902], X, 175) wrote: "In these words the biographer conveys no more than a just idea of the exquisite loveliness of the picture here presented to view."

246.35 Dr. Oliver]   For Dr. Oliver Davidson (1779–1847) see Introduction, p. lxi. The children born to Dr. and Mrs. Davidson were
as follows: Anne Elizabeth (1806–1834), Lucretia Maria (1808–1825),
Morris Miller (1810–1854), Phoebe (1810–1813), Oliver (1814–1814),
Levi Platt (1816–1843), Matthias Oliver (1819–1871), Margaret Miller
(1823–1838), and Moss Kent (1827–1836).

246.36–37 Lake Champlain]   Lake Champlain separates northeastern
New York State from the State of Vermont. Plattsburgh is the county
seat of Clinton County, New York.

247.37 a lady in Canada]   The lady was Margaret's sister, Anne Elizabeth Townsend (1806–1834). See note 255.10–11.

248.9 the Saranac]   The Saranac River flows from Saranac Lake in the
Adirondacks into Lake Champlain at Plattsburgh.

248.36 from nature up to nature's God]   Compare Alexander Pope's
An Essay on Man, Epistle IV, lines 331–32.

249.34–35 Thomson's Seasons]   James Thomson (1700–1748), English
poet, published *The Seasons* in 1730.

249.35 Pleasures of Hope]   Thomas Campbell (1777–1844), Scottish
poet, published *The Pleasures of Hope* in 1799.

249.35 Cowper's Task]   William Cowper (1731–1800), English poet,
published *The Task* in 1785.

249.36 Milton, Byron, and Scott]   The references are to John Milton
(1608–1674), English epic poet; George Noel Gordon, Lord Byron
(1788–1824), English poet; and Sir Walter Scott (1771–1832), Scottish
poet and novelist.

249.43 "lisp in numbers,"]   The quotation is from Alexander Pope's
Epistle to Dr. Arbuthnot, Prologue to the Satires, lines 127–28.

252.13 rival, Elizabeth]   During the reign of Elizabeth I (1533–1603)
Mary, Queen of Scots (1542–1587) was imprisoned for nineteen years
and then executed.

253.4 an English gentleman]   In a letter dated February 16, 1842,
Fanny Calderón de la Barca wrote to William Hickling Prescott, "I
received . . . the Life of Margaret Davidson in Vera Cruz. . . . The person
mentioned as her English friend is Mr. Schenley" (*The Correspondence
of William Hickling Prescott, 1833–1847,* ed. Roger Wolcott [Boston.
1925], p. 287).

253.27 Saratoga Springs]   In the nineteenth century Saratoga Springs
was a fashionable health spa in eastern New York, thirty-three miles
north of Albany, the state capital. In the following sentence New York
means New York City.

255.10–11 daughter, Mrs. T——]   Anne Elizabeth, the eldest Davidson
daughter, married the Reverend Micajah Townsend in 1823. According
to C. M. Day, *History of the Eastern Townships* (Montreal, 1869),

p. 277, Townsend was an American, whose father, Micah Townsend, was secretary of the state of Vermont. The Reverend Townsend served three Episcopal churches in Caldwell Manor (Seigniory of Foucault) and Christie Manor (Seigniory of Noyan), just north of the United States border.

255.28 Addison] Joseph Addison (1672–1719) was an English essayist.

257.3–4 Champlain, &c.] Missisquoi Bay (Missisqui in old maps), which lies in both Vermont and Lower Canada, is connected to Lake Champlain by the Missiquoi River. St. Johns (or Saint-Jean) is a city on the Richelieu River, twenty-one miles southeast of Montreal. Alburgh is a town in Vermont on the Canadian border. Champlain is a town in New York State on the Canadian border.

257.27 round thee flow."] Of this poem Poe (*Works*, X, 177) wrote: "... we look around us in vain for anything composed at eight years, which can bear comparison with the lines subjoined; ..."

257.34 a family party] According to Margaret's journal, p. 1 (see note 245.30), "Left Caldwells Manor on friday May 31st 1833, in company with my Father my brother and Sister Towsend, a young lady, and my little nephew, my Mother and myself made up the party...."

258.2 "School for the Blind,"] "This week my dear friends took me to the blind school, poor creatures how I pity them, yet they do not seem unhappy. they laugh at each others mistakes, and guilty [*sic*] and cheerfulness prevails among them, they all seem particularly delighted when noticed by strangers, when their sweet infant voices were raised above in simple hymns I felt that there were many who might envy them, however their situation may be; the instructor seems kind, and no doubt they feel towards him the affection of children, to an indulgent father..." ("Journal," pp. 15–16).

258.2 "Deaf and Dumb Asylum;"] "Mrs Broun and her tuo [*sic*] daughters with Miss Stansbury (who had been an instructress) invited me to go with them, to the deaf and dumb institution, with this I was much pleased I expect it is much more difficult to instruct these scholars than the blind, they have no idea of words since they never heard them spoken, they cannot know the meaning of sound or speech, and it must be a hard task to teach them; we examined all, our limited time would permit, and returned delighted with our excursion—" ("Journal," p. 16).

258.3 Black Hawk] Black Hawk (1767–1838), a chief of the Sac Indians, led a rebellion in 1832 against the removal of Indians from Illinois.

258.22 the following night."] The paragraph is from Margaret's "Journal," pp. 16–17. See Textual Commentary, pp. 628–30.

260.20 village of Ballston] Ballston Spa is six miles southwest of Saratoga Springs. Before the Civil War it was a fashionable resort.

260.28 MY NATIVE LAKE] Of this poem a reviewer writing in *The New World* (June 5, 1841), 381, said: "Are not the following lines, written by this baby, when her heart was full of sorrow at being obliged to leave the shore of her native lake, 'beautiful exceedingly.' By what modern 'poetess' have they, in their pure and simple depth of feeling, been excelled?" Poe (*Works*, X, 177) also thought this poem "remarkable."

262.12 Blair, Kaimes, and Paley] Hugh Blair (1718–1800), a Scottish preacher, published his *Lectures on Rhetoric and Belles Lettres* in 1783. Henry Home, Lord Kames (1696–1782), Scottish philosopher, published his *Elements of Criticism* in 1762. Blair and Kames belonged to the so-called Scottish "common sense" school of philosophy and aesthetics, which was popular in America from 1810 to 1835. William Paley (1743–1805), English theologian, published his *Principles of Moral and Political Philosophy* in 1785 and his most popular work, *Natural Theology, or Evidences of the Existence and Attributes of the Deity* in 1802.

262.24 Virgil] Publius Vergilius Maro (70 B.C.–19 B.C.), Roman poet, is best known for his *Aeneid*.

262.32 death of her sister] Mrs. Townsend died on April 19, 1834. Dr. Davidson was with his daughter at the time of her death. On April 18, 1834, he wrote from Caldwell Manor to his wife: "Our dear Daughter is yet alive, but gradually sinking to rest–..." (manuscript letter in possession of Rutgers University Library).

267.5 'Belshazzar's Feast,'] For the story of Belshazzar's feast see Dan. 5. Margaret's interest in this subject may have been stimulated by Washington Allston's painting of the same title, which was left unfinished at the time of his death in 1843. In 1836 there was public criticism of Allston for not having finished this work, which he had started some years before his return to America in 1818, and for which ten men had agreed to pay $1,000 each and had already paid deposits. There is no reference to the painting in the poem. Irving was a friend of Allston, and Morse had studied art under him.

267.6 'Boabdil el Chico,'] The title of the poem is "Boabdil el Chico's Farewell to Granada." Margaret drew her subject from Irving's *Conquest of Granada*.

267.18 Mohawk river] The Mohawk River, the largest tributary of the Hudson, rises in central New York and flows into the Hudson at Cohoes.

267.35 Sound, or East River] The East River, which connects Upper New York Bay and Long Island Sound, separates Manhattan and the Bronx from Long Island.

267.36 Moss Kent] Moss Kent (1766–1838), lawyer and congressman

(1813–1817), was the brother of the more famous James Kent, who published his *Commentaries on American Law* from 1826 to 1830. James Kent presided at the public dinner given for Irving when the latter returned from Europe in 1832.

268.37 Mrs. Willard] Emma Hart Willard (1787–1870), teacher and writer, was a pioneer in education for women. In 1814 she opened a school for women in Middlebury, Vermont, and in 1821 moved it to Troy, New York. She wrote the poem "Rocked in the Cradle of the Deep."

272.1–2 English gentleman] See note 253.4.

272.36 Hell Gate] Hell Gate is a channel that connects the East and Harlem Rivers. See Irving's "Hell-Gate" in *Tales of a Traveller*.

272.39 Ready Money Prevost] This is a character in Irving's "The Devil and Tom Walker," which was included in *Tales of a Traveller*. According to David S. Wilson, coeditor with Brom Weber of the Twayne edition of *Tales of a Traveller*, the name was spelled in four different ways in the five earliest editions: Ready-money Provost, Ready Money Prevost, Ready Money Provost, and Ready-Money Provost.

272.42 Kidd the pirate] William Kidd (ca. 1645–1701), a British privateer, was arrested in 1699 on charges of piracy, tried, and hanged. See Irving's "Kidd the Pirate" in *Tales of a Traveller*.

274.6 he died] This was Moss Kent Davidson (1827–1836).

274.17 her eldest brother] This was Morris Miller Davidson (1810–1854).

277.9 be made immortal."] These verses are from John Milton's *A Mask Presented at Ludlow Castle (Comus)*, lines 455–63.

279.22 Dutchess County] Dutchess County, so spelled in Rand McNally's *Standard World Atlas* (New York, 1956), is in southeastern New York State on the east bank of the Hudson River.

282.9 Lithgow] Mrs. Davidson's mother, Phoebe Smith Miller, was the daughter of Judge Isaac Smith of Lithgow, Dutchess County. Margaret was apparently visiting relatives here.

282.16 West Point] According to George W. Cullum, *Biographical Register of the Officers and Graduates of the U. S. Military Academy at West Point . . .* (New York, 1868), p. 546, Levi Platt Davidson was admitted to the Academy on July 1, 1833, and was graduated in 1837 forty-seventh in a class of fifty. As a second lieutenant, he served at several frontier posts and was promoted to the rank of first lieutenant. After only three years of military service he went on sick leave, and he died at the age of twenty-five in 1842. Levi was also an aspiring poet. One of his poems, "Longing for the West," was published in the *Southern Literary Messenger* (February, 1843). See Evert A.

and George Duyckinck, *Cyclopaedia of American Literature* (Philadelphia, 1881), II, 328, n.

282.17 brother M.] This was probably Morris. Poughkeepsie is the county seat of Dutchess County.

282.29 in its wings."] See *Malachi*, IV, 2.

286.19–20 happy one] The truth of Irving's assertion can be testified to by reading Margaret's journal, especially pp. 13–14.

287.24 in its inspiration] Poe (*Works*, X, 178) quoted this paragraph and italicized the last sentence. He added: "The nature of inspiration is disputable, and we will not pretend to assert that Mr. Irving is in the wrong. His words, however, in their hyperbole, do wrong to his subject, and would be hyperbole still, if applied to the most exalted poets of all time."

291.28 Mrs. Hemans] Felicia Dorothea Hemans (1793–1835) was an English poet. A reviewer in *Arcturus* 2 (July, 1841), 126, thought Margaret "resembled Mrs. Hemans in the early possession" of "the rhythmical process" and the "talent of story-telling."

294.17 as the song goes] The song is "Home, Sweet Home," from John Howard Payne's *Clari, The Maid of Milan* (1823). Payne and Irving collaborated in writing plays in Paris in 1824.

294.18 June, 1837] This date probably applies to the following quotation. The previous excerpt was dated April 2, 1837 (292.16).

294.23 brother graduates] See note 282.16.

295.24 now and then.'] These lines have not been identified.

296.20–21 a Mr. and Mrs. H.] In 1833 in Saratoga Springs Margaret wrote in her journal (p. 11) of a Mrs. Hart, "a lady from Utica who treats me with much attention, and I am become quite attached to her. . . ." See also Margaret's account of her walk with Mrs. Hart ("Journal," pp. 12–13). There is no evidence that Mrs. Hart was the Mrs. H. mentioned here. See note 341.20: "Mr. and Mrs. H. came from Ballston. . . ."

299.28 Cousin] Victor Cousin (1792–1867) was a French philosopher.

300.2 Condillac's Ancient History] Étienne Bonnot de Condillac (1714–1780), French philosopher, was a disciple of John Locke.

300.3 Gibbon's Decline and Fall] Edward Gibbon (1737–1794), English historian, published *The Decline and Fall of the Roman Empire* (1776–1788).

300.4 Josephus] Flavius Josephus (37–95 A.D.) was a Jewish historian and soldier.

300.28 animal magnetism] A reviewer in *The New World* 2 (June 5, 1841), 381, wrote: "How much more good sense—how much more of a philosophic mind—how much more of freedom from that prejudice which rejects what is new because it is incomprehensible—how much more of a prophetic spirit, is displayed in what the child writes about 'Animal Magnetism' than in the opinions and verdicts often pronounced by the wise among grown men!"

301.38 'which casteth out fear.'] See 1 John 4:18.

302.30 Lockhart's Life of Scott] John Gibson Lockhart (1794–1854), Scottish editor and novelist, published his life of Sir Walter Scott in seven volumes in 1837–1838. Lockhart was Scott's son-in-law.

311.17 Lenore] For Poe's opinion of this poem see Introduction, pp. xlv–xlvi.

312.29 Mrs. Jameson] This is possibly Anna Jameson (1794–1860), the Irish art critic and author who published *Characteristics of Shakespeare's Women* in 1832.

312.36 'the waters of Helicon'] This quotation has not been identified.

312.40 'streams more salubrious'] This quotation has not been identified.

314.40 Brother M.] This was probably Morris. Matthias at this time was working as a civil engineer in Sing Sing (i.e., Ossining), New York. See unpublished letter from Margaret to Matthias, April 16, 1838 (Rutgers University Library).

314.43 Lake George] Lake George was the scene of several battles during the French and Indian War. In James Fenimore Cooper's *The Last of the Mohicans* Lake George was called Lake Horican.

315.3 Saratoga] Saratoga, now called Schuylerville, is about ten miles east of Saratoga Springs. On October 17, 1777, General Burgoyne surrendered his forces at Saratoga, which is now a national historical park.

315.14 by Mr. Ware] William Ware (1797–1852), a Unitarian clergyman and novelist, published *Letters of Lucius M. Piso from Palmyra to His Friend Marcus Curtius at Rome* in 1837. Later this novel was retitled *Zenobia*.

315.18–19 queen Zenobia] Queen Zenobia of ancient Palmyra conquered Egypt and most of Asia Minor and was in turn conquered by the Romans in 272.

319.11 or grey] "Black spirits and white, red spirits and gray, / Mingle, mingle, mingle, you that mingle may" (Thomas Middleton, *The Witch*, IV, 3).

320.10 a skillful physician] In a letter postmarked in Ballston May 16, (1837?) to her father in Peekskill, Margaret referred to a Dr. Gruman, who was then attending her mother (manuscript letter, Rutgers University Library). See 329.29, where Margaret refers to "Dr. M——."

321.3 Mrs. H.] See note 296.20–21.

323.30 young friend H."] 324.16 indicates that she was writing to her cousin Kate.

326.10–11 two of her brothers] These were probably Morris, who lived in New York City, and Matthias, who was working at Ossining.

326.11 West Chester county] Westchester County in southeastern New York is the county in which Irving's Sunnyside is located.

326.14 Singsing steamer] Sing Sing, now named Ossining, is a town on the Hudson River not far from Tarrytown in Westchester County.

326.28 Croton] The Croton is a short river which flows into the Hudson near Ossining. The Croton aqueduct, built in 1837–1842, supplies water to New York City. Margaret's brother Matthias worked on the Croton Aqueduct project.

327.17 Ichabod's adventure] The reference is to Irving's tale "The Legend of Sleepy Hollow" in *The Sketch Book*. Margaret was visiting Sleepy Hollow, which is in North Tarrytown. Irving is buried in the cemetery of the Dutch Reformed Church in Sleepy Hollow.

327.27–28 poor Andre's capture] John André (1751–1780) was the British officer who negotiated with Benedict Arnold, commander of West Point, for the betrayal of the Point. André was captured in North Tarrytown by three men, one of whom was John Paulding, an uncle of James Kirke Paulding. See Irving's *Life of George Washington*, Vol. IV, chap. IX.

327.37 M.] This was probably Matthias.

332.6 a young officer] This was Levi. See note 282.16.

338.13 an epistle from that lady] This letter, dated "Lenox 9 Decr '38," is in the possession of the Rutgers University Library.

338.16 deeply affecting.] For Poe's opinion of the following letter see Introduction, p. xlv.

339.39 Mr. Babcock] The Reverend D. Babcock of Ballston Spa came to Saratoga Springs on Sunday afternoons to conduct services at the Bethesda Episcopal Chapel (*Reminiscences of Saratoga*, comp. Cornelius E. Durkee; reprinted from *The Saratogian*, 1927–1928).

340.9 in the skies."] The quotation is the first two lines of an old Methodist hymn by Isaac Watts. The editor acknowledges with thanks the receipt of this information from the Reverend Albert T. Strobel, minister of the Puffer Methodist Church, Morrisville, Vermont, and the Reverend W. J. Fillier, retired Methodist minister.

341.20 Mr. and Mrs. H.] See note 296.20–21

343.1 the grave yard] Margaret is buried in Greenridge Cemetery in Saratoga Springs. Mrs. Tsing S. Chu, Director of the Saratoga Springs Public Library, kindly supplied the following information in a letter to the editor dated October 2, 1967: "The cemetery plot is a large, circular one, enclosed by an ironwork fence. There is a tall, central monument, set on a double pedestal topped by a Doric-like, fluted shaft, with the inscription: 'The Brothers of Margaret Miller Davidson have erected this structure as a testimony of their affection. She was the daughter of Dr. Oliver and Mrs. Margaret Davidson. Died at Saratoga Springs Nov. 25, 1838. Aged 15 years and 8 months.'" Also buried in the plot are Dr. and Mrs. Davidson and Margaret's brothers Morris and Levi. On July 8, 1841 Levi wrote a letter from Saratoga to Matthias, still employed as a civil engineer at Sing Sing (Ossining), in which he said: "I do not know that you have been made aware of our late conversations with regard to a monument to Margaret. Morris & myself thought that it should be erected by her brothers, & that you would join us in our views. I sent down yesterday a plan of a monument which I designed, with inscriptions & full directions for the manufacturer.... I thought the monument ought to be elegant & costly rather than otherwise, both on accout [sic] of our regard for the person beneath it, and because, now her name has become a public one, the monument will necessarily excite observation & remark, and become in a measure a standing evidence of the capacity & magnitude, of our own tastes & views as well as fraternal affection. I think the idea conveyed by the design a pretty one. it is a white marble cubic plinth, surmounted by a *broken* Corinthian or fluted column. The broken column is appropriate to one who was cut off before her career was finished, & the fluted white column has always been emblematic of female grace. I do not know where I got the idea, but I saw one similar in some cemetary in Europe & it struck me at the time as very beautiful, on one side of the plinth is to be engraved a harp unstrung down of her poetry & on the other the inscription" (manuscript letter, in possession of Rutgers University Library).

TEXTUAL COMMENTARY

In choosing the copy-text for the *Biography of the Late Margaret Miller Davidson* the editor has no choice but to accept the first edition published by Lea and Blanchard in 1841, for Irving wrote this book from memoranda supplied him by Mrs. Davidson; and neither his manuscript nor her notes have been found.

THE TEXTS

In the discussion which follows the symbols used to designate previously published editions are those given in the List of Abbreviations, page 611.

Lea and Blanchard's first edition was printed by C. Sherman & Co. The number of copies in the edition is not known; but by July 21, 1841, Irving was in correspondence with Lea and Blanchard about a second edition. According to his letter of instructions,[1] he left to the discretion of the publisher the number of copies to be printed. He did not anticipate any "alterations" and said that any corrections to be made might be indicated in a letter.

The second edition, also published by Lea and Blanchard and printed by C. Sherman & Co. in 1841, contains no major revisions but does reveal twenty-three substantive variations and more than four hundred variations in accidentals.

In 1842 Lea and Blanchard published a third edition, also printed by C. Sherman & Co. It contains one major addition: the paragraph beginning "We here interrupt..." (332.5) and the poem "To My Soldier Brother in the Far West" which follows. In addition, there are many changes in both substantives and accidentals.

In 1843 Lea and Blanchard published another edition, labeled as a "New Edition, revised." This was stereotyped by J. Fagan and printed by T. K. and P. G. Collins. It continues many of the variations introduced in 1842, corrects several errors that crept into 42, and introduces new variations. There is no evidence that Irving had a hand in this edition.

In 1845 a reimpression of the 1843 edition, stereotyped by J. Fagan, was published by Lea and Blanchard. Reimpressions of 43 appeared in 46, 47, and 48.

1. See Introduction, p. xlvii.

In 1851 what appears to have been a reimpression of the 43 edition was published by Clark, Austin & Co., New York; and reimpressions of this edition appeared in 1852 and 1854.

The 1843 English edition, printed by B. Clarke of Silver Street, Falcon Square, and published by David Bogue, though a new setting, bears a striking resemblance to the 1842 edition. When, for example, 41a, 42, and 43 differ from 41 and from each other, 43E usually follows 42; (e.g., compass. (41, 41a); compass! (42); compass? (43); compass! (43E) (324.18). 43E also introduces new variations.[2]

Authorized editions published during Irving's lifetime were collated according to the following pattern:

1. Two sight collations of the first Lea and Blanchard edition (41) (University of Wisconsin copy) with another 41 (Columbia University copy)
2. One sight collation of 41 (Wisconsin) with another 41 (Kleinfield)
3. One machine collation of 41 (Wisconsin) with another 41 (University of Texas copy)
4. Two sight collations of 41 (Wisconsin) with 41a
5. Two machine (pp. 1–106) and sight (pp. 107–52) collations of 41 (Wisconsin) with 42 (Wisconsin)
6. Two sight collations of 41 (Wisconsin) with 42 (Columbia University copy)
7. Two sight collations of 41 (Wisconsin) with 43 (Columbia University copy)
8. One sight collation of 41 (Wisconsin) with 43E
9. One sight collation of 42 (Wisconsin) with 45 (University of Wisconsin, Milwaukee)
10. One machine collation of 45 (University of Wisconsin, Milwaukee) with 47 (Texas copy)
11. One machine collation of 47 (Texas) with 51 (Texas)[3]

TREATMENT OF SUBSTANTIVES

"I am not aware of any alterations ⟨to be made⟩ necessary or advisable in the second edition; if there are any corrections they will be very trifling and may be specified in a letter, but I do not think there will

2. Although *BAL* points out that the "earliest English edition noted was advertised by Wiley and Putnam as the *third edition*" in the Atheneum of May 14, 1842, no such edition has been located. 43E symbolizes the 1843 edition published in London by David Bogue, apparently the first English edition.

3. Copies for these collations are recorded by library name and call number, or name of the present owner, together with whatever identifying marks can be noted: (1) 41 (Univ. of Wisc. C23564): 8° (7⅝ x 4⅝): ⟨1⟩⁴ 2–10⁸ ⟨11⟩⁸ 12–38⁸ *plus* ⟨24⟩⁴,

be any." That is what Irving wrote in his letter to Lea and Blanchard on July 21, 1841; but, if he did specify such changes, the letter has not been found.[4] Nevertheless, although there are no major revisions in the second edition (41a), one finds twenty-three substantive variations. The question is: Are all of these variations authentic authorial revisions? The fact of the matter is that sixteen of the twenty-three changes appear in quotations from Margaret's poetry and letters and in quotations from Mrs. Davidson's notes. If there were a probability that Irving proofread copy by comparing it with his manuscript, one could regard the revisions as corrections of errors. However, it seems more likely that he merely read the galley sheets and, failing to distinguish between his own passages and quotations from sources, made corrections from memory or from a desire to improve the style of the essay.[5] While this procedure would be valid in dealing with those parts he himself wrote, it is not acceptable in the passages acknowledged as quotations.

Without a manuscript or any other reliable printing to consult, therefore, the editor must regard the first edition as closer to the sources than any later editions would be. For this reason variations in 41a in quoted material have been rejected. Thus Margaret's sentence "Mother's health is not as good as when you was here" (268.18) is adopted in preference to the 41a correction of the grammar ("were here").[6] So with passages quoted from Mrs. Davidson's memos: "spirit," (319.41) has been preferred to "spirits;" in 41a. Exceptions to this policy are those variations which correct obvious printer's errors in 41; e.g., "by" / "my" (260.34)

---

i.e., 8 pages of ads, unpaged and undated, *plus* $\langle 25 \rangle^4$, i.e., 4 blank leaves of end papers [signed regularly on 1, except that 1 and 11 are unsigned], 180 leaves; pp. $\langle$i half title$\rangle$ $\langle$ii blank$\rangle$ $\langle$iii title$\rangle$ $\langle$iv copyright and printer$\rangle$ $\langle$v contents$\rangle$ vi–vii $\langle$viii blank$\rangle$ $\langle$9 Biography$\rangle$ 10–152 $\langle$153 Remains$\rangle$ $\langle$154 blank$\rangle$ $\langle$155 text$\rangle$ 156–359 $\langle$360 blank$\rangle$ *vs.* 41 (Columbia Univ. 812D281/L3); (2) 41 (Univ. of Wisconsin) *vs.* 41 (H. L. Kleinfield's uncataloged copy); (3) 41 (Univ. of Wisconsin) *vs.* 41 (Univ. of Texas, uncataloged); (4) 41 (Univ. of Wisconsin) *vs.* 41a (Library of Congress PS/1513/.D92A12/1841a); (5) 41 (Univ. of Wisconsin) *vs.* 42 (Univ. of Wisconsin Y / D2845): 8° (7⅜₆ x 4⅞₆) (because rebound and trimmed); (6) 41 (Univ. of Wisconsin) *vs.* 42 (Columbia Univ., Park Benjamin Collection 812D283/L); (7) 41 (Univ. of Wisconsin) *vs.* 43 (Columbia Univ 812D281/L31); (8) 41 (Univ. of Wisconsin) *vs.* 43E (Univ. of Wisconsin CA 914); (9) 42 (Univ. of Wisconsin) *vs.* 45 (Univ. of Wisconsin-Wilwaukee PS/1513/D92/A12/1845); (10) 45 (Univ. of Wisconsin-Milw.) *vs.* 47 (Univ. of Texas 60–1846); (11) 47 (Texas) *vs.* 51 (Univ. of Texas 60–1847).

4. Quoted by permission of The Carl H. Pforzheimer Library. See Introduction, p. xlvii.

5. See Textual Commentary for *Goldsmith*, pp. 432–33.

6. In a letter to her brother Matthias, dated April 16, 1838, Margaret wrote: "... you was vexed ..." (manuscript letter, Rutgers University Library).

and "not" / "now" (323.29). Variations in substantives in Irving's own prose have been accepted as probably authorial: e.g., "her mother" / "the mother" (245.38) and "scenery of" / "scenery on" (267.18). One variation which appears twice ("set up" / "sit up") is accepted in Irving's prose (286.37) but not in the quotation from Mrs. Davidson (266.37).

In the third edition (42) appears one major addition, consisting of a paragraph and thirty-four lines of poetry (332.5–36; 333.1–13). A footnote explains that the poem was found "since the publication of the first edition of this memoir." Irving should have written, "since the publication of the second edition," for the insertion does not appear there. At any rate, this revision has been accepted as Irving's. There are also forty-three substantive variations, all but ten of which appear in quoted passages and are, therefore, rejected. One exception is "bid you" / "bid me" / "bid you" (341.1), where the 41a reading has been retained (see Discussions of Adopted Readings). Although revisions of words in passages of Irving's prose have, in general, been accepted, several have not. For example, the word "narrations" in 41 (252.30) has been adopted in preference to 42's "narration" because the context suggests that Irving used the word as a synonym for "stories." No obvious reason for a change was found in "these" / "those" (254.31). Interestingly enough, in a quoted passage (268.30) Mrs. Davidson wrote, "On one of those occasions," and the word "those" was changed to "these" in 42. In both instances the original form has been adopted in preference to the change in 42.

Approximately thirty new subsantive variations appeared in 43. No evidence has been found that Irving requested changes in this edition. Six of the new variations represent a rejection of revisions in 42 and a return to the original 41 form accepted in T. Examples are "the cough" (41, 41a) / "her cough" (42) / "the cough" (43) (269.35); "Cold icy cloud" (41) / "icy cloud" (41a, 42) / "cold icy cloud" (43) (308.19). Fifteen of the new variations, being in quoted passages, have been rejected, such as "harp" (41, 41a, 42) / "heart" (43) (278.11). Three variations occurred in the passage added in 42 (332–33). One of them— "frontier post" (327.7)—has been accepted in preference to 42's "frontier part," which probably reflects a misreading of Irving's handwriting. The other two have been rejected. The phrase "And the clouds" (332.17) was changed in 43 to "And clouds," but Margaret's rhythm requires the word "the." In 332.29 the words "have met" were changed to "have been." Since the original wording is as meaningful as the revision, the 42 reading has been retained.

One new variation in 43 presents a special problem. In 41 Mrs. Davidson is quoted as saying: "It was the last piece she ever wrote, except a parody of four lines of the hymn ... " (337.38–338.1). This sentence

was retained in 41a and 42, but in 43 the word "parody" was changed
to "paraphrase." The question is: Did Mrs. Davidson write the word
"parody"; and, if so, did she not know she was in error, or was it a slip
of the pen? Was it Irving or the printer who eventually discovered the
error? As will be seen in the discussion of accidentals, Mrs. Davidson's
prose has been retained with all the grammatical errors in the first edition.
To be consistent, one might be expected to allow this misused word
to remain also. However, a study of several letters in Mrs. Davidson's
handwriting[7] shows that, although she did not always spell correctly and
had little sentence sense, she did use words correctly. In the quotation
under discussion she was dealing with the approaching death of her
daughter and at the time of writing was presumably still under the emotional strain of the girl's death. If indeed she wrote "parody" for "paraphrase," it is an understandable error. Since Irving was in effect func-
tioning as an editor, he should have caught this error in the first place.
Furthermore, although there is no evidence that Irving requested changes
in 43, neither is there any evidence that he did not. He may possibly
have noted this error and pointed it out to the publisher. It is significant
that 43E, which normally followed 42, changed "parody" to "paraphrase"
even though 42 did not notice it. For all of these reasons the 43 revision
has been accepted in T.

No new substantive variations appear in 45, 47, or 51; but about
eighteen are found in 43E. For example: "Biography" / "Memoir" (245.1);
"felt it a" / "felt it to be a" (311.39); and "Dr. M.——" / "dear M——"
(329.29). None of these revisions has been adopted in T, since there is
no evidence that Irving had a hand in the English edition.

All variants from 41 which have been adopted are included in the
List of Emendations, and many of them have been explained in the Discussions of Adopted Readings. Substantive changes in later editions
which have not been adopted are included in the List of Rejected
Substantives.

TREATMENT OF ACCIDENTALS

Although it is possible to accept some substantive revisions in 41a and
42 because of Irving's statement that, if any changes were required, he
would probably supply them in a letter, it is less easy to do so in the case
of accidentals. Irving's known tendency to ignore accidentals when
reading proof gives the editor little confidence that in this respect he
had suddenly become watchful in this the least of all his works.

More than four hundred variations in accidentals occurred in 41a.

7. See p. 630.

Most of them were carried on in 42, where, in addition, approximately three hundred more such variations appeared. Some of the changes in 42 represent a rejection of the 41a form and a return to the original version (e.g., "sure" / "sure," / "sure" [286.35]); others represent a further modification (e.g., "nigh," / "nigh,-" / "nigh-" [323.14]).

Comparatively few changes in accidentals were made in 41a and 42 in those passages presumably written by Irving or, at least, not enclosed in quotation marks. Of the variations in spelling only one has been accepted—"Leonore" / "Lenore" (311.17, 20, 27)—because the table of contents and the poem itself indicate that "Lenore" is the correct spelling. The other changes have been rejected: e.g., "wrapt" / "wrapped" (248.28); "ecstasy" / "ecstacy" (249.17); and "apostrophies" / "apostrophes" (343.28). In the latter instance, since the singular form listed in Webster (1806) is "apostrophy," Irving's plural has been accepted. The name "Ready Money" (272.39) in 41 has been accepted in preference to the hyphenated form in 41a (see Explanatory Notes, 272.39).

One aspect of spelling presents a special problem: the *or* / *our* endings. In the first two-thirds of 41 the English *our* form is consistently used. Suddenly one finds "labors" (310.34), which was changed to "labours" in 41a; and from then on, seventeen instances of the *or* ending found in 41 were changed to *our* in 41a. Three options are open to the editor: to adopt the 41a revisions to make the *our* endings consistent throughout the essay, to change all such words to the American (*or*) form, or to allow the inconsistencies in 41 to remain. Since this biography was written several years before the Author's Revised Edition was projected, in which American spelling was adopted by Putnam, the first option would seem to be the most practical. Yet the nature of the problem raises several questions of interest. For two-thirds of the book the printer consistently used the English spelling. Why at that point did he suddenly shift to the American form? Was a new typesetter assigned to the job, one who was committed to American spelling? The fact that in 41a the printer changed the American rather than the English forms suggests that Lea and Blanchard had not yet accepted American spelling as house policy. Without the manuscript at hand it is futile to speculate about which spelling Irving used or whether he wrote both interchangeably as he did in the *Goldsmith* manuscript. The few extant holograph documents do show, however, that Margaret used both endings: "honor," "honour," "labourers," "ill-humor," "neighboring," "endeavouring," "colour," and "coloured." Only one such word appears in Mrs. Davidson's letters—"honor"—but she also wrote "faver" in place of "favor." From this evidence it is quite probable that the sources contained both *or* and *our* forms, which were regularized to some degree in 41 and even more so in 41a and later editions. For these reasons the decision has been to allow the inconsistent forms in 41 to remain in T.

Of two variations in capitalization, both in 42, one—"green mountains" / "Green Mountains" (254.26)—has been accepted (see Discussions of Adopted Readings); the other—"New York" / "new York" (295.27)—has been rejected as an obvious error.

As for punctuation, whoever was responsible for changes in 41a and 42 seems to have been motivated less by a reasoned policy than by the inspiration of the moment. Thus in two instances in which 41 set off a prepositional phrase in commas ("lest, by" [247.33]; "evinced, from" [248.24]), 42 removed one of the pair. In another instance in which a comma was not used in 41 ("look by" [276.8]) 42 added one. One parenthetic expression not set off ("of course" [253.30]) has commas added in 42; another which is punctuated ("one, also," [262.37]) has the commas removed in 41a and 42. In one instance where 41 inserts a comma between subject and verb; ("daughter," [311.18]), 41a and 42 omit it; in another where there is no comma ("shores" [272.37]), 42 adds one. In a third instance all three editions use a comma in this position ("river," [267.18]). In these passages of Irving's prose the punctuation in 41 has been retained except for a few instances, which are explained in Discussions of Adopted Readings.

By far the greater number of variations in accidentals occurs in quoted passages. To what degree Margaret's poems and letters and Mrs. Davidson's memoranda were edited for the first edition there is no way of knowing without any of this source material available. It is possible, however, to gain some idea of how material was used and of the writing habits of both Margaret and her mother from a study of a few original papers that have survived.

One of these documents is Margaret's journal.[8] Although it was written five years before her death, her prose is not very different from that of the letters included in the biography; in fact, it displays much the same precocity as do the letters. In the same notebook, following the journal, are six pages of poems written in her hand.

In the biography (p. 258) Irving included details of the trip recorded in the child's journal, but only one passage appears as a direct quotation (258.8–22). A comparison of this paragraph in the book with the corresponding passage in the journal offers an insight not only into Margaret's prose style but also into the way in which sources were used in the biography. In the journal the paragraph reads:

On the 25th of June I saw, and shook hands with the famous Black Hawk the Indian Chief, the Enemy of our nation, who has

8. See Introduction, pp. xlii–xliii.

massacred our patriots, murdered our Women and helpless children, Why is he treated with so much attention by those whom he has injured? it Cannot surely arise from benevolence, it must be policy but I Cannot understand it; his Son, the Prophet, and others who accompanied him, interested me more than the Chief himself, his Son no doubt was a fine specimen of Indian beauty, he had a high brow piercing black Eyes, long black hair, which hung down upon his back, and upon the whole I think he was ↑well↓ suited to captivate an Indian Maiden; The Prophet we found surveying him self in a looking glass undoubtedly wishing to shew himself to the best advantage to the fair assembly before him, the rest were dozing on a sofa, but they were waked sufficiently to shake hands with us and others who had Enough Courage to approach so nearthem [sic]—Black Hawk himself was less prepossessing in his manners and features, than the rest though None were particularly beautiful, all but the Chief wore blankets Ear rings necklaces and ribbons of Every Colour pined to their backs, which made them look very singular—we soon returned and if I remember, dreamed of them the following night—

Whoever transcribed this paragraph for publication made significant changes. The past tense of the journal version was changed to present tense in the biography. Words were added ("himself to" / "himself off to" [258.19]); some were changed ("had Enough Courage," / "had the courage" [258.21]). A passage (258.22) was omitted without any indication being given in the text. This single example gives one little confidence that the passages quoted from Margaret's letters, which have not been found, represent faithfully what the child actually wrote.

Margaret's handwriting in the journal is clear and precise. She used and spelled correctly such words as "verdant," "dilemma," "imperceptible," "magnanimous," and even "recollections," a word that Irving never mastered. On the other hand, she misspelled such words as "propped" (proped), "servant" (searvant), "sketch" (schetch), and "height" (heighth). Like Irving, she often wrote the letter w to resemble a u in such words as "down" and "two"; and in words ending in a double l (e.g., "chill") the second l looks like an e. Also like Irving, she omitted the apostrophe from possessive nouns. She was erratic in capitalization ("friday," "Steamboat"), and her initial e's are normally in capital form.

An analysis of the first ten pages of the journal reveals some of her peculiarities in accidentals. On these ten pages alone one finds fifty-three sentence errors, of which thirty-eight are of the comma-splice variety. In ten others she used a dash, in three both comma and dash, and in two no punctuation at all. In addition, in five sentences she used a dash instead of a period as end punctuation. In nine compound sentences there is no punctuation preceding the coordinate conjunction, but she did punctuate parallel structures thirteen times. In two series she did not punctuate the final element; in a third she did. Three times she put a comma between subject and verb. One absolute construction is punctuated; another is not. She punctuated five restrictive clauses but did not punctuate three nonrestrictive ones.

Lest one suppose that these findings are useless because of the age of the child when she wrote the journal, we have two of her extant holograph letters, neither of which was used in the biography. One was written to her father in May, 1837, four years after the journal; the other was written to her brother Matthias on April 16, 1838, five months before she died.[9] The two letters, which total five pages, demonstrate that Margaret's accidentals had changed very little from the time she was ten. In the first letter there are fifteen sentence errors, thirteen of which contain commas, the other two no punctuation at all. In the second letter there are thirteen sentence errors, all but one having dashes, the other a comma. So it is with other habits. She still punctuates parallel structures and puts a comma between subject and verb. An increasing number of sentences end with a dash rather than a period.

Also extant are three holograph draft letters written by Mrs. Davidson. The first is a copy of a letter to Judge Abraham Smith, dated Ballston Spa, April, 1824. This date is undoubtedly in error, for the end of the letter was written on the reverse of a letter from Mr. Davidson to his wife, dated Caldwell's Manor, April 18, 1834. The second appears to be an undated letter to Matthias. The third, to Miss Anicartha Miller, is dated Saratoga, November 26, 1838, the day after Margaret died.[10] These three letters total about six pages. Granted that these are drafts and that one was written at a time of great sorrow, yet one finds the same peculiarities in accidentals as those in Margaret's writing, and others as well: close to thirty sentence errors, the mark between clauses being dashes rather than commas; the punctuation of parallel structures; commas omitted from nouns of address and compound sentences; dashes used for end punctuation; and quotation marks either used erratically or omitted altogether.

These findings suggest that the errors of both Margaret and her mother were habitual; and, although these documents were not the ones quoted in the biography with the exception of the paragraph from the journal, one might suppose that the memoranda given to Irving contained the same kinds of mistakes in similar degree. To take sentence errors alone,

9. Both letters are in the possession of the Rutgers University Library.
10. All three letters are in the possession of the Rutgers University Library.

one notes in 41 five such errors in pages 1 to 100 and twenty-two in pages 101 to 152. It would seem that Irving—or the printer—began by correcting such errors in the source but became less zealous in this respect as the work progressed. In 41a and 42 none of the five errors appearing in pages 1 to 100 was corrected, but eleven of the twenty-two in the remaining fifty-two pages were corrected in 41a and six more in 42. Without the manuscript or the sources it is impossible to know whether any particular error was originally Margaret's or her mother's, or whether any correct form was the result of Irving's editing or the printer's correction. There is a very real possibility that Mrs. Davidson edited Margaret's poems and letters before giving them to Irving. Of the poetic fragments composed in the last weeks of Margaret's life, Mrs. Davidson wrote: "I copy these little effusions with all their errors; there is a sacredness about them which forbids the change even of a single letter" (334.3–5). The implication is that such a prohibition did not necessarily apply to the earlier poems or, for that matter, the letters. Errors in accidentals in quoted passages of 41 have, therefore, been retained except in quotation marks, which are explained below.

There is little consistency in the variations in punctuation. In some instances both 41a and 42 omitted commas in restrictive clauses where 41 had used them (e.g., "friend," / "friend" [323.19]), and they added commas in restrictive clauses where 41 had not used them (e.g., "anecdotes" / "anecdotes," [325.10]). Sometimes 41a accepted the original punctuation, but 42 changed it (e.g., "and, although" / "and although" [248.40]). The only consistency in the use of colons and semicolons lies in the perversity with which 41a, 42, or both changed the form used in 41 (e.g., "own;" / "own:" [292.23]; "prudent:" / "prudent;" [323.23]). In these variations in accidentals between 41, 41a and/or 42 the 41 reading has been retained.

One area of accidentals in which corrections made in 41a and 42 and even in later editions have been accepted is quotation marks. In the early part of the biography Irving maintained a fair balance between paraphrasing and quoting his sources, and the quotations are properly designated. As he proceeded, he gradually increased the number and length of the quoted portions until at last he gave up, for the most part, the illusion of writing a biography and merely added paragraph after paragraph from the source without even the benefit of quotation marks. An attempt was made in 41a and 42 and later editions to add the missing marks, but not all omissions were supplied. Sometimes the lack causes the reader no problem, as in the long one-paragraph letter (314.15–315.31), which is separated by a space at the beginning and end. This has not been changed in T. At other times, however, while there is no problem at the beginning of a quotation (e.g., Margaret's letter, 323.31), real confusion exists at the end (325.5) because in the very next line a quotation from Mrs. Davidson's memo begins. Here the quotation marks added in 43 have been adopted in T. From 327.42 there is complete chaos, so much so that later editions made no attempt to resolve the muddle; indeed, only 43E had the temerity to attack it. In the interest of providing a readable text, these missing quotation marks have been adopted from later editions or, in several instances, supplied by the editor where no correction was ever made.

In a related matter the first six passages of quoted poetry in 41 were enclosed in quotation marks. Then the house style changed, and marks were not generally used. In this respect the inconsistency in 41 has been retained.

The area in which 41a made its greatest number of revisions in punctuation is Margaret's poetry, particularly in the end-line position where more than fifty changes were noted. Actually there is little theoretical justification for the punctuation in 41. Most lines end in a comma, a period, or no mark at all, regardless of what follows. Exclamation points are frequent. In 41a the printer apparently tried to make the punctuation consonant with the ideas expressed, but consistency does not prevail there either. These revisions have been rejected.

Fortunately, one poem which Margaret wrote in the notebook following her journal was included in the biography (259.37–260.14); and a comparison of the original poem with the 41 version reveals the kind of editing that was done in the first edition, though not who did it. Following is the journal version:

HOME—

I would fly from the City, would fly from its care,
To my own native plants & my flow'rets so fair,
To the cool grassy shade, and the rivulet bright,
Which reflects the pale moon, on its bosom of light;
Again would I view the old cottage so dear,
Where I Sported a babe without sorrow or fear,
I would leave this great City, so brilliant & gay,
For a peep at my home, on this fine summer day,
I have friends whom I love, and would leave with regret
But the love of my home—oh! tis tenderer yet,
There a sister reposes unconcious in death,
It was there she first drew, and there yielded her breath
Attentive I listen to pleasures sweet call
But my oun darling *home* it is dearer than all

The first thing to be noted is that four lines were added (260.9–12) and the word "cottage" changed to "mansion" (260.1), and this suggests that Margaret later revised the notebook version. This raises a number of questions: Did she revise the accidentals too? Did her mother blue-pencil the copy before submitting the poem to Irving? Was it Irving or the printer who edited the poem? Whoever made the changes, some of them seem desirable, notably the end punctuation of lines at 260.1, 4, 5, 6, 7, 8, 13, and 14; but others are of questionable value, such as the end punctuation of 260.29. The comma added in 41 to 260.2 was apparently designed to set off the prepositional phrase rather than to clarify "Where I sported a babe." As Margaret wrote the line and as it is reproduced in 41, the word "babe" is the direct object of "sported" rather than the appositive of "I," which the context suggests was the intended meaning. Even though a comma was placed after "sported" in 41a, the 41 version has been retained.

Spelling in the quoted passages in 41 has been adopted, even to several outright errors (e.g., "nurseling" [314.9]; "inseperable" [341.31]). Neither 41 nor 41a was consistent in spelling the past tense of verbs: e.g., "pardoned" / "pardon'd" (251.22); "charm'd" / "charmed" (265.35); "past" / "passed" / "pass'd" (306.10); "passed" / "pass'd" (308.19). One incorrect verb form used by Mrs. Davidson and never corrected in later editions is "dare permit" (299.20–21). It has been retained in T. The word "wo" is consistently so spelled in 41 except in 333.18, where it appears as "woe." In 41a this was changed to "wo." Beginning in 43 the word in all usages became "woe," even in 43E which normally followed 42. The original form has been retained.

One area of spelling remains to be mentioned—compounds and possible compounds. Regardless of whether these appear in Irving's prose or the quoted passages, there is no way of telling who was responsible for the forms adopted. Here again there is little consistency. The largest such group is composed of words compounded with "self." Of the eighteen instances noted, five appearing in Irving's prose and two in quotations from Margaret's work are hyphenated. Of the remaining nine found in quotations from Mrs. Davidson's memoranda, six are hyphenated and three are not. She hyphenates "self-examination" three times but writes the two-word form in a fourth usage. She hyphenates "self-deception" and "self-possession" but not "self condemnation" and "self knowledge." Other inconsistencies appear. Margaret hyphenates "much-loved"; her mother does not. Mrs. Davidson hyphenates "re-united"; Margaret writes "reunited." Five times Margaret writes "footsteps" and then in a sixth instance "foot-steps." In one poem she writes "for ever more," in another "for evermore." Irving hyphenates "bed-room," but Mrs. Davidson writes "sick room" and "sick chamber." These variations have been left as they were in 41, even in such a one as "easy-chair" (340.26), where the first syllable comes at the end of the line, the word having been written without the hyphen in two other usages.

All variants in accidentals from the 41 edition which have been adopted have been included in the List of Emendations, and several have been explained in the Discussions of Adopted Readings. No silent corrections have been made.

DISCUSSIONS OF ADOPTED READINGS

The adopted readings discussed in this list are those which are preceded by an asterisk in the List of Emendations. The editor's decisions to amend or not to amend are based on her acceptance or rejection of the variant reading as Irving's.

The page and line figures are keyed in each case to a word or words in the text to which the discussion or comment refers. A bracket separates the key word or words from the comment that follows. A key to identifying symbols used in referring to previously published editions of *Margaret Davidson* is given on page 611.

245.23 eye still gleamed] Although Irving's revisions, probably made in a letter to the publisher, are not extant, it is likely that substantive changes were his rather than the printer's.

245.38 the mother,] The original "her" referred to "Lucretia" in the same line. The change is accepted as probably Irving's.

247.39 lessons] This is accepted as a probable authorial revision.

250.4 exclaimed—] In only one other instance in 41 (305.32) is there no punctuation of the word preceding quoted poetry, and there too a dash was added in 42. In thirty other instances noted, a period is used sixteen times, a semicolon eight times, a dash four times, a comma once, and an exclamation point once.

252.12 Mary, Queen] Although in general variations in punctuation in passages of Irving's prose have been rejected as probably being the work of the printer rather than the author, this one is accepted because it corrects an outright error.

254.26 Green Mountains] Irving often wrote capital *G* like a slightly larger lowercase *g*, and it is often difficult to distinguish between his lowercase *m* and capital *M*. It is quite probable that the printer misread the handwriting here. Since Irving capitalized the other geographical names in the paragraph, the correction of this name in 42 seems legitimate and is, therefore, accepted.

254.38 " 'Behold] The revision in 42 is acceptable because the poem represents a quotation within a quotation.

258.40 this! Do] Irving used dashes in dialogue to indicate a new speaker. Since here in 41 the dash appeared in the middle of a speech, the correction in 42 has been adopted.

260.34 my] The word "by" in 41 is an obvious typographical error. Compare 260.40, 261.6, 261.12.

266.37 set up]   Since this appears in a quotation from Mrs. Davidson's notes, the revision in 41a is rejected. Compare 256.30.

273.12 were not to be]   The omission of "to" in 41 was probably a printer's error.

280.3 for the eagle's]   Since Margaret's verse is metronomic in its regularity, the omission of "the" in 41, 41a, and 42 would seem to have been a printer's error not noted in the first three editions. The 43 reading is, therefore, adopted.

286.37 sit up]   This has been accepted as a probable Irving revision, but compare 266.37, where "sit up" has been rejected in favor of "set up" in 41 because it appears in a quotation from Mrs. Davidson's notes.

292.14 poetry?"]   To this point Irving meticulously placed quotation marks around passages taken verbatim from Mrs. Davidson's memoranda, but from here on he became increasingly careless. Some were added in 41a and later editions. See Textual Commentary, pp. 631–32.

305.30 exclaimed–]   See above, 250.4.

306.10 past]   Margaret's misspelling has been allowed to stand. See Textual Commentary, p. 633.

307.34 wrote, 'The bell! it hath ceased.]   The sentence as it appears in 41 is obviously in error. The revision in 41a was probably Irving's. Compare 309.3.

311.17 Lenore.]   The word is so spelled in the table of contents in 41 and in all later editions examined.

311.36 "MY DEAR]   Although the absence of the quotation mark in 41 does not cause confusion, the lack of one at the end of the letter (312.41) does. Quotation marks have, therefore, been added both here and at the end of the letter.

319.3 "I now]   Normally when Irving included a letter with the salutation, he did not use quotation marks. On the other hand, when he included extracts (e.g., 299.43) or when he omitted the salutation (e.g., 316.1), he did use them. The present instance presents a special problem. Notice that 318.37 ends a quotation from Mrs. Davidson. This is followed by three lines in the author's own voice. Then 319.3 begins a quotation from Margaret's letter, which ends at 319.40 and is immediately followed by another quotation from Mrs. Davidson. Without quotation marks at 319.3 and 319.40 real confusion exists. The 41a reading is, therefore, adopted.

319.26 hands]   The context suggests that the singular form in 41 was a printer's error.

319.40 ink."]   See 319.3.

320.2 nature]   The period in 41 appears to be a typographical error.

321.2 face.]   The quotation mark in 41 is an error which was never corrected. It belongs in the next line before the word "On." That this paragraph continues the quotation is obvious from the word "our" in line 4.

323.17 herself,"] This is the only instance in which the comma was omitted before explanatory words added by Irving. Even when quotation marks were omitted, the comma in this position was used (e.g., 327.42–"epistles,"). For this reason the 41a revision has been accepted.

323.29 now] The context indicates that the word "not" in 41 was an error.

323.31 "Saratoga,] The quotation mark is needed here to avoid a problem at the end of the letter (325.5) because in the next line (325.6) another quotation begins.

329.19 "The following] The quotation mark is needed because this paragraph is a continuation of the quotation in the previous paragraph.

332.4 prose."] The quotation mark is needed here because of the following material, inserted in 42, which breaks Mrs. Davidson's narrative.

332.7 frontier post] This paragraph and the following poem were added in 42. The word "part" in 42 was probably a misreading of Irving's handwriting. The context requires the word "post."

333.18 wo,] Margaret used this word over and over again in her poetry, always to this point so spelled. The change in 41a from "woe" in 41 in this usage appears to be valid.

335.1 THE NATURE OF THE SOUL.] In 41 this was set in capital and lowercase letters as the first line of the poem. It seems to have been a printer's error, corrected in 41a and accepted as such in T.

337.1 breathe] Since in the poems at the end of her journal Margaret used both "breathe" and "breath" correctly, the assumption is that the misspelling here was a typographical error. The 41a revision has, therefore, been adopted.

338.1 paraphrase] See Textual Commentary, pp. 625–26.

341.1 to bid me] The "you" in 340.42 suggests that the "you" here in 41 was in error. The correction in 41a has, therefore, been adopted.

343.22 endeavoured] This is accepted as a probable authorial revision.

LIST OF EMENDATIONS

These notes identify all emendations of the copy-text. The numbers before each note indicate the page and line. Epigraphs, author's chapter or section summaries, texts, quotations, and footnotes are included in the line count. Only running heads and rules added by the printer to separate running heads from the text are omitted from the count.

The reading to the left of the bracket is the portion of the text under consideration or discussion and represents an accepted reading that differs from the copy-text. The source of the reading is identified by symbol after the bracket. The reading after the semicolon is the rejected reading of the copy-text and any other text in which that reading occurs; if other alternatives are also available, they are recorded following that reading.

The swung (wavy) dash ∼ represents the same word, words, or characters that appear before the bracket, and is used in recording punctuation variants; the caret ∧ indicates that a mark of punctuation is omitted. T signifies that a decision to emend or not to emend has been made on the authority of the editor of the Twayne edition. These decisions are based upon the editor's acceptance or rejection of the variant as Irving's. Some of these editorial decisions are explained in the Discussion of Adopted Readings, which include decisions to emend as well as some decisions not to emend. Discussion is identified by an asterisk °.

A key to identifying symbols used in referring to the editions of *Margaret Davidson,* as well as to Irving's sources, is given on page 611.

°245.23	eye still gleamed] 42; ∼ ∼ beamed 41, 41a
°245.38	the mother,] 41a, 42; her ∼, 41
°247.39	lessons] 41a, 42; letters 41
°250.4	exclaimed—] 42; ∼∧ 41, 41a
°252.12	Mary, Queen] 41a; ∼∧ ∼ 41, 42
°254.26	Green Mountains] 42; green mountains 41, 41a
°254.38	" 'Behold] 42; "∼ 41, 41a
255.4	Bethlehem!'] 42; ∼!" 41, 41a
256.15	" I'll] 42; "I'll 41, 41a
256.22	dear!' "] 42; ∼!" 41, 41a
258.34	direction,] 41a, 42; directions, 41
°258.40	this! Do] 42; ∼!—Do 41, 41a
°260.34	my] 41a, 42; by 41

261.13   disappointed at] 42; ～ in 41, 41a
266.28   foreboding] 41a, 42; forebodings 41
267.18   scenery on] 41a, 42, 45; ～ of 41
*273.12   were not to be] 41a, 42; were not be 41
*280.3   for the eagle's] 43; for eagle's 41, 41a, 42
282.29   'to] 41a; "to 41, 42, 45
282.29   wings.'] 41a; ～." 41, 42, 45
286.16   we should] 42, 45, 43E; we would 41, 41a
286.19   though brief,] 41a; though a brief, 41, 42, 45, 43E
*286.37   sit up,] 41a, 42; set up, 41
287.30   this] 41a, 42; this· 41
*292.14   poetry?"] 41a, 42; ～?ᴧ 41
292.40   preparing] 41, 42, 45; prepared 41a
295.34   a short] 42; some ～ 41, 41a
297.5   the tears,] 42; her ～, 41, 41a
*305.30   exclaimed—] 42; ～ᴧ 41, 41a
*307.34   wrote, 'The bell! it hath ceased.] 41a, 42; wrote. The
                bell hath ceased. 41
311.11   enjoyment.' "] 41a, 42; ～." 41
*311.17   Lenore.] 41a, 42; Leonore. 41
311.20   Lenore] 41a, 42; Leonore 41
311.27   Lenore] 41a, 42; Leonore 41
*311.36   "My Dear] T; ᴧ～ ～ 41, 41a; "～ dear 42, 43, 45
311.37   "I wish] 42; ᴧ～ ～ 41, 41a
312.36   'the waters] 42, 43, 45; "～ ～ 41, 41a
312.36   Helicon'] 42, 43, 45; ～" 41, 41a
312.40   'streams more salubrious'] 42, 43, 45, 43E; "～ ～ ～"
                41, 41a
312.40   spring."] 42; ～·ᴧ 41, 41a
313.26   "Dear] 42; ᴧ～ 41, 41a
313.30   account,] 41a; ac-/rount, 41; accountᴧ 42, 43, 45
314.1   "Ah,] 42; ᴧ～, 41, 41a
314.12   misery."] 42; ～·ᴧ 41, 41a
316.16   'phiz, phiz'] 41a; "～, ～" 41; '～, ～,' 42
*319.3   "I now] 41a, 42; ᴧ～ ～ 41
319.4   'This] 41a, 42; "～ 41
319.6   blessing'—] 41a, 42; ～"— 41
319.10   'black] 41a, 42; "～ 41
319.11   grey,'] 43; ～," 41; gray,' 41a, 42
319.20   'What] 41a, 42; "～ 41
319.21   raise,'] 41a, 42; ～," 41
*319.26   hands] 41a, 42; hand 41
*319.40   ink."] 41a, 42; ～·ᴧ 41

320.2	nature] 41a, 42; ~. 41
*321.2	face.] T; ~." 41, 41a
321.3	"On] T; ∧~ 41, 41a
321.3	'Parting Word'] T; "~ ~" 41, 41a
*323.17	herself,"] 41a, 42; ~∧" 41
323.20	everything,] T; ~. 41; every thing, 41a, 42
*323.29	now] 41a, 42; not 41
*323.31	"Saratoga,] 43; ∧~, 41, 41a, 42
323.32	"June] 43; ∧~ 41, 41a, 42
324.13	'Nonsense,] T; "~, 41; "~!∧ 41a, 42; '~! 43
324.13	sentimental;'] T; ~;" 41; ~!" 41a, 42; ~!' 43
324.25	"June 2d.] T; ∧~ 2d. 41, 41a, 42; "~ 2nd. 43E
325.5	in it."] 43; ~ ~.∧ 41, 41a, 42
325.6	"The time] 43E; ∧~ ~ 41, 41a, 42, 43
326.4	New York."] 43E; ~ ~.∧ 41, 41a, 42, 43
327.42	"In these] 43E; ∧~ ~ 41, 41a, 42, 43
327.42	epistles,"] 43E; ~,∧ 41, 41a, 42, 43
327.42	"there] 43E; ∧~ 41, 41a, 42, 43
328.13	"On the] 43E; ∧~ ~ 41, 41a, 42, 43
328.19	'Oh,] 43E; "Oh, 41, 41a, 42, 43
328.27	I am.'] T; ~ ~.∧ 41; ~ ~." 41a, 42
328.32	'she] 43E; "~ 41, 41a, 42, 43
328.34	again.'] 43E; ~." 41, 41a, 42, 43
*329.19	"The following] T; ∧~ ~ 41, 41a
329.23	"'As to] T; "∧~ ~ 41, 41a
330.2	you.'] T; ~,∧ 41; ~." 41a, 42
330.3	"From] 43E; ∧~ 41, 41a, 42, 43
330.8	'I] 43E; "I 41, 41a, 42, 43
330.9	mother.'] 43E; ~." 41, 41a, 42, 43
330.25	'Mamma,] 43E; "~, 41, 41a, 42, 43
330.27	end.'] 43E; ~." 41, 41a, 42, 43
330.28	'And] 43E; "~ 41, 41a, 42, 43
330.31	being?'] T; ~?" 41, 41a
330.35	'Oh my mother,'] 43E; "~ ~ ~." 41, 41a, 42, 43
330.35	'I] 43E; "I 41, 41a, 42, 43
330.37	life __.'] T; ~ __." 41; ~ __." 41a; ~ __∧" 42
331.20	on the subject,] 41a, 42; on the the ~, 41
*332.4	prose."] 42; ~.∧ 41, 41a
*332.7	frontier post] 43; frontier part 42
332.15	'Tis] 42; 'T is 43
332.17	And the clouds] 42; And clouds 43
332.19	'Tis] 42; 'T is 43
332.29	have met] 42; have been 43

332.33   years] 42; ⁓, 43
333.9   rest] 42; ⁓, 43
333.13   "The following fragments," continues Mrs. Davidson,
                "appear] 42; The following fragments appear 41, 41a
*333.18   wo,] 41a, 42; woe, 41
333.21   tone."] 41a, 42; ⁓.ᴧ 41
333.36   "These] 43E; ᴧ⁓ 41, 41a, 42, 43
*335.1   THE NATURE OF THE SOUL.] 41a, 42; The nature
                of the soul, 41
335.26   "As the] T; ᴧ ⁓⁓ 41, 41a, 42
336.26   "About] T; ᴧ⁓ 41, 41a, 42
336.35   'Not] T; "⁓ 41, 41a, 42
336.35   mother!'] T; ⁓!" 41, 41a, 42; ⁓!ᴧ 43, 45
*337.1   breathe] 41a, 42; breath 41
337.35   "It was] 43E; ᴧ⁓ ⁓ 41, 41a, 42, 43
*338.1   paraphrase] 43; parody 41, 41a, 42, 45
338.1   'I would] 43E; "⁓ ⁓ 41, 41a, 42, 43
338.2   always,'] 43E; ⁓," 41, 41a, 42, 43
338.6   tears."] 42; ⁓.ᴧ 41, 41a
340.14   'Mother,] 41a, 42; "⁓, 41
340.15   short.'] 41a, 42; ⁓." 41
340.40   her,] 41a, 42; here, 41
*341.1   to bid me] 41a; to bid you 41, 42, 45
341.7   neighborhood] T; neigh-/horhood 41; neighbourhood
                41a, 42
341.25   her a late] 41a, 42; her a a late 41
342.7   said, 'I] 41a, 42; ⁓, ᴧI 41
342.8   oppression.'] 41a, 42; ⁓.ᴧ 41
342.9   'Margaret] 41a; ᴧ⁓ 41, 42, 45
342.10   mother.'] 41a; ⁓.ᴧ 41, 42, 45
343.3   "A few] 41a, 42; ᴧ⁓ ⁓ 41
343.3   departure,"] 41a, 42; ⁓,ᴧ 41
343.4   "I was] 41a, 42; ᴧ⁓ ⁓ 41
343.8   'For] 41a, 42; "For 41
343.9   Private.'] 41a; ⁓." 41; private.' 42
343.16   of divine grace."] 41a; ⁓ ⁓ ⁓.ᴧ 41; of the divine grace."
                42; of the Divine grace. 43E
*343.22   endeavoured] 42; attempted 41, 41a

LIST OF REJECTED SUBSTANTIVES

This list provides a historical record of substantive variants in the authorized texts which appeared during Irving's lifetime but which were not adopted for the Twayne text.

The numbers before each entry indicate the page and line number. The reading to the left of the bracket is the word or words accepted from the copy-text. The source or sources of the reading are identified by the symbol after the bracket. The reading after the semicolon indicates the rejected form, the sources of which are identified by symbol.

A key to identifying symbols used in referring to previously published editions of *Margaret Davidson*, as well as to Irving's sources, is given on page 611.

vi.4–5	of the late] 41, 41a; of 43E
vi.6	Miller] 41, 41a; M. 43E
245.1	BIOGRAPHY] 41, 41a; Memoir 43E
248.30	shower,"] 41, 41a; showers," 42
252.30	narrations.] 41, 41a; narration. 42, 43, 45, 43E
254.31	these] 41, 41a; those 42, 43, 45, 43E
256.27	set] 41, 41a, 42, 43; sit 43E
258.41	replied she] 41, 41a; she replied 43E
264.15	those] 41, 41a; these 42, 43, 45, 43E
266.37	set up] 41; sit up 41a, 42, 43, 45, 43E
268.17	was] 41; were 41a, 42, 43, 45, 43E
268.29	those] 41, 41a; these 41, 43, 45, 43E
269.35	the cough] 41, 41a, 43, 45; her ⌐ 42, 43E
277.28	angel] 41, 41a; angels 42; angels' 43, 45, 43E
278.11	harp] 41, 41a, 42, 43E; heart 43, 45
278.36	stars] 41, 41a, 43, 45, 43E; star 42
279.31	thy valley,] 41, 41a; the ⌐ₐ 42, 43, 45, 43E
281.14	the pure] 41, 41a, 42, 45; their ⌐ 43E
281.27	to be an almost invariable] 41, 41a; to be almost an invariable 42, 43, 45, 43E
282.6	say she] 41, 41a, 42, 43E; ⌐ that she 43, 45
282.15	with dear brother,] 41, 41a; ⌐ my ⌐ ⌐ₐ 42, 43, 45, 43E
282.22–23	flowers as] 41, 41a; ⌐ are as 42, 43, 45, 43E
285.2	world,] 41, 41a, 42, 45; worlds 43E
285.8	Too pure to sin,] 41, 41a, 43, 45, 43E; Too pure too sin, 42

285.11	or] 41, 41a, 42; and 43, 45, 43E
286.4	purer] 41, 41a, 42, 43E; tender 43, 45
286.5	tender] 41, 41a, 42, 43E; purer 43, 45
287.36	aught] 41, 41a, 42, 45; ought 43E
290.19	thee,] 41; thine, 41a, 42, 43, 45, 43E
291.17	this case] 41, 41a, 43, 45, 43E; his ～ 42
291.37	know of no] 41, 41a, 42, 45; know no 43E
292.37	e'er] 41, 41a, 42; e'en 43, 45, 43E
294.17	goes. * * * *] 41, 41a, 42; goes. 43, 45, 43E
294.17–18	home, sweet, sweet home!'] 41, 41a, 42, 43, 45; home, sweet home!" 43E
294.21	I can] 41, 41a; I may 42, 43, 45, 43E
295.15	recollection] 41, 42, 45; recollections 41a
295.29–30	her helpless] 41, 41a, 42, 45; her as helpless 43E
299.15	to a] 41, 41a, 42, 45; with a 43E
300.4	not quite finished] 41, 41a, 42, 43E; not finished 43, 45
300.25	that we might both] 41, 41a; ～ ～ both might 42, 43, 45, 43E
300.35	may all be] 41, 41a; may be all 42, 43, 45, 43E
303.35	is a something] 41, 41a, 42, 43, 45; is something 43E
304.11	heart-awakening] 41, 41a, 42 43, 45; heart-awaking 43E
305.30	again and again,] 41, 41a, 43, 45; again and again∧ 42; again and again and again, 43E
306.4	wake to hope and glee,] 41, 41a, 42, 43E; wake to youthful glee, 43, 45
*306.10	past] 41; pased 41a; pass'd 42, 43, 45, 43E
306.10	awaken'd] 41, 41a, 42, 43E; waken'd 43, 45
307.6	cords] 41, 41a, 42, 43, 45; chords 43E
308.19	the cold icy cloud] 41, 43, 45; the icy cloud 41a, 42, 43E
308.28	their] 41, 41a; thine 42, 43, 45, 43E
310.14	The health] 41, 41a, 42, 43E; To the health 43, 45
310.30	adapt] 41, 43, 45; adopt 41a, 42, 43E
311.25	the sofa,] 41; her ～ 41a, 42, 43, 45, 43E
311.26	wile away] 41, 43E; while away 41a, 42, 43, 45
311.39	felt it a] 41, 41a, 42, 43, 45; felt it to be a 43E
312.15	or a consumption] 41, 41a; or consumption 42, 43, 45, 43E
315.6–7	present even that] 41, 41a, 42, 43E; present that 43, 45
316.5–6	could have found no better way] 41, 41a; could have no better way 42, 43, 45, 43E
317.2	anticipation] 41, 41a, 42, 45; anticipations 43E
317.30	quench it,] 41, 41a; quench, 42, 43, 45, 43E
319.37	written you a] 41, 41a; written a 42, 43, 45, 43E

323.24–25	gratify her and] 41, 41a; gratify and 42, 43, 45, 43E
324.4	till] 41, 41a, 42, 45; until 43E
324.14	streak] 41, 41a, 42, 45; freak 43E
325.10	whilst] 41, 41a; while 42, 43, 45, 43E
326.36	around] 41, 41a, 42, 45; round 43E
326.43	especial] 41; special 41a, 42, 43, 45, 43E
327.20	rising] 41; running 41a, 42, 45
327.28	valleys] 41; valley 41a, 42, 45
327.33	a most] 41; the ~_∧ 41a, 42, 43, 45, 43E
328.28	support] 41, 41a, 43, 43E; suppress 43, 45
328.36	and a depression] 41, 41a; and depression 42, 43, 45, 43E
329.28	criterion] 41, 41a, 42, 45; criterions 43E
329.29	Dr. M———] 41, 41a, 42, 45; dear M——— 43E
329.34	is the contrary,] 41, 41a, 42, 43E; is contrary, 43, 45
330.33	and friend,] 41, 41a; and a friend, 42, 43, 45, 43E
330.42	hope] 41, 41a, 42, 43E; hopes 43, 45
331.10	pang. Many] 41, 41a, 42; pang. [*paragraph*] "Many 43, 45
331.17–18	one, yet] 41, 41a, 42, 43E; one, and yet 43, 45
331.25	although] 41, 41a; though 42, 43, 45, 43E
331.33	although] 41, 41a; though 42, 43, 45, 43E
331.35	hear] 41, 41a, 42, 45; bear 43E
332.17	And the clouds] 42, 43E; And clouds 43, 45
332.29	have met] 42, 43E; have been 43, 45
334.31	strain] 41, 41a; strains 42, 43, 45, 43E
336.36	room, placed] 41, 41a; room, and placed 42, 43, 45, 43E
337.35	regain] 41, 41a; gain 42, 43, 45, 43E
338.8	our request,] 41, 41a, 42, 43E; our own request 43, 45
339.3	in bed,] 41, 41a; in my bed, 42, 43, 45, 43E
339.27	herself. Oh!] 41, 41a; herself. [*paragraph*] "Oh! 42, 43, 45
340.26	She had] 41, 41a, 42; *paragraph* ~ ~ 43, 45
340.28	*paragraph* "On] 41, 41a; [*No paragraph*] _∧On 42, 43, 45
341.19	In] 41, 41a, 42; *paragraph* "In 43, 45
341.39–40	asleep. My] 41, 41a; asleep. [*paragraph*] "My 42, 43, 45
341.8	her quiet as] 41, 41a; her as quiet as 42, 43, 45, 43E
343.8	around] 41, 41a, 42, 45; round 43E
343.16	of divine grace.] 41; of divine grace." 41a; of the divine grace." 42, 43, 45; of the Divine grace. 43E
343.34	sorrow] 41, 42, 45; sorrows 41a

LIST OF COMPOUND WORDS
HYPHENATED
AT END OF LINE

List I includes all compound and possible compound words that are hyphenated at the end of the line in the copy-text. In deciding whether to retain the hyphen or to print the word as a single-word compound (without the hyphen), the editor has made her decision first on the use of each compound word elsewhere in the copy-text; or second, when the word does not appear elsewhere in the copy-text, on Irving's practice in other writings of the period (chiefly *A Tour on the Prairies*, 1835; *Goldsmith*, 1849; and *Mahomet*, 1849–1850); or finally, if the word does not appear in Irving's other writings of the period, on contemporary American usage, chiefly as reflected in Webster's dictionary of 1806. Each word is listed in its editorially accepted form after the page and line numbers of its appearance in the T text.

List II presents all compounds, or possible compounds, that are hyphenated or separated as two words at the end of the line in the T text. They are listed in the form in which they would have appeared in the T text had they come in mid-line.

LIST I

248.23	themselves	307.29	Farewell
250.4	landscape	313.35	highway
252.9	sometimes	315.19	reperusing
255.6	outstrip	319.7	pathway
272.33	overgrown	319.22	bed-clothes
281.37	self-deception	324.19	understand
284.4	self-denial	325.17	bedside
293.4	farewell	331.12	Heretofore
299.43	bookworm	334.3	outpourings
301.21	self-examination	340.2	henceforth
301.39	all-imposing	340.26	easy-chair
305.15	fireside		

LIST II

248.29–30	sunshine	255.9–10	therefore
250.12–13	without	259.21–22	playwrights

645

266.37–38　irksome
272.31–32　poetical-looking
274.7–8　　herself
299.16–17　writing-table
300.30–31　understand
320.8–9　　however
321.4–5　　throughout

326.27–28　breakfast
326.41–42　ourselves
329.40–41　horseback
335.27–28　self-examination
336.32–33　overcome
340.24–25　something

INDEX